WITHDRAWN

Vatican II and the Collects for Ordinary Time

A Study in the Roman Missal (1975)

Gerard Moore, sm

Vatican II and the Collects for Ordinary Time

A Study in the Roman Missal (1975)

Gerard Moore, sm

Catholic Scholars Press
San Francisco - London - Bethesda
1998

Library of Congress Cataloging-in-Publication Data

Moore, Gerard, 1956-
    Vatican II and the collects for ordinary time : a study in the
    Roman Missal (1975) / Gerard Moore.
      p. cm.
    Includes bibliographical references and index.
    ISBN 1-57309-217-7 (alk. paper). -- ISBN 1-57309-216-9 (pbk. :
    alk. paper)
    1. Collects. 2. Catholic Church. Ordo Missae. I. Title.
    BX2015.7.M66   1998
    264'.0201--dc21   98-20607
                                                   CIP

Copyright 1998 by Gerard Moore

All rights reserved. Printed in the United States of America. No part of this book may be used or reproduced in any manner whatsoever without written permission except in the case of brief quotations embodied in critical articles and reviews.

Editorial Inquiries:
International Scholars Publications
7831 Woodmont Avenue, #345
Bethesda, MD 20814

To order: (800) 55-PUBLISH

with thanks to Veronica my mother,
my companions Gerald and Michael, and colleague James
Tua nos, quaesumus, Domine, gratia semper et praeveniat et sequatur ac bonis operibus iugiter praestet esse intentos (Dom XXVIII).

TABLE OF CONTENTS

LIST OF TABLES — xv

LIST OF ABBREVIATIONS — xvii

COMMENDATORY PREFACES

AUTHOR'S PREFACE

INTRODUCTION — 1

PART ONE

HISTORICAL AND METHODOLOGICAL PRINCIPLES

CHAPTER ONE. 'COLLECT STYLE' ORATIONS AND THE FIRST PRESIDENTIAL PRAYER OF THE MASS IN EARLY ROMAN LATIN EUCHOLOGY — 9

Introduction	9
The 'Collect style' Oration of the Roman Liturgy	10
Name and Function of the 'collect style' prayer	10
The structure of the 'collect style' prayer	13
The style of the 'collect style' prayer	16
The extensive use of 'collect style' prayers in early Roman, Latin liturgy	17
The earliest instances of the 'collect style' of prayer in early Roman, Latin liturgy	19
Elements operative in this development	20

The First Presidential Prayer of the Ancient Roman Latin Mass: the 'Collect'	23
The place of the first presidential prayer in the liturgy	24
The overall shape of the oration.	25
The origin and function of the first Presidential prayer of the Mass: Four Theories	28
(a) *Collecta* as the *oratio ad collectam*	28
(b) The presidential oration as the conclusion of a litany	28
(c) The first presidential prayer serves to introduce the lessons	28
(d) The 'collect' as the conclusion of the entrance rites	31
(e) Summary	32
Conclusion	33
CHAPTER TWO. THE COLLECT IN THE MISSAL OF PAUL VI	35
Introduction	35
The Revision of the Roman Missal	36
The work of the *Consilium*	36
The principles and methods used in the revision of the Missal	38
(a) The style of Roman prayer	38
(b) The principles of revision	38
(c) The methods of revision	39
The Sundays of Ordinary Time in the Missal of Paul VI	41
Interpretative keys to the Missal: the General Instruction and the General Norms	41

	vii
The Feast of Sunday in the General Norms	43
The meaning of Ordinary Time in the General Norms	43
The Character, Place and Function of the Collect in the Mass	46
The nature of the Mass as a sacrifice	46
The role of the priest in the Mass according to the the General Instruction	49
The nature of the Eucharist as a public and communal act of worship according to the General Instruction	51
The collect as a 'presidential' prayer	53
The place of the collect in the Mass according to the General Instruction	55
The framework of the collect according to the General Instruction	57
The function of the collect	58
(a) The function of the silence	58
(b) The function of the collect oration	60
The function of the collect in the ancient Roman, Latin liturgy and in MR(1975): A comparison	65
Conclusion	67
The focus of our study	67
CHAPTER THREE. METHOD FOR THE STUDY OF THE COLLECTS	69
Introduction	69
Establishing the 'Text'	70

Preliminary considerations: the 34 collects for the Masses of Ordinary Time	70
The 'text' of the collect in the Missal of Paul VI	71
The original text	72
The history of the text	73
Establishing the 'best textual witness'	75
Summary	77
Establishing the Meaning of a Liturgical Text	77
The original historical and liturgical context of each prayer	78
(a) The original historical context	78
(b) The original liturgical context	78
(c) The limits of this approach	79
The structure of the prayer	79
The meaning of the prayer from an analysis of its vocabulary	81
(a) Liturgy as a priviliged locus	81
(b) The relationship of liturgical texts to the scriptures	82
(c) The integrity of liturgical traditions	82
(d) Factors governing the choice of examples	82
(e) Examples from outside liturgical and scriptural sources	83
(f) Research instruments	84
The impact of modifications made to the original prayer	84
The theology of the prayer	86
Resumé of the structure of each analysis	86
Summary	88

The Organization of the Analyses of the 34 Collects into Chapters	88
Conclusion	90

PART TWO

THE ANALYSES OF THE SUNDAY COLLECTS FOR ORDINARY TIME

CHAPTER FOUR. PRAYERS FROM THE *VERONENSIS*: THE COLLECTS FOR SUNDAYS IV, VIII, XVIII, XXIV, XXV, and XXXIII

	95
Introduction	95
The collect for Sunday IV	99
The collect for Sunday XXXIII	116
The collect for Sunday XXV	127
The collect for Sunday XVIII	148
The collect for Sunday VIII	179
The collect for Sunday XXIV	201

CHAPTER FIVE. PRAYERS FROM THE EASTERTIDE LITURGIES OF *REGINENSIS* 316: THE COLLECTS FOR SUNDAYS VI, X, XI, XII, XIV, XV, XXI, XXIII and XXIX

	219
Introduction	219
The collect for Sunday XXIII	223
The collect for Sunday XIV	236
The collect for Sunday XV	252
The collect for Sunday XXI	268

The collect for Sunday X	281
The collect for Sunday XXIX	294
The collect for Sunday XI	302
The collect for Sunday XII	311
The collect for Sunday VI	323

CHAPTER SIX. PRAYERS FROM THE MASSES FOR THE ORDINARY SUNDAYS THROUGHT OUT THE YEAR IN *REGINENSIS* 316: THE COLLECTS FOR SUNDAYS IX, XX, XXII, XXVI, XXVII, XXX, XXXI and XXXII   339

Introduction	339
The collect for Sunday XX	342
The collect for Sunday XXII	351
The collect for Sunday IX	366
The collect for Sunday XXVI	375
The collect for Sunday XXVII	387
The collect for Sunday XXXI	401
The collect for Sunday XXX	410
The collect for Sunday XXXII	420

CHAPTER SEVEN. PRAYERS FROM THE GREGORIAN SACRAMENTARIES: THE COLLECTS FOR WEEK I, THE SUNDAYS II, III, V, VII, XVII, XXVIII and WEEK XXXIV   437

Introduction	437
The collect for Sunday III	444

The collect for Week I	457
The collect for Sunday II	469
The collect for Sunday V	484
The collect for Sunday VII	498
The collect for Sunday XVII	511
The collect for Sunday XXVIII	536
The collect for Week XXXIV	543

CHAPTER EIGHT. PRAYERS FROM THE AMBROSIAN SOURCES: THE COLLECTS FOR SUNDAYS XIII, XVI and XIX 559

Introduction	559
The collect for Sunday XIX	569
The collect for Sunday XVI	587
The collect for Sunday XIII	599

PART THREE

THE RELATIONSHIP OF THE CHRISTIAN PEOPLE TO GOD

INTRODUCTION	617
CHAPTER NINE. THE THEOLOGY OF GOD	621
Introduction	621
The theology of the divine 'name'	621
(a) The primary expressions of God's Name	622
(b) Subsidiary titles	624

(c) The trinitarian structure of 'naming' God	625
(d) Summary	627
The divine attributes	627
(a) *Pietas*	628
(b) *Misericordia, miserari*	628
(c) *Fortitudo*	630
The work of God	630
(a) Creation, providence and government as complementary	630
(b) God's work of redemption	634
(c) God's fulfillment of his works in eternity	639
(d) Conclusion	640
Qualities of God's actions	640
(a) Abundant generosity	640
(b) Perfection in goodness	641
(c) Ordered and provident	642
Conclusion	642
CHAPTER TEN. THE CHRISTIAN LIFE IN GRACE	645
Introduction	645
The community of the church: a people of grace	646
(a) *Ecclesia*	646
(b) *Populus Dei*	647
(c) *Familia tua*	647
(d) *Famuli tui*	647
(e) *Filii*	648
(f) Those who make Christian profession	648
(g) Summary	649

The Christian life as a life of love and service of God expressed in worship	649
(a) Love and service	649
(b) Worship	650
The necessity of grace in the love and service of God	653
The impediment of sin	654
(a) The motivation of the prayers	654
(b) The description of sin and its effects	655
(c) The intensity of the struggle against sin	657
The portrayal of lived grace	657
(a) Following the divine precepts	657
(b) Good works	657
(c) What is humanly involved in doing good works	658
(d) Biblical images of life in grace	659
(e) Eschatological quality	660
(f) Summary	660
The relationship of the church to the world	661
(a) God's power and government over all creation	661
(b) The world, *mundus*	662
(c) The relationship between the church and the world	663
(d) Summary	664
Conclusion	664

CHAPTER ELEVEN. EVALUATION OF THE MISSAL OF PAUL VI.. 667

Introduction	667
The collation of the prayers as collects for the Sundays of Ordinary Time	667

The new context of the prayers in the
  Missal of Paul VI 667

A critique of the collects for the Sundays in
  Ordinary Time 670

    (a) The General Instruction of the Missal 671
    (b) Critique furnished from Dumas 673

Concluding remarks and proposals for
  further research 678

    (a) The original function of the first
    presidential prayer in early Roman Latin
    liturgy: some concluding remarks 678

    (b) The function of the collect in the
    Missal of Paul VI: some concluding
    remarks and proposals for further
    investigation 680

APPENDIX

  I   Collects for the Sundays in Ordinary Time
       in MR(1975) 683

  II   Collects for the Sundays in Ordinary Time:
       Original Source, and Position in MR(1570)
       and MR(1975) 689

  III   The *Cursus* in the Collects for Ordinary
       Time in MR(1975) 695

BIBLIOGRAPHY 705

INDEX ONE Vocabulary in the Collects for Ordinary Time   721

INDEX TWO Key Latin terms 727

INDEX THREE Scripture (Vulgate) references 731

LIST OF TABLES

Table

1.	The structure of each analysis	86
2.	The arrangement of the analyses into chapters	89
3.	The sources of the collects from the Gregorian Sacramentaries	441
4.	The sources of the prayers A 1019 - A 1023	514
5.	Sources of the Mass of which *H 894* is the collect	544
6.	Sources of the collect for Sunday XIX: *super sindonem* Triplex 1494	566
7.	Sources of the collect for Sunday XVI: Final prayer *Orationes in die secundo in laetanie*	567
8.	Sources of the collect for Sunday XIII: First prayer *Orationes in die tertio in laetanie*	568

LIST OF ABBREVIATIONS

A	The Sacramentary of Angoulême (Ed. P.Saint-Roch, <u>Liber Sacramentorum Engolismensis</u>)
Ariberto	The Sacramentary of Ariberto (Ed. A.Paredi, "Il Sacramentario di Ariberto")
Bergom	*Sacramentarium Bergomense* (Ed. A.Paredi, <u>Sacramentarium Bergomense</u>)
Biasca	The Sacramentary of Biasca (Ed. O.Heiming, <u>Das Ambrosianische Sakramentar von Biasca</u>)
Bruylants	P.Bruylants, <u>Les oraisons du Missel Romain</u>
DACL	<u>Dictionnaire d'Archéologie Chrétienne et de Liturgie</u> (Eds. F.Cabrol and H.Leclerq)
G	The Sacramentary of Gellone or the *Gellonensis* (Ed. A.Dumas, <u>Liber Sacramentorum Gellonensis</u>)
GIRM	General Instruction of the Roman Missal
H	*Hadrianum* (Ed. J.Deshusses, <u>Le Sacramentaire Grégorien</u>)
L	*Veronensis* (Ed. C.Mohlberg, <u>Sacramentarium Veronensis</u>)
LMS	The Mozarabic Sacramentary (Ed. M.Férotin, <u>Liber Mozarabicus sacramentorum</u>)
MP	Bruylants, <u>Les oraisons du Missel Romain</u> II.
MF	*Missale Francorum* (Ed. C.Mohlberg, <u>Missale Francorum</u>)
Milan	The Sacramentary of Milan (Ed. J.Frei, <u>Das Ambrosianische Sakramentar D 3-3</u>)
MR(1570)	The Missal of Pius V (<u>Missale Romanum ex decreto Sacrosancti Concilii Tridentini restitutum, Pii V iussu editum</u>)

MR(1975)	The Missal of Paul VI (*Missale Romanum Ex Decreto Sacrosancti Oecumenici Concilii Vaticani II Instauratum Auctoritate Pauli PP. VI Promulgatum*)
P	*Paduensis* (Ed. J.Deshusses, *Le Sacramentaire Grégorien*)
PL	Patrologia Latina (Ed. J.P.Migne)
S	The Sacramentary of St. Gall (Ed. C.Mohlberg, *Das fränkische Sacramentarium Gelasium*)
SC	*Sacrosanctum Concilium*
Sp	The Supplement to the Hadrianum (Ed. J.Deshusses, *Le Sacramentaire Grégorien*)
TDNT	*The Theological Dictionary to the New Testament* (Eds. G.Kittel, Vols 1-4; G.Friedrich, Vols. 5-9)
Triplex	*Sacramentarium Triplex* (Ed. O.Heiming, *Das Sacramentarium Triplex*)
V	*Reginensis* 316 or the Gelasian Sacramentary (Ed. C.Mohlberg, *Liber Sacramentorum Romanae Aeclesiae Ordinis Anni Circuli*)

COMMENDATORY PREFACE

In times of liturgical change, historical studies take on a new importance. They give us insight into our traditions in ways that help us both appreciate their riches and find some freedom in appropriating what they offer into different religious and cultural contexts.

One of the challenges of the contemporary liturgical renewal in Catholicism is that of finding good prayer forms. A first effort has been to translate the Latin heritage, a work that in some respects is not yet adequately finished. The second effort, hardly begun, is to compose new prayers. To be successful, both tasks require a good understanding of the tradition. Gerard Moore's study of the Collects for Sundays in Ordinary Time serves these purposes well.

Translations of liturgical prayer can be undertaken in too narrow a way, relying too much on dictionary definitions of terms. By studying the sources, and comparing the use of words in different contexts, Moore gives new appreciation of the meanings of both words and phrases in the original Latin texts, steeped as they are in the historical development of the Roman liturgy. He also draws attention to the rhetorical devices used in composing prayers, so that we understand better how the form of a prayer carries its meaning.

His study also helps in the composition of new prayers because it reveals the religious and cultural world in which prayer composition takes place. As the works shows, there is a theology of church encased in these prayers, which has to do with a people's relations to God, to the world around them, and to each other. There is a religiously cultural vision of God, the universe and society, as well as an ethical standard of living, embodied in the prayers. In many respects, their theology reveals a world in which we no longer live. However, in transposing into a new key for the composition of liturgical prayers we need to be aware that the whole universe of cultural and religious meaning comes to play in them, in a way that compares with the Roman world to which the prayers studied by Moore belong.

Moore's work is painstaking and careful in its examination of the prayers and of their sources. It is done with a keen attention to the variety of sources used, to literary forms, to the transposition of standard terms, and to liturgical, religious and cultural contexts. It is an exemplary study, of the kind of which we need many more in order to engage well in a grasp of our tradition and in the process of liturgical change and inculturation.

David N. Power, O.M.I.
Shakespeare Caldwell-Duval Distinguished Professor of Theology
The Catholic University of America
Washington, DC

COMMENDATORY PREFACE

Just as it was a privilege to be a reader for Dr. Gerard Moore's doctoral thesis here at The Catholic University of America, so it is a privilege to write this commendatory preface for its publication. In a world that often communicates by "sound bite" and which often is divided into ideological camps, it is a rare work that can be commended for its profound depth (while being eminently readable) and its prudent and judicious conclusions. Dr. Moore's work in the Sunday collects is both profound and prudent, as it is astute and (appropriately) ambitious. In addition to the contribution which it makes to a theological understanding of the collects presently prayed at Sunday Eucharist it also makes a contribution ot the evolution of liturgical method itself. Let me illustrate each of these.

In chapters one through three Dr. Moore appropriately summarizes and assesses what we know about and can assert regarding the theology of the collect as one kind of presidential prayer. Here he asserts what we can say for sure about this prayer and what needs to be left open in light of his meticulous and precise study of each collect, which study includes historical background, lexical adjustments the collect experienced through history leading to a consideration of its present text and meaning in the context of Sunday Eucharist. This Herculean task occupies chapters four through eight. His work here is, in my estimation, without parallel or peer in the English-speaking liturgical world. In addition, his contribution to the still evolving field of liturgical science in the way he utilizes historical sources (interpreting them in their proper socio-political and ecclesial contexts) and interprets them theologically for (the seemingly modest) conclusions in chapters nine through eleven is most significant. There are times when liturgical historians and liturgical theologians are pitted against each other, or at least when history and theology seem to clash when liturgical method is employed. Dr. Moore steers a moderating and imitable course here in the way both are utilized to give insight into what these prayers say about God, the church and the liturgy at which they are prayed. At the same time his work includes a most beneficial evaluation and critique of the present Missal. The brevity of this last chapter (eleven) should not be mistaken as a cursory job. In fact the work accomplished here offers some of the more important critiques of the present liturgical texts in general and makes a significant contribution to appreciating the theological value of the present reform. At the same time Dr. Moore sets our sights on ongoing liturgical reform of the rites now in use.

This is a hefty tome. The entire work deserves the careful study of liturgists, academicians and pastoral theologians. Parts One and Three are also highly recommended to all who engage in liturgical ministries as these chapters tell us clearly what we are doing when we engage in the act of Sunday Eucharist. I look forward to the application of the method used here to other projects both by Dr. Moore and those whom he teaches. He will be a wise mentor if he encourages others to use the method utilized here. He will also be a master teacher who leads his students both to use and to surpass him, that is to improve on the work in liturgical method so significantly undertaken here.

Rev. Dr. Kevin W. Irwin
The Catholic University of America

AUTHOR'S PREFACE

This study took shape as a doctoral dissertation in the Department of Theology, School of Religious Studies, Catholic University of America. It could not have been brought to fruition without the guidance, critical and scholarly comment, and availability of my director Dr. David N. Power, O.M.I.. Invaluable were the diligent reading and perceptive commentary provided by Dr Kevin W. Irwin and Dr Gerard Austin O.P.. The staff at Mullen Library, especially Bruce Miller and the team in the Theology/Philosophy Reserve, were particularly helpful and encouraging.

As the revitalization of the Roman liturgy gathers pace, our study of the texts themselves appears to be languishing. There is a certain inevitability about this. Liturgical method is undergoing thorough reappraisal. New areas of study are being explored around culture, sociology, participation, posture, dance, translation, and the form of rites, to name a few. Yet at the same time, critical editions of sacramentaries, prayers, blessings and the like, along with concordances, are now becoming available to the textual scholar. My hope is that, alongside these new fields, this work will contribute to our understanding of how orations function in the liturgy, the breadth of historical, theological and cultural riches they carry, and 'world' they name for us. Some prayers we will find comforting, others alien, still others transforming. The more clearly we understand the 'stones' upon which our liturgy is built, their form, function and heart, the more persuasively we can repolish, refine, or replace them, and the more boldly we can pray.

Gerard Moore sm
Thursday October 23, Twentyninth Week in Ordinary Time, 1997

INTRODUCTION

As part of the renewal of the liturgical books called for by the Second Vatican Council, the Roman Missal has undergone substantial revision. This has included a revision of the presidential prayers assigned to the priest. Given the central role of the Missal in the worship of the Church, especially as the *ecclesia* works to renew itself in response to the Council, these prayers merit comprehensive study.

In recent studies on these orations much attention has been given to the prefaces and eucharistic prayers[1], the prayers over the gifts[2], and to the postcommunion prayers[3], especially for Masses for the Proper of Seasons. By

---

[1] For example, E.Mazza, The Eucharistic Prayers of the Roman Rite, translated by M.J.O'Connell from the Italian Le Odierne Preghiere Eucharistiche, Bologna: Centro Editioriale Dehoniano, 1984 (New York: Pueblo Publishing Company, 1996); L.Soubigou, A Commentary on the Prefaces and the Eucharistic Prayers of the Roman Missal, translated by J.A.Otto from the French Les préfaces de la liturgie - étudiés, prêchées, méditées, I, II, Paris: P.Lethielleux (no year given) (Collegeville: The Liturgical Press, 1971); and A.Ward and C.Johnson, The Prefaces of the Roman Missal: a source compendium with concordance and indices (Roma: Tipografia Poliglotta Vaticana, 1989).

[2] See W.Haunerland, Die Eucharistie und ihre Wirkungen im Spiegel der Euchologie des Missale Romanum, Liturgiewissenschaftliche Quellen und Forschungen, Band 71 (Münster: Aschendorff, 1989); and J.Janicki, "Le orazioni 'super oblata' del ciclo 'de tempore' secundo il 'Missale Romanum' di Paolo VI," (diss., Pontifico Ateneo S. Anselmo, Roma, 1977).

[3] See See W.Haunerland, Die Eucharistie und ihre Wirkungen im Spiegel der Euchologie des Missale Romanum; and T.A.Krosnicki, Ancient Patterns in Modern Prayer, The Catholic University of America Studies in Christian Antiquity, No. 19 (Washington: The Catholic University of America Press, 1973).

contrast, little attention has been paid to the 34 collects allocated for the Sundays of Ordinary Time[4].

Many of the collects for Ordinary Time, like many of the prayers in the current Missal, are also found in its predecessor, the Roman Missal of Pius V. There are a number of studies and excursions on the prayers of that Missal, inclusive of those orations which have been incorporated into the Missal of Paul VI. These studies, however, are of varying usefulness. Some are scholarly[5], while others are primarily works of piety and devotion[6]. None of

---

[4]See A.M.Caron, "Eucharistic mystery: Spring of new Life. A study in Liturgical Theology," (Ph.D diss., Drew University, 1987); K.H.Hughes, "The Opening Prayers of 'The Sacramentary': A Structural Study of the Prayers of the Easter Cycle," (Ph.D. diss., University of Notre Dame, 1981); T.Manu, "Le thème de la vie dans l'euchologie du missel romain de Paul VI: Collectes, Prières sur les Offrandes, Postcommunions," (diss. Pontifico Ateneo S. Anselmo, Roma, 1977); J.Miazek, "La 'colletta' del 'proprio de tempore' nel 'Missale Romanum' di Paolo VI," (diss. Pontifico Ateneo S. Anselmo, Roma, 1977); J.Pascher, Die Orationen des Missale Romanum Papst Pauls VI, IV Teil, Im Jahreskreis (St Ottilien: EOS Verlag, 1983); and L.Weiss, "Die Orationen im Missale Romanum von 1970," (diss. Albert-Ludwigs-Universität, Freiburg, 1978).

[5]See L.Brou, Les oraisons de dimanches après la Pentecôte: Commentaire liturgique, Paroisse et Liturgie no. 38 (Bruges: Apostolat Liturgique Abbaye de Saint-André, 1959); M.Bruns, "The Language of the Roman Missal. Part I: Sunday and Ferial Masses of Advent," (Ph.D. diss., St Louis University, 1947); "Commentaire des collectes dominicales du missel romain," in Travaux liturgiques, I (Louvain: Abbaye du Mont César, 1955), 199-266; F.M.Gerdes, "The Language of the Roman Missal. Part III: Second Sunday after Epiphany to Quinquagesima Sunday," (Ph.D. diss., St Louis University, 1968); M.Haessly, Rhetoric in the Sunday Collects of the Roman Missal: With Introduction, Text, Commentary and Translation (St Louis: Manufacturers Printery, 1938); P.Schorlemmer, Die Kollektengebete mit Texte, Übersetzung und einem Glossar (Gütersloh: Bertelsmann, 1928); M.Sweeney, "The Language of the Roman Missal. Part IV: The Sunday Masses of Lent," (Ph.D. diss., St Louis University, 1969); J.White "The Language of the Roman Missal Part II: Masses of the Christmas Season," (Ph.D. diss., St Louis University, 1951).

them, however, is without some insight. Because a vast number of traditional Roman prayers were incorporated into the worship books of the Church of England, studies of some of the collects with which we are concerned are to be found in Anglican worship commentaries[7].

Despite the existence of these various commentaries on some of the prayers, there is need for a new study. The orations now have been given a new context within the Missal of Paul VI itself, which has bearing on their meaning. Recent scholarship has produced an array of critical editions of the ancient liturgical texts, accompanied by comprehensive concordances, enabling a further, more textually sure level of investigation than was possible earlier. The development of liturgical theology has called forth the need for a theology that is expressive of the content of the prayers, while respectful of their genre precisely as prayers.

This study, in focussing on the collects for the Sundays of Ordinary Time, will attempt to ascertain their liturgical theology of the relation of the Christian people to God. This relationship, in fact, appears to be one of the central concerns reflected in these orations.

---

[6] See M.A.Chapman, The Prayer of Faith: Brief sermon outlines for the Sundays of the Year, on the orations or collects of the Mass (London: B.Herder Book Co., 1928); M.Haessly, Reflections on the Sunday Collects of the Roman Missal (St Meinrad: A Grail Publication, 1947); and C.C.Martindale, The Prayers of the Missal I: The Sunday Collects (New York: Sheed and Ward, 1937).

[7] See E.M.Goulburn, The Collects of the Day: An Exposition Critical and Devotional of the Collects appointed at the Communion, Vol II (New York: E.& J.B.Young & Company, 1881). For a study of collects in current Anglican liturgy see M.R.Dudley, The Collect in Anglican Liturgy: Texts and Sources 1549-1989, Alcuin Club Collection (Collegeville: The Liturgical Press, 1994).

The structure of the work:

Our study has been divided into three parts. Part I is on the nature of the collect and on the method to be used in its study. It has three chapters. The first deals with the origins, shape and role, in early Roman liturgy, of the prayer that is now referred to as the collect. Chapter two examines the shape and function of the collect as interpreted by the Missal of Paul VI. Chapter three contains a discussion of the method utilized in the analysis of each of the 34 collects, and the rationale for their compilation into separate chapters.

Part II consists of the studies of each of the 34 individual collects for the Sundays of Ordinary Time. These analyses have been allocated into five chapters, primarily determined according to the earliest liturgical source in which the prayers are to be found. Each chapter is prefaced by a brief introduction offering a description of the original liturgical source, and commenting on any particular features to which attention needs to be drawn.

A comprehensive presentation of the relation of the Christian people to God as this emerges from the study of the collects is taken up directly in Part III. This section of the dissertation opens with an Introduction that sets forth an analysis of the understanding of worship contained in the prayers, and its implications for presenting the theology of grace therein. Chapters nine and ten are concerned with developing a liturgical theology of the relationship of the people to God expressive of the content of the prayers, relating this to their genre precisely as public prayers and acts of worship. The final chapter of the dissertation contains an evaluation of the Missal, offers a critique of how the relation of the Christian people to God is expressed in the collects, and comments on further questions opened by our examination of the orations.

A number of appendices and an index have been incorporated into the back of the dissertation. It is the author's hope that they will be of service to the reader, and act as a stimulant to further research.

Two points warrant notice in this introduction. One is the discrepancies in Latin spelling across the critical editions of the early liturgical sources, the

Latin Vulgate bible, and the *editio typica* of the Missal of Paul VI. The rule applied throughout this study has been to remain faithful to the spelling and the text, even when corrupt, as found in the critical edition of that text. Where necessary, important textual variations are adverted to in a footnote.

The second is the use of inclusive language when reference is made to God. While this may be desirable for a range of reasons, the sheer weight of references to God, divine actions and attributes in the prayers proved to be overwhelming, making any attempt at avoiding the use of masculine pronouns for God seem too artificial and contrived. The reader, then, will encounter throughout the text references to God using masculine pronouns and pronominal adjectives.

PART ONE
HISTORICAL AND METHODOLOGICAL PRINCIPLES

CHAPTER ONE
'COLLECT STYLE' ORATIONS AND THE FIRST PRESIDENTIAL PRAYER OF THE MASS IN EARLY ROMAN LATIN EUCHOLOGY

INTRODUCTION

The first presidential prayer of the Masses in the Missal of Paul VI is called the collect (*collecta*)[1]. It is the product of a distinctive genre of Christian prayer that first appeared in fifth century Rome. On establishing itself as a central feature of Roman worship, this form of prayer has maintained to the present a preeminent position in western euchology. The genre has come to be known as the 'collect style' of prayer. At the same time, the term 'collect' has come to specify one particular example of this genre, the presidential prayer that precedes the lessons of the Mass. The word *collecta*, however, does not regularly occur in early latin Roman texts, where *oratio* is more common.

This chapter has two tasks. In the first instance it will examine the names, structure, rhetorical style, use and origins of the 'collect style' of oration. The second part of the chapter has as its particular focus the first presidential prayer of the Mass in early Roman latin euchology. This section will consist of an analysis of the place of the collect in the Mass, its structure, origin and function.

---

[1] MR(1975) Institutio Generalis Missalis Romani, § 10, § 32.

Much of the material below is dependent on two earlier studies, one by G.G.Willis[2] and the other by K.Hughes[3], which set out in some detail the state of the question concerning the origins, function and structure of the collect of the Roman Mass.

THE 'COLLECT STYLE' ORATION OF THE ROMAN LITURGY

Name and Function of the 'collect style' prayer:

The 'collect style' of prayer takes its name from Gallican usage. Capelle has pointed out that *collectio* is used in Gallican books such as the Missale Gothicum, the Bobbio Missal and the Sacramentary of Autun as a technical term to designate the variable prayers in the Mass and Office[4]. He further shows that a host of writers, from Cassian (360-436) to Walafrid Strabo (c.808-849) offer common witness to the function of the collect[5]. According to the testimony of these ancient authors, the collect is a prayer made by the priest on behalf of the community, which, coming at the end of a litany, psalm, or short period of silent prayer, serves to sum up (*colligere*) the

---

[2]G.G.Willis, "The Variable Prayer of the Roman Mass," in Further Essays in Early Roman Liturgy, Alcuin Club 50, (London: SPCK, 1968), 91-131. He maintains much the same positions in a later work published after his death, G.G.Willis, A History of the Early Roman Liturgy to the Death of Pope Gregory the Great, Henry Bradshaw Society, Subsidia 1 (London: The Boydell Press, 1994), 61-77.

[3]K.H.Hughes, "The Opening Prayers of 'The Sacramentary': A Structural Study of the Prayers of the Easter Cycle" (Ph.D diss., University of Notre Dame, 1981). The first chapter of Hughes' dissertation, which itself has much in common with Willis, discusses the origin of the various 'collect style' prayers, as well as the names, functions, structure, style and content of the collect of the Mass.

[4]B.Capelle, "Collecta," Travaux liturgiques de doctrine et d'histoire, II (Louvain: Abbaye du Mont César, 1962), 195.

[5]Ibid, 196.

petitions which the people have made. Its essential nature is that of petition. First the term *collectio* and then, later, the present term *collecta*, were derived from this usage of the verb *colligere*.

The equivalent term in Roman usage came to be the noun *oratio*[6], a word which appears to be derived from the priest's invitation to the community to pray collectively, *oremus*[7]. *Oratio* was still used as a designation of the opening collect in the Missal of Pius V.

A second, Roman, origin of the term *collecta* is found in the writings of Bernhold of Constance (c.1050-1100). After giving the above meaning of *collecta*, he adds a second, less definitive (*videntur*) view. The excerpt is from *Cap.III, De prima in missa oratione* of his *Micrologus*:

> *Sequitur oratio quam collectam dicunt, eo quod sacerdos, qui legatione fungitur pro populo ad Dominum (II Cor, V), omnium petitiones ea oratione colligat atque concludat. Illae tamen orationes specialius collectae vocari videntur quae, apud Romanos, super collectam populi fiunt, dum colligitur ut procedat de una ecclesia in aliam, ad stationem faciendam*[8].

---

[6]For a summary of the prayer designations used in Rome see Willis, "The Variable Prayers," 103-105.

[7]There has been some question over the origin of the term *oratio*. Its derivation from *oremus* is espoused by C.Mohrmann. She disputes the claim by Jungmann that the designation of the prayer as an *oratio* indicates that the prayer has, to a certain extent, the character of classical Roman public discourse (*oratio*). She does not dispute, however, that the orations are written according to a definite formal, rhetorical style. See C.Mohrmann, <u>Liturgical Latin: Its Origins and Character</u> (Washington DC: The Catholic University of America Press, 1957), 74. For Jungmann's position see J.A.Jungmann, <u>The Mass of the Roman Rite: Its Origins and Development (Missarum Sollemnia)</u> I, trans. F.Brunner from <u>Missarum Sollemnia</u>, Vienna: Herder Verlag, 1949, German Revised Edition, 1949 (Westminister MD: Christian Classics Inc., 1992), 360.

[8]The prayer which follows is called the collect because the priest, who by delegation is the representative of the people before God, in that oration collects and brings to conclusion the petitions of all. Nevertheless, those prayers which seem more properly to be called collects, according to the

In the second etymological account, *collecta* stands for the *plebs collecta*, gathered to set off in procession to the stational church. The sense of *collecta* here is not that of a prayer which takes up and concludes the prayer of all, but of a prayer over those gathered[9]. Capelle has shown that the weight of evidence points clearly to the first of Bernhold's two derivations as the most probable origin of the present day term 'collect'[10].

However, Bernhold's speculation is also of value. While it does not indicate the origins of the term, it is a pointer to the variety of functions that one prayer could come to fulfill. Once a prayer was introduced, it could carry several meanings, not all of which flow organically from its original purpose. It is possible, then, that the term *collecta* denoted two primary functions. The sense of *collecta* as derived from *colligere* points to the prayer's function in gathering and concluding the petition of the assembly. This is a feature common to all 'collect style' prayers. The sense of *collecta* as *plebs collecta* indicates that the prayer served to gather and unite those assembled into a single worshipping community. This sense would be especially applicable to the opening presidential prayer of the Mass. These considerations will be taken up below in the discussion of the function of the collect in the Roman Mass.

Romans, are made over the gathering of the people when it gathers so that it may proceed from one church to another, in order to carry out the stational liturgy.
Bernhold of Constance, Micrologus de Ecclesiasticis Observationibus, PL 151, 979.

Bernhold goes on to give the example of the collect over the people gathered at the church of St. Anastasia before they depart for the stational liturgy to be held at the church of St. Sabina. See the *Hadrianum* 35, Feria IIII, (H 153). The liturgy is that of the opening day of the lenten fast.

[9] This view has had the support of such commentators as Bona, Mabillon, Duchesne and Batiffol. See Capelle, "Collecta," 192-193.

[10] Capelle, "Collecta," 198-199.

The structure of the 'collect style' prayer:

The 'collect style' prayer has a quite simple and almost austere structure and style[11]. Yet the prayer form is capable of enormous flexibility.

Most commonly the prayers contain an (a) address to God[12], (b) a motivating clause which refers to some attribute or saving act of God or recalls some aspect of human existence, (c) a petition, and (d) a purpose clause[13]. The opening prayer for Sunday XXVI in the Missal of Paul VI (originally V 1198) provides a good illustration of this format:

(a) ADDRESS TO GOD: *Deus,*

(b) MOTIVATING CLAUSE: *qui omnipotentiam tuam parcendo maxime et miserando manifestas,*

---

[11] The 'collect style' prayer is not the only form of prayer in the Roman Mass. Other distinctive styles are evident in the Roman Canon, the prefaces and various poetic elements in the liturgy. For consideration of these prayer forms see Mohrmann, Liturgical Latin, 62-73, 77-82. See also by the same author "Le latin liturgique," La Maison-Dieu, (1950/23): 1-30, especially 16-28.

[12] Almost invariably the early Roman, Latin orations are addressed to the first person of the Trinity. See Jungmann, The Mass of the Roman Rite I, 379-380; and also his The Place of Christ in Liturgical Prayer, trans. A. Peeler from Stellung Christi im liturgischen Gebet, Münster: Aschendorff, 1925, 2nd German Edition revised 1962 (Staten Island N.Y.: Alba House, 1965), 105-123.

[13] There is substantial agreement on what constitutes the structure of the 'collect style' prayers, though different authors prefer different terminologies. See the discussion of the various schema of the structure of the orations in Hughes, "The Opening Prayers of 'The Sacramentary'," 30-40. Hughes herself shows a preference for the schema developed by Haessly. See M. Haessly, Rhetoric in the Sunday Collects of the Roman Missal, (St Louis: Manufacturers Printery, 1938), 13-17. The schema adopted in this study is closest to that described in some detail in Willis, "The Variable Prayers of the Roman Mass," 118-119, and subseqently neatly summarized in Willis, A History of Early Roman Liturgy, 65.

(c) PETITION: *multiplica super nos gratiam tuam,*

(d) PURPOSE CLAUSE: *ut ad tua promissa currentes, caelestium bonorum facias esse consortes.*

There are variations to this basic framework. The motivating clause is not always retained, as in the opening prayer for Sunday XVIII in the Missal of Paul VI (originally L 887). This prayer also contains a double petition *adesto ... largire,* a double purpose clause, and a description of the community:

(a) ADDRESS: *domine,*

(b) 1ST PETITION: *Adesto famulis tuis,*

    MAIN PETITION: *et   perpetuam benignitatem largire poscentibus*

(c) PURPOSE: *ut his ...*
et grata restaures,
et restaurata conserves,

(d) DESCRIPTION: *qui auctore te gubernatore gloriantur.*

In other orations the petition stands without a consequent purpose clause. This can be seen in the opening prayer for Sunday IV in the Missal of Paul VI (originally L 432). This prayer also has two petitions and lacks a motivating clause:

(a) ADDRESS: *Domine Deus noster*

(b) PETITION: *concede nobis ... ut*
tota mente veneremur,
et omnes homines rationabili
diligamus affectu.

The ordering of the structural elements is also variable. In the opening prayer for Sunday XII (originally V 586), the motivating clause, *quia numquam ...*, follows the petition, *sancti nominis tui ...*, while the address, *Domine*, is positioned within the petition. The prayer can be set out as follows:

(a) PETITION: *Sancti nominis tui, (Domine) timorem pariter et amorem fac nos habere perpetuum,*

(b) ADDRESS: *Domine*

(c) MOTIVATION: *quia numquam tua gubernatione destituis, quos in soliditate tuae dilectionis instituis.*

In his examination of the structure of the 'collect style' prayers, Jungmann concluded that those prayers with motivating clauses and purpose clauses were an amplification of a simpler, more original form containing only an address and petition[14]. Mohrmann, however, offers a different view[15]. She points to an earlier study of pagan, Roman prayers by Rheinfelder[16], in which he shows that the motivating clause was a standard feature of such prayers. In this view, the simpler format is a modification of the more complex, original structure. Rheinfelder's study opens the way to two further conclusions. Firstly, a predecessor of the Roman, latin, Christian 'collect style' prayer is Roman pagan prayer. Secondly, this style of prayer has a typical Roman character and appeal[17].

---

[14]Jungmann, The Mass of the Roman Rite I, 374-375.

[15]Mohrmann, Liturgical Latin, 75-77.

[16]H.Rheinfelder, "Zum Stil der lateinischen Orationem," Jahrbuch für Liturgiewissenschaft 11 (1931): 20-34.

[17]Mohrmann holds the view that prayers which consist of an address and relative clause are typical of general human prayer: "In my opinion, however, we are here concerned with a very widespread, almost general, human euchological form which is to be found, among other places, in the Greek epic" (Liturgical Latin, 76).

The style of the 'collect style' prayer:

The 'collect style' orations not only had a certain shape but were written in a particular style. They are precise, concise, sober prayers, devoid of overly exuberant, emotive or ostentatious elements. The prayers are replete with stylistic elements from the rhetorical traditions of Rome. Mohrmann makes the point thus:

> In the close-knit, well-composed phrases of the Roman Orations, in which the celebrant resumes, as it were, the prayer of the faithful, we find traces of the style processes of the art of polished speech, taught and practiced for centuries in the schools of Rome.[18]

In particular, the 'collect style' orations were written in accordance with the rules of the Roman rhetorical device known as the *cursus*[19]. By arranging the accents in the last syllables of a literary unit or clause according to a fixed set of rules (the *cursus*), the prayer took on a certain rhythm and harmony. This thoroughly and distinctly Roman style is a central feature of the 'collect style' prayers. The chief forms of Roman *cursus* operative in the present opening prayers for Ordinary Time in the Missal of Paul VI are laid out in Appendix III, entitled "The *cursus* in the Collects for Ordinary Time in MR(1975)."

---

[18] Mohrmann, Liturgical Latin, 75. See also the description offered by T.Klauser, A Short History of the Western Liturgy, trans. J.Halliburton from Kleine abendländische Liturgiegeschichte: Bericht und Besinnung, Bonn: Peter Hanstein Verlag, 5th German edition, 1965 (New York: Oxford University Press, 1969), 40. For a study of the rhetorical elements in the opening prayers of the Missal of Pius V, see Haessly, Rhetoric in the Sunday Collects of the Roman Missal.

[19] For a summary description of the three chief forms of cadences in the Roman *cursus* see Jungmann, The Mass of the Roman Rite I, 376-377. See also Hughes, "The Opening Prayers of 'The Sacramentary'," 42-43. For a more complete study of the *cursus* in litugical texts see E.Vacandard, "Le cursus: son origine, son histoire, son emploi dans la liturgie," Revue des questions historiques 78 (1905): 59-102; and H.Leclerq, "Cursus," DACL III, 3193-3205.

The extensive use of 'collect style' prayers in early Roman, Latin liturgy:

The earliest extant collections and books of the Roman latin liturgy already reveal the 'collect style' of prayer in full flower. In these texts the prayer form is fully developed in terms of structure and rhetorical style. As such, it is utilized in a variety of contexts in the liturgy. The two earliest extant collections of latin, Roman Mass prayers, the sixth century *Veronensis*[20] and the seventh century *Reginensis* 316[21] contain a wealth of different 'collect style' prayers for each Mass: collects, *orationes super sindonem*, *super oblata*, postcommunion prayers, and prayers *super populum*. Similar prayers are also provided for the Office[22]. 'Collect style' orations are utilized to precede both

---

[20]L.C.Mohlberg, L.Eizenhöfer, and P.Siffrin, ed. Sacramentarium Veronense, Rerum Ecclesiasticarum Documenta, Series Maior, Fontes I (Roma: Casa Editrice Herder, 1956). For a brief review of this text see the Introduction to Chapter Four, 115.

[21]L.C.Mohlberg, L.Eizenhöfer and P.Siffrin, ed. Liber Sacramentorum Romanae Aeclesiae Ordinis Anni Circuli (Cod. Vat. Reg. 316), Rerum Ecclesiasticarum Documenta, Series Maior, Fontes IV (Roma: Casa Editrice Herder, 1960). For a brief review of this text see the Introduction to Chapter Five, 274.

[22]For example see the collection in the *Veronensis* entitled XVIII,xxxi *Orationes matutinas uel ad vesperum* (L 587 - L 590) and the set in *Reginensis* 316 entitled I,lvi *Incipiunt orationes paschales uespertinales* (V 516 - V 540).
These orations appear to have a different place in the office from the so called 'psalm prayers', prayers which were said at the conclusion of each psalm in the Office. For early latin examples of psalm prayers see A.Wilmart, The Psalter Collects: From V-VIth Century Sources (Three Series), The Henry Bradshaw Society, No 83, edited by L.Brou (London: 1949). For further commentary see C.Mohrmann, "A Propos des collectes du psautier," Vigiliae Christianae 6 (1952):1-19.
Two marks which serve to distinguish the psalm prayers (also referred to as 'collects') from the 'collect style' orations we are describing are the clear allusion in the psalm prayer to the psalm it concludes and the general absence of the *cursus* from some whole series of the prayers. On the other hand, the liturgical function of these prayers is much the same as that of 'collect style' prayers in the ancient sacramentaries. These psalm prayers are prayers of petition said by the president of the liturgical assembly and offered after the

the *Reginensis* 316 Easter Vigil readings (I,xliii, V 431) and Pentecost Vigil readings (I,lxxvii, V 618)[23]. As well, in that sacramentary each Vigil reading is concluded with a 'collect style' prayer (Easter V 432 - V 442, Pentecost V 619 - V 622). The prayers which come after each reading usually contain an allusion to that reading, as seen in 'psalm prayers'. The same 'collect style' of prayer acts as a conclusion to each petition in the *Reginensis* 316 Good Friday liturgy (*Reg.* 316, I,xli, V 401, V 403, V 405 ... V 417).

Furthermore, individual prayers also show themselves to be remarkably adaptable to differing liturgical contexts, as shown by the way they are constantly redeployed in different situations. Whereas the collect prayers for the Vigils of Easter and Pentecost, and for the Good Friday petitions, are rarely, if ever, used outside those very specific contexts, the same conservatism is not found with regard to the Mass and Office collects. As will be shown below, across various Roman liturgical sources, the same prayer can be found as an opening prayer or as a *super sindonem*, as an Office prayer or an oration *super oblata*, as a prayer *super populum* or as an opening prayer, as a *super sindonem* or as a postcommunion[24].

---

recitation of each psalm. In this the psalm prayer brings together and concludes the prayer of the assembly.

[23]The custom of a collect before the readings for the Good Friday, the Easter Vigil and the Vigil of Pentecost appears to have been a characteristic of the presbyteral, rather than the papal liturgy. Such a prayer is not attested to in descriptions of the corresponding papal ceremonies. See A.Chavasse, Le Sacramentaire Gélasien (Vaticanus Reginensis 316): Sacramentaire presbytéral en usage dans les titres romains au VIIe siècle (Tournai: Desclée & Cie, 1958), 92, 106. Note however that the Ember Day vigils in *Reginensis* 316 (I,xix, I,lxxxiii, II,lx, II,lxxxv), the *Hadrianum* (44, 117, 166, 191) and the *Paduensis* (XL, CVIII, CLXVIII, CCI) all contain an opening collect. See the tables drawn up by Chavasse in Le Sacramentaire Gélasien, 110-111.

[24]See below, 674.

The versatility and flexibility of the 'collect style' prayer is clear. While maintaining a set framework and style, the prayer was capable of being structured in a variety of ways, and was seen as fitting to be utilized in a range of liturgical contexts.

The earliest instances of the 'collect style' of prayer in early Roman, Latin liturgy:

The Roman 'collect style' oration first appears quite late in the development of Christian liturgy. The opening presidential oration of the Mass is not attested to before the middle of the fifth century[25]. There is a degree of evidence that St Leo (pope 440-461) was composing 'collect style' prayers to serve as variable orations for particular Masses[26]. Certainly by the close of the fifth century Pope Gelasius (492-496) composed complete Masses whose opening prayer, *super sindonem*, prayer over the gifts, postcommunion and *super populum* were all written in 'collect style'[27].

The very nature of the *Veronensis* as a sixth century collection of earlier, disparate *libelli* points to both the creation of new 'collect style' prayers for each liturgy, and to a desire to compile them for reference or reuse[28]. Such compiling may also be a reflection of the status of the author and the superior quality of the prayers. A number of orations in the

---

[25] See Willis, "The Variable Prayers of the Roman Mass," 112-116.

[26] Hughes, "The Opening Prayers of 'The Sacramentary'," 13-16.

[27] These Masses also included a preface. For a study of the Masses of Pope Gelasius, see G.Pomarès, Gélase Iᵉʳ: Lettre contres les lupercales et dix-huit messes du sacramentaire Léonien, introduction, texte critique, traduction et notes de G.Pomarès, Sources Chrétiennes 65 (Paris: Les Éditions du Cerf, 1959).

[28] For example in the *Veronensis* there are nine Masses for Christmas, fourteen for the feast of St Laurence, and twenty eight for the feast of Sts. Peter and Paul. See Willis, "The Variable Prayers of the Roman Mass," 93.

Veronensis collection are found in the slightly later presbyteral sacramentary *Reginensis* 316. The existence of such a working sacramentary in the seventh century already indicates a movement away from the creation of fresh prayers for each liturgy, a preference for well styled prayer formulae, and a willingness to use well written prayers in diverse liturgical contexts[29].

These two sacramentaries, then, witness to the fact that between the mid-fifth century and the time of Pope Gelasius a remarkable feat of liturgical adaptation and inculturation had been brought to a rich conclusion. During that period the Roman liturgy was embellished by the inclusion of variable presidential prayers set into the structure of the Mass. A vast number of these prayers, composed in classical Roman rhetorical style, were of such stylistic and theological quality that they were written down, copied, collected, and reused.

Elements operative in this development:

The exact impetus which, in the fifth century, gave rise to the variable prayers of the Roman Mass, written in this particular 'collect style', remains unknown. However a number of factors emerge as influential in the development of this style of prayer.

Perhaps the first, though very general, factor is the Roman church's response to the new freedom and public status it gained with the promulgation of the Edict of Milan (313). One of the effects of Constantine's decree was the gradual elaboration and development of the liturgy. Christian worship in

---

[29] It seems that not all presiders were equally adept at coping with the demands of composing prayers afresh for each liturgy. Hughes lists a series of citations from Augustine and various late fourth and early fifth century African Synods dealing with both the inadequacies in freely composed prayers, as well as the corrective measure of compiling standard collections of texts. See Hughes, "The Opening Prayers of 'The Sacramentary'," 8-10.

Rome became an open, public event, which eventually displaced the pagan cult as the official worship of the city itself[30].

A second effect of the Edict, again gradual in its implementation, was that the decrease in power of the Roman pagan cult left Christians free to reappraise the value of elements of Roman tradition, religious language and rhetoric. Previously these traditions had been in direct competition with Christianity, and so were seen to be dangerously laden with pagan connotations. With the decline of paganism, Christians were more able to reappropriate into their worship various features of Roman tradition and rhetoric[31]. The introduction into the Mass of variable, 'collect style' prayers such as the opening prayer, *super sindonem, super oblata,* postcommunion, and *super populum* took place as part of the response of Roman Christians to this changed situation.

At the same time Christian authors had been turning their attention to the question of the sense and function in Christian writings of the stylistic traditions of classical Roman literature[32]. According to Lactantius, a polished

---

[30] Jungmann comments that in the course of the fifth and sixth centuries, a time of continuous upheaval and calamity in Rome, Roman worship actually grew in splendour. He attributes this to the fact that the papacy and the church were the one only remaining glory of that once dominant city. See Jungmann, The Mass of the Roman Rite I, 59.

[31] For a study of the ready adoption by Christians of elements of classical Roman rhetoric and literary style, especially elements traditionally found in Roman pagan prayer, see the article by Mohrmann on the stylistic qualities of the Roman Canon. She further observes that, whereas the Romans freely utilized pagan styles of prayer, they were more reserved towards the introduction of the vocabulary typically found in pagan orations. See Mohrmann, "Quelques observations sur l'évolution stylistique du canon de la Messe romain," Vigiliae Christianae 4 (1950): 1-19. A parallel process is evident in the adoption by church dignitaries of the ceremonial dress and accoutrements of the Roman court. See Klauser, A Short History of the Western Liturgy, 32-37.

[32] For the following discussion see Mohrmann, Liturgical Latin, 46-59.

traditional style could be of service in the conversion of intellectuals to the faith. However, for Hilary of Poitiers elegance of style has rich theological connotations in that it showed God reverence and honour. Mohrmann points out that fifth century Christians were quite at home with the use of highly stylized language in prayer[33]. Though such language could not be easily understood[34], it was felt to ably reflect the sacral style deemed to be appropriate for divine worship.

The import of the linguistic shift in Rome from Greek as the liturgical language to the predominance of Latin must be taken into consideration. Though both languages may have been in use in Rome for some time, the definitive shift to Latin as the official liturgical language seems to have taken place by the end of the fourth century[35]. With the change from Greek came the further possibility of developing new prayers and forms of prayer appropriate to the structures, style and religious traditions of the belatedly adopted language.

---

[33]Ibid., 60-61.

[34]This point should not be overemphasized. While modern post Reformation sensibilities place much emphasis on hearing and understanding each word, this was not necessarily a major concern of earlier Christians. On the other hand, it should not be too quickly concluded that the early prayers were unintelligible. The presence of the *cursus* in the oration means that certain expressions and endings would have clearly rung in the minds (and hearts) of the hearers. Clearly those orations written for special circumstances, such as those composed by Gelasius against the celebration of the Lupercalia by Christians (see the study of the collect for Sunday IV, originally L 432, below, 121), would have been somewhat pointless if their meaning was unintelligible to the assembly. A final consideration is that the collect, as the prayer which took up and gathered the petitions of those present, functioned in and with the prayers of the whole assembly. The faithful did not need to fully understand the presidential oration to know that their prayers were being brought to conclusion and placed before God.

[35]Mohrmann dates the transition period between 360 and 382. See Mohrmann, Liturgical Latin, 50. See also Willis, The Development of the Roman Mass, 21-22.

In summary, the end of the fifth century in Rome already saw a profusion of 'collect style' orations, along with their complete integration into the structure of the Mass in the newly developed, variable prayers. While no single cause has been put forward to explain this development, a number of factors have been identified as playing a part. The development of the Christian liturgy as it became both public and official worship, the Christian appreciation of classical rhetorical style, the shift from Greek to Latin as the language of Roman liturgy, and the traditional freedom of presiders to compose prayers all contributed to some degree. Furthermore, the emergence of able composers such as Gelasius, the compilation of superior texts into standard reference collections, and the willingness to reuse well composed prayers, ensured that a copious number of 'collect style' prayers were written, preserved and continuously used.

The somewhat abrupt, yet abundant, emergence of the 'collect style' prayer is then the fruit of a longer period of adaptation and inculturation. The Roman liturgy was reworked and reshaped to include a whole series of variable presidential prayers for each Mass. Among these the 'collect style' orations were written in the rhetorical conventions of classical, Roman literature. These prayers were quickly accepted, prized and compiled. In this way they became the norm for subsequent variable presidential prayers in Western euchology.

THE FIRST PRESIDENTIAL PRAYER OF THE ANCIENT ROMAN LATIN MASS: THE 'COLLECT'

Our study is concerned with only one of these variable, 'collect style' orations, the first presidential prayer of the Mass. This prayer, however, has become so representational of the genre that it is now generally known simply as the 'collect'.

The place of the first presidential prayer in the liturgy:

The first presidential prayer of the Mass immediately preceded the readings. This can be seen in the Order of the Mass set out in the opening pages of the *Hadrianum*. There the Mass is described as beginning with an introit, followed by the *Kyrie*. Next came the *Gloria* if appropriate. This was followed by the *oratio*, which we call the collect, which was in turn followed by the first reading[36].

A second witness to the existence of this prayer in the Mass is found in *Ordo* I, which contains directions for the celebration of the papal Mass as was the custom around the year 700[37]. Following an extensive description of the Pope's arrival, preparations, the entrance procession, and the *Kyrie* litany, the text continues:

> *Quando vero [laetaniae] finierint, dirigens se pontifex contra populum incipit <u>Gloria in excelsis Deo</u>. Et statim regerat se ad orientem usquedum finiatur. Post hoc dirigens se iterum ad populum dicens: <u>Pax vobis</u>, et regerans se ad orientem dicit: <u>Oremus</u>, et sequitur oratio. Post finitam sedit. Similiter episcopi vel presbiteri sedent*[38].

---

[36] *Hoc est inprimis introitum qualis fuerit statutis temporibus siue diebus festis seu cottidianis, deinde kyriae eleison. Item dicitur gloria in excelsis deo, si episcopus fuerit, tantummodo die dominico, siue diebus festis; a praesbyteris autem minime dicitur nisi solo in pascha. Quando uero laetania agitur neque gloria in excelsis deo neque alleluia canitur. Postmodum dicitur oratio, deinde sequitur apostolum. Item gradalem seu alleluia. Postmodum legitur euanglium ....* (1, *Qualiter Missa Romana caelebratur*, H 2).

[37] See M.Andrieu, <u>Les Ordines romani du haut moyen âge</u> 2: Les textes (Ordines I-XIII), Spicilegium Sacrum Lovaniense 23 (Louvain, 1948/60), 65-108. For a summary of the *Ordo*, along with some commentary, see Klauser, <u>A Short History of the Western Liturgy</u>, 60-70.

[38] When [the litany] will have finished, the Pope, turning towards the people, begins the *Gloria*. He at once turns back to the east until the *Gloria* is finished. After this he once more faces the assembly, saying: "Peace be with you," then again facing the east says: "Let us pray." The oration follows. After it is finished he sits. At that time the bishops and presbyters also sit (*Ordo* I, 53).

The ministers do not sit, however, until the faithful have made their response in the form of an *Amen*[39].

Two things are especially worthy of note in this description. Firstly, the oration is followed by a change of posture. This is an indication that one phase of the liturgy has been brought to a close, and that another is about to begin[40]. The opening presidential prayer, then, serves to bring to a conclusion, if not to a climax as well, the entrance rite. Secondly, there is no mention of the silence between the call to prayer, *oremus*, and the presidential prayer. This may indicate that the silence had already been dropped at papal Masses, perhaps to help shorten the service.

These rubrics, then, are a further pointer to the function of this oration. Here it appears to serve as the prayer which concludes the act of assembling the community. As a single community, ministers and people, they are united in prayer in the first presidential oration of the liturgy.

The first presidential prayer of the ceremony, the first occasion on which the president prayed on behalf of the gathered community, served as the climax and conclusion of the opening rites. This would justify the use of the term *collecta* to refer to the gathering of the people.

The overall shape of the oration:

This opening prayer was set within a larger framework, as already indicated above in *Ordo* I. This setting consisted of a call to prayer by the president, silence in which the faithful made their petition, the collect prayer

---

[39] An alternative rubric reads here: *non [pontifex] sedit antequam dicant, post orationem primam, Amen* (*Ordo* I, 53).

[40] For an examination of the significance of such gestures in assessing the structure of a rite, see M.Searle, "Semper Reformanda: The Opening and Closing Rites of the Mass," in Shaping English Liturgy: Studies in Honor of Archbishop Denis Hurley, ed. P.Finn and J.M.Schellman (Washington: The Pastoral Press, 1990), 53-92.

said by the president, the closing formula which began with the preposition *per*, and the people's final response *Amen*.

The rubric for the entrance of the presider and the opening of the liturgy for the Good Friday ceremony in *Reginensis* 316 is most instructive for determining the framework of a presidential prayer (*Reginensis* 316, I,xli *Incipit ordo de feria VI Passione Domini*)[41]. Since the Good Friday service has neither introit, *Kyrie* nor *Gloria*, the presider's prayer opens the liturgy. The rubrics are as follows.

> At the ninth hour, all proceed to the church, and the holy cross is placed over (upon?) the altar. The priest comes from the sacristy, with those in holy orders, proceeding in silence and without chant. They come before the altar, where the priest calls on all to prayer, each according to his ability: *Oremus*. The deacon directs all to kneel: *Flectuamus genua*. And after a little while he directs them to rise: *Levate*. The priest then says the oration (V 395-396)[42].

The president calls the assembly to prayer. The congregation's special posture[43] highlights the centrality of the prayers of the entire community. The presidential oration gathers and concludes the prayer of the assembly.

Note that this prayer serves a dual function. It is both the prayer which collects the petitions of the faithful (*collecta* as *colligere*), and the prayer which concludes the introductory rites of the liturgy. From this second point we can

---

[41]For a study of this rite, see Chavasse, Le Sacramentaire Gélasien, 91-93.

[42]*Ora nona procedunt omnes ad aecclesiam; et ponitur sancta crux super altare. Et egreditur sacerdos de sacrario cum sacris ordinibus cum silentio nihil canentes, et ueniunt ante altare, postolans sacerdos pro se orare et dicit: Oremus. Et adnuntiat diaconus: Flectamus genua. Et post paululum dicit: Leuate. Et dat Orationem*: .... (V 395).

[43]The particular posture adopted during the collect varied for the season, and varied throughout the centuries. Kneeling was eventually omitted at Eastertide and on Sundays because it reflected a penitential character inappropriate to those feasts. See Jungmann, The Mass of the Roman Rite I, 367-372.

see that the context of the presider's prayer in the Good Friday ritual as a whole indicates that the prayer functions to gather and unite the community. This is the sense of *collecta* as *plebs collecta*.

Almost without exception, in the ancient Roman sacramentaries each *oratio, super sindonem, super oblata,* postcommunion, and *super populum* closed with a formula introduced by the preposition *per*[44]. Some prayers read *per Dominum*, or *per eundem Dominum nostrum*. The formula itself appears to be nowhere written out in full, though the *Veronensis* postcommunion from a Mass for the Ascension reads *per eundem Iesum Christum dominum nostrum* (L 174).

A more complete witness to this type of formula can be found in the writings of Fulgentius (d. 533), a North African bishop. In his *Epistola 14*, Fulgentius is faced with a series of questions from the Deacon Ferrandus. The deacon's fourth question, which concerns the expression which closes the presidential prayer, sets out the formula as follows:
Per Iesum Christum Filium tuum Dominum nostrum, qui tecum vivit et regnat in unitate Spiritus sancti[45].

It is reasonable to conclude, then, that in the early Roman latin liturgy the opening prayer was brought to a close by a formula which invited the mediatorship of Christ and praised the Trinity.

In response to the presidential prayer, the community replied *Amen*[46], thus ratifying the prayer.

---

[44]The following is based on the more detailed discussion in Jungmann, The Place of Christ in Liturgical Prayer, 114-118, 200-208.

[45]Fulgentius, Epistola XIV, PL 65, 424, § 35.

[46]See Jungmann, The Mass of the Roman Rite I, 236, 384.

The origin and function of the first presidential prayer of the Mass: Four Theories

The origin and original function of what is now called the collect of the Mass remain clouded. Four theories have dominated the field of discussion[47].

(a) *'Collecta' as the 'oratio ad collectam'*

One theory, already alluded to in the above discussion of the etymology of *collecta*, suggests that the Mass collect developed from the Roman *oratio ad collectam*. This prayer was said at the church of the *collecta* where the community gathered to begin the procession to the stational church of the day where the liturgy was to be celebrated[48]. With the demise of the practice of first gathering at the *collecta* church, the prayer was transfered to the beginning of the Mass in the stational church. The weakness of the theory is that these *collecta* were only occasional, and cannot account for the inclusion of the prayer in all sets of Mass prayers.

(b) *The presidential oration as the conclusion of a litany*

A second theory is that the collect brought to a conclusion the *Kyrie* litany. However, it seems that the introduction of a litany to this part of the liturgy postdates the presence of the opening presidential prayer.

(c) *The first presidential prayer serves to introduce the lessons*

Willis himself favours the view that the first presidential prayer is related to the readings which follow it[49]. He views the prayer as a Roman borrowing and development of a model found in the Alexandrian rite, where

---

[47] These four theories are well set out by both Willis and Hughes. The reader is referred to Willis, "The Variable Prayers of the Roman Mass," 108-112 and Hughes, "The Opening Prayers of 'The Sacramentary'," 27-30.

[48] As well as H 153, the example given by Bernhold of Constance, see the *oratio collecta* for the Mass, *Hadrianum*, 27 *Oratio ad collectam ad Sanctam Adrianum*, H 123.

[49] Willis, "The Variable Prayers of the Roman Mass," 110-112, and Willis, A History of the Early Roman Liturgy, 64.

the readings were prefaced by an invariable prayer[50]. This prayer, proclaimed by the president on behalf of the assembly, sought the purifying and strengthening grace of the Spirit so that the community may hear the readings worthily and be well instructed by them. Willis finds further evidence for the connection of the prayer to the readings that follow it in the Syrian ordination rites of the later fourth century described in the Apostolic Constitutions VIII. There, in the rite for each order, a prayer immediately precedes the lessons. Because each rite has its own prayer, Willis views the oration as variable. However the prayers are not written in Roman 'collect style'.

The connection between these prayers and the opening presidential prayer of the Roman Mass, and subsequently the relationship between that oration and the readings that follow, appear too tenuous. The hypothesis does not explain how a fixed prayer became a prayer which was variable not only for each rite but for each celebration of the Mass. Nor does it account for the

---

[50]The earliest example of such a prayer is the "First Prayer of the Lord's (Day)" from the Sacramentary of Serapion. Willis gives the greek text as found in F.X.Funk, Didascalia et Constitutiones Apostolorum I, 158. See Willis, "The Variable Prayers of the Roman Mass," 110, footnote 5. Dix offers the following translation, repeated by Hughes:

> We beseech Thee, Father of the Only-begotten, Lord of the universe, Artificer of creation, Maker of the things that have been made; we stretch forth clean hands and unfold our thoughts unto Thee, O Lord. We pray Thee, have compassion, spare, benefit, improve, increase us in virtue and faith and knowledge. Visit us, O Lord: to Thee we display our own weaknesses. Be propitious and pity us all together. Have pity, benefit these people. Make it gentle and sober-minded and clean; and send angelic powers that all this Thy people may be holy and reverend. I beseech Thee send 'holy Spirit' into our mind and give us grace to learn the divine scriptures from (the) Holy Spirit, and to interpret cleanly and worthily, that all the laity here present may be helped; through Thy Only-begotten Jesus Christ in (the) Holy Spirit, through Whom to Thee be glory and might both now and to all the ages of the ages, Amen.

See G.Dix, The Shape of the Liturgy, 2nd edition with additonal notes by P.V.Marshall (New York: The Seabury Press, 1945/1982), 447 and Hughes, "The Opening Prayers of 'The Sacramentary'," 14, footnote 25.

completely different literary style of the Roman prayer. As well, the opening presidential orations of the Roman Mass seem to bear no trace of specific petitions for the grace to hear the readings themselves. Finally, examination of the contents of the orations themselves shows that there is only a weak relationship between individual opening prayers and actual scripture pericopes. This last point will be taken up in further detail below.

A related theory, which Willis does not support, is that a 'collect style' oration originally followed each reading, as seen in the vigils of Easter and Pentecost. In time the reading was moved back so that the prayer came to precede the lesson.

This theory has little to recommend it. There is a scarcity of textual or patristic evidence to support this proposed transference of the readings. Moreover, the prayers which follow the ancient Easter and Pentecost Vigil readings most usually contain clear references to the readings. As well, the sacramentary tradition has treated these orations with remarkable reverence. They are rarely, if ever, used outside of their context as prayers following the vigil readings. Such conservatism does not sit too easily with transferring the lesson to a place after the prayer. Nor is such restraint evident in the way the liturgical tradition has treated presidential prayers in general. As will be seen in the analyses below, the same oration is often used in positions other than that of the opening prayer of the Mass, and can also be found in Masses for a variety of seasons and liturgical contexts. It is very unlikely then that the opening presidential prayer of the Mass is descended from prayers which followed the readings.

While the Roman liturgists may have been inspired by an (Alexandrian) practice of a presidential prayer immediately prior to the readings, there is little to suggest that the prayer functioned in view of the readings.

(d) *The 'collect' as the conclusion of the entrance rites*

The fourth hypothesis is that of Jungmann[51]. He proposes a neat schema in which what he calls the collect, secret and postcommunion each brought to a conclusion the three processions: entrance, presentation of the gifts, and communion. Each of these potentially tedious liturgical events was covered by a chant. Thus the three processions were enhanced by the addition of an antiphon and a collect, and through this a 'soft point'[52] of the developing Roman liturgy was solidified. As to the function of the oration, in Jungmann's view, the prayer served mainly to draw the introductory rite to a conclusion.

An examination of the place of the prayer in early Roman Easter and Pentecost Vigil services lends some support to Jungmann's contention that the oration he calls the collect brings to a close the introductory rites. In the Gelasian sacramentary both the vigils of Easter (*Reginensis* 316, I,xliii) and Pentecost (*Reginensis* 316, I,lxxvii) open with a prayer (V 431 and V 618 respectively). This opening prayer is not found in the corresponding vigils of the Gregorian sacramentaries, the *Hadrianum* (84, 110 respectively) and the *Paduensis* (LXXIIII, CIII respectively). As noted earlier, Chavasse concludes that the presence of such a prayer is a characteristic of the vigils celebrated in the Roman presbyteral, titular churches[53]. For our purposes, the presence of this oration is a further indication that the opening prayer is not attached to the lessons which follow. Furthermore, it is an indication that the first presidential prayer served to bring opening rites to a conclusion.

---

[51] See Jungmann, Public Worship: A Survey, trans. C.Howell from Der Gottesdienst der Kirche, Innsbruck: Verlangsantalt Tyrolia, 1955; (Collegeville: The Liturgical Press, 1957), 94-95.

[52] The terminology is that of Robert Taft. See his article "The Structual Analysis of Liturgical Units: An Essay in Methodology," in Beyond East and West: Problems in Liturgical Understanding, NPM Studies in Church Music and Liturgy (Washington: The Pastoral Press, 1984), 161.

[53] Chavasse, Le Sacramentaire Gélasien, 92, 106.

This usage of an oration in the Gelasian Easter and Pentecost vigils has parallels in the above mentioned order of service for the Good Friday liturgy in the same Sacramentary.

Further corroboration for this role of the collect is found in the above mentioned Ember Day Vigil liturgies in *Reginensis* 316, as well as in the *Hadrianum* and the *Paduensis*. In each of these sacramentaries there is a prayer preceding the first lesson, and as well an oration that follows each reading. The first presidential prayer has no direct connection with the readings, a feature already seen in the Gelasian Easter and Pentecost Vigil ceremonies.

Jungmann makes two further points which are relevant to determining the function of the opening prayer. Firstly, the oration is primarily a prayer of petition[54]. It functions to gather and conclude the petitions of the faithful (*collecta* as *colligere*)[55]. Secondly, the prayer is the first place, and until the *secreta*, the only place, in which the president of the assembly steps before the congregation to speak[56]. For Jungmann, this is a clue that this presidential prayer is the climax of the ceremony of entry. This point alludes to the function of the prayer uniting those present into a single worshipping community. This is the sense of *collecta* as *plebs collecta*.

(e) *Summary*

Our discussion of the four theories of the origin and function of the opening presidential prayer has reached some tentative conclusions. The first is somewhat negative. The inspiration for and original intention of the opening presidential prayer remains unknown. However, following Jungmann's hypothesis, this prayer soon, if not originally, served to bring to a conclusion

---

[54] Jungmann, The Mass of the Roman Rite I, 374.

[55] Ibid, 361.

[56] Ibid, 359.

the opening rites of the Mass. More specifically, as the first presidential prayer of the Mass, the oration brought these rites to their climax, gathering those assembled, ministers and people, into a single worshipping community. At the same time, the nature of the opening prayer as a prayer of petition indicates that the oration originally functioned to gather and conclude the prayer of all those in the congregation. The prayer, then, appears to have two primary functions, one flowing from its nature as petition (*collecta* as *colligere*), the other from its context in the Mass as the climax of the introductory rites (*collecta* as *plebs collecta*). In calling the prayer *collecta* the Missal of Paul VI seems to be espousing this meaning.

However, the prayer is also open to other functions. From its context in the Mass, the prayer would be the first occasion in the liturgy to announce the particular feast, season or special circumstance that was being celebrated by the community. The place of the prayer immediately prior to the readings means that the oration could also be used to open to the assembly a theme present in the readings.

CONCLUSION

In this chapter we have attended to two tasks. The first was to examine the name, structure, style, use and origins of the 'collect style' oration itself. It was seen that the 'collect style' oration is a prayer of petition. It has a specific, though flexible, structure, and as well is written in the style of classical, Roman, Latin, rhetorical tradition. The genre was developped in Rome in the second half of the fifth century. While no single cause has yet been put forward to explain its development, the prayer form is a remarkable witness to a fertile period of liturgical adaption and inculturation. During that period the Roman Mass was reshaped with the addition of a whole series of variable, presidential, 'collect style' prayers, constructed around the conventions of classical, Roman literature.

The focus of our study then shifted to a study of one of these particular 'collect style' prayers, the opening presidential prayer of the Roman Mass. Account was taken of the oration's use, structure, origins, function and content. The exact origin of the prayer remains unknown. However, the prayer appears to have two primary functions, one deriving from the nature of the prayer itself (*collecta* as *colligere*), the other deriving from the context of the prayer at the conclusion of the introductory rites (*collecta* as *plebs collecta*). Though Bernhold of Constance may not have been completely accurate over the etymology of the term *collecta*, he does seem to have identified the two poles which come into play in the opening presidential prayer of the liturgy.

At the same time, secondary functions could accrue to the prayer. The opening presidential prayer was in a position to interpret for the assembly the liturgical or historical context in which the particular celebration took place. Similarly, it could also help prepare the assembly to be attentive to the scriptures which followed. These possible functions, however, would appear to be at most secondary.

CHAPTER TWO
THE COLLECT IN THE MISSAL OF PAUL VI

INTRODUCTION

The first document to emerge from the Second Vatican Council (1962-65), the Constitution on the Sacred Liturgy[1], was devoted to the task of the renewal and growth of the liturgy (SC, § 1)[2]. The Constitution set out a number of general norms to guide the process (SC, § 22-25). The Council Fathers sought a renewal that would both preserve sound liturgical traditions and allow room for the legitimate development of new forms (SC, § 23). They directed that this be done using a twofold approach. On the one hand, there would first be a thorough investigation, theological, historical and pastoral, of the individual parts of the liturgy. On the other hand, changes were only to be made when there was a real and proven need for them (SC, § 23). Any such new forms ought to grow organically out of the forms already in the tradition (SC, § 23). As well, any reform ought to grow from, and foster a love of, the scriptures (SC, § 24). The revision of the liturgy

---

[1] Sacrosanctum Concilium, December 4, 1963: Acta Synodalia Sacrosancti Concilii Oecumenici Vaticani Secundi, II, vi (Roma: Typiis Polyglottis Vaticaniis, 1973), 409-497. The Latin text with English translation is also found in N.Tanner, Decrees of the Ecumenical Councils II (Washington DC: Georgetown University Press, 1990), 820-843. The Constitution will be referred to hereafter by the initials SC. Any translations are from the text in Tanner, unless otherwise stated.

[2] ... *suum* [*sacrosanctum concilium*] *esse arbitratur peculiari ratione etiam instaurandam atque fovendam liturgiam curare* (SC, § 1) ([The Holy Council] therefore, and with quite special reason, sees the taking of steps towards the renewal and growth of the liturgy as something it can and should do.)

necessarily entailed the revision of the official liturgical texts (SC, § 25), including the Roman Missal.

In this chapter we will focus first on this revision of the Roman Missal, and then, more particularly, on the character, place, framework and function of the collect for the Sundays of Ordinary Time in the revised liturgy of the eucharist.

THE REVISION OF THE ROMAN MISSAL

The work of the *Consilium*:

The reform of the rite of the Mass was directly addressed in paragraph 50 of the Constitution on the Liturgy. This section set down six requirements of any revision[3]:

(1) that the distinctive character of each part, as well as their interconnections, appear clearly;

(2) that a devout and active participation of the faithful be made easier;

(3) that the rites be simplified;

(4) that doublets and less useful additions be eliminated;

(5) that worthwhile elements lost in the course of time be restored;

(6) that the substance of the rites be faithfully maintained.

The task of renewing the liturgy was carried out by a special commission (*Consilium*), the *Consilium ad exsequendam Constitutionem de*

---

[3]This summary is taken from A.Bugnini, The Reform of the Liturgy: 1948-1975, trans. M.J.O'Connell from La riforma liturgica (1948-1975), Roma: Edizione Liturgiche, 1983 (Collegeville, Minnesota: The Liturgical Press, 1990), 339. Bugnini's interpretations and views are of considerable importance since he was the secretary of the *Consilium ad Exsequendam Constitutionem de Sacra Liturgia*, the *Consilium* with the responsibility for implementing the reform of the Roman liturgy.

sacra liturgia, constituted by Paul VI on Jan 25, 1964[4]. The plan which the *Consilium* followed divided the work of reform into separate tasks, each of which was allocated to a specific group (*Coetus*)[5]. The revision of the order of the Mass was given to *Coetus* 10[6], while *Coetus* 18bis was concerned with the revision of the prayers and prefaces. It is this second group that is of most interest to the present study, since it was their role to revise the presidential prayers, including the collects, for use in Mass and the Office.

The membership of *Coetus* 18bis consisted of P.Bruylants (relator), G.Lucchesi (secretary), A.Rose, W.Dürig, H.Ashworth, G.A.Gracias, A.Dumas. On Fr.Bruylants' death in October 1966, A.Rose became the relator[7]. Dumas later published three articles which are significant for understanding the compilation of the Missal. One detailed the sources of the new or revised presidential prayers and prefaces[8]. A second dealt with questions of translation[9]. The third set out the principles and methodology of the revision[10]. It is to this third article that we will now turn.

---

[4]Paul VI, motu proprio Sacram liturgiam, January 25, 1964: Acta Apostolica Sedis 56 (1964): 139-144. For a translation see A.Flannery, Vatican Council II: The Conciliar and Post Conciliar Documents (New York: Costello Publishing Company, 1975/1986), 41-44.

[5]For a discussion of the plan see Bugnini, The Reform of the Liturgy, 60-68.

[6]For a list of the members of this group see Bugnini, The Reform of the Liturgy, 337 footnote 1.

[7]Ibid., 397 footnote 10.

[8]A.Dumas, "Les sources du Missel romain," Notitiae 7 (1971): 37-42, 74-77, 94-95, 134-136, 276-279, 409-410.

[9]A.Dumas, "Pour mieux comprendre les textes liturgiques du Missel romain," Notitiae 6 (1970): 194-213.

[10]A.Dumas, "Les oraisons du nouveau Missel romain," Questions liturgiques 52 (1971): 263-270.

The principles and methods used in the revision of the Missal:

In his article "Les oraisons du nouveau Missel romain" Dumas summarily sets out the principles and methods which guided the *Consilium* as it sought to undertake its brief to revise the Missal. He comments on three areas: the *Consilium's* understanding of the style characteristic of Roman prayer, the principles for revision of the prayers, and the manner in which the revisions were accomplished.

(a) *The style of Roman prayer*:

The revisors wished to remain faithful to the characteristics of the Roman style of prayer. The three outstanding and complementary qualities of Roman prayer were seen to be its clarity (*clarté*), concentratedness of form (*densité*), and its sobriety (*sobriété*)[11].

(b) *The principles of revision*:

The three principles which guided the revision were described as veracity (*vérité*), simplicity (*simplicité*), and pastoral sensitivity (*sens pastoral*)[12]. A number of factors are mentioned under the heading of veracity. The compilers of the Missal sought to be true to the best witness of a text. Secondly they wished to restore each text to its true nature and appropriate liturgical context. Thirdly, historical veracity was restored by removing any mention of hagiographical legends in the prayers. In the main this point concerned the revision of the calendar and the prayers of the sanctoral. Fourthly, the compilers wished to restore the veracity of a prayer's inspiration and style. This included the deletion of allusions to fasts that were no longer observed, the omission of excessive rhetorical elements, and ensuring all orations were addressed to the Father. The fifth and final factor was that the prayers should be theologically correct (*la vérité théologique*).

---

[11] Ibid, 263.

[12] Ibid, 263-266.

The second principle operative was that of simplicity. In conformity with the style of Roman prayer, the orations were to be clear and to the point, somewhat like Dumas' idea of a good homily[13].

The third principle guiding the revision was that the orations should be sensitive to the pastoral needs of contemporary Christians and the contemporary world[14]. Through this principle, the revision of the liturgy was seen to be able to take place in fidelity to the pivotal concerns of the Second Vatican Council[15]. Dumas cites an application of this principle which is of direct concern to our study. Out of consideration for this pastoral sense, the prayers set in place for the Sunday liturgy were allocated to that position on account of the richness of their doctrine and the clarity of their expression[16].

(c) *The methods of revision*:

Dumas also describes the manner and means whereby the revision was accomplished in accordance with the above principles[17]. He deals, in this section of the article, with the choice of texts, their adaptation, and the creation of new texts. Under the choice of texts he makes three points[18]. Firstly, texts from the former Missal, where necessary restored to their best textual witness, were utilized in the new Missal. Secondly, when further texts were necessary, they were chosen largely from the oldest Roman books, the

---

[13] "*Il suffit donc que chaque prière exprime l'essentiel de son contenu, sans répétitions ni détours, obéissant aux principes requis pour une bonne homélie: avoir quelque chose à dire, savoir le dire, s'arrêter après l'avoir dit*" (Dumas, "Les oraisons," Questions Liturgiques 52 (1971): 265.

[14] Ibid, 266.

[15] SC, § 4.

[16] Dumas, "Les oraisons," QL 52 (1971): 266.

[17] Ibid, 266-270.

[18] Ibid, 266-267.

Veronensis and *Reginensis* 316. Some were also taken from the Gregorian sacramentaries, the *Hadrianum* and the *Paduensis*, as well as from the mixed Gelasian Sacramentary of Angoulême. Thirdly, on rare occasions, prayers were imported from other sources, such as the *Bergomense*, the Mozarabic Sacramentary, and the *Missale Gothicum*.

Under the rubric of adaptation[19], certain ancient texts were modified so as to make them more appropriate for contemporary Christian sensibilities. For example, the radical opposition between earth and heaven, often found in ancient prayers in expressions such as *terrena despicere et amare caelestia*, was seen to be no longer appropriate.

Dumas also described the means employed for the creation of new texts[20]. In creating new prayers, the compilers kept to the fore the desire to ensure a sense of unity and harmony between the new Missal and its predecessors. New prayers were formed using five methods: centonization using ancient prayers, prayers formed from the Vulgate translation of the scriptures, prayers formed from patristic writings, prayers formed from ecclesiastical documents, such as the documents of Vatican II, and finally the creation of completely new prayers. This last method was reserved for situations for which there were no equivalents in earlier sacramentaries.

In the concluding chapter of this study we will return to the principles and means outlined by Dumas so as to ascertain how successfully they were employed with regard to the collects for the Sundays of Ordinary Time[21].

---

[19]Ibid, 267-268.

[20]Ibid, 269-270.

[21]See below, 673.

One of the fruits of the labour of the *Consilium* was the Missal of Paul VI, promulgated by Pope Paul VI on April 3rd, 1969[22]. Later emendations resulted in the 1975 *Editio altera typica*, the text for our study[23]. It is to this 1975 Missal that we now turn to examine the place and function of the collect for the Sundays of Ordinary Time.

THE SUNDAYS OF ORDINARY TIME IN THE MISSAL OF PAUL VI

Interpretative keys to the Missal:
the General Instruction and the General Norms

The Missal of Paul VI provides two interpretative keys for understanding the rites, functions of the ministers and participants, the environment for worship, and the liturgical year as they are set out in the sacramentary. The new Missal opens with a General Instruction[24], whose role

---

[22] Paul VI, Constitutio Apostolica Missale Romanum April 3, 1969: MR(1975), 11-16. This text will be referred to as Constitutio Apostolica Missale Romanum.

[23] For a list of these emendations, none of which are pertinent to our study, see Sacra Congregatio pro Cultu Divino, "De editione typica altera Missalis Romani et Gradualis simplicis," Notitiae 11 (1975): 290-337.

[24] "Institutio Generalis Missalis Romani", MR(1975) 19-91. The *Institutio* will be known in this study as either the General Instruction or GIRM, its English acronym. Unless otherwise noted, all translations of this text will be from the following official, English language edition of the Roman Missal: The Sacramentary, revised according to the second typical edition of the Missale Romanum (1975), March 1, 1985, for use in the dioceses of the United States of America, trans. prepared by the International Committee on English in the Liturgy (Collegeville: The Liturgical Press, 1985). Henceforth this text will be referred to as The Sacramentary (USA/ICEL, 1985).

is set out in the Apostolic Constitution[25] which promulgated the Missal itself. The role of the General Instruction is as follows:

> *Nunc vero, ut novam Missalis Romani compositionem, summis saltem lineamentis, quasi praefiniamus, in primis animadvertimus, Institutione Generali, qua in libro tamquam prooemio usi sumus, novas normas eucharistici sacrificii celebrandi proponi, sive quoad ritus persolvendos et officia uniuscuiusque astantis et participis propria, sive quoad suppellectiles et loca rei divinae peragendae necessaria* (MR(1975), 13).[26]

Following the General Instruction are the General Norms for the Liturgical Year and Calendar[27], preceded by the *Motu Proprio*[28] by which they were decreed. The purpose of the Calendar and General Norms is to govern the arrangement of the liturgical year:

> *... novum Calendarium Romanum generale a Consilio ad exsequendam Constitutionem de sacra Liturgia compositum, itemque normas*

---

[25]Constitutio Apostolica Missale Romanum, MR(1975), 11-16. All translations of this text, unless otherwise noted, are taken from The Sacramentary (USA/ICEL, 1985).

[26]Now, however, our purpose is to set out, at least in broad terms, the new plan of the Roman Missal. We therefore point out, first, that a General Instruction, for use as a preface to the book, gives the new regulations for the celebration of the eucharistic sacrifice. These regulations cover the rites to be carried out and the functions of each minister or participant as well as the furnishings and the places needed for divine worship.

[27]"Normae Universales de Anno Liturgico et de Calendario," MR(1975) 100-125. These will be referred to throughout as the General Norms. All translations of this text, unless otherwise noted, are taken from The Sacramentary (USA/ICEL, 1985).

[28]Paul VI, Motu proprio Mysterii Paschalis, February 14, 1969: MR(1975) 97-99. All translations of this text, unless otherwise noted, are taken from The Sacramentary (USA/ICEL, 1985).

universales ad ordinationem anni liturgici spectantes, Apostolica Nostra auctoritate approbamus[29].

Together GIRM and the General Norms provide the understanding of the meaning of the holy day Sunday, the sense of Ordinary Time, and the nature and function of the collect that has guided the reform of the Missal. Each of these topics, which form part of the background to our study, will now be examined.

The Feast of Sunday in the General Norms:

According to the General Norms, Sunday is ranked as the first holy day of all[30]. The reason given for this is that Apostolic tradition, in cognizance of the day of Christ's resurrection, established Sunday, the Day of the Lord, as the first day of the Christian week. Furthermore, the General Norms add that on that day each week the church celebrates the Paschal mystery[31].

The meaning of Ordinary Time in the General Norms:

The General Norms show that the church's liturgical year is divided into seasons. The aim of this yearly cycle is that the community celebrate the entire mystery of Christ, from his incarnation to Pentecost, and to the

---

[29] We approve the new Roman Calendar drawn up by the Consilium and also the general norms governing the arrangement of the liturgical year (Mysterii Paschalis, MR(1975), 98).

[30] General Norms, § 4.

[31] For the broad range of understandings of the feast of Sunday in the Christian tradition see W.Rordorf, Sunday: The History of the Day of Rest and Worship in the Earliest Centuries of the Christian Church, trans. A.A.K.Graham from Der Sonntag: Geschichte des Ruhe- und Gottesdiensttages im altesten Christentum, Zürich: Zwingli Verlag, 1962 (Philadelphia: The Westminister Press, 1968) and R.Taft, "Sunday in the Byzantine Tradition," in Beyond East and West: Problems in Liturgical Understanding, 31-48.

expectation of his coming[32]. Apart from the season named Ordinary Time, *Tempus "per annum"*, each of the seasons is seen to have its own distinct character, *indoles*. Because *indoles* is an important term for understanding the role of the collect in the Mass as set out in GIRM, its use here deserves some consideration.

The word appears twice in the General Norms. The first instance is with reference to the twofold character of the season of Advent: "*Tempus Adventus duplicem habet indolem* ... "[33]. Advent is described as a time of devout preparation for the solemnity and a time of joyful expectation of the second coming of Christ. The paragraph dealing with Advent continues:

> ... *est enim tempus praeparationis ad sollemnia Nativitatis, in quibus primus Dei Filii adventus ad homines recolitur, ac simul tempus quo per hanc recordationem mentes diriguntur ad expectationem secundi Christi adventus in fine temporum. His duabus rationibus, tempus Adventus se praebet ut tempus devotae ac iucundae exspectationis*[34].

Here *indoles* has the sense of the particular mystery a season celebrates, and as well, the particular character of that celebration.

The same sense can be found a few paragraphs later, where the General Norms set out an understanding of Ordinary Time. The paragraph reads:

> *Praeter tempora propriam indolem habentia, triginta tres vel triginta quattuor supersunt hebdomadae per anni circulum, in quibus non celebratur peculiaris mysterii Christi aspectus; sed potius ipsum*

---

[32]General Norms, § 17.

[33]General Norms, § 39.

[34][Advent has a twofold character] as a season to prepare for Christmas when Christ's first coming to us is remembered; as a season when that remembrance directs the mind and heart to await Christ's Second Coming at the end of time. Advent is thus a period for devout and joyful expectation.

mysterium Christi in sua plenitudine recolitur, praesertim vero diebus dominicis. Huiusmodi periodus, tempus "per annum" nuncupatur (§ 43)[35].

In the General Norms, then, the term, *indoles*, refers to the way the church celebrates that specific aspect of the mystery highlighted by the particular season. The particular *indoles* of the mystery is seen to establish the particular *indoles* of the celebration. As noted above, Advent has a dual character, devotion and joyful expectation. The Easter season has the character of joyful celebration, as if the whole fifty days were one great feast[36]. Lent is marked by recalling one's baptismal commitment and doing penance[37].

The Sundays of Ordinary Time are described as having no single, determinative *indoles*. Rather, they are devoted to the celebration of the mystery of Christ in all its fullness. However, it can be concluded from the above that in the General Norms, the nature of Sunday itself as both the Day of the Lord and the first day of the Christian week, highlights the celebration of the resurrection.

As set out by the General Norms, the character (*indoles*) of the Sundays in Ordinary Time ought, then, reflect firstly the celebration of the resurrection, and secondly the celebration of the mystery of Christ in all its fullness.

Having established the Missal's understanding of the feast of the Sundays in Ordinary Time, attention will now be directed to the collect of the Mass itself.

---

[35] Apart from those seasons having their own distinctive character, thirty-three or thirty-four weeks remain in the yearly cycle that do not celebrate a specific aspect of the mystery of Christ. Rather, especially on the Sundays, they are devoted to the mystery of Christ in all its aspects. This period is known as Ordinary Time (General Norms, § 43).

[36] General Norms, § 22.

[37] General Norms, § 27.

THE CHARACTER, PLACE AND FUNCTION OF THE COLLECT IN THE MASS

According to the General Instruction, the collect is a prayer of petition, said by the priest in the name of the community, which brings to conclusion the introductory rites of the Mass. To understand its function, it is necessary to consider how the instruction interprets each of the following key features: the nature of the Mass as a sacrifice, the role of the priest in the Mass, the communal nature of the Mass as an act of worship, the collect as a priestly prayer said in the name of the community, the place of the collect in the introductory rites, and the shape and function of the collect. These will now be examined.

The nature of the Mass as a sacrifice:

We will open our study of the character, place and function of the collect in the Mass by examining the understanding of the sacrificial nature of the Mass as interpreted by the General Instruction. This is essential for an appreciation of the view in the Instruction of the functions of the priest and of the assembly.

In paragraph 2 of the Introduction (*Prooemium*) the General Instruction affirms the sacrificial nature of the Mass. There the Mass is said to be the sacramental renewal of the sacrifice of the cross. It is the sacrifice of praise and of thanksgiving, of propitiation and satisfaction:

> *Ita in novo Missali lex orandi Ecclesiae respondet perenni legi credendi, qua nempe monemur unum et idem esse, excepta diversa offerendi ratione, crucis sacrificium eiusque in Missa sacramentalem renovationem, quam in Cena novissima Christus Dominus instituit Apostolisque faciendam mandavit in sui memoriam, atque proinde*

missam simul esse sacrificium laudis, gratiarum actionis, propitiatiorium et satisfactorium (Prooemium, § 2.)[38]

The same paragraph gives an outline of the role of the priest in the sacrifice of the Mass. The priest, in keeping anamnesis or memory during the Eucharistic prayer, is said to address God in the name of the whole people, render thanks, and offer the living and holy sacrifice. The sacrifice offered is described as the oblation of the church as well as the offering of the victim by whose sacrifice God wished to be pleased. The priest also prays that the body and blood of Christ may be a sacrifice acceptable to the Father, and so salvific for the whole world:

> ... *in his* [*in Precibus Eucharisticis*] *enim sacerdos, dum anamnesin peragit, ad Deum nomine etiam totius populi conversus, ei gratias persolvit et sacrificium offert vivum et sanctum, oblationem scilicet Ecclesiae et hostiam, cuius immolatione ipse Deus voluit placari, atque orat, ut Corpus et Sanguis Christi sint Patri sacrificium acceptabile et toti mundo salutare* (Prooemium, § 2).[39]

In paragraph 4 of the Introduction to the General Instruction, the priest is described as the one who, during the Mass, offers the sacrifice in the person of Christ, and presides over the assembly of the holy people: *qui in persona*

---

[38] Thus in the new Missal the Church's rule of prayer is in accord with the constant rule of its faith, by which we are assuredly taught that the sacrifice of the cross and its sacramental renewal, which Christ instituted at the Last Supper and mandated that his apostles should do this in his memory, are one and the same sacrifice, though they differ in respect to the mode in which they are offered. Accordingly, the Mass is at one and the same time the sacrifice of praise and thanksgiving, the sacrifice of propitiation and of satisfaction. (The translation is the author's.)

[39] [In the Eucharistic prayer] while he performs the anamnesis, the priest, addressing God in the name of all the people, renders thanks to him and offers the living and holy sacrifice, namely the oblation of the Church and the victim, by whose sacrifice God wished to be pleased, and the priest prays that the Body and Blood of Christ may be an acceptable sacrifice to the Father and salvific for the whole world.
(The translation is the author's.)

Christi sacrificium offert coetuique populi sancti praesidet (Prooemium, § 4).[40]

The priest's sacerdotal power is understood to be a continuation of the power of Christ, the High Priest of the New Testament: *atque ipsa [sacerdotalis] potestas ... quae est continuatio potestatis Christi, Summi Pontificis Novi Testamenti* (Prooemuim, § 4).[41]

It can be inferred that the priest's role as presider of the community's worship follows from the sacerdotal power to offer the sacrifice in the name of the whole church bearing the person of Christ.

This understanding of the role of the ministerial priesthood is said to shed light on the meaning of the royal priesthood of all believers, *regale sacerdotium fidelium* (Prooemium, § 5). The faithful are said to offer a spiritual sacrifice, *sacrificium spiritale*, which, through the ministry of the priest, is taken up wholly into union with the sacrifice of Christ, the one mediator:

> *id est regale sacerdotium fidelium, quorum sacrificium spiritale per presbyterorum ministerium in unione cum sacrificio Christi, unici Mediatoris, consummatur* (Proemium, § 5)[42].

In summary, the General Instruction's explanation of the sacrificial nature of the Mass immediately raises the questions of the roles in the Mass of the priest and of the faithful. The sacerdotal power of the priest is a continuation of the High Priestly power of Christ. By reason of this power,

---

[40]who offers the sacrifice in the person of Christ and presides over the assembly of the holy people.
(The translation is the author's.)

[41]And this priestly power ... is a continuation of the power of Christ, the High Priest of the New Testament.
(The translation is the author's.)

[42]This is the royal priesthood of believers. Through the ministry of the presbyters the spiritual sacrifice of the royal priesthood of believers is taken up wholly into union with the sacrifice of Christ, the one Mediator.
(The translation is the author's.)

the priest, bearing the person of Christ, offers the sacrifice. In doing so the priest joins the spiritual sacrifice of the priestly people to the sacrifice of Christ, the one mediator. On account of this the priest presides over the worship of the community.

In light of this understanding of the sacrificial nature of the Mass we will now consider in further detail what is said concerning the function of the priest in the Mass.

The role of the priest in the Mass according to the General Instruction:

The Introduction to the General Instruction describes the function of the priest as follows. The priest is the one who offers the sacrifice in the person of Christ, and so presides over the assembly of the holy people. The priest's sacerdotal power is a continuation of the power of Christ, the High Priest of the New Testament.

The function of the priest is referred to on a number of other occasions in the General Instruction.

Paragraph 7 of the General Instruction states that the priest holds the person of Christ, and presides over the celebration of the Lord's Supper:

In Missa seu Cena dominica populus Dei in unum convocatur, sacerdote praeside personamque Christi gerente, ad memoriale Domini seu sacrificium eucharisticum celebrandum (GIRM, § 7)[43].

Though the role of the priest is set within the ecclesial worship of the people of God, even when the participation of the faithful is not possible, the Eucharist remains an act of Christ and the church in which the priest always (*semper*) acts for the salvation of the people:

... *aliquando non possible haberi* [*participatio fidelium*], *eucharistica*

---

[43]In the Mass, or the Lord's Supper, the people of God are called together into one, with the priest as president holding the person of Christ, so that they may celebrate the memorial of the Lord or the eucharistic sacrifice. (The translation is the author's.)

> *celebratio sua efficacia et dignitate semper est praedita, quippe quae sit actus Christi et Ecclesiae, in quo sacerdos semper agit pro salute populi* (GIRM, § 4)[44].

In the properly 'presidential' prayers, the priest, who presides over the assembly as the one who holds the person of Christ, directs the prayers to God in the name of the whole of God's holy people and of those present:

> *Hae preces [orationes praesidentiales] a sacerdote, qui coetui personam Christi gerens praeest, ad Deum diriguntur nomine totius plebis sanctae et omnium circumstantium* (GIRM, § 10)[45].

The General Instruction's understanding of the role of the priest in the Mass is most fully set out in § 60. The apposite section reads:

> *Etiam presbyter, qui in societate fidelium sacra Ordinis potestate pollet sacrificium in persona Christi offerendi, exinde coetui congregato praeest, eius orationi praesidet, illi nuntium salutis proclamat, populum sibi sociat in offerendo sacrificio per Christum in Spiritu Sancto Deo Patri, fratribus suis panem vitae aeternae dat, ipsumque cum illis participat. Cum igitur Eucharistiam celebrat, debet Deo et populo cum dignitate et humilitate servire, et in modo se gerendi et verba divina proferendi praesentiam vivam Christi fidelibus insinuare* (GIRM, § 60)[46].

---

[44] Even when it is not possible for the faithful to participate, the eucharistic celebration retains it efficacy and dignity since clearly it is an act of Christ and the Church, in which the priest always acts for the salvation of the people. (The translation is the author's.)

[45] These presidential prayers are said by the priest, who, holding the person of Christ, presides over the assembly. They are directed to God in the name of the entire holy people and of those present.
(The translation is the author's.)

[46] The priest also [i.e. as well as the bishop] in the company of the faithful enjoys the sacred power to offer the sacrifice in the person of Christ. Hence, he presides over the assembly, presides over its prayer, proclaims to it the good news of salvation, associates the people with himself in offering the sacrifice through Christ in the Spirit to God the Father, gives the bread of eternal life to his brothers, and shares in it himself with them. When therefore he celebrates the Eucharist, he must serve God and the people with dignity and humility, and in his way of acting and of proclaiming the word of God,

In the Mass, then, the priest offers the sacrifice in the person of Christ (*in persona Christi*). Because of this (*exinde*) he also presides over the gathered assembly, leads their orations, and proclaims the message of salvation. The priest unites the community to himself in offering the sacrifice to God through Christ in the Spirit. As well, he gives to his brothers and sisters the bread of eternal life, and shares himself with them in it. Note that the priest's role is set within an ecclesial context of the community of brothers and sisters gathered in Christ offering sacrifice to God. However this is always dependent on the fact that he is empowered to act in the person of Christ.

From this examination, it can be seen that the General Instruction highlights three particular functions of the priest in the Mass. The priest holds the person of Christ, and in virtue of this presides over the assembly and directs the prayer to God in the name of the whole of God's people and of those present. This is set within the context of the Eucharist as an action of Christ and the church. What the General Instruction says about the nature of the Eucharist as a public and communal act will now be addressed.

<u>The nature of the Eucharist as a public and communal act of worship according to the General Instruction</u>:

The communal and public nature of the Eucharist as an act of worship is set forth in § 5 of the Introduction to the General Instruction[47]. There it is stated that the celebration of the Eucharist is the action of the whole church; *namque celebratio Eucharistiae est actio Ecclesiae universae*[48]. On account of

---

express for the faithful the living presence of Christ.
(The translation is the author's.)

[47]Prooemium, §5, 21.

[48]The celebration of the Eucharist is the action of the whole church. (The translation is the author's.)

this the participants should carry out each of the parts, and only those parts, which are theirs by virtue of their place (*gradus*) in the people of God: *in qua [celebratio Eucharistiae] unusquisque solum et totum id agat, quod ad ipsum pertinet, respectu habito gradus eius in populo Dei*[49].

This point is taken up again in § 58 of the General Instruction. Each member of the congregation is said to have the right (*ius*) and duty (*officium*) to participate in the celebration according to his or her order (*ordo*) and office (*munus*):

> *In coetu, qui ad Missam congregatur, unusquisque ius habet et officium participationem suam afferendi diverso modo pro diversitate ordinis et muneris* (GIRM, § 58).[50]

Paragraph 5 of the Introduction to the General Instruction underscores the nature of the Eucharist as an ecclesial act of worship. In the Eucharist, Christ is said to gather and nourish this people chosen by God (*populus Dei*) and purchased in Christ's blood. As a people, the faithful are called to offer the prayer (*prex*) of the whole human family to God. Their petition, then, is a central aspect of the Eucharist. At the same time, the *populus Dei*, by offering Christ's sacrifice, renders its thanks to Christ for the mystery of salvation. Finally, the holy people of God grow in unity and holiness as a people through its active, conscious and fruitful participation in the celebration. The paragraph reads:

---

[49][In the celebration of the Eucharist] each and every one should do only but all those parts that pertain to him or her by virtue of his or her place within the people of God.
(The translation is the author's.)

[50]Each person in the assembly gathered for the Mass has the right and duty to participate in different ways on account of their order or office. (The translation is the author's.)

The General Instruction goes on to give a more detailed explanation both of the duties (*officium*) and ministries (*ministerium*) of those in sacred orders (§ 59-61), and of the duties (*officium*) and offices (*munus*) of the people of God (§ 62-64).

*Hic enim populus est populus Dei, Sanguine Christi acquisitus, a
Domino congregatus, eius verbo nutritus, populus ad id vocatus, ut
preces totius familiae humanae ad Deum admoveat, populus, qui pro
mysterio salutis gratias in Christo agit eius sacrificium offerendo,
populus denique, qui per communionem Corporis et Sanguinis Christi in
unum coalescit. Qui populus, licet origine sua sit sanctus, tamen per
ipsam participationem consciam, actuosam et fructuosam mysterii
eucharistici in sanctitate continenter crescit* (Proemium, § 5, 21)[51].

The Introduction to the General Instruction, then, brings out the ecclesial and public nature of the Eucharist as an act of worship. It is that action of the entire ecclesial community in which the church, as a royal priesthood, unites its spiritual sacrifice with that of Christ, the one mediator. It is the work of the people of God itself, a people which has been gathered by the Lord and nourished by him in the Eucharist. In the Eucharist, the faithful give thanks by offering Christ's sacrifice. As well, they bring before God the prayer of the whole human family. Finally, through their active participation they grow in holiness.

Since the collect is a public prayer said by the priest, we will now examine the General Instruction's understanding of the 'presidential' prayers of the Mass, and the collect in particular.

The collect as a 'presidential' prayer:

The prayers and parts of the Mass assigned to the priest are described in GIRM § 10-13. The preeminent prayer of the priest is the eucharistic prayer.

---

[51]For this people is the people of God, purchased by the Blood of Christ, gathered together by the Lord, fed by his word. They are a people called so that they might offer to God the prayer of the whole human family, a people who give thanks for the mystery of salvation in Christ by offering his sacrifice, a people who are made one through communion in the Body and Blood of Christ. They are a people who, although a holy people from their origins, nevertheless through their conscious, active and fruitful participation in the mystery of the Eucharist, grow continuously in holiness.
(The translation is the author's.)

Second to this, however, are the collect, prayer over the gifts, and postcommunion[52]. These prayers are described as follows:

> *Hae preces [collecta, super oblata, post communionem] a sacerdote, qui coetui personam Christi gerens praeest, ad Deum diriguntur nomine totius plebis sanctae et omnium circumstantium. Merito igitur "orationes praesidentiales" nominantur* (§ 10)[53].

The description sets out a number of the aspects of these 'presidential' prayers which include the collect. They are prayers directed towards God in the name of the entire church, as well as in the name of the gathered assembly: *in nomine totius plebis sanctae et omnium circumstantium*. In praying the oration the priest presides over the assembly, holding the person of Christ: *qui coetui personam Christi gerens praeest*.

The presidential prayers, then, appear to have a number of functions. First and foremost the presidential prayers are prayers of the one who holds the person of Christ, and on account of this presides. The presidential prayers also place before God the prayer of the community. As well, they set the prayer of the community within the context of the prayer of the whole church. Moreover, the prayer of the community includes prayer for the whole human family.

---

[52]GIRM, § 10.

[53]Next are the prayers: the opening prayer or collect, the prayer over the gifts, and the prayer after communion. These prayers are said by the priest, who, holding the person of Christ, presides over the assembly. They are directed to God in the name of the entire holy people and of those present. Thus there is good reason to call them "the presidential prayers" (GIRM, § 10). (The translation is the author's.)

This description is based on SC, § 33.

The place of the collect in the Mass according to the General Instruction:

As set out in the General Instruction, the Mass is a single, unified act of worship[54]. Though it has two central parts, the liturgy of the Word and of the Eucharist, they are seen to be so closely and firmly (*arcte*) joined together that they form one united celebration. This ritual also has certain opening and closing rites. The collect has been given its place among these opening rites.

The General Instruction clearly distinguishes the Introductory Rites (*Ritus initiales*) from the Liturgy of the Word (*Liturgia verbi*). The Introductory Rites are discussed in a special section (§ 24-32) under the heading III *De Singulis Missae Partibus* A) *Ritus initiales*. The rites consist of the introit, salutation, penitential rite, *Kyrie*, *Gloria* and the collect[55]. As a single introductory ritual, they are said to have their own particular character (*character*) and purpose (*finis*). Paragraph 24 reads:

> *Ea quae liturgiam verbi praecedunt, scilicet introitus, salutatio, actus paenitentialis, Kyrie, Gloria et collecta, characterem habent exordii, introductionis et praeparationis.*
> *Finis horum rituum est, ut fideles in unum convenientes communionem constituant et recte ad verbum Dei audiendum digneque Eucharistiam celebrandam sese disponant* (GIRM, § 24)[56].

Their character in relationship to the Mass is to begin the celebration (*exordium*), introduce the rite (*introductio*), and to prepare the faithful to hear the Word and celebrate the Eucharist (*praeparatio*). Their purpose is twofold.

---

[54]This paragraph is based on GIRM, § 8.

[55]GIRM, § 24.

[56]The parts preceding the liturgy of the word, namely the entrance song, greeting, penitential rite, *Kyrie*, *Gloria* and the opening prayer or collect, have the character of a beginning, introduction, and preparation.

The purpose of these rites is that the faithful coming together take on the form of a community and prepare themselves to listen to God's work and celebrate the eucharist properly (GIRM, § 24).

Note that this translation, from <u>The Sacramentary</u> (USA/ICEL, 1985) reads *collecta* as 'opening prayer or collect'.

Firstly they act to convene the faithful into a single community (*in unum convenientes communionem constituant*). Secondly, they seek to dispose the faithful to hear God's word in uprightness (*recte*), and offer worship worthily (*digne*). As can be seen, the collect brings these introductory rites to a conclusion.

As the first presidential prayer of the Mass, then, the collect is also, in effect, the culmination of the introductory rites. Thus, it serves to mark the unity of the people and priest in the presence of Christ, with the priest, in the person of Christ, offering prayer to God in the name of the community and of the church.

It is interesting to note the way the General Instruction is quite reserved in the way it names the collect. In § 10 the prayer is referred to only as a *collecta* and a presidential prayer, *oratio presidentialis*.

While our study concentrates only on the *Editio Typica* of the Missal note that there is a further conflation of names for the collect when the vernacular translations of the Missal are taken into account. In the Sacramentary approved for use by the Bishops of the United States the translation of GIRM § 10 reads "the opening prayer or collect" where the latin simply reads *collecta*. Throughout the Sacramentary the collect is referred to as the "opening prayer". In the Missal approved for French speaking countries GIRM § 10 reads *c'est-à-dire la prière d'ouverture (collecta)*, while in the Mass texts of the Missal itself the heading over the collect is simply *Prière*. The German language Messbuch translates *collecta* in GIRM § 10 as *Tagesgebet*, and as well uses this word as the title in the prayer text. The Dutch Altaarmissaal translates *collecta* in GIRM § 10 as *het (openings-)gebed*, while it uses the general *Gebed* in the Mass text. The Italian Missal has a slightly different approach. Whereas its translation of GIRM § 10 reads *l'orazione di inizio (o colletta)*, the title *colletta* is used in the Mass texts. The Spanish language Missal for Mexico remains the closest to the Latin, translating *collecta* in GIRM § 10 with *oración colecta*, and retaining that title for the Mass texts. Each of these titles offers an interpretation of the function of the prayer.

All this reflects some hesitation over the function of the prayer, and some reserve over the adoption of *collecta*. As seen in Chapter One, this hesitation has its roots in the earliest liturgical sources. The Roman preference was to describe the prayer as an *oratio*, though the prayer is rarely given a title in the earliest Roman sacramentaries. The Gallican sacramentaries, on the other hand, preferred the designation *collecta*. The Missal of Pius V uses *oratio*[57].

The framework of the collect according to the General Instruction:

The collect prayer is set within the following framework (GIRM, § 88):

(a) The priest invites the community to pray: *Oremus*,

(b) The priest and assembly together pray in silence for a short time: *et omnes una cum sacerdote ad breve tempus silentes orant*,

(c) The priest says the collect prayer, which is concluded with a trinitarian formula[58],

(d) The people give their acclamation by responding *Amen*.

---

[57]For the contemporary Missals see Missel Romain (Paris: Desclée-Mame: 1974); Messbuch, Herausgegeben im Auftrag der Bischofskonferenzen Deutschlands, Österreichs und der Schweiz sowie der Bischöfe von Luxemburg, Bozen-Brizen und Lüttich (Köln: Benziger, 1975); Altaarmissaal vor de Nederlandse Kerkprovincie, (Nationale Raad voor Liturgie, 1979); Messale Romano: Riformato a Norma dei Decreti del Concilio Ecumenico Vaticano II e Promulgato da Papa Paolo VI (Roma: Conferenze Episcopale Italiana, 1973); and Misal Romano: Reformado segun las Normas de los decritos del Concilio Ecumenico Vaticano II y Promulgado por el Papa Pablo VI, Edicion tipica aprobada por la Conferencia episcipal Mexicana (México: Conferencia Episcopal Mexicana 1993).

[58]For these formulae see GIRM, § 32.

The function of the collect:

The General Instruction all too briefly makes a number of points about the function both of the silence and of the collect oration itself. The apposite section of the text reads:

> *Deinde sacerdos populum ad orandum invitat; et omnes una cum sacerdote parumper silent, ut conscii fiant se in conspectu Dei stare, et vota sua in animo possint nuncupare. Tunc sacerdos profert orationem, quae solet "collecta" nominari. Per eam indoles celebrationis exprimitur et precatio verbis sacerdotis ad Deum Patrem, per Christum in Spiritu Sancto, dirigitur.*
> *Populus precationi se coniungens, illique assentiens, acclamatione Amen suam facit orationem* (GRIM, § 32).[59]

In order to fully understand the function of the collect as set forth in the General Instruction, we will have to investigate both the role ascribed to the silence and that ascribed to the collect oration itself.

(a) *The nature and function of the silence*:

The silence of the community is an action of the gathered community. It is entered into at the invitation of the priest (*sacerdos*) presiding over the worship: *sacerdos populum ad orandum invitat*. As well, the silence is kept by the priest and people together: *et omnes una cum sacerdote parumper silent*.

The function of the silence is twofold. During this time the worshipping community are invited to become conscious that they stand in the sight of God, and as well to formulate within themselves their desires and

---

[59] Then the priest invites the people to pray, and all, together with the priest, keep silence for a short time, so that they may become conscious that they stand in the sight of God, and may formulate their prayers of homage and desire. Then the priest proclaims the prayer, which it is customary to name the collect. Through it the character of the celebration is expressed, and the entreaty is directed in the words of the priest to the Father, through Christ in the Holy Spirit.
 The people make the prayer their own and give their assent by the acclamation, *Amen* (GIRM, § 32).
(The translation is the author's.)

prayers of homage: *ut conscii fiant in conspectu Dei stare, et vota sua in animo possint nuncupare.*

The terms *in conspectu Dei, vota,* and *in animo nuncupare* bear the sense of public acts of worship. *In conspectu Dei* is quite common in the Vulgate translation of the psalms, themselves prayers of the Israelite cult. Its use can be seen in Ps 118:169-170, where it describes the desire of a member of the assembly to bring his entreaty and petition (*deprecatio, postulatio*) before God:

"*Appropinquet deprecatio mea in conspectu tuo, Domine; iuxta eloquium tuum da mihi intellectum. Intret postulatio mea in conspectu tuo, secundum eloquium tuum eripe me*" (Ps 118:169-170)[60].

Votum carries the threefold sense of a public vow, supplication and also praise and homage[61]. These meanings appear to come into play in the Vulgate translation of Ps 115:18: "*Vota mea Domino reddam in conspectu omnis populi eius in atriis domus Domini, in medio tui, Ierusalem.*"

The verb *nuncupare* is very rarely used in Christian liturgical Latin[62]. It is, however, found in classical Latin. There the expression *vota nuncupare* is used to designate the vows made during public worship by civil officials

---

[60] See also Ps 140:2, and as well Ap 15:4, where the sense is of public adoration: *Omnes gentes ... adorabunt in conspectu tuo.*

[61] A.Blaise, Dictionnaire latin-français des auteurs chrétiens (Turnhout: Brepols, 1964), 860.

[62] The verb is not found in the Schnitker and Slaby concordance of the Missal of Paul VI, nor in the Blaise study of the principal vocabulary of the prayers of the latin liturgy. It is noted only once (G 2053) in the Deshusses concordance of the early sacramentaries. See T.A.Schnitker and W.A.Slaby, Concordantia Verbalia Missalis Romani (Münster: Aschendorf, 1983), and A.Blaise, Le vocabulaire latin des principaux thèmes liturgiques (Turnhout: Brepols, 1966), and J.Deshusses and B.Darragon, Concordances et tableaux pour l'étude des grands sacramentaires, III, 3, Spicilegii Friburgensis Subsidia 13, (Fribourg, Suisse: Éditions Universitaires, 1982), 189.

(counsels, magistrates) in connection with the execution of their offices[63]. Note here that *nuncupare* was not used in any of the draft schemata for the General Instruction[64]. The preferred expression in the drafts was *et vota sua in animo possint efformare*[65]. It is possible, then, that the last minute substitution of *nuncupare* in place of *efformare* was aimed at highlighting the communal dimension of the silent petitions of the faithful. The substitution, though, is not entirely successful. Given the public nature of *nuncupare*, the expression *in animo possint nuncupare* is something of a contradiction.

In spite of this, the text's interpretation of the silence is clear. During this time of quiet the whole assembly are invited to make themselves conscious that they, as a worshipping community, are in the presence of God (*in conspectu Dei*). At the same time, they are invited by the priest to formulate their prayers of supplication, praise and homage.

(b) *The function of the collect oration*:

The collect oration itself is said to have two functions. The collect both expresses the character (*indoles*) of the celebration, and is a priestly prayer (*verbis sacerdotis*) of intercession and mediation (*precatio*) directed to God

---

[63]See J.Facciolati, A.E.G.Forcellini, and J.Furlanetti, Lexicon Totius Latinitatis, III (Patavii: Typis Seminarii MDCCCLXXI), 413. See also F.Blatt, ed. Novum Glossarium Mediae Latinitatis, M-N (Hafniae: Ejnar Munksgaard, MCMLIX-MCMLXIX), 1532-1535.

[64]There are five *Schemata* dealing with the General Instruction amongst the documents of the *Consilium*: *Schemata* 250, (12/X/1967), *Schemata* 264 (18/XII/1967), *Schemata* 273 (15/II/1968), *Schemata* 282 (21/III/1968), and the final draft *Schemata* 301 (15/XI/1968). For a complete list of the *Schemata* of the *Consilium* see P.Marini, "Elenco degli 'Schemata' del 'Consilium' e della Congregazione per il Culto Divino (Marzo 1964 - Febbraio 1975)," Notitiae 18 (1982): 487-539.

[65]See *Schemata* 264, III,A,6, and §32 in *Schematae* 273, 282, and 301.

through Christ in the Spirit. The General Instruction reads:

> *Per eam [collecta] indoles celebrationis exprimitur et precatio verbis sacerdotis ad Deum Patrem, per Christum in Spiritu Sancto, dirigitur. Populus precationi se coniungens, illique assentiens, acclamatione Amen suam facit orationem* (GIRM, § 32).

Both of these functions will now be examined. The sense of *indoles* will be clearer if it is examined second. In the General instruction, the collect is said to address intercession and petition (*precatio*[66]), by the word of the priest, to God the Father through Christ in the Spirit: *precatio verbis sacerdotis ad Deum Patrem, per Christum in Spiritu Sancto, dirigitur*. According to the General Instruction, then, the collect is essentially a prayer of petition and mediation.

The collect is also said to function to express the *indoles* of the celebration. Though this ascription is not found in the first draft of the General Instruction[67], it is present in the second and subsequent drafts[68].

The meaning of *indoles* when applied to the liturgical seasons has been studied above. There it was seen that *indoles* has the sense of the particular mystery a season celebrates, and as well the particular character (joy, expectation, penance ...) of that celebration. The Sundays of Ordinary Time have no particular *indoles*, rather they are devoted to the mystery of Christ in all its fullness.

---

[66] For the liturgical sense of *precatio* as intercessory prayer see Blaise, Vocabulaire, § 100. The noun *precator* means intercessor. The conjunction of *precatio* and *sacerdos* underscores the mediating role of the priest. The use of *precatio* in the text was, like the use of *nuncupare*, a last minute change. The fifth draft, *Schemata* 301 (§ 32) reads *prex*. The substitution of *precatio* strengthens the nature of the collect as a public prayer of petition and mediation.

[67] See *Schemata* 250, III,A,6.

[68] See *Schemata* 264, III,A,6.

Indoles is also used in the General Instruction, where it is associated with the communitarian nature of the celebration of the Eucharist. In an earlier section (§ 14), the Instruction insists on the importance of the dialogues between celebrant and congregation, as well as on the importance of the acclamation of the congregation, because the celebration of the Mass ought to have, of its nature, a communal character (*indoles*): *Cum Missae celebratio natura sua indolem "communitariam" habeat*" (GIRM, § 14)[69]. This communal character, then, refers both to the unity of those gathered and to their communion with the priest.

The nature of the collect prayer expresses something of the *indoles* of the celebration. The collect is an action of the gathered community, priest and people united in the sight of God. The silence and the collect oration itself together form a communal act of petition and praise (*nuncupare vota*), in which the prayer of each member of the community is offered to God through the mediating prayer (*precatio*) of the priest (*sacerdos*). The nature of the collect indicates, then, that the character of the celebration is one of public worship in which the petitions and praise of the united assembly and of each of its members are offered to God through the mediating prayer of the priest.

In light of these various meanings of *indoles* in the General Instruction and in the General Norms, it can be seen that the collect expresses the *indoles* of the celebration in four ways. As a presidential prayer made up of an invitation, communal silence, oration and acclamation, the collect reflects the communitarian character of the Mass. Furthermore, it expresses the nature of Christian worship as an act of the united assembly offering praise and petition to God through the mediatory prayer of the priest. During particular seasons, the collect also functions to express the particular mystery being celebrated, along with the attitude and disposition with which it ought be celebrated.

---

[69]Since by nature the celebration of Mass has the character of being the act of a community (GIRM, § 14).

This understanding of the collect's functions fits well with the stated character (beginning, introduction and preparation) and purpose (assembly of the community, disposition of the celebration) of the introductory rites. The relationship between the collect and the particular mystery being celebrated works to introduce the mystery, prepare the community for the particular celebration, and dispose the minds of those gathered towards the mystery. Clearly this function is most operative during particular seasons, for feasts, and for votive Masses. The same can be said for the relationship between the collect and the particular character in which the Mass is celebrated. Also clear is the underlying character of the collect as a prayer which convenes those gathered into a single community in union with the priest to offer praise and make petition to God. This unity is broadened when account is taken of the fact that the presidential prayer is also seen as a prayer said in the name of the entire church. Furthermore, the petition of the community and church includes prayer for the whole human family. In this it unites the assembly to the needs and intentions of the whole of humanity.

What could be made more explicit in the General Instruction is the relationship between the *precatio* of the priest and the silent *vota* of the assembly. Our vocabulary analysis shows that the link is expressed through the public nature of *nuncupare* and *vota*, and the intercessory sense of *precatio*. Within the context of the Mass as an act of public worship, the intercessory prayer of the priest mediates the petition, praise and homage of the gathered community. This understanding underlines the mediatory role of the priest.

A study of the earlier drafts of the General Instruction points to a degree of confusion about the relationship between the people's silent petition and the presidential oration. In the first draft, *Schemata* 250, the link is not clear. Using language reminiscent of ancient writers such as Bernhold of Constance, the draft states that the people's *Amen* concluded (*concludere*) and confirmed the presidential prayer. However, for Bernhold, it was the priest's prayer which concluded (*concludere*) and gathered (*colligere*) the people's petitions. The apposite section of the *Schemata* text reads:

"*Post aliquod temporis spatium, quo omnes in silentio orant, sacerdos profert orationem, quam populus concludit confirmatque acclamando 'Amen'*" (*Schemata* 250, A,III,6)[70].

The second draft, *Schemata* 264, clearly understands that one function of the collect is to gather (*colligere*) the prayer of the whole community. The *Amen* is seen to serve to conclude (*concludere*) the whole prayer:

"*Tunc sacerdos profert Orationem, quae 'Collecta' nominatur; per eam totius communitatis oratio quodammodo colligitur, indoles celebrationis exprimitur ... Populus precatione se uniens, illique et assentiens acclamatione 'Amen' orationem concludit*" (*Schemata* 264, III,A,6)[71].

However, by the third draft (*Schemata* 273), and consequently in all the remaining drafts and the resultant General Instruction, three significant changes have been put into effect. Firstly, the function of the collect as gathering (*colligere*) the silent prayer of the faithful has been dropped. Secondly, the people's *Amen* no longer concludes (*concludere*) the prayer. Rather, it is through their *Amen* that the people join with and assent to the priest's prayer, which he offers in his public role. Thirdly, the two verbs most associated in ancient writing with the function of the collect, *concludere* and *colligere*, have

---

[70] After a certain length of time, during which all pray in silence, the priest says the oration which the people conclude and confirm by the acclamation 'Amen'.

[71] Then the priest says the Oration, which is called the 'Collect'; through the collect the prayer of the whole community is joined together in a certain measure, the character of the celebration is expressed ... The people conclude the prayer by their acclamation 'Amen', thereby uniting themselves to the petition and assenting to it.

both been removed from the text. The apposite section of the *Schemata* 274 reads:

> *Tunc sacerdos profert orationem, quae communiter 'collecta' nominatur; per eam indoles celebrationis exprimitur et prex verbis sacerdotis ad Deum Patrem, mediante Christo in Spiritu Sancto dirigitur. Populus precationi se uniens, illique assentiens acclamatione 'Amen' orationem suam facit (Schemata 274, § 32)*[72].

It appears, then, that the General Instruction has highlighted the role of the collect precisely as a presidential and mediatory prayer. In doing this, it emphasises the priestly nature of the collect oration.

There is also a second area of confusion. The General Instruction does not show how the two functions it ascribes to the collect, expressing the character of the celebration and making petition, are related to each other. There is no indication as to which is primary, or indeed as to how they are linked.

The function of the collect in the ancient Roman, Latin liturgy and in MR(1975): A comparison:

There are a range of similarities and differences between the function of the collect in the early Roman, Latin liturgy and in the Missal of Paul VI. These are most conveniently set out in the shape of a comparative table. In the final chapter of this study we will use the information gathered from our analysis of the collects of the Sundays in Ordinary Time to determine whether those collects do, in fact, carry out these functions[73]. The similarities and differences can be set out as follows:

---

[72] Then the priest offers the oration, which generally is called the 'collect'. Through the collect the character of the celebration is expressed and a prayer by the words of the priest is directed to the Father by the mediation of Christ in the Holy Spirit. The people make the oration their own by uniting themselves to it and assenting to it through their acclamation 'Amen'.

[73] See below, 678ff..

	ANCIENT ROMAN COLLECTS	MR(19750
PRES. PRAYERS	*A prayer said by the priest on behalf of the community.*	(i) A prayer directed to God in the name of the whole church, as an act of public worship, (ii) and in the name of the gathered community, (iii) manifests for the community that Christ, the only mediator, presides in the person of the priest, (iv) the prayer of the community includes prayer for the whole human family, (v) marks unity of people and priest in presence of Xt.
SILENCE	*The faithful make their petitions.*	(i) The members of the assembly become conscious that they stand in the sight of God in an act of public worship, (ii) the faithful formulate within themselves prayers of supplication, praise and homage.
COLLECT ORATION	*(1) Gathers (colligere) the petitions of the community and concludes (concludere) them, (2) gathers the assembly into a single, worshipping community (collecta as plebs collecta).*	(i) Concludes the Introductory Rites, which open the liturgy, introduce the ritual, and prepare the faithful for its worthy celebration. (ii) expresses the character (*indoles*) of the celebration, (iii) is a priestly prayer of petition which mediates the petition, praise and homage of the assembly.
AMEN	*Ratifies and confirms the prayer of the president.*	The faithful unite themselves to the prayer of the priest, making it their own.

CONCLUSION

This chapter has sought to place the collect oration for the Sundays in Ordinary Time within their broader context as part of the revision of the liturgy stemming from the renewal of the church desired by the Second Vatican Council. In doing so we first examined the principles and method which guided the revision of the Missal. Then, using the General Instruction of the Missal and the General Norms of the Liturgical Year and Calendar, we analysed the meaning of the feast of Sunday and the season of Ordinary Time as understood by the Missal. Finally the General Instruction and General Norms were used to establish the character, place and function of the collect in the new sacramentary. A brief comparison between the functions of the collect in the ancient Roman, Latin liturgy and the Missal of Paul VI closed off the chapter.

Focus of our study:

The focus of our study is the actual text of the collect prayers for Ordinary Time, excluding the common trinitarian concluding formulas. Specifically these texts are studied with a view to analysing what they, as a collection of prayers, say concerning the relationship of the Christian people to God. As an analysis of the texts themselves, this study puts to one side the many questions concerning the function, structure and nature of that part of the Mass known as the collect. However it is the hope of the author that a close study of the prayer texts themselves will be relevant for any discussion of the broader questions concerning the place and function of the collect in the Mass.

In the next chapter we will turn our attention to the method of textual analysis employed in this study.

CHAPTER THREE
METHOD FOR THE STUDY OF THE COLLECTS

INTRODUCTION

The task of this chapter is to set forth the method used both to analyse each of the collects, and to determine the arrangement of the individual studies into separate chapters. The present chapter, then, deals with the principles upon which the method is based, their practical application to our study, and the principal research tools utilized.

The relationship of the Christian people to God implied in each prayer can only be discussed once the **meaning** of the **text** has been opened up. These methodological considerations are necessarily concerned with two pivotal issues. First, it is necessary to establish the 'text' that is to be studied. The second issue is the development of a method that is suitable for analysing the meaning of such a 'text'.

The shape of the methodological investigation pursued here will roughly correspond to the framework subsequently employed in the analysis of each collect. This serves a number of purposes. It clarifies the function of each step of an actual analysis, highlights its methodological presuppositions, and provides an opportunity to name the principal research tools appropriate for that part of the study. As well it points to the coherence of the framework as a whole.

The headings and subdivisions which usually structure each collect study are as follows:

PRAYER (as it stands in the Missal of Paul VI): Latin text and translation

THE PRAYER IN THE ORIGINAL SOURCE

USE [of the original prayer] IN OTHER SOURCES

USE [of the original prayer] IN THE MISSAL OF PAUL VI

CHANGES FROM THE ORIGINAL

ANALYSIS OF THE ORIGINAL SOURCE
Origin:
Grammatical structure:
Vocabulary:
Meaning of the prayer:

ANALYSIS OF THE WORDS AND PHRASES IN THE COLLECT IN THE CONTEXT OF THE MISSAL OF PAUL VI

THE RELATIONSHIP OF THE PEOPLE TO GOD

FREER TRANSLATION OF THE PRAYER

The question of the establishment of the 'text' is the principal concern of the first five sections. The meaning of the 'text' is considered in the sections dealing with the analysis of the original source and the analysis of the collect in the context of the Missal of Paul VI. It is to the question of the 'text' that we first turn.

ESTABLISHING THE 'TEXT'

Preliminary considerations: the 34 collects for the Masses of Ordinary Time:
The precise focus of our study is the relationship between the Christian people and God set forth in the collects for the Sundays of Ordinary Time in the Missal of Paul VI (1975). In this Missal 34 Masses have been allocated to cover the weeks of Ordinary Time. Entitled the *Missae Dominicales et*

Cotidianae[1], they form a coherent, clearly defined unit in the new Missal. Each Mass is typically titled, for example, *Dominica XXIV Per Annum*, here using Week 24.

There are two exceptions to this. The Sunday which opens the season is devoted to the celebration of the feast of the Baptism of the Lord. However that week is counted as the first week of the season, and a Mass text has been provided for daily celebrations[2]. This Mass is called *Hebdomada I Per Annum*. It has been included in our study because it clearly belongs among the Masses of Ordinary Time. Similarly, Ordinary Time is brought to a close with the celebration of the solemnity of Christ the King on the Sunday of the last week of the season[3]. A Mass, entitled *Hebdomada XXXIV Per Annum* has been provided for the remaining ferial days of the week. For the sake of completeness, this Mass has also been included in our study.

As has been seen in the previous chapter, that part of the Introductory Rites which falls under the name *Collecta* itself has a number of components. It consists of the president's invitation to prayer (*Oremus*), a period of silence, the collect oration and trinitarian formula said by the priest, and the people's acclamation *Amen*. While each of these parts makes some comment on the relationship of the Christian people to God, only the contribution made by the collect oration itself will be the focus of our study.

The 'text' of the collect in the Missal of Paul VI:

The analysis of each collect opens with the text of the prayer as found in the 1975 *editio typica altera* of the Missal of Paul VI. Each text is

---

[1] MR(1975), 340.

[2] See MR(1975), 339.

[3] The title reads *Dominica ultima per annum, Domini Nostri Iesu Christi Universorum Regis, Sollemnitas*, MR(1975), 380-381.

accompanied by a literal translation. As well, since a number of prayers are used on more than one occasion in the Missal, the liturgical context of each usage is given. The implication is that the liturgical context of a text, as well as the text itself, offers a contribution to the meaning of the prayer[4]. The 'text' of each collect, then, includes both the text of the prayer and its context in the Missal.

The original text:

Secondly, the earliest known text of the prayer, along with its original liturgical context, is given. When necessary, a literal translation of this prayer is included. The supposition underlying this step is that the range of meanings carried by an oration can be seen more clearly when viewed in the light of the meanings the prayer has held throughout its history. Two things are noted in this section of the analysis of each collect. Attention is given to the differences between the original and current prayer in terms of structure, vocabulary and phrases, and the differences in liturgical context are highlighted. The factors which contribute to the 'text' of the original oration, then, also contribute to the 'text' of the present collect.

The standard tool for ascertaining the original sources of the current prayers in the Missal is the series of articles by Dumas entitled "Les sources du Missel romain."[5]

---

[4]For a study of the complex interrelationship between 'text' and 'context' in liturgy see K.Irwin, <u>Context and Text: Method in Liturgical Theology</u>, A Pueblo Book (Collegeville: The Liturgical Press, 1994), especially 176-218.

[5]See Dumas, "Les sources du Missel romain," <u>Notitiae</u> 7 (1971):37-42, 74-77, 94-95, 134-136, 276-279, 409-410.
During preparation of this manuscript a more up to date study has appeared, C. Johnson, "Sources of the Roman Missal (1975): Proprium de Tempore, Proprium de Sanctis," <u>Notitiae</u> 32 (1-2-3/1996): 7-180. Like Dumas, it does not always give the earliest source or sources for some of the prayers studied here.

The history of the text:

Along with the earliest source of a text and its context in that source, there is also provided a brief account of the use made of the text throughout the liturgical tradition. The particular relevance of the textual history of the prayer is taken up below. However, it can be remarked here that the way an oration has been used in the various liturgical sources offers insight into two points that are of some concern to our study. This historical picture reveals the path the oration has traced from its earliest textual witness into the Missal of 1570, and subsequently the Missal of Paul VI.

The two standard reference works for this task are Bruylants' two volume Les oraisons du Missel Romain[6], and Moeller's volumes of prayers in the Corpus Orationum series[7] of the Corpus Christianorum. The Bruylants' text, for a long time the only such comprehensive resource available, gives the major Roman, Frankish Gelasian, and Gallican sources of all the orations of the 1604 edition of the Roman Missal of 1570. It also contains those feasts added later[8]. The Moeller series attempts to set out the sources of the orations from as many as possible of the western liturgical texts up through, but not including, the Missal of Paul VI. Although already amounting to five volumes covering over 3,500 prayers, the series is still not completed.

In order to render this material both servicable and manageable, it has been employed in the following manner. Following Bruylants' lead, our

---

[6] P.Bruylants, Les oraisons du Missel Romain: texte et histoire, Vol. I: Tabulae synopticae fontium Missalis Romain indices, Vol. II, Orationum textus et usus juxta fontes (Louvain: Centre de Documentation et d'Information Liturgiques Abbaye du Mont César, 1952).

[7] E.Moeller, J-M.Clément et B.Coppieters 't Wallant, eds., Corpus Orationum, t.1 A-C, orationes 1-880, t.2 D, pars prima, orationes 881-1707, t.3 D, pars altera, 1708-2389, t.4 E-H, orationes 2390-3028, t.5 I-O, orationes 3029-3699, Corpus Christianorum 160- (Turnhout: Brepols, 1992-).

[8] Bruylants, I,ix.

sketch of a text's history will concentrate on the major early Roman, Frankish Gelasian and Gallican sources, as well as on the appropriation of the prayer into the Roman Missal of Pius V. The Corpus Orationum volumes have been used to supplement this material. They are especially of service in that they point out where Mass prayers have been used as prayers for the Office, and vice versa. When a text is not listed in Bruylants, the occasions of its use are taken from Moeller. When a prayer is not found in either work, other references, such as the concordances by Siffrin[9] or Deshusses and Darragon[10], have been consulted.

The search for the history of a text raises two problems. Of minor concern, though of practical importance, is the lack of a standardized set of abbreviations for liturgical texts across the various concordances. The following method has been employed in this work. When a list of texts is taken from an author, in particular Bruylants, Moeller or Siffrin, the abbreviations used by that author are given. If, however, a more recent critical edition of a text pertinent to our study has been published[11], the new reference number will be placed in square brackets following the apposite

---

[9]P.Siffrin, Liber sacramentorum Romanae Aeclesiae (Cod. Vatican. Regn. Lat. 316) Sacramentorum Gelasianum: Konkordanztabellen zu den lateinischen Sakramentarien, 2, Rerum Ecclesiasticarum documenta, Series minor: Subsidia studiorum, 5 (Roma: Casa Editrice Herder, 1959).

[10]J.Deshusses, and B.Darragon, eds., Concordances et tableaux pour l'étude des grands sacramentaires: Vol. I Concordance des Pièces; Vol. II Tableaux synoptiques; Vol. III pts. 1-4, Concordance Verbale; Spicilegii Friburgensis Subsidia, nn. 9-14 (Fribourg, Suisse: Éditions Universitaires, 1982-83).

[11]In particular, the most recent critical editions of the *Hadrianum* and the Supplement of Aniane in J.Deshusses, ed., Le Sacramentaire Grégorien: Ses principales formes d'après les plus anciens manuscrits I, Spicilegium Friburgense 16 (Fribourg, Suisse: Éditions Universitaires, 1979), and the *Corpus Christianorum* edition of the *Gellonensis*, A.Dumas, ed., Liber Sacramentorum Gellonensis, Textus, Corpus Christianorum, Series Latina, 159 (Turnhout: Brepols, 1981).

reference. In the general text of our study, initials and abbreviations will correspond to those listed in the List of Abbreviations at the beginning of this work.

The second problem is of far more importance methodologically. It concerns the question of the role the history of the prayer throughout the liturgical tradition plays in determining the meaning of that prayer as it stands in the Missal of Paul VI. It is to this question that we now turn.

Establishing the 'best textual witness':

In the previous chapter we examined the principles which guided the *Consilium* in its task of the revision of the Roman Missal. As set out in the article by Dumas, the opening point under the first general principle, the principle of veracity (*vérité*), dealt with the question of the original text of a prayer (*Le texte lui-même*). The paragraph reads:

> *Lorsque le texte du Missel s'était corrumpu au cours de siècles, on l'a toujours restauré selon les meilleurs témoins. Voir, par exemple, la prière sur les offrandes du dimanche de Pâques, où l'inutile et pascitur redevient renascitur* (V 470)[12].

Three points in particular can be taken from this statement. One is that, for the compilers of the Missal, the history of a prayer through the centuries reveals the processes of corruption of the original text. The second is that the best witnesses of an oration were, seemingly, those which most accurately reflected the earliest text. The third is that it is the best text of the earliest source of a prayer which provides the basis for the prayer in the Missal of Paul VI.

---

[12]When the text of the Missal has been corrupted in the course of the centuries, it has always been restored according to the best textual witnesses. See for example the prayer over the gifts for Easter Sunday, where the redundant *et pascitur* has been reestablished as *renascitur*.
Dumas, "Les oraisons du nouveau Missel romain," Questions Liturgiques 52 (1971): 263.

The second point under the principle of *Vérité*, entitled *La nature des textes*[13], allows for the same sort of claims with regard to the context of the prayer in the Mass. Not only are texts restored to the best witness of the original, but also to their true nature (*vrai nature*) in the Mass, for example as collects or as prayers over the gifts. Again what is valuable here is that it is the best text and original context in the Mass that provide the basis for the prayer in the revised Missal.

Some of these points may well be open to debate both in theory and in their application in the revision of the Missal. Nevertheless, the principle of ensuring veracity through using the best witness of the earliest text is extremely helpful in determining the role of the history of a prayer and its pertinence for a study of its meaning in the Missal of Paul VI.

The principle establishes the primacy of the original prayer for understanding the prayer in the current Missal. The later history of the prayer is comprised of its possible adaptation, recontextualization, corruption and correction throughout the liturgical tradition. This history, however, does not provide the main interpretative bridge between the earliest use of the oration and the prayer's present use in the Missal of Paul VI. Rather, the prayer's position in the current Missal is said to be a direct appropriation of the prayer from its earliest and best source. Consequently the meaning of the prayer is largely dependent upon its context within the original source and its new context within the revised Missal. Any meanings which have accrued to the prayer over the course of the intervening centuries have been, to a degree, bypassed by this application of the principle of *verité*.

However, they have not been completely forgone. Traces of any development in the meanings of words and expressions may well be found in prayers from later sources that also have been incorporated into the Missal. As well, they may be contained in those prayers written for the Missal. These

---

[13]Ibid., 262-263.

developments, then, will come to light when the vocabulary of the prayers is studied from within their new context as collects in the Missal of Paul VI.

On some occasions a prayer in the new Missal will actually be composed of two ancient prayers[14]. In those cases, the best textual witness of both ancient orations will be studied.

Summary:

Our discussion of the issues surrounding the establishment of the correct text and its context have led to an important methodological conclusion. Determining the meaning of a prayer in the Missal of Paul VI involves a twofold process. The first step is to determine the meaning of the best textual witness of a prayer from within its context in the original source. The second step is then to see whether the prayer's new context in the Missal of Paul VI adds any meanings or offers any further interpretations of the prayer beyond those found in the original oration. The larger 'text' of our study comprises, in fact, two texts, the best witness to the original prayer in its original context and the collect in the Missal of Paul VI.

Having established the 'text' of our study, our attention will now focus more directly on the methodology employed to discover the range of meanings carried by a prayer.

ESTABLISHING THE MEANING OF A LITURGICAL TEXT

The meaning of each text, both the original prayer and the current collect, emerges from consideration of a number of factors. It involves (i) a review of the original historical and liturgical context of the prayer, (ii) a consideration of the structure of the prayer text itself, and (iii) a study of the

---

[14] The collect for Sunday XXV is composed from orations L 493 and LMZ 1374. See below, 127.

words and expressions used in that oration. In this section we will deal with these three points, first in relation to the original prayer, and then with regard to the collect in the current Missal. Our starting point will be the role played by a study of the original historical and liturgical context of each prayer.

The original historical and liturgical context of each prayer:

(a) *The original historical context*

There is a small number of the Sunday collects for which it is possible to reconstruct their probable, original, historical context. In the main, these are the orations appropriated into the Missal from the *Veronensis*[15]. This is helpful for understanding the meaning of the prayer. It provides a sense of the original intention of the author, who is addressing a defined audience within a specific historical circumstance. As well, it points to specific meanings and connotations of words and expressions that are typical of the works of that author. This further enables the prayer to be set within the broader literary context of the writer's other prayers and works.

(b) *The original liturgical context*

Whether the author is known or not, the liturgical context of a prayer plays a role in indicating the meaning of a prayer. The liturgical context of a prayer is established by examining (i) the place of the prayer in the liturgical action (as a collect, secret etc.), (ii) the particularity of the liturgical action itself (Mass, Office, Good Friday service, Lent, Advent etc.), and (iii) the relation of the prayer to the collection as a whole. Understanding this broader context aids in clarifying the sense of the references within the prayer. For example the images of light in a prayer during the Easter Vigil recall the risen Christ, the defeat of death and darkness, and the new creation in the new light. The use of this same symbol in orations for the morning Office is more immediately related to the dawning of the day, which dispells the night and its

---

[15]The studies of these orations are found in Chapter Four.

terrors. The liturgical context indicates that the immediate reference of the symbol of light is quite different, though not unrelated to other uses.

(c) *The limits of this approach*

This approach to the meaning of a collect is quite limited. As is mostly the case, the author and historical circumstances surrounding the prayer's origins remain unknown. On a number of occasions the liturgical context of a prayer is not clear. More importantly, the same prayer can be found in a variety of contexts even in the same early sacramentary[16]. Once a prayer has been uttered, and especially written down, it assumes an independence and a 'distance' from its author's original intention, original audience and original setting[17]. Many prayers from the earliest collections were freely reappropriated and adapted into differing liturgical and historical contexts.

The historical and liturgical context of a prayer, then, are helpful in determining what meanings are being actualized in that oration. However, the meaning of the prayer cannot be reduced to the original intention of the author, even when that is known, or to the earliest known liturgical context in which the oration is used.

The structure of the prayer:

The structure of the prayer makes essential contributions to the meaning of an oration. The structure establishes the range of possible relationships and dynamics between the various words, phrases, expressions, symbols and allusions that constitute the oration itself. In doing so, it also sets the

---

[16]See Appendix II "Collects for the Sundays in Ordinary Time: original source, and position in MR(1570) and MR(1975)."

[17]For a discussion of the implications of the 'gap' between a text and its origins when written texts have broken their initial link with the intention of the author, with the original audience, and with the situation common to the parties, see P.Ricoeur, Interpretation Theory: Discourse and the Surplus of Meaning (Fort Worth: Texas Christian University Press, 1976), 35, 75f.

parameters in which the probable and fitting interpretation of the prayer can take place[18]. Furthermore, the pattern around which a prayer is constructed can itself introduce elements that are part of its meaning. The collect for Sunday IV provides a good example of this[19]. That oration was clearly modelled on the New Testament injunction to love God and neighbour. The collect, then, through the appropriation of this allusion, is an attempt to associate its primary concerns, worship of God and moral behaviour, with the greatest of all the Christian commandments.

Our study of the structure of each collect includes the indentification of (i) the various elements in the prayer, (ii) the constructions through which they are joined, and (iii) the relationships which are established between the various constructs. It also contains, where appropriate, references to parallel structures in other prayers and scriptural texts. These parallels serve to highlight any added dimensions that the structure itself may carry. As well, they serve to emphasise, by comparison, the special aspect or meaning the structure may bring to light when used in this particular way. A more complete rationale for using parallel texts specifically from the liturgical sources and the scriptures is offered in the following section "The meaning of a prayer from the analysis of its vocabulary."

The key reference for studying the structure of the prayers which have come into the new Missal from amongst the collects of the Missal of Pius V is M.Haessly's Rhetoric in the Sunday Collects of the Roman Missal[20]. Also helpful were the Deshusses and Darragon concordance of the Roman, Frankish

---

[18]For some discussion of the place of the 'construction' of the text in enabling a written work to have a 'closed chain of meaning', see Ricoeur, Interpretation Theory, 81f.

[19]See below, 99.

[20]M.Haessly, Rhetoric in the Collects of the Sunday Missal (St Louis: Manufacturers Printery, 1938).

Gelasian and Gallican liturgical sources, and the Dutripon concordance of the Vulgate translation of the scriptures[21].

The meaning of the prayer from an analysis of the vocabulary:

The greater part of each analysis of a collect is taken up with a study of the vocabulary of the prayer. This undertaking has been based on the methodological principle that the meaning of a word, expression or construction in a liturgical text is best understood through an examination of the use of that word, expression or construction in liturgical texts themselves.

(a) *Liturgy as a privileged locus of theology*

The act of liturgy itself is a privileged ecclesial, and hence hermeneutical, locus[22]. As such, the vocabulary used in liturgical prayer assumes added symbolic dimensions and referents not necessarily present in its non-liturgical usage. As well, the continuous liturgical use of words and expressions, along with their adaption and reappropriation into other prayers, together build up over time the range of connotations that the vocabulary used in the liturgy may carry. Furthermore, the specific context in which this vocabulary is used and reused remains the liturgy itself. The prayers are

---

[21]F.P.Dutripon, Bibliorum Sacrorum Concordantiae: Vulgatae Editionis, editio octava (Paris: Bloud et Barral, 1880; reprint New York: Georg Olms Verlag, 1976).

There are a number of concordances to the Vulgate scriptures. This concordance was chosen on account of its ease in use and current availability. The edition of the latin Vugate scriptures used throughout the study is A. Gramatica, Bibliorum Sacrorum Iuxta Vulgatam Clementinam, Nova Editio (Roma: Typis Polygolottis Vaticanis, MCMXLVI). This edition was chosen because its text is consistent with the Dutripon concordance. However, reference will be made to other versions of the Vulgate where there are disputes concerning the rendition of a specific pericope or word. An example of this is found in the use of either *rationabilis* or *ratio* in 1 Pet 2:2. See the study of the collect for Sunday IV, below, 109, fn 29.

[22]See Irwin, Context and Text, 44-46.

composed by worshippers for the purpose of worship. It is only appropriate, then, that the vocabulary of the prayers of the liturgy be understood primarily through an examination of its use in the liturgical texts themselves.

(b) *Relationship of liturgical texts to the scriptures*

There are two corollaries to this principle. Firstly, since the liturgy and the scriptures are essentially related, the language of the liturgy resonates strongly with the language of the bible[23]. Our study of the liturgical sense of a term, then, will also take into account any biblical resonances the word or expression may carry.

(c) *The integrity of liturgical traditions*

Secondly, the liturgical meaning of words and expressions accumulates in liturgical traditions over time. This is an important methodological consideration. The meanings of words in the earliest strata of Roman liturgical texts, the *Veronensis* and *Reginensis* 316, are best understood in the light of those texts. Later Roman works, such as the *Hadrianum* and the *Paduensis*, build upon these earlier texts. Similarly, care must be taken not to confuse the different liturgical traditions. There is no necessarily uniform development of the range of meanings associated with the same word across the various early Roman, Mozarabic, Gallican and Ambrosian liturgical traditions. Each tradition may form its own particular connotations and nuances. However, in later mixed sacramentaries, such as the Ambrosian sacramentaries or the mixed Frankish Gelasian sacramentaries such as the Sacramentary of Angoulême, the influence of the different traditions is operative in the hybrid texts.

(d) *Factors governing the choice of examples*

Our vocabulary analysis, then, will pay attention to the way individual words and expressions are appropriated into a range of prayer constructs and

---

[23]The relationship of the early Latin translations of the scriptures to liturgical Latin is taken up in Mohrmann, Liturgical Latin. See also A.Blaise, Le Vocabulaire latin des principaux thèmes liturgiques (Turnhout: Brepols, 1966).

liturgical contexts. The focus of the vocabulary study, however, is not to establish the range of meanings a given word or expression may have in the broader liturgical usage. Rather it is to elucidate the meaning of that vocabulary in the prayer text that is itself the object of our study.

Consequently the examples utilized in the vocabulary analysis exhibit the following features. They are from texts of the same or a related liturgical tradition which are either contemporary with or earlier than the prayer being studied. They have been chosen because their structure, vocabulary and/or liturgical context have parallels with the vocabulary in question, which aid in understanding the range of meanings this vocabulary connotes. They are, also, a limited, but hopefully judicious, selection from a greater number of possible examples. Other examples that are also explanatory, but the addition of which would overly burden the text, are sometimes mentioned in footnotes.

(e) *Examples chosen from outside liturgical or scriptural sources*

On occasion, however, references are made to non-liturgical and non-scriptural sources[24]. In some cases this involves offering further background on words taken over into liturgical usage from pagan Roman religious and civil vocabulary[25]. Occasionally patristic texts are called upon to show how an expression may have been typical of a certain author[26], or to show more clearly

---

[24]Especially helpful here are the various studies in C.Mohrmann, Études sur le latin des chrétiens (Roma: Edizione di Storia e Letteratura, 1958); B.Botte and C.Mohrmann, L'Ordinaire de la messe; texte critique, traduction et études, Études liturgiques publiées sous la direction du Centre de Pastorale Liturgique et de l'Abbaye du Mont César, 2 (Paris: Les Éditions du Cerf, 1953); and M.P.Ellebracht, Remarks on the Vocabulary of the Ancient Orations in the Missale Romanum, Latinitas Christianorum Primaeva, Fasc.XVIII, Second Edition (Nijmegen-Utrecht: Dekker and Van De Vegt, 1966).

[25]For example see the study of *familia*, below, 487.

[26]For example the expression *et dictis exsequamur et factis* in the collect for Sunday VII was typical of the writings of Pope Gelasius. See below, 504.

how the meaning of a word in later patristic writings differed from its liturgical usage[27]. It will also be noted where an expression in a prayer is closely related to decrees from church Councils or Synods[28].

(f) *Research instruments*

The task of finding suitable examples was, in the main, achieved through the use of the Dutripon Vulgate concordance, and the Deshusses and Darragon concordance of early liturgical texts. The study of the one Mozarabic text was facilitated by the index to the Ferotin edition of the sacramentary[29]. The analysis of the Ambrosian texts was greatly aided by the concordance to the Sacramentarium Triplex[30]. Two further works were of particular importance in establishing the variety of meanings and allusions attached to liturgical vocabulary. Constant reference is made to Blaise's Le vocabulaire des principaux thèmes liturgiques, as well as to Ellebracht's Remarks on the Vocabulary of the Ancient Orations of the Missale Romanum.

The impact of modifications made to the original prayer:

Our study of the 'text' deals, in fact, with two prayers. One is the original prayer, set within its context in an early sacramentary. The other is the prayer as it stands in the Missal of Paul VI. Each will have to be analysed separately. Two factors are operative in the analysis of the later oration.

---

[27] See the study of *rationabilis*, below, 108.

[28] The collect for Week I has some affinities with an anti-Pelagian canon from the early 5th century Council of Mileve. See below, 462.

[29] M.Ferotin, ed., Le Liber mozaribicus sacramentorum et les manuscrits mozarabes, Monumenta Ecclesiae Liturgica, VI, (Paris: 1912).

[30] O.Heiming, ed., Das Sacramentarium Triplex: Die Handschrift C 43 der Zentralbibliothek Zürich, 2 Teil: Wortschatz und Ausdrucksformen, Corpus Ambrosiano Liturgicum I, Liturgiewissensschaftliche Quellen und Forschungen 49 (Münster: Aschendorff, 1968).

Even when the text in the new Missal is exactly the same as the original, its meaning is affected by its context in the new Missal. In the first instance, consideration must be taken of the impact of its liturgical context as a collect for a Sunday in Ordinary Time. As well, the collect may be utilized in other contexts in the revised sacramentary, contexts which in turn offer another interpretation of the prayer[31]. Added to this is that the Missal of Paul VI may have introduced new meanings to some of the words and expressions of the original prayer. This can come about when words and expressions are either utilized in different situations or have been placed in relationship with other terms[32]. The new Missal may also retain meanings and connotations not present in the original source, but which developed through usage in later sources. Thus, even when an ancient prayer is placed unmodified in the Missal of Paul VI, it is, in a sense, a different prayer.

On a number of occasions the original prayer has been modified, and reads differently from the best textual witness in the original source. In order to adjudge the meaning of the new, modified prayer, additional steps are necessary. Each of these changes themselves must be analysed, if possible, in terms of their historical origins, liturgical contexts and use in the liturgical tradition. Only on doing this can the meaning of the modified prayer be ascertained.

The primary instrument used in this study for researching the range of meanings carried by words and expressions in the revised Sacramentary is the

---

[31] The collect for Sunday VIII is utilized in a second, quite different context in the Missal, which in turn offers an interpretation of the prayer. See below, 197.

[32] Again, using the collect for Sunday VIII as an example, the sense of God's direction (*dirigere*) unto righteousness is broadened, in the revised Missal, to include the order of justice and peace. See below, 195.

concordance of the Roman Missal of 1975 edited by T.A.Schnitker and W.A.Slaby[33].

Note, however, that there is a large degree of continuity in meaning between the ancient sacramentaries and the new Missal. A vast number of prayers in the Missal of Paul VI are originally from the ancient sources. This was a clear intention of the compilers of the Missal[34]. To further underline this continuity, any of those prayers from the early sacramentaries used in our study as examples and which also have been incorporated into the Missal of Paul VI are so marked in a footnote.

The theology of the prayer:

The final section of each analysis examines those theological implications that pertain to the relationship of the Christian people to God, as these emerge from the meaning of the prayers. As well, a freer translation of the prayer will be offered. This translation attempts to take into account the meanings that have been uncovered in the course of the analysis.

Resumé of the structure of each analysis

The analysis of each collect is usually set out according to the following framework:

TABLE 1. THE STRUCTURE OF EACH ANALYSIS

HEADING	CONTENT
PRAYER	The collect as it stands in the Missal of Paul VI, along with a literal translation.

---

[33]T.A.Schnitker and W.A.Slaby, Concordantia Verbalia Missalis Romani (Münster: Aschendorff, 1983).

[34]See Dumas, "Les Oraisons du Missel romain," Questions Liturgiques 52 (1971): 266-269.

ORIGINAL SOURCE	The earliest witness to the prayer, its liturgical context, and a literal translation if necessary.
USE IN OTHER SOURCES	A brief history of the prayer in the major Roman, Frankish Gelasian and Gallican sources up to and including the 1604 edition of the 1570 Missale Romanum.
USE IN THE MISSAL OF PAUL VI	A list of any further contexts in the revised Missal into which the collect, or the original source, have been incorporated.
CHANGES FROM THE ORIGINAL	A detailing of the changes made to text and liturgical context of the original prayer.

ANALYSIS OF THE ORIGINAL SOURCE

<u>Origin</u>:	Where known, the conjectured original historical context is described.
<u>Grammatical structure</u>:	A study of the oration's grammatical structure.
<u>Vocabulary</u>:	A study of the prominent vocabulary of the prayer.
<u>Meaning of the prayer</u>:	The meaning of the prayer in light of the above analysis.

ANALYSIS OF THE WORDS AND PHRASES IN THE COLLECT IN THE CONTEXT OF THE MISSAL OF PAUL VI

This section discusses any new meanings introduced to the original prayer both through the new context of the prayer in the revised Missal, and through any modifications of the text of the original prayer. Where applicable, attention will be given to the <u>Origins</u>, <u>Grammatical structure</u>, <u>Vocabulary</u> and <u>Meaning</u> of these alterations.

THE RELATIONSHIP OF THE PEOPLE TO GOD

The theology of grace in both the original prayer and the collect in the current Missal.

FREER TRANSLATION OF THE PRAYER

A translation of the collect which attempts to take into account the material generated from the study of the prayer's meaning.

Summary:

In accordance with the principles and methodology outlined above, the meaning of a liturgical text emerges from a consideration of (i) the historical background to the original prayer, (ii) its original liturgical context along with the history of the prayer through the sources, (iii) the structure of the prayer, and (iv) the meanings of its words and expressions in the light of their liturgical usage. The principle operative here is that the vocabulary and structure of liturgical texts are best understood when examined from within their context in the liturgical tradition itself. Since the 'text' of each collect in the Missal of Paul VI is in fact two prayers, the original prayer in its context and the collect in the Missal, the methodology is employed twice in each study.

THE ORGANIZATION OF THE ANALYSES OF THE 34 COLLECTS INTO CHAPTERS

The analyses of the 34 collects are not presented in this study according to their order in the Missal of Paul VI. Rather, they are grouped, with some exceptions[35], firstly according to the sacramentary in which the original text is found, and secondly according to their liturgical context in that sacramentary. Admittedly this approach is somewhat unwieldly, especially since the collects have a definite order in the Missal of Paul VI. However it is in line with the methodological principles around which the study is built.

Since the liturgical meanings of a word or expression accumulate through usage over time, it is most appropriate to study the vocabulary and meanings of the earliest texts first. As well, texts which belong to each liturgical tradition are grouped together. This is a secondary consideration for

---

[35] The reasons for such exceptions are set out in the Introduction to that set of collects.

our particular study, however, since almost all our prayers are either from Roman sources or from Ambrosian sources which themselves are heavily influenced by Roman texts.

Each set of texts is prefaced by a brief introduction, outlining the history of the text, the critical edition used in this study, and other methodological and historical considerations pertinent to that set of orations.

The arrangement of the 34 collects into separate chapters is set out in the following table.

TABLE 2. THE ARRANGEMENT OF THE ANALYSES INTO CHAPTERS

CHAPTER	SOURCE	REFERENCE NUMBER IN SOURCE	WEEK IN MR (1975)
4	*VERONENSIS*:		
	Collects ascribed to Pope Gelasius (d. 496).	L 432	IV
	Collects ascribed to Pope Vigilius (d.555), set out in their probable chronological order.	L 486	XXXIII
		L 493	XXV
		L 887	XVIII
		L 633	VIII
		L 1045	XXIV
5	*REGINENSIS* 316:		
	Paschales vespertinales: Dominica post clausum paschae.	V 522	XXIII
		V 541	XIV
		V 546*	XV
		V 551	XXI
		V 556	X
		V 561	XXIX
		V 566	XI
	Dominica post Ascensa Domini.	V 586	XII
		V 587	VI

6	*REGINENSIS* 316		
	Orat. et preces Dom. Diebus.	V 1178	XX
		V 1182	XXII
		V 1186	IX
		V 1198	XXVI
		V 1201	XXVII
		V 1206*	XXXI
		V 1209*	XXX
		V 1234	XXXII
7	The *HADRIANUM* and the *PADUENSIS*: (their order is determined by their place in the Sacramentary of Angoulême).	P 52, H 85, A 91	III
		P 66, H 86, A 114	I
		H 922, A 129	II
		P 201, H 228, A 213	V
		P 112, H 911, A 226*	VII
		P 517, A 1019	XVII
		H 966, A 1396	XXVIII
		P 748, A 1487	XXXIV
8	Ambrosian sources: *SACRAMENTARIUM TRIPLEX* Sat. in Easter Week		
		Triplex 1494*	XIX
	2nd Rogation Day	Triplex 1744	
	3rd Rogation Day	Triplex 1750	XVI
			XIII

* Denotes that the prayer listed is not the original source. See the Introduction to that chapter.

CONCLUSION

In this chapter we have examined the primary methodological principles upon which the framework of the following analyses is based. These issues also have been used to determine the rationale behind the grouping of the different collect studies into chapters.

The two pivotal issues are the establishment of the actual 'text' that is to be studied, and secondly, the development of a methodology suitable for investigating the meaning of such a 'text'. It is only when the meaning of a text is set forth that an adequate understanding can be reached of the theology of grace the text contains.

The 'text' of our study was found to be, in fact, two texts, each of which had two components. They were the original text in its original context, and the text of the current collect within its context in the Missal of Paul VI. The collects themselves were appropriated more or less directly from the best witness of the original prayer in its original context in the Mass. On account of this the history of the prayer in the liturgical tradition throughout the intervening centuries, while remaining of some importance, became a quite secondary factor in determining the meaning of the 'text'.

With the 'text' established, the chapter addressed the question of developing a suitable methodology. The approach taken was that the meaning of the prayer emerges (i) from a consideration of the original historical and liturgical context of the prayer, (ii) from a study of the structure of the oration itself, and, most importantly, (iii) from an analysis of its vocabulary. This process had to be entered into for both the original prayer in its original context, and for the collect in its context in the Missal of Paul VI. Central to this process is the principle that the words, expressions and structures of liturgical texts are best understood from within the liturgical tradition itself. Two corollaries of this principle are evident. One is that liturgical texts and the scriptures are closely related. The second is that the meaning of words and expressions accumulates in each tradition over time. This takes place both through repeated usage and through reappropriation into different liturgical texts and contexts. The collects in our study have been grouped in terms of their earliest source and original context in that source on the basis of this second corollary.

Throughout the chapter, the primary research instruments used in the various parts of each analysis have been named. Two tables are to be found towards the end of the chapter. The first sets out the structure upon which each analysis of a collect is based. The second table displays the arrangement of the 34 collects into their respective chapters.

PART TWO
THE ANALYSES OF THE SUNDAY COLLECTS FOR ORDINARY TIME

CHAPTER FOUR
PRAYERS FROM THE *VERONENSIS*:
THE COLLECTS FOR SUNDAYS IV, VIII, XVIII, XXIV, XXV and XXXIII

INTRODUCTION

Towards the end of the fourth century an as yet unexplained development in Western liturgy took place[1]. As distinct from the liturgies of the Eastern churches, each Mass of the temporal and sanctoral cycle became fitted with a proper set of texts for the presider. In some centres, however, the anaphora remained unchanged. These Mass formulae were written down and collected in leaflets or *libelli missarum*. Each *libellus* contained the presidential prayers, excluding the canon, for the Masses for particular celebrations from a particular church. These *libelli* were preserved, compiled, and later reused, sometimes with modifications, in other contexts.

THE *VERONENSIS*:

The earliest available collection of Latin Roman *libelli* is the late sixth century compilation known variously as the Leonine Sacramentary, the *Sacramentarium Veronensis*, the *Veronensis* or the Verona Collection of *Libelli*

---

[1]This material is based upon C.Vogel, Medieval Liturgy: An Introduction to the Sources, revised and translated by W.G.Storey and N.K.Rasmussen from Introduction aux sources de l'histoire du culte chrétien au moyen âge, Spoleto: Centro italiano di studi sull'alto medioevo, 1981, NPM Studies in Church Music and Liturgy (Washington D.C.: The Pastoral Press, 1986), 34-59. See also Chapter One above, on the origins of the 'collect style' oration.

Missarum. For our purposes we will use the title the *Veronensis*. The critical edition of this text is that of Mohlberg[2].

Vogel describes the *Veronensis* as follows:

> The *Veronensis* is a private collection of authentically Roman *libelli* preserved in the Lateran archives after they had been partially adapted from papal use for the presbyters of the Roman *tituli*[3].

Though the *libelli* are Roman, the single existing manuscript of this collection appears to have been transcribed outside of Rome, probably in Verona itself. The text is not an official sacramentary, but rather a loosely organized, private collection of Mass prayers. The *libelli* themselves seem to have been compiled in the fifth and sixth centuries. If that is the case, then these prayers take us back to the earliest prayer forms of the Latin Roman liturgy.

There are four features of particular interest concerning the arrangement of the *libelli* in the compilation. Firstly, the Masses are all arranged according to the months of the civil year. Unfortunately, the months of January, February and March are missing from the manuscript. Secondly, there are, within the months, different sets of Masses for the same feast. For example, under the month of May there are six sets of Masses for the Ascension[4]. As well, there are 28 sets of prayers for the feast of Sts. Peter and Paul, with other Mass sets and prayers interpolated into this series[5]. Thirdly, there are collections of Masses thought to be composed or used by various popes. In

---

[2]L.C.Mohlberg, L.Eizenhöfer, and P.Siffrin, eds., Sacramentarium Veronense, Rerum Ecclesiasticarum Documenta, Series Maior, Fontes I (Roma: Casa Editrice Herder, 1956).

[3]Vogel, Medieval Liturgy: An Introduction to the Sources, 38-39.

[4]*Veronensis*, VIII, *Praeces in Ascensa Domini*, L 169-L 186.

[5]*Veronensis*, XV, XVI. See Vogel, Medieval Liturgy: An Introduction to the Sources, 44.

particular there appear to be seventy Masses from the time of Pope Vigilius (537-555), and a number from Pope Gelasius (492-496). These Masses are scattered in groups throughout the compilation[6]. Fourthly, many of the Mass sets in the *Veronensis* are incomplete. However, a full complement of variable presidential prayers for a Mass appears to consist of two orations before the offering of the gifts, seemingly an opening *oratio* and a prayer *super sindonem*, a prayer over the gifts, a preface, postcommunion, and a prayer *super populum*. Note that there are no designations in the text which identify a prayer specifically as a *super sindonem* or postcommunion etc..

ORATIONS FROM THE *VERONENSIS* IN THE MISSAL OF PAUL VI

Amongst the collects for Ordinary Time in the Missal of Paul VI are nine orations first encountered in the *Veronensis*. They are the collects for Sundays IV (L 432), VIII (L 633), XV (L 75), XVIII (L 887), XXIV (L 1045), XXV (L 493), XXX (L 598), XXXI (L 574), and XXXIII (L 486).

In this chapter we will be concerned only with the collects for Sundays IV (L 432), VIII (L 633), XVIII (L 887), XXIV (L 1045), XXV (L 493) and XXXIII (L 486)[7]. These fall into two categories. The collect for Sunday IV (L 432) appears to have been composed by Pope Gelasius[8]. It is one prayer from a series of Masses written to counter Christian participation in the celebration in Rome of the pagan festival of Lupercalia. The other five collects are most probably prayers from the pen of Pope Vigilius[9]. Their

---

[6]Vogel, Medieval Liturgy: An Introduction to the Sources, 42-43.

[7]The collect for Sunday XV is studied in chapter six, and the collects for Sundays XXX and XXXI in chapter seven. The reasons for this are set out in the introduction to those chapters.

[8]See below, 99.

[9]For details, see the section in each prayer analysis that examines the historical origins of the prayer.

original historical context appears to be the siege of Rome by the Arian Ostrogoths under Witiges (537-538).

As explained above in the chapter on the methodology employed for the study of the collects, these prayers will be studied in their probable chronological order[10]. In view of this, our study begins with the analysis of the collect for Sunday IV, an oration ascribed to Pope Gelasius. This will be followed by the studies of the collects for Sundays XXXIII, XXV, XVIII, VIII and XXIV.

---

[10]See above 88-90.

COLLECT FOR SUNDAY IV

PRAYER

Concede nobis, Domine Deus noster, ut te tota mente veneremur, et omnes homines rationabili diligamus affectu.

Grant to us, Lord our God, to worship you with all our mind and to love all people with spiritual affection.

ORIGINAL SOURCE

Veronensis: *Super sindonem* for Mass XVIII,iii, item alia 2, *Juli, Incipiunt orationes et praeces diurnae* (L 432).

USE IN OTHER LITURGICAL SOURCES

The prayer does not appear in any other liturgical sources.

CHANGES TO THE ORIGINAL SOURCE

The only change is the replacement of the *et ... et* construction with the simple conjunction *et*. This change is not attested to in the earlier editions of Ballerini[1] or Feltoe[2].

ANALYSIS OF THE PRAYER IN THE ORIGINAL SOURCE

<u>Origin</u>:

Pomarès[3] identifes the prayer as from a series of Masses written by

---

[1] <u>Liber Sacramentorum Romae Ecclesiae: Omnium vetustissimus S. Leoni Papae in vulgatis tributis</u>, PL, 55, 66.

[2] C.L.Feltoe, <u>Sacramentarium Leonianum</u> (Cambridge: At the University Press, 1896), 57.

[3] G.Pomarès, <u>Gélase Ier: Lettre contres les lupercales et dix-huit messes du sacramentaire Léonien</u>, introduction, texte critique, traduction et notes de G.Pomarès, Sources Chrétiennes 65 (Paris: Les Éditions du Cerf, 1959).

Pope Gelasius I (pope 492-496) to counter the celebration by Christians of the pagan Roman festival of Lupercalia, usually held in mid-February[4]. Our prayer was written for the Sunday liturgy of January 29, 495, just over two weeks before the festival was to take place[5]. The festival of Lupercalia was an ancient Roman tradition with a long, unclear and complicated history. At base are the metaphors of purification of the city from hostile forces and, from 276 B.C.E., the fructification of barren women. A central action of the celebration was the whipping of women by the *Lupercali*, a group of men. In ancient times the *Lupercali* were naked or dressed in a form of wolf costume, though after the time of Augustus (sometime after 44 B.C.E.) they dressed in goat skins. The festival persisted until the time of Gelasius, when it apparently had the following features. Prior to the festival the *Lupercali* would deliberately set about to seduce women. Then, as part of the festival, they would publicly denounce the women as having been seduced. These women, or perhaps others as well, once slandered publicly, would be either partially or fully stripped and subsequently whipped, to the delight of the crowd. The *Lupercali* also had affinities with the underworld, and as seducers took on the aspect of *incubi*. As such their seducing of the women also carried a sense of the continuing fertility of Rome as based in the activities of the ancestors, the *parentalia*. The divulging of names and sins, and the whipping done by these representatives of the underworld, had a salutary significance not unrelated to the pagan notion of public confession and penance to secure salvation.

There was much for Gelasius to object to in the festival. It involved a general level of drunkeness and lascivious behaviour. Furthermore, there were

---

[4]The main sources for this section are Pomarès and A.W.J.Holleman, Pope Gelasius I and the Lupercalia (Amsterdam: Adolf M. Hakkert, 1974), especially the summary of the book, 146-155.

[5]Pomarès, Gélase, 142.

the sexual sins of the *Lupercalia* and the slander and whipping of women. Because of its relationship to the forces of the underworld, it could not simply be seen as a piece of ancient Roman folklore, but remained a pagan ritual. Its metaphor of purification and fertility meant that there was a form of salvation and healing outside the Christian economy. It was clear to Gelasius that the participation of Christians in such an event was far from being harmless participation in a local folk custom. It compromised the worship of God, the love of God, and the love of neighbour.

Grammatical structure:

The prayer is made up of (a) a simple address, followed by (b) a twofold petition introduced by *concedere* and an *ut* clause of request:

(a)   Address: *Domine deus noster*

(b)   Petitions: *concede nobis ... ut*
                   et te tota mente veneremur
                   et omnes homines rationabili diligamus
                   affectu.

The petitions are held in parallel by an *et ... et* construction. Worship of God and love of all other humans are related to each other, and sought together.

Prominent vocabulary: The entire construction *Domine deus noster ... rationabili diligamus affectu*, and the words and expressions *concedere, domine deus noster, venerari, tota mens, diligere,* and *rationabilis affectus*.

Our analysis of the vocabulary will begin with the verb of petition *concedere*.

Concede[6]

Along with a variety of verbs (*prosequi, dare, effundere, infundere, inserere, largiri, multiplicare, tribuere, praestare, adiciere*), *concedere* signifies God's act of giving, of granting[7]. It is normally followed by such words as *quaesumus* or *propitius*. In some prayers this dependence is brought out in the address to God. In our collect the use of the imperative is quite direct.

The faithful seek two interconnected petitions. Because of the scriptural basis underlying the pair of requests, we will first examine the biblical import of the whole petition before going on to analyse the liturgical sense of each word and phrase.

Domine deus noster, ut et te tota mente veneremur, et omnes homines rationabili diligamus affectu

The prayer is evocative of the Gospel episode in which Jesus is questioned concerning the greatest commandment of the Law. He answers by joining two Old Testament injunctions concerning the obligation to love God[8] and to love one's neighbour[9], establishing that the entire law hangs on love of God and of neighbour:

"'*Diliges Dominum Deum tuum ex toto corde et in tota anima tua et in tota mente tua.' Hoc est maximum mandatum. Secundum autem simile est huic:*

---

[6] For examples of the use of *concedere* see Deshusses, Concordances, III, 1, 291-300.

[7] Blaise, Vocabulaire, § 65, § 67, §68. He translates these terms by *accorder* and *donner*.

[8] "*Audi, Israel: Dominus Deus noster Dominus unus est. Diliges Dominum Deum tuum ex toto corde tuo et ex tota anima tua et ex tota fortitudine tua. Eruntque verba haec, quae ego praecipio tibi hodie, in corde tuo ...*" (Dt 6:4-6).

[9] "*Diliges amicum tuum sicut teipsum, Ego Dominus*" (Lv 19:18).

'Diliges proximum tuum sicut teipsum.' In his duobus mandatis universa lex pendet et prophetae" (Mt 22:37-40)[10].

The Lucan parable of the Good Samaritan (Lc 10:29-37) shows that 'neighbour' refers to all humans.

Gelasius has reworked the Gospel passage, applying the greatest commandment to the situation he is facing.

A number of further points can be made from a study of the prayer's vocabulary, beginning with the verb *venerari*. Note, however, that the address, *Domine deus noster*, is lifted directly from the biblical text.

Veneremur[11]

The term has been introduced into Christian liturgical vocabulary from pagan Roman ritual language. In Roman cultic vocabulary *venerari* meant to honour the gods with reverence and ritual service so that they might be moved to grant the favours requested[12].

This verb is not usually associated, in Christian euchology, with direct acts of homage to God. Rather it is normally applied to the veneration of the saints, or to the veneration implied in carrying out mandates such as the lenten fast.

In a *Veronensis* collect, the faithful petition that they may commemorate with full devotion the anniversary of the deaths of the apostles Peter and Paul, by whose teachings the world has been prepared to confess the one God. In this act of veneration, the church prays that the two apostles will continue from heaven to promote on earth the confession of the divine unity:

---

[10]The pericope is also found in Mr 12:29-31 and Lc 10:27-28.

[11]For further examples of the use of *venerari* see Deshusses, Concordances III, 4, 426-429. See Blaise, Vocabulaire, § 16, § 20.

[12]Ellebracht, Remarks on the Vocabulary of the Orations in the Missale Romanum, 150-151.

"*Omnipotens sempiterne deus, da populis tuis praecipuorum apostolorum Petri et Pauli natalem diem plena deuotione uenerare; ut quorum doctrinis ad confessionem deitatis unius institutus est mundus, ipsorum nunc quoque suffragiis diuinae pareat unitati*" (L 342)[13].

The carrying out of the lenten fast also falls within the ambit of *venerari*. The salvific fast is understood to help dispose the hearts of the people to receive the paschal mystery with worthy minds, and to take up a continuous increase of devotion. The prayer reads:
"*Exercitatio ueneranda, domine, ieiunia [ieiunii] salutaris pupuli tui corda disponat, ut et dignis mentibus suscipiat paschale mysterium et continuate deuotionis sumat augmentum*" (V 235)[14].

The use of *venerari* in our collect is highly unusual in that God is the direct object of the verb. This is found in only a few of the prayers in the Deshusses concordance[15], and not at all in the Missal of Pius V[16]. This serves to emphasize that all actions of veneration must ultimately show honour to God and bring the faithful closer to the ways of God. By replacing the scriptural

---

[13] All powerful, eternal God, grant to your people to venerate with the fullness of devotion the day of the birth [into eternal life] of your principal apostles Peter and Paul, so that the world, instructed by their teachings concerning the confession of the one God, may now also be subject to the divine unity by the favourable intercessions of these same ones.

[14] May their worship through the salutary fast dispose the hearts of your people, Lord, so that they both may receive the paschal mystery with worthy minds, and may receive an increase of their continued devotion.
This prayer, slightly modified, has been incorporated into the Missal of Paul VI: MR(1975) Fer III hebd., IV Quadr., Collecta, 211.

[15] For example, see L 422, which is also a Gelasian anti-Lupercalia prayer (Pomarès, Gélase, 93), and the collect L 877, which is examined below, 111.

[16] Ellebracht, Remarks on the Vocabulary of the Ancient Orations in the Missale Romanum, 150.

'love of God' with the 'worship of God', the prayer highlights that worship belongs to God alone. As well, it points up that all acts of worship must be in line with the underlying commandment to love God totally. Furthermore, Gelasius is making it clear that those who engage in the festival of the Lupercalia are neither loving nor worshipping God as Christians ought.

This worship of God is further described as done *tota mente*, which will now be examined.

Tota mente[17]

This phrase reflects the biblical text on which the collect is modelled. The sense of *mens*, mind, is that of the 'interior dispositions' of the human person.

This can be seen in the following Christmas prayer, where the faithful petition spiritual joys so that their inner dispositions may be congruent with the worship that they are carrying out. The prayer reads:
"*Presta, quaesumus, domine, spiritualibus gaudiis nos repleri, ut quae actu gerimus, mente sectemur*" (L 1320)[18].

Mens can also be used to refer to the common inner disposition of the whole people. This can be seen in the following *Reginensis* 316, *super sindonem* where it is asked that the people may have a mind that is willingly devoted to God's majesty, even as it seeks to placate him for its sin.
"*Da, quaesumus, domine, hanc mentem populo tuo, ut quae ad te placandum necessitate concurrit, maiestati tuae fiat etiam uoluntate deuotus*" (V 1219)[19].

---

[17] For further examples of the use of *mens* see Deshusses, Concordances III, 3, 53-62.

[18] Grant, Lord, that we may be replenished with spiritual joys, so that what we carry out in our actions we may pursue with our minds.

[19] Give to your people, Lord, this mind, that when by necessity it pursues what placates you, it may become in will devoted to your majesty.

In our collect, *tota mente* refers to the disposition of the church as a body, and is an encapsulation of Mt 22:37. The community must be one in its worship, and totally dedicated to God's service.

The second petition in the prayer is that the faithful may be able to love all humans with spiritual affection, *omnes homines rationabili diligamus affectu*. This will now be examined, beginning with the verb *diligere*. *Diligamus*[20]

Diligere encompasses all aspects of divine love, and of that human love which is congruent with God's love.

In the Vulgate translation of the scriptures, *diligere* is used to describe the Father's love for the Son, and the divine love for believers:
"*Sicut dilexit me Pater, et ego dilexi vos. Manete in dilectione mea, dixit Dominus*" (Jo 15:9).

In the liturgical sources, the verb describes the scope of God's love for all creation. The *oratio super sindonem* in a Mass for Charity recalls in its address clause that God created humankind with such love that he also redeemed them from their wickedness. In the light of this, the faithful ask that they may be given the ardour of this very love, so that led on by divine example, they may repay good for evil. The prayer reads:
"*Deus, qui cum omnes creaturas diligens feceris, in eam indulgentiam hominum [in ea indulgentia hominem], ut etiam illum ab impietatibus redemeris, condedisti: da seruis tuis hanc caritatis affectum, ut bona pro malis rependere tuo incitentur exemplo*" (V 1328)[21].

---

[20]For further examples of the use of *diligere* see Deshusses, Concordances III, 1, 503-504.

[21]God, who, when you made all creatures in love, created humankind with such indulgence that you would redeem it even from its impieties, give to your servants this affect of love, that by your example they may be spurred on to repay good for evil.

The object of Christian love, in L 432, is all humanity, *omnes homines*. Whereas the expression *tota mente* reflects that totality with which Christians love, *omnes homines* means that this love can have no exceptions. Such love is exemplified in the story of the Good Samaritan, which in Luke's Gospel immediately follows the pericope concerning the 'Greatest Commandment'[22].

This love is further descibed as *rationabili affectu*. Both these terms will be explored, beginning with the sense of *affectus*.

(Rationabili) affectu[23]

Affectus denotes a tangible inner affection that leads a person to action.

The preface of a Mass celebrating the anniversary of a bishop's consecration contains the only other example of *rationabilis affectus*. The bishop desires to be subject in affection to all, and prays that harmful pride of power may not raise him up, but rather that the administration of charity according to the law may make him modest. The oration reads:

"*Uere dignum: teque profusius implorare ... Et qui loco ceteris praesidemus, cunctis rationabili subdamur affectu. Nec nos extollat noxia potestatis elatio, sed potius modestos efficiat administratio legitima caritatis*" (L 1005)[24].

The affect of Christian love extends to all. It includes returning good for evil, and accepting the correction extended by enemies:

"*Domine, sancte pater, omnipotens aeternae deus, da seruis tuis hunc caritatis*

The text in Moeller reads ... *in ea indulgentia hominem, ut etiam illum* ....
See Moeller, Corpus Orationum II, D, Orationes 881-1707, oration 1515, 288.

[22] Lc 10:25-37.

[23] For further examples of the use of *affectus* see Deshusses, Concordances III, 1, 64-67.

[24] ... and may we who in our place preside over others, be subject in spiritual affection to all. Nor may the harmful pride of power raise us up, but rather may the legitimate administration of love made us modest.

affectum, ut bona pro malis reddere tuo incitentur exemplo, et de inimicis suis correctionem magis cupiant quam ultione gaudere" (L 602)[25].

In L 432, *affectus* is qualified by the adjective *rationabilis*.

Rationabili[26] (affectu)

In early Christian writing, the Greek λογικον was transposed into Latin as *rationabilis*. However it retained the Greek meaning of 'spiritual,' that is in keeping with the realm of the Spirit, rather than the Latin sense of 'rational', 'according to reason'[27]. *Rationabilis* was later replaced by *purus*, a word avoided by the early Christians because of its association with pagan worship.

In the Vulgate translation of the Letter to the Romans[28], Paul urges the community to live lives that are a spiritual service (*rationabile obsequium*) to God. Such lives are according to the highest aspects of human nature, pleasing to God, and in conformity to the will of God rather than in conformity to the behaviour of the world. The passage reads:

"Obsecro itaque vos, fratres per misericordiam Dei, ut exhibeatis corpora vestra hostiam viventem, sanctam, Deo placentem, rationabile obsequium vestrum. Et nolite conformari huic saeculo, sed reformamini in novitate sensus

---

[25] Lord, holy father, all powerful eternal God, give to your servants this affect of love, that they may be spurred on by your example so as to pay back good things for evil, and that they may rather desire to receive correction from their enemies than rejoice in revenge over them.

[26] For further examples of the use of *rationabilis* see Deshusses, Concordances III, 4, 24-25.

[27] C.Mohrmann, "*Rationabilis - Logikos*", in Études sur le latin des chrétiens (Roma: Edizioni di Storia e Lettura, 1958), 179.

[28] For further commentary on this passage, see J.A.Fitzmyer, Romans, The Anchor Bible (New York: Doubleday, 1993), 639-641.

vestri, ut probetis quae sit voluntas Dei bona et beneplacens et perfecta" (Rm 12:1-2).

The adjective is also found in the Vulgate translation of 1 Peter, where the author reminds the community of the meaning of charity. The letter encourages the members of the community, as new born children in the Word, to love each other intensely from the heart, and to rid themselves of such things as spite and deceit. In this way they seek the spiritual milk (*rationabile lac*) that leads to salvation. The passage reads:

"*Animas vestras castificantes in oboedientia caritatis, in fraternitatis amore, simplici ex corde invicem diligite attentius; renati non ex semine corruptibili, sed incorruptibili per verbum Dei ... Deponentes igitur omnem malitiam et omnem dolum et ... sicut modo geniti infantes, rationabile sine dolo lac concupiscite, ut in eo crescatis in salutem* (1 Pt 1:22-2:2).[29]

On occasions St. Ambrose (339-397) used *rationabilis* to mean spiritual[30], as in this passage from his commentary on Ps 118, which evokes 1 Peter, and where the spiritual is that which is drawn from the scriptures:

"<u>Oculi quoque eius sicut colombae</u>. *Oculi sunt uiri uidelicet spiritualibus*

---

[29]There is some confusion in the Latin Vulgate translation and transliteration of this piece of scripture. One Latin Vulgate (B.Fischer, I.Gribomont, H.F.D.Sparks, W.Theile, eds. <u>Biblia Sacra Iuxta Vulgatam Versionem</u>, Editio Altera Emendata Tomus II Proverbia-Apocalypsis, Stuttgart: Wüttembergische Bibelanstalt, 1975) uses *ratio* in place of *rationabilis*. The 1946 Nova Editio of the Latin Vulgate reads *rationabile* (A.Gramatica, ed. <u>Bibliorum Sacrorum Iuxta Vulgatam Clementinam</u>, Nova Editio, Roma: Typis Polyglottis Vaticanis, MCMXLVI). The Greek text reads λογικον (logikon) (L.Aland et alia, eds. <u>The Greek New Testament</u>, United Bible Societies, in cooperation with the Institute for the New Testament Textual Research, Münster/Westphalia, Third Edition (Corrected), Stuttgart: Biblia-Druck GmbH, 1983).

[30]Mohrmann, "*Rationabilis - Logikos*," 184-186.

ornati sensibus, qui ad uidenda mysteria sunt acuti et parati ad penetranda scripturae secreta diuinae, rationabili lacte fungentes ... "[31]

On other occasions he employs *rationabilis* in its Roman juridical and philosophical sense of 'reasonable', 'rational', 'conformed to the essence of a thing'[32], in line with general Christian usage. Mohrmann is under the impression that in a number of cases, Ambrose wants to bring the Christian sense of 'spiritual' to bear on the profane usage[33]. He also brings something of the profane sense into the Christian.

The adjective *rationabilis* retained the sense of 'spiritual' in liturgical usage, while indicating that it is spiritual because it is in conformity to God's good pleasure. Meditating on what is spiritual, on what is pleasing to God, leads to following God both in word and deed:

"*Praesta, quaesumus, omnipotens deus, ut semper rationabilia meditantes quae tibi sunt placita et dictis exequamur et factis*" (V 1521)[34].

---

[31] *His eyes are as those of a dove* (Cn 5:12). The eyes are those of a man who is adorned with the spiritual senses, eyes which are keen to perceive mysteries, and ready to penetrate the secrets of divine scripture, drawing forth spiritual milk ....
Ambrose, Expositio Psalmi XXVIII: (Litterae XII-XXII), Sancti Ambrosii Episcopi Mediolanensis Opera 10 (Milano: Biblioteca Ambrosiana, 1987), 15, 13.

[32] Botte disputes this last connotation. See B.Botte and C.Mohrmann, L'Ordinaire de la messe: texte critique, traduction et études (Paris: Éditions du Cerf, 1953), 117f.

[33] Mohrmann, "*Rationabilis - Logikos*," 185.

[34] Grant, we beg all powerful God, that always meditating on spiritual things, we may carry out by words and deeds the things that are pleasing to you.
This prayer has been incorporated into the Missal of Paul VI: MR(1975), Dom. VII per annum, Collecta, 346. For a study of this collect see below, 498.

In the Roman Canon, *rationabilem* is coupled with *acceptabilem* to describe God's action over the oblation. God is requested to make the oblation blessed, approved, ratified, spiritual and acceptable so that it may become for the community the body and blood of Christ. As approved and ratified, the spiritual and acceptable oblation is right and fitting because it is in line with God's will:

"*Quam oblationem tu, deus, in omnibus, quaesumus, benedictam, ascriptam ratam rationabilem acceptabilemquae facere digneris, ut nobis corpus et sanguis fiat dilectissimi filii ...*" (V 1248)[35].

Spiritual actions are those actions which are in accord with the divine will, as seen in the following *Veronensis* collect. This oration provides a direct parallel with L 423. In the collect, as in L 423, Christians are called to love all humans with a spiritual love, a love that is in accord with the greatest commandment, and is total (*tota mens*) and sincere (*sincera mens*). Note also that the collect, as mentioned above, associates the verb *uenerari* with the worship of God. The oration reads:

"*Da nobis, domine, rationabilem, quaesumus, actionem; ut te solum sincera mente uenerantes, et fiducialius quae tua sunt postulemus, et facilius adsequamur*" (L 877)[36].

In summary, the adjective *rationabilis* denotes what is pleasing to God, is in accordance with his will and command, and constitutes 'pure worship'. With its references to the Letter to the Romans and the First Letter of Peter, as

---

[35] Grant, Lord, we ask you, to make this offering wholly blessed, approved, ratified, spiritual and accepable so that it may become for us the body and blood of your dearly beloved Son ...
See MR(1975) Ordo M. cum populo, Prex euch. I, Quam oblationem, 451.

[36] Give to us, Lord, spiritual worship, so that worshiping you alone with sincere minds, may we both ask confidently for what are your things, and more easily put them into effect.

well as its liturgical currency, the use of *rationabilis* reinforces the contrast between the authentic Christian worship in relation to love of God and neighbour, and the participation of Christians in the pagan festival. The adjective gives an added dimension to Gelasius' argument by invoking the scriptural writings of the twin pillars of the Roman church, two powers more potent than the Roman ancestors.

By using the phrase *diligere rationabili affectu*, Gelasius is expressing that love of neighbour should be carried out with a true spiritual integrity that follows Christ's own example, is according to the revealed will and ordinance of God, and is not compromised by false worship.

Meaning of the prayer:

The prayer is an adaptation of the great commandment (Mt 22:37-40), arranged to emphasize that love of God involves uncompromised worship practices. It echoes a section in the Vulgate translation of Paul's Letter to the Romans in which Paul emphasizes right worship as conformity to the ways of God in line with the highest aspects of human nature. There are also reminders of the injunction to love as found in the Vulgate translation of the First Letter of Peter.

The oration calls on God to bestow the twin graces of wholehearted, authentic worship, and of sincere and active love towards all others. The prayer braids together worship and charity. Both worship and love are according to God's will and commandment.

ANALYSIS OF THE WORDS AND PHRASES IN THE COLLECT IN RELATIONSHIP TO THE MISSAL OF PAUL VI

This *super sindonem* has been retrieved from the *Veronensis* for inclusion as a collect in the Missal of Paul VI. Though the sense of a contrast with pagan feasts is no longer present, the underlying biblical injunction remains as its focal point. The new context in the revised Missal does not give rise to any major shifts in the meaning of the vocabulary. The unrestricted love of others is open to quite a variety of contexts, but will always be kept in conjunction with the love and zeal for God's worship.

The verb *venerari* retains its distinctive focus in the prayer[37]. While it occurs 58 times in various forms in the new Missal, the collect for Sunday IV remains the sole instance where God is the direct object of the verb.

THE RELATIONSHIP OF THE CHRISTIAN PEOPLE TO GOD
The prayer in its original context:

In its original context, this prayer served as a powerful reminder of the relationship of the members of the Roman community to the Christian God with regard to both their worship and behaviour. The prayer inextricably intertwined authentic worship of God, Christian love of God, and true love of neighbour.

Love and worship are reciprocal. Authentic worship of God knows no compromise with pagan customs and beliefs which lie outside the dominion of God. There is no room for partaking in supposedly benign customs, much less immoral and sinful practices. This is forcefully expressed in two ways. One is the use of God as the direct object of *venerari*. The second is the justaposition of *venerari* with *diligere*, which stresses that anything that is less than authentic worship is a refusal to love God completely. Furthermore, worship by Christians is inauthentic when it compromises love of neighbour. True love of God, authentic worship, and God-like love of neighbour are all necessary, and are related one to the other.

---

[37] For the use of *venerari* in the Missal, see Schnitker and Slaby, Concordantia, 2764-2766.

The use of *diligere* signifies that the love Christians must show cannot be differentiated from the scope of God's own loving. This love must be for the true good of the other, a properly spiritual love, in accord with the highest aspects of human nature. Love of neighbour is also to be without compromise or reticence. It is to be extended to all. Clearly the women victims are meant here. However the debate within the Roman Christian community was acrimonious, and there is a sense here in which Gelasius is calling his opponents to charity towards him and his supporters, as well as to authentic love of the victims[38].

The adjective *rationabilis* as a qualificative of Christian love links that love even more closely to divine worship, since it is necessarily in conformity with God's will and ordinance. In concentrating on worship, Gelasius is making the claim that all grace, especially that associated with the work and continuing care of the ancestors, lies within the scope of God's own economy of salvation. The help of the ancestors is not a grace over and above what God does, rather it can only be given in true worship of God and is only fruitful in authentic love of neighbour. In fact, true worship and authentic love are understood through the founding apostles of the church of Rome, Peter and Paul, rather than through the ancestors.

The unmodified use of the imperative *concede* reinforces the community's dependence on God for all salutary and worthy things.

The prayer in the Missal of Paul VI:

Removed from its original context, the collect has lost a little of its immediacy. As a collect in Ordinary Time, the prayer insists that true worship

---

[38] See Pomarès, Gélase, 36f, and Hollemann, Pope Gelasius I and the Lupercalia, 61f.

and authentic love of neighbour are both demanded, and are both according to God's commandment and will as known in revelation.

The transposition of *venerari* into the great commandment serves to remind the community that authentic worship belongs with authentic love. The love of God and the worship of God belong together.

Alongside love and worship of the divine is love of neighbour. This love is *rationabilis*, 'spiritual' love. Such love is founded in and imitative of God's own love for every person. It is centred in what is most noble in human nature. As well, it is grounded in God's command and ordinance.

FREER TRANSLATION OF THE COLLECT

Concede nobis, Domine Deus noster, ut te tota mente veneremur, et omnes homines rationabili diligamus affectu.	Grant to us that we may worship you, our Lord and God, with our whole heart and soul and mind, and that we may love all others with the warmth of your love, and in accordance with your will.

COLLECT FOR SUNDAY XXXIII

PRAYER

Da nobis, quaesumus, Domine Deus noster, in tua semper devotione gaudere, quia perpetua est et plena felicitas, si bonorum omnium iugiter serviamus auctori.	Give to us, Lord our God, to rejoice always in devotion to you, because happiness is everlasting and complete, if we serve continuously the author of all good things.

ORIGINAL SOURCE

Veronensis: Collect for Mass XVIII, xiii, *Julio, incipiunt orationes et praeces diurnae* (L 486).

There are no changes from the original prayer.

USE IN OTHER LITURGICAL SOURCES

This prayer, with some adaptations, appears in H 928, P 939, A 1973, Ph 1418[1]. H 928 and Pa 939 read:

Fac nobis, quaesumus, domine deus noster, in tua deuotione gaudere: quia perpetua est et plena felicitas, si bonorum omnium seruiamus auctori. Per.

---

[1] See Deshussses, Le Sacramentaire grégorien, 326 where he lists the liturgical sources for H 928. The collect as it stands in the *Veronensis* is not listed in any other liturgical sources by Siffrin or Moeller, et alii: see P. Siffrin, Sacramentarium Veronense (Leonianum): Konkordanztabellen zu den römischen Sakramentarien 1, Rerum Ecclesiasticarum Documenta, Series Minor: Subsidia Studiorum 4 (Roma: Casa Editrice Herder, 1958) 45; and E. Moeller, I. Clément, and B. Coppieter 'T Wallant, Corpus Orationum II D, oration 934, 35.

ANALYSIS OF THE PRAYER IN THE ORIGINAL SOURCE
Origin[2]:

This mass was one of a series probably written by Pope Vigilius while Rome was under siege by the Arian Ostrogoths under Witiges. Chavasse places it as the Mass for either August 23rd or 30th in the year 537[3]. The siege will not end until early March 538. The Mass corresponds to a period of hope for the Romans in the war. They had just come through a famine and pestilence in July, and are greeted with the encouraging news that imperial troops have disembarked at Naples and are on their way to relieve the city. In the face of a possibly immanent victory Vigilius fears the community will fall away from its devotion to the liturgy and praise of God. This particular Mass is replete with reminders to the community that as the fortunes of the city improve their gratitude ought increase rather than decrease. This is especially clear in the *super sindonem*:

"*Quaesumus, omnipotens deus, ne ad dissimulationem tui cultus prospera nobis collata succedant, sed ad gratiarum actionem tibi propinsius exhibendam potius nos semper accedant:*" (L 487)"[4].

The origins of the prayer reveal two foci: gratitude for God's bounty, and a concern lest such gratitude be short lived.

---

[2]This section is dependent on the research of Chavasse. See A. Chavasse, "Messes du Pape Vigile (537-555) dans le Sacramentaire Léonien," Ephemerides Liturgicae 64 (1950): 161-213.

[3]Ibid, 191-192.

[4]"We ask you, all powerful God, that these transpirings that are favourable for us may not result in the disregarding of your worship, but rather may lead us on to continually expressing favourably our thanksgiving to you."
See also the preface of the Mass, L 489.

Grammatical Structure:

The collect is made up of two balanced sections. The first consists of a simple invocation and a petition:

domine deus noster   *da nobis .. in tua semper devotione gaudere*

The second section gives the reason for the request, at the same time restating the petition:

quia perpetua est et plena felicitas   *si bonorum omnium iugiter serviamus auctori.*

The phrases *in tua devotione gaudere* and *servire auctori bonorum omnium* are in parallel. The petition - *da semper gaudere, iugiter serviamus* - is the means which, if granted, will bring about the desired end of the praying community: *perpetua et plena felicitas*.

Vocabulary:

Prominent vocabulary: *gaudere, devotio, felicitas, plenus, perpetuus, servire, auctor*.

We will begin our vocabulary study with an analysis of the petition [*da nobis*] ... *in tua semper deuotione gaudere*.

In tua semper deuotione gaudere

Gaudere[5]

The verb *gaudere* denotes the Christian response to living within the bounteous effects of God's love. It is closely associated with the worship and devotion of the church in response to salvation from God.

---

[5]For examples of the use of *gaudere* see Deshusses, Concordances III, 2, 194-197.

In the Vulgage translation of the New Testament, the verb *gaudere* is used when Paul is urging the community in Thessalonika to rejoice continually, even though they had been beset with hardships (1 Th 3:1-5). He brings together, in the admonititon which closes 1 Thessalonians, constant rejoicing, unceasing prayer, and thanksgiving in all things as actions that God wills in Christ[6]:

"*Semper gaudete. Sine intermissione orate. In omnibus gratias agite: haec est enim voluntas Dei in Christi Iesu in omnibus vobis*" (1 Th 5:16-18).

No matter what the community faces, there is always cause for rejoicing because of what God has done in Christ.

In a collect for a lenten Mass which is concerned with the fast[7], the community asks that it may rejoice in the full effects of the fast as it takes up the paschal observances:

"*Obseruationis huius annua caelebritate laetantes, quaesumus, domine, ut paschalibus actionibus inherentibus plenis eius effectibus gaudeamus*" (V 99)[8].

Rejoicing (*gaudere*) is connected with joyfully (*laetantes*) celebrating the feast,

---

[6]For the textual basis for the connection between these three admonitions and critical comment see D.Williams, 1 and 2 Thessalonians, New International Biblical Commentary (Peabody, Massachusetts: Hendrickson Publishers, 1992), 99-100; L.Morris, The First and Second Epistles to the Thessalonians, revised edition (Grand Rapids, Michigan: William B. Eerdmanns Publishing Company, 1991), 171-175; and B.Johanson, To All the Brethren: A text-linguistic and rhetorical approach to I Thessalonians (Stockholm: Almqvist & Wiksell International, 1987), 138-139.

[7]The *super sindonem* for the Mass reads "*Adesto, domine, supplicantionibus nostris, et hoc sollemne ieiunium ....*" (V 100).

[8]"Rejoicing in the annual celebration of this observance [the fast], we ask Lord, that, adhering to the paschal celebrations, we may rejoice in their full effects."
This prayer is also found in the Missal of Paul VI: MR(1975) Sabb. hebd. III Quadr., Collecta, 207.

and the effects of the paschal observances and the lenten fast, which are themselves part of the continuing work of salvation in Christ.

A December collect links the trust and rejoicing of the community with God's oversight, goodness, propitiation and unceasing protection:
"*Deus, qui conspicis, quia in tua pietate confidemus, concede propicius, ut de caeleste semper proteccione gaudeamus*" (V 1157)[9].

The fellowship of heaven is a state of rejoicing. The collect for the feast of Saints Felicissimus and Agapitus (August 6) asks God to grant that the faithful may rejoice in the heavenly companionship of those two saints whom the community is venerating. The prayer sets together praise (*magnificantes*) of God's clemency, worship, the veneration of the saints, and rejoicing in the complete fellowship of heaven:
"*Magnificantes, domine, clementiam tuam, supplices exoramus, ut qui nos sanctorum tuorum frequentibus facis nataliciis interesse, perpetuis tribuas gaudere consortiis*" (L 733)[10].

Through God's safekeeping and his salutary assistance, the faithful ask to rejoice in his perpetual favours both in mind and body:
"*Conserua, domine, populum tuum, et quem salutaribus praesidiis non desinis adiubare, perpetuis tribue gaudere beneficiis et mentis et corporis*" (L 70)[11]. This *super populum* conjoins rejoicing of the faithful with God's safekeeping,

---

[9] God, you watch over us because we trust in your goodness, grant, propitiously, that we may rejoice always in your heavenly protection.

[10] Glorifying your clemency, Lord, we humbly pray that you, who enable us to take part in the celebration of the entry into eternal life of your saints [Felicissimus and Agapitus], may grant us to rejoice in everlasting companionship with them.
See also L 1175.

[11] Preserve your people Lord, and grant them, whom you never cease from assisting with salutary helps, to rejoice with perpetual favours in mind and body.

his salvific assistance, and perpetual favour in mind and body.

In summary, the rejoicing of the Christian community is a response to and an exulting in the favour and propitiation God has shown them through salvation in Christ. The faithful celebrate their joy most particularly in their worship and acts of devotion. Their rejoicing, involving both mind and body, takes place within the context of the community. The celebration that is begun on earth is fulfilled in the complete fellowship with the saints in heaven. Our collect particularly relates *gaudere* to the *devotio* of the community.

Devotione[12]

The noun *devotio* is discussed below in the study of the collect for Sunday VIII (L 633)[13]. Summarizing that discussion here, *devotio* denotes an inner attitude of devotion to God, and is also used to describe the acts of devotion themselves, such as the Mass, fasting, penance. The devotion of the community, and its expression in worship and acts of piety, bring unity, security, and tranquillity to the community.

In the phrase *in tua semper devotione gaudere* the prayer focuses on the worship and devotion of the community. Worship is a communal response to God's unceasing protection, assistance, favour and propitiation in Christ. It is expressed in unceasing prayer, thanksgiving, celebration, praise, veneration of the saints, and paschal observances such as the fast. Worship brings unity, security and tranquillity to the community. The prayer sets in parallel the unceasing rejoicing, worshipping and devotion of the community with the continuous worship of the author of all good things, and relates both to everlasting and full happiness, *perpetua et plena felicitas*.

---

[12]For examples of the use of *devotio* see Deshusses, Concordances III, 1, 461-465.

[13]See below, 189.

Perpetua et plena felicitas

Felicitas[14]

In the liturgical sources *felicitas* denotes the beatitude enjoyed by the saints in heaven.

This can be seen in a preface, where *felicitas* is coupled with *beatitudo*, and describes the heavenly state of the saints. It is the ground for their intercession on behalf of the church, and of the church's devotion to them:
"*Uere dignum: te in tuorum glorificantes confessione sanctorum, qui mirabili dispensatione sapientiae tuae et illis beatitudinem sempiternam, et fragilitati nostrae congrua praeparasti subsidia, ut quos ad te placandum praeuideris dignos, eorum qui tibi placuerunt dignis praecibus propitiatus intenderis. Unde supplices inploramus, ut sicut illos manet aeterna felicitas, sic pro nobis eorum depraecatio continuata non desit:*" (L 120)[15].

In L 486, *felicitas* is qualified by the adjective *perpetua* to underline its everlasting quality. It is also qualified by *plena* which denotes a spatial sense[16]. Its occurrence in the prayer points to the expectation of such blessedness on the part of those who serve (*servire*) God in worship and honour him as the author (*auctor*) of all good things.

If Chavasse's dating is correct the prayer contrasts the present calamities besetting the city with the perpetual and full happiness that comes

---

[14]For examples of the use of *felicitas* see Deshusses, Concordances III, 2, 129-130. Blaise, Vocabulaire, associates *felicitas* with *beatitudo*. See § 299.

[15]It is truly right and fitting to glorify you in your saints. In the marvellous dispensation of your wisdom, you prepared eternal beatitude for the saints and fitting assistance for our human weakness, so that you might propitiously look upon the worthy prayers of those who were pleasing to you, those whom you will have foreseen as pleasing to you. From this we humbly ask that in the same way as eternal happiness abides in them so also may their continuous intercession on our behalf be present.

[16]For an example of this usage of *plena* see L 249.

from unceasing worship. Our study will now turn to the verb *servire*.
Iugiter serviamus[17]

This verb is analysed below in the study of the collect for Sunday XXIV (L 1045)[18]. Summarizing that discussion here, *servire* is especially connected with worship and church office. In that collect, the more wholeheartedly the community enters into worship of God the more fully it will feel the effects and power of God's favour. Whatever else it experiences, as long as it carries out true worship it knows that it enjoys God's mercy and favour.

In L 486, *iugiter servire* is in parallel with rejoicing in continuous devotion. It is more specifically related to worship's recognition of God as the source of all good things (*bonorum omnium auctor*). This gives a particular tone to their service and worship.

Auctor

The understanding of God as *auctor* is discussed in the study of the collect for Sunday XVIII (L 887)[19]. Summarizing that discussion here, it means first that God is source and origin of what is good. From this it follows that God exercises continuous care, exemplified in his protection, governing and healing.

In L 486, worship and devotion are rendered to God as the author of all good things and the one from whom the faithful expect true happiness. The prayer has brought together God's authorship, true devotion and the expectation of eternal happiness.

---

[17]For examples of the use of *servire* see Deshusses, Concordances III, 4, 222-224.

[18]See below, 212.

[19]See below, 161.

Meaning of the Prayer:

The immediate petition of the prayer is that God may grace the church with that joy which comes from unceasing devotion. In the second clause of the prayer, such devotion is described as the service of the One who is author of all good things. For that reason it is what guarantees full and unending happiness.

The church's worship on earth is a response in grace to God's propitiation and favour. Furthermore it is an experience of the fulfilment of God's wise dispensation since it mirrors the full and perfect rejoicing that characterizes the state of heaven. As such it is a participation in the fellowship of the saints.

In the probable historical context of the siege, with some hope for peace in sight, the prayer sets before the community the importance of worship, devotion and service to God. It reminds them of the participation in heaven that worship anticipates, of the gifts that it brings, and of its overriding significance whether in times of war, hope or prosperity. Victory should bring an increase in worship and thanksgiving, rather than a slackening off, as Vigilius seemed to fear. Yet the blessing and happiness of peace can in no way compare to the full and complete happiness of heaven that is glimpsed in worship. Regardless of either victory or defeat, because the faithful now live in Christ, they have true cause to rejoice constantly, pray and give thanks in response to God's will.

ANALYSIS OF THE WORDS AND PHRASES IN THE COLLECT IN RELATIONSHIP TO THE MISSAL OF PAUL VI

The most original form of this prayer has been placed in the Missal. This highlights those aspects of the original collect which were modified in later sources, but restored to the prayer for the current Missal. God is called upon to give (*da*) to the community rather than to make (*fac*) the community rejoice in worship. This emphasizes the graciousness of God's action and the freedom of the community. The rejoicing and the serving are to be continuous (*semper, iugiter*). This indicates that they are always at play in the lives of Christians.

The private prayer of thanksgiving after Mass from St Thomas Aquinas reflects the vocabulary of the collect being studied. It associates eternal rejoicing (*gaudium sempiternum*), abundance (*plena*), and happiness (*felicitas*) with the feast of eternal life in God:

"... *Et precor te ad illud ineffabile convivium me peccatorem perducere digneris, ubi tu, cum Filio tuo et Spiritu Sancto, Sanctis tuis es lux vera, satietas plena, gaudium sempiternum, iucunditas consummata et felicitas perfecta*" (MR(1975) Gratiarum actio post M., Or. S. Thomae de Aquino, 935)[20].

As a private prayer, it points to the communal liturgy of the eucharist as an anticipation of the feast of heaven.

RELATIONSHIP OF THE CHRISTIAN PEOPLE TO GOD

With regard to the relationship of the Christian people to God, the collect focuses on the worship and devotion of the community.

Christian worship is marked by joy. In their worship the faithful recognize and rejoice in the propitiation and favour God has shown them through salvation in Christ. This rejoicing grounds all their devotion, veneration, fasts and observances. It bears fruit, bringing unity, peace and tranquillity to the community. Yet, regardless of all circumstances, the simple

---

[20] ... And I pray that you [God] deign to lead me, a sinner, to that ineffable feast, where you, with your Son and Holy Spirit, are, for the saints, the true light, bountiful abundance, eternal joy, complete delight, and perfect happiness.

fact of salvation in Christ is cause for constant rejoicing, prayer and thanksgiving.

The prayer links the worship and devotion of the community to the complete and full happiness that is found in heaven. Worship is a participation in and an anticipation of eternal beatitude. The prayer urges the faithful to rejoice with unceasing (*semper*) devotion and to serve continuously (*iugiter*), so that every moment of their lives may be characterised by worship and devotion, and so by participation in the divine. While the lifting of the siege may bring some happiness to the community, it is in worship and devotion that true, full and everlasting happiness is tasted. In this sense, the response of the Christian community to God in worship transcends their immediate historical circumstances and is related most directly to salvation in Christ, eternal beatitude and the communion of the saints.

All authentic worship itself comes from God, who is the author of all good things, and specifically of sincere devotion and the peace that comes from it. Because it comes from God, he will bring it to fullness in heaven.

FREER TRANSLATION OF THE COLLECT

Da nobis, quaesumus, Domine	Give to us, Lord our God, to
Deus noster, in tua semper	rejoice in continuous worship and
devotione gaudere, quia perpetua	devotion. Our happiness will be
est et plena felicitas, si bonorum	everlasting and full if, without
omnium iugiter serviamus auctori.	ceasing, we serve you, the author
	of everything that is good.

COLLECT FOR SUNDAY XXV

PRAYER

Deus, qui sacrae legis omnia constituta in tua et proximi dilectione posuisti, da nobis, ut, tua praecepta servantes, ad vitam mereamur pervenire perpetuam.

God, who established all the ordinances of the sacred law upon love of you and love of neighbour, grant to us that, observing your commandments, we may merit to come to eternal life.

ORIGINAL SOURCE

This prayer was created for the Missal of Paul VI by combining two prayers from the ancient sources[1], the *Veronensis* and the *Liber Mozarabicus Sacramentorum*[2]. The two original prayers are:

---

[1] Antoine Dumas, "Les sources du Missel romain (III)," Notitiae 7 (1971): 95.

[2] M. Férotin (ed.), Le Liber mozarabicus sacramentorum et les manuscrits mozarabes, Monumenta Ecclesiae Liturgica 6 (Paris: Librairie de Firmin-Didot et Cie, 1912).

Deus, qui sacra legis omnia constituta in tua et proximi dilectione posuisti: da nobis horum propitius efficientiam mandatorum: quia inpossible sibi nullus excusat, quod tanta breuitate concluditur, tanta aequitate percipitur: per. (L 493).

God, who established all the sacred precepts of the law in love of God and love of neighbour, propitiously give to us the power to carry out these mandates, because no one may plead the excuse that it is impossible for him to do, what is encapsulated with such brevity, and is conceived in such justice.

Veronensis: *Super sindonem* for Mass XVIII, xiiii, item alia 2, Iulio, Incipiunt orationes et praeces diurnae (L 493).

Placabilis Domine, qui es pax certa et caritas indisrupta, pacem nobis omnibus largire plenissimam: ut pacifici tua seruantes precepta, ad vitam mereamur peruenire perpetuam. (LMZ 1374).

Peace-giving Lord, who is certain peace and unbroken love, bestow the fullness of peace on us in all things, so that, observing your commandments in peace, we may merit to come to eternal life.

Liber Mozarabicus Sacramentorum: CLIV, Mass In VIII Dominica de Quotidiano, Prayer *Ad Pacem* (LMZ 1374).

USE IN OTHER LITURGICAL SOURCES

Neither the *super sindonem* from the *Veronensis* nor the *ad pacem* prayer from the Mozarabic liturgy appear in other liturgical sources.

CHANGES FROM THE MOST ORIGINAL SOURCE

Veronensis: The invocation *Deus, qui..* and the opening of the petition *da nobis* have been used unchanged, the remainder of the prayer being discarded. In the original version *sacra* modified *constituta*, whereas in the new collect it modifies *legis* in the genitive, *sacrae*. In the source, the institutions of the law are sacred, in the new Missal the law itself.

Mozarabic: Only the purpose clause of the petition has been retained *ut .. perpetuam*. One modification has been made. The reference in the clause to peace has been dropped, with *pacifici seruantes* reading simply *servantes*.

ANALYSIS OF THE PRAYERS IN THE ORIGINAL SOURCES
Methodological note:

Because this collect from the Missal of Paul VI is a combination of two different prayers some modification to the usual methodology is necessary. Each of the two original sources will be examined in terms of origin, structure vocabulary, and meaning. In the section on vocabulary attention will be given to those words which either appear in the later composite collect or which require further explanation to more clearly elucidate the sense of the original. Where possible the words in the Mozarabic Sacramentary will be analysed in terms of their usage in the sources of that distinctive liturgical tradition. Unfortunately no definitive concordance is presently available for either the sacramentary or the Mozarabic Ordines[3], and the general indexes in the Férotin editions are not exhaustive. Their aim was to give the range of uses of some expressions, pointing up distinctive nuances in the Mozarabic liturgical

---

[3]M. Férotin, <u>Le Liber ordinum en usage dan l'église wisigothique et mozarabe d'Espagne du cinquième au onzième siècle</u>, Monumenta Ecclesiae Liturgica 5 (Paris: Librairie de Firmin-Didot et Cie, 1904).

tradition[4]. Only two words from our prayer, *vita* and *pacificus*, fall into this category. It is presumed then that the other words in the prayer do not have nuances that are particular to the Mozarabic liturgy, and that they can be analysed using the Roman sources. Nevertheless, wherever possible examples are given from the Mozarabic Sacramentary.

A) ANALYSIS OF THE PRAYER IN THE ORIGINAL SOURCE: L 493
Origin[5]:

This prayer is dated by Chavasse as from the Mass of September 6, 537, during the siege of Rome by the Visigoths. From the Romans' perspective the war was entering a more hopeful stage with the possible arrival in Rome of the imperial troops that had recently landed in Naples and were heading towards the city.

The prayer is a *super sindonem* in a set of Mass prayers which is part of a grouping of 33 Masses, making up section XVIII of the Veronensis and placed under the month of July. This grouping contains nine Masses from Pope Gelasius (d.496), 23 from Pope Vigilius (d.555) during the siege, and one thanksgiving Mass from Vigilius written following the closure of hostilities. The Masses from Pope Gelasius and the thanksgiving Mass have been inserted at various points throughout the larger group, interrupting the sequence of these siege Masses.

Grammatical structure:

The collect has two parts: (i) an invocation of God and a clause which

---

[4]Férotin, Le Liber mozarabicus sacramentorum et les manuscrits mozarabes, 1001-1002.

[5]This section is dependent on A. Chavasse, "Messes du Pape Vigile (537-555) dans le Sacramentaire Léonien," Ephemerides Liturgicae 64 (1950): 187-192.

motivates the petition by looking to past divine action, and (ii) a petition along with a further motivation clause, reflecting the attractiveness of God's twofold mandate:

(i)	Address:	*Deus*	
	Motivation:	*qui*	*sacra legis omnia constituta in tua et proximi dilectione posuisti*
(ii)	Petition:	*da nobis*	*horum propitius efficientiam mandatorum*
	Motivation	*quia*	*inpossibile sibi nullus excusat, quod tanta breuitate concluditur, tanta aequitate precipitur.*

The address focusses on God's ordaining all the sacred precepts of the law to the commandment to love God and neighbour. The petition is based in the motivating clause. Because God is the author of the law, and ordained all sacred ordinances in love of God and neighbour, then God can be properly asked to give the power to keep the divine mandates. The *quia* clause brings in a second line of argument in support of the petition. This law of love is compelling for humans. No one can plead the excuse that it is impossible to keep when it is fashioned with such simplicity and informed by such equity.

Vocabulary:

Prominent expressions and vocabulary: *ponere, in tua et proxime dilectione, sacrum constitutum, lex, aequitas.*

Posuisti[6]

Our word study will begin with the verb *ponere*, which expresses that the divine commandments and mandates were established in love of God and

---

[6] For further examples of the use of *ponere* see Deshusses Concordances III, 3, 399-400.

neighbour, and are ordained towards bringing about this love.

In a *super sindonem* God is addressed as the one who has placed the fullness of the commandments in love of God and of neighbour. On account of sin, the faithful ask God to let his love, which cleanses from sin, abound in them:

"Deus, qui plenitudinem mandatorum in tua et proximi dilectione posuisti: hanc nobis gratiam largire propitius, ut quia in multis offendimus, tua caritas abundet in nobis, per quam peccata mundantur" (L 599)[7].

According to L 493, God is invoked as the one who has ordained all the commandments of the holy law towards love of God and neighbour. The community asks for the grace to carry out the mandates both because the laws are God's, and because they are appealing, encapsulated as they are in such brevity and informed by such justice. The divine law of love of God and neighbour will now be examined.

In tua et proximi dilectione

This phrase is taken directly from the scriptures. In the old law, the love of God was the first of all commandments (Dt 6:4-6)[8], and the members of the chosen people were to love each other (Lv 19:17-19)[9], and the stranger

---

[7]God, who established the abundance of your mandates in love of you and of neighbour, grant propitiously to us this grace, that because we offend in many things, your love, through which sins are cleansed, may abound in us.

[8]*"Audi, Israel: Dominus Deus noster Dominus unus est. Diliges Dominum Deum tuum ex toto corde tuo et ex tota anima tua et ex tota fortitudine tua. Eruntque verba haec, quae ego praecipio tibi hodie, in corde tuo."* (Dt 6:4-5).

[9]*"Non oderis fratrem tuum in corde tuo, sed publice argue eum, ne habes super illo peccatum. Non quaeras ultionem nec memor eris iniuriae civium tuorum. Diliges amicum tuum sicut teipsum. Ego Dominus. Leges meas custodite"* (Lv 19:17-19).

dwelling among them (Lv 19:34)[10], with the same
love that they held for their own selves.

For Jesus, the whole Law and the prophets, the entire Old Testament revelation of God, depends entirely upon these two commandments (Mt 22:37-40)[11]. They are the key to entry to eternal life (Lc 10:25,28)[12]. The neigbour is exemplified in the parable of the good Samaritan (Lc 10:29-37).

The liturgical sources take up Jesus' teaching. As expressed in L 599, used earlier with respect to *ponere*, the fullness of the commandments is established in love of God and neighbour[13].

Collect L 432, incorporated into the Missal of Paul VI as the collect for Sunday IV in Ordinary Time, braids love of God and neighbour with uncompromised worship of God[14]. It connects worship and charity, both of which are the central focus of God's commandments.

In L 493, love of God and neighbour are the two greatest commandments of the old law. No love of God is complete without love of

---

[10]"*Si habitaverit advena in terra vestra et moratus fuerit inter vos, non exprobetis ei; sed sit inter vos quasi indigena, et diligetis eum quasi vosmetipsos; fuistis enim et vos advenae in terra Aegypti*" (Lv 19:33-34).

[11]" '*Diliges Dominum Deum tuum ex toto corde et in tota anima tua et in tota mente tua.*' *Hoc est maximum mandatum. Secundum autem simile est huic: 'Diliges proximum tuum sicut teipsum*'" (Mt 22:37-40). This passage has synoptic parallels: Mr 12:29-31, Lc 10:27-28. These pericopes have been discussed already in Collect IV.

[12]The question of entry into eternal life provides the setting for the parallel passage in Luke: "*Et ecce quidam legis peritus surrexit tentans illum et dicens: Magister, quid faciendo vitam aeternam possidebo? ... [Jesus] Dixitque illi,: Recte respondisti: hoc fac et vives,*" (Lc 10:25,28). See also Mr 12:34.

[13]See also L 440.

[14]See also L 422, and the study of Collect for Sunday IV in Ordinary Time, above 102.

neighbour. For Jesus, living them out brings the believer to eternal life. In the *super sindonem*, the sacred mandates are ordained towards and subsumed into love of God and love of neighbour. Love of God includes and is exemplified in uncompromised worship.

Sacra legis omnia constituta

In L 493, the context of the prayer points to *constituta* as the individual ordinances that detail the divine law. By qualifying *constituta* with *sacra*, the *super sindonem* emphasises that all the divine mandates are ordained to love of God and neighbour. This law of love is praised for its brevity and justice (*aequitas*). We will now turn to the meaning of God's *aequitas* in early Roman euchology.

Aequitate[15]

Though *aequitas* is not retained in the collect for the Missal of Paul VI, it is an important component in the original prayer in that it relates the commandment to love God and neighbour to God's justice.

The scriptures link God's justice with the reign, judgement and righteousness of God and of Christ.

In Ps 78 God's judgement and reign is characterized by *aequitas*:

"*Flumina plaudent manu simul, montes exsultabunt a conspectu Domini, quoniam venit iudicare terram. Iudicabit orbem terrarum in iustitia et populos in aequitate*" (Ps 97:8-9).

As part of the proof that the Son is greater than the angels, the Letter to the Hebrews links the Son's reign (*thronus, regnum*) with God's justice (*aequitas*), righteousness (*iustitia*) and hatred of injustice (*iniquitas*):

"*Ad filium autem: 'Thronus tuus, Deus, in saeculum saeculi, virga aequitatis virga regni tui. Dilexisti iustitiam et odisti iniquitatem*'" (Heb 1:8-9).

---

[15]For further examples of the use of *aequitas* see Deshusses, Concordance III, 1, 51.

In a preface, God is praised as the source of all wisdom and providential ordering (*ratio*)[16]. In this providence humans have been created as spiritual beings (*rationales*) who share in God's wisdom and ordering. The more Christians participate in God, and remain in this divine likeness, the more they remain on the path of justice and in the order of truth:

"*Uere dignum: qui cum summa sis ratio nosque rationales efficeris, certum est, et tanto nos a tua participatione discedere, quantum ab aequitatis tramite deuiamus; et tantum in tua similitudine permaneamus, quantum non dibellimur ab ordine ueritatis*" (L 1077)[17].

God's justice is related to his order of truth, and both are expressions of his all encompassing ordering and providence. Human actions which are in accord with divine order are themselves well ordered, and correspond to God's justice and truth. Note the parallel with the use of *rationabilis* in the collect for Sunday IV (L 432). There the faithful ask for the grace to love all people with spiritual affection (*rationabili affectu*), where the adjective *rationabilis* denotes what is pleasing to God, and in accord with his will and command.

In L 493, God's holy mandates, ordained to love of God and neighbour, are conceived in and possessed by justice. They reflect God's ordering, order of truth, and his justice. In their obedience to the commandments human beings act in concert with God's providential order, justice and truth. Christians cannot excuse themselves from carrying out the

---

[16] The divine *ratio* is related to God's wisdom (*sophia*), ordering and providence. See A.Blaise, Dictionnaire latin-français des auteurs chrétiens, 696.

[17] It is right and fitting to give you praise: Since you are the source of all wisdom and providential ordering, and you made us spiritual beings, it is certain, that the more we forsake participation in you, the more we deviate from the path of justice, and the more we remain in your likeness, the less we are driven from the order of truth.

sacred precepts when they embody such ordering, truth, and justice, and bring about participation in the likeness of God in humanity.

Meaning of the prayer:

In the first section of the prayer God is addressed as the one who has established the Law and its precepts. They are all subordinated to love of God, with its connotation of pure worship, and to love of neighbour. The precepts reflect the supreme wisdom and providence of God by which all things are ordered. In obeying his mandates, the human mind and will participate in divine providence and so in that order of justice and truth which God has established.

The remainder of the prayer is a petition for the power to live out the sacred mandates of the law. Christians cannot complain that they are impossible to keep, encapsulated as they are with such economy, yet epitomizing the equity and justice of God.

God's commandments are an expression of his love, justice, truth, and providential ordering. Sharing in God's image and partaking in true worship, the community follows the order established in the law. For those who wish to truly love God and their fellow humans the divine mandates are not to be neglected, whether in the midst of the siege, or in hope of imminent relief.

B) ANALYSIS OF THE PRAYER IN THE SOURCE: LMZ 1374
Origin[18]:

The exact historical origins of this prayer remain unknown, as indeed they remain for most of the prayers of the Mozarabic Sacramentary. They are

---

[18] The following is based on Férotin, Le Liber mozarabicus sacramentorum et les manuscrits mozarabes, xiv-xvii. This section of Férotin is later reproduced by E. Bourque, Étude sur les sacramentaires romains: les textes primitifs, Pt I (Roma: Pontificio Instituto di Archeologia Cristiana, 1948), 25f.

of Spanish provenance and probably were written well before the beginning of the eighth century. They could be quite ancient since there are no offices in honour of such Spanish saints as St. Leander (c.550-600/601) and St. Isidore (c.560-636), and even the prayers for the feasts of St. Jerome (c.342-420) and St. Augustine (354-430) seem to be of a different and later style compared to those in honour of the ancient martyrs.

Grammatical structure:

The prayer is made up of (i) an address to God with motivating clause, and (ii) a petition with a purpose clause:

(i) Address: *placibilis domine*

Motivation: *qui es pax certa et caritas indisrupta*

(ii) Petition: *largire plenissimam pacem nobis omnibus*

Purpose: *pacifici servantes tua precepta mereamur peruenire ad uitam perpetuam.*

There is a balance in the structure of the prayer brought about through the notion of peace:

Divine realm:	God is peace,
Human realm:	Petition for God to bestow that peace,
Human realm:	The community acts out of that peace, keeping the divine precepts,
Divine realm:	The believer enters the realm of peace.

With the provision of peace by God, the believer is enabled to observe God's commandments and so enter eternal life with God.

Vocabulary:

Prominent expressions and vocabulary: *pacificus, servire, tuum preceptum, pervenire, mereri, ad vitam perpetuam.*

Our vocabulary analysis for this section of the prayer will begin with the meaning of the adjective *pacificus* in the expression *pacifici tua seruantes precepta*.

Pacifici tua seruantes precepta

Pacifici[19]

Though not included in the Collect in the Missal of Paul VI *pax* and *pacificus* form the bridge between the parts of the original prayer, and qualify the keeping of God's precepts.

The word *pacificus* has been studied in Collect VIII[20]. However in the Mozarabic Sacramentary there is a prayer *ad pacem* included as one of the Mass prayers. The following analysis further explores the use of *pax* and *pacificus* in this context. These prayers link the love of peace and life in peace with overcoming sin, good will, worship and obedience to God's precepts.

In a prayer *ad pacem* from the Mass for the first day of Lent, the faithful are reminded of the prophet Elijah. He travelled for forty days and nights on the nourishment of a single meal from God. His journey, divinely commanded, took him from despair in the wilderness to encounter with God at Horeb[21]. For the remainder of his life he then fasted spiritually until he merited to ascend to heaven. The faithful pray for the grace of the prophet that they may overcome the delights of the flesh. Through this grace, the faithful ask to be moderate in all things, peace loving, and able to follow the heavenly precepts:

"*Deus, cui transferendus Elias quadraginta dierum ieiunium consecrauit et*

---

[19] For other examples of the use of *pacificus* in the Mozarabic Sacramentary see LMZ 1188 and LMZ 1446. For other sources see Deshusses, Concordances 111, 3, 278-279.

[20] See below, 185.

[21] 3 Rg 19:1-8 (1 Kgs 19:1-8).

spiritaliter donec ad caelestis mereretur ascendere ieiunavit: prophetalem quaesumus gratiam dona populis christianis, in quia superemus delectationes carnis et sanguinis. Fac in omnibus et per omnia continentes; fac pacificos; fac precepta celestia seruantes: quibus et in hoc sacrificio benignus appareas, et humiliter te invocantibus propitiatus occurras" (LMZ 321)[22].

In the preface, peace is related to the fast and disciplining fleshly delights, contentment in all things and through all things, following God's precepts, and God's favourable and propitious presence in the sacrifice and worship. This presence is in response to the humble petition of the faithful. Note that while Elijah fasted spiritually up until the day he merited to ascend to heaven, all his actions take place in God's power and reflect the prophet's obedient listening to God[23].

Another *ad pacem* prayer names God as the abundance of all good things and as unfailing love of the saints. He is asked to provide for the community concord marked by good will. This good will enables the faithful in peace to follow and do continuously God's precepts:

"Deus, bonorum omnium copia et sanctorum indeficiens caritas, presta nobis in bona uoluntate concordiam: ut tua semper pacifici sequamur et faciamus precepta" (LMZ 1125)[24].

---

[22] God, to whom Elijah, while journeying in response to your summons, consecrated a fast of forty days and then fasted spiritually until he merited to ascend to heaven, give to your people the prophet-like grace in which we may overcome the pleasures of flesh and blood. Make us restrained in all things and through all things, make us peace loving, make us to follow your precepts: may your favour be evident to us in this sacrifice and may you come propitiously to meet us as we humbly call upon you.

[23] For the Elijah cycle of stories 3 Rg 17:1 - 4 Rg 2:18 (1 Kgs 17:1 - 2 Kgs 2:18).

[24] God, store of all good things, and unfailing love of the saints, grant us concord in good will, so that, peaceful, we may always follow and do your

In summary, peace and living in peace is associated with concord in good will, obedience to God's precepts, self discipline through fasting and moderation, contentment, and God's presence in worship. It operates at the personal and ecclesial level of human existence. In LMZ 1374 peace is related to keeping the divine commandments, *tua seruantes precepta*.

Tua servantes precepta[25]

The keeping of God's commandments is a divine teaching, and is conjoined with grace, peace, wholehearted devotion and harmony in the community.

The spirit of grace and peace enables believers to be totally devoted to God and live in harmony with each other. In this way they keep (*servare*) the heavenly commandments, which are based in love of God and neighbour:

"*Deus, qui aeclesiam tuam in dilectione[m] tuae diuinitatis et proximi cuncta seruare caeles<t>ia mandata docuisti: da nobis spiritum pacis et gratiae, ut uniuersa familia tua et toto tibi sit corde deuota, et pura sibi uoluntate concordet*" (L 971)[26].

In a preface, love of God and neighbour are seen as the two precepts (*preceptum*) which fulfill the entire law. The prayer echoes the interchange of love of God and worship of God found in L 432, the source of Collect IV in the Missal of Paul VI. Obedience is related to receiving good things in the present and in eternity:

"*Uere dignum: qui sic rationabilem non deseris creaturam, ut et quibus modis*

---

precepts.

[25] For further examples of the use of *servare* see Deshusses Concordances III, 4, 226-227, and for *praeceptum*, III, 3, 432-434.

[26] God who taught your church to keep all the heavenly mandates in love of your divinity and of neighbour, give us the spirit of peace and grace, so that your whole family may be devoted to you with all their heart, and may live in harmony with a pure will.

placere tibi, et qualiter possit inpetrare quae poscit ostendas; praecipiens ut te principaliter toto corde uenerantes, consequenter et uniuersos homines, sicut nosmet ipsos tamquam consortes nostri generis diligamus; tunc circa eos uerum probantes affectum, ut quemadmodum nos purgari desideramus a uitiis, ita et eorum quos amamus optemus. Quibus praeceptis duobus totam legem sine difficultate conplentes, bona praesentia sumamus et aeterna" (L 422)[27].

Note that the spiritual, rational nature of humanity is related to God's showing them how to please him and how to obtain what they request, by the practice of true love.

In LMZ 1374, the phrase *pacifici tua seruantes precepta* brings forward obedience to God's precepts with special reference to their fulfillment in love of God and of neighbour, the worship and devotion of the faithful, peace and harmony amongst the community, self-discipline and receiving good things in the present and in eternal life. Keeping the divine precepts has an ecclesial context, and belongs with the peace, harmony, worship and devotion of the ecclesial community. Because Christian obedience reflects the image of God in humanity itself, and his justice and truth, it relates the individual believer, the community and all humankind, and leads towards God's plan for all creation.

Specifically in our prayer, the peaceful observance of God's precepts is further related to the attainment of eternal life, *ad vitam mereamur pervenire perpetuam*. This expression will now be examined.

---

[27][God], you do not desert spiritual creatures and you show them both how to please you and how your creatures are able to obtain what they request. You command that, first and foremost venerating you with all our hearts, consequently we might love all humans, loving all with whom we share humanity just as we love ourselves. And concerning the demonstration of true affection, you command that we desire those we love to be purged from their sins in whatsoever way we would wish to be purged from our sins. May we, fulfilling the whole law without difficulty by those two precepts, take up good things in the present and in eternity.

Ad vitam mereamur pervenire perpetuam[28]

Pervenire and *mereri* emphasize the actions of the community as they live out their salvation in God through their worship and obedience to the mandates. Though to merit means etymologically to earn or deserve, the meriting and attaining of the community take place wholly within the context of God's work in the cross and the resurrection of Christ.

In a blessing for the Saturday Mass preceding the Octave of Easter, the faithful merit to obtain future rewards within the context of salvation in the cross of Christ:

"Dei Patris Filius, qui peccata nostra per corpus suum cruci adfixit, suo carnes uestras adfigat amore. Amen.

Quique uos filios redemptionis sibi adoptauit ex gratia, nulla uos patiatur se iudicante mancipari gehenna. Amen.

Quo saluate per crucem, ad futuram quandoque mereamini peruenire mercedem. Amen." (LMZ 683)[29].

Conjoined with salvation through the cross is Christ taking upon himself the sins of the faithful, his continuous love for believers, their adoption out of his favour as children of the redemption, their judgement unto mercy rather than punishment, and their meriting to obtain eternal rewards.

In an Easter Sunday *super sindonem*, God is addressed as the one who gladdens the community by the annual solemnity of the resurrection of the

---

[28]For further examples of the use of *pervenire* see Deshusses Concordances III, 3, 359-362, and for *mereri* III, 3, 63-70.

[29]May the Son of God the Father, who affixed our sins to the cross through his body, affix your flesh by his love.
May he who, in his favour, adopted you for himself as children of redemption, suffer not one of you to be delivered to Gehenna.
When the time comes may you merit to obtain the eternal reward, in him whom you are saved through the cross.

Lord. On account of this, the community prays, that, through the celebrating of the resurrection, they may merit to come through to eternal joys:

"*Deus, qui nos resurrectionis, dominicae annua solempnitate laetificas, concide propicius, ut per temporalia festa quae agimus peruenire ad gaudia aeterna mereamur*" (V 464)[30].

In a prayer over the elect who are undertaking the catechumenate, God is requested to guard them through the power of the cross of Christ. Through this power, the community asks that these elect may preserve the beginnings of the abundance of glory in themselves through adherence to God's mandates, and so merit to come through to the glory of regeneration.

"*Praeces nostras, quaesumus, domine, clementer exaudi et hos electos tuos crucis dominicae, cuius inpraessione signamur, uirtute custodi, ut magnitudinis gloriae rudimenta seruantes per custodiam mandatorum tuorum ad regeneracionis peruenire gloriam mereantur*" (V 286)[31].

Summarizing the above, the phrase *ad vitam mereamur pervenire perpetuam* values the actions of the community in their worship and keeping the commandments, but sets them wholly within the context of salvation in the cross of Christ, his continuous love, adoption, redemption and merciful judgement.

In LMZ 1374, the faithful ask God, whom they call upon as certain peace and true love, for the fullness of peace. God's peace provides the

---

[30] God, who gladdens us by the annual solemnity of the resurrection of the Lord, grant propitiously that, through the temporal festival which we celebrate, we may merit to come to eternal joys.
This prayer is included in the Missal of Paul VI: MR(1975) Fer. IV infra oct. Paschae, Collecta, 295.

[31] Mercifully hear our prayer, Lord and guard these your elect by the power of the cross of the Lord, by the seal of which we are signed, so that preserving the beginnings of the abundance of glory, they may merit to come through to the glory of your regeneration through the keeping of your mandates.

context for them to be able to keep the commandments and merit to obtain eternal life. This context of the divine gift of peace is related to salvation in Christ. It is grounded in his love, adoption, redemption, and merciful judgement for believers.

The meaning of the prayer:

The prayer, relating God's peace to his love, asks him to bestow on the community the fullness of his peace. This peace and love is related to obedience to God's mandates, self-denial, worship, peace and harmony, and receiving good things in the present and in eternity. The *ad pacem* prayer more specifically concentrates on the peace which is associated with keeping God's mandates, which themselves are ordained towards love of God and neighbour. Through this obedience in peace and love, the faithful ask that they may merit to reach eternal life. They can only merit this in the context of God's love, peace, and bestowal of peace through salvation in Christ.

ANALYSIS OF THE COLLECT FROM THE MISSAL OF PAUL VI

The composite collect forms a new prayer, centred around the observance of the commandments, which are subsumed in the commandment to love God and neighbour. The community prays that their obedience may lead to obtaining eternal life.

Grammatical structure:

The collect contains (i) an address to God with a motivating clause, and (ii) a twofold petition:

(i)   Address: *Deus*

      Motivation: *qui sacrae legis omnia constituta in tua et proximi dilectione posuisti,*

(ii)   Petition: *da nobis   ut*

                         servantes tua praecepta,

                         ad vitam mereamur pervenire perpetuam.

The first petition *servantes* provides the means for the fulfilment of the second petition *mereamur pervenire*.

The motivational clause of the collect echoes Matthew's account of the questions about the greatest commandment (Mt 22:37-40). The petition reflects the concerns underlying Luke's account, where a lawyer, attempting to test Jesus, wants to know what he must do to possess eternal life (Lc 10:25). For Jesus, love of God and neighbour lead to eternal life (v.28).

Meaning of the prayer:

The prayer gathers together the different versions of Jesus' commandment to love God and neighbour. The divine law is sacred, with all of its mandates ordained towards love of God and neighbour. Living out the divine precepts, itself a gift from God, leads to gaining eternal life.

The great commandment is itself a reflection of God's truth, justice and provident governance, which provides the image for the rationality which God planted in humanity. Living out the divine image and its truth and justice involves love and worship of God, and charity towards all others, towards the 'neighbour'.

Obedience to God's precepts is an ecclesial action, and is associated with peace and harmony in the community, worship, self-denial, fasting, moderation and receiving God's gifts in the present and in eternity.

This obedience is meritorious for eternal life because it is wholly set within the peace and love of God, the salvation brought about in Christ through his cross, his continuous love, adoption, redemption and merciful judgement towards the community.

RELATIONSHIP OF THE CHRISTIAN PEOPLE TO GOD

In the relationship of the Christian people to God, God ordains his mandates and the sacred law to love of God, with its connotations of true worship of God, and love of neighbour. The term 'neighbour' intends all humanity, as in the parable of the Good Samaritan.

The divine mandates themselves reflect God's provident ordering, truth and justice. Human reason is the divine image implanted at creation. To obey the mandates, ordained as they are towards love and worship of God and charity towards all, is to relate to God through participation in the divine image, to walk in his justice and live in his order of truth.

Obeying God's precepts on earth is conjoined in the Christian community with true worship, peace and harmony, self-denial, fasting, moderation, and receiving God's gifts. Obedience is not simply an individual action, but is part of the identity, harmony and worship of the church itself, and a reflection of God's order of truth and way of justice for all humanity and creation.

The obedience which leads to eternal life is possible only within the relationship to God established in Christ. The relationship is one of peace, marked by God's love, redemption, adoption and merciful judgement in Christ.

FREER TRANSLATION OF THE COLLECT

Deus, qui sacrae legis omnia constituta in tua et proximi dilectione posuisti, da nobis, ut, tua praecepta servantes, ad vitam mereamur pervenire perpetuam.

God, who established the mandates of holy law to serve love of God and neighbour, grant that by keeping your precepts we may deserve to come to everlasting life.

COLLECT FOR SUNDAY XVIII

PRAYER

Adesto, Domine, famulis tuis, et perpetuam benignitatem largire poscentibus, ut his, qui te auctorem et gubernatorem gloriantur habere, et grata restaures, et restaurata conserves.

Be present, Lord, to your servants, and bestow your unending favour on the ones beseeching you, so that for these servants who glory to have you as their originator and governor, you may restore what is pleasing to you and you may preserve what you have restored.

ORIGINAL SOURCE

Adesto, domine, famulis tuis, et opem tuam largire poscentibus; ut his, qui auctore te gubernatore gloriantur, et creata restaures, et restaurata conserues (L 887).

Be present Lord to your servants, and bestow your help on those beseeching you, so that, for those who glory in having you as their originator and governor, you may restore what has been created and preserve what you have restored.

Veronensis: Final prayer in Mass XXVII,v, *item alia, Septembri, Admonitio ieiunii mensis septimi et orationes et praeces* (L 887).

USE IN OTHER LITURGICAL SOURCES

As noted by Bruylants[1], the prayer is found in these sources:

Feria IV post Dominicam II Quadragesimae: V(I.22;p32) [V 182], Pr (56,4), X (56,4),

Feria V post Dominicam III Quadragesimae: P(220),

Feria V post Dominicam II Quadragesimae, Super populum, A(393), S(344), COR(49,4)[H 220], N(56), Q(40v), 1474(78), 1570, 1604, as well as in the following uncritical editions G(64,4)[G 377], Z(283).

The prayer is used twice in the Missal of Paul VI. Besides being the opening prayer for Sunday XVIII in Ordinary Time it is also among the Orationes Super Populum[2]. Except for the addition of the word *feliciter* and the replacement of *his* with *iis*, this *super populum* is the same as the original source L 887. The most significant difference between the two uses of the prayer in the Missal of Paul VI is the replacement of *creata* with *grata* in the collect.

CHANGES FROM THE MOST ORIGINAL SOURCE

The liturgical context of the prayer has changed. Originally a final prayer over the people for a Sunday during the September fast, it was handed on through the liturgical sources as a lenten prayer. In the Missal of Paul VI it is used as an opening collect for a Sunday in Ordinary Time, as well as being placed among the generic prayers over the people at the end of the Mass.

---

[1]Bruylants II, 23. For a more exhaustive list of sources, manuscripts and variations see Moeller, Corpus Orationum I, A-C Orationes 1-880, Oration 95, 50; and Deshusses, Le Sacramentaire Grégorien, 145, footnote to H 220.

[2]MR(1975), Orationes super populum 8, 508: *Adesto, domine, famulis tuis, et opem tuam largire poscentibus; ut iis, qui te auctore et gubernatore feliciter gloriantur, et creata restaures, et restaurata conserues: per Christum.*

Throughout the manuscript tradition the text of the prayer has undergone various modifications which have influenced the present form of the collect. *Opem tuam* has become *perpetuam benignitatem*, a modification present in many sources: X(56,4), COR(49,4)[H 220], N(56), Q(40v), 1474(78), 1570, 1604, G(64,4)[G 377][3]. The phrase *qui auctore te gubernatore gloriantur* now reads *qui te auctorem et gubernatorem gloriantur habere*, a variation seen in some manuscripts of the Gregorian Sacramentaries[4]. *Creata restaures* has become *grata restaures*, a modification found in V(I.22;p32)[V 182], Pr(56,4), and P(220)[5]. Other manuscripts read *congregata, congrata* or *agnita*, and one manuscript replaces *conserves* with *gubernas*.[6] The *super populum* for Feria V post Dominicam II Quadragesimae in the Roman Missal of Pius V incorporates *perpetuam benignitatem*, however it also reads *congregata restaures*. The collect as it stands in the Missal of Paul VI is a revised version of the original source, modified in the light of the prayer's textual tradition.

The interplay in the sources between *opem tuam, perpetuam benignitatem, perpetuam pacem,* and *perpetuam veniam,* between *creata, grata, congregata, congrata* and *agnita,* and between *conserves* and *gubernas* highlights God's continuous help in the face of sin, the restoration of what is pleasing to God, and his ongoing preservation and guidance of what has been restored. These themes fit well with the Christian fast and the season of Lent.

---

[3]Bruylants II, 23.

[4]Deshusses, Le Sacramentaire Grégorien, 145, footnote to H 220.

[5]Bruylants II, 23.

[6]Deshusses, Le Sacramentaire Grégorien, 185, footnote to H 220.

ANALYSIS OF THE PRAYER IN THE ORIGINAL SOURCE
Origin:

The exact historical background of this prayer is not known with certainty. According to Chavasse[7] section XXVII of the *Veronensis* unites two collections of Mass formulae. Masses i to viii are Masses for the fast of the seventh month (September). Masses viiii to xiiii are a collection of Masses for the fast of the tenth month (December). Chavasse attributes both collections to the pen of Pope Vigilius (537-555) for the following reasons. The heading for section XXVII employs the word *admonitio*, which appears in the *Veronensis* only in Masses by Pope Vigilius.[8] The introduction to the section (L 860) and the opening Mass set (L 861-866) contain references that could refer to the siege of Rome by the Arian Ostrogoths under Witiges, indicating in that case that the orations are from the September of 537[9]. Furthermore Vigilius has borrowed prayers from XXVII,xii and xiii (L 933-37 and L 938) to compose a later Mass XXVIIII,xi (L 1027-1033) which Chavasse dates the third Sunday after Easter, March 25, 538.[10] This borrowing indicates that the two collections of Masses in XXVII were established collections. Such borrowing

---

[7] A. Chavasse, "Messes du Pape Vigile (537-555) dans le Sacramentaire Léonien," Ephemerides Liturgicae 64 (1950): 180.

[8] A. Chavasse, "Messes du Pape Vigile (537-555) dans le Sacramentaire Léonien," Ephemerides Liturgicae 66 (1952): 213, footnote 78.

[9] "*Annua nobis est, dilectissimi, ieiuniorum .. et praesentibus periculis exui*" (L 860),
"*Populi tui, deus, defensor et rector .. et ab infestis hostibus liberemur*" (L 862).

[10] Chavasse, "Messes du Pape Vigile," Ephemerides Liturgicae 64 (1950): 182.

is consistent with authorship by Vigilius, since he occasionally redeployed prayers he had previously composed into other Masses.[11]

There is then a strong possiblity that our prayer, L 887, is part of a collection written by Pope Vigilius for the September fast. The first prayer of this collection was written during the siege of 537. Some prayers from the collection for the December fast also predate the lifting of the siege as their later re-use by Vigilius shows. Though it is possible that L 887 may have its origins in the Masses for the fast during the particular September of the siege this cannot be affirmed with any certainty since there is no indication of the war in either the prayer itself or in the other prayers in that particular set.

Once established in the September collection of Masses for the September and December fast the prayer was incorporated in other liturgical books as a lenten prayer.

Grammatical Structure:

This prayer is a well balanced, taut prayer. It is made up of four parts, (a) an address, (b) two petitions, (c) two interconnected purpose clauses, and (d) a description of the praying community:

(a)	Address:	*domine*
(b)	1st Petition:	*Adesto famulis tuis*
	Main Petition:	*et opem tuam largire poscentibus*
(c)	Purpose clauses:	*ut his ... et grata restaures,*
		et restaurata conserves
(d)	Description:	*qui auctore te gubernatore gloriantur.*

---

[11]Chavasse, "Messes du Pape Vigile," Ephemerides Liturgicae 66 (1952): 147f.

Each part is made up of two elements which are grammatically parallel, and in which the second element takes up and continues the first: God's presence (*adesse*) is continued in his bestowing (*largire*), God's authorship (*auctor*) is carried forward in his governing (*gubernator*), God's restoration (*restaurare*) is carried forward in his preserving (*conservare*). Further examination of the purpose clause and the description of the community reveals a parallelism between *auctor* and the verb *creare*, and also between *gubernator* and the verbs *restaurare* and *conservare*. The *et ... et* construction in the purpose clauses especially highlights the faithful's desire that God safeguard what he restores.

The clause *qui auctore te gubernatore gloriantur* provides the motivation for the petition. In their glorying in God as their creator and governor, the faithful view themselves as his servants (*famuli tui*) who confidently make supplication (*poscentes*). Precisely because of their belief that God is both *auctor* and *gubernator* they are confident in seeking the restoration of all created things and God's subsequent guardianship over them.

Vocabulary:

Prominent vocabulary: *Adesse, famulus, largire, ops, poscere, gloriari, auctor, gubernator, restaurare, creare, conservare, gratum, benignitas*.

Our vocabulary study will follow the structure of the prayer, beginning with an examination of the petition *adesto ... opem tuam largire*, and of the petitioners *famuli tui, poscentes*. Then the discussion will move to the descriptive clause which contains the motivation for the petitions. Finally, the two purpose clauses will be analysed. The prayer opens, then, with God's servants calling on him to be present (*adesse*) to them.

Adesto[12]

God's presence is linked with and effected through his works. It is God's response to the prayers, trust, hope and service of the faithful, which he propitiously receives.

God's presence, preservation (*conservare*), perpetual help (*auxilium*) on earth, and eternal life are linked in the following prayer over the people in a Mass for the fast of the fourth month. Note that divine preservation entails help in the present and obtaining eternal grace:

"*Adesto, domine, populis tuis tua protectione fidentibus, et tuae se dexterae suppliciter inclinantes perpetua defensione conserua. Percipiant, quaesumus, domine, uitae praesentis auxilium, et gratiam repperiant sempiternam*" (L 231)[13].

In being present to them, God gives help to the supplicants or to those for whom supplication is made. The first is exemplified in a lenten collect (V 137), where God's presence works to remake (*reficere*) the minds of the supplicants through the effect of the commandments (the fast):

"*Adesto, quaesumus, omnipotens deus, ad [ac] ieiunio corporali mentem nostram operibus tuorum refice mandatorum*" (V 137)[14].

However, in a collect from a Mass in time of war, the supplicants request God to be present to the leaders of the empire, and through his

---

[12]For further examples of the use of *adesse* see Deshusses, Concordances III, 1, 39-42.

[13]"Be present Lord to the people who trust in your protection and preserve by perpetual defense those who humbly bow before your power. May they receive, Lord, help for the present life, and may they obtain eternal grace." For a similar dynamic, linking God's presence (*adesse*), his recreation (*recreare*) and subsequent defense (*defendere*) of the faithful, see L 548.

[14]Be present all powerful God, and in bodily fast remake our minds by the works that you command.

presence offer inspiration and strength:

"*Deus, in te sperantium salus et seruientium fortitudo, suscipe propitius praeces nostrae et romani imperii adesto rectoribus, ut tuis consiliis inspirati tua opitulatione muniti aduersum omnia resistere sibi arma praeualeant*" (V 1498)[15].

In L 887, God's presence is in response to the prayer of the petition of his servants, and is linked with and effected through the bestowing of divine help. This bestowal is expressed in the verb *largire*.

Largire[16]

God, who is in need of no gifts, bestows all gifts, and through them brings salvation, a fact to be recognized even when gifts are offered to him. This is clearly seen in the following prayer over the gifts from the *Veronensis*:

"*Deus qui, cum muneribus nullis indigeas, ipse nobis munera concta largiris: accipe propitius, quae de tuis donis tibi nos offerre uoluisti; non solum nostrae reputans deuotioni quae tua sunt, sed etiam per haec nos ad caelestia regna perducens*" (L 551)[17].

In collect L 887, the people's prayer, God's presence and God's bestowal of gifts are related. The gifts are here described as *opes tua*, and as the restoration and conservation of what God has created.

---

[15]God, salvation of those who hope in you and strength of those who serve you, propitiously hear our prayers and be present to the leaders of the roman empire, so that inspired by your counsels and fortified by your help they may prevail to resist against all arms.

[16]For further examples of the use of *largire* see Deshusses, Concordances III, 2, 443-446.

[17]God, who stand in need of no gifts, you yourself bestow all gifts on us. Accept propitiously that which from your gifts you wish us to offer you; not only accounting what are your things for our devotion, but also leading us to the heavenly kingdom through these things.

Opem tuam[18]

God's help is characterized by bounteousness (*benignus*), goodness (*pietas*), mercy (*misericordia*), and propitiation (*propitiatio*). It covers a wide range of gifts, including the response to grace, healing in the present and rejoicing in the life to come. Furthermore, it is linked with the people's prayers and trust.

In a prayer over the people, God's help is bestowed on sinners out of his favour (*benignus*), so as to bring sincere devotion, healing (from sin) and eternal rejoicing:

"*Succurre, domine, quaesumus, populo supplicanti, et opem tuam tribue benignus infirmis; ut sincera tibi mente deuoti, et praesentis uitae remediis gaudeant et futurae*" (L 937)[19].

God's help is related to his mercy (*misericordia*) and clemency (*propitiatus*). Note that God is present (*adesse*) in the exercise of his mercy to the people who trust in him. The prayer reads:

"*Adesto, domine, plebi tuae, et in tua misericordia confidenti opem tuae propitiationis inpende*" (L 654)[20].

The believer requires God's help even to take hold of the assistance that he offers, as seen in this *super populum*. The prayer links God's help with his grace and goodness (*pietas*) and with the people's supplication and trust:

---

[18]For further examples of the use of *ops* see Deshusses, Concordances III, 3, 261-262. *Ops*, as an expression of God's help, is frequently employed with the verb *largiri*. See Blaise, Vocabulaire, § 71.

[19]Hasten to the aid of your supplicating people Lord, and out of your favour bestow your help on the weak, so that devoted to you with sincere minds, they may rejoice in your remedies in the present life and in the life to come.

[20]Be present Lord to your people, and since it trusts in your mercy, pour out on it the bounty of your propitiation.

"*Auxiliare, domine, supplicibus tuis, ut opem tuae gratiae consequantur, qui in tua pietate confidunt*" (L 666)[21].

In L 887, God's help, in response to the people's petition, is requested so as to restore created things and preserve them as restored. If Chavasse's dating is correct this help is given to those who carry out the fast, even while in the midst of civil strife. The faithful's trust and petition is set forth in the pair of terms *famuli tui* and *poscentes*.

Famulis tuis[22]

The noun *famulus* is used in the liturgical sources for anyone who presently is a member of the community, for those who bear ecclesial office, for those in orders, and for the faithful who have died. It is extended to Old Testament figures as well.

In a lenten prayer it denotes all who are reborn in Christ. It is linked with both the worship and service they owe God, and the rejoicing that such service brings. The prayer reads:

"*Omnipotens sempiterne deus, da, quaesumus, uniuersis famulis tuis plenius adque perfectius omnia festi paschalis introire mysteria, ut incunctanter pia corda cognoscant, quantum debeant de confirmata in Christo renascentium glorificatione gaudere*" (V 349)[23].

Famulus is used of anyone dedicated to God's service, as in these prayers, one for a deceased bishop and the other which remembers the prayers

---

[21] Help, Lord, your supplicating people, that those who trust in your compassion may obtain the help of your grace.

[22] For further examples of the use of *famulus* see Deshusses, Concordances III, 2, 111-126.

[23] All powerful God, give to all your servants to enter more fully and perfectly into the entire mystery of the paschal feast, so that pious hearts may know without hesitation how much they ought to rejoice regarding the confirmed glorification of those being reborn in Christ.

of King David:

"*Praesta, quaesumus, domine, ut anima famuli tui illius episcopi quam in hoc saeculo commorantem sacris muneribus decorasti, caelesti sede gloriosa semper exultet*" (V 1633)[24].

"*Multiplica, domine, super nos misericordiam tuam et praeces nostras propitius exaudire dignare, sicut exaudisti famulum tuum regem David ...*" (V 1570)[25].

Famulus is an important word in denoting people's relation to God, since it designates an attitude of constant service and rejoicing, along with a sense of divine election. In L 887 the community are God's servants (*famuli tui*) who glory to have him as their originator and governor, and beseech (*poscere*) his aid. They are helped by the restoration of all created things from their fallen state and their ensuing preservation from sin.

Poscentibus[26]

The verb *poscere* is one of a range of verbs used in the liturgical sources to designate petition. Other verbs include *orare, precari, petere, postulare, quaesere, rogare*[27].

In a prayer *super populum*, *poscere* is conjoined with the humble entreating (*supplex*) of the church for the help (*auxilium*) of God's blessing.

---

[24]"Lord, may the soul of your servant and bishop n., which during its stay in this world you distinguished with sacred gifts, exult unceasingly at the glorious heavenly throne."
This prayer, modified to apply to a priest rather than a bishop, is included in the Missal of Paul VI. See the Mass MR(1975) Pro sacerd. def. 1, Collecta, 900.

[25]Multiply your mercy over us Lord, and deign propitiously to hear our prayers, just as you heard the prayers of your servant King David ....

[26]For further examples of the use of *poscere* see Deshusses, Concordances III, 3, 412-414.

[27]Blaise, Vocabulaire, § 76-82.

This help is extensive, covering pardon, instruction in good works, consolation in temporal needs, and reaching and partaking in eternal life:

"*Consequatur, domine, quaesumus, tuae benedictionis auxilium, quod supplex poscit aeclesia: percipiat indulgentiam, boni [bonis] operis instruatur, temporalium necessitatum consolatione respiret, ad gaudia sempiterna perueniat et adsumat aeterna*" (L 503)[28].

In L 887, God's presence and bestowal of bounty is in response to the prayer of his servants, who are described as *poscentes*. This designates dependence, as well as a devout and humble attitude of prayer and supplication.

Before continuing on into the oration's purpose clause, the preceding material will be quickly summarized. The faithful, as God's *famuli*, are characterized by an attitude of constant service and rejoicing, and a sense of divine election. As humble supplicants, they call on God to be present to them, and to effect this presence through the bestowal of his help. Such divine assistance, however, is marked by bounty and goodness. It is offered out of God's mercy in light of his propitiation, and it aims to bring the faithful to eternal beatitude. Already from the two petitions, it is becoming clear why the community describes itself as those *qui auctore te gubernatore gloriantur*, a clause which will now be examined, beginning with the verb *gloriari*.

Gloriantur[29]

This verb is used in the Vulgate latin translation of Romans 5:1-11, where Paul glories in three aspects of faith; reconciliation in Christ, hope in

---

[28]Lord, may the church obtain the help of your blessing, which it asks in humility. May it receive pardon, be instructed in good works, be refreshed by the consolation of needed temporal things, and may it come through to everlasting joys and receive the things of eternity.

[29]For further examples of the use of *gloriari* see Deshusses, Concordances III, 2, 218-219.

present trials, and a share in God's eternal glory[30].

In the liturgical sources the community glories in events that show forth the salvation God has wrought. This can be seen in a Christmas prayer *super populum*, where the faithful glory in the birth of the divine son who is their lord. Those who glory in this event look for an increase of faith and security, for protection through God's governance (*gubernare*), and for the hope of eternal life:

"*Largire, quaesumus, domine, famulis tuis fidei et securitatis aumentum: ut qui de natiuitate domini nostri tui filii gloriantur, et aduersa mundi te gubernante non sentiant, et quae temporaliter celebrare desiderant, sine fine percipiant*" (L 1243)[31].

Through the gift of total trust, the faithful glory in God who does not desert them. The opposite to glorying in God is proud presumption, which he resists:

"*Da nobis, domine, quaesumus, in te tota mente confidere; quoniam sicut superbis in sua uirtute praesumentibus semper obsistis, ita non deseris in tua misericordia gloriantes*" (L 540)[32].

---

[30] "*Iustificati ergo ex fide pacem habeamus ad Deum per Dominum nostrum Iesum Christum, per quem et habemus accessum per fidem in gratiam istam, in qua stamus et gloriamur in spe gloriae filiorum Dei. Non solum autem, sed et gloriamur in tribulationibus scientes quod tribulatio patientiam operatur .. Non solum autem, sed et gloriamur in Deo per Dominum nostrum Iesum Christum, per quem nunc reconciliationem accepimus*" (Rm 5:1-11).

[31] Bestow on your servants an increase of faith and security, that those who glory in the birth of our Lord and your Son, with you governing may not suffer the adversities of the world, and what they desire to celebrate in the present time, may they receive without end.

[32] Give us, Lord, to trust you with all our minds, because just as you always withstand the proud who presume in their own strength, so you do not desert those who glory in you.

In summary, glorying in God is connected to humble realization of sinfulness, trust in the mercy and compassion of God, and faith in the security, hope, guidance and worship that comes in the reconciliation brought by Christ. Glorying in God on earth is fulfilled in sharing in his glory in heaven. In L 887, the community, God's servants calling on him in their need, glory in God as the one from whom they have their origin and from whom they expect provident governance. The verb *gloriari* connects these two titles to God's salvific acts in Christ, and to God's ongoing work in the whole of creation. The appellation *auctor* will be examined first.

Auctor[33]

Through the title *auctor* the faithful understand God to be the source of all life and goodness. On account of this, the community turns to him for help to remain within this goodness.

In a post communion, God is addressed as *auctor* of peace and at the same time as an originator who loves the peace of which he is the source. Thus he can be asked to defend it:

"Deus, auctor pacis et amator, quem nosse uiuere, cui seruire regnare est, protege ab omnibus inpugnationibus supplices tuis, ut qui defensione tua fidemus, nullius hostilitatis arma timeamus" (V 1476)[34].

In another prayer, the title *auctor* denotes God as the origin of mercies and of goodness. In this capacity he is asked to look upon the fasts and bring healing of conscience to sinners:

---

[33]For further examples of the use of *auctor* see Deshusses, Concordances III, 1, 138-139.

[34]"God, author and lover of peace, whom to know is to live, to serve whom is to rule, protect your suppliants from all attacks so that we who trust in your defense, may fear the arms of no adverse action."
This prayer is included in the Missal of Paul VI. See the Mass, MR(1975) Temp. belli vel eversionis, Collecta, 825.

"*Deus, omnium misericordiarum ac bonitatis auctor, qui peccatorum remidia ieiuniis orationibus et aelymosinis demonstrasti: respice propitius in hanc humilitatis nostrae confessionem, ut qui inclinamur consciencia nostra, tua semper misericordia eregamur*" (V 249)[35].

As author and lover of peace, author of all mercies, author of all goodness, God is continually engaged in the protection of the faithful, their healing and their being raised up. He provides even the remedies for sins in fasts, prayers and alms. The word *auctor* thus designates God as source of life, and as source of all that is good in the life of Christians, who readily turn to him for forgiveness and care. In L 887, God's guidance and governing closely follows upon his authorship.

Gubernator[36]

The noun *gubernator* is listed by Deshusses and Darragon as occuring in only three prayers. However the related verb *gubernare* is indexed in over 60 prayers. In the liturgical sources, the action designated as *gubernare* completes and continues other actions.

In a Christmas prayer *ad populum*, *gubernare* is associated with *tueri* and *perficere*. The oration links the economy of grace that is celebrated in the feast of the Nativity with those actions by which God safeguards, sanctifies, governs and perfects the people:

"*Populum tuum, domine, quaesumus, tueantur sanctificent et gubernent*

---

[35] "God, author of all mercies and all goodness, who established the remedies for sins in fasts, prayers and alms, look propitiously upon this confession of our humility, that we who are bowed down in our conscience may always be raised up by your mercy."
This prayer is included in the Missal of Paul VI. See the Mass, MR(1975) Dom. III in Quadr., Collecta, 200.

[36] For further examples of the use of *gubernator* and *gubernare* see Deshusses, Concordances III, 2, 242-43.

aeternumque perficiant tam deuotionibus acta sollempnibus, quam natalitiis agenda diuinis Iesu Christi domini nostri" (V 16)[37].

The invocation in a prayer for a Mass celebrating the anniversary of the bishop's ordination sets God's governing within the context of his love of and fidelity to fallen creation. In spite of its debasement and displacement, God neither disdains nor despises creation. Rather he rouses and raises up a people. The prayer sets the people who have been roused up in parallel with the things that are most base yet which God does not disdain. Further, the people who are raised up parallel the things that have been thrown down yet which God does not abandon. The first petition of the prayer asks God to support and govern this people. They readily petition God's governing because they are confident that what God loves, is faithful to and raises up, he will continue to support and guide. The prayer points up two aspects of this governance. Firstly it affects the life of the church, including the choice, ordination and rule of bishops. Secondly, in its use of *gubernare* the prayer contrasts the lowliness of creatures, which includes the person of the bishop, with the work of God.

"*Domine, sancte pater, omnipotens deus, qui dignaris infima et abiecta non despicis: adtolle quos suscitas et guberna quos eriges. Da mihi famulo tuo sufficientiam commissi moderaminis. Da aeclesiae tuae pacem, cui me praeesse uoluisti; ut in uno eodemque spiritu sit tibi grata deuotio et plebis et praesulis*" (L 963)[38].

---

[37]We beseech you, Lord, that both the acts of devotion solemnly celebrated, and what was set to be enacted through the divine birth of our Lord Jesus Christ, may safeguard, sanctify, and govern your people, and perfect it in eternity.

[38]Lord, holy Father, all powerful God, you neither disdain what is most base nor despise what has been thrown down. Support those you rouse and govern those you raise up. Give to me, your servant, sufficient means of

In a lenten *super sindonem*, the providence of God's compassion is sought to restore, renew, protect, govern, and bring to the portals of eternal life:

"*Reparet nos, quaesumus, domine, semper et innouet tuae prouidentiae pietatis, que fragilitatem nostram et inter mundi tempestates protegat et gubernet et in portum perpetuae salutis inducat*" (V 130)[39].

In summary, the verb *gubernare* is one of a number of words which denote God's continuous guidance, strengthening, protection and perfection of the church. It is an effect of and expression of the divine love in which God created all things, brought salvation from sin, and renewed the human community. Amidst the sin and temptation of life on earth, God's governance guides the life of the church, keeps it in truth and leads it to eternal life. The church's euchology links it with a broad range of God's actions in the life of the church, amongst which are the restoration (*restaurare*) and renewal (*renovare*) of the faithful, their sanctification and perfection, and the provision of such gifts as good government (*moderamen*) and peace. The very need for God's continuous guidance is a constant reminder to the church of its dependance on God and its proclivity to sin.

With the pairing of *auctor* and *gubernator* in the clause *auctore te gubernatore gloriantur*, the oration invokes a sweeping range of ongoing actions beginning with the fact that God is source and origin of all that is good. The divine actions associated with these and kindred terms manifest the continuous presence of the love of God for humanity. This underpins the faith

---

government. Give peace to your church, which you wish me to lead, so that in one and the same spirit both people and bishop may give you thankful devotion.

[39] Lord, may the providence of your compassion restore and renew us, and may it protect and govern our human fragility amongst the storms of the world and lead it up to the door of eternal salvation.

and hope of Christians in the face of sin and tribulation. Trapped by sin and helpless by their own efforts alone, the faithful glory only in salvation in Christ and the hope and strength this gives in tribulation. The combination of *auctor* and *gubernator* invoke all that God has brought forward and continues to support and love; his creation, peace, mercy, goodness, remedies for sins, healing and protection. Conjoined with God's governing is the rousing of what has been thrown down, and its being restored, renewed, guarded, sanctified, strengthened and supported.

In L 887, the ecclesial community glories in the God who faithfully saved and governs what he created in his love. In light of this, they petition God on behalf of all created things. They ask him to restore all that he has created, and to preserve it in this restored state. This conjunction of the verbs *creare*, *restaurare* and *conservare* will now be analyzed.

Creata[40]

In the Vulgate translation of the scriptures, the verb *creare* and the noun *creatura* are applied in two contexts. They refer to God's original act of creation, as set forth in the Genesis narratives. They are also applied to the new creation brought forth by Christ's work of reconciliation. In Christ, the old creation, subject to sin, has passed away, and all things have been made new. This new creation shares in the freedom of the glory of God's children. The early liturgical sources reflect both applications of *creare*.

The scriptures open with God's creation of all that exists, its inherent goodness, and God's pleasure in it.

"*In principio creavit Deus caelum et terram .. Viditque Deus cuncta quae fecerat, et erant valde bona*" (Gn 1:1-31).

---

[40]For further examples of the use of *creare* see Deshusses, <u>Concordances</u> III, 1, 388-389.

However, in the wake of the sin of Adam and Eve, all creation suffers, with the earth also cursed:

"*Adae vero dixit: Quia audisti vocem uxoris tuae et comedisti de ligno, ex quo praeceperam tibi ne comederes, maledicta terra in opere tuo..*" (Gn 3:17)[41].

Through the reconciliation brought about by Christ all things are made new:

"*Si qua ergo in Christo nova creatura, vetera transierunt ecce facta sunt omnia nova; omnia autem ex Deo, qui nos reconciliavit sibi per Christum et dedit nobis ministerium reconciliationis*" (2 Cor 5:17-18).

In Christ creation itself will be freed from the corruption of sin, and will share in the liberty of the glory of the children of God:

"*Quia et ipsa creatura liberabitur a servitute corruptionis in libertatem gloriae filiorum Dei*" (Rm 8:17).

In a prayer for the blessing of the baptismal font during the Easter Vigil, *creare* signals the creation of a new people from the womb of the baptismal font. It is connected with God's presence in the sacraments, the spirit of adoption which he sends, and the work of the minister which God completes:

"*Omnipotens sempiternae deus, adesto magne pietatis tuae mysteriis, adesto sacramentis et ad creandos nouos populos, quos tibi fons baptismatis parturit, spiritum adoptionis emitte et quod humilitatis nostrae gerendum est ministerio, tuae uirtutis conpleatur effectus*" (V 444)[42].

---

[41] Also Gn 5:29.

[42] "All powerful eternal God, be present to the mysteries of your great goodness, be present to these sacraments, and to create new people whom the font of baptism brings forward from its womb, send the spirit of adoption, and may the effect of your power make complete that which is done by the ministry of our humble person."

This prayer, with *recreandos* replacing *creandos*, is included in the Missal of

Creation and restoration are brought together in a prayer for the reconciliation of minors rebaptized from heresy. This work of creation (*creare*) and redemption (*reparare*) are predicated of God who is called *conditor* and *redemptor*. Redemption restores in the first creation the image and likeness of God. By reason of sin even children are caught up in the need for forgiveness, and by the work of the enemy, heresy embroils the young, who cannot free themselves from it but need God's grace and pardon. Note the symmetry between creation, redemption, pardon and church membership, as well as that between the words *conditor* and *redemptor*, *reparare* and *creare*. The prayer reads:

"*Deus humani generis conditor et redemptor, deus qui facturam similitudinis et imaginis tuae secundum diuicias bonitatis in id reparas quod creasti: respice propicius super hunc famulum tuum, ut quidquid ignoranciae ipsius necessitas hostilitatis influxit, indulgencia tuae pietatis ignosce, ut in eo cui adhuc intelligencia integra non suppetit, nihil reputetur ad culpam, sed aeclesiae membrum remissionis tuae benignitate reputetur*" (V 688)[43].

In a preface for the December fast, God is asked to preserve the community which he has restored by Christ's passion. The prayer brings together creation, restoration, merciful forgiveness, preservation, liturgical celebration and eternal life:

"*Vere dignum: qui creasti tui beata passione nos reparas: conserva in nobis*

Paul VI. See MR(1975) Vig. pasch., Or. post litanias, si adsunt baptt., 282.

[43] God, creator and redeemer of the human race, God who according to the riches of your goodness restores the handiwork of your image and likeness in that which you created: look with pardon upon this your servant, in whom full intelligence is not yet sufficient, so that whatever danger of ignorance has influenced him by the work of the enemy may not be reputed to him as fault, but, by the goodness of your remission, he may be counted a member of your church.

operam misericordiae tuae, ut in huius celebritate mysterii per<pe>tua deuotione uiuamus:" (L 941)[44].

The doxology *per quem* in the Roman Canon reflects God's creative activity in Christ. The prayer affirms God's entire action of unceasingly creating, sanctifying, vivifying, blessing and bestowing all things on the community, and relates them to Christ, creator and redeemer. Note that here, what is offered to God comes from God, and what is bestowed on the worshippers in creation is even more fully blessed. The doxology reads: *"Per quem* [Christ] *haec omnia, domine, semper bona creas sanctificas uiuificas benedicis et praestas nobis"* (V 1254)[45].

In summary, in the liturgical sources the verb *creare* enfolds God's original act of creation, his work of restoration in the redemption wrought by Christ, and his continuous creating, sanctifying, blessing, vivifying and bestowing in Christ. Creation, recreation, and the restoration of God's image bespeak forgiveness, freedom from sin, baptism and worship.

In L 887, the verb *creare* denotes all that God created, which in turn he is asked to restore (*restaurare*).

---

[44] "You who created us, you restore us by the blessed passion of your [Son]. Preserve in us the works of your mercy, so that we may live in perpetual devotion by the celebrating of this mystery.

[45] "Through whom you constantly create, sanctify, vivify, bless and establish all these good things for us."
Some commentators think that the *Per quem* is the conclusion of a blessing of natural produce which on occasion took place at this point in the canon. If so, then the blessing is in concert with L 887, since in both the restoration of creation in Christ is associated with the renewed community. See Joseph A. Jungmann, The Mass of the Roman Rite II, 259-64; and Enrico Mazza, The Eucharistic Prayers of the Roman Rite, 87.

Restaures, restaurata[46]

In the mystery of the incarnation, the old and earthly law has ceased, and the human condition has been brought forth in a new heavenly restored nature, as seen in this Christmas preface:

"*Vere dignum: nos sursum cordibus erectis diuinum adorare mysterium, quo humana conditio ueteri terrenaquae lege cessante noua caelestisquae substantia mirabiliter restaurata profertur, ut quod magno die munere geritur, magnis ecclesiae gaudiis caelebretur*" (V 14)[47].

God restores human creatures both inwardly and outwardly. The fast, an external passing thing imposed by God, holds the people back from bodily pleasures, and even strenghtens them. On the other hand, God restores them internally, giving them spiritual purpose and the desire for eternal realities:

"*Plebem tuam, domine, quaesumus, interius exteriusque restaura; ut, quam corporeis non uis delectationibus inpediri, spiritali facias uigere proposito; et sic rebus foueas transituris, ut tribuas potius inherere perpetuis*" (L 1020)[48].

In a *super populum* from a Mass concerned with the pardon of sins God is addressed as *creator* and *reparator*, connecting his work of restoration with his creative activity. The *instituta bona* which God wishes to give to his

---

[46]For further examples of the use of *restaurare* see Deshusses, Concordances III, 2, 218-219. Our prayer appears to be the only one in the sources indexed by Deshusses which applies *restaurare* beyond humanity to the broader sense of all created things.

[47]It is right and fitting that, with hearts raised up, we adore the divine mystery, by which the human condition, with the old and earthly law ceasing, is brought forth wonderfully restored as a new and heavenly nature, so that the worship and service of this great day may be celebrated by the great joy of the church.

[48]Restore your people Lord both internally and externally so that since you do not wish it to be held back by bodily delights, you may bring it to thrive by spiritual purpose. Thus may you comfort it by passing things, so that you may grant it to cling rather to perpetual things.

people are set in parallel with what has been restored (*restaurata*):
"*Creator populi tui, deus, adque reparator: tuere supplices, tuere misericordiam postulantes; ut + satisfactio<ne> pro se intercedente sanct<or>um ill<or>um + et instituta bona recipiant, et restaurata custodiant*" (L 56)[49].

The eucharist and fasting are sources of restoration for the believer. According to a lenten offertory prayer, the eucharist more swiftly restores what the fast had begun:
"*Sacrificia, domine, propensius ista restaurent, quae medicinabilibus sunt instituta ieiuniis*" (V 280)[50].

In summary, the verb *restaurare* harks back to the original creation in goodness, and refers to what has been restored of that creation through the reconciliation Christ has wrought. The work of restoration by God's power continues through the fasts and liturgies of the church, and in the intercession of the saints. In particular the liturgical euchology applies the verb *restaurare* to the restoration of humanity through baptism.

In L 887, God's restoration is directed towards all created reality. This divine action is there related to the divine epithets, *auctor* and *gubernator*. The second of the oration's purpose clauses seeks that God preserve (*conservare*) what he has so graciously restored.

---

[49]God, creator and restorer of your people; safeguard those who ask your mercy, so that seeking satisfaction through the intercession of the saints N. they may receive the good things instituted for them, and may keep them once they have been restored.

[50]May these sacrifices more quickly restore those things which have been begun by the healing fasts.

Conserves[51]

The verb *conservare* is another verb related to creation and restoration, and used to express the extent of God's action. The three verbs complement each other. To keep or preserve follows on creation and restoration.

In the Letter to Jude, God is said to preserve from sin and lead into the presence of his glory:

"*Ei autem qui potens est vos conservare sine peccato et constituere ante conspectum gloriae suae immaculatos in exaltatione in adventu Domini nostri Iesu Christi*" (Ju 24).

In a prayer over the wine mixed with water used in the the consecration of an altar, God's preserving is conjoined with his creating, giving spiritual blessing, sending the Spirit, and bestowing eternal salvation:

"*Creator et conservator humani generis, dator graciae spiritalis, largitor aeternae salutis: tu permitte spiritum tuum super uinum cum aqua mixtum, ut arma<ta> uirtute caelestis defensionis ad consecracionem huius aeclesiae vel altaris proficiat*" (V 691)[52].

The above prayer, and almost all instances of *conservare* in the early sources apply God's safeguarding to the human race or the Christian community[53]. Only rarely are created things the object of God's preservation[54]. The prayer which concludes the readings in the Pentecost Vigil in *Reginensis*

---

[51]For further examples of the use of *conservare* and *conservator* see Deshusses, Concordances III, 1, 335-336.

[52]Creator and preserver of the human race, giver of spiritual grace, bestower of eternal salvation: send your spirit over this wine mixed with water, so that armed by the power of heavenly defense, it may bring about the consecration of this church or altar.

[53]See also V 200, V 453, and V 454,

[54]It seems the only such occasions in the *Veronensis* and *Reginensis* 316 are L 887 and V 623.

316 is motivated by the community's belief that God restores (*reparare*) all that has fallen (*conlapsa*), and safeguards what he has restored. Note however that the focus of the prayer remains on the restoration of humanity in baptism. This can be seen in the structure of the prayer, where the *conlapsa* that are restored are set in parallel with the people renewed by baptism, and God's ongoing preservation is paralleled by his inspiration and direction of the baptized. The oration reads:

"*Domine Deus uirtutum, qui, conlapsa reparas et reparata conseruas, auge popuos in tui nominis sanctificatione renouandos, ut omnes qui diluintur sacro baptismate, tua semper inspiratione dirigantur*" (V 623)[55].

The verb *conservare* denotes God's ongoing concern for and action on behalf of the people he has created, saved from sin, and restored. In liturgical euchology, God's upholding and preserving is associated with a broad variety of graces, amongst which are the gift of the Spirit, consolation, inspiration and direction. Through this preserving action, the renewed community is enabled to remain in its state of restoration, and can be brought to eternal life.

In L 887, the clause *creata restaures, et restaurata conserves* relates God's restoration and preservation to all created things. From the entire economy of God's creative and redemptive love in Christ, the faithful glory in God as creator, author, restorer, governor, preserver. The prayer relates these titles, and their ecclesial context, to the whole of creation, asking God to restore and preserve all created things for the faithful. Included here is the concept of creation narrated in Genesis. The prayer focuses on God's restoring all things to their biblical pristine goodness, of which humankind, made in the image and likeness of God, is the crowning achievement. If the historical

---

[55]God of all powers, who restores fallen things and preserves what has been restored, increase the people being renewed in the blessing of your name, so that all who are washed in sacred baptism may be directed always by your inspiration.

context of the prayer is the seige of Rome by the Arian Ostrogoths, the *creata* to be preserved would include the order of peace, orthodox belief, and the (disrupted) liturgy of the church.

Meaning of the Prayer:

The main thrust of the prayer takes its focus from the faithful's acclamation of God as their *auctor* and *gubernator*. In light of this, they are confident that he will be present to them, and grant his bountiful assistance. In particular they request that God, in his government, restore and preserve as restored, what he as *auctor* created.

However, the broader liturgical usage of the terms *auctor*, *gubernator*, *creare*, *restaurare* and *conservare*, when applied to God, bespeaks a far richer understanding of the oration. Together they put forward God's entire economy of creation, salvation and renewal.

The pair *auctor* and *creare*, associated with other epithets such as *conditor*, point to the original creation narrated in Genesis, the ongoing creation of all that is good, and to the recreation in Christ of sinful humanity and sin-damaged creation. Implicit in the divine creative activity is God's continuing care and maintenance of what he has established in love. The church's euchology expresses this through terms like *reparator*, *redemptor*, *gubernator* and *amator pacis*.

Our prayer associates God's authorship with his restoration, governorship and preservation of all he has made. These actions betoken the whole range of activities that God has undertaken to overcome sin and bring humanity and all created things back to their original goodness. The verb *restaurare* points up the mystery of the incarnation, and the reconciliation of all things in Christ. It is further linked with baptism, the liturgy and devotions of the church, and the intercession of the saints. Similarly, God's governance and preservation denote the consolation, inspiration, direction, healing and sanctification that God provides to protect the faithful from sin and to lead them to eternal life.

The *super populum* neatly summarizes all this as *opem tuam*, a term which reflects the bounty, goodness, mercy and propitiation that suffuses the divine economy of creation, salvation and restoration. All this is paralleled in the glorying of the faithful, a glorying that illuminates their own sinfulness while proclaiming their hope in Christ's reconciliation, its effects in the present, and its promise of eternal glory.

In the original prayer, the concern of the community arising from the siege is set within this context. If God remains present to the church, he will continue his creative and providential work, whatever the plight of the people. It is not surprising that the restoration of an original order of peace and security be uppermost in their minds. If God restores it, he can also be depended upon to preserve it.

ANALYSIS OF THE WORDS AND PHRASES IN THE COLLECT IN RELATIONSHIP TO THE MISSAL OF PAUL VI

The vocabulary of the *super populum* has retained the same meaning within its new context as a collect in the Missal of Paul VI. This is corroborated by the fact that a number of the prayers used in the above analysis of L 887 are also to be found in the Missal. The collect, however, contains two terms not found in the original prayer: *grata* has been substituted for *creata*, and *perpetuam benignitatem* for *opem tuam*. The effect of these two substitutions will now be examined.

Grata[56]

By substituting *grata* for *creata* the Missal of Paul VI loses some of the resonance of what is understood by creation in the early sources. The substitution emphasises God's pleasure in his work rather than the work itself.

The adjective *gratus*, in its various forms, is used 30 times in the Missal of Paul VI[57]. In the large majority of these prayers, twenty of which are offertory prayers, the adjective refers to what is pleasing and acceptable to God, God's name or God's majesty.

The passion of Christ, as pleasing to God's majesty, brought salvation for the whole world:
"Munera supplicantis Ecclesiae, Domine, in conspectum maiestatis tuae ascendant accepta, cui pro totius mundi salute grata exstitit Filii tui passio gloriosa" (MR(1975) Pro evangelizatione populorum B, Super oblata, 815)[58].

While some of the resonance of creation is lost in the collect, the Missal of Paul VI maintains a connection between *grata* and *creata* by retaining the original prayer, L 887, in the Missal as a *super populum*[59].

In Collect XVIII, *grata* refers to all that God created and which God 'saw to be good'[60]. The shift from *creata* to *grata* emphasises that what was originally created found favour with God. This parallels the use of *perpetua benignitas* over *opes tuae*.

---

[56] For examples of the use of *gratus* in the Missal of Paul VI see Schnitker and Slaby, Concordantia, 1065.

[57] Ibid.

[58] Lord, to whom the glorious passion of your Son was pleasing for the salvation of the whole world, may the gifts of your suppliant church ascend as an acceptable offering in the sight of your majesty.

[59] RM(1975), Orationes super populum 8, 508.

[60] "*Viditque Deus cuncta quae fecerat, et erant valde bona*", Gn 1:31.

Perpetuam benignitatem[61]

The noun *benignitas*, as used in the Vulgate translation of the scriptures, is associated with God's redemptive compassion and kindness.

In the Letter to Titus, God the Father's benevolence (*benignitas*) and kindness (*humanitas*) in compassion (*misericordia*) through Christ brought salvation, rebirth and renewal in the Spirit, and made the baptized heirs of the hope of eternal life:

"*Cum autem benignitas et humanitas apparuit Salvatoris nostri Dei, non ex operibus iustitiae, quae fecimus nos, sed secundum suam misericordiam salvos nos fecit per lavacrum regenerationis et renovationis Spiritus sancti, quem effudit in nos abunde per Iesum Christum salvatorem nostrum ut iustificati gratia ipsius heredes simus secundum spem vitae aeternae*" (Tt 3:4-7).

For Paul in the Letter to the Romans, God's *benignitas* is linked with his abundant goodness, tolerance and forbearance:

"*An divitias bonitatis eius et patientiae et longanimitatis contemnis? Ignoras quoniam benignitas Dei ad paenitentiam te adducit?*" (Rm 2:4).

This noun appears 16 times in the Missal of Paul VI[62]. It is applied to God's favour which gives salvation in spite of what humans deserve[63], and as

---

[61] For examples of the use of *benignitas* in the Missal of Paul VI see Schnitker and Slaby, Concordantia, 213.

[62] Ibid.

[63] "*Munera, Domine, tuis altaribus adhibemus de beatorum apostolorum Petri et Pauli sollemnitatibus gloriantes ut quantum sumus de nostro merito formidantes, tantum de tua benignitate gloriemur salvandi*" (MR(1975) M. in Vig. Ss Petri et Pauli, app., Super oblata, 571). Translation: We put the gifts on your altars, Lord, glorying in the solemnities of the blessed apostles Peter and Paul. May we glory in being saved by your goodness as much as we tremble concerning our own merits.

well denotes the favour out of which God propitiously brings a harvest of fruit from the earth[64].

In our collect from the Missal of Paul VI *perpetuam benignitatem* is the unending favour of God. It is linked with his mercy, salvation in Christ, regeneration in baptism through the Spirit, repentance, the fruitfulness of the earth and eternal life. The compilers of the Missal have preferred this over the original *opem tuam*. While the *ops* of God is characterized by mercy, bounty and ubiquity, the use of *perpetua benignitas* has a strong correspondence to the economy of creation and salvation found in the combination of *auctor* and *gubernator*, and to the fruitfulness of creation.

The change, then, to *perpetua benignitas* further specifies what is implicit in *ops tua*, parallels the modification of *creata* to *grata*, and highlights the divine benevolence and love out of which God creates, governs, restores, and preserves.

RELATIONSHIP OF THE CHRISTIAN PEOPLE TO GOD

The Christian community exists in and exemplifies the divine economy of creation, salvation, restoration and preservation. This economy is expressed through the liturgically established vocabulary which has surfaced in the analysis of the oration. The words *auctor, creator*, along with *conditor* amongst others, point to initial creation, recreation in Christ, and God's continuous provision of good things. This ongoing divine fidelity to what God loves is encountered in the conjunction of the words *restaurare, gubernare* and

---

[64] "*Benedictionem tuam, Domine Deus, super populum tuum propitiatus infunde, quatenus, dante te benignitatem, terra nostra proferat fructus suos, quibus ad honorem sancti tui nominis grata semper mente fruamur*" (MR(1975) Aliae orr., in conserendis agris B, Collecta, 831). Translation: Pour your blessing propitiously, Lord God, over your people, that in as much as you bestow your kindness, our land may bring forth its fruit, by which we may rejoice always with grateful minds to the honour of your holy name.

conservare. They reflect the bounty of God's favour, mercy and propitiation. Throughout the early liturgical sources these features are linked with such appellations as *reparator, redemptor, amator*, and so connote sanctification, vivification, protection and support. Our oration sets the relationship of the Christian people to God within this context of the restoration and preservation of all created things, and especially of humankind, destined for eternal life.

In response, the members of the church see themselves as servants, devoted to God in worship and rejoicing, and confident in his favour. As servants, they glory in God, a response in which they remain mindful of their sin, yet rejoice in reconciliation, in the restoration and preservation of all created things, and in the hope of sharing in eternal glory.

FREER TRANSLATION OF THE COLLECT

Adesto, Domine, famulis tuis, et perpetuam benignitatem largire poscentibus, ut his, qui te auctorem et gubernatorem gloriantur habere, et grata restaures, et restaurata conserves.

Hear us your servants Lord, and in answer to our prayers, bestow upon us your continuous graciousness. We are the people whose glory it is to know you are the source of all things and that you guide us with ever vigilant care. For our sake restore to perfection all the things that you made in your love, and keep in your love all that you have so graciously restored.

COLLECT FOR SUNDAY VIII

PRAYER

Da nobis, quaesumus, Domine, ut et mundi cursus pacifico nobis tuo ordine dirigatur, et Ecclesia tua tranquilla devotione laetetur.

Give to us Lord both that the course of world events may be directed for us by your peaceful order and that your church may rejoice in tranquil devotion.

ORIGINAL SOURCE

Veronensis: *Super sindonem* for Mass XVIII, xxxviiii, Julio, incipiunt orationes et praeces diurnae, L 633.

USE IN OTHER LITURGICAL SOURCES

As noted by Bruylants[1], the prayer is also found in these sources: Dominica IV post Pentecosten: Pr(147,1), A(1054), S(947), P(535), OR(169)[Sp 1141], X(255,1), N(138), Q(140), 1474(262), 1570, 1604, and in the unedited sources: G(175,1)[G 1174], Z(709), PaAng(216); Incipiunt orationes quotidianae, COR(202,54)[H 929].

CHANGES FROM THE ORIGINAL SOURCE

The only change concerns the address. The original source reads *Da nobis, domine deus noster.* The present invocation, *Da nobis quaesumus Domine*, follows that found in Sp 1141 (though the earlier P 535 reads *domine quaesumus*).

---

[1]Bruylants II, 170. For a more exhaustive list of sources, manuscripts and variations see Moeller, Corpus Orationum, II, D Pars prima Orationes 881-1707, Oration 899, 14; and Deshusses, Le Sacramentaire Grégorien, 393, footnote to Sp 1141.

ANALYSIS OF THE PRAYER IN THE ORIGINAL SOURCE[2]

Origin:

Chavasse concludes that this collect was written for the papal Mass of Sunday February 14th., 538 (Quinquagesima Sunday)[3]. The siege of Rome by Witiges, king of the Arian Ostrogoths, was continuing, and an uneasy truce had been broken three times in the previous month. Not only was the siege threatening the city, but it also was disrupting the lenten fast and the preparation of the community for the celebration of Easter. This is reflected in the collect of the Mass, where the term *institutum* refers to the fast[4]: "*Annue, quaesumus, omnipotens deus, ut sacramentorum tuorum gesta recolentes, et temporali securitate releuemur, et erudiamur legalibus institutis:*" (L 632)[5].

Grammatical structure[6]:

The prayer consists of (a) a simple address introducing (b) an *ut* clause containing two petitions.

(a) Address: *Da nobis, quaesumus, Domine,*

(b) 1st Petition: *ut et mundi cursus pacifico nobis tuo ordine dirigatur,*
2nd Petition: *et Ecclesia tua tranquilla devotione laetetur.*

---

[2]For a study of this prayer see A.Bastiaensen, "Sur quelques oraisons du Missel Romain," in <u>Mélanges Christine Mohrmann: Nouveau recueil offert par ses anciens élèves</u>, (Utrecht/Anvers: Spectrum Éditeurs, 1973), 157-163.

[3]A.Chavasse, "Messes du Pape Vigili (537-555) dans le Sacramentaire Léonien," <u>Ephemerides Liturgicae</u> 64 (1950): 183-187.

[4]Ibid., 184.

[5]Grant, we ask you, almighty God, that as we recall what you have done through your mysteries, we may both be assuaged by temporal security and instructed by the fasts which have been legally instituted.

[6]For a more thorough grammatical analysis see M. Haessly, <u>Rhetoric in the Sunday Collects of the Roman Missal</u>, 80-82.

The petitions stand in parallel and are joined by an *et .. et* construction. The granting of the second petition is dependent on the first. Peace is asked specifically for the church of Rome (*nobis*). Only with this specific peace established can the second petition bear fruit.

Vocabulary:

Prominent vocabulary: *dirigere, cursus, mundus, ordo, pacificus, laetari, devotio, tranquillus.*

The first petition is that God direct the course of world events in his peaceful order. Our analysis of this request will commence with the verb *dirigere*.

Dirigatur[7]

The verb is found a number of times in the Vulgate translation of the scriptures[8]. In Genesis, Abraham's senior servant, preceded on his journey by Yahweh's angel, sets out to find a wife for Isaac, and is led to Rebekah (Gn 24:1-67)[9]. When he has negotiated the marriage with her family, they press him to stay for a number of days. However, in spite of their objections, he wishes to set out immediately. He does not want to delay the return journey because God is directing (*dirigere*) his way:

---

[7] For further examples of the use of *dirigere* see Deshusses, Concordances III, 1, 505-507.

[8] Bastiaensen, "Sur quelques oraisons du Missel Romain," 159.

[9] For Westermann the story centres around God's direction in the lives of this small community: "At the same time God's hand takes on an all-embracing importance; the success or failure of the commission depends on whether God grants success or not. Ch. 24 then becomes a 'guidance narrative' whose purpose is to attest the hand of God in the life of a small community and thus in personal life", C.Westermann, Genesis 12-36, translated by J.J.Scullion from Genesis (Kapitel 1-11), Neukirchen-Vluyn: Neukirchener Verlag, 2nd German edition, 1976 (Minneapolis: Augsburg Publishing House: 1985), 382.

"*Nolite, ait, me retinere, quia Dominus direxit viam meam*" (Gn 24:56).

In this story, God directs the events which lead to the fulfillment of the divine promises (v.7) made to Abraham and his people.

The verb is also found in the Vulgate translation of Psalm 5, where those who love and worship God are directed in the way of righteousness in God's sight. There they believe they will find protection from their enemies:
"*Domine, deduc me in iustitia tua, propter inimicos meos dirige in conspectu tuo uiam meam*" (Ps 5:9).

At the birth of John the Baptist, according to the Vulgate translation of Luke's Gospel, Zachariah prophesies that his child will herald one sent from God. This child, the coming Lord, is said to be the one who will bring light to those sitting in darkness and fear of death, and direct (*dirigere*) their feet into the way of peace:
"*Per viscera misericordiae Dei nostri, in quibus visitavit nos oriens ex alto; illuminare his qui in tenebris et in umbra mortis sedent, ad dirigendos pedes nostros in uiam pacis*" (Lc 1:78-79).

God is believed to direct the faithful into the way of peace, taking them out of sin and death.

In summary, God's direction leads to righteousness, the fulfillment of the divine promises, and protection from enemies, sin and death.

In the liturgical sources, the church has a priviliged place in God's directing the divine dispensation:
"*Dirige domine, quaesumus, aeclesiam tuam dispensatione caelesti; ut quae ante mundi principium in tua semper est praesentia praeparata, usque ad plenitudinem gloriamque promissam te moderante perueniat*" (L 921)[10].

---

[10]Direct your church Lord, we ask, by your heavenly dispensation, that the church, which was prepared always in your presence before the beginning of the world, may reach, through your guidance, right to the promised fullness and glory.

The church, prepared in God before the beginning of the world, is fulfilled through the world. In the divine dispensation, God directs the church to its promised fullness and glory. Note that God's direction (*dirigere*) is in concert with his dispensation (*dispensatio*).

In L 633, the focus of God's direction is the course of world events, the *cursus mundi*.

Cursus mundi

Cursus[11]

In a passage from the Vulgate translation of the Book of Judges, the course (*cursus*) and order (*ordo*) of the created heavens are under God's command, and are used by him to vanquish Israel's enemies and bring the chosen people peace. Deborah and Barak sing a victory song after triumphing over Yahweh's enemy Sisera, the commander of the Canaanite army. The song rejoices that even the heavens took part in the battle, holding their course (*cursus*) and order (*ordo*) while fighting against the king[12]:

"*De caelo dimicatum est contra eos: stellae manentes in ordine et cursu suo adversus Sisaram pugnaverunt*" (Jd 5:20).

In the liturgical sources, God is said to rule the course (*cursus*) of all the heavens and all movements of the times, as seen in a prayer from a Mass celebrating the first birthday[13] of a child:

"*Deus, qui saeculorum omnium cursum ac momenta temporum regis, exaudi*

---

[11]For further examples of the use of *cursus* see Deshusses, Concordances III, 1, 402.

[12]The song verse alludes to the type of help celebrated in Js 10:10-14, where the heavens aid Israel through sending hailstones, and by delaying the setting of the sun, giving Israel more time to kill their enemies.

[13]The post communion makes this clear: "*.. qui famulum tuum illum ad hanc diem natalis sui genuini exempto anno perducere dignatus es ....*" (V 1460).

nos propicius, et concede, ut famuli tui illius, cuius hodie natalem diuinae caelebramus consecracione mysterii, longeuam ei largiaris aetatem, quatenus fidei eius augmentum multisquae annorum curriculis haec solem[p]nitatis devotio perseueret" (V 1457)[14].

The divine rulership of the course of all events extends to the life of each person. Through the *devotio* of the sacred mystery the community pray that the course of the child's life will be long and that his or her faith will grow.

In summary the ordering of the world and the course which events take, whether in nature or in human life, are under God and directed by God, according to divine dispensation. We will now turn our attention to the sense of *mundus* operative in the prayer.

Mundus[15]

Mundus can have the general sense of the sphere of human existence and activity.

In a prayer for a Mass for peace (*Reginensis* 316 III,lvi), God is the creator of the world (*mundus*), and the order (*ordo*) of the heavens runs its course according to his will. Accordingly, God is asked to bestow the tranquillity of peace in the present so that the people can rejoice with unceasing exultation in the divine mercy:

"Deus, conditor mundi, sub cuius arbitrio omnium saeculorum ordo decurrit, adesto propitius inuocationibus nostris et tranquillitatem pacis praesentibus

---

[14] God, you who rule the course of the heavens and the movements of the times, hear us favourably and grant that you may bestow long life to your servant *illius*, the day of whose birth we celebrate today with the consecration of the divine mystery, that the devotion of this solemn feast may lead to an increase of his faith through the cycle of many years.

[15] For further examples of the use of *mundus* see Deshusses, Concordances III, 3, 122-126.

concede temporibus, ut in laudibus misericordiae tuae incessabile exultatione laetemur" (V 1473)[16].

The tranquil peace that God grants the world is evidence of the divine favour and mercy, and leads to unceasing praise and exultation. It is a peace that the community desires to enjoy in its own times.

As creator and ruler, God directs the course of nature and of human events to his peaceful ordering (*tuus pacificus ordo*) for the sake of his people (*nobis*), who have the sense of living their own lives in dependence on this order. The divine *ordo* will now be examined.

Tuo pacifico ordine
Ordine[17]

As seen in V 1473 above, in association with *mundus*, the order of the heavens runs its course through the free choosing of God, who created all things. *Ordo*, then, refers to the comprehensive ordering of God in which all things run their course. It is qualified, in our oration, by the adjective *pacificus*.

Pacifico[18]

Pacificus and the synonym *tranquillus* refer to both civil peace and to inner peace.

In a preface, the community pray that God, who guards the faithful in divine mercy from adversaries of the body, will also guard them from enemies

---

[16] God, creator of the world, under whose free choice the order of all the heavens runs its course, be present favourably to our prayers and grant the tranquility of peace in these present times, so that we may rejoice in praises of your mercy with unceasing exultation.

[17] For further examples of the use of *ordo* see Deshusses, Concordances III, 3, 270-271.

[18] For further examples of the use of *pacificus* see Deshusses, Concordances III, 3, 278-279.

of the mind. As well, they ask that God make inwardly peaceful those who have been given tranquillity in external affairs:

"*Vere dignum: clementiam tuam toto corde poscentes, ut qui nos a corporalibus tueris aduersis, ab hostibus quoque mentis expedias; et quos exteriore tribuis tranquillitate gaudere, interius facias esse pacificos*" (L 1024)[19].

In the sphere of imperial politics Constantine was called *fundator pacis*, *pacificus princeps*, *conservator pacis*[20], the term applying also to any one of his successors. There was a strong correlation between the *ordo romanus*, the *ordo christianus* and the *ordo pacis*. Pope Vigilius, besieged by Arian Ostrogoths and under pressure from the emperor in Constantinople, was faced with protecting the city, preserving the orthodoxy of the faith, and walking the balance between the Byzantine court and the Roman church. In another of his collects from the same period, the peaceful order of God included the protection of the Roman name:

"*Propitiare, domine, in te confidentibus populis, et ad custodiam Romani nominis dexteram tuae protectionis extende; ut regnum maiestati tuae deditum tua semper sit uirtute defensum*:" (L 1128)[21].

Later manuscripts, dependent on Benedict of Aniane, no longer read

---

[19] It is right and fitting: ... asking your mercy with all our hearts, that as you guard from bodily dangers, you may deliver us also from enemies of the mind, and that you may make inwardly peaceful those whom you grant to rejoice in outer tranquility.

[20] This section closely follows Bastiaensen, 160ff. For a list of texts dealing with the siege and the enemies of Rome see A.Chavasse, "Messes du Pape Vigile," Ephemerides Liturgicae 66 (1952): 168-170.

[21] Be favourable, Lord, to the peoples trusting in you and extend the right hand of your protection towards the care of the Roman name, so that the kingdom dedicated to your majesty may be always defended by your power.

pacifico ordine, but have the less imperial, but perhaps no less political, *pacifice dirigatur*.

God's peaceful order is that arrangement of events which make up the course of world affairs. As directed by God, it opens into the way of righteousness, opposes sin and death, and has as its goal the inner peace of believers and the worship and devotion of the church. It has sometimes been understood to have been expressed in a particular political ordering, identified with the chosen people in the scriptures, and later with the Christian Roman empire.

In L 633, God is asked to direct world events in his peaceful order. The community especially desires peace because it enables them to worship unhindered by strife and unrest. Their second petition, to which we will now turn, is that the church may rejoice in tranquil devotion, *et ecclesia tua tranquilla deuotione laetetur*.

Laetetur[22]

The rejoicing (*laetari*) of the faithful is especially linked with acts of worship.

In a post communion, the faithful pray that they will not be silent in God's praises. They celebrate joyfully (*laetantes*) because God, delivering them from the bad things which they deserved, has given them good things: "*Laudes tuas, domine, non tacemus: quia nos a malis quae merebamur expediens, bona tua prestas celebrare laetantes*" (L 572)[23].

---

[22] For further examples of the use of *laetari* see Deshusses, Concordances III, 2, 438-440.

[23] We do not leave unsaid your praises Lord: because you, delivering us from the bad things we were meriting, give us good things to celebrate rejoicing.

On the feast of St Laurence, the collect prays that the celebration of the passion of the martyr may make the community rejoice, and lead them to sufficient contemplation of the martyrdom:

"*Beati Laurenti nos faciat, domine, passio ueneranda laetantes et ut eam sufficienter recolamus efficiat*" (V 988)[24].

In a collect for the Mass of the apostles and martyrs Philip and James, God is the wondrous splendour of the saints who consecrated the day of their martyrdom. God is requested to give the church to rejoice on the anniversary of such a great feast, so that the church may be helped nearer his mercy by the example and merits of the two apostles:

"*Deus, qui es omnium sanctorum tuorum splendor mirabilis quique hunc diem beatorum apostolorum Philippi et Iacobi martirio consacrasti, da aecclesiae tuae de natalicia tantae festiuitatis laetare, ut apud misericordiam tuam et exemplis eorum et meritis adiuuemur*" (V 860)[25].

The verb *laetari*, then, is especially connected with worship. Praising God, remembering the saints and rejoicing in God's gifts lead the church to express its rejoicing in worship, itself a gift. Through rejoicing, the community comes closer to God's mercy, contemplates further the acts of the saints, and is helped by their example and merits. The community is named the *ecclesia*, a term which deserves some consideration.

---

[24] May the passion of St Laurence, which we venerate, make us rejoice, and may it bring about that we recollect it sufficiently.

[25] God, you who are the splendour of all your saints, and who consecrated this day by the martyrdom of the blessed apostles Phillip and James, give to your church to rejoice on the birthday of such a great feast, so that we may be helped nearer your mercy both by their example and their merits.

Ecclesia[26]

Ecclesia is a latin transcription of the greek εκκλησια. The noun is used in the scriptures to denote both the assembled congregation, and, as well, the entire church. The local assembly understood itself to be a representation of the whole church. The key feature of the term is that it is a reminder that God is the one who assembles the community for worship.

In L 633 the assembly seek to rejoice in tranquil devotion, *tranquilla deuotio*. The meaning of *deuotio* will be discussed first.

Devotione[27]

The noun *devotio* was appropriated into Christian liturgical usage from pagan cultic language[28]. It originally meant an action whereby one would deliver oneself and or an enemy into the hands of the gods of the Underworld in order to save one's country. By transference it came to describe dedication to the gods.

In Christian liturgical language, *devotio* denotes an inner attitude of devotion to God[29], and also is used to describe the acts of devotion themselves which express this attitude. It is used in this sense to describe the Mass, penance, fasting.

Devotio refers to the eucharist in the conclusion of the preface in a Mass in honour of the apostles Peter and Paul, where the *devotio* which

---

[26]For examples of the use of *Ecclesia* see Deshusses, Concordances III, 2, 5-12. For a study of the term see K.L.Schmidt, "καλεω, κτλ," TDNT III, 501-536. See also Ellebracht, Remarks on the Vocabulary of the Ancient Orations in the Missale Romanum, 5-7.

[27]For further examples of the use of *devotio* see Deshusses, Concordances III, 1, 461-465.

[28]Ellebracht, Remarks on the Vocabulary of the Ancient Orations in the Missale Romanum, 97-100.

[29]See V 1457 in the above discussion of *cursus*.

celebrates their triumph is the sacrifice of praise being offered:

"*Uere dignum: teque laudare mirabilem deum in sanctis tuis .. Huius igitur triumphi diem hodierna deuotione celebrantes hostias tibi, domine, laudis offerimus*" (L 285)[30].

In a prayer for the dead, *devotio* refers to the affect which motivated the acts of penance and, as well, to the actual performance of the penance carried out in the course of the life of the deceased:

"*Animae famuli tui, quaesumus, domine, per haec sacrificia redemptionis, aeternae remissionem tribue peccatorum, ut deuotio paenitentiae, quam gessit eius affectus, perpetuae salutis consequatur effectum:*" (L 1145)[31].

Note the interplay between the affect in the believer and the effect for which the prayer asks.

In a preface for the December fast *devotio* covers the act of fasting and the inner devotion that motivates it:

"*Vere dignum: glorificantes et de praeteritis creatorem ... sed exhibita potius sollemni deuotione ieiunii, cum subsidiis corporalibus profectum capiamus animarum:*" (L 913)[32].

Devotio is also related to *tranquillitas* and *pax*.

In a prayer over the gifts, God is invoked as the author of sincere devotion and peace. The people pray that with this gift they may venerate God's majesty

---

[30]It is worthy to praise you wonderous God in your saints ... Therefore, celebrating the day of their triumph by this day's devotion, we offer to you the sacrifices of praise.

[31]Bestow, Lord, eternal remission of sins to the soul of your servant through these sacrifices of redemption, so that the devotion of penance, which his love brought him to perform, may reach the effect of eternal salvation.

[32]It is fitting: praising the creator for past things ... but rather by the devotion shown in the solemn fast, may we, with these bodily aids, receive the progress of our souls.

fittingly, and that their participation in the sacred mystery may lead to unity of mind in the community:

"*Deus, auctor sincerae deuotionis et pacis, da quaesumus, ut et maiestatem tuam conuenienter hoc munere ueneremur, et sacri participatione mysterii fideliter sensibus uniamus*" (L 1047)[33].

Fitting worship expresses the gift of sincere devotion. According to this prayer unity in the community flows from participation in the sacred mystery.

Worship works to bring about *tranquillitas* and security, which in turn serve worship:

"*Vere dignum: tua nobis enim munera conferri posse confidimus abundantiam deuotionis et pacis, ut et securitatem tribuat recte curata religio, et sacris sollemnitatibus famuletur concessa securitas |:tranquillitas:|:*" (L 640)[34].

In summary, the devotion of the community and its expression in worship and acts of piety bring unity, security and tranquillity to the community, and are, in turn, enhanced by this security and tranquillity. This devotion includes both inner sentiment and outward action. In L 633, *deuotio* is qualified by the adjective *tranquilla*.

---

[33]God, author of sincere devotion and peace, grant that we may venerate your majesty fittingly by this gift, and that by participation in the sacred mystery, we may faithfully join together in our minds.
This prayer is used a number of times in the Missal of Paul VI: MR(1975) VII die infra oct. Nat. Domini, Super oblata, 161; MR(1975) Sabb. temp. Nat., Super oblata, 176; MR(1975) Dom XXIII per annum, Super oblata, 362.

[34]It is fitting ... we trust that your gifts can confer on us an abundance of devotion and peace, so that rightly administered worship may bestow security, and the granted security (tranquility) may favourably serve sacred solemnities.

Tranquilla[35]

Both the adjective *tranquillus* and the noun *tranquillitas* are rarely used in the Vulgate translation of the scriptures[36]. *Tranquillus* appears in a passage from the First Letter of Timothy which reflects the intention of the prayer under consideration. The author urges the community to pray for everyone, including kings and those in power, so the faithful can lead tranquil and quiet lives in all devotion (*pietas*) and propriety. According to the Letter, a quiet and tranquil life in civil peace sets the grounds for devout and moral living. The passage reads:

"*Obsecro igitur primum omnium fieri obsecrationes, orationes, postulationes, gratiarum actiones pro omnibus: pro regibus et omnibus qui in sublimitate sunt, ut quietam et tranquillam vitam agamus in omni pietate et castitate*" (1 Tm 21-2).

Tranquillus and its cognate *tranquilitas* are somewhat more common in the early liturgical sources. In a prayer over the gifts for a Mass during the September fast, the heavenly gifts of the eucharist are said to be best received in tranquility of mind and thought, a tranquillity which comes through God's protection of believers from sin:

"*Multiplices, domine, incursos quas mundus ingerit tu repelle; ut haec dona caelestia / tranquillis cogitationibus capere ualeamus*" (L 889)[37].

Tranquil and serene times, along with favourable weather, bring the produce of the earth to maturity. This, in turn, leads the community to praise

---

[35]For further examples of the use of *tranquillus* and *tranquillitas* see Deshusses, Concordances III, 4, 376-377.

[36]*Tranquillitas* is used 5 times, and *tranquillus* only twice. See Dutripon, Bibliorum Sacrorum Concordantiae, 1375.

[37]Repel, Lord, the manifold incursions which the world brings upon us, so that we may be able to receive these heavenly gifts with tranquil thoughts.

God, as seen in the following blessing for the new produce:
"*Benedic, domine, hos fructos nouos uuae sive favae, quos tu, domine, per rorem caeli et inundantiam pluuiarum et tempora serena atquae tranquilla ad maturitatem perducere dignatus es, ad percipiendum nobis cum gratiarum actione:*" (V 1603)[38].

Tranquillus also describes the way God works in bringing about the recreation of all created reality in Christ. According to the prayer after the first reading of the Easter Vigil, the first creation account, God's work in creating and redeeming the world through Christ has this quality:
"*Deus inconmutabilis uirtus, lumen aeternum, respice propicius ad tocius aeclesiae tuae mirabile sacramentum et opus salutis humane perpetuae disposicionis effectu tranquillus operare, totusque mundus experiatur et uideat deiecta erige, inueterata nouari, et per ipsum redire omnia in integrum, a quo sumpseret principium:*" (V 432)[39].

In tranquillity, God works the effect of his perpetual disposition, bringing about the salvation of humanity and the renewal of creation. This divine work underlies the prayer being considered, where God directs events in his peaceful ordering to bring about tranquil worship.

---

[38]Bless, Lord, this new produce of berry or beans, which you, through the dew of heaven and the overflowing rain and serene and tranquil times, deigned to bring to maturity, so that we can receive them with thanksgiving.

[39]God, unchangeable strength, eternal light, look down favourably onto the marvellous mystery of your entire church, and in tranquillity bring about the work of human salvation by the effect of your perpetual disposition, that the whole world may experience and see what has been thrown down raised up, the old made new, and all things return to their original state through him, from whom it had taken its origin.
This prayer is also found in the Missal of Paul VI: MR(1975) Vig. pasch., Or. post VII lectionem, 279.

The adjective *tranquillus* decribes a state or time characterized by political peace, serenity, fruitfulness, freedom from sin, and peace of mind which lays the grounds for devout, quiet and moral living, the reception of heavenly gifts, and for unhindered praise. It is a reflection of the divine tranquillity in which God worked creation and recreation in the divine dispensation.

In L 633 *tranquilla devotio* is worship which bears the marks of tranquil times and tranquil hearts, and is reflective of God's own tranquil activity. The collect asks God to provide a time of civil peace in which fitting worship and devotion, especially the fast, can take place and be effective. Worship and devotion themselves work to bring about peace, security, unity and tranquillity. The tranquil devotion of the church parallels the peaceful ordering of the world.

Meaning of the Prayer:

During the uneasy truce of the siege, the Pope prays that God's order may prevail. The weight of the events endured by the community is having an impact at a number of levels. The siege, the uncertainty and tension of the truce, and its ramifications for the relationship between Rome and Constantinople are causing anguish and hardship for the city. This political scenario raises unsettling theological questions. How can God's ordering of the whole course of world events permit the diminishment of the honour due to the church of Rome, the triumph of Arian heretics over orthodox churches, and the endangerment of the 'divine' *pax romana*? At another level the current conditions are endangering the worship of God, and specifically here the carrying out of the lenten fast. This worship is the very reason for the existence of the church, and hence to be submitted to God's care and protection, lest it be impeded by an absence of peace.

In the face of all this the collect asks that God's order of peace be reasserted over the course of world events, with particular reference to the disorder brought about by the military accomplishments of the 'barbarians' who are also heretics. Secondly it asks that the church, living in this civil peace, may carry out its worship and devotion. This worship is at present disrupted and disturbed. Only a return to peace will bring about the conditions for right worship and devotion, the direct and immediate concern of the collect.

ANALYSIS OF THE WORDS AND PHRASES IN THE COLLECT IN RELATIONSHIP TO THE MISSAL OF PAUL VI

The ancient collect, used repeatedly throughout the liturgical sources, has come into the Missal of Paul VI virtually unchanged. Some further remarks on the use of the vocabulary within the Missal can be made. Since the Missal incorporates the collect as part of the concluding prayer in an Advent set of General Intecessions[40], the Missal itself offers an interpretation of the prayer as a whole.

Two words whose meaning are enlarged when seen in their context in the Missal of Paul VI are the verb *dirigere* and the adjective *pacificus*. This will now be examined.

Vocabulary:

Dirigo[41]

In the scriptures and the ancient liturgical sources, God's direction leads to righteousness. The Missal of Paul VI broadens this to include justice.

---

[40]MR(1975) Specimina or. univers., temp. Adv., 923-24.

[41]For examples of the use of *dirigere* in the Missal of Paul VI see Schnitker and Slaby, Concordantia, 560-562.

In the entrance antiphon for a Mass for the preservation of peace and justice, the people pray that God will direct them in the way of righteousness (*iustitia*):

"*Da pacem, Domine, sustinentibus te, et exaudi orationes servorum tuorum, et dirige nos in viam iustitiae.*" (MR(1975) Pro pace et iustitia servanda, Ant. ad intr., 821)[42].

The antiphon is a modified form of Ecli 36:18-19 (Sir 36: 18-19)[43]. The meaning of *iustitia*, living according to God's law and righteousness, is broadened to include the order of justice and peace, the theme of the Mass.

Pacifico[44]

The adjective *pacificus* undergoes a shift in usage in the Missal. Alongside its application to spiritual and civil peace it is applied to the gifts prayed over at the offertory, and, more importantly, to the self-offering of Christ on the Cross. On the Cross, Christ, the spotless victim, offered himself for peace and accomplished the sacraments, the mystery, of human redemption:

"*VD .. ut, seipsum in ara crucis hostiam immaculatam et pacificam offerens, redemptionis humanae sacramenta perageret ....*" (MR(1975) D. n. Iesu Christi univ. Regis, Praef. propr., 381)[45].

---

[42] Give peace to the people whom you sustain, Lord, and hear the prayers of your servants, and direct us in the way of righteousness.

[43] "*Da mercedem sustinentibus te, ut prophetae tui fideles inveniantur, et exaudi orationes servorum tuorum, secundum benedictionem Aaron de populo tuo, et dirige nos in viam iustitiae*" (Ecli 36: 18-19/Sir 36:18-19).

[44] For examples of the use of *pacificus* in the Missal of Paul VI see Schnitker and Slaby, Concordantia, 1762.

[45] ... [so that] offering himself, on the altar of the cross, a spotless and peacemaking victim, he accomplished the mysteries of human redemption.

The peace of Christ includes peace for the victims of war and disorder. This can be seen in the following prayer over the gifts in a Mass for refugees and exiles, where the oblation is described as a peaceful offering that brings communion of minds and an increase in love:

"Domine, qui tuum voluisti Filium ponere animam suam, ut in unum tuos dispersos filios congregaret, praesta, ut haec pacifica oblatio communionem obtineat animorum, et caritatem fraternitatis adaugeat" (MR(1975) Pro profugis et exsulibus, Super oblata, 836)[46].

While the term *pacifica oblatio* is not found in the ancient Roman liturgical sources, it is common in the Vulgate translation of the Old Testament. There it denotes the *selamim* offering, an offering made in thanksgiving and recognition for the peace and well-being that God has given[47].

In the case of this collect, the *pacificus ordo* is that ordering which brings peace. In the context of the Missal of Paul VI, it refers back to the cross of Christ, more immediately to the action of the eucharist, and can carry reference to the order of peace of which the world stands in need.

The Collect as interpreted by the Missal itself:

The Missal itself interprets the collect by incorporating it into the concluding prayer for an Advent General Intecessory rite (MR(1975) Specimina or. univers., temp. Adv., 923-24). The opening prayer focusses the

---

[46] Lord, you who wanted your Son to lay down his soul, that he might gather your dispersed people into one, grant, that this peacemaking offering may obtain the union of souls, and increase love of neighbour.

[47] For some Old Testament examples see Lv 3:1, the many occasions throughout Lv 7:11-34 and Nm 7, Jd 20:26, 21:4, I Reg (1 Sam) 10:8, 11:15, II Reg (2 Sam) 6:17, and Ez 45:15. For exegetical commentary see J. Milgrom Leviticus 1-16, The Anchor Bible, (New York: Doubleday, 1991), especially on pages 217-225; and Baruch A. Levine, Numbers 1-20, The Anchor Bible, (New York: Doubleday, 1993): 224f.

rite on the coming of Christ. Just as Jesus came in his day to bring good news to the poor and bring healing to the contrite of heart (Lc 4:18)[48], so now the mercy of Jesus is implored for the present time to bring salvation to those in need:

"*Adventum Domini nostri Iesu Christi, fratres carissimi, votis omnibus praestolantes, ipsius misericordiam impensius imploremus, ut, sicut ipse ad evangelizandum pauperibus et sanandos contritos corde venit in mundum, ita, nostris quoque temporibus cunctis egentibus velit praebere salutem*" (MR(1975) Specimina or. univers., temp. Adv., A, 923)[49].

Four sets of two petitions each arise out of this prayer, requesting a variety of gifts for the church and the world: that Christ visit and always guard the church, and fill its leaders with grace, that the present times be tranquil (*tranquilla*), and that rulers govern according to Christ's will, that the Lord remove all disease, famine, and tribulation, that the persecuted may be left free, and that the faithful may be witnesses of Christ's love before all, remain in the truth and vigilant in awaiting Christ's return.

The concluding prayer brings all these petitions within the perspective of the collect under investigation. In this prayer, God is addressed as the one who wants all to be saved and no one to be lost. He is asked to hear the prayers of the people, and respond by granting that world events be directed by God's peaceful order, and that the church rejoice in tranquil devotion:

"*Omnipotens sempiterne Deus, qui salvas omnes et neminem vis perire, exaudi*

---

[48] "*Spiritus domini super me; propter quod unxit me, evangelizare pauperibus misit me, sanare contritos corde*" (Lk 4:18).

[49] Dear brothers, awaiting the coming of our Lord Jesus Christ with every prayer, we implore his mercy more earnestly, that just as he himself came into the world to bring the good news to the poor and healing to the contrite of heart, in that way also may he wish to furnish salvation to all those in need in our time.

preces populi tui et praesta, ut et mundi cursus pacifico nobis tuo ordine dirigatur, et Ecclesia tua tranquilla devotione laetetur" (MR(1975) Specimina or. univers., temp. Adv., F, 924)[50].

Accordingly, God's peaceful order for the world is a gift of salvation for all from Christ's mercy, given both for those in need (*cuncti egentes*), and for the sake of the church (*nobis .. dirigatur*). The petitions relate God's peaceful ordering more closely to the life, works, and future coming of Christ, paralleling the references to Christ carried in *pacificus*. The divine order is also more clearly related to concerns for justice, paralleling the development of *dirigere*. The Advent context of the prayer is a reminder that both the peaceful order and tranquil worship will only be completed in Christ.

RELATIONSHIP OF THE CHRISTIAN PEOPLE TO GOD
The prayer in its original context:

The church's worship and devotion is tranquil and untroubled when the world is at peace, established in righteousness, and freed from sin and death. Civil unrest disturbs worship and devotion, and interrupts the church's praise. God's own order of world events is one of civil peace for the sake of the church, precisely so that the faithful may fulfill their mission of worship. Worship and peace both fall under God's order, with God establishing peace so that the church may worship.

The Prayer in the Missal of Paul VI:

While the Missal of Paul VI gives a more Christological focus to God's peaceful order, the dynamics of the prayer remain unchanged. The church is

---

[50]Almighty eternal God, you who save all and wish none to perish, hear the prayers of your people and grant, that both the course of world events may be directed by your peaceful order for us, and that your church may rejoice in tranquil devotion.

able to rejoice in tranquil, fruitful devotion, worship that mirrors God's own creative and restorative tranquillity and rejoicing, when there is peace in the course of worldly events. While including righteousness, the Missal also sees this peace in terms of Christ's mercy, his salvation for all in need, and in terms of justice.

FREER TRANSLATION OF THE COLLECT

Da nobis, quaesumus, Domine, ut et mundi cursus pacifico nobis tuo ordine dirigatur, et Ecclesia tua tranquilla devotione laetetur.

Give to us your people, Lord, a world made peaceful in your plan of love, so that in it your church may delight in uninterrupted devotion.

COLLECT FOR SUNDAY XXIV

PRAYER

Respice nos, rerum omnium Deus creator et rector, et, ut tuae propitiationis sentiamus effectum, toto nos tribue tibi corde servire.

God, creator and ruler of all things, look down upon us and grant that we may serve you with all our heart, so that we may feel the effect of your merciful favour.

ORIGINAL SOURCE

Veronensis: Collect for Mass XXVIIII, xiiii, item alia 1, Septembri, L 1045. One of fifteen masses without a title of the same type as the *Orationes et Praeces Diurnae* of Group XVIII (L 1015-1102)[1].

USE IN OTHER LITURGICAL SOURCES

The prayer is not used in any other liturgical source.

CHANGES FROM THE MOST ORIGINAL SOURCE

The only change made is the rearrangement of *"ut et"* to *"et, ut"*. This change already appears in the earlier editions of Ballerini[2], and in C.L.Feltoe[3].

---

[1] Vogel, Medieval Liturgy: An Introduction to the Sources, 46.

[2] Liber Sacramentorum Romae Ecclesiae: Omnium vetustissimus S. Leoni Papae in vulgatis tributus, PL, 55, 125.

[3] C.L.Feltoe, Sacramentarium Leonianum, (Cambridge: At the University Press, 1896): 134.

ANALYSIS OF THE PRAYER IN THE ORIGINAL SOURCE

Origin:

This prayer is from a set of Masses that appeared as a collection either during the time of Pope Vigilius (537-555), the reign of Pelagius I (556-561) or early in the pontificate of John III (561-574)[4]. Chavasse[5] dates the prayer itself as from the Mass for May 9, 538, the fifth Sunday after Easter, one of nine Masses composed by Vigilius during the period immediately following the deliverance of Rome from the invasion by Witiges, the Arian Ostrogothic king. The siege was lifted on March 4 of that year.

Grammatical Structure:

The prayer is made up of (a) an address containing the motivation for the petition, and (b) two petitions (*respice* and *tribue*), the second of which contains (c) a purpose clause.

(a) Motivating address: *rerum omnium Deus creator et rector.*
(b) 1st Petition: *Respice nos,*

  Main Petition: *et toto nos tribue tibi corde servire,*
(c) Purpose: *ut tuae propitiationis sentiamus effectum.*

There are a number of features to note in the structure of the prayer. The address conjoins two divine titles, *creator* and *rector*. The comunity's faith in God's creating and governing power motivates it to seek his propitiation. Feeling the effect of divine propitiation is related to the whole-heartedness of the faithful's worship.

---

[4]Vogel, <u>Medieval Liturgy: An Introduction to the Sources</u>, 58, footnote 124.

[5]A.Chavasse, "Messes du Pape Vigile (537-555) dans le Sacramentaire Léonien," <u>Ephemerides Liturgicae</u> 64 (1950): 182.

Vocabulary:

Prominent vocabulary: *creator, rector, respicere, sentire, effectus, propitiatio, servire, totum cor.*

Our analysis will begin by examining the oration's address, *rerum omnium deus creator et rector*, which provides the motivation of the prayer.

Rerum omnium deus creator et rector

In the liturgical sources, God's role as creator is intimately connected with the restoral of the people from sin, their preservation in grace, and their life in heaven. Correspondingly, God's rulership is especially a governing of what has been restored, so that the faithful do not fall away from God but come to eternal life. Words such as *creator, rector, conditor, reparator, conservator*, occur in Latin prayers in such a way that they complement one another, in expressing God's relationship to the world. Our first step will be to analyse the use of *creator* in the early euchology.

Creator[6]

According to a burial prayer, God, creator and founder of all things, is the beatitude of the saints and will call the dead man to be present at the final resurrection:

"Deus, qui uniuersorum creator et conditor es, qui cum sis tuorum beatitudo sanctorum, praesta nobis petentibus, ut animam fratri nostri illius corporis nexibus absolutam in prima sanctorum tuorum resurrectione fatias praesentari." (V 1619)[7].

---

[6] For further examples of the use of *creator* see Deshusses, Concordances III, 1, 382-383.

[7] God, who are the creator and maker of everything that is, who, since you are the beatitude of your saints, grant to us who petition you, that you may grant the soul of our brother N___, now set free from the restraints of the body, to be present at the final resurrection of your saints.

Here, God's creating and founding work underpins the heavenly beatitude of the saints and their participation in the final resurrection.

The *super populum* from a Mass for a martyr associates the faithfuls' reception and guardianship of the good things God has instituted and restored with his power as their creator and restorer. In this prayer God's creative activity is said to be brought to completion in the mercy and restoration granted to sinners[8]. In relation to L 1045, it is helpful to note that the people look for mercy from their creator and restorer, paralleling the petition for God's *propitiatio* in L 1045. The prayer reads:

"*Creator populi tui, deus, adque reparator: tuere supplices, tuere misericordiam postulantes, ut satisfactio pro se intercedente sanctum illum et instituta bona recipiant, et restaurata custodiant*" (L 56)[9].

God is addressed as creator, preserver, the giver of grace and the dispenser of salvation in a blessing over the water and wine used in the consecration of an altar during the consecration of a new basilica. He sends the Spirit over the mixture of wine and water, used in consecrating the church or altar, providing the power of heavenly defence:

"*Creator et conservator humani generis, dator graciae spiritalis, largitor aeternae salutis: tu permitte spiritum tuum super uinum cum aqua mixtum, ut*

---

[8] See also V 28, a prayer from the office for the nativity, in which God's role as creator is complemented by his role as restorer of human nature: "*Deus creator humani reformatorqui naturae ..*" (V 28).

[9] God, creator and restorer of your people, listen to our supplication, look upon those who call on your mercy, so that, there may be satisfaction for the sake of your people from the intercession of this saint and may your people both receive the good things you established, and may guard what has been restored.

arma <ta> uirtute caelestis defensionis ad consecracionem huius aeclesiae vel altaris proficiat" (V 691)[10].

In this blessing of a place dedicated to worship, God's work as creator is put in the context of God's preserving, giving grace and bestowing eternal salvation. Together they provide, in the Spirit, a protected space in which God can be worshipped.

God's activity as creator in the order of sin and salvation extends to the restoration of the people, their continual preservation in grace, salvation and worship, and their ultimate establishment in beatitude and the final resurrection. In L 1045, however, God is not only addressed as *creator* but also as *rector*.

Rector[11]

The title *rector* gives consideration to God's continuing guidance of the affairs of humankind, and most particularly those of the Christian community. This rulership is connected to his restoration of the human race from sin.

In the words of an Easter collect, God is the one who restores and rules the human race. As such, God is asked to increase the church through the entry of new members, and to increase the devotion of all members:

"Deus, [qui] humani generis es et reparator et rector, da, quaesumus, aecclesiam tuam et noua prole semper augeri et deuocionis cunctorum crescere filiorum" (V 510)[12].

---

[10]Creator and preserver of the human race, giver of spiritual grace, bestower of eternal salvation, may you send your Spirit over the wine mixed with water, so that, by the well armed power of heavenly defense, it may avail unto the consecration of this church or altar.

[11]For further examples of the use of *rector* see Deshusses, Concordances III, 4, 31-32.

[12]God, you who are the restorer and ruler of the human race, grant, we ask, that your church may always be increased by new offspring, and there

In another prayer, God's work as ruler is conjoined with his presence as protector, guardian, sustainer, and giver of eternal life:
"*Tu esto, quaesumus, domine, populi tui munimen et custus, ut uitae praesentis sustentator et rector, ut conlator aeternae*" (L 544)[13].

It can be seen, then, that God's governing is placed alongside what he does in creating, guarding, protecting, strengthening the people, and will be completed with the gift of eternal life. No one title stands alone, but all titles complement each other.

In collect L 1045 the titles of *rector* and *creator* bring together God's activities of creating, restoring, and ruling all things, and bringing them to fulfillment. The prayer particulary relates these to God's *propitiatio*, a term that has to do with sin. This makes it clear that *rector* and *creator* fit readily with other titles such as *reparator* and *munimen*. Worship too is established in God's creative work and fostered in the divine governing and mercy.

Having called upon God as *creator* and *rector*, the community make their petition, *respice nos* ....

Respice[14]

According to Ellebracht[15] *respicere* in pagan prayer meant a call for a favourable glance from the gods, a glance that already contained a token of acceptance. This meaning of the verb is also applied to God in its use in the

---

may be an incease of the devotion of all its children.

[13]May you be, Lord, the protector and guardian of your people, so that you may be the sustainer and ruler of [its] present life, and the bringer of eternal life.

[14]For further examples of the use of *respicere* see Deshusses, Concordances III, 4, 73-77.

[15]Ellebracht, Remarks on the Vocabulary of the Ancient Orations in the Missale Romanum, 89f.

Vulgate. In the liturgical sources it is used in this sense in prayers over the gifts. In other prayers, such as L 1045, the imperative *respicere* has the broader signification of God regarding favourably in order to help. Connected in the prayer to *propitiatio*, God's intervention is related to the people's efforts to make reparation, and to God's own mercy.

In L 1045, the assembly's petition is that they may feel the effect of God's propitiation, *tuae propitiationis sentiamus effectum*. Our study of this clause will commence with the verb *sentire*.

Tuae propitiationis sentiamus effectum
Sentiamus[16]

This verb has the sense of experiencing God's salvific acts and feeling deeply their effects.

In a postcommunion, the reception of the sacraments enables the faithful to feel in mind and body the remedy that leads to glory:

"*Sentiamus, domine, quaesumus, tui perceptione sacramenti subsidium mentis et corporis; ut in utroque saluati de caelestis remedii plenitudine gloriemur*" (L 630)[17].

Communion is felt as a remedy in the whole person. Feeling this remedy leads to giving glory.

Similarly, in another postcommunion, the entire liturgical action restores the mind and body. The faithful pray that they may feel the effect of the celebration in which they engage:

---

[16] For further examples of the use of *sentire* see Deshusses, Concordances III, 4, 215-217.

[17] By the reception of your sacrament, Lord, may we feel help of mind and body, so that, saved in both we may glory in the fullness of the heavenly remedy.
This prayer has been incorporated into the Missal of Paul VI: MR(1975) Fer. II hebd. I Quadr., Post comm, 186.

"*Sit nobis, domine, reparatio mentis et corporis caeleste mysterium, et cuius exequimur actionem, sentiamus effectum*" (L 580)[18].

Sentire, then, refers to the divinely guaranteed interior experience that results from an external action, primarily that of worship. In L 1045 *sentire* is related to the noun *effectus*.

Effectum[19]

This noun describes a dynamic spiritual power within the person or community[20].

In a collect for a Mass for charity, God, who makes all things for good to those who love God, is asked to grant to the hearts of the faithful the inviolable effect of love. In this effect, no temptations are able to change the

---

[18]Lord, may the heavenly sacrament be for us healing in mind and body, and may we feel the effects of what we carry out in this action.

[19]A number of studies of *effectus* have been made. See O.Casel, "Beiträge zu römischen Orationen", Jahrbuch für Liturgiewissenschaft 11 (1931): 35-45, and W.Diezinger, Effectus in der römischen Liturgie (Bonn: Peter Hanstein Verlag GMBH, 1961). A summary can be found in Ellebracht, Remarks on the Vocabulary of the Ancient Orations in the Missale Romanum, 122f. For further examples of the use of *effectus* see Deshusses, Concordances III, 2, 14-17.

[20]There is some interplay and interchange in the sources between *effectus* - an agent active in the person, and *affectus* - a feeling in the person (See the study of Collect IV). In a prayer for the dead, it is asked that, through the sacraments and remission of sins, the affect and the devotion of penance may attain the effect of salvation:
"*Animae famuli tui, quaesumus, domine, per haec sacrificia redemptionis aeternae remissionem tribue peccatorum, ut deuotio paenitentiae, quam gessit eius affectus, perpetuae salutis consequatur effectum:*" (L 1145).
The interchange is evidenced when the same prayer is sometimes written with either *effectus* or *affectus* when it appears in a different liturgical source, or even when it appears more than once in the same source: "*Sumptis muneribus domine quaesumus, ut cum frequentatione mysterii, crescat nostrae salutis effectus*" (Sp 1134, H 807, G 1755), whereas the text reads "*Sumptis .. affectus*" in V 590 and G 1092.

desires which God has inspired:

"*Deus, qui diligentibus te facias cun[c]ta prodesse, da cordibus nostris inuiolabilem caritatis effectum, ut desideria de tua insperatione concepta nulla possint temptacionum mutari*" (V 1323)[21].

Worship has an effect in believers. According to a collect for a daily Mass, the God of salvation grants to the people the affect of supplicating and worshiping. The community prays that they will also receive the effect of divine favour: "*Adiuba nos, deus salutaris noster; et quibus supplicandi tibi prestas affectum, tribue tuae propitiationis effectum*" (L 504)[22].

The effect of God's favour is felt through worship, which itself arises from the desire for worshipping that God places in the community. Here 'affect' denotes what is felt in the heart of the believer, and is completed by the 'effect', the external reality brought about by God's merciful favour.

A secret for Eastertide also points up the relationship between worship and receiving divine effects. Reviewing the offerings of Easter, the faithful desire to obtain the effect of what they celebrate in the act of worship: "*Paschalis hostias recensentes quaesumus, domine, ut quod frequentamus actu, conpraehendamus effectum*" (V 491)[23].

God's effects are dynamic and powerful, and can be felt in the heart. The liturgy is a locus for receiving divine effects, both in the sense that what is carried out externally in the liturgical action may be effective in believers themselves, and also in that the effects of God's favour are bestowed through

---

[21] God, you who make all things to be of benefit to those who love you, give to our hearts the inviolable effect of your love, so that no temptations may be able to change the desires received from your inspiration.

[22] Help us, God of our salvation, and to those to whom you grant the affect of offering you supplication, may you bestow the effect of your propitiation.

[23] Recalling to mind the Paschal offering, Lord, we ask that we may take hold of the effect of what we carry out in action.

worship. In the prayer under consideration, the effect has to do with God's propitiation (*propitiatio*).

Propitiationis[24]

Propitiatio is an action exhibiting an attribute of God, and comprehends favour arising out of divine mercy and forgiveness towards those who have sinned.

The preface L 566 lays out the breadth of God's favour. Without this favour, what is pleasing to God and salutary for humans cannot be desired, wished for, pursued, begun, or completed. God's favour is felt in every desire and action which is in line with God's will:

"*Uere dignum: cuius propitiationem in hac primum parte sentimus, cum ea, quae tibi sunt placita et nobis salutaria, desideramus adpetere. Dum enim sine te nihil recti uelle possimus aut agere aut perficere, indubitanter est gratiae, quidquid conuenienter operamur*" (L 566)[25].

However, *propitiatio*, *propitius* and *propitiatis* also serve to designate a petition for pardon[26].

According to a secret for a Sunday Mass, the salutary offering brings about the purgation of sins and is a propitiation of God's power:

"*Concede nobis, domine, quaesumus, ut haec hostia salutaris et nostrorum fiat*

---

[24]For further examples of the use of *propitiatio*, *propitius* and *propitio* see Deshusses, Concordances III, 3, 508-518.

[25]It is right and fitting: whose propitiation we feel in the first place, when we desire to seek the things which are pleasing to you and salvific for us. For, since without you we are unable to wish for, do or bring to completion anything that is upright, whatever we do that is fitting is undoubtedly done by grace.

[26]See Blaise, Vocabulaire, § 278.

purgatio delictorum et tuae propitiacio potestatis" (V 1215)[27].

The *Hanc igitur* inserted in the canon for a Mass for the dead, offers the oblation for the sake of the soul of the one who has died, requesting God to receive the offering as a propitiation, and to bestow the largesse of divine mercy so that, cleansed by these sacrifices, the departed may be freed from the chains of death and brought through to life:

"*Hanc igitur oblationem illius famuli tui, quam tibi offeret pro animam famuli tui illius, quaesumus, domine, propitiatus accipias, et miserationum tuarum largitate concedas, ut quidquid terrena conuersatione contraxit, his sacrificiis emendetur, ac mortis uinculis absolutis transitum mereatur ad uitam*" (V 1213)[28].

Summarizing, then, *propitiatio* means divine favour, and it also carries the sense of God being propitiated and bestowing merciful favour in response to those acts of worship addressed to the cause of the sinner in seeking divine favour.

In collect L 1045, the faithful request to feel the effect of God's favour and pardon, the merciful favour that arises from God's roles as *creator* and *rector*. The divine favour and pardon are necessary that they may be able to worship well, but on the other hand, God is asked to grant heartfelt worship (*toto corde servire*) so that they may experience his merciful favour.

---

[27] Grant to us, Lord, that this salutary offering may be both the purgation of our sins and the propitiation of your power.
This prayer has been incorporated into the Missal of Paul VI: MR(1975) Fer. III hebd. III Quadr., Super oblata, 203.

[28] Therefore we ask you, Lord, that you may accept propitiously the offering of this your family, which it offers to you for the soul of your servant N___, and grant in the magnitude of your mercy that whatsoever he brought about in his earthly life may be cleansed by these sacrifices, and with the chains of death loosened, he may merit a passage to life.

Toto corde servire

Servire[29]

In classical Latin, the verb *servire* is applied to the actions of worshippers who offer service to the gods. This was readily taken over into Christian usage. The concept of humans as God's servants is found frequently in the Vulgate translation of the scriptures[30].

For Paul, Christians are servants of righteousness. They no longer serve sin, but serve righteousness unto sanctification:

"*Liberati autem a peccato servi facti estis iustitiae .. ita nunc exhibete membra vestra servire iustitiae in sanctificationem*" (Rm 6: 18-19).

In the liturgical sources contemporaneous with the prayer being analysed, service to God is especially connected with worship and the fulfillment of church offices.

A lenten secret prays that the people may always serve God's altars worthily, and be saved by continuous participation in worship:

"*Concede nobis, misericors deus, et dignae tuis seruire semper altaribus et eorum perpetua participatione saluari*" (V 71)[31].

Service includes fulfilment, through grace, of the tasks of the various orders of the church. The Good Friday petitions include a prayer for all the orders in the church, that by the gift of divine grace, they may faithfully serve the church that God rules and sanctifies:

---

[29] For further examples of the use of *servire* see Deshusses, <u>Concordances</u> III, 4, 222-224.

[30] Ellebracht, <u>Remarks on the Vocabulary of the Ancient Orations in the Missale Romanum</u>, 56.

[31] Grant to us, merciful Lord, that we may serve your altars worthily, and be saved by our continuous participation in worship.
This prayer has been incorporated into the Missal of Paul VI: MR(1975) Fer. VI hebd. V Quadr., Super oblata, 222.

"*Ominpotens sempiterne deus, cuius spiritu totum corpus ecclesiae sanctificatur et regitur, exaudi nos pro uniuersis ordinibus supplicantes, ut gratiae tuae munere ab omnibus fideliter seruiatur.*" (V 405)[32].

Authentic service of God's majesty comes from a sincere heart, and is in concert with a will devoted to God:
"*Omnipotens sempiterne deus, fac nos tibi semper et deuotam gerere uoluntatem et maiestati tuae sencero corde seruire*" (V 561)[33].

It is worth noting that the sense of *servire* is broadened in the slightly later Roman Papal sacramentary, the *Hadrianum*. There the sense of *servire* not only includes not only worship but obedience to the commandments. In a *super populum* for a Mass at the stational church of Cosmos and Damien during Lent, God is requested that the divine favour increase the people subject to God, and that they may always serve the divine mandates:
"*Subiectum tibi populum quaesumus domine propitiatio caelestis amplificet, et tuis semper faciat seruire mandatis*" (H 247)[34].

---

[32] All powerful, eternal God, by whose Spirit the whole body of the church is sanctified and ruled, hear our supplication for all the orders of your church, so that, by the gift of your grace, your church may be served faithfully by all. This prayer has been incorporated into the Missal of Paul VI: MR(1975) Fer. VI in Pass. Domini. Or. pro omnibus fidelibus, 253.

[33] Almighty, eternal God, may we always have a will devoted to you and serve your majesty with a sincere heart.
This prayer is also used in the Missal of Paul VI: MR(1975) Dom. XXIX per annum, Collecta, 368. For a study of this collect see below, 294.

[34] Lord, may your heavenly favour increase the people subject to you, and may it make them always serve your mandates.
Note here a play on the verbs *servire* and *servare*. The latter, meaning to keep or preserve, is used in connection with obedience to God's mandates. This can be seen in the expression *tua precepta seruantes*, which has been analysed in the study of the collect for Sunday XXV. See above, 140. See also L 971 and V 447.

The prayer has been incorporated into the Missal of Paul VI: MR(1975)

The sense of *servire* here is that of life in obedience to God's mandates, though the connection with *propitiatio* remains. God's merciful favour increases the church through Baptism, and enables the growing community, old members and new alike, to live out their baptism through obedience to the divine mandates.

Our collect qualifies *servire* with the phrase *toto corde*.

Toto corde[35]

Toto corde echoes the great commandment to love God and neighbour without reserve. This precept has already been examined in Collect IV.

A prayer from a Mass in a monastery links running to God with all one's heart to serving God with a mind subject to him, imploring his mercy, and continuously rejoicing in divine favours:

"*Fac, quaesumus, domine, famulos tuos toto semper ad te corde concurrere, tibi subdita mente servire, tua misericordia suppliciter implorare et tuis iugiter beneficiis gratulare*" (V 1430)[36].

The expression *totum cor* bears the sense of the entire person, devoted fully to serving God. Furthermore, the heart is the locus of God's active *propitiatio*, which works the remedies of divine loving kindness, dispelling any darkness of sin that remains.

In collect L 1045 divine effects and divine favour are felt in the heart. Worship and service made in the heart allow the believer to feel inwardly the effects of the divine *propitiatio*. Through the gift of heartfelt worship the

---

Orr. super populum, II, 508.

[35] For further examples of the use of *cor* see Deshusses, Concordances III, 1, 363-369.

[36] Lord, make us, your servants, to run to you always with all our hearts, to serve you with minds subject to you, to humbly supplicate and implore your mercy, and to continuously rejoice in your divine favour.

faithful hope to realize the effect of divine mercy. This takes place in the heart, the inner being of the worshipper, where the baptized desire the favour and mercy of God be active. The elements of propitiation and heartfelt devotion are blended in the prayer.

Meaning of the prayer:

As *creator* and *rector*, God creates, restores, guides and bestows eternal salvation out of the divine favour and merciful pardon. These actions provide the basis for worship. The divine merciful favour has a dynamic effect which can be felt in the human heart. In the collect, the community request that God give them the gift of wholehearted worship so that they may more fully feel the effects of God's merciful favour.

ANALYSIS OF THE WORDS AND PHRASES IN THE COLLECT IN RELATIONSHIP TO THE MISSAL OF PAUL VI

The verb *servire* undergoes further expansion in the Missal of Paul VI.

The collect of the Mass for the priest St Camillus de Lellis celebrates especially his love for the sick, echoing Jesus' admonition that whatever is done to the least in love is done to God[37]. The prayer asks for the spirit of divine love so that through serving God in others, the faithful may come to heaven;

"Deus, qui sanctum Camillum presbyterum caritatis in infirmos singulari gratia decorasti, eius meritis, spiritum nobis tuae dilectionis infunde, ut, tibi in

---

[37] *"Et respondens rex dicet illis: Amen, dico vobis, quandui fecistis uni ex his fratribus meis minimis, mihi fecistis"* (Mt 25:40)

fratribus servientes, ad te, hora exitus nostri, securi transire possimus" (MR(1975) S. Camili de Lellis, Collecta, 577)[38].

God is served through acts of charity performed out of the spirit of divine love, in accord with the passage of the last judgement in Mt 25:31-46.

Meaning of the prayer:

The dynamic of the prayer remains unchanged. Though the Gregorian sources and the Missal of Paul VI have added the dimensions of obedience and service in charity to *servire*, the context of the prayer as a collect for the eucharist means that the primary focus of prayer remains the worship of the community. However, this worship is now linked to obedience to the commandments and to deeds of charity.

THE RELATIONSHIP OF THE CHRISTIAN PEOPLE TO GOD
The prayer in its original context:

In the face of the devastation of the seige, the city of Rome began to rebuild itself and sought to reinterpret its relationship to the divine. The prayer sets the relationship of the Christian people to God within the favour and merciful pardon (*propitiatio*) of God, which underlies all divine creating and guiding, and which is lived out primarily in true Christian worship.

While the siege brought both physical and spiritual hardship to the community, the prayer centres on worship as the locus of experiencing the divine *propitiatio*. The more wholeheartedly the community enters into worship, the more fully it will feel the effects and power of God's favour. Whatever else it experiences, as long as it carries out true worship it knows

---

[38] God, you who adorned St Camillus with the grace of an especial love for the sick, by his merits pour upon us the spirit of your love, so that, serving you in our brothers and sisters, at the hour of our passing, we may be able to come to you in safety.

that it enjoys God's mercy and favour. Worship serves as a reassurance in the face of other difficulties.

The prayer in the Missal of Paul VI:

As a Sunday prayer in Ordinary Time, the historical context of Virgilius' attempt to build up the worship of Rome following the war is left behind. Nevertheless, as a collect for the celebration of the eucharist, the worship context and the dynamic of the prayer remain the same. The more completely the community participates in the liturgy, the more fully the members feel the effect of God's favour, mercy and pardon. Now, instead of being linked to the need for assurance in face of hostile threats, true worship is linked with obedience to God's commandments and with Christian charity.

The expanded notion of service in the Missal of Paul VI allows this worship dynamic to be incorporated into a variety of ecclesial and social contexts. The relationship remains marked by the divine *propitiatio*, whereby God acts favourably towards a sinful people.

FREER TRANSLATION OF THE COLLECT

Respice nos, rerum omnium Deus creator et rector, et, ut tuae propitiationis sentiamus effectum, toto nos tribue tibi corde servire.

God, you create and guide everything that is. Look favourably upon us. May we worship and serve you with all our hearts, and through our service, experience the power of your favour and pardon.

CHAPTER FIVE
PRAYERS FROM THE EASTERTIDE LITURGIES OF *REGINENSIS* 316:
THE COLLECTS FOR SUNDAYS VI, X, XI, XII, XIV, XV, XXI, XXIII, XXIX

INTRODUCTION[1]

The production and compilation of *libelli Missarum* gave rise to the Sacramentary. The Sacramentary was designed as a presider's book, containing all, and only, the texts the presider needed for the celebration of the Eucharist, as well as the other liturgical events at which the presider would officiate. These included, among others, the Good Friday service, the liturgy of the Hours, the dedication of churches, and the consecration of virgins.

REGINENSIS 316

The earliest extant example of a Roman Sacramentary is the document known as *Codex Vaticanus Reginensis latinus* 316. It is variously named as the Gelasian Sacramentary, the Old Gelasian Sacramentary, or *Reginensis* 316. In this study it will be referred to as *Reginensis* 316. The critical edition is that of Mohlberg[2].

---

[1] This section closely follows Vogel, Medieval Liturgy: An Introduction to the Sources, 64-70. For the most complete study of *Reginensis* 316 see Chavasse, Le Sacramentaire Gélasien.

[2] L.C.Mohlberg, L.Eizenhöfer and P.Siffrin, eds. Liber Sacramentorum Romanae Aeclesiae Ordinis Anni Circuli (Cod. Vat. Reg. 316), Rerum Ecclesiasticarum Documenta, Series Maior, Fontes IV (Roma: Casa Editrice

The manuscript appears to have been copied around the year 750 at the nunnery of Chelles, outside Paris. It is a Frankish recension of a Roman book. The text is divided into three parts, with the temporal and sanctoral cycles kept separate. Each Mass has two prayers before the *secreta*, apparently an opening presidential prayer of the Mass, and an *oratio super sindonem*. There is also an *oratio postcommunionem*, and occasionally a preface and *oratio ad populum*.

Though the book contains a number of Frankish additions, the substratum of the text is Roman. Furthermore, the Roman substratum itself appears to be an organized compilation of various *libelli* belonging to different periods and representing Roman presbyteral and papal usage. This earlier Roman prototype was probably compiled in Rome somewhere between 628 and 715, from whence copies were carried across the Alps under private initiative. These were widely used in Gaul. They were an important source for several Gallican sacramentaries, such as the *Missale Gothicum*, the *Missale Gothicum vetus*, and the *Missale Bobbiense*. As well they were a significant influence in the development of what are known as the Frankish Gelasian sacramentaries, such as the Sacramentary of Gellone and the Sacramentary of Angoulême.

ORATIONS FROM THE EASTERTIDE LITURGIES OF *REGINENSIS* 316 IN THE MISSAL OF PAUL VI

Eighteen orations from *Reginensis* 316 have been incorporated into the collects for the Sundays of Ordinary Time in the Missal of Paul VI. They fall into three distinct groups. Nine have been taken from the liturgies during Eastertide, including the Easter vespers and the Mass for the Sunday after the Ascension. This group will be treated in the present chapter. Eight prayers have been introduced into the new Missal from the set of 16 Masses for the Sundays of the year which open Book III of *Reginensis* 316. These will be

---

Herder, 1960).

studied in the following chapter. One prayer, the collect for Sunday VII, is the first presidential prayer for Mass III,lxvi (V 1521) entitled *Orationes in Contencione ad Missas, Item Alia Missa*. This prayer will be studied in Chapter Seven[3].

Chapter Five is concerned with the collects for Sundays VI (V 587), X (V 556), XI (V 566), XII (V 586), XIV (V 541), XV (V 546), XXI (V 551), XXIII (V 522) and XXIX (V 561). The collect for Sunday XXIII (V 522) was originally a prayer for vespers during Eastertide. The collects for Sunday XII and VI were originally the opening presidential oration and the *oratio super sindonem* respectively for the Mass I,lxv, entitled *Orationes et Praeces Dominica Post Ascensa Domini*. The remaining prayers are the first presidential prayers of the six Masses which followed the octave of Easter. These Masses are typically named as the Masses of the Sundays *post clausum paschae*. According to Chavasse, these six formed a distinct set of Masses later incorporated into *Reginensis* 316 as a group[4].

Amongst these six prayers, the collect for Sunday XV warrants special consideration. The oration is first met as an opening presidential prayer in the *Veronensis* Mass, VIII,xx (L 75). The Mass appears to be one of that series composed by Gelasius to combat the celebration in Rome of the pagan festival of the Lupercalia[5]. However, because the oration's incorporation in the Missal of Paul VI seems to be dictated more by its presence among these six *Reginensis* 316, Eastertide Sunday Masses than by its place in the *Veronensis*, it will be studied in this chapter.

---

[3]The reasons for this are set out in the introduction to Chapter Seven. See below, 557.

[4]Chavasse, Le Sacramentaire Gélasien, 241-244.

[5]For details see the study below, 254.

The analyses of these orations have been arranged below according to the order in which the prayers appear in *Reginensis* 316. Our study will commence with the collect for
Sunday XXIII, followed by the collects for Sundays XIV, XV, XXI, X, XXIX, XI, XII and VI.

COLLECT FOR SUNDAY XXIII

PRAYER

Deus, per quem nobis et redemptio venit et praestatur adoptio, filios dilectionis tuae benignus intende, ut in Christo credentibus et vera tribuatur libertas, et hereditas aeterna.

God, through whom redemption comes for us and adoption is bestowed upon us, look favourably upon the children of your love, so that to those who believe in Christ, true freedom and eternal inheritance may be granted.

ORIGINAL SOURCE

Deus, per quem nobis et redemptio venit et praestatur adoptio, respice in opera misericordiae tuae, ut in Christo renatis et aeternam tribuatur hereditas et vera libertas[1].

Reginensis 316: prayer from the set of orations for vespers during Paschaltide, I,lvi, *Incipiunt orationes paschales uespertinales* (V 522).

USE IN OTHER LITURGICAL SOURCES

As noted by Siffrin[2], the prayer also appears in these liturgical sources: A 821, G 67r [G 785], G 68v [G 815], S 620, s 16, CO 93,4 [H 427], P 364,

---

[1]God, through whom redemption comes to us and adoption is bestowed upon us, look upon the works of your mercy, so that to those who have been reborn in Christ, eternal inheritance and true freedom may be granted.

[2]P.Siffrin, Konkordanztabellen zu den römanischen Sakramentarien II, Liber Sacramentorum Romanae Aeclesiae, 66. For a more complete list of sources, manuscripts and liturgical contexts see Moeller, Corpus Orationum, II D, Orat. 881-1707, oration 1310, 208-209.

F 779, B 626, Ga G 288³, Ga V 224 *a*⁴.

The oration is usually found as a prayer for vespers during the Easter season.

The substance of the oration forms the basis of a blessing for the Resurrection (Sp 1758)⁵.

USE IN THE MISSAL OF PAUL VI

This collect for the Mass of Sunday XXIII in Ordinary Time appears unmodified as the collect for the Mass of Sunday V in Easter⁶, and as the collect for the Mass of Saturday, week II in Easter⁷.

The above mentioned blessing for the Resurrection (Sp 1758) is also found in the Missal of Paul VI as a solemn blessing for Paschal time: MR(1975) Benedd. in fine M., Bened. soll., temp. pasch., 6, 498.

---

³"*Omnipotens sempiterne deus, per quem nobis redemptio praestatur et adoptio, respice in opera pietatis tuae et, quae dignatus es conferre, conserva, ut in Christi renatis aeterna tribuatur hereditas et vera libertas*" Missa paschalis, III feria, collect (Ga G 288).

⁴"*Deus, per quem no<bi>s redemptio praestatur et adoptio, erege ad te tuorum corda credentium, ut omnis rege[ne]rati sacro baptismate adpraehendam mente, quod misteriis susceperunt*" Collecta item Missa Pasch. VI Fer., (Ga V 224).

⁵*Deus qui per resurrectionem unigeniti sui uobis contulit et bonum redemptionis et decus adoptionis, suae uobis conferat praemia benedictionis. Amen.*
Et quo redimente perceptistis donum perpetuae libertatis, eo largiente consortes efficiamini aeternae hereditatis. Amen.
Et cui consurrexistis in baptismate credendo, adiungi mereamini in caelesti regione bene uiuendo. Amen.
Quod ipse praestare dignetur qui cum patre (Sp 1758).

⁶MR(1975) Dom. V Paschae, Collecta, 303.

⁷MR(1975) Sabb. post domm. II, IV et VI Paschae, Collecta hebd. II, 322.

CHANGES FROM THE ORIGINAL

The liturgical context of the prayer has been altered. Originally a prayer for vespers in Eastertide, it functions in the Missal of Paul VI as a Sunday Mass collect for Ordinary Time, and as a collect for a Sunday Mass and a weekday Mass in Eastertide.

Two changes have been made to the original text. The petition has been changed from *respice in opera misericordiae tuae* to *filios dilectionis tuae benignus intende*. While the modification weakens the sense that it is God's work, it does highlight the love which underlies the divine work of redemption and adoption. The change also emphasises the faithful's status as beloved, adopted children (*filii dilectionis*).

The faithful are described as *in Christo credentibus* rather than *in Christo renatis*. Here there is a shift away from God's work (*renasci*) to the work of believers (*credere*). The prayer no longer carries any direct allusion to the baptismal rite celebrated during the Easter Vigil.

These modifications of the original text make their first appearance in the Missal of Paul VI.

ANALYSIS OF THE PRAYER IN THE ORIGINAL SOURCE
Origin:

Research to date has revealed very little about the historical origin of this set (I,lvi) of vesper prayers in *Reginensis* 316. There are indications that they are from a Roman, non-monastic Office[8].

Methodological Note:

From the ensuing investigation of the structure of the oration it seems that the structure, vocabulary and content of the prayer are very dependent on

---

[8] A. Chavasse, Le Sacramentaire Gélasien, 454-455.

the Letter to the Galatians. This necessitates a modification in the usual methodology. The grammatical structure and vocabulary will be examined together in the one section. Any additional references to the use of vocabulary in the wider liturgical sources will be added at the apposite place.

Grammatical structure and vocabulary:

Prominent vocabulary: *redemptio, venire, adoptio, praestare, respicere, opus, misericordia, renasci, tribuere, hereditas, libertas.*

The prayer consists of three sections, (a) an address to God with motivating clause, (b) a general petition, and (c) two purpose clauses, and a description of the community.

(a) Address: *Deus*
    Motivation: *per quem nobis et redemptio venit*
    et praestatur adoptio.

(b) Petition: *respice in opera misericordiae tuae*

(c) Community: *ut in Christo renatis*
    1st Purpose: *et aeternam tribuatur hereditas*
    2nd Purpose: *et vera libertas [tribuatur].*

The motivating clause contains an *et ... et* construction, conjoining *redemptio* and *adoptio*. The two purpose clauses are also set within an *et ... et* construction, conjoining *hereditas* and *libertas*. Note the parallelism across the two sets of clauses between *redemptio* and its fruit *libertas*, and *adoptio* and its consequence *hereditas*. The phrase *in opera misericordiae tuae* embraces redemption, adoption and rebirth (baptism).

The outstanding feature of the prayer is its reflection of the Pauline matrix of redemption, adoption, baptism, inheritance and freedom. When examined more closely it is clear that the structure, vocabulary and content of the prayer closely resemble certain passages in Paul's Letter to the Galatians.

The following four features of the collect can be found in the Vulgate translation of Galatians (i) the conjunction of redemption (*redemptio*) and adoption (*adoptio*), (ii) the association between baptism and inheritance, (iii) the conjunction of inheritance (*hereditas*) and liberty (*libertas*), and (iv) the relationship between the pair redemption/adoption and the pair inheritance/liberty. The Galatians background to each of these four pairings will now be examined, beginning with the pair *redemptio* and *adoptio*.

(i) *Redemptio/adoptio*: Through redemption (*redimere*) by Christ from the law, comes adoption by God as children (*adoptio filiorum*) and as heirs (*heredes*):

"*ut eos qui sub lege erant redimeret, ut adoptionem filiorum reciperemus. Quoniam autem estis filii, misit Deus Spiritum Filii sui in corda vestra clamantem: Abba. Pater. Itaque iam non est servus, sed filius. Quod si filius, et heres per Deum*" (Gal 4:5-7).

(ii) Baptism[9] and inheritance: Those who are baptized in Christ become heirs (*heredes*) to the promise first made to Abraham:

"*Quicumque enim in Christo baptizati estis Christum induistis ... Si autem vos Christi, ergo semen Abrahae estis, secundum promissionem heredes*" (Gal 3:27-29).

(iii) *Hereditas/libertas*: Both the status of being an heir, and the gift of liberty from enslavement, come from being the free children (the children of the free woman) of God's promise (*filii liberae*). The free offspring share in the freedom by which Christ freed all who believe in him:

"*Sed quid dicit Scriptura? 'Eice ancillam et filium eius'; non enim heres erit filius ancillae cum filio liberae. Itaque, fratres, non sumus ancillae filii, sed liberae, qua liberate Christus nos liberavit*" (Gal 4:30-31).

---

[9]For the connection between baptism and rebirth (*renasci*) see Blaise, Vocabulaire, § 332, § 333, § 336.

(iv) *Redemptio/adoptio* and *hereditas/libertas*: It can be seen from the above that adoption and baptism provide the connection between redemption on the one hand, and the pairing of *hereditas* and *libertas* on the other.

Clearly, the structure of the prayer closely follows Paul's discussion in Galatians of redemption, adoption, baptism, inheritance, and freedom. Further examination of Galatians, as well as Romans, clarifies the Pauline meaning of *hereditas* and *libertas*.

Hereditas

The inheritance is the fulfillment of the promises made to Abraham (Gal 3:14,29)[10], which are now shared by those who believe in Christ. Reception of the inheritance comes through entry into the kingdom of God (Gal 5:21)[11]. In the early liturgical euchology, *aeterna hereditas* denotes participation in eternal life[12].

Libertas

Redemption, baptism and adoption enable the believer to live in the manifold freedom (*libertas*) by which Christ frees and which he bestows[13]. First and foremost, freedom in Christ is an internal freedom, in which the

---

[10]"*ut in gentibus benedictio Abrahae fieret in Christo Iesu, ut pollicitationem Spiritus accipiamus per fidem*" (Gal 3:14), "*Si autem vos Christi, ergo semen Abrahae estis, secundum promissionem heredes*" (Gal 3:29).

[11]"... *Quae praedico vobis, sicut praedixi, quoniam qui talia agunt, regnum Dei non consequentur*" (Gal 5:21).

[12]Blaise, Vocabulaire, § 296. For further examples of the use of *hereditas* see Deshusses, Concordances, III, 2, 251.

[13]For the close connection in Galations between redemption from the law and the moral life of freedom see, F. Matera, Galatians, Sacra Pagina Vol. 9, (Collegeville: Liturgical Press, 1992), 192-198.

Spirit of Christ shapes the life of the believer in the freedom of Christ[14]. Freedom in the Spirit includes liberation from the diabolical forces that rule the world[15]. It denotes freedom from the carnal desires of the flesh, which, when unfettered, lead ineluctably to sin (Gal 5:13)[16]. Most manifestly for Paul, Christ brings liberation from the old Law. The Law was ultimately oppressive because of its failure to get to the root of sin and death (Gal 3:13)[17]. This is more fully elaborated by Paul in Rm 5:12-7:24. The freedom which Christ brings is freedom in the Spirit to serve one another in love (Gal 5:13-14)[18]. It

---

[14] See Rm 8:1-13, especially v.2. The passage juxtaposes the freedom in the Spirit with its effects, freedom from the law of sin and death (v.2) as well as the gifts of life and peace (v.6). For commentary see Fitzmyer, Romans, 482-483.

[15] "*Ita et nos, cum essemus parvuli, sub elementis mundi eramus servientes*" (Gal 4:3). See also Gal 4:9-10.
For commentary on the diabolical nature of these forces see H.D.Betz, Galatians: A Commentary on Paul's Letter to the Churches in Galatia, Hermenia, ed. H.Koester, (Philadelphia: Fortress Press, 1979), 204-205. Matera holds a different view. He reads the verse as pointing to humanity's subjection to rudimentary religious principles, such as the Law and its obligations. What is common to both interpretations is that these elements, whether diabolical or religious, hold sway over the people. Only in Christ is their bondage broken, and a new, deeper relationship of freedom established. See Matera, Galatians, 148-158.

[16] "*Vos enim in libertatem vocati estis, fratres, tantum ne libertatem in occasionem detis carnis, sed per caritatem spiritus servite invicem*" (Gal 5:13). See also Gal 5:17-21.

[17] "*Christus nos redemit de maledicto legis ....*" (Gal 3:13).

[18] "*... tantum ne libertatem in occasionem detis carnis, sed per caritatem spiritus servite invicem. Omnis enim lex in uno sermone impletur: 'Diliges proximum tuum sicut te ipsum.'*" (Gal 5: 13b-14).

is manifest in the fruits of the Spirit; love, joy, peace, patience, kindness, goodness, trustfulness, gentleness and self-control (Gal 5:22)[19].

The use of *libertas* in the early liturgical sources reflects this Pauline understanding. A study of *libertas, liberare* and *liber* in the early euchology is found in the analysis of the collect for Sunday XXXII[20]. Summarizing that discussion here, *libertas* connotes the internal freedom to act in the Spirit, freedom from sin and the power of the devil, freedom from civil strife and misfortune, and, less frequently, freedom from external pressures and limitations. Of these four, the first is the most central.

Various combinations of the themes of redemption, adoption, baptism, inheritance, and freedom are present in other Pauline writings. In Romans, adoption as God's children makes Christians heirs of God and coheirs with Christ (Rm 8:14-15,17)[21]. As already noted, believers live in the freedom of life in the Spirit, in which they are both free from sin and death, and freed for life and peace (Rm 8:2,6)[22]. They receive this freedom through baptism (Rm 6:3-9).

---

[19] "*Fructus autem spiritus est caritas, gaudium, pax, patientia, benignitas, bonitas, longanimitas, mansuetudo, fides, modestia, continentia, castitas*" (Gal 5:22).

[20] See below, 420.

[21] "*Quicumque enim Spiritu Dei aguntur ii sunt filii Dei. Non enim accepistis spiritum servitutis iterum in timore, sed accepistis spiritum adoptionis filiorum in quo clamamus: Abba, Pater ... Si autem filii, et heredes: heredes quidem Dei, coheredes autem Chisti ....*" (Rm 8:14-15,17).

[22] "*Nihil ergo nunc damnationis est iis qui sunt in Christo Iesu, qui non secundum carnem ambulant; lex enim spiritus vitae in Christo Iesu liberabit me a lege peccati et mortis ... nam prudentia carnis mors est, prudentia autem spiritus vita et pax*" (Rm 8:1-2,6). See also Rm 7:24.

The blessing which opens the Letter to the Ephesians (Eph 1:3-14) combines adoption as children (*adoptio filiorum*) in Christ (v.5)[23], redemption (*redemptio*) and the remission of sins (v.7)[24], and the Spirit as the pledge of the eternal inheritance (*hereditas*)(v.13-14)[25].

Respice in opera misericordiae tuae

The collect's petition shows no clear dependence on the Letter to the Galatians. It does, however, echo various verses from the psalms, notably Ps 68:17 and Ps 89:16:

"*Exaudi me, Domine, quoniam benigna est misericordia secundum multitudinem miserationum tuarum respice*" (Ps 68:17),

"*Respice in servos tuos et in opera tua et dirige filios eorum*" (Ps 89:16).

Respice

The verb *respicere*, commonly found in the psalms and liturgical sources, has been analysed in the study of the collect for Sunday XXIV[26]. *Respicere* conveys the faithful's humble request that God turn his favourable gaze towards them in response to their supplication.

In opera misericordiae tuae

This expression is found in a *Reginensis* 316 lenten collect, V 334. There *opus* refers to God's work of restoration of his people through the passion of Christ. The prayer reads:

---

[23] "*qui praedestinavit nos in adoptionem filiorum per Iesusm Christum in ipsum, secundum propositum voluntatis suae*" (Eph 1:5).

[24] "*in quo habemus redemptionem per sanguinem eius, remissionem peccatorum secundum divitias gratiae eius*" (Eph 1:7).

[25] "*in quo et vos, cum audissetis verbum veritatis, evangelium salutis vestrae, in quo et credentes signati estis Spiritu promissionis sancto, qui est pignus hereditatis nostrae, in redemptionem adquisitionis, in laudem gloriae ipsius*" (Eph 1:12-13).

[26] See above, 206.

"*Omnipotens sempiterne deus, qui Christi tui beata passione nos reparas, conserua in nobis opera misericordiae tuae, ut in huius caelebritate mysterii perpetua deuotione uiuamus*" (V 344)[27].

Similarly *opus* is used to designate God's works of redemption, righteousness and loving kindness, as in *opus redemptionis nostrae* (L 93), and *opera iustitiae tuae adque pietatis*" (L 266).

God's mercy, *misericordia*, is discussed in the study of the collect for Sunday XXVI[28]. There it is seen that the divine mercy is the primary expression of God's love in Christ towards the faithful. It is known to the faithful in their experience of the defeat of sin and death, restoration and being raised up, and the promises of eternal life.

In V 522, the phrase *opera misericordiae tuae* has a double reference. Clearly it refers to the believers, who through baptism, have entered into the community formed by God's actions in Christ of redemption and adoption. At the same time it emphasises that their baptism, freedom, redemption and adoption are God's doing, his *opus*.

Meaning of the prayer:

The prayer is a recapitulation of the Pauline economy of salvation in Christ. The oration is motivated by the people's faith that they have been redeemed in Christ, and as well been offered a new status as adopted children of God. They have embraced this new relationship with God through their baptism. Freedom in Christ, redemption, adoption and baptism are

---

[27] All powerful, eternal God, who restores us by the blessed passion of your Christ, preserve in us the work of your mercy, so that in the celebration of this mystery, we may live in perpetual devotion.
With some modifications this prayer has been incorporated into the Missal of Paul VI: MR(1975) Fer. VI in Pass. Domini, Post comm., 264.

[28] See below, 378.

experienced as acts of God's mercy. The faithful's petition is that God continue to turn his mercy towards them, and in doing so grant them true freedom and eternal inheritance. These gifts are the direct continuation of redemption and adoption.

True freedom involves internal freedom in the Spirit, as well as liberation, in Christ, from death and sin, evil, and the oppressive weight of the old Law. In this freedom, Christians serve one another in love, their lives manifesting the fruits of the Spirit. Through their liberty in Christ, the faithful partially experience the inheritance that their adoption promises. They receive the fullness of this inheritance in heaven, where, living the fullness of life in Christ and the Spirit, they will live as children of God, free from all sin and death.

ANALYSIS OF THE WORDS AND PHRASES IN THE COLLECT IN THE CONTEXT OF THE MISSAL OF PAUL VI

The modifications made to the oration, while still reflecting the Pauline pattern behind the prayer, have brought some changes to the focus of the collect.

The replacement of *in opera misericordiae tuae* with *filios dilectionis* to some degree strenghtens the Pauline connections. The use of *filii* carries forward the relationship forged by God in our adoption. As seen above, God's mercy (*misericordia*) is the primary expression of God's love (*dilectio*) for his people. These changes to the petition, then, further highlight the Pauline themes of God's love and his adoption. Yet the same change also weakens the prayer to a degree. The expression *opera misericordia tuae* emphasises that redemption was God's work.

The substitution of *in Christo renatis* with *in Christo credentibus* has an effect on the prayer. The use of *credentes* stresses the action of the faithful as believers. On the other hand it puts less accent on the work done by God. In this sense the change is in line with the substitution of *filii dilectionis* for *opera misericordiae tuae*. Moreover, there is a loss of the explicit mention of baptism. This weakens the connection between *redemptio/adoptio* and *libertas/hereditas*, and in so doing, lessens the relationship of the prayer to the framework and content of the Letter to the Galatians.

The reasons for this change are not evident. In the Missal of Paul VI the description of the faithful as *renati* is mainly restricted to prayers for Lent, Easter and Pentecost[29]. In light of this the change is a little out of place, since our collect is also the collect for the fifth Sunday after Easter, and for the Mass of Saturday of week two in Eastertide[30].

There are a number of prayers, however, in which baptism and belief are set side by side. This can be seen in two of the prayers listed above as dependent on our collect[31]. An Easter collect sets *credentes* and *renati* in parallel. The prayer reads:

"*Deus, qui credentes in te fonte baptizmatis innovasti, hanc renatis in Christo concede custodiam ....*" (MR(1975) Sab. post domm. III et V Paschae, Collecta hebd. III, 331)[32].

---

[29]*Renasci* is found 18 times in the Missal of Paul VI. Thirteen of these are from orations in Lent, Eastertide and Pentecost, two are connected with baptism and confirmation, and there is one prayer each in the Mass for the feast of the Baptism of the Lord and the Mass of Sts. Joachim and Anne. The only one in Ordinary Time is in a blessing *super populum*, which itself has Paschal references: (MR(1975) Orr. Super populum, 18, 509). See Schnitker and Slaby, Concordantia, 2169-2170.

[30]MR(1975) Dom. V Paschae, Collecta, 303, MR(1975) Sabb. post domm., II, IV et VI, Collecta hebd. II and MR(1975) Benedd. in fine M., Bened. soll., temp. pasch., 6, 498.

[31]See Ga V 224 and Sp 1758, whose texts are above, 224, fn 4, fn 5.

[32]God, who renewed those who believe in you by the font of baptism, guard those who have been reborn in Christ ....

In the other change to the prayer, the verb *intendere* has much the same sense as *respicere*[33].

RELATIONSHIP OF THE CHRISTIAN PEOPLE TO GOD

Those who believe in Christ enter into a relationship with God as his adopted children and heirs, and in the freedom of the Spirit. God makes this offer out of his love and mercy, and effects it through redemption in Christ. The faithful take up their new status as adopted children through baptism, and maintain it in the constancy of their faith. As the prayer stands in the Missal of Paul VI the expression of the theology of baptism is diminished.

As God's children in faith, believers live in the freedom that Christ brings, as well as in the hope of the eternal inheritance which is now their due. Their lives in freedom are taken up in a love and service of one another which is characterized by the fruits of the Spirit, themselves a foretaste of eternal life.

FREER TRANSLATION OF THE COLLECT

Deus, per quem nobis et redemptio venit et praestatur adoptio, filios dilectionis tuae benignus intende, ut in Christo credentibus et vera tribuatur libertas, et hereditas aeterna.

God, you bring about our redemption and adopt us as your own. Look down kindly upon us, the children of your love. Grant that we who believe in Christ may live in true freedom and reach the inheritance that you have promised us.

The prayer, with slight variations, is first found in *Reginensis* 316 as a *Super sindonem* from the Mass of Friday in Easter week (V 490).

[33] See Ellebracht, Remarks on the Vocabulary of the Ancient Orations in the Missal Romanum, 88-89.

COLLECT FOR SUNDAY XIV

PRAYER

Deus, qui in Filii tui humilitate iacentem mundum erexisti, fidelibus tuis sanctam concede laetitiam, ut, quos eripuisti a servitute peccati, gaudiis facias perfrui sempiternis.

God, who in the humility of your Son raised up the fallen world, grant holy joy to your faithful, so that you may make enjoy in eternal delights those whom you rescued from the slavery of sin.

ORIGINAL SOURCE

Deus, qui in filii tui humilitatem iacentem mundum erexisti, laetitiam concede <fidelibus tuis>, ut quos perpetuae <mortis> eripuisti casibus, gaudiis facias sempiternis perfruere (V 541).

God, who in the humility of your son raised up the fallen world, grant joy to your faithful, so that you may make enjoy in eternal delights those whom you have rescued from the calamities of eternal death.

Reginensis 316: Collect from the Mass, I,lvii, Orationes et preces dominicum post octabas paschae (V 541).

USE IN THE MISSAL OF PAUL VI

This collect for the Mass of Sunday XIV in Ordinary Time is also the opening prayer for the Mass of Tuesday, Week IV in the season of Easter[1].

---

[1] MR(1975) Fer. II post domm. II, IV et VI Pascha, Collecta, hebd., IV, 315.

USE IN OTHER LITURGICAL SOURCES

As noted by Bruylants[2], the collect is also found in the following sources:

Dominica II post Pascha: Pr(109,1), A(892), S(687), P(390), OR(166)[Sp 1114], X(111,1), N(123), Q(126), 1474(225), 1570, 1604, as well as in these uncritical editions G(116,1)[G 861], Z(544), FrSal 1(IX,1), PaAng(147).

In letania maiore ad sanctum laurentium. Alia missa Pr(120,1).

Incipiunt orationes et missae dominicales quotidianae Gregorii papae, Pr(233,1). Note that this third appearance in the Prague Sacramentary falls outside the paschal season.

CHANGES FROM THE ORIGINAL SOURCE

There are two changes to the original text.

The major change occurs in the purpose clause of the prayer. The clause *quos perpetuae mortis eripuisti casibus* has been modified to *quos eripuisti a servitute peccati*. This change is not found in any of the sources. This modification substitutes servitude to sin for its consequences, eternal death.

The second change is that *laetitiam* has become *sanctam laetitiam*. In a number of the ancient sources[3] and in the earlier Roman Missal, *laetitia* was qualified by *perpetua*, contrasting the petition for perpetual joy with the calamity of perpetual death. The insertion of *a servitute peccati* has removed this contrast. The introduction of *sancta* emphasizes the eucharistic context of the community's joy.

---

[2]Bruylants, II, 364. For a more detailed list of sources and manuscripts see Moeller, Corpus Orationum III, D, Orat 1708-2389, oration 1737, 13.

[3]For example A 892 and G 861.

ANALYSIS OF THE PRAYER IN THE ORIGINAL SOURCE

Origin:

According to Chavasse[4], this Mass is one of a pre-existing group of six Masses for the Sundays after Easter, which were later incorporated as a group into *Reginensis* 316. He argues from a degree of correspondence between the Masses and the Epistle and Gospel readings for the Sundays after Easter current in Rome before the end of the sixth century.

Grammatical structure[5]:

The collect consists of (i) an address, with a clause containing the motivation for petitioning God, and (ii) the petition itself, followed by a purpose clause.

(i) Address: *Deus*
 Motivation: *qui in filii tui humilitatem iacentem mundum erexisti*

(ii) Petition: *laetitiam concede fidelibus tuis*
 Purpose: *ut quos perpetuae mortis eripuisti casibus gaudiis facias sempiternis perfruere*

The prayer is constructed around a cluster of parallels and contrasts. *Filii humilitas/ iacens mundus*: The free humbling of the divine Son in love[6] is set in contrast with the lowering of the creation due to its sin in pride[7]. The

---

[4]Chavasse, Le Sacramentaire Gélasien, 241-44.

[5]See also, M.Haessly, Rhetoric in the Sunday Collects of the Roman Missal, 62.

[6]This image is taken from Ph 2:8-9: "*Humiliavit semetipsum factus oboediens usque ad mortem, mortem autem crucis. Propter quod et Deus exaltavit illum et donavit ille nomen, quod est super omne nomen*".

[7]Adam and Eve succumb to the temptation to be like gods (Gn 3:5). They eat the forbidden fruit despite the threatened punishment of death for such an

fallen state of the world is a state of death.

Iacentem mundum/ erexisti: Through the Son's obedience unto death, God raises up the fallen world.

Erexisti/ eripuisti: God's snatching the community from perpetual death parallels his raising of the fallen world.

Perpetua mors/ sempiterna gaudia: The most central contrast in the prayer is between the effects of sin and the effects of salvation. The state of the world in sin is a state of unremitting death. Death has a complete and perpetual hold over humanity and creation. It has the same duration and depth as the life intended by God for creation. This forms a stark contrast with the everlasting joys of life in God.

Laetitia/ sempiterna gaudia: God's salvific action of raising up the fallen world is already a cause for joy. Just as death, the present condition due to sin, carries over into eternity, so too does the joy of salvation. The experience of it on earth is an anticipation of life in eternal joy.

Vocabulary:

Prominent vocabulary: *humilitas, iacere, erigere, mundus, laetitia, mors, casus, gaudium, perfrui.*

In filii tui humilitatem iacentem mundum erexisti:

Humilitatem[8]

In the Vulgate translation of the scriptures, the verb *humiliare* is used to describe the self-abasement of Christ set forth in Philippians 2:6-9. The

---

offense (Gn 3:3). Their sin of pride leads to the state of death. See also Rm 5:12.

[8]For further examples of *humilitas* see Deshusses, Concordances III, 2, 282-84. Collect V 329 speaks of Christ's *humilitas* as an example for humankind.

humilitas of the Son denotes his free divesting of his divinity, his incarnation, and redemptive death on the Cross. On account of this scandalous death, God exalts Jesus:

"*Qui, cum in forma Dei esset, non rapinam arbitratus est esse se aequalem Deo, sed semetipsum exinanivit formam servi accipiens, in similitudinem hominum factus et habitu inventus ut homo. Humiliavit semetipsum factus oboediens usque ad mortem, mortem autem crucis. Propter quod et Deus exaltavit illum et donavit illi nomen, quod est super omne nomen*" (Ph 2:6-9).

In collect V 541, this self-humiliation is invoked as the act in which God raised up the fallen world.

Iacentem mundum[9]

This phrase denotes the state of the world in ruin because of its rejection of its place in God's design. In the prayer the fallen state of the world parallels existence in perpetual death. The phrase is also closely linked with the notion of 'darkness' and the rejection of the 'light'. These images need to be analysed together.

The image of darkness is synonymous with the rejection of God, while the image of light is very closely associated with creation. The first act of creation was the creation of light, its blessing, and separation from the darkness (Gn 1:3-4). The creation of light is the founding act of creation. In the original goodness, all subsequent creation was created in the light and belongs in the light. Consequently, rejection of God entails a preference for the darkness of the abyss (Gn 1:2) over the goodness of the entire creation (Gn 1:31). The 'fallen' state of the world involves the rejection of its place in creation, the rejection of the light, and the embracing of the darkness.

---

[9] For further examples of the use of *iacere* see Deshusses, Concordances III, 2, 285. For *mundus*, III, 3, 122-26.

The phrase *iacentem mundum* occurs in the invocation which opens a blessing of the Paschal candle during the Easter Vigil. There the fallen state of the world is associated with existence in darkness. God's saving action of covering the world with light so as to make it newly visible is linked with his original intentions as creator (*conditor*), author of light (*auctor*), artisan (*fabricator*), and source of light (*exordium*). The liturgical setting of the prayer places God's saving actions in the context of the Paschal mystery: "*Deus, mundi conditor, auctor luminis, siderum fabricator, deus qui iacentem mundum in tenebras luce perspicua retexisti, deus, per quem [in]effabili potentia omnia claritas sumpsit exordium ...*" (V 426)[10].
Erexisti[11]

The verb denotes God's act of raising up the fallen world, carried out in view of Christ's self-abasement, obedience and death. Further, it parallels God's work of snatching humanity from perpetual death. The past tense underscores that God has already carried this out. It already constitutes a source of joy for those on earth.

A similar phrase, *deiecta erigi* is found in an Easter Vigil prayer which follows the reading of the Genesis creation account. There God's act of raising up what sin has thrown down is placed alongside the renewal of what has grown old (in sin), and the return of all things to their pristine integrity in God and Christ. Note that this restoration to the original blessing is related to God as eternal light, and is ascribed to his providence:
"*Deus inconmutabilis uirtus, lumen aeternum, respice propicius ad tocius*

---

[10] God, creator of the world, author of light, shaper of the stars, who, by your light, made visible the world that had fallen into darkness. You are the God through whom, by your ineffable power, all splendour has received its beginning ...

[11] For further examples of the use of *erigere* see Deshusses, Concordances III, 2, 39.

aeclesiae tuae mirabile sacramentum et opus salutis humane perpetuae disposicionis effectu tranquillus operare, totusque mundus experiatur et uideat deiecta erigi, inueterata nouari, et per ipsum redire omnia in integrum, a quo sumpseret principium" (V 432)[12].

The invocation, *in filii tui humilitatem iacentem mundum erexisti*, encapsulates the drama of creation, sin and redemption. Though the world ever remains God's creation, its fallen condition is a rejection of its place in God. In its sin, creation enters a state of death. This rebellion is also imaged as a state of ruin and darkness. God, however, in continuity with his work as creator, artisan, and author and source of light, did not reject creation. In the free self-abasement of Christ, which encompasses his incarnation, obedience as human and redemptive death, God raised up the world. He freed it from its subjection to endless death. Creation is renewed and restored to its original state in God and Christ. In Christ's obedience and death comes God's propitiation and his work of human salvation. Motivated by God's overwhelming acts of salvation, the faithful ask for the gift of joy, which results from the overcoming of the death which follows sin.

Laetitiam[13]

In the liturgical sources the nouns *laetitia* and *gaudium* are both used to express the joy of Christians. They are often associated with the idea of

---

[12]God, unchangeable strength, eternal light, look down favourably onto the marvellous mystery of your entire church, and in tranquillity bring about the work of human salvation by the effect of your perpetual disposition, and may the whole world experience and see what has been thrown down raised up, the old made new, and all things return into their original state through him from whom it had taken its origin.

[13]For further examples of the use of *laetitia* see Deshusses, Concordances III, 2, 437-38. See also the study of *gaudium* in the analysis of Collect XXXIII, above 118.

celebration, especially the celebration of the Paschal mysteries[14]. The verb *gaudere* has been analysed in the study of Collect XXXIII. Summarizing that discussion here, the rejoicing of the Christian community is a response to and an exulting in the favour and propitiation God has shown them through salvation in Christ. The faithful celebrate their joy most particularly in their worship and acts of devotion. Their rejoicing, involving both mind and body, takes place within the context of the community. This celebration, which is begun on earth, is fulfilled in the complete fellowship with the saints in heaven.

In V 541, the faithful request the gift of joy as their response to salvation in God and Christ. The Christian community rejoices that the world has been raised out of death. In spite of creation's sin, God, in the redemptive *humilitas* of Christ, has carried forward his work as creator, artisan and author of light. This is the ultimate ground of all Christian joy. From the structure of the prayer itself, the joy which the community petitions is expressed as an anticipation of the eternal joy, given to those whom God has saved from eternal death.

Quos perpetuae <mortis> eripuisti casibus

The fallen state of the world parallels the state of perpetual death. It is an eternal, all-encompassing state, devoid of life, yet filled with turmoil. As such it is in direct and complete contrast to the eternal joys of heaven. The faithful are those who have been snatched from this death.

---

[14] See Blaise, Vocabulaire, § 9. For specific examples of the use of *laetitia* see 1 Pt 1:8-9 and V 486.

Perpetuae mortis casibus[15]

The term *perpetua mors* denotes the eternal death to which humanity is subject because of its fall. The fall itself is the ultimate consequence of sin. Encompassing more than physical death, it is death as contrasted with life in God and life in Christ.

In the Pauline letters, death, the result of sin, is the state of human separation from God that has engulfed the entire human race:
"*Propterea, sicut per unum hominem peccatum in hunc mundum intravit, et per peccatum mors; et ita in omnes homines mors pertransiit, in quo omnes peccaverunt*" (Rm 5:12)[16].

Death is also a state of profound inner wretchedness and anxiety, in which the very being of the person is torn apart by sin. Nothing good emerges, and every will and action leads to frustration:
"*Non enim quod volo bonum hoc facio, sed quod nolo malum hoc ago ... Infelix ego homo! quis me liberabit de corpore mortis huius? Gratia Dei per Iesum Christum Dominum nostrum. Igitur ego ipse mente servio legi Dei, carne autem legi peccati*" (Rm 7:19,24-25).

Humanity, under the shadow of death, lives in a darkness that is only dispelled by the compassionate actions of God in Christ. The light Christ brings overcomes the darkness and shows the way of peace:
"*Per viscera misericordiae Dei nostri, in quibus visitavit nos oriens ex alto; illuminare his qui in tenebris et in umbra mortis sedent, ad dirigendos pedes nostros in viam pacis*" (Lc 1:78-79)[17].

---

[15]For further examples of the use of *mors* see Deshusses, Concordances III, 2, 107-110. For *casus*, III, 1, 231.

[16]The passage is development of Gn 3:17,19.

[17]The preface L 1247 takes up this image.

The adjective *perpetua* qualifies *mors*. It brings to the fore the finality and completeness of the destruction that sin has wrought. By way of contrast, however, it highlights the enormity of salvation, and the unending, perfect joy of life in God. The noun *casus* further reinforces the magnitude of the destruction that sin has brought upon human nature.

Eripuisti[18]

God's work of deliverance is first and foremost deliverance from perpetual death. In V 541 it parallels his work of raising the fallen world in view of the Son's *humilitas* and death. Existence in God's deliverance is a life of continuous joy. It is life in the fullness of all goodness, as in the original creation.

In a prayer *super populum* from a Mass commemorating a martyr, God is asked to bring to the fullness of good things those he has snatched from all evil (*a malis omnibus clementer ereptos*). Evil is identified with death and mortality. It is further associated with the imagery of darkness. Through God's intervention, existence in death and evil (*mala*) is replaced by life in the perfection of goodness (*bona*), just as in V 541 perpetual death gives way to eternal joy:

"*Tuere, domine, supplices tuos, sustenta fragiles, purga terrenos; et inter mortalium tenebras mortales ambulantes tua semper luce uiuifica, adque a malis omnibus clementer ereptos ad summa bona peruenire concede*" (L 46)[19].

Note that the perfection of goodness is an allusion to that of original creation.

---

[18] For further examples of the use of *eripere* see Deshusses, Concordances III, 2, 39-40.

[19] Protect your suppliants Lord, sustain the weak and purify those who dwell on the earth. Give life by your light always to us mortals, walking amidst the darkness of all that is subject to death. In doing so grant that those you have rescued mercifully from every evil may come to the perfection of everything that is good.

The complete clause *quos perpetuae mortis eripuisti casibus* qualifies the faithful as the community that has been snatched from the perpetual death which is the state of the fallen world, brought about by sin. Death, in tandem with sin, extends to the entire creation and humanity across all the ages. Creation has rejected its place in God. At the level of human existence, those who live in the death of sin live in continuous inner turmoil. The qualification *perpetua* emphasises the depth and finality of this death. Associated with the metaphor of death are the images of ruin and darkness.

The very magnitude of the lifelessness, turmoil and destruction of death from sin serves to highlight the graciousness of God's salvation. The faithful have been snatched from death. This is already a cause for rejoicing on earth, a rejoicing which anticipates the unending joy of heaven. This state of rejoicing further reinforces the tragic nature of perpetual death.

Gaudiis facias sempiternis perfruere

Eternal joy is the joy of heaven. It is able to be attained only because God has delivered the faithful from sin and danger, and provides ongoing help, as seen in this preface:

"*Uere dignum: per quem nos eruis a peccatis, a periculis exusi, et ad gaudia sempiterna perduces*" (L 584)[20].

The verb *perfruere* implies a nuance of duration and perfection in the experience of eternal joy in heaven.[21]

The clause *gaudiis facias sempiternis perfruere* contrasts the joy of heaven with the perpetual death from sin. The contrast reflects the wondrous nature of the salvation that comes from God's compassion and forgiveness in Christ. Eternal joy is the unhindered fulfillment of that same joy felt by the

---

[20]It is right and fitting to give you praise Lord. Through Christ you rescue us from sin, deliver us from danger, and lead us to everlasting joy.

[21]Blaise, Vocabulaire, 298, fn 14.

church on earth. The source of this joy is the realization of the magnitude of what God has freely done for them, and their experience of worshipping and living in the community of the renewed creation.

Meaning of the prayer:

The collect is a petition for joy as the community, in the light of Christ's self-abasement, reflects on God's gracious act of saving all creation, especially humanity, from perpetual death. This state is the ultimate consequence of sin. It is the unceasing rejection of life in God, and results in the ruined, fallen state of creation, and constant turmoil in the human heart. More forcefully it is a permanent state, affecting all aspects of existence with a dread finality. In the scriptures and liturgical sources, it is often accompanied by the image of darkness.

The faithful request joy because death has not had the final word. Through the lowering of Christ, God has already raised up the fallen world and delivered the faithful from eternal death. In place of *perpetua mors* God grants the unending enjoyment of eternal delights. The joy which Christians experience merely anticipates the joy of eternal life. Just as their existence in death on earth due to sin would have carried over into eternity, so now their present joy in God's deliverance presages their future eternal joy.

ANALYSIS OF THE WORDS AND PHRASES IN THE COLLECT IN RELATIONSHIP TO THE MISSAL OF PAUL VI

Vocabulary:

The two changes in the prayer require comment.

The replacement of *perpetuae mortis casibus* with the phrase *a servitute peccati* brings about a change in the sense of the prayer. The wording of the new phrase reflects the contrast found in Rm 6:16 between servitude to sin, which leads to death, or service in obedience, which leads to righteousness[22]. The revision gives more emphasis to the cause of the fallen condition of creation, and links Christ's *humilitas* with freedom from the bondage of sin. This freedom also carries with it the sense of free and pleasing obedience to God, as is reflected in the collect for the Mass of the confessor Raymond of Penyafort:

"*Deus, qui beatum Raimundum presbyterum insignis in peccatores misericordiae virtute decorasti, eius nobis intercessione concede, ut, a peccati servitute soluti, quae tibi sunt placita liberis mentibus exsequamur*" (MR(1975) S. Raimundi de Penyafort, Collecta, 515)[23].

The modification weakens the prayer. It draws attention to the state of bondage rather than the more deeply troubling state of existence in perpetual death. The force of the prayer's structure is also weakened. The parallel between the fallen world and bondage (not qualified as *perpetua*) to sin falls short of the image of the fallen world as caught in perpetual death. Nor does bondage to sin form a fitting contrast with eternal joy. As seen above in the Vulgate translation of Romans 6:16, the scriptural contrast is with service in obedience, rather than joy. The language of the prayer is no longer eschatological. It no longer links the loss of the life of creation and the beginning of death in sin, nor the life brought through death in Christ's humility and the death which is without end[24].

---

[22]"*Nescitis quoniam cui exhibetis vos servos ad oboediendum, servi estis eius, cui oboeditis, sive peccati ad mortem sive oboeditionis ad iustitiam?*" (Rm 6:16). See also vv. 17-20.

[23]God, you made your priest St Raymond renowned by virtue of his mercy towards sinners. Grant that by his intercession, we who have been freed from slavery to sin, may freely accomplish what is pleasing to you.

[24]This substitution seems to show the same timidity in the face of the language of eternal death that is found in the changes made to the euchology of

The second change is the qualification of *laetitiam* with the adjective *sanctam*. The Gallican influenced sources broadened the scope of *laetitia*, identifying it with a range of earthly blessings, including an abundance of food, health, and peace.[25] However the adjective *sancta* brings to the fore the liturgical context of rejoicing. The only other appearance of *sancta laetitia* in the Missal of Paul VI is in the collect for the feast of Sts. Peter and Paul, where the 'reverent and holy joy' is the joy which comes in the celebration of the feast:

Deus, qui huius diei venerandam sanctamque laetitiam in apostolorum Petri et Pauli sollemnitate tribuisti, da Ecclesiae tuae eorum in omnibus sequi praeceptum, per quos religionis sumpsit exordium" (MR(1975) M. in die Ss. Petri et Pauli, app., Collecta, 572)[26].

This focus on worship relates the rejoicing of the community more closely to the experience of worship. Christians should be marked by the joy that is experienced in worship. Yet this rejoicing is now linked to pleasing obedience.

---

the Ordo Exsequiarum. See W.D.V.Antonio, "The Euchological Texts of the Ordo Exsequiarum of 1969," Ephemerides Liturgicae 107 (1993): 289-311.

[25] See G 2821, G 1976, and G 2033.

[26] "God, you have given us the reverent and holy joy that comes from worship in today's feast of the apostles Peter and Paul. Grant that your church may follow their teaching in all things since we received the foundations of the faith through them."
A similiar conjunction of the adjectives *sancta* and *veneranda* is found in L 1273.

RELATIONSHIP OF THE CHRISTIAN PEOPLE TO GOD

The prayer in its original context:

Sin condemned creation and humanity to a state of perpetual death. It is a state of fallenness, turmoil and darkness that is without end. It endures beyond the moment of physical death, as an empty and lifeless contrast to the fullness of eternal life enjoyed in God and Christ.

God's deliverance of humanity from death is already a cause for joy on earth. While the conditions and consequences of sin may still encompass the faithful, the dread finality of death and sin has been overcome. The Christian community, then, ought be characterized by joy because such death no longer has the final word. Their rejoicing in salvation while on earth is a participation in and anticipation of the rejoicing in heaven.

Salvation is entirely and gratuitously the work of God, a work already brought about. The absolute hold that death had is a reminder of the magnitude of salvation. God's actions have been accomplished in the mystery of Christ's humility and redemptive death. The focus of the prayer, however, is joy that God has done what only God could do, release creation from death due to sin.

The prayer in the Missal of Paul VI:

The prayer as it stands in the Missal of Paul VI is weakened due to its loss of the vigorous eschatological perspective of creation, sin, death and salvation. Rather, the fallen world is held in bondage to sin. The metaphor of captivity does not bear the dread or *gravitas* of the metaphor of eternal death. The collect now understands the contemporary community to be held in chains of sin. It is in a state of disobedient service and toil. Such bondage does imply a fallen state. However, the prayer no longer comments on the absolute effects of sin in creation and humanity. It steers away from sin and death as essentially loss of life, as a state of turmoil, and as unending, dreadful rejection of eternal life and joy. In the revised prayer, sin has lost its force as death. The joy of the community reflects its obedient service and righteousness.

The response of the faithful in joy is even more closely associated with worship. The liturgy is the most fitting form of celebration of deliverance. The Christian life ought be marked by the joy celebrated in the liturgy. This rejoicing in the liturgy grounds the future rejoicing in heaven.

FREER TRANSLATION OF THE COLLECT

Deus, qui in Filii tui humilitate iacentem mundum erexisti, fidelibus tuis sanctam concede laetitiam, ut, quos eripuisti a servitute peccati, gaudiis facias perfrui sempiternis.	God, you have raised the fallen world in the humility of your Son. May your faithful be filled with devout joy, so that those you have delivered from the bondage of sin may enjoy unending delight.

COLLECT FOR SUNDAY XV

PRAYER

Deus, qui errantibus, ut in viam possint redire, veritatis tuae lumen ostendis, da cunctis qui christiana professione censentur, et illa respuere, quae huic inimica sunt nomini, et ea quae sunt apta sectari.

God, you show the light of your truth to those who stray so that they may be able to return to the way, give to all who are counted among those who make Christian profession, both to reject those things which are hostile to the name Christian, and to follow those things which are suitable to it.

ORIGINAL SOURCE

Deus, <qui> errantes ut in uia posse redire ueritatis lumen ostendis, da cunctis qui christiana professione censentur, et illa respuere qui huic inimica sunt nomini et ea quae sunt apta sectari: Per (L 75).

Veronensis: Collect for the Mass, XX, <Item Alia>, April (L 75).

Reginensis 316: Collect for the Mass, I,lviii, Item II Dom. post clausum Paschae (V 546).

The opening *qui* clause is in need of some restoration. Capelle[1] prefers to render it *Deus, qui errantes ut in via[m] possint redire*, where *errantes* is the subject of *possint*. Mohlberg[2] seems to concur. The Missal of Paul VI follows

---

[1] B.Capelle, "Messes du Pape S. Gélase dans le Sacramentaire Léonien", Revue bénédictine 56 (1945-46): 12-15. See also Capelle's earlier article on this collect, "La collecte du troisième dimanche après paques, dans le missel romain", Revue bénédictine 41 (1929): 171-173.

[2] See the comment in Mohlberg, Liber Sacramentorum Romanae Aeclesiae (*Reg.* 316), 11.

the Supplement to the Hadrianum: *qui errantibus ut in via[m] possint redire* (Sp 1117).

USE IN THE MISSAL OF PAUL VI

This collect for the Mass of Sunday XV in Ordinary Time is also the opening prayer for the Mass of Tuesday, Week III in the season of Easter[3].

USE IN OTHER LITURGICAL SOURCES

As noted by Bruylants[4], the collect is also found in these sources: Dominica III post Pascha: Pr(111,1), A(910), S(705), P(396), OR(166)[Sp 1117], X(112,1), N(123), Q(126), 1474(226), 1570, 1604, and in these uncritical editions G(120,1), Z(549), PaAng(162), Dominica I post sancti Angeli Pr(195,1).

Almost every manuscript places the prayer as a collect in the season of Easter. Apart from the original context of the prayer, which is discussed below, two other contexts are worth noting. In the Prague Sacramentary, the collect is used twice. One occurrence is in Easter. The second, as the first Sunday after the feast of St Michael, lies outside the season of Easter. The six Sundays after the feast of St Michael precede the Sundays of Advent. This provides a precedent for the position in Ordinary Time of the prayer in the Missal of Paul VI. The second context to note is the use of the prayer in connection with the Praemonstratension Divine Office: *Praeparatio divini officii <oratio> pro errantibus*, Praem I[5].

---

[3]MR(1975) Fer II post domm. III et V Paschae, Collecta hebd., III, 325.

[4]Bruylants, II, 336. For a more complete listing of manuscripts and sources see Moeller, <u>Corpus Orationum</u> II, D, Orat 881-1707, oration 1582, 317.

[5]Moeller, <u>Corpus Orationum</u>, II, D, 317.

CHANGES FROM THE ORIGINAL SOURCE

In addition to the restoration of the text, the only other change between the original and the collect in the Missal of Paul VI is the modification of *veritatis* to *veritatis tuae*, following V 546.

While the current version of the prayer reads *in viam ... redire*, much of the manuscript tradition, inclusive of the earlier editions of the Roman Missal, reads *in viam ... redire iustitiae*[6].

ANALYSIS OF THE PRAYER IN THE ORIGINAL SOURCE
Origin:

The *Veronensis* Mass XX has been a cause of some speculation. It is both out of place amongst the April Masses for martyrs, and contains only four prayers. Capelle has established its Gelasian authorship[7], and Pomarés has placed it as the Mass of January 1, 495, the first in a series which envisages the approaching Roman pagan/folk festival of Lupercalia, till then held annually on the ides of February[8]. The Mass XX was displaced from the rest of the series in the compilation of the *Veronensis*, and placed among the April prayers.

As noted in the study of Collect IV[9], Gelasius opposed the festival not only on the grounds of the lack of charity inherent in its customs and the licentious behaviour of the participants, but also because it celebrated, as still active, the power of the ancient Roman gods. For Gelasius the festival implied

---

[6] For example G 925, A 922, Sp 1117, and MR(1570) Dom. III post Pascha .

[7] Capelle, "Messes du Pape S. Gélase," Revue bénédictine 56 (1945-46): 12-40.

[8] G. Pomarès, Gélase, 82-84, and 142.

[9] See above, 99.

a means of grace outside the Christian economy of salvation. His position was unequivocal: the festival was not merely a piece of folklore re-enacted annually, but a pagan celebration incompatible with the teachings and lifestyle of Christianity.

The collect (L 75) of Mass XX was borrowed to serve as the opening prayer (V 546) of a Mass found in *Reginensis* 316 for the third Sunday in Easter. According to Chavasse[10], this Mass itself is one in a cohesive layer of Easter texts placed as a whole in *Reginensis* 316. Since the collect's inclusion in *Reginensis* 316, it has been almost exclusively used in Masses for the season of Easter.

As one of these Easter Masses, the collect contains an echo of the Epistle of the day. As postulated by Chavasse[11], the readings of the day would have been 1 Pt 2:21-25 and Jo 10:11-16. While the theme of the good shepherd is paramount in the Gospel, and reflected in the Epistle, the Epistle speaks of the straying (*errantes*) sheep[12]. This will be taken up below.

Grammatical structure[13]:

The prayer is made up of (i) an address with a motivation clause, and (ii) a twofold petition on behalf of all the faithful.

(i)   Address: *Deus,*

Motivation: *qui errantes in via posse redire veritatis lumen ostendis.*

---

[10]A. Chavasse, Le Sacramentaire Gélasien, 241-44.

[11]Ibid., 244.

[12]"*Eratis enim sicut oves errantes, sed conversi estis nunc ad pastorem et episcopum animarum vestrarum*" (1 Pt 2:25).

[13]See also Haessly, Rhetoric in the Sunday Collects of the Roman Missal, 63.

(ii) Beneficiaries: *da cunctis*   *qui christiana professione censentur*

    Petition: *et*   *illa respuere qui huic inimica sunt nomini*
    Petition: *et*   *ea quae sunt apta sectari.*

The two petitions are in tandem.

The motivation for the collect is the faithful's belief that God shows the light of his truth so that all who are astray are able to return to his way. In view of this, the faithful petition on behalf of all Christians for the grace to shun what is inimical to the name Christian, and follow what is fitting to it. Because God brings those who stray back to the way, he can certainly be relied upon to uphold in truth those who actually profess his way.

Vocabulary:

Prominent vocabulary: *via, lumen, veritas, errare, censere, christiana professio, respuere, nomen, inimicus, sectari.*

Qui errantes ut in via[m] possint redire, veritatis lumen ostendis

    The study begins with the address clauses of the prayer since they provide the motivation for the petitions. These clauses rest on the metaphors of the way (*via*), light (*lumen*) and truth (*veritas*). These images are often found together in the scriptures and the liturgical sources. Their conjunction can be seen in this verse from Ps 118: "*Lucerna pedibus meis verbum tuum et lumen semitis meis*" (Ps 118:105). The psalm associates God's word with his truth (v.89-90). Note also that in the psalm, the choice for God's path is at the same time a rejection of the paths of evil (v.101) and iniquity (v.104). This corresponds to the two petitions in L 75.

    The New Testament writings apply these three images to Christ. He is the light which overcomes all darkness (Jo 1:4, 9). In another Johannine passage, Christ is the embodiment of the way (*via*), truth (*veritas*) and life (*vita*) (Jo 14:6). Life in his light (*lux*) is characterized by love (1 Jo 2:9), goodness, righteousness and truth (Eph 5:8-9).

The liturgical usage of this set of images is exemplified in the following two prayers for morning office[14]. As seen in Ps 118 above, they reflect the complete incompatibility between God's way (*via*), light (*lux*) and truth (*veritas*), and the ways of error (*error*) and falsehood (*falsitas*):

"*Emitte quaesumus, domine, lucem tuam in cordibus nostris et mandatorum tuorum luce perpetua, et [ut] in uia tua ambulantes nihil patiamur errorem*" (V 1582)[15],

"*Ueritas tua, quaesumus, domine, luceat in cordibus nostris et omnis falsitas destruatur inimici*" (V 1583)[16].

The conviction of the faithful is that God shows the light of his truth in such a way that even those who stray are brought back to it.

Errantes[17]

The verb *errare* and the noun *error* are used to designate departure from God's ways, such as heresy, schism, participation in immoral and pagan practices, and disobedience. Those who stray (*errare*) by following paths other than God's fall into error, and walk in sin, darkness and death. Yet, associated with the deviation of humanity from God's ways is the divine will that all humanity be saved.

---

[14]For an oration which associates the light of truth with Christ see V 11.

[15]Lord, send your light into our hearts and, walking by the perpetual light of your mandates in your way, may we suffer no error.

[16]Lord, may your truth shine in our hearts and may all falsehood of the enemy (devil) be destroyed.

[17]For further examples of the use of *errare* and *error* see Deshusses, Concordances III, 2, 40-41.

The collect echoes the last verse of the probable Easter lectionary reading (1 Pt 2:21-25) for the Mass. This verse itself is based in Is 53:6[18], where the verb *errare* implies following paths other than God's. Precisely because these paths are not God's they lead to iniquity. In the Isaiah passage, God's response to humanity's deviation from his ways is the justification of the many through the suffering of his servant (Is 53:11). In the reading from 1 Peter, it is through Christ that the wandering sheep have returned to the shepherd and guardian of their souls.

In the liturgical sources, *errare* and the noun *error* are applied to various situations which place Christians at odds with their membership of the church. In the following prayer for heretics and schismatics from a Good Friday liturgy, the noun *error* is used to denote the wrong beliefs of heretics and schismatics, who themselves are described as straying *(errantes)*. The way of heresy and schism is associated with the deceptions of the devil. In contrast, the way of truth is linked with membership of the catholic and apostolic church. As in collect L 75, the paths of truth and error are mutually exclusive. Note that the petition is set within the context of the faithful's belief that God wishes all to be saved and no one to be lost. The oration reads:

"Oremus pro heredicis et scismaticis, ut deus et dominus noster eruat eos ab erroribus et ad sanctam matrem aeclesiam catholicam atque apostolicam reuocare dignetur ... Omnipotens sempiterne deus, qui omnes saluas et niminem uis perire, respice ad animas diabolica fraude deceptas, ut omni

---

[18]*"Omnes nos quasi oves erravimus, unusquisque in uiam suam declinavit, et posuit Dominus in eo iniquitatem omnium nostrum"* (Is 53:6).

heredica peruersitate depulsa errancium corda resipiscant et ad ueritatis tuae redeant firmitatem" (V 412-413)[19].

For Pope Gelasius, *error* particularly denotes the sacrilegious participation in pagan practices, which has a debilitating effect on morals[20]. Error is avoided by living in the light of the commandments, as seen above in the morning oration V 1582.

Error is used to describe the state of human existence outside of God, a state of perpetual death. This is brought out in the preface for the Easter Mass (I,lviii) of which the prayer being studied (V 541) is the collect. The preface affirms God's universal saving actions in Christ in the face of humanity's straying from God and entrapment in perpetual death. Freedom from unending death is set in parallel with the gift of eternal life. The preface reads: *"Uere dignum: per Christum dominum nostrum. Qui humanis miseratus erroribus per uirginem nasci dignatus est, et per passionem mortis a perpetua nos morti liberauit, ac resurrectione sua aeternam nobis contulit uitam. Quem laudant angeli"* (V 549)[21].

---

[19]Let us pray on behalf of heretics and schismatics, that our Lord and God may deliver them from all error and deign to call them back to the holy, catholic and apostolic, mother church ... All powerful and almighty God, who saves all and wishes no one to perish, look toward the souls of those deceived by the deceit of the devil, so that when all perversity of heresy has been driven out, the hearts of those in error may repent and may return to the steadfastness of your truth.

[20]See L 76, L 77 and L 78, which accompany the collect L 75. See also Capelle, "Messes du Pape S. Gélase," Revue bénédictine 56 (1945-46): 19.

[21]"It is right and fitting to give praise, through Christ our lord, who, out of compassion for humanity's wanderings from God's way, deigned to be born of the virgin, and through his passion and death freed us from perpetual death, and conferred eternal life on us by his resurrection. The angels praise him." Note that *error* is translated as 'wanderings' since it is in parallel with *errantes* in the collect of the Mass.
With some slight adjustments, this prayer has been incorporated into a preface

The invocation *qui errantes ut in via[m] possint redire, veritatis lumen ostendis* reflects God's desire to save those of his people who stray. Those who follow paths other than God's, whether through heresy, schism, sacrilege, immorality or disobedience, exist in falsehood, darkness and perpetual death[22]. Their ways are inimical to the ways of God. God, however, meets their deviation by ever showing the light of truth which enables them to return to his path, which is revealed in Christ, his death and resurrection, and in the church.

In light of their belief in God's desire to bring to his way all who have strayed into darkness, falsehood and perpetual death, the faithful pray that God will bestow gifts so that those who, by their Christian profession, are to be counted among the members of the church, may remain on his path, or if they have strayed, return to his path.

Da cunctis qui christiana professione censentur, et illa respuere qui huic inimica sunt nomini et ea quae sunt apta sectari:

We will examine this section of the prayer by first analysing the expression *Christiana professione censentur*.

Christiana professione censentur

The vocabulary of the prayer in relationship to the writings of Gelasius has been studied by Capelle[23] and to a lesser extent Pomarés[24]. Pomarés concerns himself only with Gelasius' letter against the Lupercalians. The extensive parallels between his prayers and writings reveal the typical Gelasian

---

in the Missal of Paul VI: MR(1975) Ordo M. cum populo, Praef. II de domm. per annum, 413.

[22]The concept of perpetual death, *mors*, has been studied in the analysis of the collect for Sunday XIV. See above 244.

[23]Capelle, "Messes du Pape S. Gélase," Revue bénédictine 56 (1945-46): 18-20.

[24]Pomarés, Gélase, 82-83.

vocabulary in L 75. Various combinations of the words *professio, christiana, nomen, censere* and *inimicus* are common throughout his writings, while *christiana professio* is found in the letter against the Lupercalians, and *censere* and *respuere* are employed together frequently. This vocabulary will now be examined.

Censentur[25]

The collect's petition is made on behalf of those who are reckoned among (*censeri*) the people who have made Christian profession. A similar use of the verb *censere* can be seen in this *super sindonem* from a Mass for the dead:

"*Maiestatem tuam, domine, supplices exoramus, ut animae famulorum famularumquae, tuarum ab omnibus quae per humanitatae conmiserunt exute, in tuorum censeantur sorte iustorum*" (V 1672)[26].

Christiana professio[27]

The verb *censere* is qualified by the phrase *christiana professione*, indicating that the faithful are reckoned according to their Christian profession. Two interconnected themes seem to be attached to this notion of profession; the baptismal profession of faith, and commitment to a way of life.

---

[25]For further examples of the use of *censere* see Deshusses, Concordances III, 1, 241.

[26]Lord, we your supplicants pray that the souls of your servants, freed from all the things which they incurred on account of their humanity, may be counted among the company of your righteous.
See also L 1248 and L 1154.

[27]For further examples of *professio* see Deshusses, Concordances III, 3, 496. For the phrase *christiana professio* in Gelasius' letter against the Lupercalians, see Pomarés, Gélase, 186.

Pomarés claims that *christiana professio*, when found in Gelasius' anti-Lupercalian letter and Masses, refers to the profession of baptismal faith[28]. The opening clauses from L 623, a preface from one of his anti-Lupercalian Masses, appears to bear this out. The text reads:

"*Uere dignum: suppliciter exorantes, ut omnis a nostro discedat corde profanitas, et quod professione respuimus, actione uitemus: quia nimis est exsecrandum, ut cum uanae superstitionis ipsos quoque remoueris sectatores, a fidelibus tuis diabolica figmenta tractentur ...*" (L 623)[29].

It would seem that the renunciation of Satan, conjoined with the profession of faith is in mind, since that is the specific act of rejection preliminary to the profession of faith. Pomarés himself translates *professio* as 'Christian profession' (*profession chrétienne*)[30]. Note also that profession involves commitment to a way of life. In parallel to the collect being studied, what is rejected (*respuere*) by profession is to be avoided in action.

Capelle argues for extending the meaning of *censere* in L 75 beyond this sense. Because the verb is used in the passive and followed by an ablative, he understands it to include the idea of being 'judged by', in this case by Christian profession[31].

---

[28] Pomarés, Gélase, 192-193, fn 3.

[29] It is right and fitting to praise you: We humbly ask that all profanity leave from our hearts, and that we may avoid in practice what we shun in our profession. This is because it is an exceedingly detestable thing that, when you have displaced the followers of empty superstitions, the pagan celebrations are taken up by your own faithful ...

[30] Pomarés, Gélase, 228.

[31] Capelle, "Messes du Pape S. Gélase," Revue bénédictine 56 (1945-46): 19,32.

Nomen[32]

Nomen refers to the appellation Christian. The concept of *nomen* has been studied as part of the analysis of the collect for Sunday XII. It is seen there that *nomen* denotes the essence or being of a person or thing. Collect L 75 appears to be the only instance in the early orations and in Gelasius' letter against the Lupercalians where *nomen* is linked with *christiana*. The early orations, however, contain many examples of a parallel form, *Romanum nomen*[33]. Moreover, both the phrases *nomine censeri*[34] and *christianum nomen*[35] are found in other works by Gelasius, as well as in writings he is said to have drafted.[36] In L 75, the *nomen* 'Christian' points to the essence of Christian profession, both in terms of baptism and commitment of a way of life.

---

[32]For examples of the use of *nomen* see Deshusses, Concordances, III, 3, 167-175.

[33]See, among others, L 480 and L 1128.

[34]"*Johannes archdiaconus Falerionensis urbis eversionem ecclesiae ab eo, qui praesulis nomine censetur, effectam grandi nobis supplicatione conquestus est ...*". (Trans.: John, the Archdeacon of the city of Faleriae, has complained to us with great supplication following his eviction from the church, where he is reckoned as its leader.)
This example is from Fragment 22 of the *Epistolarum Fragmenta* of Pope Gelasius, published in A.Thiel, Epistolae Romanorum Pontificum Genuinae, vol. 1 (Brunsbergae: Eduardi Peter, 1868), 496.

[35]"*Quae modis omnibus est amovenda pernicies, ne per Christiani nominis institutum aut aliena pervadi, aut publica videatur disciplina subverti ....*"
(Trans.: That evil ought be done away with using every means, lest, through the institution of the Christian name, either a foreign discipline may appear to have pervaded, or the public discipline may appear to be subverted.)
This example is from *Epistola* 14:14 of Pope Gelasius. See Thiel, Epistolae Romanorum Pontificum Genuinae, 370.

[36]Capelle lists a selection of examples for both phrases. See Capelle, "Messes du Pape S. Gélase," Revue bénédictine 56 (1945-46): 19.

The petition asks that those who have professed Christian faith be given the graces both to reject what is inimical to the name Christian, and to follow what is appropriate to it.

Inimica respuere ... apta sectari

The context of the prayer and the above analyses demarcate what is appropriate from what is hostile to Christian commitment. The inimical represents a choice in will and action away from God's path and from participation in the church. It marks a preference for falsehood, darkness and perpetual death over God's truth and eternal life. Joining in pagan practices, immorality, heresy, schism, disobedience all oppose Christian commitment and lead away from truth. On the other hand, things that are appropriate to the name Christian are characterized by love, goodness, righteousness and truth. They are in harmony with God's mandates.

The prayer sets *respuere* and *sectari* in an *et .. et* construction. For those who wish to live in truth, there can be no tolerance of deceit and sin, nor any reluctance to carry out what is fitting.

The petiton *da cunctis qui christiana professione censentur, et illa respuere qui huic inimica sunt nomini et ea quae sunt apta sectari* is a reminder that while believers enter God's paths through their profession of faith, they only remain in the light through their loving adherence to truth. This obedience is itself a gift from God. It involves both discerning and following what is appropriate and spurning what is seen to lead away from truth. The faithful are confident in their petition because of their conviction that God offers the light of truth to all. This grounds their hope that all who already profess the way of Christ will be given the grace to remain in truth.

Meaning of the prayer:

The meaning of the prayer rests in the petition that those who have made Christian profession may be kept from following errant ways. Their

Christian profession is a public reckoning by which they reject their former straying from God's way, acknowledge his truth, and are now known by the name 'Christian'. This name, however, must not only be professed but necessarily lived out appropriately. What is inimical to it must be shunned, and what is appropriate to it must be carried out. The confidence of the baptized that God will grant their petition stems from their faith that he constantly works to enable those who stray to return to the truth.

The historical and liturgical contexts of the prayer bear this out. Gelasius, the probable author, was engaged in a polemic with Christians who publicly defended and participated in the festival of the Lupercalia. He notes with abhorrence that even though God had brought pagan Rome from its errant ways to the true path, those who now bear the name Christian were intent on taking up the pagan celebrations (L 623). For Gelasius, Christian profession involves the renunciation of sacrilegious beliefs (the power of the ancestors to bring salvation) and practices. This is lived out both through rejecting festivals and rites that are contrary to baptismal commitment and by doing what is appropriate.

The liturgical context of the prayer as a collect in Easter offers the possibilitiy of a different perspective. The invocation of God's universal salvific will echoes the paschal mystery being celebrated. The image of light recalls the splendour of the resurrection through which the darkness is illuminated by the truth of Christ. It recalls Christ's triumph over all that leads to darkness, sin and perpetual death. The *christiana professio* is a reminder of the Easter baptism of the neophytes, and indeed of the baptism of all the members of the community. The petition corresponds to the guidance and strength that the newly baptized will need to live out their new commitment.

ANALYSIS OF THE WORDS AND PHRASES OF THE COLLECT IN THEIR CONTEXT IN THE MISSAL OF PAUL VI

Vocabulary and meaning of the prayer:

The scope of the adjective *christianus* is extended in the Missal of Paul VI to all Christian churches. The *super oblata* of a Mass for Christian Unity confirms that Christians are already united in their common baptism[37]. The post communion of that same Mass associates the clause *omnes qui christiano gloriantur nomine* with all baptized Christians, regardless of their particular ecclesial affiliation[38].

RELATIONSHIP OF THE CHRISTIAN PEOPLE TO GOD

God is the way, truth and light of the Christian people in their life on earth. While the faithful's profession of God's name, however, is marked by their wandering from his paths, God continuously works to bring all who stray back to his truth. Foundational in the Christian relationship to God is that God does not abandon anyone who strays from God's path.

---

[37]"*Quam tibi, Domine, offerimus hostiam et purificationem conferat, et omnes uno baptismate coniunctos eorundem mysteriorum tandem participes efficiat*" (MR(1975) Pro unitate christianorum, C, Super oblata, 812), (Trans: Lord, may the offering which we offer to you both confer purification, and make all who have been joined in one baptism at length to be sharers of these same mysteries.)
For the appearance of *baptisma* in the Missal of Paul VI, where it is used 35 times, see Schnitker and Slaby, Concordantia, 179-180.

[38]The prayer reads: "*Sacramenta Christi tui sumentes, quaesumus, Domine, ut in Ecclesia tua sanctificationis gratiam renoves quam dedisti, et omnes qui christiano gloriantur nomine in unitate fidei tibi servire mereantur*" (MR(1975) Pro unitate christianorum, C, Post comm., 813), (Trans: On receiving the sacraments of your Christ, Lord, we ask that you renew in your church the grace of sanctification which you gave, and that all who glory in the name Christian may merit to serve you in unity of faith.)

The prayer raises two aspects concerning the profession of the name Christian. Firstly it refers back to baptism as that public moment of confession through which one is accounted a member of the church. Secondly, the collect makes it clear that the baptismal profession of faith has implications for the behaviour of the believer. Bearing the appellation Christian implies both doing what is appropriate to that name, and rejecting what is inimical to it.

As the prayer stands in the Missal of Paul VI, it carries a significant ecumenical dimension. By praying for all who profess the name Christian, the collect links the local community gathered in the eucharist with the whole body of Christian believers. The oration envisions the Christian people as all those who have undertaken baptism, and who profess it with congruent behaviour.

FREER TRANSLATION OF THE COLLECT

Deus, qui errantibus, ut in viam possint redire, veritatis tuae lumen ostendis, da cunctis qui christiana professione censentur, et illa respuere, quae huic inimica sunt nomini, et ea quae sunt apta sectari.

God, you show the light of your truth to whoever strays from your path so that they might return. Give to all who confess their baptism in Christ, both to despise what is inimical to the name they profess and to carry out whatever is fitting to it.

COLLECT FOR SUNDAY XXI

PRAYER

Deus, qui fidelium mentes unius efficis voluntatis, da populis tuis id amare quod praecipis, id desiderare quod promittis, ut, inter mundanas varietates, ibi nostra fixa sint corda, ubi vera sunt gaudia.

God, who makes the minds of the faithful to be of one will, give to your people to love what you command, and desire what you promise, so that, amidst the inconstancy of the world, there our hearts may be fixed where there are true joys.

USE IN THE MISSAL OF PAUL VI

This collect for the Mass of Sunday XXI in Ordinary Time is also the opening prayer for the Mass of Tuesday, Week V in the season of Easter[1].

ORIGINAL SOURCE

Reginensis 316: Collect for the Mass I,lviiii, Tertia Dominica post clausum Paschae (V 551). The only change from the original collect is the correction of *uoluntati* to *voluntatis*.

USE IN OTHER LITURGICAL SOURCES

As noted by Bruylants[2], the collect is used in these sources: Dominica IV Post Pascha: Pr(114,1), A(922), S(726), P(411), *OR*(167)[Sp 1120], X(113,1), N(124), Q(126v), 1474(228), 1570, 1604, and in these

---

[1]MR(1975): Fer II post domm. III et V Paschae, Collecta hebd., V, 325.

[2]Bruylants, II, 342. For a more complete listing of sources and manuscripts see Moeller, Corpus Orationum II D Orationes 881-1707, oration 1633, 338.

uncritical editions G(129,1)[G 925], Z(554), FrSal 3(23,1).

The prayer has been very rarely used outside Easter. It appears in a *Missa in venerationem unius apostolis*, (GregorTc 1956), and has been incorporated into preface A 1250 for hebdomada XIIII post Pentecosten.

ANALYSIS OF THE PRAYER IN THE ORIGINAL SOURCE

Origin:

The collect served as the opening prayer of a Mass for the fifth Sunday in Easter. This Mass is identified by Chavasse[3] as one of a cohesive layer of texts placed as a whole in *Reginensis* 316. Since its inclusion in *Reginensis* 316, the collect has been used, with very few exceptions, in Masses for the Easter season

Grammatical structure:[4]

The prayer consists of three parts, (a) an address to God with motivating clause, (b) a set of petitions, and (c) a purpose clause within the petition.

(a) Address: *Deus,*
    Motivation: *qui fidelium mentes unius efficis voluntatis,*

(b) Petitions: *da populis tuis*
    id amare quod praecipis
    id desiderare quod promittis,

(c) Purpose: *ut, inter mundanas varietates,*
    ibi nostra fixa sint corda,
    ubi vera sunt gaudia.

---

[3]Chavasse, Le Sacramentaire Gélasien, 241-44.

[4]See Haessly, Rhetoric in the Sunday Collects of the Roman Missal, 65-68.

The structure of the prayer works to bring out the meaning of the collect. In this section, the following features will be commented on: the *ibi ... ubi* construction, the parallel between *amare* and *desiderare*, the relationship between heart (*cor*), mind (*mens*) and will (*voluntas*), and the parallel between the motivating clause and the purpose clause.

The purpose clause is built around an *ibi ... ubi* construction. This is very rare in the liturgical sources[5]. The construction parallels Jesus' teaching, as set out in both Matthew and Luke, that where one's treasure is, there one's heart is to be found:

"*Thesaurizate autem vobis thesauros in caelo, ubi neque aerugo neque tinea demolitur, et ubi fures non effodiunt nec furanter. Ubi enim es thesaurus tuus, ibi est et cor tuum*" (Mt 6:20-21)[6]. In Matthew, the context suggests that true treasure accrues when Christians carry out good works (almsgiving, prayer, fasting) for God's glory (they are done in secret) rather than for human praise. Luke's account has a more direct anti-wealth thrust. Material possessions ought be sold for the sake of the needy, because riches seduce the heart from God's riches. For both Gospels, human treasures, whether human praise or material wealth, are illusory. They do not last. Only heavenly treasures are lasting. Both Gospels draw the same conclusion. Those whose hearts are set on passing worldly treasures do not have their hearts set on God and his lasting treasures. It is the desire of the heart, not actions, appearances or wealth, that is central to attaining eternal treasures.

The purpose clause of the collect is built around this saying. The lasting true joys of heaven (*vera gaudia*) are in contrast to the vicissitudes and changing circumstances of living in the world (*mundanae varietates*). As in

---

[5]For two less crisp examples in the Gallican influenced sources see G 2406 and G 2097.

[6]See also Lc 12:33-34.

the Gospel pericopes, the attitude of the heart is the primary concern of the prayer. However, the collect substitutes joy (*gaudium*) for the Gospel emphasis on treasure. The grace to fix one's heart on the true joys amidst the inconstancy of the world is the subject of the collect's petition.

The petition consists of two *id ... quod* clauses, set in tandem:

    id amare   *quod praecipis*
    id desiderare   *quod promittis*.

Relating this double petition to the purpose clause, the faithful seek that their hearts and wills may be fixed on the divine precepts and promises. These correspond to true joys, and are in contrast to the *mundanae varietates*. It is love of God's commands and desire for God's promises that gives stability in the midst of the changing realities of the world.

The pairing of *amare* and *desiderare* brings together heart and will. The faithful wish to love the precepts and to long for the promises with an ardent will. It should be noted here that in the liturgical sources the nouns 'heart' and 'mind' are interrelated. While *mens*[7] highlights reflection and decision, and *cor*[8] affection and desire, both terms are used to denote the inner self of the believer. The combination of *amare* (heart) and *desiderare* (will), and their implicit relationship to 'mind', serve to bring out the parallel between the collect's invocation of God and its purpose clause.

The invocation puts forth the faith of the community in God's power to unite the minds of the faithful in one will. The purpose clause has as its concern hearts fixed on true joys. Set in parallel, the minds (and hearts) of

---

[7]*Mens* has been discussed in the study of the collect for Sunday IV. See above 105.

[8]*Cor* has been discussed in the study of the collect for Sunday XXIV. See above 214.

Christians are of one will when their hearts (and minds) are set on true joys. The sense of the prayer follows from this.

Motivated by the fact that God is the one who unites the minds of the faithful into one will, the community asks for the gifts that will enable them to set their hearts on true joys. True joys on earth are found in God's commands and promises. Consequently they ask that they may love what God commands and ardently long for what he promises.

From this analysis it can already be seen that the unity of will amongst the faithful is one of love, expressed through love of the precepts, desire for the promises, and hearts set on true joys. This is what gives constancy and security to Christian people among the changing things of the world.

Vocabulary:

The sense of the prayer can be found mainly through the analysis of its structure. In view of this, the vocabulary study will concentrate on using the scriptures and liturgical sources to bring out the further nuances and relationships that the words and phrases carry.

Prominent vocabulary: *voluntas, praecipere, desiderare, promittere, varietas, mundanus, gaudium*.

Our study begins by examining the unity of will put forward in the motivating clause *qui fidelium mentes unius efficis voluntatis*.

Unius voluntatis

Unity of will signifies pursuit of a common end, whether good or bad. An Advent postcommunion prayer is also concerned with unity of will amongst the Christian family. The prayer's petition for a common will in Christ is linked with the performance of good works (*opera iusta*) and the common entry into God's kingdom:

"*Da, quaesumus, omnipotens deus, cunctae familiae tuae hanc uoluntatem in Christo filio tuo domino nostro uenienti in operibus iustis aptos occurrere, et*

[*ut*] *eius dexterae sociati regnum mereantur possidere caelesti"* (V 1139)[9].

In V 551, the community of the faithful in one will is related to the love of God's precepts and the desire for his promises. They are united in the pursuit of this one purpose.

Id amare[10] *quod praecipis, id desiderare quod promittis*

Things associated in this set of petitions are found in a number of other prayers: the parallel between *amare* and *desiderare*, the relationship between the precepts and the promises, and love for the precepts. These will be explored following some initial comment on the verbs *praecipere*[11], *desiderare*[12] and *promittere*[13].

As seen in the study of the collect for Sunday XXV, all God's precepts (*quod praecipis*) are themselves ordained towards love and worship of God, and love of neighbour. It is most appropriate that the precepts themselves be loved, since they direct the faithful towards love by doing God's bidding. The verb *desiderare* evokes the scriptural longing of the human heart for God and the things of God (Ps 41:2, Ps 118:20,131). God's promise (*quod promittis*) is

---

[9]All powerful God, grant to your family this will in Christ your son our Lord who is to come, that, made worthy by good works, they may run to meet him, so that, united at his right hand, they may merit to possess the kingdom of heaven.

[10]The verb *amare* is discussed in the study of the collect for Sunday XII. See below, 320.

[11]The divine precepts have been analysed as part of the study of the collect for Sunday XXV. See above 140.

[12]For further examples of *desiderare* see Deshusses, Concordances III, 1, 444-445. The collect under analysis appears to be the only example where the desire of the faithful is linked directly to what God has promised.

[13]For further examples of *promittere* see Deshusses, Concordances III, 3, 504.

principally eternal beatitude in heaven[14].

Amare ... desiderare: A prayer for travellers also conjoins love (*diligere*) of what the divine law commands and desire (*desiderare*) for where it leads. Living a blameless life (*via inmaculatorum*) is equated with love for the precepts and desire for their goal. The precepts lead to the beatitude that comes from God:

"*Deus, vere beatitudinis auctor atque largitor, dirige nos in eam quam inmaculati ambulant uiam, ut testimonia legis tuae piis cordibus exquirentes perseueremus et diligere quod praecipiunt, et desiderare quo ducunt*" (V 1321)[15].

Praecipere ... promittere: Receiving the divine promises follows upon obedience to God's commands:

"*Proficiat, quaesumus, domine, fidelis populus tuae pietatis instinctu, et salubri conpunctione deuotus, gratanter quae praecipis exsequatur, ut quae promittis accipiat*" (L 1122)[16].

The obedience that brings entry to the promises entails love of what God commands:

"*Omnipotens sempiterne Deus, da nobis fidei spei et caritatis aumentum; et ut mereamur adsequi quod promittis, fac nos amare quod praecipis*" (L 598)[17].

---

[14]See Blaise, Vocabulaire, § 303 and § 44.

[15]God, author and bestower of true beatitude, direct us in that path which the blameless walk, so that, diligently scrutinizing the commandments of your law with devout hearts, we may continue steadfastly both to love what they command and to desire where they lead.

[16]Lord, may your faithful people go forth under the impulse of their love for you, and devout in their salutary remorse, may they more thankfully follow what you command, so that they may receive what you promise.

[17]"Almighty eternal God, give us an increase in faith, hope and charity, and so that we may merit to reach what you promise, make us love what you

In summary, while noting the relationship between God's precepts and his promises, the focus of the petitions falls on the attitude of the faithful towards them. From the structure of the collect, it appears that true joy embraces both promises and precepts. In asking for the gift to love the precepts and to desire the promises to which they lead, the baptized seek to set their hearts and minds on what are both true and joyful. The unity of the faithful in one will flows from such an orientation of the hearts of believers. It leads to the true joys, which are eternal, beyond the vicissitudes of this world.

The petition for the twofold gift of love of the precepts and desire of the promises is entirely fitting. The precepts themselves are ordained to love and worship of God and neighbour. The divine promises, attained through the love exemplified in the precepts, are fulfilled in eternal life in the God who is love. Already, the faithful have their hearts fixed on true joys.

Inter mundanas varietates

The phrase *inter mundanas varietates* describes the context in which the Christian people live their earthly life. The inconstancy and change found on earth of itself is not conducive to unity of will among the faithful nor to their apprehension of true joys.

Varietates[18]

The Letter of James contrasts what is unchanging with what is subject to change. The unchanging God (*non datur transmutatio*) is the source of only what is good and perfect. Both *transmutatio* and *vicissitudo* mean change. They are used to denote the mutability of all created things, even the heavenly

---

command."
This prayer is also found in the Missal of Paul VI: MR(1975) Dom. XXX per annum, Collecta, 365.

[18]For further examples of the use of *varietas* see Deshusses, Concordances, III, 4, 421.

lights (*lumina*). By implication, what is subject to change is open to evil. The connection with our prayer is twofold. Firstly, the *vicissitudinis obumbratio* is similar to the *mundana varietas*. Secondly, only God, the unchanging source of all that is good, is the guarantor of true joys[19]:

"*Omne datum optimum et omne donum perfectum desursum est, descendens a Patre luminum apud quem non est transmutatio nec vicissitudinis obumbratio. Voluntarie enim genuit nos verbo veritatis, ut simus initium aliquod creaturae eius*" (Jc 1:17-18).

In a prayer for travellers, *varietas* refers to the changes and inconstancy that occur in life on earth. The premise of the prayer is that earthly vicissitudes may be offset by divine help and protection:

"*Adesto, domine, subplicationibus nostris et uiam famuli tui illius in salutis tuae prosperitatis dispone, ut inter omnes uitae huius uarietatis tuo semper protegatur auxilio*" (V 1314)[20].

Mundanas[21]

The changeableness of earthly things (*res mundanae*) is in contrast to the perpetual nature (*perpetua*) and goodness of the things that come from God. This is seen in a collect from a Mass in the December fast. Note that God provides fitting things (*aptanda*), and in particular the *devotio* of the fast, which lead the faithful through the world's inconstancy towards the unchanging

---

[19]For critical commentary see M.Dibelius, James: A Critical Commentary on the Epistle of James, Hermeneia, ed. H.Koester, translated by Michael A. Williams from Brief des Jakobus, Göttingen: Vandenhoeck & Ruprecht, 1964, 11th revised edition prepared by H.Greeven (Philadelphia: Fortress Press, 1976), 100-103.

[20]Hear our supplications, Lord, and arrange the path of your servant ___ in the richness of your salvation, so that amidst the changes of this life he may always be protected by your help.

[21]For further examples of the use of *mundanus* see Deshusses, Concordances, III, 3, 120.

good things:

"*Deus, qui singulis quibusque conpetenter aptanda temporibus sempiterno cernis intuitu: da nobis, quaesumus, ut cum rerum uicissitudine mundanarum ad bona quoque perpetua piae deuotionis crescamus accessu*" (L 1294)[22].

The other prayers of this Mass (LXIII), particularly the preface (L 1297) and the *super populum* (L 1299), also contrast earthly change and eternal joy. In parallel with L 1294, they express the belief that God provides support on earth which brings the faithful to the unchanging and eternal[23].

The phrase *inter mundanas varietates* connotes the changeability and inconstancy of life on earth. This mutability is in contrast to the stability and eternity of life in God. In the midst of the vicissitudes of earthly life, the faithful ask to have a heart and mind fixed on true joys through the gift of love of God's precepts and desire for his promises.

While not invoked specifically in this prayer, the adjective *mundanus* and the noun *mundus* also can carry a pejorative sense[24]. In biblical (Vulgate) and liturgical sources they can signify the desire for what is false, sinful and earthly over what is true, good and divine. This further sense gives more weight to the need for the faithful to fix their hearts on true joys.

---

[22]God, who in your eternal provision discern what is appropriate to each and every age, grant us, we beseech you, that despite the change of earthly things we may grow toward the attainment of unending good by an increase in loving devotion.

[23]The preface L 1297 emphasises communion: "*et per eum ciuum ... perueniamus ad uictum sine fine mansurum.*" The *super populum* (L 1299) reads: "*ut transeuntium rerum necessaria consolatione foveat, et fiducialius ad aeterna contendat.*"

[24]See Blaise, Vocabulaire, § 502.

Vera gaudia[25]

From the structure of the prayer we have seen that true joy is assured to those who love what God commands and desire what he promises.

The following prayer over the gifts contrasts the notion of false joys, which it relates to the contagion of sin, with eternal life, which is the fruit of God's promises. Joy embraces the precepts as well as the promises. True joy is to love God's commands (*veritas*) rather than to follow other ways to pleasure (*falsa gaudia*):

"*Ut tibi grata sint, domine, munera populi tui, ab omni, quaesumus, eum contagio peruersitatis emunda; nec falsis gaudiis inherere patiaris, quos ad ueritatis tuae praemia uenire promittis*" (L 517)[26].

The preface (L 518) of the same Mass (XVIII)[27] connects false joys with the deceit of the devil (*diabolica simulatio*).

In V 551, the qualification of *gaudium* with *verum* serves to bring out the changeableness of the world. As well, it relates the divine precepts and the promises to the truth of God's teaching. This provides the faithful with further grounds for loving and desiring them.

---

[25] For further examples of *gaudium* see Deshusses, Concordances, III, 2, 197-200. This seems to be the only example of *verum gaudium*. The more particular use of *gaudium* to describe eternal life has been analysed in the study of the collect for Sunday XIV. See above 246.

[26] "Cleanse the gifts of your people from all contagion of perversity Lord, so that they may be pleasing to you. May you not allow to cling to false joys those whom you promise to come to the rewards of your truth."
This prayer is also found in the Missal of Paul VI: MR(1975) Fer. V hebd. III Quadr., Super oblata, 205.

[27] According to Pomarès this Mass is from the pen of Pope Gelasius, written following the celebration of the festival of the Lupercalia. In light of this, the *falsa gaudia* indicate rejoicing in teachings which are counter to the faith, as well as the moral depravity that the festivities entailed. See Pomarès, Gelasius, 108-110.

Meaning of the prayer:

Motivated by the fact that God is the one who unites into one will the minds of the faithful, the community asks for the gifts that will enable them to set their hearts on true joys. True joys are found in God's commands and promises. Consequently believers ask that they may love what God commands and ardently long for what he promises. When the hearts of the faithful love these true joys, then their minds are united in one will.

This meaning of the prayer is carried into the Missal of Paul VI unaltered.

RELATIONSHIP OF THE CHRISTIAN PEOPLE TO GOD

The relationship of the Christian people to God is lived out in a world in which change and vicissitude are constants. Amidst this unstable and transitory environment the community is united in one will when their hearts and minds love what God commands and desire what he promises. Through this love and desire, the hearts of the faithful are fixed on true joys, and the community is one in God and one in what it pursues. This gives the community stability and direction in the midst of constant change.

Love of the precepts and desire for the promises is an entirely fitting response to God's own love for the faithful, which is evidenced in his precepts, promises and the unity of the community. The precepts are ordained towards love of God and neighbour, while the promises denote complete fellowship with the God who is love. Despite the inconstancy of life on earth, love of the precepts and desire for the promises already offers a foretaste, albeit transitory, of the joys and unity of heaven.

FREER TRANSLATION OF THE COLLECT

Deus, qui fidelium mentes unius efficis voluntatis, da populis tuis id amare quod praecipis, id desiderare quod promittis, ut, inter mundanas varietates, ibi nostra fixa sint corda, ubi vera sunt gaudia.

God, you form the minds of the faithful into a single will. Grant that we may love your precepts and long for your promises, so that depite living amidst the inconstancies of the world, our hearts may be fixed where your true joys are to be found.

COLLECT FOR SUNDAY X

PRAYER

Deus, a quo bona cuncta procedunt, tuis largire supplicibus, ut cogitemus, te inspirante, quae recta sunt; et, te gubernante, eadem faciamus.

God, from whom all good things come, bestow upon your supplicants, that by your inspiration we may be concerned with right things, and by your guidance do them.

ORIGINAL SOURCE

Reginensis 316: A collect for the Mass Quarta Dominica Post Clausum Paschae, Book I,lx (V 556).

In the only change from the original, *tuis largire supplicibus* has replaced *largire supplicibus*, a modification already present in the Missal of Pius V. As the *tui supplices*, the believers know they belong to God, and so may be confident of receiving good things from him. In light of the scriptures, they should be even more confident in entreating God since he gives every good gift to his faithful (Mt 7:7-11).

USE IN OTHER LITURGICAL SOURCES

As noted by Bruylants[1], the prayer has been used as a collect for the Easter season in these sources:
Dominica V post Pascha: Pr (117,1), A (944), S(748), P(424), *OR*(167)[Sp 1123], X(114,1), N(125), Q(127), 1474(229), 1570, 1604, as well as in the uncritical editions: G(134,1)[G 949], Z(568),
In Vigilia Ascensionis: Q(128:rubr.) 1474(232), 1570, 1604.

---

[1]Bruylants II, 129. For a more detailed listing of sources and manuscripts, see Moeller, <u>Corpus Orationum</u> II D, Orationes 881-1707, oration 1085, 109.

In two manuscripts the prayer is used in a Mass outside the Easter season: *Alia oratio cottidiana*: Ménard 199 B, Ratisb 2490.
It also is found as a prayer for laudes: *Feria IV in L.mo, oratio in laud.*, Bergom 1558.

ANALYSIS OF THE PRAYER IN THE ORIGINAL SOURCE

Origin:

According to Chavasse[2], this Mass is one of a pre-existing group of six Masses for the Sundays after Easter, which were later incorporated as a group into *Reginensis* 316. Chavasse argues from a correspondence between the Masses and the Epistle and Gospel readings for the Sundays after Easter current in Rome before the end of the sixth century that the Masses can be dated to that period or later. There is a resonance of the proposed Epistle in the collect. The prayer invokes God as the one from whom good things come, while the Epistle describes God as the unchangeable source of all that is good and perfect, and of only what is good and perfect (Jc 1:17)[3].

Grammatical structure:[4]

The prayer consists of (a) an address and motivating clause, and (b) a twofold petition. The petition is made on the grounds that good things proceed from God.

---

[2]Chavasse, Le Sacramentaire Gélasien, 241-44.

[3]"*Omne datum optimum et omne donum perfectum desursum est, descendens a Patre luminum apud quem non est transmutatio nec vicissitudinis obumbratio*" (Jc 1:17). This text has also been discussed in the study of the collect for Sunday XXI. See above 348.

[4]For a more complete analysis of the grammatical structure of the prayer see Haessly, Rhetoric in the Sunday Collects of the Roman Missal, 68-69.

(a) Address: *Deus*
    Motivation: *a quo bona cuncta procedunt*

(b) Petition: *tuis largire supplicibus*
                 ut cogitemus, te inspirante, quae recta sunt
                 et, te gubernante, eadem faciamus.

The two petitions are set in parallel, an arrangement which serves to emphasize various aspects of the prayer. Firstly, knowing what is upright implies doing that same thing. Secondly, God's grace accompanies every upright human action.

Christian's action	God's action	object
cogitemus	*te inspirante*	*quae recta sunt*
faciamus	*te gubernante*	*eadem.*

Thirdly, the structure of the petition further emphasises the need for God's grace. While human actions frame the opening (*cogitare*) and closing (*facere*) of the clause, the centre of the petition is taken up with God's works and design: *inspirare, recta, gubernare*.

A fourth point is that the sequence of the petition reflects the movement, on both the divine and human planes, from initiating an action to completing it:

God's inspiring	leads to	God's governing:
thinking what is right	is brought to completion by	correspondingly doing that same thing.

Doing what is right under God's guidance is the endpoint of a process that commences with thinking what is right under God's inspiration.

There is a further parallel between *bona* and *recta*. The upright things (*recta*) carried out in thought and deed under God's inspiring and governing correspond to the good things (*bona*) which proceed from God. Just as God brings forth what is good, the faithful, under God's inspiration and governance, can bring forth what is upright.

Vocabulary:

Prominent vocabulary: *bonus, procedere, largire, supplex, rectus, cogitare, inspirare,* and *gubernare.*

Our study opens with a discussion of the collect's motivating clause *a quo bona cuncta procedunt.* The clause connotes God's original act of creation, the goodness that continues to flow from him, and his work of salvation.

Bona cuncta

It is clear from the first creation narrative in Genesis (Gn 1) that everything that came forth from God's initial act of creation is good[5]. The proposed reading for the Mass further declares that everything that is good and perfect, and only what is good and perfect, comes from God (Jc 1:17)[6].

Procedunt[7]

The verb *procedere* connotes both the goodness and salvific nature of what comes forth from God. In the New Testament *procedere* is associated with the divine teaching that gives life (Mt 4:4), and the salvific sending of Christ (Jo 8:42)[8] and the Holy Spirit (Jo 15:26)[9].

---

[5] "*Viditque Deus cuncta quae fecerat, et erant valde bona*" (Gn 1:31).

[6] The collect for Sunday XXII contains a similar motivating clause: "*Deus virtutum, cuius est totum quod est optimum ...*" See also L 881, L 1146, and Blaise, Vocabulaire, § 147.

[7] For further examples of the use of *procedere* see Deshusses, Concordances III, 3, 491-492.

[8] "*... ego enim ex Deo processi et veni; neque enim a meipso veni, sed ille me misit*" (Jo 8:42).
There is some slight correspondence between the notion of Jesus proceeding

In Collect V 556, the invocation suggests the entire work of creation, salvation and ongoing preservation. The substantive *bona* has the sense of the goodness of the original creation and the goodness of all present things. The verb *procedere* has the further sense of God sending forth not only created things, but salvation through divine teaching, Christ and the Holy Spirit. The community makes its petition confident that God, on account of his works of creation, salvation and continuous help, will respond to their prayer. Their request is marked with due humility (*supplices*) in the face of such unmitigated goodness.

The collect's petition uniquely combines two constructions that are found independently in a number of early orations. One is the conjunction of thought (*cogitare*) and action (*facere*) in doing what is good and upright. Since this sets forth the actual petition it will be examined first. The second is the relationship between God's inspiring (*inspirare*) and governing (*gubernare*).

Cogitemus ... quae recta sunt ... eadem faciamus
Cogitemus[10] *... faciamus*

A number of prayers in the liturgical sources focus on the unity of thought (*cogitare*) and action (*facere, agere*) in doing what is good (*bona*) or upright (*recta*). The collect L 638 closely parallels the prayer under consideration, though it is more emphatic that without God humans can do

---

from the Father and the proposed Gospel for the Mass (Jo 16:23-30) as conjectured by Chavasse. In the Gospel passage, the word used is *exire* rather than *procedere*, i.e. to go forth.

[9] "*Cum autem venerit Paraclitus, quem ego mittam vobis a Patre, Spiritum ueritatis qui a Patre procedit ...*" (Jo 15:26).

[10] For further examples of the use of *cogitare* see Deshusses, Concordances III, 1, 274.

nothing good[11]. The same can be seen in collect L 1015[12], where thinking (*cogitare*) and doing (*agere*) what is good (*bona*) corresponds to God's will.

The verb *cogitare* warrants further attention. In L 1015 it connotes not only the act of thinking but of solicitous reflection and pondering. The oration's petition calls for a spirit of reflection (*spiritus cogitandi*) that results in living according to God's ways. Much the same use of *cogitare* can be seen in Paul's discussion of the advantages of remaining unmarried in the First Letter to the Corinthians (1 Cor 7:32-34), as translated in the latin Vulgate. The text parallels solicitude about the Lord's affairs with being concerned about them (*cogitare*). The sense of the passage is not of anxiety about, but rather of giving attention to and concerning one's mind with the things of the Lord[13]. In the Vulgate the pericope reads:

"*Volo autem vos sine sollicitudine esse. Qui sine uxore est sollicitus est quae Domini sunt, quomodo placet Deo. Qui autem cum uxore est sollicitus est quae sunt mundi, quomodo placeat uxori et divisus est. Et mulier innupta et*

---

[11] "*Presta nobis, domine, quaesumus, auxilium gratiae tuae; ut sine qua nihil boni possumus, eadem largiente dignae quae tua sunt et cogitatione [cogitare] ualeamus et facere*" (Trans: Grant us Lord the help of your grace so that, through the fitting bestowal of your grace, we, who without you are able to do nothing good, may be able both to think and to do those things that are yours.)

[12] "*Largire nobis, domine, quaesumus, spiritum cogitandi quae bona sunt promptius et agendi, ut qui sine te esse non possumus, secundum te uiuere ualeamus*" (L 1015) (Trans: Grant to us, Lord, a spirit of thinking on what are good, and of eagerly doing them, so that we, who are not able to exist without you, may be able to live according to you.) See also V 1190.
This prayer is also found in the Missal of Paul VI: MR(1975) Fer. V hebd. I Quadr., Collecta, 189.

[13] For critical comment, see W.F.Orr and J.A.Walther, 1 Corinthians, The Anchor Bible (New York: Doubleday and Company Inc., 1976), 219.

virgo cogitat quae Domini sunt, ut sit sancta corpore et spiritu; quae autem nupta est cogitat quae sunt mundi, quomodo placeat viro" (1 Cor 7:32-34). In V 556 this note of solicitude is underscored in two ways. Firstly *cogitare* is related to God's inspiration, which itself carries the sense of continuing animation towards an end. Secondly there is a parallel between *cogitare* in the collect and the verb *desiderare* in the post communion (L 560) of the same Mass (I,lx): *"cogitemus ... quae recta sunt ... faciamus"* and *"desiderare quae recta sunt et desiderata percipere"*. This association of the two verbs brings out that *cogitare* denotes more than an individual act of thought. Rather it involves more complete consideration of the particular object. Our oration pairs this solicitude with action (*facere*), and associates them with upright things (*recta*).

Quae recta sunt

The notion of upright things is discussed in the analysis of the collect for Sunday VI[14], where it was seen that human actions that are upright correspond to what is righteous in God's sight. In V 556, *recta* is applied to both thorough consideration and action.

There are a number of points to note concerning the conjunction of *cogitare, facere* and *recta* in V 556. The pairing between *cogitare* and *facere* is made complete in the use of *eadem*. There ought be no inconsistency in heart, mind and will between being solicitous about what is upright and doing it. From the structure of the prayer, *recta* is set in parallel with *bona*. Christian actions in grace that are *recta* correspond with the *bona* that come from God. In this correspondence the faithful participate in the creative and salvific work of God. Just as God brings forth all good things, the faithful, too, bring forth upright things when they ponder and then do what is right. The prayer emphasises the need for God's grace. Attentive concern for what is

---

[14]See below, 330.

upright requires God's inspiring. Doing the same calls for God's governing. These two graces will now be discussed.

Te inspirante ... te gubernante

The conjunction of *inspirare* and *gubernare* serves to bring out that God's grace precedes, underlies and brings to completion all upright human actions, and in our case considering and doing what is upright. Furthermore, it implies God's ongoing commitment to what he inspires. A number of early orations set these verbs in apposition. Before studying their conjunction, there is some value in looking at both *inspirare* and *gubernare* separately.

Te inspirante[15]

The verb *inspirare* denotes God's creative inspiring and animating. It also carries the implication that God will sustain what he brings to life. This can be seen in the second Genesis creation account (Gn 2:4-24). The verb *inspirare* is used in the Vulgate bible to describe God's privileged enlivening of the first human being by the giving of his own breath (Gn 2:7)[16]. This inspiring to life is followed by his completion of creation for the sake of the first human. In light of this passage, it can be seen that what God inspires is privileged, is in line with his goodness, and is supported by his ongoing creative work.

The liturgical sources take up both the relation of God's inspiration to what is good, and God's fidelity to what he inspires. A prayer over the deceased invokes God as the one who inspires everything that is good in the human heart. The community's hope is that what God inspired in the deceased

---

[15] For further examples of the use of *inspirare* see Deshusses, Concordances III, 1, 444-445.

[16] "*Formavit igitur Dominus Deus hominem de limo terrae et inspiravit in faciem eius spiraculum vitae, et factus est homo in animam viventem*" (Gn 2:7).

while still living will be salutary after his death:

"*Deus, a quo inspiratur humanis cordibus omne quod bonum est: sicut animae famuli tui paenitentiam uelle donasti, sic indulgentiam tribue miseratus optatam*" (L 1146)[17].

A *super populum* expresses the confidence that God will provide the graces which he has inspired the faithful to request. The prayer associates this trust with God's propitiation:

"*Adsit, domine, quaesumus, propitiatio tua populo supplicanti, ut quod te inspirante fideliter expetit, tua celeri largitate percipiat*" (L 168)[18].

The verb *inspirare* is linked with the Holy Spirit in the Vulgate translation of the scriptures. The faithful can speak of God only under the inspiration of the Holy Spirit (2 Pt 1:21)[19]. The liturgical sources, however, do not seem to emphasize any direct association between the verb *inspirare* and the Holy Spirit[20].

In V 556, God's inspiring is the grace which enables the faithful to think over and ponder what is upright. The collect sets this inspiration in tandem with divine governance (*gubernare*).

---

[17]God, by whom everything that is good in the human heart is inspired: just as you gave to the soul of your servant to wish to do penance, so may you mercifully bestow the hoped for pardon.

[18]May your propitiation be present to your suppliant people Lord, so that what they petition faithfully under your inspiration, they may receive in your swift bounty.
This prayer is also found in the Missal of Paul VI: MR(1975) Specimina or. univers., temp. per annum II, or. sacerd. concl., 929.

[19]"*Non enim voluntate humana allata est aliquando prophetia, sed Spiritu sancto inspirati locuti sunt sancti Dei homines*" (2 Pt 1:21).

[20]The liturgical sources and the early Christian authors preferred to use *flare* and *flatus* when speaking of the Holy Spirit. See Blaise, Vocabulaire, § 217, fn 1.

Te gubernante

The noun *gubernator*, and the verb *gubernare* have been discussed in the analysis of the collect for Sunday XVIII[21]. Summarizing that discussion here, the verb *gubernare* is one of a number of words which denote God's continuous guidance, strengthening, protection and perfection of the church. It is both an effect and expression of the divine love in which God created all things, brought salvation from sin, and renewed the human community. Amidst the sin and temptation of life on earth, God's governance guides the life of the church, keeps it in truth and leads it to eternal life. The early Roman euchology links it with a broad range of God's actions in the life of the church, amongst which are the strengthening of the Holy Spirit (*roborare*), the sanctification of the faithful, and the gifts of good government (*moderamen*) and peace. In V 566, God's governing is sought to guide Christian actions so that the faithful may seek and do what is right (*recta*).

Inspirante ... gubernante

The relationship between God's inspiring and governing, which parallels the relationship between God's inspiring and sustaining seen in the second Genesis creation account, is found in other early orations. It is clearly seen in a blessing for consecrated virgins. There, because God inspires this good in the community, the faithful confidently petition that he will provide the means to sustain and safeguard the women being consecrated:

"... *ut uirginitatis sancte propositum, quod te inspirante suscipiunt, te gubernante custodiant*" (L 1103)[22].

---

[21]See above, 162.

[22]The complete prayer reads: "*Respice, domine, propitius super has famulas tuas, ut uirginitatis sancte propositum, quod te inspirante suscipiunt, te gubernante custodiant*" (L 1103), (Trans: Lord, watch propitiously over these your servants, so that under your governance they may keep the vow of holy virginity which they undertook through your inspiration.)

It is also found in a *super populum* for the feast of John the Baptist "... *ut ad promissiones tuas te inspirante currant, te gubernante perueniant*" (L 256)[23].

In V 556, the verbs *inspirare* and *gubernare* are paired to denote the graces the community petition to allow them to think what is right and to do it. The faithful realize that they can only think what is right if God inspires them, and that they can only do the same thing if God governs them. The oration sets this divine inspiration and governance within the broader context of the good things that come from him. God's inspiration itself underlies the formation of the first human, and the subsequent making of all creation in which humanity and created things are sustained as good. Because of this, the community is confident that whatever God inspires, he will govern to its appropriate conclusion. This conjunction of *inspirare* and *gubernare*, along with its relationship to God's creative work (*bona procedere*), mirrors the pairing of *auctor* and *gubernator* found in the collect for Sunday XVIII (L 887)[24].

Meaning of the prayer:

The meaning of the collect emerges from the twofold petition. The faithful seek that, with God's inspiration, they may think on what is upright, and with God's governance that they may do it. Considering what is upright ought to result in doing it, while God's inspiring is brought to completion in

---

[23]The complete prayer reads: "*Quos tuos effices, domine, tua pietate circumtege, et fragilibus sanctorum omnium praetende subsidia; ut ad promissiones tuas te inspirante currant, te gubernante perueniant*" (L 256), (Trans: Lord, cover with your mercy, those whom you form as your own, and extend to the weak the help of all the saints, so that under your inspiration they may run to your promises, and by your governance they may reach them.)

[24]See above, 164.

his governing. Under God's inspiring and governing, the upright actions that come from the faithful are congruent with the good things that come forth from God. In this way Christians participate in God's salvific work.

The scriptural and liturgical usage of the vocabulary enriches the meaning of the prayer. The good things that proceed (*procedere*) from God not only bespeak God as the source of creation, perfection and goodness, but also as the source of salvation. Christ, the Holy Spirit and divine teaching come forth from God to bring salvation.

God's inspiring (*inspirare*) and governing (*gubernare*) reflect this goodness and salvation. God's inspiring implies both the goodness of what he inspires and his willingness to support it as good. As such it is the basis for his governing.

RELATIONSHIP OF THE CHRISTIAN PEOPLE TO GOD

The relationship of the Christian people to God ought to be characterized by a unity of thought and deed in what is upright. Christian reflection and consideration of what is *recta* ought to lead to its being done. However, only in grace can there be this congruence between and among heart, mind, will and action. The heart and mind can only be solicitous about what is right under God's inspiration, and carry it through under his governance. Both are necessary.

When the faithful avail themselves of this grace, their thorough consideration and consequent actions are congruent with, and participate in, God's creative and salvific work. Just as all good things, and only good things, come forth from God, so too will what is upright come forth from the faithful when they both think and do what is upright.

The confidence of the faithful that their petitions for upright things are heard stems from the fact that God is the source of all that is good. Furthermore, God unceasingly continues to act (*inspirare, gubernare*) in the fallen world to ensure the goodness and uprightness of human thought and action.

In the light of the goodness that God creates and sustains, believers are both humble and suppliant (*supplices*). Because of sin they realize that nothing upright or good can come from them alone. Yet because they know that they come from God and are his people (*tui supplices*), they are confident that God will inspire and hear their prayer for what is upright.

FREER TRANSLATION OF THE COLLECT

Deus, a quo bona cuncta procedunt, tuis largire supplicibus, ut cogitemus, te inspirante, quae recta sunt; et, te gubernante, eadem faciamus.

God, from whom everything that is good comes forth, we humbly entreat you. Inspire us that we may be concerned about what is right, and guide us that we may act accordingly.

COLLECT FOR SUNDAY XXIX

PRAYER

Omnipotens sempiterne Deus, fac nos tibi semper et devotam gerere voluntatem, et maiestati tuae sincero corde servire.

All powerful, eternal God, make us always both have a will devoted to you, and to serve your majesty with sincere hearts.

ORIGINAL SOURCE

This prayer occurs in three places in *Reginensis* 316, with only slight grammatical variations:

Omnipotens sempiterne Deus, fac nos tibi semper et devotam gerere voluntatem, et maiestati tuae sencero corde servire. Per Dominum.

Collect for the Mass Quinta Dominica Post Clausum Paschae, Book I,lxi (V 561),

Super sindonem for the Mass Item Alia Missa, Book III,viiii (V 1210). The text reads *maiestatem tuam*. Note that the collect (V 1209) for this same Mass has been incorporated into the Missal of Paul VI as the collect for Sunday XXX[1].

A post communion prayer among many following the Incipit Canon Accionis, Book III, <XVII> (V 1264). The text reads *famulari* rather than *servire*.

USE IN OTHER LITURGICAL SOURCES

As noted by Bruylants[2], the prayer has also been used as a collect, a *super sindonem* and as a post communion prayer. It has been found in a

---

[1] See below, 410.

[2] Bruylants II, 762.

variety of liturgical seasons:

Dominica infra Octavam Ascensionis: S(781), P(448), OR(168)[Sp 1126], X(117,1), N(127), Q(130), 1474(235), 1570, 1604, as well as the following uncritical editions G(142,1)[G 986], Z(599), FrAug(III,1).

Dominica V post Epiphaniam: G(35,1)[G 206].

Dominica IV post clausum Paschae: G(134,1¹)[G 950].

Orationes et preces cum canone per dominicis diebus, V(III,9,2;p.229) [V 1210].

Dominica XV post Pentecosten: Pr(198,1), A(1274), G(218,2)[G 1403], Z(808), S(1133).

Postcommuniones post canonem: V(III,16;p.237) [V 1264], Pr(236,4), A(1775), Z(1097).

ANALYSIS OF THE PRAYER IN THE ORIGINAL SOURCE

Origin:

According to Chavasse[3], the Mass I,lxi is one of a pre-existing group of six Masses for the Sundays after Easter, which were later incorporated as a group into Regenensis 316. Chavasse argues from a correspondence between the Masses and the Epistle and Gospel readings for the Sundays after Easter current in Rome before the end of the sixth century that the Masses can be dated to that period or later.

Grammatical structure[4]:

The prayer is made up of (a) a simple address, acclaiming God's power and eternity, and (b) a twofold petition:

---

[3]Chavasse, Le Sacramentaire Gélasien, 241-44.

[4]For a more complete analysis see Haessly, Rhetoric in the Sunday Collects of the Roman Missal, 70-71.

(a) Address: *Omnipotens sempiterne deus*

(b) Petitions: *fac nos tibi semper
                    et devotam gerere voluntatem
                    et maiestati tuae sencero corde seruire.*

The two petitions are in parallel:

et	tibi	devotam voluntatem	gerere
et	maiestatis tuae	sincero corde	servire.

The *semper et ... et* construction emphasizes that both the gifts of a devoted will and a sincere heart are necessary, and need to be present at all times (*semper*).

The meaning of the prayer is apparent from the structure and internal logic of the petitions. Service of God's majesty with a sincere heart is a gift that can come about when the will is completely devoted to God. On the other hand, the gift of a will devoted to God is expressed in sincere service of God's majesty.

There is a contrast implied in the prayer between the power, eternity and majesty of God and the lowliness of the faithful, who respond by seeking simply to have a will devoted to God and to offer the service of a sincere heart. Even these are gifts from God (*fac nos*), of which the faithful are in constant (*semper*) need.

Vocabulary:

Prominent vocabulary: *voluntas, devotus, gerere, servire, cor, sincerus,* and *maiestas*.

Tibi devotam gerere voluntatem

The first of the collect's two petitions is that God grant his faithful a will (*voluntas*[5]) devoted to him (*tibi*). The relationship between the will and service is brought out in *super populum* V 1219. The oration contrasts *necessitas*[6] and *voluntas*. While the need (*necessitas*) of the faithful itself incites them to please God, the prayer asks that they go beyond this to willing service:

"*Da, quaesumus, domine, hanc mentem populo tuo, ut quia ad te placandum necessitate concurrit, maiestati tuae fiat etiam uoluntate deuotus*" (V 1219)[7].

The verb *concurrere* denotes the acting together of both the people's mind and will, and so recalls what is asked in Collect XXI about the unity of the will.

In qualifying the people as *devotus*[8], the collect asssociates this with *voluntas* or willing action. *Devotus* is the adjective that corresponds to the noun *devotio*[9], which itself has been analysed as part of the discussion of the collect for Sunday VIII[10]. Drawing on this study, it can be seen that a devoted will is one that is totally given over to God in a way that is characterized by an attitude of deep veneration and worship.

---

[5]The noun *voluntas* has been examined as part of the analysis of the collect for Sunday XXI. See above, 272.

[6]For examples of *necessitas* see 1 Jo 3:17 and V 411.

[7]Give to your people, Lord, this mind, that, since it strives to please you by reason of its need, the people may also be devoted to you with its will.

[8]There seem to be only two examples where *devota* is associated with *voluntas*, our collect V 561, and V 1219 used above.

[9]Blaise, Vocabulaire, § 21.

[10]See above, 189.

From its context in the prayer, the verb *gerere*[11] means to have or to bear. The faithful pray that they may have a will devoted to God. This use of *gerere* is quite unusual in the ancient liturgical sources, however it does occur in other latin writings[12].

In summary, the first petition asks that the members of the community may always have a will that is unreservedly devoted to God. With such a will their actions can be pleasing to him. This request is set in tandem with a second petition to always serve God's majesty with a sincere heart. Such service exemplifies a will devoted to God.

Maiestati tuae sencero corde servire

The verb *servire* has been studied in the analyses of the collects for Sunday XXIV (L 1045) and Sunday XXXIII (L 486)[13]. The verb is especially concerned with service as worship and the fulfillment of church offices. In the prayer being analysed, the service to God's majesty is modified by the phrase *sincero corde*.

Cor has been analysed as part of the study of the collect for Sunday XXIV[14]. Though it particulary denotes the seat of love and affection within the person, it more generally points the whole of the inner human, heart, soul and mind. In the collect, *cors* is qualified by *sincerus*.

---

[11]For further examples of the use of *gerere* see Deshusses, Concordances III, 2, 209-210.

[12]See Ellebracht, 102-103, who testifies to the rarity of this usage. She gives the further examples L 239, L 324 and L 530. See also Haessly, Rhetoric in the Sunday Collects of the Roman Missal, 143-44.

[13]See above, 212.

[14]See above, 214.

The adjective *sincerus* has been examined in the analysis of Collect VI (V 587)[15]. Summarizing that discussion here, *sincerus* denotes that disposition of the mind and heart which is willingly open and wholeheartedly devoted to what is justifying in the sight of God. It, too, is especially linked with worship. The petition directs service with a sincere heart towards God's majesty.

In the ancient liturgical sources *maiestas*[16] is a quality possessed by God alone, refering especially to his power[17]. More generally however, *maiestas tua* is used along with the personal pronouns *te* and *tibi*, and the more abstract *nomen tuum*, as a liturgical term for addressing God[18]. This usage is exemplified in collect L 1057. Note that here serving (*famulari*) God at all times parallels unceasing praise of God's majesty:

"*Protector in te sperantium deus, presta, quaesumus, ut maiestatem tuam sine cessatione laudemus; et ut tibi possimus iugiter famulari, salutem nobis tribue mentis et corporis*" (L 1057)[19].

---

[15]See below, 332.

[16]For further examples of the use of *maiestas* see Deshusses, Concordances III, 3, 11-16. For commentary on the early Christian and liturgical use of *maiestas* see C. Mohrmann, "Note sur doxa" in Études sur le latin des chrétiens, 284, and B. Botte and C. Mohrmann, "Maiestas", in L'Ordinaire de la messe: texte critique, traduction et études (Paris: Éditions du Cerf, 1953), 111-113.

[17]Ellebracht, Remarks on the Vocabulary of the Ancient Orations in the Missale Romanum, 40.

[18]See Blaise, Vocabulaire, § 22.

[19]Protector of those who hope in you, grant that we may praise your majesty unceasingly, and, so that we may be able to serve you always, grant us health in mind and body.

In V 561 *maiestas tua* and the pronoun *tibi* are in parallel. Together they set forth that God is the proper object of the devotion of the will and service from a sincere heart.

In summary, the clause *maiestati tuae sencero corde servire* is a petition for the gift of wholehearted, undivided service and worship of God in heart, mind and soul. Such service and worship can only come about when the will is devoted to God.

Meaning of the prayer:

The prayer is made up of a pair of interconnected petitions. The faithful request both that they may always have a will that is devoted to God and that they may always worship and serve God with a sincere heart. Their worship and service is truly sincere when aligned with a will that is wholly devoted to God. On the other hand, a will devoted to God finds expression in service and worship with a sincere heart. This is the proper attitude in face of the power, eternity and majesty of God. The conjunction of *voluntas* and *cor* envisions the complete person; will, heart, soul, mind and body. The service envisaged in the prayer is primarily worship.

There seem to be no significant shifts in the meaning of the prayer when it is set within the context of the Missal of Paul VI.

RELATIONSHIP OF THE CHRISTIAN PEOPLE TO GOD

Service and worship with a sincere heart is underpinned by a will that is completely devoted to God. The devotion of the will to God is expressed in sincere and heartfelt service and worship, involving heart, soul, mind and body. On the other hand, it is this devotion of will and sincerity of heart that makes service and worship pleasing to God. Yet this devotion and sincerity are themselves first gifts from God.

FREER TRANSLATION OF THE COLLECT

Omnipotens sempiterne Deus, fac nos tibi semper et devotam gerere voluntatem, et maiestati tuae sincero corde servire.

Almighty, eternal God, form our will so that we are constantly devoted to you. May we always serve and worship you with sincere hearts.

COLLECT FOR SUNDAY XI

PRAYER

Deus, in te sperantium fortitudo, invocationibus nostris adesto propitius, et, quia sine te nihil potest mortalis infirmitas, gratiae tuae praesta semper auxilium, ut, in exsequendis mandatis tuis, et voluntate tibi et actione placeamus.

God, the strength of those who hope in you, propitiously hear our invocations, and, because without you mortal weakness is able [to do] nothing, grant always the help of your grace, so that in following your commandments we may be pleasing to you both in will and in action.

ORIGINAL SOURCE

Reginensis 316: Collect for the Mass I,lxii, Sexta Dominica post clausum Paschae (V 566).

The original text stands in the Missal of Paul VI with only one modification. The clause *gratiae tuae praesta semper auxilium* has replaced the original petition *praesta auxilium gratiae tuae*. The change lends further emphasis to the continuous (*semper*) need for God's help in the face of the weakness due to subjection to death. The adverb *semper* does not seem to be present in earlier sources.

USE IN OTHER LITURGICAL SOURCES

As noted by Bruylants[1], the collect has also been used in these sources: Various Dominica post Pentecost: S(858), P(505), *OR*(168)[Sp 1129],

---

[1] Bruylants, II, 230. For a more complete listing of sources and manuscripts see Moeller, Corpus Orationum II, D, 881-1707, oration 1245, 180.

X(251,1), N(135), Q(139), 1474(254), 1570, 1604 and these unedited sources G(156,1)[G 1076], Z(655), Par(17).

The more complete list in Moeller reveals that the prayer has also been used as an offertory prayer and as a prayer for the office:

Missale dominicalis II, secreta, Bobbio 507,

Alia oratio in quadragesima ad missam sive ad vesperum, vigilias quam etiam ad matutinum, Milano 58.

ANALYSIS OF THE PRAYER IN THE ORIGINAL SOURCE

Origin:

The collect served as the opening prayer of a Mass for the seventh Sunday in Easter, one Mass in a cohesive layer of texts placed as a whole in *Reginensis* 316, and identified as such by Chavasse[2].

Grammatical structure[3]:

The prayer is made up of two sections. The first section (a) contains an address to God with motivating phrase:

(a) Address: *Deus*,
Motivation: *in te sperantium fortitudo*.

The second section (b) consists of two petitions and two clauses. The *ut* clause sets out the purpose of the petitions, while the *quia* clause establishes the necessity for making petition in the first place.

(b) Petition 1 *adesto propitius invocationibus nostris*,
Petition 2 *praesta auxilium gratiae tuae*,
Necessity: *quia sine te nihil potest mortalis infirmitas*,
Purpose: *ut in exequendis mandatis tuis et uoluntate et actione placeamus*.

---

[2]Chavasse, Le Sacramentaire Gélasien, 241-44.

[3]For a more complete analysis see Haessly, Rhetoric in the Collects of the Roman Missal, 73-75.

The *et...et* construction in the purpose clause indicates that compliance with God's mandates that is not freely willed is not acceptable to God. On the other hand, the willingness to obey is only pleasing when expressed in actual obedience.

In the face of their own weakness which leads to death, the faithful put their hope in God. They invoke him in the belief that he is the source of their strength and courage. Their petition is that their obedience be characterized by a unity of will and action in what is pleasing to God.

Vocabulary:

Prominent vocabulary: *fortitudo, sperare, invocatio, adesse, propitius, infirmitas, mortalis, exsequi, mandatum, voluntas, actio, placere* and the phrase *sine te nihil potest*.

Our study will commence with an analysis of the motivating clause, *in te sperantium fortitudo*, with its focus on God's *fortitudo*.

Fortitudo[4]

In the psalms, *fortitudo* particularly designates the powerful help, protection and guardianship God offers his people[5]. However, when ascribed to humans, *fortitudo* denotes that power in the soul which enables the person to overcome adversity[6]. The early euchology invoked God as the *fortitudo* of the faithful. The baptized, aware of their own human weakness, looked to God and the sacraments as the source of their moral strength, courage and inner

---

[4]For further examples of the use of *fortitudo* see Deshusses, Concordances III, 2, 176-77.

[5]See Blaise, Vocabulaire, § 156 & 489 footnote 1. In Ps 27:8, God is viewed as the people's strength and protector (*protector*), while in Ps 58:17, God is invoked as the strength and guardian (*susceptor*). See also Ps 60:4 and Acts 6:8.

[6]See Jb 6:11.

fortitude[7]. Analogously, God was invoked to be a source of strength and courage for leaders in times of war (V 1494, V 1498).

The collect V 1364 sheds further light on the prayer being studied. This oration links the strength God gives with his consolation[8]. Together they are related to the strengthening (*munire*) and restoration (*reparare*) of fallen human nature. In parallel with V 566, God is invoked as the source of fortitude and consolation by those (the *humiles* and the *fideles*) who approach God in recognition of their human weakness (*humana fragilitas*). Note also that God's presence and help are associated both with his propitiation and the faithful's supplication. The prayer reads:

"*Deus, humilium consolator et fidelium fortitudo, propitius esto subplicibus, ut humana fragilitas, quae per se procliuis est ad labendum, per te semper muniatur ad standum; et quae per se prona est ad offensam, per te semper reparetur ad ueniam*" (V 1364)[9].

In V 566, God is addressed as the source of courage and moral strength for those who hope in him. The faithful place their hope in God on account of the powerlessness (*sine te nihil potest*) to do good that comes from their mortal weakness (*mortalis infirmitas*). Their hope is that, in his propitiation, God will hear (*adesto*) their invocations and respond with his help. This petition, and the phrase *mortalis infirmitas*, will now be examined.

Adesto propitius inuocationibus nostris et quia sine te nihil potest mortalis infirmitas praesta auxilium gratiae tuae

---

[7]See Blaise, Vocabulaire, § 489. For specific examples see L 749, L 876.

[8]See also V 411.

[9]God, consoler of the humble and strength of the faithful, be propitious to your supplicants, so that human fragility, which of itself is inclined to falling, through you may be ever strengthened to remain upright, so that what of itself is prone to offense, through you may always be restored to pardon.

The petition *adesto invocationibus ... praesta auxilium* is similar to that found in the collect for Sunday XVIII (L 887)[10]. In both collects, God's presence is in response to the invocation of those who hope in him. It is linked with and effected through the bestowal of divine help. Our collect, however, also links God's presence and help with his propitiation[11]. This is quite common in the liturgical sources[12]. The noun *invocatio* and its cognate *invocare* are commonly found in the Vulgate translation of the scriptures[13]. God's people are frequently described as invoking God's name in prayer: *et nomen Domini invocabo* (Ps 115:13,17)[14]. The context for the hope and petition of the community is its powerlessness (*sine te nihil potest*) in the face of its *mortalis infirmitas*.

Quia sine te nihil potest

The clause *quia sine te nihil potest* evokes Jesus' discourse on the true vine in John's Gospel. The relevant verse reads:

"*Ego sum vitis, vos palmites; qui manet in me, et ego in eo, hic fert fructum multum, quia sine me nihil potestis facere*" (Jo 15:5).

From the whole passage (Jo 15:1-17) it can be seen that the faithful bring forth lasting fruit that is acceptable to God only when they act in concert

---

[10] "*Adesto, domine, famulis tuis, et opem tuam largire poscentibus ...*" See above, 154.

[11] The adverb *propitius* has already been discussed as part of the investigation of the noun *propitiatio* in the analysis of the collect for Sunday XXIV (L 1045). See above, 263. For further examples of the use of *propitius* see Deshusses, Concordances III, 3, 513-518.

[12] See L 670, V 1473.

[13] For the use of *invocatio* see Dutripon, Bibliorum Sacrorum Concordantiae, 691-692.

[14] See also Ac 2:21 and Rm 10:13.

with Jesus. Outside of him, however, they can do 'nothing' acceptable to God.

This *quia* clause has many parallels in the early orations. They all attempt to express the faithful's utter dependence on God as they attempt to do what is upright (*recta*), righteous (*iustum*) and worthy (*dignum*)[15]. The implication from the purpose clause in our collect is that the faithful, of themselves, can do nothing pleasing (*placere*) to God. This is on account of their *mortalis infirmitas*.

Mortalis infirmitas[16]

In the Vulgate translation of the Letter to the Romans, the weakness (*infirmitas*) that Christians feel (Rm 8:26) is due to the effects of sin and death that remain within them even after baptism (Rm 8:10)[17]. The early orations use *infirmitas* in a similar way to denote the inability of the faithful to carry out their duty towards God[18]. Collect V 566 further qualifies this *infirmitas* as *mortalis*, as leading to death (*mors*). This oration appears to be the only example of *mortalis infirmitas* in the early sources.

'Death' (*mors*) has been studied in the analysis of the collect for Sunday XIV (V 541)[19]. Summarizing that discussion here, human existence is subject to death because of sin. The noun *mors* and its adjective *mortalis* encompass more than physical death, referring to death as contrasted to life in God and in

---

[15]See L 566 (*recta*), L 1174 (*iustum*), and L 970 (*dignum*).

[16]For further examples of the use of *infirmitas* see Deshusses, Concordances III, 2, 355-56. For *mortalis*, III, 3, 110-111.

[17]For commentary see J.A.Fitzmyer, Romans, 517.

[18]Ellebracht, Remarks on the Vocabulary of the Ancient Orations in the Missale Romanum, 181.

[19]See above, 244.

Christ. In life on earth, 'death' is a state of profound inner wretchedness and anxiety. Ultimately it is a permanent condition from which humans are unable to extricate themselves.

At the centre of collect V 566 stands the community's admission of its own weakness, the consequence of which is wretchedness and death. In face of this, they request the grace of unity between will and action in their obedience to God's mandates.

In exequendis mandatis tuis, et voluntate tibi et actione placeamus

The divine mandates have been discussed in the analyses of the collects for Sundays IV, XXI and XXV[20]. Summarizing that discussion here, the entire content and design of the precepts is focused on love. All God's mandates are ordained towards love and worship of him and love of neighbour. Pleasing obedience (*exsequendis*) consists first and foremost in love for the commandments, a love which is duly expressed in carrying them out. Genuine obedient love of the precepts, itself a gift from God, is pleasing to him and leads to eternal life.

Our collect highlights the relationship between the love which the mandates embody, and the will and actions of the faithful. Human will and deeds are pleasing to God when they express a loving desire for God's designs, effected in acts of genuine loving obedience. Both are necessary. The more the faithful truly follow God's law, the more their minds and actions conform to God's love, and so are pleasing to him.

Preface L 566 provides a parallel with our collect. It it is clear in the preface that only God's grace can assure the necessity of will (*velle*) and deed (*agere*) in what is pleasing to God. As pleasing to God, this comprehensive obedience is salvific (*salutaria*), a sure antidote then for *mortalis infirmitas*. Note also that these graces are linked with God's propitiation:

---

[20]See especially, 102, 273 and 140.

"*Uere dignum: cuius propitiationem in hac primum parte sentimus, cum ea, quae tibi sunt placita et nobis salutaria, desideramus adpetere. Dum enim sine te nihil recti uelle possimus aut agere aut perficere, indubitanter est gratiae, quidquid conuenienter operamur*" (L 566)[21].

Meaning of the prayer:

The meaning of the collect is found in its purpose clause. The community requests the grace both to freely will what God commands and to put his mandates into effect. Only in such a conjunction of will and deed is their obedience pleasing to God. Since what is pleasing to God is also salvific, such willing and active obedience is in direct contrast to the proclivity to death which constantly weighs down the baptized.

Realizing their own powerlessness to do anything pleasing of themselves, the faithful put their hope in God. They trust that he will be the source of that courage and strength which will enable them to will and do what is acceptable, in following his commandments.

There are no significant changes to the vocabulary or to the meaning of the prayer in the Missal of Paul VI. The addition of the adverb *semper* further emphasizes the insistent tendency to death endemic in the baptized.

RELATIONSHIP OF THE CHRISTIAN PEOPLE TO GOD

Despite their membership of the body of Christ, Christians remain in a state of weakness, prone to disobedience. Any actions they take independent

---

[21] "It is right and fitting ... We feel your propitiation [God] before all else when we desire to strive for what are pleasing to you and salvific for us. Since without you we can neither will what is right, nor perform any action or bring it to completion, it is without doubt that whatever we do that is fitting comes from your grace."
See also V 439 and L 995.

of God inevitably lead them to death, to a wretched existence outside of God, grace and goodness. Acknowledging their inconstancy and feebleness, the faithful place their hope in God. They look to him as the source of their strength, courage and consolation, through which comes help, strengthening and restoration. God's commandments have their part to play in this. They direct the faithful towards authentic love of God and neighbour, guiding their wills and actions so that they may be pleasing to God.

The collect also comments on the nature of Christian obedience. It is only pleasing to God when it involves both freely willing God's precepts and putting them into effect. Such salutary compliance can only come about with God's help, which itself is given in the light of his propitiation.

FREER TRANSLATION OF THE COLLECT

Deus, in te sperantium fortitudo, invocationibus nostris adesto propitius, et, quia sine te nihil potest mortalis infirmitas, gratiae tuae praesta semper auxilium, ut, in exsequendis mandatis tuis, et voluntate tibi et actione placeamus.

God, strength of those who hope in you, attend favourably to our prayers. Send the help of your grace always, because in our weakness and subjection to death we can do nothing without you. Grant that our will and our actions may be intent on pleasing you as we live out your mandates.

COLLECT FOR SUNDAY XII

PRAYER

Sancti nominis tui, Domine, timorem pariter et amorem fac nos habere perpetuum, quia numquam tua gubernatione destituis, quos in soliditate tuae dilectionis instituis.

Lord, make us have, in equal measure, continuous fear and love of your holy name, because you never abandon in your government those whom you establish in the steadfastness of your love.

ORIGINAL SOURCE

Sanctae nominis tui, domine, timorem pariter et amorem fac nos habere perpetuum, quia nunquam tuam gubernationem distitues, quos in soliditate tuae dilectionis institues: per.

Reginensis 316: Collect for the Mass I, lxv, Orationes et Praeces Dominica Post Ascensa Domini (V 586).

Note that the *super sindonem* of this Mass (V 587) is incorporated in the Missal of Paul VI as the collect for Sunday Week VI in Ordinary Time.

USE IN OTHER LITURGICAL SOURCES

As noted by Bruylants[1], the collect is also found in these sources: Dom. infra Oct. Ssimi Corporis Christi, secunda post Pentecosten: S(870), Pr(139,1), OR(168)[Sp 1132], C(252,1), N(136), Q(139), 1474(259), 1570, 1604, and these unedited sources G(159,1)[G 1088], Z(661), Dom. post Ascensa Domini: Pr(124,1).

An eighth century (?) liturgical fragment reveals the prayer was utilized at vespers for the feast of the Ascension: A. Bannister, "Liturgical Fragments,"

---

[1]Bruylants, II, 1033. He also alludes to, but forgets to include, A 993.

The Journal of Theological Studies 9 (1908): 411[2].

CHANGES FROM THE ORIGINAL

There are a few minor grammatical corrections. *Sanctae* now reads *sancti* and *gubernationem* has been changed to *gubernatione*, as already witnessed in A 993. *Distitues* and *institues* have become *distituis* and *institiuis*, changes found in Pr(124,1), Pr(139,1) and A 993.

ANALYSIS OF THE PRAYER IN THE ORIGINAL SOURCE

Origin:

The collect is the opening prayer for a Mass which, according to Chavasse[3], displays the characteristics typical of the Masses in *Reginensis* 316. He accords it no specific date or historical context, though the Mass may be quite ancient. The prayer *ad populum* of the Mass appears to come from an ancient liturgical source because of its reliance on a pre-Vulgate version of the scriptures[4].

Grammatical structure:

The prayer consists of two parts. The first contains (a) an address to God and the petition. The second (b) sets out the reason which motivates the petition.

---

[2] The fragment has been appended to the Mohlberg edition of *Reginensis* 316, where the oration is numbered V 1806$_7$. It is named as Bonifatius 61 in the bibliography of Moeller's Corpus Orationum series. See the study of collect VI, 411.

[3] Chavasse, Le Sacramentaire Gélasien, 246.

[4] A.Dold, "Stark auffällige, dem Altgelasianum und dem Pragense nahe Sakrementar-Texte im CLM 28547," Ephemerides Liturgicae 66 (1952): 344-348.

(a) Address: *Domine*
    Petition: *Sanctae nominis tui, timorem pariter et amorem fac nos habere perpetuum.*

(b) Motivation: *Quia nunquam tuam gubernationem destitues, quos in soliditate tuae dilectionis instituas.*

The prayer contains two sets of pairs which derive some of their vibrancy from their seemingly antithetical nature. The petition sets *timor* and *amor* together. The First Letter of John holds them in opposition[5]. There is no room for fear (*timor*) in the presence of love (*caritas*). On the other hand, it is said that fear of the Lord is the beginning of wisdom (Ps 110:10). The collect pursues this second approach. It requests an equal measure of both fear and love. In the motivating clauses, the verbs *instituere* and *destituere* are paired. By qualifying *destituere* with the adverb *nunquam*, both verbs emphasize the fidelity of God to what he establishes in love.

The liturgical context of the Ascension adds a further dimension to both pairings. The conjunction of *timor* and *amor* recalls the awe and fear of the disciples on those occasions in the Gospels when the Jesus they loved revealed himself to them in his glory[6]. The joining of *destitues* and *instituas* brings to the fore the issue of God's ongoing presence and governing in the church while the community itself celebrates Jesus' physical departure from the earth to take his place in heaven. This contrast is also present in the *super sindonem* of the same Mass (V 587)[7].

---

[5]*Timor non est in caritate; sed perfecta caritas foras mittit timorem, quoniam timor poenam habet; qui autem timet non est perfectus in caritate* (1 Jo 4:18).

[6]See such narratives as the calming of the storm Mr 4:35-41, the walking on the water Mr 6:45-52, and the Transfiguration Mr 9:2-8.

[7]V 587 has been incorporated in the Missal of Paul VI as the collect for Sunday Week VI in Ordinary Time.

In view of their faith that God does not desert those whom he has established in the steadfastness of his love, the faithful ask for the gifts of unceasing fear and love.

Vocabulary:

Prominent vocabulary: *instituere, dilectio, soliditas, destituere, gubernatio, nomen, timor, amor.*

We begin a study of the vocabulary by examining the clause *quos in solidate tuae dilectionis institutis*, since it provides the major motivation for the prayer's petition.

Dilectionis[8]

This noun is associated with *amor* and *caritas*, as the verb *diligere* is associated with *amare*[9]. In the Vulgate translation of John's Gospel, *dilexit* is used to translate ἠγάπησεν where it refers to God's love in sending the Son into the world (Jo 3:16). This same verb is used to express the mutual love between Father and Son (Jo 15:9).

In early liturgical orations, *diligere* is seldom used of God's love for the world or for the church. In the one instance found in the *Veronensis* (L 1061), it is associated with God's chastisement of sinners, as in the Vulgate translation of Heb 12:6. It is used more readily to express the faithfuls' love of God[10]. On the other hand, the adjective *dilectissimus* applied to the Son, readily expresses the mutual relation between Father and Son (L 552).

In V 586, the love whereby God establishes and governs the church is the motive which moves it to implore the gifts of *timor* and *amor*.

---

[8]For further examples of the use of *dilectio* see Deshusses, Concordances III, 1, 502. For *diligere* see III, 1, 503-504.

[9]See Blaise, Vocabulaire, § 150.

[10]See Blaise, Vocabulaire, § 46.

Soliditas[11]

The collect V 586 appears to provide the only example of the expression *soliditas dilectionis* in early liturgical sources. The word *soliditas*, however, is used to formulate the understanding that the firmness of the church's foundation comes from the fact that it is grounded in God's action. This is found in the preface:

"*Uere dignum: qui aeclesiam tuam in apostolica soliditate fundatam ab infernarum erues terrore portarum, et [ut] in tua ueritate persistens nulla recipiat consortia perfidorum*" (L 310)[12].

Instituues[13]

The verb *instituere* and the noun *institutor* are employed to signify the belief that it is God himself who establishes the church as his people, and that his gracious action is its constant ground. This may be said in a general way, as when God is invoked as *populi institutor et rector* (L 379)[14]. It may also be related to specific moments in the church's life, as in the way the following prayer associates God's establishing action with the sacraments:

---

[11] For further examples of the use of *soliditas* see Deshusses, Concordances III, 4, 259.

[12] "Worthy are you of praise: You deliver your church, which you founded in solidity on the apostles, from the terror of the gates of the underworld, so that, perservering in your truth, it may have no fellowship with the perfidious."
This preface serves as a source for the collect for the feast of St. Leo the Great in the Missal of Paul VI: MR(1975) S. Leonis Magni, Collecta, 639.

[13] For further examples of the use of *instituere* and *institutor* see Deshusses, Concordances III, 2, 374-6.

[14] The prayer reads: "*Populi tui, deus, institutor et rector, peccata quibus inpugnantur expelle, ut semper et tibi placitus et tuo munimen [munimine] sit securus*" (L 379), (Trans: Lord, founder and ruler of your people, drive out the sins by which it is assailed so that it may always be pleasing to you and secure in your protection).

"*Adesto, domine, fidelibus tuis, et quos caelestibus instituis sacramentis, a terrenis conserua periculis*" (L 873)[15].

In V 586, God's love is invoked as the motivating force behind the divine action of establishing and governing the church.

Nunquam tua gubernatione destituis

God's action in governing the church is associated in the prayer's motivating clause with the love whereby he founds the church.

Gubernatione[16]

This word has been studied in analyzing the Collect for the eighteenth Sunday[17]. Summarizing that discussion here, God's governing is one in a continuous and interconnected set of actions in his work in creation and salvation. It takes up and continues his creating. God loves and remains committed to what sin has caused to fall. His governing reveals this love and is connected with his raising up, guarding and strengthening.

Destitues[18]

The verb *destituere* is qualified by the adverb *nunquam* and the expression is used to show the constancy of God's loving governance. The verb is paired with the verb *instituere* in the construction of the prayer, to show how the two divine actions are related.

This is expressed in similar language in a preface for the September fast (L 909) where *gubernatio* is linked, as here, with *destituere*:

---

[15] Be present Lord to your people, and those whom you establish in the heavenly sacraments, may you preserve from earthly dangers.

[16] For further examples of the use of *gubernator* and *gubernare* see Deshusses, Concordances III, 2, 242-243.

[17] See above, 162.

[18] For further examples of the use of *destituere* see Deshusses, Concordances III, 1, 447.

"*Uere dignum: qui sempiterno consilio non desinis regere, quod creasti ... certi, quod qui iniustos malosque non deseris, multo magis quos tuos esse tribuisti clementi nullatenus gubernatione destituas*" (L 909)[19].

While in this prayer, God is praised primarily for the governance of the church which he has founded, it is also recalled that he does not abandon even the unrighteous and the wicked. This is further evidence of the constancy of his love.

In V 586, the petition is placed first, unlike the unsual construction of collects. What is asked is couched in the words: *sancti nominis tui timorem et amorem*, which will now be explored for their meaning.

Sancti nominis tui ... timorem pariter et amorem fac nos habere perpetuum.
Nominis[20]

The expression the 'name' of God, his *nomen*, is a hebraism transposed into the Vulgate scriptures[21] and common in the liturgical sources. In Hebrew thought the 'name' expresses the being and the essence of a person or deity[22]. In the New Testament, Jesus is the revelation of God's 'name' to those God

---

[19]It is right and fitting to praise you God who, in your eternal counsel, do not cease to rule what you have created ... Certainly, since you do not desert the unrighteous and the wicked, even more so will you never foresake by you governance, those you have granted to be your people.

[20]For further examples of the use of *nomen* see Deshusses, Concordances III, 3, 167-175.

[21]For critical commentary see H.Bietenhard, "ὄνομα, κτλ.," TDNT V, 242-283.

[22]See Lv 18:21, Lv 20:3, Ps 102:1-5.

gave him (Jo 17:6). The liturgical sources simply borrowed the hebrew expression to serve as a designation of God[23].

In the collect V 586, the divine name signifies the God who does not abandon the people he has established in his love. He is the object of the people's petition for the gifts of fear and love.

Timorem[24]

In the Vulgate scriptures the noun *timor* is used to translate the Greek Septuagint use of φόβος, the reverence and submission of the faithful in the face of God's power, holiness and majesty[25]. This religious response is expressed in piety, obedience and wisdom.

Psalm 21 connects fear of God (*timor*), itself a mark of the chosen people, with praise of God:
"*Qui timetis Dominum laudate eum; universum semen Iacob, glorificate eum:*" (Ps 21:24).

Fear of God and love (*diligere*) of God are set together in the pericope Dt 10:12-13, where they are associated with wholehearted and unstinted service, worship and obedience:
"*Et nunc, Israel, quid Dominus Deus tuus petit a te, nisi ut timeas Dominum Deum tuum et ambules in viis eius et diligas eum ac seruias Domino Deo tuo*

---

[23]There are many examples of this. In an offertory prayer from a Mass for martyrs, to praise God is to praise his name:
"*Magnificamus domine, nomen tuum, omnipotens et misericors deus ....*" (L 84), (Trans: We glorify your name, almighty and merciful God ....) Also see Blaise, Vocabulaire, § 22.

[24]For further examples of the use of *timor* see Deshusses, Concordances III, 4, 367.

[25]For critical commentary see G.Wanke, "φοβεω, κτλ.," TDNT IX, 189-219.

in toto corde tuo et in tota anima tua custodiasque mandata Domini et caeremionias eius, quas ego hodie praecipio tibi, ut bene sit tibi?"

Reverential and pious fear is the beginning of wisdom (Ps 110:10), its fullness, expression and blessing (Ecli 1: 11-40). As is the case with wisdom, piety and reverence are connected with knowledge and insight (Pro 2:5-6). Furthermore, *timor* is associated with godly leadership. In Is 11:1-9 it is one of the seven gifts[26] through which the messianic leader will bring righteous judgement, justice for the poor, and universal peace.

This Isaian text was subsequently incorporated into the baptismal liturgy in the prayer for consignation by the bishop. There 'fear of God' is a gift which enables the faithful to live out their regeneration in baptism and the Spirit:

"*Deus omnipotens, pater domini nostri Iesu Christi, qui regenerasti famulum tuum ex aqua et spiritu sancto quique dedisti ei remissionem omnium peccatorum: tu, domine, emitte in eum spiritum sanctum tuum paraclytum et da ei spiritum sapientiae et intellectus, spiritum consilii et fortitudinis, spiritum scientiae et pietatis; adimple eum spiritum timoris dei et domini nostri Iesu Christi; et iube eum consignari signum crucis in uitam aeternam ....*" (V 615)[27].

---

[26]In the hebrew text there are only six gifts. However, the Septuagint and Vulgate both translate 'piety' twice. In v.2 the Vulgate uses *pietas*, while in v.3 it reads *timor Domini*. See Edward J. Kissane, The Book of Isaiah, vol 1 (Dublin: The Richardson Press, 1941), 142.

[27]"Almighty God, father of our Lord Jesus Christ, you regenerated your servants through water and the Spirit, and you gave them remission of all sins. Lord send on them your Holy Spirit the Paraclete, and give them the spirit of wisdom, and understanding, the spirit of counsel and fortitude, the spirit of knowledge and devotion; fill them with the spirit of fear of God and of our Lord Jesus Christ; and bid them to be signed by the sign of the Cross unto eternal life."
See also V 451 for a similar usage, and V 684 where the same prayer is used

Amorem[28]

Love for God is expressed in the liturgical sources by the noun *amor*, the related nouns *caritas, dilectio, pietas* and *devotio*, and the verbs *amare* and *diligere*[29]. The love of believers for God is a response to his love. It encompasses love and worship of God, and love of neighbour.

Timorem et amorem

The conjunction of fear and love of God has been seen above in Dt 10:12-13, where it denoted whole-hearted, zealous service, worship and obedience. The same pairing is also found in a small number of early orations[30]. In a Pentecost prayer, both fear and love of God's name are based in the recognition that God is the source of all mercy:

"*Domine, deus noster, cuius est prima causa miserendi, qua nomen tuum timeamus et amemus, cordibus nostris miseratus infunde, ut quae tibi non placent refutantes, sincera tibi uoluntate subdamur*" (L 189)[31].

In a blessing for virgins (L 1104), fear and love are related in a highly expressive way through the petition:

"... *Amore te timeant, amore tibi serviant ...*" (L 1104)[32].

Here it is clearly highlighted that love is the basis of fear of the Lord,

---

as a blessing for those being taken into the church from heresy.

[28]For further examples of the use of *amor* and *amare* see Deshusses, Concordances III, 1, 87-88.

[29]Blaise, Vocabulaire, § 46.

[30]See also V 1361.

[31]Lord God, you are the beginning and source of compassion, by which we may fear and love your name. In your mercy, pour into our hearts that we, refusing what is not pleasing to you, may be subject to you in sincerity of will.

[32]... May they fear you [God] in love, and serve you in love ....

and of his service.

In the phrase *timorem pariter et amorem fac nos habere perpetuum*, the collect brings together two fundamental Christian responses to the recognition that the faithful are established and guided in God's love. Along with the gift of reverent and dutiful obedience in the face of such love, the prayer asks for an equal measure of the gift of love. The love of the community is the fitting response desired by God. Pious, reflective observance is never absent from such love.

The community calls on God to grant that this devotion and love for him may constantly (*perpetuum*) abide in them, enabling them to continually remain within the love and salvation God brought and continues to bring. Together, piety and love engender, and are expressed in, a commitment to sincere worship, obedience, wisdom, love of neighbour and the building of the messianic kingdom. This pairing of *timor* and *amor* recalls the conjunction of worship and love of God found in the collect for Sunday IV (L 432)[33].

Meaning of the prayer:

The faithful petition God to give them continuously, and to the same degree, fear and love of him. Their fear, which comes from their love, is expressed in their reflective piety, service, worship and obedience. Together *timor* and *amor* establish the grounds for all good human actions. The baptized request these two gifts as a response to the depth of God's love for them. The community has been founded in the steadfastness of divine love. Their foundation is set in the core of God's own existence as the God who is love. There can be no more sure foundation. Because they have been instituted in God's love, they will never be abandoned by God's guidance.

---

[33] See above, 102.

There are no significant shifts in vocabulary or meaning as the prayer stands within the new context of the Missal of Paul VI.

RELATIONSHIP OF THE CHRISTIAN PEOPLE TO GOD

The Christian people exist in and through the steadfast firmness of God's love. They are established in the core of God's existence.

The prayer focuses particularly on the active fidelity of God's love which sustains the relationship of the people to God. He continues to govern the people he establishes in love, never abandoning them. God's governance is founded in his love, while the sacred mandates of his law are all ordained towards love. The post Ascension liturgical context of the prayer, with its anticipation of the feast of Pentecost, would point to the guiding presence of the Holy Spirit in the church.

The church is characterized by both fear and love of God. The pious devotion and observance of the community is based in its love for God. Through the gift of fear the faithful humbly acknowledge God's steadfast love, mercy and deliverance, and respond with devout service. This response is the heart of their worship, the source and inspiration of their wisdom, and the impulse that directs them to build the kingdom.

FREER TRANSLATION OF THE COLLECT

Sancti nominis tui, Domine, timorem pariter et amorem fac nos habere perpetuum, quia numquam tua gubernatione destituis, quos in soliditate tuae dilectionis instituis.

Lord, you never abandon nor do you cease to guide the people you have formed in the absolute strength of your love. Grant that we may never cease to hold your name in both awe and love.

COLLECT FOR SUNDAY VI

PRAYER

Deus, qui te in rectis et sinceris manere pectoribus asseris, da nobis tua gratia tales exsistere, in quibus habitare digneris.	God, who declare that you abide in upright and sincere hearts, give to us by your grace to be as those in whom you deign to dwell.

USE IN THE MISSAL OF PAUL VI

A modified form of this collect features in the Missal as the collect for a Mass in the Common of Virgins:

Deus, qui te in puris manere cordibus asseris, da nobis, beatae N. virginis intercessione, per gratiam tuam tales exsistere, in quibus habitare dignere. Per Dominum. (MR(1975) Commune virgg. 3, Collecta, 710).

In line with a theme of the Common, the prayer focuses on purity of heart as a grace which forms the faithful to be a people in whom God deigns to dwell.

ORIGINAL SOURCE

Reginensis 316: *Super sindonem* for the Mass I, lxv, *Orationes et Praeces Dominica Post Ascensa Domini* (V 587).

The original prayer stands in the Missal of Paul VI with only slight modifications to spelling and grammar. Where the present prayer reads *in rectis et sinceris pectoribus*, the original reads *rectis ac senceris pectoribus*. As well *asseris* has been preferred to *adseris*, and *exsistere* to *existere*.

Note that the collect from this same Mass is incorporated in the Missal of Paul VI as the collect for Sunday Week XII in Ordinary Time. Both prayers reflect the feast's concern with Christ's departure from the earth in his ascension to the Father in heaven, and God's ever abiding presence in the Christian community on earth.

The prayer occurs a second time in *Reginensis* 316 as the *super sindonem* in a Mass for the September fast: Mass II,lx, *Oraciones in Ieiunio Mensis Septimi* (V 1038). There it contains one variation. The adjective *rectus* has been dropped. God declares that he remains in sincere hearts. In the collect (V 1037) of the same Mass, the community have asked for the grace to take up and carry out the fast with appropriate piety and devotion. Through these two prayers, the Mass links sincerity of heart with fitting celebration of the *devotio* of the fast.

USE IN OTHER LITURGICAL SOURCES

As noted by Siffrin[1], the prayer appears in these sources:
Dominica in octava Pentecostes *seu* I post Pentecosten;
super sindonem: B 779,
Dominica *seu* hebdomada III post Pentecostes;
collect: A 994, G 1089, S 871, P 508,
super sindonem: B 788,
prayer *ad populum*: F 1550.

Though originally a *super sindonem* for the feast of the Ascension, the liturgical sources have made use of this prayer for the Masses after Pentecost. Its use in the Missal of Paul VI is in line with this.

Note also that the oration, along with the collect from the same Mass, is used as prayers for vespers: *Orationes in vigilia ad Ascensionem Domini,*

---

[1] The sources noted are from P.Siffrin, Konkordanztabellen zu den römanischen Sakramentarien II, Liber Sacramentorum Romanae Aeclesiae, 74. For the liturgical context of each prayer, as well as a more complete list of sources and manuscripts, see Moeller, Corpus Orationum III D, Orationes 1708-2389, oration 2128, 189-190.

advespera alia oratio, Bonifatus 61[2].

ANALYSIS OF THE PRAYER IN THE ORIGINAL SOURCE

Origin:

The prayer is from a Mass which, according to Chavasse[3], displays the characteristics typical of the gelasian Masses in *Reginensis* 316, containing a collect, *super sindonem* and a prayer *ad populum*. He accords it no specific date or historical context, though the Mass may be quite ancient. The prayer *ad populum* at least appears to come from an ancient liturgical source because of its reliance on a pre-Vulgate version of the scriptures[4].

Grammatical structure:

The prayer consists of two sections. The first (a) is made up of the address to God and the motivating clause. The second (b) contains the petition, motivated by God's declaration.

(a) Address: *Deus,*
 Motivation: *qui te rectis ac senceris manere pectoribus adseris*

(b) Petition: *da nobis tua gratia tales existere, in quibus habitare digneris.*

Both sections of the prayer are in parallel:

habitare parallels *manere*, while *tales existere* parallels *in rectis et sinceris pectoribus*.

---

[2]See Moeller, 189, and also A. Bannister, "Liturgical Fragments," The Journal of Theological Studies 9 (1908): 411.

[3]Chavasse, Le Sacramentaire Gélasien, 246.

[4]Dold, "Stark auffällige, dem Altgelasianum und dem Pragense nahe Sakramentar-Texte im CLM 28547," Ephemerides Liturgicae 66 (1952): 344-348.

The parallel between *manere* and *habitare* has scriptural associations. As shown below, in the Vulgate bible *manere* indicates the Johannine theme of God's abiding in believers, while the use of the verb *habitare* is characteristic of the Pauline understanding of the indwelling of Christ. The oration is built around this pairing. Through their interrelationship it is clear that the phrase *tua gratia tales exsistere* is in parallel with *in rectis et sinceris pectoribus*. Because God declares he dwells in upright and sincere hearts, the faithful request the gift of such hearts so that they may be the sort of community in which God dwells.

The analysis of the prayer's vocabulary will, then, begin with a study of *manere* and *habitare*. Following this it will move to examine the prayer's warrant (*adserere*), and the graces petitioned (*recta et sincera pectora, tales existere*).

Vocabulary:
Prominent vocabulary: *adserere, manere, habitare, pectus, rectus, sincerus, existere.*

The original context for our prayer, the feast of the Ascension, raises before the faithful the relationship between God's promise to remain present in the community and Jesus' return to the Father. The *super sindonem*, through its use of the scripturally charged verbs *manere* and *habitare*, stresses God's presence within the church. Since both verbs represent different scriptural traditions they will first be examined individually.

Manere[5]

In translating John's Gospel, the Vulgate uses the verb *manere* to express God's promise to remain in the hearts of believers[6]. God abides in those who confess that Jesus is the Son of God, who believe in God's love for them, and who dwell in God's love (1 Jo 4:15-16). Furthermore, remaining in God's love involves keeping his commandments (Jo 15:10), including sharing with the poor (1 Jo 3:17).

A prayer (L 169) from a Mass for the feast of the Ascension contrasts the continued presence of Christ on earth with his enthronement in heaven[7]. While in the example *manere* is applied to Christ and in V 587 it connotes God's abiding, the use of the verb in both prayers is similar. It is set within the context of the same feast, underscored by God's promise, and points up the divine indwelling in the church. The oration reads:

"*Adesto, domine, supplicationibus nostris, ut sicut humani generis saluatorem consedere tecum in tua maiestate confidimus, ita usque ad consummationem saeculi manere nobiscum, quemadmodum es pollicitus, sentiamus*" (L 169)[8].

In V 587, *manere* is paralleled by the more Pauline expression of divine

---

[5]For further examples of the use of *manere* see Deshusses, Concordances III, 3, 21-22.

[6]For further examples see Jo 6:57, Jo 15:5-7, Jo 17:21, 1 Jo 4:13, and 1 Jo 5:12. For a summary of the Johannine use of the greek *menein* (abide, remain, stay, dwell in) see R. Brown, The Gospel According to John (i-xii), The Anchor Bible, (New York: Doubleday, 1966), 510-512.

[7]It appears that there are no other prayers in the early sources, apart from L 951, that are concerned with God's dwelling (*manere*).

[8]"Lord, hear our supplications, so that, just as we trust that the saviour of humankind is seated with you in your majesty, so also may we feel that he remains with us until the end of time, just as you promised."
With slight modification this prayer is used in the Missal of Paul VI: MR(1975) Dom. VII Paschae, Collecta, 308.

indwelling *habitare*.

Habitare[9]

The verb *habitare* connotes the Pauline understanding of Christ's indwelling. It designates Christ's presence by faith (Eph 3:17), or the presence of the Spirit (Rm 8:8-9). Alternately, it can mean the presence of Christ's word (Col 3:11) or his power (2 Cor 12:9). Without Christ, sin dwells in the inner depths of the human person (Rm 7:17-19).

The liturgical sources contain two prayers which are both motivated by the fact that God dwells (*habitare*) in the saints and does not desert those with devoted hearts. In view of this, the faithful ask for assistance in the midst of earthly perils, or for freedom from earthly or carnal desire.

"*Deus, qui in sanctis habitas et pia corda non deseris, suscipe propicius oracionem nostram et tribue misericordiam tuam, ut te custode seruati ab omnibus uitae huius periculis liberemur*" (V 957)[10],

"*Deus, qui [i]n sanctis habitas et pia corda non deseris, libera nos a terrenis desideriis et cupititate carnali ut nullo in nobis regnante peccato tibi soli domino liberis mentibus seruiamus*" (V 1179)[11].

In V 587, *manere* and *habitare* parallel each other to designate God's indwelling in the hearts of the faithful. This is a common biblical and liturgical use. The same vocabulary is used to contrast God's or Christ's indwelling with the presence of sin in those who do not follow God's ways. In

---

[9] For further examples of the use of *habitare* see Deshusses Concordances III, 2, 248-249.

[10] God, who live in your saints and do not desert devoted hearts, propitiously receive our prayer and bestow your mercy, so that, with you as guardian, we may be freed from all the dangers of this life.

[11] God, who live in your saints and do not desert devoted hearts, free us from earthly desires and the cravings of the flesh, so that, when no sin reigns in us, we may serve you alone with free minds.

V 587 *manere* refers to God's word and effective promise, whereas *habitare* occurs in the petition, for among the faithful gathered, God's indwelling can only be the effect of grace. Placed in the context of the more general use of *habitare* in Christian Latin and liturgical vocabulary, the contrast with the claims of sin underlies the need to ask for the grace that assures God's presence and indwelling. God's word and effective promise, which underlie his abiding, are denoted through the verb *adserere*.

Adseris[12]

The verb *asserere* is used sparingly in the liturgical sources, indexed as it is only six times in the Deshusses' concordance. The prayer V 587 appears to be one of the very few examples where God is the subject. In this *super sindonem, asserere* serves two functions. It pinpoints the effective power of God's word or declaration. Secondly it indicates that this is the basis of God's presence, signified by the words *manere* and *habitare*. This declaration, and God's indwelling, are further related to the faithful's possession of upright and sincere hearts. Attention will now be turned to these qualities.

Rectis et senceris pectoribus

Pectoribus[13]

Like its analogue *cor*[14], *pectus* is used to designate the inner being of the person, and especially the seat of love.

In a collect for the Mass of the Easter Vigil, *pectus* is set in apposition with mind and soul to connote the whole person. Mind, heart and soul are

---

[12]For further examples of the use of *adserere* see Deshusses Concordances III, 1, 132-133.

[13]For further examples of the use of *pectus* see Deshusses Concordances III, 3, 326-327.

[14]*Cor* has been discussed in the study of the collect for Sunday XXIV. See above, 214.

renewed in baptism:

"*Omnipotens sempiterne deus, qui hanc sacratissimam noctem per uniuersa mundi spatia gloriae dominicae resurrectionis inlustras, conserua in nouam familiae tuae progeniem sanctificationis spiritum quem dedisti, ut corpore et mente renouati puram tibi animam et purum pectus semper exhibeant*" (V 453)[15].

Hearts in which God promises to abide are marked by uprightness and sincerity.

Rectis[16]

The adjective *rectus* denotes what is pleasing to God and salvific for humans. This can be seen in the following preface, which sets what is upright (*recta*) in parallel with

what is pleasing (*placita*) to God and salutary (*salutaria*) for the faithful. Upright things are the object of will (*velle*), action (*agere*) and completion of action (*perficere*). Only God (*sine te*) and his grace (*indubitanter est gratiae*) can assure the unity of will and action in what is right. The Mass formula (XVIII,xxvii) indicates the need for God's propitiation of sin if the faithful are to be given the grace to pursue what is right. This theme is incorporated into the preface quoted:

"*Uere dignum: cuius propitiationem in hac primum parte sentimus, cum ea,*

---

[15]"Almighty eternal God, you set ablaze with light throughout the entire world this most holy night of the glorious resurrection of the Lord. Preserve in the new members of your family the spirit of sanctification which you have given, so that, renewed in body and mind, they may always tender you a pure soul and a pure heart."
The same prayer, with slight modifications, is used in the Missal of Paul VI. The major change is the substitution of *puram animam et purum pectus* with *puram servitutem*: MR(1975) Vig. pascha, Collecta, 280.

[16]For further examples of the use of *rectus* see Deshusses Concordances III, 4, 32-33.

quae tibi sunt placita et nobis salutaria, desideramus adpetere. Dum enim sine te nihil recti uelle possimus aut agere aut perficere, indubitanter est gratiae, quidquid conuenienter operamur" (L 566)[17].

A collect from the *Veronensis* sets what is *recta* in parallel with what God loves as *iustitia*. At the same time, what is upright is diametrically opposed to what is evil (*perversa*), which itself parallels what God condemns as unjust (*iniusta*). When the faithful love what is upright and spurn what is evil, their actions are congruent with God's own love for what is just and his condemnation of what is unrighteous:

"Deus, qui iustitiam diligis et iniusta condemnas: da nobis, quaesumus, et amare quae recta sunt, et peruersa uitare" (L 1091)[18].

A *super sindonem* relates doing what is upright to love of integrity of conscience and of reputation:

"Fac nos, quaesumus, domine, quae sunt recta sectari, integritatem conscientiae diligere semper et famae" (L 1075)[19].

In summary, to freely pursue and love the upright is a grace given by God. To ask it, the faithful need to be confident that God propitiates sin and is ready to direct their will and action. Human actions that are upright correspond to what is righteous in God's sight, while the faithful's love for what is upright parallels God's own love for what is righteous. In this

---

[17] It is right and fitting ... We feel your propitiation [God] before all else in this respect when we desire to strive for what are pleasing to you and salvific for us. Since without you we can neither will what is right, nor perform any action or bring it to perfection, it is without doubt that whatever we do that is fitting comes from your grace.

[18] God, you love righteousness and you condemn what is unjust, grant to us both to love what is upright and spurn what is wrong.

[19] Lord, make us follow what is upright, and unceasingly love intergrity of conscience and of reputation.

correspondence, the *recta* are a fitting object of Christian love. In our oration upright hearts are further qualified as *sincera*.

Sinceris[20]

The adjective *sincerus* denotes that affection of the mind and heart which is willingly open and wholeheartedly devoted to what is justifying in God's sight. It is linked with a devoted will towards God, devoted supplication, mutual love, justifying reception of communion, and the absence of deceit.

In a collect from the Sundays after Easter, sincerity of heart is related to the service of God's majesty. It goes with a devout will:
"*Omnipotens sempiterne deus, fac nos tibi semper et deuotam gerere uoluntatem et maiestati tuae sencero corde seruire*" (V 561)[21].

A prayer *ad populum* relates sincerity of heart to love of neighbour. It too is a gift that results from devout supplication:
"*Confirma, domine, quaesumus, tuorum corda filiorum, et gratiae tuae uirtute corrobora; ut et in tua sint supplicatione deuoti, et mutua dilectione sinceri*" (L 1050)[22].

---

[20] For further examples of the use of *sincerus* see Deshusses Concordances III, 4, 244-245.

[21] "Almighty eternal God, may our wills always be devoted to you, and may we serve your majesty with sincere hearts."
This prayer is included in the Missal of Paul VI amongst the collects for the Sundays in Ordinary Time: MR(1975) Dom. XXIX per annum, Collecta, 368. See above, 294.

[22] "Lord, strengthen the hearts of your children, and invigorate them by the power of your grace, so that they may always be both devoted in supplication to you and sincere in mutual love for one another."
This prayer is incorporated in the Missal of Paul VI: MR(1975) Orr. super populum, 23, 510.

A prayer over the gifts associates sincerity of mind, the opposite of duplicity of heart, with justification. Such sincerity is a quality of worship exercised in the offering of the gifts:

"*Offerimus tibi, domine, munus, quod sicut duplici sumentes corde condemnat, ita sincera capientes mente iustificat*" (L 439)[23].

In summary, the grace of a right and sincere heart involves the complete inner being of the human person; soul, mind and heart. As upright, everything the person wills, sets in action and brings to perfection, is preceded by grace and carried through in grace. It is in harmony with the righteousness that God loves, and is salutary for the faithful. This grace is a consequence of God's propitiation of sin which Christians enter through their renewal in baptism. In their love for what is right, the faithful also desire to shun whatever is evil. *Sincerus* denotes an undivided will, devout in God's ways. This quality is particulary applied to worship. It is further applied to the love of neighbour that results from worship.

The foundation of V 587 is God's promise to abide in such a heart. In light of this, the petition requests the grace to be able to have an upright and sincere heart so that the faithful can be the sort of people in whom God dwells. *Tales existere*[24]

A similar phrase is found in the *super sindonem* for a daily Mass. God is asked to turn the hearts of his people to him so that they can be the sort of people to whom God grants perpetual favours:

"*Plebis tuae, deus, ad te corda conuerte, ut tuo munere talis existat, cui tu*

---

[23]Lord, we offer you the gift which condemns those who receive it in duplicity of heart just as it justifies those who receive it with sincere hearts.

[24]For further examples of the use of *existere* see Deshusses <u>Concordances</u> III, 2, 81-82.

perpetua beneficia largiaris" (V 1293)[25].

In the *super sindonem* V 587, the community is asking for the grace to live with upright and sincere hearts so as to be the type of people in whom God abides.

Meaning of the prayer:

The effective assertion of God that he abides in hearts that are upright and sincere motivates the faithful to petition God for the grace to have such hearts. In this gift, they are able to be the people in whom God dwells.

The verbs *manere* and *habitare*, used here in parallel, denote the presence of God's love, Christ's word and power, and the presence of the Spirit. The Ascension context would especially point to the presence of the Spirit, as well as Christ's continued presence in the church. This indwelling is the basis of the renewal of humanity in God's providential ordering. In contrast, those in whom God does not dwell exist in sin. They can do nothing that is good.

God's assertion reflects the power of his word. What God declares, he carries out.

The people in whom God abides are characterized by upright and sincere hearts. Their whole inner self, their heart (*pectus, cor*), soul (*anima*) and mind (*mens*), is included here. In their existence as upright persons, everything they will, act on and bring to perfection comes from God's grace. This grace comes as a consequence of God's propitiation of sin. Right will and right deeds are in harmony with what God loves as righteous (*iustitia*). In view of this, those in whom God dwells love what is upright because it is what God loves. At the same time they shun what is evil. A sincere heart is

---

[25]Turn the hearts of your people towards you, God, so that, by your gift, they may live as a people to whom you give eternal favours.

undivided in its desire for what is upright. It is most notably taken up with undivided worship and praise. Such sincere worship leads to love of neighbour.

ANALYSIS OF THE WORDS AND PHRASES IN THE COLLECT FROM THEIR CONTEXT WITHIN THE MISSAL OF PAUL VI

The Missal of Paul VI brings no changes to the dynamic of the prayer. Two things however will be noted here. The first is the hope of God's abiding presence is placed in some new contexts. The second is that the Missal loosens the link between sincerity of heart, uprightness of heart, and God's indwelling, again because of the contexts to which the terms apply.

As seen above, in a Mass from the Common of Virgins, purity of heart is seen as a grace which forms the faithful to be a people in whom God deigns to dwell[26].

The verbs *manere* and *habitare* are linked in a blessing at the conclusion of a nuptial Mass. In the blessing the gift of harmony in mutual love is understood as the grounds for the dwelling of the peace of Christ in the couple and its abiding in their home:
"*Deus Pater aeternus in mutuo vos servet amore concordes, ut pax Christi habitet in vobis, et in domo vestra iugiter maneat ...*" (MR(1975) In celebr. Matrimonii A, Bened. in fine M., 748)[27].

In the Missal there is a weakening of the link between sincerity, right conduct and God's indwelling. This is seen in the Good Friday petition for those who do not believe in God (*qui in Deum non credunt*). The adjective

---

[26]"*Deus, qui te in puris manere cordibus asseris, da nobis ...*" (MR(1975) Commune virgg. 3, Collecta, 710).

[27]May God the eternal Father preserve you harmonious in your mutual love so that the peace of Christ may dwell in you and abide always in your home ...

sincerus, while denoting the integrity and authenticity of their (*qui non Deum agnoscunt*) searching for God, nevertheless describes an attribute of those who do not confess God. In the Good Friday prayer, there is in reality an acknowledgement that unbelievers may not be simply dismissed as sinners. Even they may possess sincere and upright hearts. In this case, the biblical promises of indwelling cannot be evoked. This use of the term, then, does not connote the worship, devotion or righteous conduct of Christians. Hence those mentioned are not those to whom the biblical promise of indwelling was made, nor the indwelling of God[28]. The prayer reads:

"*Oremus et pro iis qui Deum non agnoscunt, ut, quae recta sunt sincero corde sectantes, ad ipsum Deum pervenire mereantur ... Omnipotens sempiterne Deus, qui cunctos homines condidisti, ut te semper desiderando quaererent et inveniendo quiescerent, presta quaesumus, ut inter noxia quaeque obstacula omnes, tuae signa pietatis et in te credentium testimonium bonorum operum percipientes, te sola verum Deum nostrique generis Patrem gaudeant confiteri*" (MR(1975) Fer. VI Pass. Dom., orat. uni. VIII Pro iis in Deum non credunt, 255)[29].

---

[28]Though *sincerus* occurs 31 times in the Missal of Paul VI, there appear to be only two other examples of this sense of *sincerus* as 'honest', 'authentic': MR(1975) Fer. VI in Pass. Domini, Or. pro iis qui in Christum non credunt, 255, and MR(1975) Ordo M. cum populo, Prex euch. IV, Intercc., 470. All three references are in prayers newly composed for the Missal. See Schnikter and Slaby, 2340-2341.

[29]Let us pray for those who do not recognize God, so that, following what is upright with sincere hearts, they may merit to come to God himself ... All powerful, eternal God, you fashioned all humanity so that in their desiring they might seek you always, and on finding you they might be at peace. Grant that among any harmful obstacles whatsoever, all people, perceiving the signs of your goodness and mercy, and as well the witness of the good works of your faithful, may rejoice to confess you alone as the true God and Father of humankind.

RELATIONSHIP OF THE CHRISTIAN PEOPLE TO GOD

The most central point that the prayer makes concerning the relationship of the Christian people to God is the community's belief in God's promise to dwell in those who live in sincerity and uprightness of heart. This abiding can be described in a number of ways, including the presence of God's love, the presence of Christ's word and power, and the presence of the Spirit. In the original context, implicit in God's indwelling is the contrast with those outside the community, in whom sin is the dominant presence. The contrast, however, has been slightly modified in the Missal of Paul VI, so that those who live with sincerity of mind and heart, though who may profess belief in God, are not classified as sinners.

The prayer notes the power and effectiveness of God's word. Because God has declared that he will remain in sincere and upright hearts, then God will do so. On the strength of this, God can be confidently petitioned to bring about those conditions in the community so that the faithful may be such a people that God will dwell in them.

FREER TRANSLATION OF THE COLLECT

Deus, qui te in rectis et sinceris manere pectoribus asseris, da nobis tua gratia tales exsistere, in quibus habitare digneris.	You assert, Lord, that you abide in hearts that are upright and sincere. By the power of your grace give us such hearts so we may be numbered among the people in whom you dwell.

CHAPTER SIX
PRAYERS FROM THE MASSES FOR THE ORDINARY SUNDAYS THROUGHOUT THE YEAR IN *REGINENSIS* 316: THE COLLECTS FOR SUNDAYS IX, XX, XXII, XXVI, XXVII, XXX, XXXI and XXXII

INTRODUCTION

The collects for Sundays IX (V 1186), XX (V 1178), XXII (V 1182), XXVI (V 1198), XXVII (V 1201), XXX (V 1209), XXXI (V 1206) and XXXII (V 1234) all belong to the series of 16 Masses which open Book III of *Reginensis* 316. These Masses are entitled *Oraciones et praeces cum canone per dominicis diebus* (V 1178-V 1241). According to Brou[1], these Mass texts were available to be used for those Sundays between the seasons of Christmas and Lent, and again between Pentecost and Advent, on which no other major solemnity or feast was celebrated. The ancient Sacramentary did not identify any of the Masses with a particular free Sunday. Because there are only 16 Masses in the series, some would have been used more than once during the course of the liturgical year. Little is known concerning the historical origins of the set as a whole.

A small number of prayers in these Masses are also found in the *Veronensis*[2]. Two are of particular interest to our study. The collect for

---

[1] L.Brou, "Étude historique sur les oraisons des dimanches après la Pentecôte dans la tradition romaine," Sacris Erudiri 2 (1949): 166-170. Chavasse follows Brou. See Chavasse, Le Sacramentaire Gélasien, 496-497.

[2] See Deshusses, Concordances II, 105-107.

Sunday XXX (V 1209) is first encountered in the liturgical sources as the first presidential prayer for the *Veronensis* Mass XVIII,xxxiii, Julio (L 598). This section of the *Veronensis* is entitled *Incipit orationes et praeces diurnae*. The collect for Sunday XXXI (V 1206) is also a first presidential prayer from a Mass in the same section of the *Veronensis*: Mass XVIII,xxviiii (L 574). Chavasse allows that both prayers were composed by Pope Vigilius for use in Masses during the siege of Rome by the Arian Ostrogoths (537-538)[3]. However, their incorporation in the Missal of Paul VI seems to be dictated more by their presence among the sixteen *Reginensis* 316 Masses for Sundays during the year than by their place in the *Veronensis*. On account of this, they have been included in this chapter.

The analyses of these orations from Book III of *Reginensis* 316 have been arranged according to their order of appearance in that liturgical source. Our study, then, will commence with the collect for Sunday XX, followed by the studies of the collects for Sundays XXII, IX, XXVI, XXVII, XXXI, XXX and XXXII.

---

[3]See below, 410, 401.

COLLECT FOR SUNDAY XX

PRAYER

Deus, qui diligentibus te bona invisibilia praeparasti, infunde cordibus nostris tui amoris affectum, ut, te in omnibus et super omnia diligentes, promissiones tuas, quae omne desiderium superant, consequamur.

God, who has prepared good things beyond our vision for those who love you, pour into our hearts the ardour of love of you, so that, loving you in all things and above all things, we may reach your promises, which surpass all longing.

ORIGINAL SOURCE

Reginensis 316: Collect for the Mass III,i, *Oraciones et Praeces per Dominicis Diebus* (V 1178).

The only modification to the original source for inclusion in the Missal of Paul VI is an adjustment of grammar and spelling, the phrase *omne desiderium* replacing *omni disiderio*. This study will follow the spelling in the Missal.

Note that in the original text it is V 1179 that is styled *collectio*, not V 1178. However, by comparison with the other formulas in this section it is probably 1178 which was the collect, and 1179 the prayer *super sindonem*.

USE IN OTHER LITURGICAL SOURCES

As noted by Bruylants[1], the prayer has also been used as a post Pentecost collect in these sources:
Dominica V post Pentecosten: Pr(154,1), A(1095), S(976), P(554),

---

[1]Bruylants, II, 323. For a more complete list of sources and manuscripts see Moeller, <u>Corpus Orationum</u> II, D, Orationes 881-1707, oration 1532, 296.

OR(170)[Sp 1144], X(256,1), N(139), Q(140), 1474(263) 1570, 1604 and in the unedited sources G(180,1)[G 1211], Z(731), PaAng(234).

ANALYSIS OF THE PRAYER IN THE ORIGINAL SOURCE

Origin:

See accompanying introductory note on this collection of Masses in *Reginensis* 316.

Grammatical structure[2]:

The prayer consists of (a) an address and motivating clause, (b) a petition, and (c) a result clause specifying two effects of granting the petition.

(a) Address: *Deus*
    Motivation: *qui diligentibus te bona invisibilia praeparasti*

(b) Petition: *infunde cordibus nostris tui amoris affectum*

(c) Result: *ut* (i) *te in omnibus et super omnia diligentes*
                 (ii) *promissiones tuas, quae omne desiderium superant, consequamur.*

In the result clause, the second effect follows as a consequence of the first. The gift of obtaining the divine promises is a consequence of loving God in all things and above all things.

The *bona invisibilia* and *promissiones tuas* are set in parallel. The good things God has prepared which are beyond human vision parallel the promises God has made which transcend human desires. Obtaining the promises brings about the apprehension of the already prepared invisible good things. By implication, the taste of the *bona invisibilia* on earth reveals the divine

---

[2]For a more complete analysis see Haessly, Rhetoric in the Collects of the Roman Missal, 82-83.

promises and excites a love for the God who offers them. This link between the *bona invisibilia*, the promises and the love of the faithful shapes the dynamic of the prayer. The *bona invisibilia* lie behind the love of the faithful for God and their faith in the promises. In turn, those who love God seek the ardour of love for God. Through the granting of this petition they receive an unsurpassable love for God which leads to obtaining the divine promises. The oration can be schematized thus:

Bona invisibilia   *parallel*   the divine promises
      ↓   ↑
<u>love</u> of the faithful   *parallels*   <u>love</u> of God in & beyond all things
      ↓   ↑
        Petition for an increase in the <u>ardour of their love</u> for God

The prayer interweaves two levels of human existence, the 'beyond' and the present. The *bona invisibilia* are beyond human sight, and bespeak promises that are beyond human desire. Yet they provide the context for human existence, and are approachable and attainable through love for God lived in the present. It is the gift of zealous and ardent love of God in the heart of the believer that enables those who love God to love God in and above all things, and thus attain the divine promises.

Vocabulary:

Principal vocabulary: *invisibilia, diligere, praeparare, cor, amor, affectus, promissio, desiderium, superare, consequi*.

The meaning of the prayer emerges from its structure. The analysis of the vocabulary serves to further clarify the terms, and especially to reveal the biblical imagery underlying the oration. Our discussion will commence with the motivating clause, *deus, qui diligentibus te bona inuisibilia praeparasti*, which introduces the two main ideas operative in the prayer, the *bona invisibilia* and the faithful's response of love. Since their love is only comprehensible in light of the revelation of the *invisibilia*, this term will be studied first.

Bona inuisibilia[3] *praeparasti*

The term *bona invisibilia* designates two interrelated notions. It parallels the divine promises, those riches of heaven that God has prepared for those who love him. They are beyond human vision and understanding. Underlying this, however, is the breadth of God's revelation and salvation.

The scriptures and the liturgical sources point out the way in which things seen and known on earth (*visibilia*) image and reveal the *bona invisibilia* that are beyond human vision. These *bona* are especially revealed in Christ, the church, its sacraments and worship, and in creation. Among the *invisibilia* they image are reconciliation, rebirth, peace, and praise of God.

The clause takes its immediate reference from 1 Cor 2:9, which sets forth what God has prepared for those who love him is beyond human comprehension:

"*sed, sicut scriptum est, quod 'oculus non vidit nec auris audivit, nec in cor hominis ascendit, quae praeparavit Deus iis qui diligunt illum'*".

Yet things that are visible open the minds of the faithful to what is beyond sight. In the Christological hymn at the beginning of the Letter to the Colossians (Col 1:15-20), Christ is the image of the invisible God (v.15). He is the first born from the dead (v.18), the one in whom all fullness dwells (v.19), and the reconciliation of all things to God (v.19). As such he points to what is beyond human sight yet presently experienced; the defeat of death, the rebirth of all humanity, the reconciliation of creation with God. The church, as his body (v.18), also images the unseen God. In the Letter to the Romans,

---

[3]For further examples of the use of the adjective *invisibilis* see Deshusses, Concordances III, 2, 404. See also Blaise, Vocabulaire, § 128, 249.

creation too can serve as pointer to the invisible God and to his power (Rm 1:20)[4].

The early orations similarly understand certain *visibilia* as aids to reaching the *invisibilia*. This is particularly so in a *super populum* for the December fast. Here the *visibilia* include the devotion of the fast (from the liturgical context), the worship itself and the feast of the incarnation[5]. The prayer reads:

"Tuere, domine, plebem tuam, et sacram sollemnitatem recolentem caelestis gratiae largitate prosequere; ut uisibilibus adiuta solaciis, ad inuisibilia bona promptius incitetur" (L 1315)[6].

In V 1178, the primary thrust of the motivating clause is that God has prepared the *bona invisibilia*, revealed as they are in Christ, the church, creation, and the liturgy, for those who love him. This love will now be examined.

Diligentibus

The faithful are described as *diligentes*, as those who love God. The love of the people for God has already been discussed in the analyses of the collects for Sundays IV and XXV[7], where it was linked directly to Jesus'

---

[4]*"Invisibilia enim ipsius a creatura mundi, per ea quae facta sunt intellecta, conspiciuntur, sempiterna quoque eius virtus et divinitas ..."* (Rm 1:20).
For a similar idea, though with more emphasis on the need for faith, see Heb 11:3.

[5]See the preface (L 1313) of the Mass (XLIII,iii).

[6]Guard your people, Lord, and, accompany it with the bounty of your grace, as it keeps this holy solemnity, so that aided by visible comforts, your people may be roused more readily to the good things that are beyond vision. See also L 1297 and L 172.

[7]For Sunday IV see above, 102, for Sunday XXV, above, 132.

restatement of the deuteronomic mandate. Christian love involves love and worship of God, and love of neighbour. Those who love God follow his mandates and commandments, which themselves are ordained towards this twofold love. As well, the commandments reflect God's own wisdom and providential ordering of all that he created in love. Thus life in love is life in God's wisdom and providence. This love for God is the grounds for entry to eternal life.

In V 1178, God's own good actions, such as the reconciliation of fallen creation, the rebirth of humanity, the restoration of peace and harmony, the possibility of true worship, have been effected by and revealed in Christ. Though their fullness remains beyond human vision, their revelation itself incites the faithful to love God. At the same time, only those whose love is in concert with God's love can partake in this fullness of revelation and salvation.

In the light of the *bona invisibilia* God has prepared and revealed, those who love him ask him to fill the faithful, heart, soul and mind, with a zealous, ardent, burning love for him: *infunde cordibus nostris tui amoris affectum*[8].

The *diligentes* seek a twofold effect from their petition for the gift of ardent love. Their ultimate desire is to obtain God's promises. They seek this through their petition for the gift to love God in and above all things.

Ut te in omnibus et super omnia diligentes

This petition evokes the deuteronomic commandment to love God (Dt 6:4-9). In the deuteronomic text, the love of God is at the centre of all the commandments, and as well involves the whole person, heart (*cor*), soul and strength. The faithful should be mindful of this love of God in every action from rising to sleeping, and in every place whether at home or on a journey.

---

[8]*Cor* has been analysed in the study of the collect for Sunday XXIV. See above 214. *Amor*, likewise has been discussed in the analysis of the collect for Sunday XII. See above 320. For *affectus*, found in the collect for Sunday IV, see above 107.

Reminders of this love should be carried in their hands and their minds, and burnished on the thresholds of their dwellings.

The petition and its deuteronomic source find a strong parallel in a prayer for the consecration of virgins (V 790)[9]. The relevant line reads: "*In te habeat omnia, quem diligere appetat super omnia ....*". Yet this sentence simply summarizies the women's desire that their whole life be centred on, dependent on and reflective of their love for God[10].

In V 1178, the ultimate end of loving God in and above all things is reaching the divine promises, which themselves are qualified as being beyond all human imagination and desire.

Promissiones tuas, quae omne desiderium superant, consequamur.

The divine *promissiones* signify eternal life in God[11]. They are marked by a divine superabundance (*superare*) which exceeds human desire

---

[9]See also L 1104, Sp 1254, G 2608-2609.

[10]"*Deus, castorum corporum benignus habitator et incorruptarum, deus, amator animarum: .. in caritate ferueat, et nihil extra te diligat; laudabiliter uiuat laudarequae non appetat. Te in sanctitate corporis, te in animi sui puritate glorificet. Amore te timeat, amore tibi seruiat. Tu ei honor sis, <tu> gaudium, tu uoluntas. Tu in merore consolacium, tu in ambiguitate consilium, tu in iniuria defensio, in tribulacione paciencia, in paupertate abundancia, in ieiunio cibus, in infirmitate medicina. In te habeat omnia, quem dilegere appetat super omnia ....*" (V 790).
Translation: God, bounteous dweller in chaste bodies and lover of incorrupt souls ... May [the one being consecrated] be fervent in love, and love nothing apart from you. May she live praiseworthily, and not desire to be praised. May she glorify you in sanctity of body and in the purity of her soul. May she fear you in love, and serve you in love. May you be her honour, her joy, her will. May you be her consolation in grief, her counsel in ambiguity, her defence against wrongdoing, her patience in tribulation, her wealth in poverty, her food in times of fast, her remedy in sickness. May she have you in all things, whom she loves above all things...

[11]The divine promises were discussed in the analysis of the collect for Sunday XXI. See above 273ff.

(*desiderium*)[12]. The ascription of these qualities to eternal life echoes a variety of scripture passages in which such excess is related to the abundance and power of God.

With regard to human *desiderium*[13], the riches of God are enough to fulfill all human longings:

"*Deus autem meus impleat omne desiderium vestrum secundum divitias suas in gloria, in Christo Iesu*" (Ph 4:19).

In the same vein, the power of God in the faithful surpasses (*facere superabundanter*) what Christians can ask or even understand:

"*Ei autem, qui potens est omnia facere superabundanter quam petimus aut intelligimus secundum virtutem quae operatur in nobis*" (Eph 3:20)[14].

In V 1178, the gift of obtaining God's promises follows from loving him in all things and above all things. Both these gifts come from the ardour of the love for God which is the object of the faithful's petition. The promises, which parallel the *bona invisibilia*, signify eternal life in God. Just as the *bona invisibilia* are beyond human ken (1 Cor 2:9), so too the divine promises, obtained through love of God, transcend every human desire.

Meaning of the prayer:

The meaning of the prayer emerges from the link between the *bona invisibilia*, the love of God above all things, and the acquisition of the divine promises which surpass all human longing. The faithful live within the revelation of God's love and goodness. The *visibilia*, chiefly God's self-

---

[12] Our oration appears to be the only prayer in the early sources that applies these qualities to the divine promises.

[13] For further examples of the use of *desiderium* see Deshusses, Concordances III, 2, 443.

[14] See also Ph 4:7.

revelation in the incarnation but also inclusive of the church, the liturgy, and creation, point to the *bona invisibilia* which will be fully revealed in eternal life. In response, the faithful seek to love God in and above all things, in line with the deuteronomic mandate. Love is the first and deepest response of the Christian to God. Through such an all-encompassing love for God, the baptized seek to attain eternal life, the promises which are beyond human desire.

ANALYSIS OF THE WORDS AND PHRASES IN THE COLLECT IN RELATIONSHIP TO THE MISSAL OF PAUL VI

The placement of the prayer in the Missal of Paul VI has brought about no major change to the vocabulary and meaning of the collect.

Worth noting is that, in the Missal, to love God above all things is related to the *devotio* of self denial:

"*Deus, qui beato Antonio abbati tribuisti mira tibi in deserto conversatione servire, eius nobis interventione concede, ut, abnegantes nosmetipsos, te iugiter super omnia diligamus*" (MR(1975) S. Antonii, Collecta, 516)[15].

RELATIONSHIP OF THE CHRISTIAN PEOPLE TO GOD

The church lives within the economy of revelation, in which the *visibilia*, chiefly the incarnation, the church and creation, reflect the as yet unseen good things that God has set in store for those who love him. These divine promises are beyond all human longing.

From within this world of revelation, the faithful relate to God in total and all-encompassing love. They seek to love him in and above all things.

---

[15] God, who granted to Blessed Abbot Anthony the wondrous marvels of serving you in prayer (*conversatio*) in the desert. Through his intercession on our behalf, grant that, practising self denial ourselves, we may constantly love you above all things.

This love, itself a gift from God, is a response to his revelation. As well it is the basis of their hope of entry into the promised eternal life.

FREER TRANSLATION OF THE COLLECT

Deus, qui diligentibus te bona invisibilia praeparasti, infunde cordibus nostris tui amoris affectum, ut, te in omnibus et super omnia diligentes, promissiones tuas, quae omne desiderium superant, consequamur.	God, you have prepared good things beyond the measure of our minds for those who love you. Flood our hearts with an ardent love for you. Lead us to love you in all things and beyond all things, so that we may gain your promises, which surpass all we could ever want or desire.

COLLECT FOR SUNDAY XXII

PRAYER

Deus virtutum, cuius est totum quod est optimum, insere pectoribus nostris tui nominis amorem, et praesta, ut in nobis, religionis augmento, quae sunt bona nutrias, ac, vigilanti studio, quae sunt nutrita custodias.

God of all powers, of whom is everything that is perfect, insert into our hearts the love of your name, and grant that with an increase in devout observance you may nourish what is good in us and in our zealous vigilance keep what has been nourished.

ORIGINAL SOURCE

Deus virtutum, cuius est totum quod est optimum, insere pectoribus nostris amorem tui nominis et praesta, ut et nobis relegionis aumentum quae sunt bona nutrias ac vigilantia studium quaesomus nutrita custodias.

    Reginensis 316: Collect for the Mass III,ii, Oraciones et Praeces per Dominicis Diebus (V 1182).

USE IN OTHER LITURGICAL SOURCES

    As noted by Bruylants[1], the collect is found in these sources: Dominica VI post Pentecosten, V(III.2,1;p.225) [V1182], Pr(158,1), A(1116), S(990), P(564), OR(170), X(257,1), N(140), Q(140V), 1474(265), 1570, 1604, as well as in these sources which do not have critical editions: G(183,1), Z(736), PaAng(245), Par(28).

    The prayer is found amongst the prayers after Mass in two sources:

---

[1]Bruylants, II, 467. For a more complete listing of sources and manuscripts see Moeller, <u>Corpus Orationum</u> III, D, Orationes 1708-2389, oration 2210, 228.

Preces post missam, alia oratio West II 526, West III 1365.

CHANGES FROM THE ORIGINAL

The Missal of Paul VI renders the prayer as it is found in the *Paduense* (P 564) and the Sacramentary of Angoulême (A 1116). The corrupt text of *Reginensis* 316 has been corrected accordingly: *et nobis* has become *in nobis, relegionis augmentum* has become *religionis augmento, uigiliantia studium* has become *vigilanti studio*, and *quaesomus* has been corrected to *quae sunt*[2]. This study will follow the corrected spelling as found in the Missal of Paul VI.

The prayer appeared in the Supplement to the Hadrianum (Sp 1147) and in the Missal of Pius V (Sixth Sunday after Pentecost) in a modified form:
.. *praesta et nobis religionis augmentum; ut, quae sunt bona nutrias ac pietatis studio, quae sunt nutrita custodias.*

ANALYSIS OF THE PRAYER IN THE ORIGINAL SOURCE
Origin:
See the accompanying introductory note to this series of prayers in *Reginensis* 316.

Grammatical structure[3]:

The collect is made up of three parts, (a) an address with motivating clause, (b) two connected petitions, and (c) two purpose clauses which amplify the second petition.

---

[2] For further discussion see L. Brou, Les Oraisons des dimanches après la Pentecôte: Commentaire Liturgique, Paroisse et Liturgie 38 (Bruges: Abbaye de Saint-André, 1959), 33.

[3] For a more complete analysis see Haessly, Rhetoric in the Sunday Collects of the Roman Missal, 84-86.

(a)	Address	*Deus virtutum*
	Motivation	*cuius est totum quod est optimum*
(b)	1st Petition	*insere pectoribus nostris amorem tui nominis*
	2nd Petition	*et praesta*
(c)	Purpose	*ut* (i) *in nobis religionis augmento, quae sunt bona nutrias*
		ac (ii) *(in nobis) vigilanti studio, quae sunt nutrita custodias.*

The motivating clause associates God's goodness with his power. Together they provide the basis for the confidence of the faithful in the goodness of what God gives and his power to give it. The two petitions are connected. The granting of the second is dependent on the fulfillment of the first. God nourishes what is good, and guards what is so nourished, when the hearts of the faithful are full of love of his name. At the same time, love of God's name is itself a good which is nourished by the *augmentum religionis* it has inspired and by perseverance in it (*uigilanti studio*).

The construction of the two purpose clauses is also instructive. By the increase of devotion and religious observance, God is asked to nourish what is good in the heart. Then, by his care, exercised through the people's zealous perseverance in their devotion, God is petitioned to protect what is thus nourished. God's guardianship protects what he has nourished. These *bona* in the hearts of the faithful are related to the perfection that comes from God.

The prayer is replete with biblical phrases. The appellation *dominus virtutum* is common in the Old Testament. The motivation clause draws its inspiration from the Letter of James (Jc 1:17). The notion of God's *nomen* is an Old Testament hebraism that found its way into liturgical language. It denotes God's self or God's essence. God's vigilant care is also echoed in the psalms (Ps 126:1).

Vocabulary:

Prominent vocabulary: *virtutes, optimum, pectus, nomen, amor, religio, nutrire, vigilans studium, custodire.*

The vocabulary study will begin with the conjunction of God's power and goodness found in the motivating clause. This pairing grounds the community's confidence both in the gifts that come from God, and in God's power to respond to their petitions.

Deus virtutum[4]

The appellation *Deus virtutum* is an important title of God with biblical origins. It is used in the Vulgate Old Testament to translate the greek Κύριος τῶν δυνάμεων[5]. In Old Testament thought this phrase denoted the victorious cosmic king surrounded by his heavenly host, ever ready to fight the battles with chaos, and on the historical plane, ever ready to fight on behalf of his people. Examples of this can be found in the Psalms. In Ps 23, the *dominus virtutum* (v.10) is acknowledged as creator and ruler of all things and people (v.1-2). In light of this, the faithful worship (v.4) and seek his blessing and mercy (v.5)[6]. This earlier conception provides the basis for the later New Testament and early Christian understanding of God as the one to whom all

---

[4]For further examples of the use of *virtus* see Deshusses, Concordances III, 4, 464-472.

[5]The hebrew transliteration reads Yahweh Sabaoth, which itself is translated by a variety of interchangeable latin and greek phrases including *Dominus exercituum* (Is 2:12, Jr 5:14), Κύριος παντοκράτωρ (Jr 5:14), Κύριος σαβαώθ (Is 2:12) and *Dominus Sabbaoth* (Jr 11:20). For critical commentary see C.L.Seow, "Hosts, Lord of," in D.N.Freeman, ed., The Anchor Bible Dictionary III (New York: Doubleday, 1993), 304-307.

[6]See also Ps 58:6, Ps 79, Ps 83.

powers (*virtutes*) are subject, and as well whose power is at work in the liturgy and human affairs[7].

The New Testament writings specifically reveal Christ's share in God's supremacy over all powers. Through Christ's death and resurrection, God has made all powers (*virtutes*) subject to him (1 Pt 3:22). In Ephesians, God has placed Christ above every power (*virtus*) and name (*nomen*) (Eph 1:20-21). For Paul in Romans, no powers (*virtutes*) can separate the faithful from the love (*caritas*) of God in Christ (Rm 8:38-39).

The title *Deus virtutum* is found in the liturgical sources. In a prayer which concludes the Pentecost vigil readings, the appellation is connected with the work of reparation, sanctification and preservation:

"*Domine deus virtutum, qui, conlapsa reparas et reparata conseruas, auge populos in tui nominis sanctificatione renouandos, ut omnes qui diluintur sacro baptismate, tua semper inspiratione dirigantur*" (V 623)[8].

Note the dynamic in the motivation clause. What God has restored he maintains as restored. Consequently those who are being renewed in baptism confidently petition God to continue to send them the graces which are appropriate to their renewed state. In V 1182 a similar dynamic is at work in the purpose clauses. The faithful are confident that if God bestows an increase

---

[7]For commentary on this understanding of God's power at work in human affairs, see Ellebracht, Remarks on the Vocabulary of the Ancient Orations in the Missale Romanum, 127-129.

[8]God of all powers, who restore what has fallen and preserve what you have restored, increase the people to be renewed in the sanctification of your name, and may all who are washed by sacred baptism be directed always by your inspiration.

of religious observance to nourish what is good in them, then he can be counted upon to watch over what has been nourished[9].

In V 1182, God's power is conjoined with the belief that he is the source of all that is good.

Cuius est totum quod est optimum[10]

As noted above, this descriptive clause is reminiscent of Jc 1:17. The goodness that comes from God has already been examined in a number of prayers[11]. Summarizing that material here, the clause evokes the goodness of initial creation, and the continuing good things that proceed from God inclusive of salvation in Christ and the Spirit. Furthermore the passage from James also implies that only what is good comes forth from the unchanging God.

The title *deus virtutum* ascribes to God supreme power over all powers, and over all that exists. Among the demonstrations of his power are his works of reparation, sanctification and preservation. In V 1182, the phrase *cuius est totum quod est optimum* draws out some of the implications of the title. From God's power comes everything that is good and perfect, and only what is good and perfect. Both God's power and goodness evoke reference to his works of salvation. At the level of human existence, whatever is good in the human heart comes from God, and so can be nourished and preserved by God. Motivated by God as the source of all power and unchanging goodness, the faithful ask that he will insert in their hearts the love of his name.

---

[9] See also L 1229, where God is addressed as *Omnium uirtutum, deus, bonorumque largitor* ....

[10] For further examples of the use of *optimus* (*bonus*) see Deshusses, Concordances III, 1, 199.

[11] A closer study of the pericope from James can be found in the analysis of the collect for Sunday XXI. See above, 348. Commentary on the *bona* that come from God can be found in the study of the collect for Sunday X. See above 284.

Insere pectoribus nostris tui nominis amorem

The terms in the petition have been analysed elsewhere. The noun *pectus* has been discussed in the study of the collect for Sunday VI[12]. It denotes the human person, heart, soul and mind. God's *nomen*, and the phrase *tui nominis amor* were examined in the analysis of the collect for Sunday XII. There it was seen that the divine *nomen*, a biblical term, indicates God's self, essence and revelation[13]. In the study of the collect for Sunday IV it was noted that love for God is especially expressed in worship and in love of neighbour[14]. In V 1182 the first petition requests heartfelt love for God, whose unmatched power is expressed in his overwhelming goodness.

The love of the divine name is the fundamental thrust of Christian life, as here requested of God who rules all powers, and by divine power works in the human heart. From within this love and reverence, by which the faithful seek the glory of God's name, Christians may, by religious observance, be nourished in what is good and, by their vigilance, safeguarded in this good.

Religionis augmentum quae sunt bona nutrias

Religionis[15] *augmentum*

In pagan Latin, *religio* meant the performance of religious rites, ceremonies and observances. Connected with it were the qualities of awe and reverence, along with a conscientious regard for one's duties. On its appropriation into Christian liturgical language, *religio* denoted religious observance and practice, inclusive of worship and good actions.

---

[12] See above, 329.

[13] See above, 317.

[14] See above, 102f.

[15] For further examples of the use of *religio* see Deshusses, Concordances III, 4, 54-55.

The Letter of James describes the *religio* which is pure in God's sight. It involves charity towards widows and orphans in their need, and guarding oneself from worldly contamination (Jc 1:26-27)[16].

In a *super populum*, *religionis augmentum* is equated with the exercise of good works (*pia opera*), God being the author of all the good that humans do. The granting of good gifts is associated with the faithful's increase in observance and devotion:

"*Adesto, domine, propitius plebi tuae; et ut eam perpetua bonitate non deseras, piis operibus indesinenter exerce: quia omnia dona prestabis, quibus concesseris religionis aumentum*" (L 670)[17].

Note that the collect (L 665) of this Mass (XVIII,xli) is concerned with the people's devotion to the name of God.

In a preface, the gift of an increase of *religio* is associated with devoted celebration of the Paschal Mystery[18]:

"*Uere dignum: suppliciter exorantes, ut et securitatem nobis temporum tribuas et religionis aumentum, quo magnum pietatis tuae sacramentum et quietis celebremus mentibus et deuotis*" (L 1125)[19].

---

[16]"*Si quis autem putat se religiosum esse non refrenans linguam suam, sed seducens cor suum, huius vana est religio. Religio munda et immaculata apud Deum et Patrem haec est: visitare pupillos et viduas in tribulatione eorum et immaculatum se custodire ab hos saeculo*" (Jc 1:26-27).

[17]Be present Lord propitiously to your people, and so that you may not desert them in your perpetual goodness, engage them unceasingly in good works: because you will furnish all gifts for those whom you have granted an increase in observance and devotion.

[18]For the reference to the Paschal Mystery see the collect (L 1123) for the Mass (XXXII,iii).

[19]It is right and fitting ... humbly praying that you bestow on us security in our age and an increase in observance, by which we may celebrate the great sacrament of your merciful goodness with tranquil and devoted minds.

In V 1182 the requested increase in the observance of worship and good works is understood to nourish (*nutrire*) what is good (*bona*) in the human person. First among these goods is love of God's name.

Nutrias[20]

The verb *nutrire* is not found in the *Veronensis*[21], and is quite rare in *Reginensis* 316 (V 166, V 470, V 1604). While it can denote God's fruitful nourishment of the harvest crops (V 1604), it is used most especially to denote the refreshment that comes from participation in Christian worship, which in turn leads to eternal life.

In a lenten post communion, refreshment and nourishment are set in parallel. The nourishment that communion brings is associated with attaining eternal life:

"*Refecti, domine, panae caelesti, ad uitam, quaesumus, nutriamur aeternam*" (V 166)[22].

According to an Easter offertory prayer, the church is nourished through the sacrifices offered in the Mass. Here, what is nourished is firstly what has been reborn in the Paschal Mystery:

"*Sacrificia, domine, paschalibus gaudiis immolamus, quibus ecclesia tua mirabiliter renascitur et nutritur*" (V 470)[23].

---

[20]For further examples of the use of *nutrire* see Deshusses, Concordances III, 3, 190.

[21]Though for the noun *nutrimentum* see L 1303.

[22]Restored by heavenly bread, may we be nourished Lord unto eternal life.

[23]"With paschal joy we offer these sacrifices, Lord, by which your church is wonderfully reborn and nourished."
With a slight modification (*exultantes offerimus* for *immolamus*) the prayer has been incorporated into the Missal of Paul VI: MR(1975) M. in die dom. Paschae in Resurr. Domini, Super oblata, 291.

The collect V 1182 associates God's nourishing with both love for God and religious practice. Within the context of the gift of love for God's name implanted within their hearts, the faithful petition the gift of an increase in their observance and practice of worship and good works. Through such an increase they seek that God may refresh and nourish what is good in their hearts. This goodness itself comes from God, who is the source of all goodness. The oration especially associates *bona* with the gift of love of God's name. The verb *nutrire* carries with it overtones of the strengthening and nourishing that comes from worship and communion, which ultimately leads to eternal life.

Having made this request, the faithful call upon God's power and goodness once again. Just as they asked for an increase in observance and practice so that God may restore and nourish what is good in their hearts, so they now ask that they may zealously and vigilantly maintain this *religio* so that God may guard what he has nourished.

Vigilanti studio quae sunt nutrita custodias
Custodias[24]

The liturgical sources associate God's guardianship with a range of divine activities, such as his ruling, preserving, protecting, bestowing and bountiful enriching. These actions are directed towards preserving what has come from God as creator (*institutor*) and author (*auctor*).

In a prayer over the people, the petition for God to guard (*custodire*) the gifts of his grace in his people is made because God is their creator (*institutor*) and ruler (*rector*). The gifts he is asked to guard correspond to the good things (*bona*) which he as *auctor* gave them. His guardianship parallels his work of preservation and protection. In an alternative purpose clause for

---

[24]For further examples of the use of *custodire* see Deshusses, Concordances III, 1, 403-407.

the prayer, the divine guardianship parallels his bestowal of gifts and the bountiful enrichment of what he created as good:

"*Omnipotens sempiterne deus, populi fidelis institutor et rector, in familia sacramento tui nominis adquisita gratiae tuae dona custodi: ut bona, quae te auctore percipit, te protegente seruentur* |:[*aliter*] *te largiente copiosius augeantur:*|" (L 514)[25].

Note the reference to the divine *nomen*. The faithful are described as the family brought together by the sacrament of God's name (baptism).

Uigilanti[26] *studio*

The object of the church's vigilant zeal is the increase of devotion (*augmentum religio*). Liturgical euchology associates both *vigilare* and *studium* with worship and devotion, all the while stressing that they are gifts from God.

Uigilare

According to the psalms, human oversight and vigilance are in vain unless supported by God's guardianship:

"*Nisi Dominus aedificaverit domum, in vanum laboraverunt qui aedificant eam. Nisi Dominus custodierit civitatem, frustra vigilat qui custodit eam*" (Ps 126:1).

A prayer from an Advent Mass uses *uigilare* in a twofold sense. It connotes vigilance in expectation of Christ's coming, as well as watchfulness

---

[25]"Almighty eternal God, creator and ruler of your people, guard the gifts of your grace in the family you acquired by the sacrament of your name, so that the good things, which it received from you their author, may be preserved by your protection: | [alternative] may be increased bounteously by your bestowing|."
For further actions associated with God's guardianship see V 1244 and V 1558.

[26]For further examples of the use of *vigilare* see Deshusses, Concordances III, 4, 454. For *pervigil* see III, 3, 362. For *studium* and *studere* see III, 4, 288. This prayer appears to be the only use of the term *vigilans studium*.

against sin. The oration associates expectant vigilance with offering exultant praise:

"*Fac nos quaesumus, domine deus noster, peruigiles atque solicitos aduentum expectare Christi filii tui domini nostri, ut dum uenerit pulsans, non dormientis peccatis sed uigilantes et in suis inueniat laudibus exultantes*" (V 1128)[27].

In V 1128, *vigilare* qualifies the faithful's zeal (*studium*) in their religious observance. A similar type of zeal is evident in the lenten offertory prayer V 663. There, zeal of pious devotion is an attribute in believers which makes their offerings acceptable to God. It leads to an upright spirit and cleanness of heart, and to a worship offered in faith and humility:

"*Omnipotens sempiterne deus, qui non sacrificiorum ambitione placaris, sed studio piae deuotionis intendis, da familiae tuae spiritum rectum et habere cor mundum, ut fides eorum haec dona tibi conciliet, humilitas oblata commendet*" (V 663)[28].

The final petition of our oration, then, invites God to guard, rule, guide and preserve the good that the people's increased religious observance has nourished and refreshed. They ask him to achieve this through granting them vigilant zeal in their observance and practice. Through such zeal they are ever alert to avoid sin, and as well, are able to offer acceptable worship, in true faith and love of God's name.

---

[27] Make us, Lord our God, to be ever vigilant and solicitous as we await the coming of Christ, your Son and our Lord, so that when he comes knocking he may find us not sleeping in our sins, but vigilant and exalting in his praise (V 1128).

[28] Almighty eternal God, who are not pleased by the vain display of sacrifices but look upon the zeal of loving devotion, grant that your family may have an upright spirit and a clean heart, so that their faith may make these gifts agreeable to you, and their humility may entrust to you their offerings (V 663).

Meaning of the prayer:

The central petition of the prayer is that God plant deep in the hearts of the baptized the gift of love of his name. Their love is in response to their faith in the power of God over all things and in all things. This power is expressed in that unmitigated, bountiful goodness which is exemplified in the cosmic acts of creation, salvation and renewal, as well as in God's guidance and protection in their own lives.

Within the context of their love for God, the faithful further ask for an increase in their observance of worship and practice of good works. Through this religious observance they seek that God will nourish the good that is in their hearts, especially the love for God which has just been petitioned. Connected with this petition is their prayer that God will enable them to persevere with zeal in what has been undertaken. God's power and goodness are trustworthy for those who love him. They are the source of all *bona* in the human heart, and so can be counted upon to provide the means for the nourishment and care of those good things.

Zeal for God's name, heartfelt love, and constant and devout service, exist together in the lives of the Christian people, who recognize the power of God over all things working for their good.

ANALYSIS OF THE WORDS AND PHRASES IN THE COLLECT IN RELATIONSHIP TO THE MISSAL OF PAUL VI

Vocabulary and meaning of the prayer:

There are no significant changes in use of vocabulary and in the meaning of the prayer within the context of the Missal of Paul VI.

Note, however, that the post communion prayer for the same Sunday (XXII) associates communion (an act of *religio*) with the nourishment of divine love (*nutrimentum caritatis*), and relates such nourishing to an increase in good works (another act of *religio*). The prayer reads:

"*Pane mensae caelestis refecti, te, Domine, deprecamur, ut hoc nutrimentum caritatis corda nostra confirmet, quatenus ad tibi ministrandum in fratribus excitemur*" (MR(1975) Dom. XXII, per annum, post communionem, 361)[29].

THE RELATIONSHIP OF THE CHRISTIAN PEOPLE TO GOD

The relationship of God to humanity and the church is expressed in a number of ways. Most centrally it is put forward in the title *Deus virtutum*. This is further elaborated when God is designated the source of all that is good, and by implication of only what is good. More specifically, the relationship is set forth in the gifts of love and religion that are bestowed, as well as in the nurturing protection that God maintains over the people.

The Christian's relationship to God is expressed in the love of God's name, and in the practice of religion which follows on from and in turn nourishes such love. However it is also expressed in an attitude of trusting dependence that looks to God as source of all that is good, and looks to God's vigilance in nourishing and protecting the good in human hearts and the love of God's name. If the church continues in devotion and good works, it is because God gives the grace but on the other hand, grace comes only to those who practice devotion and persevere in it.

The factors that come together in this prayer to express the church's relation to God are: recognition of God's power that works in all things, love of God's name embedded in their hearts, and the constant and vigilant religious observance by which this devotion is nourished and protected.

---

[29]"Restored by the bread of the heavenly table, we pray Lord, that this nourishment of love may strengthen our hearts so that we may be aroused to serve you in our brothers and sisters."
This prayer was written for the Missal of Paul VI.

FREER TRANSLATION OF THE COLLECT

Deus virtutum, cuius est totum quod est optimum, insere pectoribus nostris tui nominis amorem, et praesta, ut in nobis, religionis augmento, quae sunt bona nutrias, ac, vigilanti studio, quae sunt nutrita custodias.

Whatever is good comes from you, God to whose power all things are subject. Implant the love of your name deep in our hearts, so that by guiding us in living devout lives, you may nourish all that is good in us, and guard what you have nourished, through our zealous perseverance.

COLLECT FOR SUNDAY IX

PRAYER

Deus, cuius providentia in sui dispositione non fallitur, te supplices exoramus, ut noxia cuncta submoveas, et omnia nobis profutura concedas.

God, whose providence in its disposition never fails, we supplicants beseech you, that you may remove everything that is harmful to us, and grant to us everything that is profitable.

ORIGINAL SOURCE

Reginensis 316: *Super sindonem* for the Mass III,iii, Oraciones et Praeces per Dominicis Diebus (V 1186).

The original has been incorporated unmodified into the Missal of Paul VI. This study will follow the spelling found in the Missal.

USE IN OTHER LITURGICAL SOURCES

As noted by Bruylants[1], the collect is also found in these sources, usually amongst the Masses for Sundays outside of a particular season: Pr(159,1), A(1125), S(999), P(567) *OR*(171)[Sp 1150], X(258,1), N(141), Q(141), 1474(266), 1570, 1604, as well as in these unedited sources: G(186,1)[G 1241], Z(744), PaAng(253), Par(29).

Note also that the collect is used as a prayer for the office: *Ordo officii per hebdomadam, sabbato, ad nocturnam, oratio*, Casin[1] 24.

---

[1]Bruylants, II, 220. For a more detailed listing of sources and manuscripts, see Moeller, Corpus Orationum II D, Orationes 881-1707, oration 1188, 154.

ANALYSIS OF THE PRAYER IN THE ORIGINAL SOURCE

Origin:

See the accompanying introductory note to this series of prayers from *Reginensis* 316.

Grammatical structure[2]:

The prayer consists of (a) an address with motivating clause, and (b) a twofold petition, requesting a double effect from God's providence

(a) Address: *Deus*
    Motivation: *cuius providentia in sui dispositione non fallitur*

(b) Petitions: *te supplices exoramus*
    ut *noxia cuncta submoveas*
    omnia nobis profutura concedas.

The structure of the paired petitions reveals their essential meaning. The opposites *noxia nobis* and *profutura nobis* are set in parallel, as are their respective verbs *submovere* and *concedere*. *Noxia* and *profutura* indicate that in the fallen state of creation, there is need for the help of God's providence in the face of human weakness. On the other hand, *submovere* and *concedere* reveal God's protection and positive action. The faithful request the removal of what is harmful and the granting of what is helpful[3].

God's unfailing *providentia* provides both the context for distinguishing what is harmful from what is advantageous, and also the grounds for the

---

[2] For a more complete grammatical analysis, see Haessly, Rhetoric in the Sunday Collects of the Roman Missal, 86-88.

[3] Other early orations contain a similar dynamic:
"... *Sed ut noxia quaeque discutias et prospera iugiter largiaris* ..." (L 571),
"*Plebs tua, domine, quaesumus, benedictionis sancte munus accipiat, per quod et noxia quaeque declinet, et optata repperiat*" (L 581). L 581 is also found in the Missal of Paul VI: MR(1975) Orr. super populum, 4, 507.

community's confidence in its supplication. The remainder of this study will be largely devoted to the analysis of the vocabulary of the motivating clause "*cuius providentia in sui dispositione non fallitur.*"

Vocabulary:

Prominent vocabulary: *providentia, dispensatio, fallere, supplex, submovere, concedere, noxius, profuturus.*

The central feature of the prayer is the faithful's belief, expressed in the motivating clause, of the unfailing providence of God.

Providentia[4]

The early Christian understanding of God's *providentia* had both an intellectual and an affective sense[5]. The intellectual sense designated the universal government of the divinity. This is reflected in the opening lines of the following preface, in which the providence by which God rules all things

---

[4]For further examples of the use of *providentia* see Deshusses, Concordances III, 3, 533-34.
While the word *providentia* most readily expresses the concept of providence, Blaise also points up other terms that carry similar meaning. He divides them into three categories: (1) expressions of God's continuous care for creation, (2) expressions of providential government, and (3) expressions of providential preordination. A number of these words occur in the Mass collects for the Sundays of ordinary time in the Missal of Paul VI, consequently relating those terms to the unfailing divine *providentia* set forth in the collect for Sunday IX. These words, with the number of the week in which the collect occurs, are as follows:
category (1); *conservare* (XVIII),
category (2); *rector* (XXIV), *gubernare* (X, XII, XVIII), *moderari* (II), *ordinare* (VIII),
category (3); nil.
Note also that, like *providentia* (L 880), both *rector* and *gubernare* are related to God's creative activity: *creator et rector, auctor et gubernator.* See Blaise, Vocabulaire, § 138-141.

[5]See Blaise, Vocabulaire, § 141.

parallels the power through which he created them:

"*Uere dignum: cuius et potentia sunt creata et prouidentia reguntur uniuersa* ..." (L 880)[6].

The more distinctly Christian contribution is the development of the affective dimension of God's providence. In the orations the intellectual sense of ordering is consistently related to God's mercy (*pietas*) and clemency (*clementia*). This is evident in the conjunction of *providentia* and *pietas* in the lenten *super populum* V 130[7]. In the prayer, merciful providence (*tuae providentia pietatis*), directed towards the aid of human weakness (*fragilitas nostra*) and effected through the lenten observances, brings restoration (*reparare*) and renewal (*innovare*). Furthermore, God's providence remains active in all difficulties, protecting (*protegere*) and guiding (*gubernare*) the faithful so as to lead (*inducere*) them to eternal salvation. The prayer reads:
"*Reparet nos, quaesumus, domine, semper et innouet tuae prouidentiae pietatis, que fragilitatem nostram et inter mundi tempestates protegat et gubernet et in portum perpetuae salutis inducat*" (V 130)[8].

In V 1186, divine, merciful providence is conjoined with the noun *dispositio*.

---

[6]"... [God] by whose power all things were created, and in whose providence they are ruled ...."

[7]See also L 271 (*clemens providentia*), L 308 (*providentiae tuae beneficia*).

[8]May the mercy accorded by your providence restore and renew us, may it protect our human weakness in the midst of the storms of this world, and may it govern and lead us, bringing us to the port of eternal salvation.

Dispositio[9]

The divine *dispositio* embraces the entire economy of creation and salvation, inclusive of the special role of the church in the work of salvation. This can be seen in the prayer which follows the Genesis creation reading in the Easter Vigil liturgy from *Reginensis* 316. The oration joins creation (from the Genesis reading), the mystery of the church, and the perpetual divine plan in which human salvation is effected. This salvation is associated, in propitiation, to the raising up (*erigere*) and renewal (*nouare*) of fallen creation (celebrated in the Vigil). The ultimate aim of God's *dispositio* is the return of all creation to its pristine origins and integrity. Note also that the divine economy is described as *perpetua*. As such it is related to the unchanging nature of God's power and the eternity of his light (*Deus inconmutabilis uirtus, lumen aeternum*) which themselves underlie the act of creation and ground God's continuous fidelity to what he has created. The text reads:

"*Deus inconmutabilis uirtus, lumen aeternum, respice propicius ad tocius aeclesiae tuae mirabile sacramentum et opus salutis humane perpetuae disposicionis effectu tranquillus operare, totusque mundus experiatur et uideat deiecta erigi, inueterata novari, et per ipsum redire omnia integrum, a quo sumpseret principium*" (V 432)[10].

---

[9] For further examples of the use of *dispositio* see Deshusses, Concordances III, 1, 513.

[10] "God, unchanging power, eternal light, look propitiously onto the wonderful mystery of all your church and tranquilly bring about the work of human salvation by the effect of your perpetual disposition, so that the whole world may experience and see the fallen raised up, the old made new, and all things return to their perfection through the one from whom they received their beginning."
The prayer is also found in the Missal of Paul VI: MR(1975) Vig. pasch., Or. post VII lectionem, 279.

The divine *dispositio* extends to the ordering of ordinary human affairs, placing all events and arrangements within the workings of salvation and grace[11]. Thus in a *secreta* from a wedding Mass, the bride is understood to have grown, developed and come to readiness for the new station of marriage all under God's *dispositio*. The expectation underlying the prayer is that what God's plan brings about God's grace will complete. As will be shown below, the preface from the same Mass links this grace to God's *providentia*. The *secreta* reads:

"*Adesto, domine, supplicacionibus nostris et hanc oblacionem famularum tuarum illarum, quam tibi offerunt pro famula tua illa, quam ad statum maturitatis et ad diem nupciarum perducere dignatus es, placidus ac benignus adsume, ut quid tua dispositione expeditur, tua gratia conpleatur*" (V 1445)[12].

As with the divine *dispositio*, divine providence is also active in mundane affairs, with the purpose of bringing salvation. The preface to the same Mass (III,lii) associates divine *providentia* and grace with the ordinary affairs of married life (the begetting of offspring), particularly forseeing the regeneration of offspring through baptism:

"*Uere dignum:* ... *Tua enim, domine, prouidentia tuaque gracia ineffabilibus modis utrumque dispensat, ut quod generacio ad mundi aededit ornatum, regeneracio ad aeclesiae perducat augmentum*" (V 1446)[13].

---

[11] For the relationship of the divine *dispositio* to ecclesial orders and offices see L 951.

[12] Hear, Lord, our supplications and, in peace and benevolence, receive this oblation of these your maidservants ___ which they offer on behalf of your handmaid ___ whom you deigned to bring to maturity and to guide through to this day of her marriage, so that what was made ready by your disposition may be brought to fulfillment by your grace.

[13] "It is right and fitting ... For your providence and your grace dispense by ineffable means to serve two purposes [*utrumque*] so that what the generation of offspring adds to the adornment of the world, the rebirth of baptism may

Together the divine *providentia* and *dispositio* denote God's merciful guidance and governance in his entire economy of creation and salvation. Divine providence includes the more intellectual action of ordering and the affective disposition of mercy. This providence is especially effected through the mystery of the church. The divine economy embraces the first creation, its renewal and restoration following sin, and the return of all things to their original perfection and goodness in God. While divine providence encompasses the entire universe and plan of salvation, it also guides all the events and orderings of human life within this plan.

Collect V 1186 further describes this conjunction of *providentia* and *dispositio* as unfailing (*non fallitur*[14]). This assures the faithful that God's merciful government and design are ever present and ever active in their lives as well as in all creation. This dependability implies a contrast between God's benevolent disposition and all other human dispensations, which remain subject to sin and unable to bring about the restoration of creation.

In the face of such power and mercy, the faithful, aware of their own fragility and weakness, present their petition in humble supplication. This note of humility, as the response of sinful humanity to God's overwhelming greatness and mercy, has already been encountered in the study of the collect for Sunday X (V 556)[15].

The church's request is that God's providence take from their midst what is harmful, and provide them with what is beneficial. The above analysis

---

lead to the growth of the church."
This prayer has been incorporated into the Missal of Paul VI: MR(1975) In celebr. Matrimonii A, Praef. propr., 745.

[14]For further examples of the use of *fallere* see Deshusses, Concordances III, 2, 102-103.

[15]See above, 285. Other examples include L 876, L 1100.

of *providentia* and *dispositio* brings more definition to *noxia* and *profutura*. Given the merciful nature of God's providence, its all embracing scope in human affairs, and its orientation towards salvation, the *profutura* have the connotation of what is congruent with restored creation and advantageous for eternal life. By contrast *noxia* connote what lead to perdition. God's providence and disposition both remove what is harmful and provide what is needful.

Meaning of the prayer:

The meaning of the prayer is established by the reference in the motivating clause to God's unfailing providence and its disposition. This determines the community's relation to God and its dependence on divine care and action. Providence denotes the people's confidence in God's merciful and beneficial rule. It also marks God's continuous care for what he created, inclusive of the restoration, renewal, guidance and protection of all things, and ultimately their return to their pristine state. All human actions fall within the ambit of the divine providential economy of grace, a disposition in which the church plays a role.

The unfailing nature of divine providence gives rise, in the community, to humility and reassurance. All human rule of itself is fallible, infected as it is by sin. Yet the baptized can be confident that in God's providence and its disposition, characterized as it is by mercy, power and love, they can always ask to be protected from harm and granted what leads to salvation.

There are no significant changes in use of vocabulary and in the meaning of the prayer within the context of the Missal of Paul VI.

THE RELATIONSHIP OF THE CHRISTIAN PEOPLE TO GOD

The Christian people relate to God within the economy of creation, salvation and the return to original goodness that has been effected in God's merciful providence and its disposition. Everything, from the entire order of creation to the ordering of human affairs, falls under the merciful rule of God, a rule that brings salvation, renewal and completion. The church, under God's government, plays a role in this plan. The unfailing nature of God's loving providence is the grounds for the church's assurance that their petitions are not in vain.

At the same time, the inerrancy and dependability of God's providence signals the ever-failing nature of human government and designs. The collect's petition, with its contrast between the *noxia nobis* and the *profutura nobis*, is also a reminder of the fallen state of the world, human proclivity to sin, and the twofold action of God in removing what is harmful and providing what is beneficial.

FREER TRANSLATION OF THE COLLECT

Deus, cuius providentia in sui dispositione non fallitur, te supplices exoramus, ut noxia cuncta submoveas, et omnia nobis profutura concedas.

God, your merciful care of your people never ceases nor falls short. Hear the prayers which we humbly presume to place before you. Take from our midst all that brings harm to us, and send every gift that is beneficial for our salvation.

COLLECT FOR SUNDAY XXVI

PRAYER

Deus, qui omnipotentiam tuam parcendo maxime et miserando manifestas, gratiam tuam super nos indesinenter infunde, ut, ad tua promissa currentes, caelestium bonorum facias esse consortes.

God, who manifest your omnipotence most especially by pardoning and showing mercy, pour unceasingly your grace upon us, so that running to your promises, you may make us partakers of the goods of heaven.

ORIGINAL SOURCE

Reginensis 316: Collect for the Mass III,vi, *Oraciones et Praeces per Dominicis Diebus* (V 1198). Unlike the other Masses for this section which have both a collect and a *super sindonem*, this Mass (III,vi) has only the one prayer, the oration being studied, preceding the *secreta* prayer.

In the main modification of the original source, the verb in the first petition *multiplica* has been replaced by *indesinenter infunde*. There is little change to the meaning of the prayer[1]. Whereas *multiplica* emphasises the abundance of divine grace, *indesinenter infunde* underscores the complete

---

[1] Blaise treats *multiplicare* (§ 67) and *infundere* (§ 66) in an extended section dealing with verbs signifying God's giving (*donner, accorder*). There seems to be little of significance to distinguish them one from the other. See Blaise, Vocabulaire, § 65-68. Perhaps the modification is chiefly stylistic, since *multiplicare* already appears twice amongst the collects for Ordinary Time (Sundays XVI, XVII), and *infundere* only on one other occasion (Sunday XX). Against this, *effundere* is found in the petition of the collect for Sunday XXVII.

dependence of the community on God's mercy and pardon. Note that the petition in MR(1570) reads *multiplica super nos misericordiam tuam*[2].

USE IN OTHER LITURGICAL SOURCES

As noted by Bruylants[3], the collect is also found in these sources: Dominica X post Pentecosten; Pr(173,1; 201,1), A(1179), S(1047), P(591) OR(172)[Sp 1159], X(261,1), N(143), Q(142), 1474(270), 1570, 1604, as well as in these unedited sources: G(198,1)[G 1332], Z(767).

In the Ambrosian sacramentary, the *Bergomensis*, the prayer served as a collect for the third of the Pentecost Rogation Days: *Orationes quae dicendae sunt in litaniis vel in vigiliis cottidianis diebus, de die tertio, alia oratio* (Bergom 727).

ANALYSIS OF THE PRAYER IN THE ORIGINAL SOURCE

Origin: See the accompanying introductory note for the Masses from this section of *Reginensis* 316.

Grammatical structure[4]:

The collect consists of (a) an address with motivating clause, (b) a petition, and (c) two interconnected purpose clauses, with the attainment of the second one dependent on the fulfillment of the first.

---

[2]This rendition, which echoes Ps 35:8, is found in some earlier manuscripts. See Moeller, Corpus Orationum III D Orationes 1708-2389, 117.

[3]Bruylants, II, 418. For a more complete list of sources and manuscripts see Moeller, Corpus Orationum III D Orationes 1708-2389, oration 1952, 116-117.

[4]For a more complete analysis see Haessly, Rhetoric in the Sunday Collects of the Roman Missal, 92-95.

(a)	Address Motivation	*Deus* *qui omnipotentiam tuam parcendo maxime et miserando manifestas,*
(b)	Petition	*multiplica super nos gratiam tuam,*
(c)	1st Purpose 2nd Purpose	*ut ad tua promissa currentes,* *caelestium bonorum facias esse consortes.*

The use of *parcere* and *miserari* in the gerund emphasises that God's pardon and mercy are effected and experienced in the present. This is further evidenced in the verb *manifestare*.

The two purpose clauses are connected. Sharing in the goods of heaven follows upon active desire (*currere*) for the promises. The promises and the *caelestium bona* are in parallel. As well, the enthusiasm, desire and effort that *currere* denotes is fulfilled in the joy of sharing in (*consortes*) the goods of eternal life. Both the running towards and participation in heavenly goods are gifts from God, consequent on his mercy and pardon. In turn, the experience of this mercy and pardon establishes the faithful's confidence that it is possible for them to enter heavenly beatitude. The study of the prayer's vocabulary makes these dynamics clearer.

Vocabulary:

Prominent vocabulary: *omnipotentia, parcere, miserari, maxime, manifestare, multiplicare, gratia, currere, promissum, consors.*

Our discussion will begin with an analysis of the motivating clause, *qui omnipotentiam tuam parcendo maxime et miserando manifestas.*

The oration expresses the people's faith that God's power (*omnipotentia*) is most fully and clearly (*maxime*) manifested (*manifestare*) in the community's experience of divine mercy (*miserari*) and pardon (*parcere*). This reflects God's power over sin and death, as well as the power of God's love for humanity in spite of their sin. The verbs are commonly found together in the scriptures and the early orations. Before examining their conjunction, they will be treated separately, beginning with the more all-embracing term *miserari*[5].

Miserando

References to God's mercy and compassion are found in overwhelming numbers in the scriptures and the early orations. One of the most comprehensive expositions is to be found in Eph 2:4-6, where God's mercy is seen to be the primary expression of God's boundless love for humanity. The Christian experience of salvation from sin and death[6], restoration in Christ, being raised up, and the promise of heaven are all an experience of God's mercy in Christ:

"*Deus autem qui dives est in misericordia propter nimiam caritatem suam, qua dilexit nos et cum essemus mortui peccatis, convivificavit nos in Christo, cuius gratia estis salvati, et conresuscitavit et consedere fecit in caelestibus in Christo Iesu*" (Eph 2:4-6)[7].

---

[5] The divine mercy is expressed through a wealth of word forms related to the verb *misereri*. Blaise lists *misericors, miserator, misereri, miseratus, misericordia*. See Blaise, Vocabulaire, § 64. The main reference works used in this study make no distinction between the scriptural and liturgical use of *misereri* and *miserari*. See Blaise, Vocabulaire, § 64, Dutripon, Bibliorum Sacrorum Concordantiae, 883-885, Deshusses (see below) and Schnitker and Slaby, Concordantia, 1482-85. For the purposes of this study, they will both be treated as having the same meaning. For further examples of the use of *misericordia, misericorditer, misericors* and *misereri* see Deshusses, Concordances III, 3, 89-100.

[6] Sin and death have been studied in the analysis of the collect for Sunday XIV. See above, 244.

[7] See also the passage Tt 3:4-6. It contains more emphasis on the regeneration of baptism and renewal in the Spirit.

As in the scriptures, the early liturgical sources repeatedly set grace within the context of God's mercy, including the averting of what sins truly deserve (L 1039), the defeat of the enemies and errors of faith (L 621), protection from *mortalitas* (L 446), and remedies for sin (L 871). A very common appellation of God conjoins his mercy and power; *omnipotens et misericors Deus*[8]. Our prayer, V 1198, links the experience of pardon (*parcere*) with this all embracing mercy.

Parcendo[9]

Though God's pardon of sin can be associated with repentance, ultimately it does not come about as a result of anything the faithful may do or offer. In Joel 2:18 it is related to God's commitment to his promise, whereby God jealously guards his sinful people because they are his. A passage from the Book of Wisdom (Sap 11:21-27) associates God's sparing and pardon with his act of creation. The excerpt states that God loves all he created, and offers pardon precisely because he loves his creation. The relevant verse reads "*Parcis autem omnibus, quoniam tua sunt, Domine, qui amas animas*" (Sap 11:27). Note further that in the passage God's mercy (*misereri*) is an expression of his creative power (v.24), a power which manifests God's love.

The use of *parcere* hints at a degree of play between our oration and the verse Rm 8:32 in the Vulgate translation of that letter. The God who did not spare his own son (Rm 8:32[10]), manifests his power in unsparing pardon and mercy (V 1198).

---

[8]For some of the many examples in the *Veronensis*, see L 84, L 121, L 122, L 172, L 188.

[9]For further examples of the use of *parcere* see Deshusses, Concordances III, 3, 284-85.

[10]"*Qui etiam proprio Filio suo non pepercit ...*" (Rm 8:32).

The conjunction of *parcere* and *miserari* points to a further scriptural play. The prophecies of doom which characterize the first section of the Book of Ezekiel are intermittently punctuated by the following refrain, in which God expresses his impending, furious punishment in response to the depth of the people's sinfulness:

"*Dicit Dominus ... et non parcet oculus meus, et non miserebor*" (Ez 5:11)[11].

Our oration stands this prophecy on its head. God's power is shown not in his ability to punish sinners, but in his forgiveness of sinners and his defeat of sin and death. The contrast with the Ezekiel formula emphasizes that mercy and pardon are at the heart of all God's actions for humanity, and constitute the prime expressions of his love and power.

God's power and mercy are conjoined in a number of prayers[12]. The divine mercy provides the context for pardon, which itself is often one in a series of divine actions. An example is the *super sindonem* V 1369, where pardon (*parcere*), support (*sustentare*), forgiveness (*ignoscere*) and sanctification (*sanctificare*) are all set together within the framework of God's mercy. The oration reads:

"*Misericors et miserator domine, qui nos parcendo sustentas et ignoscendo sanctificas, da ueniam peccatis nostris et sacramentis caelestibus seruientes ab omni culpa liberos esse concede*" (V 1369)[13].

The same can be seen in V 1365, where, within the context of mercy, pardon is linked with the forgiveness of sins and restoration[14].

---

[11]See also Ez 7:4,11; 8:18; 9:5,10.

[12]Other examples include L 509, V 239, V 1365, V 1414.

[13]God of compassion and pity, you who sustain us by pardoning and sanctify us by forgiving, grant forgiveness for our sins, and concede that we who are serving your heavenly mysteries, may be free from all fault.

[14]See also L 190, where pardon is associated with correction (*corripere*).

The conjunction of *miserari* and *parcere* connotes the deepest workings of God's love. The divine mercy is the primary expression of God's love in Christ towards sinful humanity. It is known to the faithful in their experience of the defeat of sin and death, restoration and being raised up, and the promises of eternal life. *Parcere* focuses mercy directly on the forgiveness of sin. Yet it, too, calls to mind the ever faithful love of God for his creation. The liturgical euchology does not conceive of God's pardon as an isolated event, but links it with such actions as forgiveness, support, correction, sanctification. In this way it understands pardon as one in a series of actions enabling the sinner to live within God's righteousness.

Together, the pardon and mercy of God evoke the defeat of death, and the whole economy of salvation, restoration and eternal life which God's love for sinful humanity has worked. In V 1198, the experience of this redemptive love, mercy and pardon is seen as the principle manifestation of God's power.

Manifestas[15]

The verb *manifestare* also deserves comment. Through its use in the scriptures and the early liturgical sources, *manifestare* carries not only the meaning of disclosure, but also the sense of a manifestation that is so strong it calls forth a response or witness. It also has Christological overtones. This can be seen in the Vulgate translation of John's Gospel, where the miracle at Cana, the first of Jesus' great signs, both manifests Jesus' glory and elicits the first act of faith:

"*Hoc fecit initium signorum Iesus in Cana Galilaeae et manifestavit gloriam suam, et crediderunt in eum discipuli eius*" (Jo 2:11)[16].

---

[15] For further examples of the use of *manifestare* see Deshusses, Concordances III, 3, 22.

[16] In this passage and in the one below from the Letter of John, *manifestare* is a translation of the greek ἐφανερόω. For comment on its Christological

The same heightened sense of disclosure can be seen in the opening verses of the First Letter of John. Here the manifestation of Christ, the Word of life heard, seen and touched, evokes belief and testimony (1 Jo 1:1-2). Similarly, in the liturgical sources *manifestare* connotes the powerful disclosure revealed in the incarnation (L 1266), the testimony of John the Baptist (L 252), and the witness of martyrdom (L 410).

In V 1198, *maxime manifestas*, combined with the gerunds *parcendo* and *miserando*, denotes that the principal expression of God's power is disclosed in the sinner's experience of pardon and mercy, an experience which takes in salvation from death, forgiveness, restoration, and the promises of eternal life.

In light of their experience of the power of God through his mercy and pardon of their sins, the faithful petition that he bestow the same mercy and pardon upon them: *multiplica super nos gratiam tuam*. The purpose of their request is twofold; to run to God's promises, and so come to eternal life. *Currentes*[17]

The first purpose clause expresses the desire to run towards the divine promises or the things promised: *ad tua promissa currentes*. The clause is quite common in the early orations, where it signifies the faithful's desire to reach eternal happiness[18]. As seen above in the study of the collect for Sunday XXI, the divine promises denote eternal beatitude[19]. That same study also reveals that the promises are attained through love and obedience of the divine

---

significance, see R.Brown, The Epistles of John, The Anchor Bible (New York: Doubleday & Company, Inc., 1982), 166-67.

[17]For further examples of the use of *currere* see Deshusses, Concordances III, 1, 401-402.

[18]Blaise, Vocabulaire, § 44, fn 1, and see also L 256.

[19]See above, 273.

precepts. The participle *currentes*, then, signals the promptitude of this love and obedience to the mandates. According to Blaise, it denotes a degree of fervour and eagerness, echoing Paul's image of the athlete running so as to capture the prize (1 Cor 9:24)[20]. This desire, hope and fervour for the divine is reflected in the following Christmas offertory prayer, where the conjunction of *exultare* and *currere* points to the joy and worship associated with the manifestation of redemption[21]. The prayer reads:

"*Exultantes, Domine, cum muneribus ad altaria ueneranda concurrimus: quia et omnium nobis hodie summa uotorum et causa nostrae redemptionis exhorta est*" (L 1261)[22].

In the words of V 1198, the faithful eagerly run towards the divine promises through free, eager and loving obedience to God's mandates. The gift of life in the promises is described as *caelestium bonorum ... esse consortes*.

Consortes[23]

This clause is loosely based on the Vulgate translation of 2 Pt 1:4. In the epistle, the fulfillment of the divine promises is described as a partaking in (*efficere consortes*) the divine nature. The pericope stresses the sinless

---

[20]"*Nescitis quod ii, qui in stadio currunt, omnes quidem currunt, sed unus accipit bravium? Sic currite ut comprehendatis*" (1 Cor 9:24). See Blaise, Vocabulaire, § 470, footnote 1. *Currere* is linked more directly with the divine mandates in Ps 118:32 and L 623.

[21]The relationship between the mandates and worship was brought out in the studies of the collects for Sundays IV and XXV.

[22]Rejoicing, Lord, eagerly we together approach your altars for worship, because today both the perfection of all our prayers and longings and the cause of our redemption has appeared to us.

[23]For further examples of the use of *consors* see Deshusses, Concordances III, 1, 340-341.

imperishability of the divine over and against the changeableness and corruption of what is worldly:

"... *ut per haec efficiamini divinae consortes naturae fugientes eius, quae in mundo est, concupiscentiae corruptionem*" (2 Pt 1:2-4).

The collect under consideration has replaced sharing in the divine nature with sharing in the good things of heaven[24]. A similar construction is found in the lenten collect V 129, an oration which contains a number of parallels with V 1198. Participation in the lenten fast and *devotio* (*gloriosa remedia*), itself a foretaste of heaven, is paralleled with life according to God's government, the result of which is eternal life. This relationship between participation in the remedies and God's government calls to mind the link betwen God's mandates and the promises. The remedies, as a foretaste of heaven, connote the experience of divine mercy and pardon on earth. The collect reads: "*Deus, qui nos gloriosis remediis in terris adhuc positus* [*positos*] *iam caelestium rerum facis esse consortes, tu, quaesumus, in ista qua uiuimus nos uita guberna, ut ad illam in qua ipse es luce* [*lucem*] *perducas*" (V 129)[25].

Meaning of the prayer:

The meaning of the prayer flows from the implications of the motivating clause. The divine acts of pardon and mercy connote the whole economy of God's love in Christ for sinful humanity. They express the

---

[24]According to Blaise, the expressions *caelestium bona, bona invisibilia* (Sunday XX, above, 436), and *perpetua felicitas* (Sunday XXXIII, above, 149) all refer to the eternal blessings and beatitude of heaven. See Blaise, Vocabulaire, § 299.

[25]God, who through gloroius remedies make us already partakers of heavenly things while still on earth, we ask you to govern us in this life which we live, so that you may lead us to that in which you yourself are the light. This prayer is also found in the Missal of Paul VI: MR(1975) Sabb. hebd. II Quadr., Collecta, 199.

faithful's experiences of the defeat of death and sin, and their restoration and preservation, experiences which are the foretaste and promise of eternal life. The verb *manifestare* further points to the transformative, disclosive power of this revelation in Christ of pardon and mercy amongst sinners. For the believer, this manifestation is the foremost expression of God's power.

Their experience of God's merciful pardon raises in the faithful the desire to eagerly seek the fullness which God's love promises. Their running and striving for the promises is exhibited in enthusiastic and loving obedience for God's mandates and worship. The end result of this course is a sharing in the immutable good things of eternal life. These entail the complete revelation of that divine love, whose power is most clearly shown on earth in its mercy and pardon.

The placement of the prayer within the context of the Missal of Paul VI has brought about no major change to the vocabulary and meaning of the collect.

THE RELATIONSHIP OF THE CHRISTIAN PEOPLE TO GOD

God's power is most deeply revealed in his pardon and mercy. This experience points to the entire economy of God's love and mercy in Christ, expressed in salvation from death and sin, restoration, preservation and the promise of eternal life. At the same time, this experience of the economy of mercy indicates how sin and death have overwhelmed humanity, leaving it powerless and destitute apart from God's mercy.

The manifestation of God's mercy and pardon leads the baptized to eagerly pursue, love and obey the mandates, inclusive of worship. This loving obedience offers a foretaste of heaven. Through such obedience, which itself is dependent on God's grace of pardon and mercy, the faithful no longer share in sin and death, but in the immutable goodness of eternal life.

FREER TRANSLATION OF THE COLLECT

Deus, qui omnipotentiam tuam parcendo maxime et miserando manifestas, gratiam tuam super nos indesinenter infunde, ut, ad tua promissa currentes, caelestium bonorum facias esse consortes.

God, the breadth and depth of your power is revealed to us in your pardon and mercy. Never cease to pour your grace upon your people so that as we eagerly seek your promises, you may make us partakers of heavenly things.

COLLECT FOR SUNDAY XXVII

PRAYER

Omnipotens, sempiterne Deus, qui abundantia pietatis tuae et merita supplicum excedis et vota, effunde super nos misericordiam tuam, ut dimittas quae conscientia metuit, et adicias quod oratio non praesumit.

All powerful, eternal God, who by the abundance of your loving kindness surpass the merits and the prayers of your supplicants, pour out your mercy upon us, so that you may forgive what our conscience dreads and add what our prayers do not presume to ask.

ORIGINAL SOURCE

Reginensis 316: Collect for the Mass III,vii, *Oraciones et Praeces per Dominicis Diebus* (V 1201). The prayer has been incorporated unchanged into the Missal of Paul VI, though there have been some slight corrections (*habundantia, meritis, demittas*).

USE IN OTHER LITURGICAL SOURCES

As noted by Bruylants[1], the collect is also found in these sources: Dominica XI post Pentecosten; Pr(178,1), A(1217), S(1081), P(615), OR(172)[Sp 1162], X(262,1), N(143), Q(142v), 1474(272), 1570, 1604, as well as in these unedited sources: G(205,1)[G 1375], Z(784), Par(36).

ANALYSIS OF THE PRAYER IN THE ORIGINAL SOURCE

Origin:

See the accompanying introductory note to this series of prayers in *Reginensis* 316.

---

[1]Bruylants, II, 770.

Grammatical structure[2]:

The collect consists of (a) an address to God with motivating clause, (b) a petition, and (c) two connected purpose clauses whose structure parallels that of the motivating clause.

(a) Address   *Omnipotens, sempiterne Deus*
    Motivation   *qui abundantia pietatis tuae*
                         et merita supplicum excedis
                         et vota (supplicum excedis).

(b) Petition   *effunde super nos misericordiam tuam,*

(c) 1st. Purpose   *ut*   *dimittas quae conscientia metuit,*
    2nd. Purpose   *et*   *adicias quod oratio non praesumit.*

The prayer contains a number of parallels. The first is between God's *abundantia pietatis* and his *misericordia*. The faithful pray that God will show the abundance of his loving goodness through pouring his merciful compassion upon them. Just as God's loving kindness attends to merit and to prayer, so too does his mercy. These twinned effects form the second major parallel in the prayer.

This second parallel is between the clauses which express the prayer's motivation and those which express the purpose of the prayer's petition. They can be set out as follows:

merita supplicum excedis   *dimittas quae conscientia metuit,*

vota (supplicum excedis)   *adicias quod oratio non praesumit.*

Reference to the faithful's merits parallels what conscience dreads, and similarly their *vota* and *oratio* are placed in parallel.

These parallels, then, open up the meaning of the prayer. Motivated by their belief that God's goodness is such as to exceed both their merits and their

---

[2] For a more complete analysis see Haessly, Rhetoric in the Sunday Collects of the Roman Missal, 95-98.

desires and prayers, the suppliant community petitions God's mercy. In their faith that God exceeds their merits, they petition his merciful forgiveness of the true merits their conscience dreads. As well, in their trust that God exceeds their prayers, they petition that God will mercifully add to their own prayer what they do not even dare ask or desire.

Building upon this understanding of the prayer, the ensuing vocabulary study will add the further connotations that the various words carry, and show up parallels with other orations from the early sources.

Vocabulary:

Prominent vocabulary: *abundantia, pietas, meritum, supplex, vota, excedere, effundere, misericordia, dimittere, conscientia, metuere, adicere, oratio, praesumere.*

Our study will commence with the motivating clause. At its centre is the divine *habundantia pietatis*, which is reflected in the whole mystery of creation and salvation.

Pietatis[3]

According to Blaise, perhaps the only application of *pietas* to the goodness of God in the Vulgate translation of the scriptures is found in 1 Tm 3:16[4]. In this reading of the text, God's *pietas*, a mystery, is manifested in the

---

[3] For further examples of the use of *pietas* see Deshusses, Concordances III, 3, 368-375. See also B.Botte, "Pietas", in Botte and Mohrmann, L'Ordinaire de la Messe, 141-143; Blaise, Vocabulaire, § 149; and Ellebracht, Remarks, 47-49.

[4] Blaise, Vocabulaire, § 149. For the use of *pietas* in the Vulgate translation of the scriptures see Dutripon, Bibliorum Sacrorum Concordantiae, 1063. The word is listed 23 times.

This understanding of *pietas* as the mystery of God's loving kindness may not reflect the sense of the text. The greek reads εὐσεβείας μυστήριον. In neither of the two above mentioned articles by Botte and Mohrmann nor in

salvation brought forth by Christ in his incarnation, justification, visibility to the angels, his being preached to the peoples, triumph, glorification and acceptance by humanity in faith. The verse reads:

"*Et manifeste magnum est pietatis sacramentum, quod manifestatum est in carne, iustificatum est in spiritu, apparuit angelis, praedicatum est gentibus, creditum est in mundo, adsumptum est in gloria*" (1 Tm 3:16).

The liturgical sources especially associate the divine *pietas* with the forgiveness of sin. This is evident in the motivating clause of the following *super sindonem*:

"*Deus, cuius tanta est excellencia pietatis, ut uno peccatore conuerso maximum gaudium facias in caelis habere ..*" (V 1386)[5].

Note that the other prayers of this same Mass (III,xl), especially the collect V 1385, are concerned with God's mercy (*misericordia*), goodness

---

Ellebracht's work is there mention of references from the Vulgate translation of the scriptures in which *pietas* is understood to denote the divine loving kindness. Some commentators on 1 Tm 3:16, notably Debelius and Conzelmann, understand the greek text to refer to the 'mystery of the Christian religion'. In turn they see this as a synonym for the 'mystery of faith' in Tm 3:9. Foerster sees it as the refering to the mystery of the life of Christ which is the grounds for the Christian way of living in relation to God. See M.Dibleius and H.Conzelmann, The Pastoral Epistles, Hermeneia ed. H.Koester, translated by P.Buttloph and A.Yarbro from Die Pastoralbirefe by M.Dibelius, (no publisher given) 4th revised edition by H.Conzelmann, 1966 (Philadelphia: Fortress Press, 1972), 61-63, and W.Foerster, "σεβομα", TDNT VII, 182-183.

On the other hand, the sense of *pietas* in the prayer of the early Roman, Latin euchology is usually that of God's loving kindness (Ellebracht). A reading of 1 Tm 3:16 from within this liturgical perspective could well understand *pietatis sacramentum* to connote the mystery of God's loving kindness in Christ, as seemingly Blaise has done.

[5]God, the excellence of whose loving kindness is so great that you bring about exceedingly great rejoicing in heaven at the conversion of one sinner.... The clause echoes Lc 15:7.

(*bonitas*), and forgiveness (*venia*) in the face of sin and guilt (*propriae conscienciae reatus*). The motivating clauses in the *super sindonem* and the collect hold God's *pietas* and *misericordia* in parallel.

Botte[6] shows that the divine *pietas* and *misericordia* are often synonymous in the early orations. He points to their parallelism in various expressions in the *Veronensis*:

aures misericordiae: L 655,
aures pietatis: L 450,

remedia misericordiae: L 1058,
remedia pietatis: L 1299,

in tua misericordia confidenti: L 654 (L 199, L 452, L 904),
qui in tua pietate confidunt: L 666 (L 31, L 508).

A clear example of such parallelism between God's devoted loving kindness and his pity and compassion is the doublet in L 1272. There redemption is predicated of either the divine *pietas* or God's *miseratio*. Note that Blaise translates both *misericordia* and its cognate *miseratio* as *miséricorde*[7]. The oration is the final prayer in a *Veronensis* Christmas Mass (XL,viiii):

"*Deus, qui creationem condicionis humanae diabolicis non es passus perire nequitiis, remedia tuae propitiationis exsequere; ut in eadem non praeualeat inimica subreptio, sed redemptio tuae miserationis |:pietatis:| obtineat*" (L 1272)[8].

---

[6]Botte, "Pietas", 142. Though the phrases are the same, some of the orations listed in this study differ from those Botte employs.

[7]Blaise, Vocabulaire, § 151.

[8]God, who did not suffer the creation of the human race to perish through the wickedness of the devil, accomplish the remedies of your propitiation, so that in view of those same remedies hostile deceptions may not win out, but

The prayer sets the remedies of God's propitiation and the redemption of God's *pietas/miseratio* in parallel. The feast associated the divine *redemptio* and *remedia* with the incarnation. Furthermore, God's redemption is believed to be a continuation of his commitment to what he created (*non es passus perire*). The prayer links redemption to the overcoming of the wickedness and deception of the devil.

In V 1201, God's loving goodness is associated with his power (*omnipotens*)[9]. The baptized have faith that God's goodness is of such an abundance that it exceeds both their merits (*merita*) and their prayers (*uota*): *merita supplicum excedis et uota*. This will now be examined.

Merita supplicum excedis et uota

The expression is reminiscent of the sentiment of the Vulgate translation of Ephesians 3:20:

"*Ei autem, qui potens est omnia facere superabundanter quam petimus aut intelligimus secundum virtutem quae operatur in nobis*" (Eph 3:20).

In V 1202 it is the merits and prayer of the faithful that are exceeded.

Merita excedis

The merits (*merita*) of the faithful have been discussed in the study of the collect for Sunday XXV[10]. An aspect of *meritum* points to what believers' actions earn when carried out in concert with God's grace. In V 1201, *merita excedis* is set in parallel with *dimittas quae conscientia metuit*. On the one hand, God surpasses human merits in giving reward. On the other, he forgives the sins which would deserve punishment.

---

the redemption of your mercy |:goodness:| may prevail.

[9] Note that according to the collect for Sunday XXVI, God's power is most manifest in his mercy (*miserari*). See above, 378.

[10] See above, 142.

Vota (excedis)[11]

In V 1201, not only are human merits exceeded, but also the *vota* of the supplicants. The noun *votum* is frequently used in the Vulgate translation of the scriptures, especially in the psalms, to mean public prayer[12]. *Votum* is found throughout the early orations, denoting the prayers and desires of the faithful. In V 1201, it is set in parallel with *oratio*. The clause describes the faithful as *supplices*, a term whose sense of humble supplication further underscores the inadequacy of the merits and prayers of the baptized.

In view of their faith in the abundance of God's goodness over against the inadequacy of their own merits and prayers, the suppliant community request God to pour upon them his *misericordia*. The work of this mercy is in fact to forgive the sins which impede merit.

Misericordiam tuam

As seen above in the study of the collect for Sunday XXVI[13], God's mercy is the primary expression of his boundless love for humanity. Its scope includes salvation from sin and death, restoration, raising up the fallen and the dead, and the promise of heaven, all of which come through Christ. The parallel between God's *misericordia* and *pietas* in both the liturgical euchology and V 1201 itself has already been drawn out sufficiently.

The purpose of this petition for merciful kindness is twofold; to forgive what the human conscience dreads, and to add what our prayers do not even presume to ask. Since the parallel between these two petitions and the

---

[11]For further examples of the use of *votum* see Deshusses, Concordances III, 4, 496-499. See also Ellebracht, Remarks on the Vocabulary of the Ancient Orations in the Missale Romanum, 121-122. The pagan Roman understanding of *votum* as public praise, petition or vow has been discussed in Chapter Two above, 59.

[12]See Dutripon, Bibliorum Sacrorum Concordantiae, 1475.

[13]See above, 378.

motivating clause has already been noted, each of the purpose clauses will now be examined, beginning with the first; *dimittas quae conscientia metuit.*

Dimittas[14]

The verb *dimittere* carries two related meanings which further evoke the abundance of God's *pietas* and *misericordia*. In line with its use in the Vulgate translation of the Lord's prayer (Mt 6:9-15), the verb denotes the Father's pardon and forgiveness (v.12)[15].

Moreover, as noted by Blaise[16], *dimittere* is related to the verb *remittere* and the noun *remissio*, and so connotes not only pardon for sin but the remission of debt. This can be seen in the following December preface from the *Veronensis*. Here pardon of sin is associated with remission (*relaxare*) of its penalty, and also with the justification and favouring of the forgiven sinner: *"Uere dignum: qui non solum peccata dimittis, sed ipsos etiam iustificas peccatores; et reis non tantum poenam relaxas, sed donas et praemia"* (L 1327)[17].

Conscientia[18]

Conscientia denotes the conscious moral sense of right and wrong. It is often associated with the heart, and so the inner being of the person. The

---

[14] For further examples of the use of *dimittere* see Deshusses, Concordances, III, 1, 505.

[15] *"et dimitte nobis debita nostra, sicut et nos dimittimus debitoribus nostris"* (Mt 6:12).

[16] Blaise, Vocabulaire, § 279.

[17] Worthy of praise and honour ... are you who not only pardon sins but even justify the sinners themselves, and who not only remit the punishment for those who are guilty, but even grant them rewards.

[18] For further examples of the use of *conscientia* see Deshusses, Concordances III, 1, 328-329.

scriptures, in their Vulgate translation, contrast the state of conscience (*conscientia*) of the person living in sin and wickedness with that of the person living in fidelity to God. Iniquity disturbs the conscience, leading it to fear the worst (*saeva*) (Sap 17:10)[19]. However, according to the opening passage of the First Letter to Timothy, a good conscience is related to purity of heart and sincere faith. Together they are associated with authentic love. The apposite verse reads:

"*Finis autem praecepti est caritas de corde puro et conscientia bona et fide non ficta*" (1 Tm 1:5).

Note the apposition of *cor* and *conscientia*, as well as that between *purus, bonus* and *sincerus*. This set of adjectives provides a strong contrast to the fear and dread that sin engenders in the conscience as described in V 1201.

The collect from one of a series of Masses arranged under the title *Orationes pro Caritate* in *Reginensis* 316 highlights a number of the above points. *Conscientia* and *cor* are set in apposition. Both are said to experience fear of God's gaze on account of sin. The collect relates forgiveness (*venia*) to God's propitiation, to his attention to the people's groans, and the healing of the wounds of sin. Further it matches the universality of human fault and guilt with trust in the unlimited nature of God's forgiveness. The oration reads:
"*Deus sub cuius oculis omne contrepitat [cor trepidat] et omnes conscientiae pauescunt, propitiare omnium gemituum et cunctorum medere uulneribus, ut sicut nemo nostrum liber a culpa est, ita nemo sit alienus a uenia*" (V 1360)[20].

---

[19]"*Cum sit enim timida nequitia, dat testimonium condemnationis; semper enim praesumit saeva perturbata conscientia*" (Sap 17:10).

[20]God, under whose watchful gaze every heart trembles and every conscience grows fearful, hear favourably the groans of all and heal their wounds, so that just as no one of us is free from fault, so also may no one be estranged from your forgiveness.

Note that fear and sin mentioned in the collect parallel the quality of the faithful's merits which deserve judgement (*de meritorum qualitate diffidimus, non iudicium ... sentiamus*) as set out in the *super sindonem* (V 1361) of the same Mass (III,xxxv)[21].

Metuit[22]

As already seen in the study of the structure of V 1201, the merits of the faithful and what their consciences dread are placed in parallel. They connote the fear of judgement in the hearts and consciences of believers on account of their sin. This sin is already experienced as wound and guilt.

A similar meaning of *metuere* is found in the *Hadrianum* vesper prayer for day five of Easter week. There Christian dread is associated with the consequences of that disobedience which rouse the wrath of God who brought salvation and freedom in the Paschal Mystery. Note that in this prayer, the grace (*doce nos*) to dread, along with the grace to love what God commands, are understood to enable the faithful to live in Christian freedom, and in so doing avoid sin. However, in V 1201, the faithful dread the consequences their sins have engendered. The vesper prayer reads:

"*Deus qui nobis ad caelebrandum paschale sacramentum liberiores animos praestitisti, doce nos et metuere quod irasceris, et amare quod praecipis*" (H 420).[23]

In V 1202, God is asked to forgive (*dimittere*) the sins and punishments which conscience dreads.

---

[21] Note also that the petition in the *super sindonem* V 1361 parallels that in our prayer V 1201.

[22] For examples of the use of *metuere* see Deshusses, Concordance, III,3,76-77.

[23] God, who granted us souls more free to celebrate the paschal mystery, teach us both to dread what angers you and to love what you command.

As well as the pardon and remission of what the faithful's merits truly deserve, God's merciful kindness is invoked to add to the community's prayer what they do not even presume to ask; *"adicias quod oratio non praesumit."*
Adicias quod oratio non praesumit[24]

The clause echoes two Pauline passages in the Vulgate translation of the New Testament, Rm 8:26 and Eph 3:20. The above mentioned Ephesians verse is redolent with praise of the power of God, whose actions surpass what the faithful could ever ask (or even understand)[25]. The text from Romans guarantees that the Spirit gives voice to our prayers even when human weakness leaves us unable to express our needs[26].

Other prayers in the early sources express a hesitation to presume (*non praesumere*) in making petition similar to that found in V 1201. In a post communion from a Mass for the martyr St Laurence, the community ask that the prayer of the saint, who himself is pleasing to God and whose prayer is righteous, may give what their conscience does not presume to ask. The prayer reads:

"Sancti Laurenti nos, domine, praecatio iusta tueatur; et quod nostra conscientia non praesumit, eius nobis qui tibi placuit oratione donetur" (L 765)[27].

---

[24]For further examples of the use of *praesumere* see Deshusses, Concordances, III, 3, 468.

[25]"*Ei autem, qui potens est omnia facere superabundanter quam petimus aut intelligimus secundum virtutem quae operatur in nobis .."* (Eph 3:20). See Blaise, Vocabulaire, § 68, footnote 8.

[26]"*Similiter autem et Spiritus adiuvat infirmitatem nostram: nam quid oremus sicut oportet, nescimus; sed ipse Spiritus postulat pro nobis gemitibus inenarrabilibus"* (Rm 8:26).

[27]May the righteous entreaty of St. Laurence guard us, Lord, and may what our conscience does not presume, be given us by the prayer of him who is

The noun *oratio*, with its roots in the verb *orare*[28], is very frequently found in the Vulgate translation of the scriptures, especially in the psalms[29].

What is implied in the text is that the prayer of the holy martyr is always righteous and pleasing to God, something the church on earth cannot guarantee about its own desires, merits or actions. Hence it is proper that the church does not presume to ask.

A final prayer for a Mass in the *Veronensis* (XXVIIII,xii) is based around the community's reluctance to presume on its own merits. Rather the church relies on its faith in God's mercy and bountiful forgiveness. Note that the oration sets God's *pietas* and *misericordia* in parallel. The prayer reads: *"Moueat pietatem tuam, quaesumus, domine, subiectae tibi plebis effectus, et misericordiam tuam supplicatio fidelis optineat: ut quod meritis non praesumit, indulgentiae tuae largitate percipiat"* (L 1038)[30].

In V 1202, the believers call on God's mercy to add what they do not presume to ask in prayer. This reluctance to presume fits well with their sinfulness, the merits of which their consciences dread. Note also that their

---

pleasing to you.
Note that this same prayer, when used in *Reginensis* 316 for the Vespers of the feast, reads *quod nostra conscientia non mereatur* (V 979).
    See also L 152, a prayer which forms the base of the closing prayer for the General Intercessions in Holy Week in the Missal of Paul VI: MR(1975) Specimina or. univers., in ferr. Hebd. s., Or. sacerd. concl. 927. Note that in the new prayer mention of the aid of the saints has been replaced by reference to the merits of Christ.

[28]See the discussion in Chapter One, 11.

[29]See Dutripon, Bibliorum Sacrorum Concordantiae, 992.

[30]May [this] work of the people who are subject to you arouse your loving kindness Lord, and may this faithful supplication obtain your mercy, so that what this people does not presume by its merits, it may receive by the bounty of your forgiveness.
See also L 61.

reluctance runs counter to God's invitation to make constant petition (Mt 7:7-11). That God would give what the community neither deserves of its own merits nor dares to seek is entirely congruent with the church's faith in divine mercy and loving kindness.

Meaning of the prayer:

At the heart of the prayer is the parallel between God's *pietas* and *misericordia*. Virtually synonymous, together they evoke the goodness and power of God turned towards sinful humanity in the mystery of redemption in Christ. They bespeak our salvation from sin and death, justification, restoration, healing and the promise of eternal life.

The community, confident that the power of God's loving goodness and merciful kindness exceeds human merits and prayers, invokes this goodness and mercy so that God may pardon their sins, remit the punishment that is due, and add to their prayers what they do not even dare to ask. Both the faithful's dread of judgement and their hesitancy in prayer are themselves effects of what humans have truly merited. It is in light of the inadequacy of their merits, and the dread of the punishment their sins have earned, that Christians are hesitant to ask for what they need. Their prayer, is, in effect, a humble appeal (*supplex*) to God's loving kindnes (*pietas*), mercy (*misericordia*) and forgiveness (*dimittere*). Even in this their prayer is inadequate, and reliant on the abundance of God's *pietas* to surpass it and on his mercy to add what is left unsaid.

Note also that by placing dread within the conscience, the prayer indicates that it consumes the whole inner person, heart, soul and mind.

The placement of the prayer within the context of the Missal of Paul VI has brought about no major change to the vocabulary and meaning of the collect.

RELATIONSHIP OF THE CHRISTIAN PEOPLE TO GOD

The collect sets the relationship of the Christian people to God within the economy of human salvation, restoration, forgiveness and remission, healing and eternal fulfillment brought about in Christ. This economy is the expression of God's loving kindness (*pietas*) and generous mercy (*misericordia*) toward sinful humanity.

From the side of humanity, the oration opens onto the effects of sin. The merits of human actions outside grace cause the conscience, and the whole inner person, to exist in fear of judgement and punishment. With no merits of their own, and dreading what they truly deserve, the faithful are hesitant to ask of God what they need. Christian prayer is predicated on God's salvific loving kindness and mercy. The faithful are humbly suppliant on account of their belief in God's goodness and mercy in which their sins are forgiven, their punishments waived, their prayers surpassed, and the prayers they rightly do not dare ask are made for them. True Christian prayer is an appeal to the mercy, forgiveness and generosity of God.

FREER TRANSLATION OF THE COLLECT

Omnipotens, sempiterne Deus, qui abundantia pietatis tuae et merita supplicum excedis et vota, effunde super nos misericordiam tuam, ut dimittas quae conscientia metuit, et adicias quid oratio non preasumit.

All powerful God, in your loving kindness you are generous beyond what we deserve, ask for or imagine. Pour out your gracious mercy on us who humbly call upon you. Banish the dread our conscience fears on account of our sins and the penalties they have incurred, and bolster our prayer by adding what we have not dared to ask.

COLLECT FOR SUNDAY XXXI

PRAYER

Omnipotens et misericors Deus, de cuius munere venit, ut tibi a fidelibus tuis digne et laudabiliter serviatur, tribue, quaesumus, nobis, ut ad promissiones tuas sine offensione curramus.

All powerful and merciful God, from whose gift it comes that you are served by your faithful in a fitting and praiseworthy manner, bestow upon us, we ask you, that we may run to your promises without offense.

ORIGINAL SOURCE

Veronensis: Collect for Mass XVIII,xxviiii, item alia, *Julio, Incipiunt orationes et praeces diurnae* (L 574).

Reginensis 316: *Super sindonem* for the Mass III,viii, *Oraciones et Praeces per Dominicis Diebus* (V 1206).

The prayer as it stands in the Missal of Paul VI has come down through the liturgical tradition virtually unchanged. The only modification has been the expansion of the petition *tribue* to *tribue, quaesumus, nobis*, an addition already present in *Reginensis* 316.

USE IN OTHER LITURGICAL SOURCES

As noted by Bruylants[1], the collect is also found in these sources: Dominica XII post Pentecosten; A(1248), S(1115), *OR*(173)[Sp 1165], X(263,1*mg*), N(145), Q(143), 1474(273), 1570, 1604, as well as in these unedited sources: G(213,2)[G 1371], Z(795).

---

[1] Bruylants, II, 742.

ANALYSIS OF THE PRAYER IN THE ORIGINAL SOURCE

Origin:

According to Chavasse[2] this collect most probably comes from the Mass for Sunday, November 22, 537. It is one of a collection of Masses, thought to be penned by Pope Vigilius for the Sunday Masses during the period extending from July 12, 537 till March 28, 538 inclusive. They were subsequently inserted in the *Veronensis* in the month of July. Their immediate historical context is the siege of Rome by the Arian Ostrogoths under Witiges.

Subsequently, the collect was incorporated into the series of 16 Masses which begin Book III of *Reginensis* 316, whose origin has been examined in the accompanying introductory note to this series of prayers.

Grammatical structure[3]:

The prayer consists of (a) an address to God with motivating clause, (b) a petition, and (c) a noun clause as the object of the petition. The motivating clause is unusual in the early orations in that it contains an '*ut*' clause[4], not however in this case as a purpose clause, but as a result clause.

(a) Address: *Omnipotens et misericors Deus,*
    Motivation: *de cuius munere venit,*
        ut   tibi a fidelibus tuis digne et
             laudabiliter serviatur.

---

[2]A.Chavasse, "Messes du Pape Vigile (537-555)," Ephemerides Liturgicae 64 (1950): 187-191.

[3]For a more complete analysis see Haessly, Rhetoric in the Sunday Collects of the Roman Missal, 98-100.

[4]See also the collect for Sunday XV (V 546).

(b)	Petition:		*tribue, (quaesumus, nobis),*
(c)	Request:	*ut*	*ad promissiones tuas sine offensione curramus.*

The structure of the prayer reveals a number of significant features. The address conjoins God's power and mercy, *omnipotens et misericors Deus*. The three gifts that are the subject of the prayer, worthy service, the promises themselves, and approaching them without offense, come from this divine power and mercy. The oration sets the result clause concerning praiseworthy worship, *ut ... digne et laudabiliter servire*, in parallel with the noun clause concerned with attaining the promises, *ut ... ad promissiones tuas sine offensione curramus*. Worship that is fitting and worthy, itself a gift, is in correlation with approaching God's promises without offense. The first gift, itself a foretaste of the promises[5], provides both the assurance and the motivation in seeking the second.

Vocabulary:

Prominent vocabulary and phrases: *omnipotens, misericors, munus, venire, fidelis, digne, laudabiliter, servire, promissio, sine offensione, currere.*

Our study of the prayer's vocabulary will begin with the address and motivating clause. Since a good number of the words, phrases and clauses in the oration have already been analysed earlier in this work, much of this section will simply refer to the above studies.

The address associates God's power (*omnipotens*) and mercy (*misericors*). Their relationship has been more fully explored in the analysis of

---

[5]For the idea of worship as a foretaste of heaven, see the analysis of the collect for Sunday XXXIII.

the collect for Sunday XXVI[6]. Here they are linked together as the basis for the motivating clause: *de cuius munere venit, ut tibi a fidelibus tuis digne et laudabiliter serviatur.*

De cuius munere venit

The first of these clauses, *de cuius munere venit*, emphasises that praiseworthy service is a gift from God. The dependence of the faithful on God for all good gifts has been studied in the examination of the collects for Sunday X and XXII[7]. A clause with a similar structure is found in V 522[8]. The particular gift that God is believed to offer is the ability to serve him in a fitting and praiseworthy manner. This will now be examined, beginning with *servire.*

Servire

The verb *servire* has been studied in the analysis of the collect for Sunday XXIV. It especially denotes worship and the fulfillment of church offices[9]. This sense of worship is highlighted by the adverbs *digne* and *laudabiliter.*

---

[6]See above, 377ff.

[7]See above, 284 (X) and 356 (XXII).

[8]"*Deus per quem nobis et redemptio venit et praestatur adoptio ....*" This prayer is found in the Missal of Paul VI as the collect for Sunday XXIII. See above, 223ff.

[9]A number of the prayers attributed to Pope Vigilius display a deep concern for the community's worship (*servire*), especially in relation to the disruptions caused by the siege of Rome. This concern is reflected in the above collects for Sunday VIII (L 633), XXIV (L 1045), and XXXIII (L 486). Note that the collect (V 1205) and secret (V 1207) of the same Mass (III,viii) as our prayer in *Reginensis* 316 are also concerned with the service of worship.

Digne[10]

According to Blaise[11], *digne* and the adjective *dignus*, when applied to service and worship, are comparable to *devotum* and *humile*, and are frequently found in such expressions as *digne celebrare, digne offerre,* and *digne frequentare*[12]. Worship that is rendered worthily, or *digne*, is associated with God's prior forgiveness of sin (L 704) and the preservation offered the church through the supplication of the saints (L 739). In L 574, this worship is further qualified by the adverb *laudabiliter*.

Laudabiliter[13]

The adverb *laudibiliter* is not found in the Vulgate translation of the scriptures. However, the adverb, when applied to worship, may be associated with the phrases *sacrificium laudis* (Ps 106:22) and *hostia laudis* (Ps 115:7)[14]. It appears to be found on only one other occasion in the earliest liturgical sources[15].

The other use is in a prayer for the consecration of virgins, L 1104. There the adverb has a double meaning. It describes lives that are praiseworthy for their love and devotion to God, so devoted indeed to God's

---

[10]For further examples of the use of *digne* see Deshusses, Concordances III, 1, 487.

[11]Blaise, Vocabulaire, § 2.

[12]Some examples are: *digne celebrare* L 704, L 739, *digne servire* L 1300, *digne famulari altaribus tuis* L 14.

[13]For further examples of the use of *laudabiliter* and *laudabilis* see Deshusses, Concordances III, 2, 450.

[14]See Ellebracht, Remarks on the Vocabulary of the Ancient Orations in the Missale Romanum, 193.

[15]In the Deshusses index, the adverb is listed only twice, L 574 and L 1104, while the adjective *laudabilis* is only indexed once G 2852.

service that these women seek no praise for themselves. The sense is that any such praise for them should rather be directed further to God. The appropriate section of the prayer reads: *"In caritate ferueant, et nihil extra te diligant; laudabiliter uiuant laudarique non appetant. Te in sanctitate corporis, te in animi sui puritate glorificent"* (L 1104)[16].

In summary, the motivating clause of L 574 refers to a range of features about praiseworthy worship. As a gift from God to the faithful it is characterized by humility and devotion, and carried out in a manner that deflects any praise that is its due to the praise of God. Such fitting worship is associated with God's forgiveness of sin and, as well, the supplication of the saints. In view of their trust that God's power and mercy can give this gift to the faithful, the community makes its petition: *ut ad tuas promissiones sine offensione curramus.*

Ad promissiones .. curramus

This expression has been studied in the analysis of the collect for Sunday XXVI[17]. It signals the faithfuls' love and obedience to the divine mandates and their fervent desire to enter eternal beatitude. In L 574, this love, obedience and desire is expressed in their fitting and praiseworthy worship. Note the connection between our prayer and the collects for Sunday IV (L 432), XXV (L 493) and Sunday XXXIII (L 486)[18]. Just as our collect sets worship at the heart of Christian life, together L 432 and L 493 establish that love and worship of God, and love of neighbour, are at the heart of all

---

[16] May they be fervent in love, and may they love nothing above and beyond you; may they live praiseworthy lives, yet not desire to be praised; may they glorify you in the sanctity of their bodies and in the purity of their minds.

[17] See above, 382.

[18] For studies of these collects see Chapter Four. Like L 574, both L 493 and L 486 probably were written by Vigilius.

God's precepts. In L 486, the church's joyful worship is a participation in the eternal *felicitas* of heaven. Not only, then, do Christians run towards the promises without offense through fitting and praiseworthy worship, but also such worship is a foretaste of eternal life.

Sine offensione[19]

The faithful's will and active desire (*currere*) for the promises is further characterized as *sine offensione*. In the Vulgate translation of the New Testament this phrase denotes either the avoidance of actions which, though legitimate, do not work to build up the faith of the community (1 Cor 10:31-33), or the avoidance of sinful acts (Ph 1:9-11). This second usage is taken up in the liturgical sources, as seen in the petition of this prayer from a Mass for travellers. Here sinless behaviour is associated with God's direction, protection and guidance. The petition reads: "*Deus qui diligentibus te ... dirigi uiam famuli tui illius in uoluntate tua, ut te protectore et te perduci per iusticiae semitas sine offensione gradiat*" (V 1314)[20].

In L 574, the faithful run towards God's promises without offense when their worship is fitting and praiseworthy.

Meaning of the prayer:

Through the gift of fitting and worthy worship, the faithful find both the assurance that God wills them to enter the promises and the motivation to approach them in sinless, loving obedience to the divine precepts. As well, worthy worship arouses in them a loving desire for the gift of eternal life.

---

[19] For further examples of the use of *offensio* see Deshusses, Concordances III, 3, 208.

[20] God, who for those who love you ... direct the path of your servant ___ in your will, so that with you as his protector and guide, he may walk the path of righteousness without offense.

Such proper and fitting worship connotes the faithfuls' devotion and humility in the face of their own sinfulness and God's forgiveness, their reliance on the supplication of the saints, and their desire that all praise be directed towards the one worshipped. As well it is a foretaste of eternal beatitude. Even in the face of invasion by the Arian Ostrogoths, Christian worship should not be forgotten since it is central to a life lived in God, and is a taste of true salvation. For God to grant the church that it maintain this worship, is to keep it on the way to the eternal life promised by him.

The incorporation of the collect in the collection of Masses in *Reginensis* 316, and from there into the Masses after Pentecost, has removed the immediacy which the historical context gave the prayer. However the dynamic and meaning of the prayer remain unaltered. Nor has the placement of the prayer within the context of the Missal of Paul VI brought any major change to the vocabulary and meaning of the collect.

THE RELATIONSHIP OF THE CHRISTIAN PEOPLE TO GOD

Fitting and praiseworthy worship of God is an essential aspect of loving obedience of God's mandates and loving desire for heaven. This worship is itself a gift, given to the faithful from God's power and mercy. The offering of such worship entails on the part of the faithful humility and devotion, acknowledgement of their sins, acceptance of God's forgiveness, and the aid of the saints. It keeps them on the road to the attainment of God's promises in eternal life.

FREER TRANSLATION OF THE COLLECT

Omnipotens et misericors Deus, de cuius munere venit, ut tibi a fidelibus tuis digne et laudabiliter serviatur, tribue, quaesumus, nobis, ut ad promissiones tuas sine offensione curramus.

Almighty and merciful God, only by your gracious gift can we offer you worship that renders you fitting and worthy praise. Grant us, then, this worship which enables us to run to your promises without offense.

COLLECT FOR SUNDAY XXX

PRAYER

Omnipotens sempiterne Deus, da nobis fidei, spei et caritatis augmentum, et, ut mereamur assequi quod promittis, fac nos amare quod praecipis.

All powerful, eternal God, give us an increase of faith, hope and love, and make us love what you command so that we may merit to obtain what you promise.

ORIGINAL SOURCE

Veronensis: Collect for Mass XVIII,xxxiii, *Iulio, Incipiunt orationes et praeces diurnae* (L 598). The original collect has been incorporated into the Missal of Paul VI without any major change. The verb *adsequi* in the original is now spelt *assequi*, while *aumentum* now reads *augmentum*.

The oration is used twice in *Reginensis* 316. It appears unmodified as a collect in Mass III,viiii, *oraciones et praeces cum canone per dominicis diebus* (V 1209). Note that the *super sindonem* of this same Mass has been incorporated into the Missal of Paul VI as the collect for Sunday XXIX[1]. The prayer is also used as the *super sindonem* in Mass (III,xxvi), entitled *orationes pro caritate* (V 1324). In this instance, a motivating clause has been added, and some minor changes are in evidence. The prayer reads:
"*Deus, qui iustitiam tuam elegis [tuae legis] in cordibus credentium digito tuo scribis, da nobis fidei et spei caritatisque augmentum, et ut mereamur adsequi quod promittis, fac nos amare quod praecipisti*" (V 1324)[2].

---

[1] For a study of this collect, see above, 294.

[2] God, who with your own finger write the righteousness of your law in the hearts of those who believe in you, give us an increase in faith and hope and love, and so that we may merit to attain what you promise, make us love what you commanded.

USE IN OTHER LITURGICAL SOURCES

As noted by Bruylants[3] the prayer has been used in these other liturgical sources: Dominica post Pentecosten; Pr(187,1), A(1273), S(1132), P(634), OR(173)[Sp 1168], X(264,1) N(145), Q(143v), 1474(275), 1570, 1604, as well as these unedited sources G(218,1)[G 1402], Z(807), FrSal3(26,1). *Orationes pro caritate*: G(415,3)[G 2772], S(167), X(288,1).

ANALYSIS OF THE PRAYER IN THE ORIGINAL SOURCE

Origin:

According to Chavasse[4] this collect most probably comes from the Mass for Sunday, December 20, 537, the Mass which brought to a close the December fast. The Mass, thought to be from the hand of Pope Vigilius, is one of a collection which extended from July 12, 537 till March 28, 538 inclusive, and which were inserted in the *Veronensis* in the prayers for the month of July. Their immediate historical context is the siege of Rome by the Arian Ostrogoths under Witiges.

Subsequently the collect was incorporated in a series of 16 Masses which begin Book III of *Reginensis* 316, and whose origin has been examined in the accompanying introductory note to this section.

Grammatical structure[5]:

The collect is made up of three sections, (a) an address, (b) two petitions joined by *et*, and (c) a purpose clause attached to the second petition.

---

[3]Bruylants, II, 759.

[4]Chavasse, "Messes du Pape Vigile," Ephemerides Liturgicae 64 (1950): 189.

[5]For a more detailed analysis see Haessly, Rhetoric in the Sunday Collects of the Roman Missal, 100-102.

(a) Address: *Omnipotens sempiterne Deus,*

(b) 1st Petition: *da nobis fidei, spei et caritatis augmentum,*

(c) 2nd Petition: *et   fac nos amare quod praecipis,*

(d) Purpose: *ut   mereamur assequi quod promittis.*

The first petition seeks an increase of faith, hope and love for the faithful in their present life. Joined to this by the conjunction *et* is a second petition, which has a more eschatological perspective. The faithful seek that they may love what God commands. The purpose of this second request is that they may merit to obtain what God promises.

Faith, hope and love are set together as a triad of gifts, reflecting their conjunction in 1 Cor 13:13. This suggests that the prayer is treating these three as a single collective unit.

The parallel between *quod praecipis* and *quod promittis* is similar to that found in the collect for Sunday XXI (V 551)[6]. However, L 598 posits a stronger connection between the precepts and the commands. It is in loving what God commands, itself a gift, that the believer is able to merit obtaining what God promises.

Vocabulary:

Prominent vocabulary and phrases: *fides, spes et caritas, mereri, assequi, promittere, amare, praecipere.*

Large portions of the oration's vocabulary and phrasing have already been examined earlier in this work, and so much of this section will simply refer to these studies. The triad of faith, hope and charity has not been encountered previously, however, and will be examined first.

---

[6]See above, 273.

Fidei, spei et caritatis augmentum

The conjunction of *fides*, *spes* and *caritas* echoes a number of texts in the Vulgate translation of the New Testament. Most especially it resembles 1 Cor 13:13, where they are described as the three gifts that abide (*manere*): "*Nunc autem manent fides, spes, caritas, tria haec; maior autem horum est caritas*" (1 Cor 13:13)[7].

Two complementary senses can be discerned here. Given the pericope's context as the conclusion of a discussion of the spiritual gifts, the endurance of faith, hope and love may be seen as a mark of their permanence and priority over all other, more transitory, spiritual gifts. Of these three, however, love occupies the most important place. All spiritual gifts, if held without love, are empty and of no avail (1 Cor 13:1-3). In light of L 598, the abiding nature of the three gifts, and the centrality of love, would make them the obvious basis for the petition to love what God commands.

The second sense discernible in 1 Cor 13:13 is more eschatological. Faith, hope and love can be understood as the three gifts that abide unto eternity, when faith and hope give way to vision (1 Cor 13:8,12). Again, in the light of L 598, this eschatological sense corresponds with the prayer's intention that the three virtues provide the overall context for achieving what God has promised.

In the First Letter to the Thessolonians, faith, hope and love are the protection which the Christian dons so as to remain vigilant, prepared and well defended. They lie at the heart of a life lived in anticipation of the coming of the Lord (1 Th 5:2). The apposite verse reads:

---

[7] For critical commentary on this text, see H.Conzelmann, <u>1 Corinthians: A Commentary on the First Epistle to the Corinthians</u>, Hermenia, ed. G.W. MacRae, trans. J.W.Leitch from <u>Der erste Brief and die Korinther</u>, Göttingen: Vandenhoeck & Ruprecht, 1969 (Philadelphia: Fortress Press, 1975), 229-231. The following material is based on this study.

"*Nos autem, qui diei sumus, sobrii sumus induti loricam fidei et caritatis et galeam spem salutis*" (1 Th 5:8)[8].

The scriptures, then, see the triad of faith, hope and love as the most permanent and important of all spiritual gifts in this world. They form the basis of vigilant life on earth in expectation of Christ's return. However, love, the greatest of the three, is the one that remains in eternity.

The above mentioned *super sindonem*, V 1324[9], from a Mass for charity (III,xxvi) sets these three gifts within the context of God's love, covenant, righteousness and the commandments Moses was given at Sinai. The motivating clause, *qui iustitiam tuam elegis [tuae legis] in cordibus credentium digito tuo scribis*, echoes both Dt 9:10 and Jr 31:33. The Deuteronomic text emphasises God's covenant and the Sinai commandments, while the prophet speaks of God's covenant fidelity, forgiveness, and his new covenant. From the structure of the oration, the gifts of faith, hope and love are requested in the light of the people's faith in God's covenant and forgiveness, inclusive of his law. The triad enable the faithful to respond to God's righteousness, a response which is expressed in love of the precepts. The Mass emphasises the primacy of love over faith and hope through its title *Orationes pro caritate*, the petition for the *inuiolabilem caritatis effectum* in its collect (V 1323), and the petition for *caritatis donum* in the secret (V 1325[10])[11].

---

[8]This text itself is based on Is 59:17, where it is God who is said to put on breastplate and helmet. Paul parallels the faithful's armour of faith, love and hope, with God's justice and righteousness. For critical commentary see E.Best, A Commentary on the First and Second Epistles to the Thessalonians (New York: Harper & Row, 1972), 67-70.

[9]"*Deus, qui iustitiam tuam elegis [tuae legis] in cordibus credentium digito tuo scribis, da nobis fidei et spei caritatisque augmentum, et ut mereamur adsequi quod promittis, fac nos amare quod praecipisti*" (V 1324).

[10]The offertory prayer V 1325 is included in the Missal of Paul VI: MR(1975) Pro concordia fovenda, Super oblata, 849.

In L 598, the faithful petition for an increase of these gifts which are at the basis of all response to God's forgiveness, new covenant and commandments. In connection with their increase, the community further ask to love what God commands, which is the practical way to eternal life.

Amare quod praecipis

The essential orientation of what God commands (*quod praecipis*) has been examined as part of the study of the collect for Sunday XXV (L 493 and LMZ 1374)[12]. As well, our clause itself was analyzed in the study of the collect for Sunday XXI (V 551)[13]. Summarizing that material here, God's precepts are ordained towards love and worship of him, and love of neighbour. It is most appropriate that the commandments themselves are loved since they embody God's bidding, and are the practical expression of love of God. As such, they are an experience on earth of the true joys of heaven. Furthermore, the community is united in heart and will when it loves the divine mandates. The probable original liturgical context of L 598 in a Mass which brought to a close the December fast would have served to highlight especially the particular precept of the laws and customs of the Christian fast.

In L 598, love of what God prescibes is expressed as the grounds for meriting to obtain the divine promises.

---

[11]Note that in a similar fashion the gift of love is highlighted in the *super sindonem* (L 599) of the *Veronensis* Mass (CXVIII,xxxiii) of which L 598 is the collect.

[12]For a discussion of the collect for Sunday XXV (L 493 and LMZ 1374) see above, 140. There are two connections between L 493 and the Mass of which L 598 is the collect that make L 493 a particularly apt commentary on the meaning of *quod praecipis* in our collect. Firstly, both most probably were authored by Pope Vigilius. Secondly, the motivating clause for L 493 is virtually identical to that of the *super sindonem* L 599 of the Mass: *Deus, qui plenitudinem mandatorum in tua et proximi dilectione posuisti* ....

[13]See above, 273.

Ut mereamur adsequi quod promittis

This clause is practically identical with the purpose clause from the above mentioned collect for Sunday XXV (LMZ 1374); *ut tua precepta servantes, ad uitam mereamur peruenire perpetuam*[14]. The expression *quod promittis* denotes eternal life[15]. As seen in the analysis of the collect for Sunday XXV, *mereamur pervenire* gives emphasis to the actions of the community in their obedience of God's precepts. Yet this merit and attainment of eternal life take place wholly within the context of God's work in the Cross and resurrection of Christ.

In L 598, *mereamur adsequi* similarly denotes the participation of the faithful. They are believed to merit to attain what God promises through their love of what God has commanded. This merit is set within the context of the gifts of faith, hope and love, as well as their embodiment in the gift of loving what God commands.

Meaning of the prayer:

The prayer is constituted by a series of petitions for the gifts to live in such a way on earth so as to merit to enter eternal life. The first petition is for an increase of faith, hope and love. These form the basis of a vigilant Christian life, lived in expectation of the coming of Christ. They are the most permanent of all spiritual gifts, and endure into eternal life. Among them, however, it is love which has primacy. Their presence in the faithful is the deepest expression of the community's response to God's forgiveness, covenant and commandments.

---

[14] For a study of the clause in the collect for Sunday XXV, see above, 142ff.

[15] Blaise, Vocabulaire, § 303 and § 44. See also the study of the collect for Sunday XXI, above, 273.

In conjunction with this gift, believers further ask that they love what God commands. This petition reflects both the primacy of love, and the relationship of the triad to God's covenant. The mandates themselves are directed towards love and worship of God, and love of neighbour. Love for them unites the community in heart and will, and is, as well, an experience of the true joys of heaven.

The pair of petitions for the divine gifts of faith, hope and love, and for the love of what God commands, together connote a life lived in love, worship, obedience, righteousness and unity. Through such a life, itself a foretaste of eternal life, the faithful seek to merit entry to the fullness of the divine promises.

In view of the probable history of the oration, three things can be noted. If Chavasse is correct, the Mass brought to a close the December fast[16], itself one of the precepts which are to be loved. The close of the fast presages the feast of the incarnation, the source of all faith, hope and love, and also the grounds of the divine promises.

The placement of the prayer within the context of the Missal of Paul VI has brought no major change to the vocabulary of the prayer. However, the change in liturgical context affects the meaning of the prayer.

In its original context *quod praecipis* referred directly to the fast. With the subsequent incorporation of the oration into *Reginensis* 316 as a prayer in one of the Sunday Masses this connection with the prescription to fast was broken. No longer implying the laws and practices of fasting, *quod praecipis* both took on a more general sense, and alluded to the Sunday observance. The use of the collect in Masses *pro caritate* offered an interpretation of *praeceptum* as the divine commandment to love God and neighbour.

---

[16]Chavasse, "Messes du Pape Vigile," Ephemerides Liturgicae 64 (1950): 189.

As the prayer stands in the Missal of Paul VI it continues to reflect the threefold meaning that is brought about from its context in *Reginensis* 316. It carries a reminder of the Sunday observance. At the same time the precept to love God and neighbour, the mandate to which all God's laws are ordained, is an important theme in the Sunday collects for Ordinary Time[17]. The clause also denotes general obedience to all that God commands.

RELATIONSHIP OF THE CHRISTIAN PEOPLE TO GOD

Faith, hope and love lie at the heart of the Christian response to God's forgiveness, covenant, commandments and Christ's immanent coming. They are the most permanent of all spiritual gifts, and as such form the basis of all Christian expectation for Christ and action in his name. Among the three, love has priority both since it endures beyond this life, and because no spiritual gifts in this life have value unless expressed out of love. Furthermore, the faith, hope and love of the community is connected with the love of believers for what God commands. This loving obedience is a basis for meriting to enter the divine promises, eternal life.

The oration understands Christian merit as set wholly within the economy of God's covenant and grace. The love of what God prescribes, the grounds for meriting to enter eternal life, is itself a gift of God. As well, it is an expression of the foundational divine gifts of faith, hope and love.

---

[17] See especially the studies of the collects for Sundays IV and XXV. See also the offertory prayer from a Mass for the fostering of concord: MR(1975) Pro concordia fovenda, Super oblata, 849. This prayer is a slight revision of V 1325, the *super oblata* from the *Reginensis* 316 Mass *pro caritate* (III,xxvi) of which our prayer, V 1324, was the *super sindonem*.

FREER TRANSLATION OF THE COLLECT

Omnipotens sempiterne Deus, da nobis fidei, spei et caritatis augmentum, et, ut mereamur assequi quod promittis, fac nos amare quod praecipis.

Almighty, eternal God, increase our faith, hope and love. Grant furthermore that we may love what you command, and so merit to obtain what you promise.

COLLECT FOR SUNDAY XXXII

PRAYER

Omnipotens et misericors Deus, universa nobis adversantia propitiatus exclude, ut, mente et corpore pariter expediti, quae tua sunt liberis mentibus exsequamur.

All powerful, merciful God, in your propitiation remove from us everything that is harmful, so that, freed equally in mind and body, we may pursue, with free minds, whatever pertains to your service.

ORIGINAL SOURCE

Reginensis 316: Collect for the Mass III,xv, *Oraciones et Praeces per Dominicis Diebus* (V 1234).

The prayer as it stands in the Missal of Paul VI has come down through the liturgical tradition virtually unchanged. The only modification is *propitiatus* instead of the original reading *propitiationis*, a correction already present in the *Paduensis* (P 720).

USE IN OTHER LITURGICAL SOURCES

As noted by Bruylants[1], the collect is also found in these sources: Dominica XIX post Pentecosten; A(1423), S(1278), P(720), OR(175)[Sp 1186], X(272,1), N(153), Q(148), 1474(291), 1570, 1604, as well as in these unedited sources: G(251,1)[G 1562], Z(903), FrSal 3(36,1), FrSt(XXXVII,1).

Bruylants appears to have omitted H 903.

ANALYSIS OF THE PRAYER IN THE ORIGINAL SOURCE
Origin:

See the accompanying introductory note to this series of prayers.

---

[1]Bruylants, II, 751.

Grammatical structure[2]:

The collect consists of (a) an address, (b) a petition, and (c) two purpose clauses, the second dependent on the first.

(a) Address   *Omnipotens et misericors Deus*
(b) Petition   *universa nobis adversantia propitiatus exclude,*
(c) 1st Purpose   *ut,   mente et corpore pariter expediti,*
    2nd Purpose   *quae tua sunt liberis mentibus exsequamur*

The dominance of compound verbs with the prefix *ex, excludere, expedire, exsequi,* suggests a note of intense struggle between the faithful and the *adversantia*. The opposing forces are to be utterly removed, the minds and bodies of the faithful thoroughly liberated, and God's will completely carried through. Note also the dynamic of confrontation in the petition signified by the opposition between the two prefixes, *ad*versantia and *ex*cludere.

The prayer sets in parallel *universa adversantia propitiatus excludere, mente et corpore pariter expediti,* and *liberis mentibus exsequamur.* The sense of *propitiatus* is important. The propitiation of God is associated with offense and sin. The *adversantia*, then, are spiritual adversaries which seek to lead the faithful into sin, and impede their harmony and freedom in mind and body.

The emphasis laid on the body as well as on the mind in the first clause indicates that the stress in the second clause falls on *liberis* rather than on *mentibus*. The sense of the expression is that, freed from all that afflicts the entire human person, corporal and spiritual, the faithful may go about God's will free from all encumbrance, and in harmony of mind and body. This fits with the utter thoroughness betokened by the repeated use of *ex*, and further emphasised by paralleling *expediti* with *exsequamur*.

---

[2]For a more complete analysis see Haessly, Rhetoric in the Sunday Collects of the Roman Missal, 111-113.

The prayer is one of petition. In light of God's power and mercy, the church calls upon God to remove in his mercy and forgiveness whatever is adversarial. The request is followed by two sequential purpose clauses. The first is that the granting of the petition will enable the baptized to be liberated equally in mind and body. Secondly, in such liberation the faithful desire to do God's will without hindrance.

The ensuing discussion of the prayer's vocabulary will attempt to offer greater precision to the liturgical use of *adversari* and *liber*, and as well open up the parallels found in the euchology between *adversari, propitiatus excludere, expedire* and *liberare*.

Vocabulary:

Prominent vocabulary: *omnipotens, misericors, adversari, propitiatus excludere, mens, corpus, expedire, liber, exsequi*.

The address sets together God's power and mercy, a relationship that has been discussed in the study of the collect for Sunday XXVI[3]. In light of their reliance on the divine power and mercy, the faithful make their petition that all adverse things be driven from them: *universa nobis adversantia propitiatus exclude*. Our study of the petition will begin with the substantive *adversantia*.

Adversantia[4]

The Vulgate translation of the New Testament employs the verb *adversari* and the adjective *adversarius* to connote opposition to God's way

---

[3]See above, 377ff.

[4]For further examples of the use of *adversari* see Deshusses, Concordances III, 1, 46-47.

from the devil (1 Pt 5:8)[5], the desires of the flesh (Gal 5:17)[6], disobedience and sin (1 Tm 1:9-10)[7], and those whose actions stand in the way of God's will (1 Th 2:15)[8]. The petition itself, *universa nobis adversantia propitiatus exclude*, echoes the final verse of the Lord's Prayer as found in Matthew's Gospel. Note that here the substantive *malum* is related especially to sin and temptation. As well it evokes the devil[9]. Freedom (*liberare*) is understood as freedom from evil. The verse reads:

"*et ne nos inducas in tentationem, sed libera nos a malo*" (Mt 6:13).

The orations in the early liturgical sources reflect this range in the application of *adversari*. It can denote the work of the devil (L 826), or the offenses that others do to us (L 416). A blessing (L 614) at the end of a Mass associates *adversari* with sin. In this prayer, the petition to turn away from sin is related, in God's propitiation, to the administration of solace, and the request to grant good things to both body and soul. The oration reads:

"*Exaudiat uos dominus deus noster, et pro sua quemque necessitate clamantem benignus aspiciat; solacia propitius administret, quae humana poscit infirmitas;*

---

[5]*Sobrii estote et vigilate, quia adversarius vester diabolus tanquam leo rugiens circuit quaerens quem devoret* (1 Pt 5:8). See also 2 Th 2:15.

[6]*Caro enim concupiscit adversus spiritum, spiritus autem adversus carnem: haec enim sibi invicem adversantur, ut non quaecumque vultis illa faciatis* (Gal 5:17).

[7]*sciens hoc, quia lex iusto non est posita, sed iniustis et non subditis, impiis et peccatoribus, sceleratis et contaminatis ...mendacibus et periuris, et si quid aliud sanae doctrinae adversatur* (1 Tm 1:9-10).

[8]*qui et Dominum occiderunt Iesum et prophetas et nos persecuti sunt et Deo non placent et omnibus hominibus adversantur* (1 Th 2:15).

[9]See Blaise, Vocabulaire, § 323, and § 73, fn 8.

peccata, quae aduersantur, auertat; pariterque corporibus uestris et mentibus semper profutura concedat" (L 614)[10].

In a collect of an anti-Lupercalian Mass from the pen of Gelasius[11], the destructive behaviour of *aduersantes* is seen to obstruct worship and service. From the historical context, *aduersantes* refers to those Christians who, as Christians, defended and upheld the pagan cult. In so doing, they were seen to be both engaging in immoral and uncharitable practices, and compromising their belief in salvation through Christ. It is on account of this sinful behaviour that God's appeasement (*placatus*) is called for. Freedom is equated with unhindered, pure worship. The collect reads:

"Aeclesiae tuae, domine, uoces placatus admitte, ut destructis aduersantibus uniuersis secura tibi seruiat libertate" (L 425)[12].

Note that the preface (L 428) of the same anti-Lupercalia Mass also exhibits this twofold concern over the behaviour of the *adversantes* and the need for God's appeasement. The perspective of the preface is that some Christians stray from the truth and hence God's appeasement is necessary. The baptized, however, wander on account of the falsehoods of the *adversantes* who in turn have to be cast down.

---

[10] May the Lord our God hear you, and favourably turn towards whom so ever is calling for his own necessity; may he administer the solaces which human weakness asks; may he turn away the sins which stand in opposition to him; may he grant you things that are ever advantageous, equally for your bodies and your minds.

[11] See Pomarés, Gélase, 202-204.

[12] Be appeased Lord and hear the voices of your church, so that following the tearing down of all that oppose them, they may serve you in secure freedom.
For commentary on this prayer from Gelasius, see A.Bastiaensen, "L'Église a la conquête de sa liberté: recherches philologiques dans le Sacramentaire de Vérone," in Graecitas et Latinitas Christianorum Primaeva, Supplementa III, ed. C.Mohrmann et alia (Nijmegen: Dekker & van de Vegt: 1970), 151.

A prayer which concludes a Mass for peace (*Reg* 316, III, lvi) relates *adversari* and *adversus* to the terrors of war. They are the opposite of prosperity, secure freedom, and tranquil religious observance and practice: "*Deus, qui misericordiae tuae potentis auxilium et prospera tribuis et aduersa depellis, uniuersa obstacula qui seruis tuis aduersantur expugna, ut remoto terrore bellorum et libertas securae religio sit quieta*" (V 1477)[13].

In summary, *adversantia* describes whatever brings harm to peaceful and upright human existence. At the level of human affairs, it points to whatever threatens prosperity, liberty and the tranquil practice of religion. At the deeper spiritual level, it alludes to temptation, sin, disobedience and the work of the devil. The *adversantia* affect both the body and the mind. They particularly oppose the free worship and service of God.

The sense of *aduersantia* in V 1234 is specified both by the use of *propitiatus* in the prayer itself, and by the context of the oration in the Mass as a whole. In general, the community's desire for God to be propitiated indicates that a question of sin and offense is involved. The *aduersantia* in our collect, then, refer to temptation, sin, disobedience and the work of the devil. This is further corroborated through an examination of the *super sindonem* (V 1235) for the same Mass. Where the collect deals with the forces that lead into sin, the *aduersantia*, the *super sindonem* points to the sins themselves, the trangressions and depravities of the faithful. Consequently the church asks for God's propitiation (*propitiatus*), indulgence and pardon (*venia, relaxare*). The prayer reads:

"*Da, quaesumus, omnipotens deus, sic nostram ueniam promereri, ut nostros*

---

[13]God, who, by the help of your powerful mercy, bestow prosperity and drive away adversity, storm and subdue every obstacle which stands in opposition to your servants, so that with the removal of the terror of wars, there may be both secure freedom and tranquility of religious observance.

corrigamus excessos; sic fatentibus relaxare delictum, ut coercemus in suis prauitatibus obstinatos" (V 1235)[14].

In V 1234, the church petitions God to drive out (*propitiatus*) the *adversantia*.

Propitiatus exclude[15]

Excludere has the sense of chasing out, or hunting. Along with such verbs as *liberare*, *auferre* and *eruere*, it is used in liturgical sources to denote God's work of liberation[16].

An example of this usage can be seen in the lenten *super sindonem* V 120. The faithful pray that through their participation in the self-denial (V 119) and medicine (V 212) of the fast, temptation (*manifesti hostes*) may be overcome, and the ultimate tempter, the forces of the devil (*inuisibiles hostes*) may be driven out. These adverse forces are the enemies of human weakness (*nostra fragilitas*), with its proclivity to sin. Overcoming every manifest enemy and driving out the devil are related to peace and harmony in the whole person, mind and body. The oration reads:

"Pacem nobis tribue, domine, quaesumus, mentis et corporis, ut per ieiunium

---

[14] Almighty God, grant that we may merit pardon for our sins in such a way that we may correct our transgressions, and that we may remit the offenses for those who confess in such a way that we may correct those who are resolute in their own perversity.

[15] For further examples of the use of *excludere* see Deshusses, Concordances III, 2, 59-60.

[16] See Blaise, Vocabulaire, § 73. See also the comments in Bastiaensen, "Liberté," 146-147. In particular he notes the use, in the *Vetus Latina*, of *excludere* for the exorcism of a demon: *in tuo nomine daemonia exclusimus* (Mt 7:22).

nostrae fragilitatis et manifesti subieceantur hostis [hostes] et inuisibilis [invisibiles] excludantur" (V 120)[17].

In V 1234, the petition to remove from the faithful all harmful things, most manifestly sin and the devil, is related to God's power, mercy and propitiation. The use of the present participle as a substantive, the liturgical usage of both *adversari* and *excludere*, and their opposition in the prayer, all work to emphasize the immediacy of the threat to the community. Two interconnected purpose clauses are adduced for the request; firstly that the faithful may be free in body and in mind, and, as a consequence, that they may accomplish God's will with free minds. These purpose clauses will now be examined.

Ut mente et corpore pariter expediti
Mente et corpore pariter

For convenience the conjunction of mind and body, *mente et corpore pariter*, will be examined first. As seen in earlier studies, *mens* refers to the whole inner person, mind, heart, soul[18], and even conscience[19]. The

---

[17] Bestow upon us Lord, peace of mind and body, so that through the fast both may the terrestial enemies of our weakness be brought to heel, and the spiritual ones driven out.
See also V 1538 and V 1559.
Bastiaensen offers a different approach to V 120 in his study of the almost identical L 1311, itself a prayer from the Masses for the December fast (XLIII, *In Ieunio Mensis Decimi*). In line with his reading of the early Jewish and Christian understanding of fasting as primarily a spiritual weapon, he understands *manifesti hostes* to refer to terrestial calamities and civil upheaval. In this they disturb corporeal, civil peace. The *invisibiles hostes* are spiritual enemies. The conjunction of *mens* and *corpus* is more the conjunction of the material and the spiritual spheres of existence than the inner harmony of the whole human person. See Bastiaensen, "Liberté," 146f..

[18] See the study of the collect for Sunday IV, above, 105.

[19] See the study of the collect for Sunday XXVII, above, 394.

conjunction of *mens* and *corpus* denotes the complete human being. An example of this pairing has already been seen in the present study in the *super sindonem* V 120. The importance of the well-being of both mind and body, and the harmony between them, is further emphasised by the adverb *pariter*. The prayer requests that God's propitious removal of all that is *adversantia*, of all that attempts to lead the members of the community into sin, bring liberation for the whole person, as much for the spiritual as for their bodily welfare. The advantage brought is further delineated in the liturgical usage of the verb *expedire*.

Expediti

Expedire is commonly used in the early sources to denote deliverance and liberation[20]. It is used for liberation from evil and harmful things in general, as in the phrases "*noxii omnibus expediti*" (L 4) and "*ab huius uitae periculis ... expedire*" (V 953). More regularly, however, it refers to deliverance from the effects of sin, such as mortality[21], iniquity, cupidity and guilt:

"*ut ab his iniquitatibus expediti*" (L 440),

"*mortalibus nexibus [animam] expeditam* " (L 1149),

"*a cupiditatibus terrenis expediant*" (L 1053),

"*a reatibus nostris expediat*" (V 1294).

In a number of orations, and also in V 1234, deliverance and liberation is placed with the desire to live more fully within God's way. This can be seen in the following post communion. The prayer sets together liberation from sin and obedience to the mandates. Deliverance is associated with God's

---

[20]Blaise, Vocabulaire, § 283 and § 73. In § 283, Blaise treats *liberare* and *expedire* together.

[21]For a discussion of sin and death see the study of the collect for Sunday XIV, above, 244.

clemency, while both liberation and obedience are related to God's healing work:

"*Tua nos, domine, medecinalis operatio et a nostris peruersitatibus clementer expediat et tuis faciat semper inherere mandatis*" (V 1270)[22].

Similarly, another post communion sets freedom from sin alongside fervent devotion (*in devotione currentes*). Both are associated with communion:

"*Muniat, quaesumus, domine, fideles tuos sumpta uiuificatio sacramenti et a uitiis omnibus expeditos in sancta faciat deuotione currentes*" (V 1359)[23].

In summary, the purpose clause seeks that all aspects of human existence in both the spiritual and material realms be delivered from whatsoever causes harm, particularly that which comes from sin. Deliverance from evil is often linked with the freedom to worship and live out God's mandates without hindrance.

In collect V 1234, liberation equally in mind and body is the grounds for enabling the community to follow fully and freely what God wills: *quae tua sunt liberis mentibus exsequamur.*

Quae sunt tua exsequamur

Exsequi has already been examined in the study of the collect for Sunday XI[24]. There it expresses an obedience to God's commandments which is both freely willed and put into practice (*in exsequendis mandatis tuis, et*

---

[22]Lord, may your healing work both mercifully free us from our perversity and make us always cling to your mandates.
This prayer is also found in the Missal of Paul VI: MR(1975) Dom. X per annum, Post comm., 349.

[23]May the life-giving power of the sacraments that have been received strengthen your faithful, Lord, and, delivered from all vices, may it render them fervent in their holy devotion.

[24]See above, 308.

voluntate tibi et actione placeamus). Such obedience is further described as pleasing to God. In V 1234, the verb's object is more general, *quae sunt tua*. It connotes pleasing worship and obedience to the divine mandates. As discussed above, the parallel between *mente et corpore pariter expediti* and *liberis mentibus* indicates that the stress of the purpose clause falls on the adjective *liber*.

Liberis mentibus

The New Testament understanding of *libertas* has been examined in the analysis of the collect for Sunday XXIII[25]. In this section we will examine the use of *liber, liberare* and *libertas* in the liturgical euchology[26].

Bastiaensen identifies three senses attached to the use of *liber, liberare* and *libertas* in the *Veronensis*; liberty in the civil sphere (*liberté politique*), freedom from sin and the power of the devil (*liberté religieuse*), and a more personal, interior sense of freedom from external pressures and limitations (*liberté psychologique*). The first two are by far the most common. In each of these conceptualizations freedom is not described as an end in itself, but as freedom from some sort of adversity or adversary.

The first sense of liberty concerns civil and political freedom from war and strife[27]. The overriding value of such freedom, as seen through the eyes of the early euchology, is that it offers the possibility of unhindered attendance to the tasks proper to the church, especially the liturgy. This is at the basis of the

---

[25]See above, 228ff.

[26]For further examples of the use of *liber, liberare* and *libertas* see Deshusses, Concordances, III, 3, 462-467. Some commentary can also be found in Blaise, Vocabulaire, § 283. For a detailed study of *liber, liberare* and *libertas* in the *Veronensis*, see Bastiaensen, "Liberté." Much of the following is dependent on this work.

[27]Bastiaensen, "Liberté," 122-127.

collect for Sunday VIII, discussed above[28]. Politicial and civil freedom is at the service of worship, and so points to the priority of the freedom that religion brings.

What Bastiaensen calls 'Religious' liberty involves deliverance from sin and death, and from the devil and his forces[29]. Victory has come in Christ, through whom death has been defeated and life restored (L 1137). The following postcommunion illustrates the community's faith in the power, completeness and continuing effectiveness of Christ's victory over the devil and sin. Motivated by their belief in his defeat of the devil and remission of sins, believers request that they be purged of the effects of their sin and defended from further onslaught by the forces of the devil (*hostes*). The prayer reads: "*Concede, quaesumus, domine deus noster, ut qui ad destructionem diaboli et remissionem natus est hodie peccatorum, et a culparum subreptione nos expiet, et ab hostium incursione defendat*" (V 1251)[30].

The third understanding of freedom encountered in the *Veronensis* concerns freedom from limits and constraints set upon the believer[31]. Examples of this can be found among the Masses of Pope Gelasius against the Lupercalia, where the prayers portray his desire to offer love beyond the hostility with which he has been assailed (L 414, L 450).

---

[28]See above, 179. For some other prayers along this line see L 874, L 626 and L 648.

[29]Bastiaensen, "Liberté," 127-150.

[30]Grant, Lord our God, that he, who was born so that the devil might be destroyed and sins remitted, may both cleanse us from the deception of our faults, and defend us from the incursions of the hosts of the devil.

[31]Bastiaensen, "Liberté," 150-153.

According to Blaise, *libera mens* most frequently designates the soul delivered from all spiritual impediments[32].

In V 1234, the force of the prayer's vocabulary (*adversare, excludere propitiatus, expedire*) points mainly to *liberis mentibus* as liberation from sin and the devil. This is the second meaning mentioned by Bastiaensen. God's service can be pursued with such spiritual freedom when God has driven out from all the whole of the human person all sin, all temptation and all that causes disharmony between spirit and flesh.

<u>Meaning of the prayer</u>:

The key to the prayer's meaning is in the petition. In their life on earth, the faithful are locked in continuous struggle with the various *adversantia*. The intensity of the struggle can be seen through the use of the present participle as substantive (*adversantia*), the inherent opposition signified by the prefixes *ex* and *ad* in the petition, as well as through the repeated use of the verbal prefix *ex* in the prayer itself. The oration is concerned primarily with the struggle against sin, concupiscence and the devil. In light of their faith in God's power, mercy and propitiation, the people call upon God to exert his power and drive out (*excludere propitiatus*) all that endangers the spiritual welfare of his community. God's act of removing what is harmful is often accompanied by his granting what is beneficial.

The purpose of the petition is twofold. Firstly God is asked to bring deliverance (*expedire*) in mind and equally in body. The conjunction of *mens* and *corpus* signifies the whole human person, and connotes a deep harmony amongst the many facets of the inner life of the human person. The faithful desire this freedom (*liberis mentibus*) so as to be able to carry out God's work unhindered by either spiritual foes or temptations.

---

[32]Blaise, <u>Vocabulaire</u>, § 396 fn 5.

ANALYSIS OF THE WORDS AND PHRASES IN THE COLLECT IN RELATIONSHIP TO THE MISSAL OF PAUL VI

Two words from the collect undergo something of a reduction in breadth when examined within the context of the Missal of Paul VI.

The verb *excludere* appears only twice in the Missal[33], in our collect and in a blessing which shows a close dependence on our collect[34]. In both instances its meaning remains quite general, and, though associated with God's propitiation, contains no reference to diabolical forces, as in earlier sources.

Adversari is also rare, appearing only three times in the Missal[35]. The two uses other than our prayer are both in the same Mass for those who oppress (*affligentes*) the community. There, *adversari* refers to the hostile actions which disturb the peace that should reign between the church and all others. The post communion reads:

"*Per haec pacis nostrae mysteria, da nos, Deus, cum omnibus esse pacificos, et eos qui nobis adversantur tibi gratos efficere, nobisque placatos*" (MR(1975) Pro affligentibus nos, Post comm., 853)[36].

---

[33] Schnitker and Slaby, Concordantia, 895.

[34] *Omnipotens Deus universa a vobis adversa semper excludat, et suae super vos benedictionis dona propitiatus infundat* (MR(1975) Benedd. in fine M., Bened. soll. per annum V, 502).
Translation: May the allpowerful God drive out all adversarial things from among you, and propitiously pour over you the gifts of his blessing.

[35] Schnitker and Slaby, Concordantia, 75.

[36] Through these mysteries of our peace, give us, God, peaceful relations with all peoples, and make those who oppose us thankful to you and reconciled with us.
See also the offertory prayer from the same Mass: MR(1975) Pro affligentibus nos, Super oblata, 853.

The related word *adversus* is also rare, appearing just four times in the Missal[37]. On only one of those occasions, a blessing over the water for the asperges, does *adversus* connote the opposition brought about by the devil: "... *et adversus omnes morbos inimicique insidias* ..." (MR(1975) Ordo ad faciendam et aspergendam aquam bened., Bened. aquae ad lib., 918)[38].

This narrowing of the scope of *excludere* and *adversari* indicates that the Missal of Paul VI downplays the dynamic of a profound and deadly struggle waged by the faithful in Christ against sin, death and the devil.

RELATIONSHIP OF THE CHRISTIAN PEOPLE TO GOD

The collect sets the faithful's existence on earth within the context of a thoroughgoing, vivid struggle against sin, death, the devil and his forces. This confrontation is exhibited in all aspects of the spiritual life of the human person, in mind and body equally.

The church, however, has a further perspective on this confrontation. In their faith in God, they trust in his power, mercy and propitiation to be able to drive out, equally from both mind and body, all that inhibits their freedom to love, worship and obey him. Inner harmony and spiritual freedom follow when God frees all aspects of the human person from sin, temptation and the power of the devil.

The new context of the prayer within the Missal of Paul VI has brought some modifications to the nature of the relationship. The sparing use in the Missal as a whole of the verbs *expedire* and *adversari* has weakened the metaphor of struggle and contest, especially diluting the opposition that comes from sin as death, the devil and his forces. This diminishment of

---

[37] Schnitker and Slaby, Concordantia, 75.

[38] "... against all afflictions and snares of the foe." For the use of *inimicus* for the devil see Mt 13:39 and Blaise, Vocabulaire, § 325.

eschatological tension is consistent with the downplaying of sin as death seen in the collect for Sunday XIV[39].

FREER TRANSLATION OF THE COLLECT

Omnipotens et misericors Deus, universa nobis adversantia propitiatus exclude, ut, mente et corpore pariter expediti, quae tua sunt liberis mentibus exsequamur.

God of power and mercy, drive out from among us all powers, forces and circumstances that oppose us to your love. May we be freed in soul and spirit, in body and community, so that nothing may hinder us from carrying out your will.

---

[39] See above, 248.

CHAPTER SEVEN
PRAYERS FROM THE GREGORIAN SACRAMENTARIES:
THE COLLECTS FOR WEEK I, SUNDAYS II, III, V, VII, XVII, XXVIII and WEEK XXXIV

INTRODUCTION

The sacramentaries that are covered under the term 'Gregorian' are so named because they were once thought to have been copies of a sacramentary attributed to Gregory the Great (590-604)[1]. In fact, they are different copies and redactions of the papal sacramentary used during liturgies both at the Lateran basilica and throughout the city of Rome as the city's bishops celebrated the annual round of stational liturgies. Two particular Gregorian Sacramentaries are of importance to our study, the *Hadrianum* and the *Paduensis*.

The *Hadrianum*:

The *Hadrianum* is the sacramentary sent by Pope Hadrian I (772-795) to Charlemagne (768-814) towards the end of the eighth century. The Frankish King had requested from Rome a copy of the papal sacramentary compiled by St. Gregory the Great. He desired a 'pure' text, one without any non-Gregorian additions. Charlemagne's aim was to use such an authentic papal sacramentary as a model for future liturgical reform throughout his kingdom. What he received from Hadrian was a sacramentary perhaps dating from a period slightly earlier than Hadrian I. It contained only prayers for

---

[1] The following is based on Vogel, Medieval Liturgy: An Introduction to the Sources, 79-102

those Masses and ceremonies, held in the Lateran or at the stational churches, at which the Pope presided. The critical edition of the *Hadrianum* is that of Deshusses[2].

Two features deserve some comment. Firstly, the *Hadrianum* is typical of the Gregorian sacramentaries in that there are normally only three presidential prayers for each Mass, the *oratio*, the *super oblata* and the *ad complendum* or *ad completam*. Some Masses also contain a *super populum*. Secondly, there are no Mass sets for the Sundays after Epiphany and Pentecost. However, the *Hadrianum* does contain a section, 202 *Incipiunt orationes cottidianis*, whose prayers could be used *ad libitum* for those Sundays.

The *Paduensis*:

The Sacramentary of Padua, commonly known as the *Paduensis*, is a ninth century redaction of a mid-seventh century Gregorian Sacramentary. This Roman prototype was itself an adaptation, for presbyteral use in the Vatican, of the then current papal sacramentary. The critical edition of the *Paduensis* is that of Deshusses[3].

The sacramentary has a number of features of interest to our study. As is typical of Gregorian Sacramentaries, there are usually three presidential prayers for each Mass, the *oratio*, the *super oblata* and the *ad complendum*. Some Masses are equipped with either a preface or a *super populum* or both. The Masses of the temporal and sanctoral cycles are merged into a single continuous series of Sundays and feastdays. Lastly, there is a set of fixed Mass texts for those Sundays outside of the seasons of Advent, Christmas, Lent

---

[2]J.Deshusses, Le Sacramentaire Grégorien: Ses principales formes d'après les plus anciens manuscrits, Tome I: Le sacramentaire, le supplément d'Aniane, 2me édition revue et corrigée 1979, Spicilegium Friburgense 16 (Fribourg, Suisse: Éditions Universitaires, 1971, 1979), 85-348.

[3]J.Deshusses, Le Sacramentaire Grégorien, 607-684.

and Easter, and upon which no major feast fell. There are Masses for five Sundays after Epiphany, for five Sundays after Pentecost, for six Sundays after the feast of Sts. Peter and Paul, five Sundays after the feast of St. Lawrence, and for nine Sundays after the feast of St. Michael the Archangel.

ORATIONS FROM THE *HADRIANUM* AND THE *PADUENSIS* IN THE MISSAL OF PAUL VI:

Amongst the collects for the Sundays of Ordinary Time in the Missal of Paul VI are seven orations first encountered in either the *Hadrianum* or the *Paduensis*. They are the collects for Sundays I (H 86, P 66), II (H 922), III (H 85, P52), V (H 228, P 201), XVII (P 517), XXVIII (H 966) and XXXIV (H 894, P 748). Also included in this chapter is the collect for Sunday VII (V 1521, H 911, P 112). This prayer is first met in *Reginensis* 316, where it served as a presidential prayer in a monastic Mass for an end to contention: *Missa in contencione, alia missa*[4]. However its inclusion in the Roman Missal of Pius V (Dom. V post Epip.) and subsequently as a prayer for a Sunday Mass in Ordinary Time in MR(1975) appears to be linked to the use of the prayer as a collect in the *Paduensis'* Mass for the fifth Sunday after Epiphany. Consequently these eight prayers can be grouped together in the one chapter on account of their common Gregorian origins.

There is a further reason for placing their study in the one chapter. It can be claimed that these prayers form a distinct and cohesive layer of texts among the opening prayers for Ordinary Time in the new Missal. As can be seen from the accompanying table, neither the *Hadrianum* nor the *Paduensis* contains all the prayers. Nor do these two sacramentaries always use the prayers in the same liturgical context. However, when the place of these prayers in the Frankish Gelasian Sacramentaries is taken into account, a unifying rubric can be found.

---

[4] See below, 499ff.

As is evident from the table, it is only in the Frankish Gelasian sacramentaries of Angoulême and St Gall that all eight prayers are found as Sunday Mass collects for the 'free' Sundays that occur throughout the year. From the liturgical context exemplified in the Sacramentary of Angoulême, these collects were carried across into the Roman Missal of 1570, and now stand in their present place in the Missal of Paul VI.

It can be said that while the prayers are Gregorian Roman, their unity as a distinct layer in the new Missal arises from their liturgical context in the later Frankish Gelasian Sacramentary of Angoulême. In light of this, the collects are arranged in accordance with their order in the Sacramentary of Angoulême. The first prayer to be studied will be the collect for Sunday III, followed by the collects for Sundays I, II, V, VII, XVII, XXVIII and XXXIV.

Table of the sources of the collects from the Gregorian Sacramentaries

MR 1975	P	H	Sp	A	G	Sg	MR
Dom. I	P 66	H 86	Sp 1096	A 114	G 113	S 106	Dom. Infra Oct. Epip. M 1181
	Dom I post Epip.	Item alia in Dom. (post Oct. Nat. Dom.)	Dom. I post Theo.	Dom.I post Theo.	Dom. I post Theo.	Dom. I post Teoph.	
Dom. II	*Prayer not in source*	H 922	Sp 1099	A 129	G 134	S 121	Dom. II post Epip. M773
		Incip. orat. cottd. Alia	Dom. II post Theo.	Dom. II post Theo.	Dom. II post Theo. (*Supr sin.*)	Dom. II post Teoph.	
Dom. III	P 52	H 85	Sp 1093	A 91	G 91	S 85	Dom. infra Oct. Nat. M761
	Orat. in alia Dom. (post Oct. Nat. Dom.)	Orat. in alia Dom. (post Oct. Nat. Dom.)	Dom II post Nat. Domini	Item alia Dom. (post Oct. nat. Dom.)	Item alia Dom. (post nat. Dom)	Item alia Dom. (post Oct. nat. Dom)	

Dom. V	P 201	H 228	Sp 1108	A 213	*Pray not in G*	S 193	Dom. V post Epip. & Sab. post Dom. II Quad M558
	Sabb. Quadr. II (*Sup. pop.*)	Sabb. Quadr. II (*Sup. pop.*)	Dom. V post Theo.	Dom. V post Theo.		Dom. V post Teoph.	
Dom. VII *V 1521 Missa in contencione, alia Missa*	P 112	H 911	Sp 1356	A 226	G 219 (also G 2743 Missa in Contencion after *ad complenda*)	S 206	Dom. VI post Epip. M875
	Dom. V post Theo.	Incip. orat. cottd. Alia	M. in contentione, alia -(after *ad compl*)	Dom. VI post Theo. (*Super sin.*)	Dom. VI post Theo. (*Super sin.*)	Dom. VI post Teoph. (*Super sin.*)	

Dom. XVII	P 517	*Prayer not in source*	Sp 1138	A 1019	G 1137	S 914	Dom. infra Oct. Ss. Cord.Je s., III post Pent. M911
	Ebd. IIII post Pent.		Dom. IIII post Pent.	Hebd. V post Pent.	Hebd. V post Pent.	Ebd. V post Pent.	
Dom. XXVIII	*Prayer not in source*	H 966	Sp 1177	A 1396	G 1532	S 1251	Dom. XVI post Pent. M 1150
		Orat. vesp. seu matut.	Dom. XVII post Pent.	Hebd. XX post Pent. (*Super sin.*)	Hebd. XVIII post Pent. (*Super sin.*)	Ebd. XX post Pent. (*Super sin.*)	
Dom. XXXIV	P 748	H 894	Sp 1198	A 1487	G 1621	S 1334	Dom. XXIV et ult. post Pent. M548
	Dom. VIII post Ss. Angeli	Incip. orat. cottd. Alia	Dom. XXIIII post Pent.	Hebd. XXVII post Pent.	Hebd. XXVI post Pent.	Ebd. XXVII post Pent.	
MR (1975)	P	H	Sp	A	G	Sg	MR

COLLECT FOR SUNDAY III

PRAYER

Omnipotens sempiterne Deus, dirige actus nostros in beneplacito tuo, ut in nomine dilecti Filii tui mereamur bonis operibus abundare.

All powerful eternal God, direct our actions in what is pleasing to you, so that in the name of your beloved Son we may merit to abound in good works.

ORIGINAL SOURCE AND HISTORICAL ORIGINS

The prayer has been incorporated into the Missal of Paul VI from the Gregorian sources without any change. For further comment on the original sources of the prayer, see the accompanying introductory note to this chapter.

The original liturgical context of the prayer in the sources in the Masses for January or in a Mass for the octave of Christmas highlights certain features in the oration. The recently celebrated feast of the incarnation is one of the central acts of the mystery of God's saving will, his divine *beneplacitum* (Eph 1:9). Furthermore, the beginning of the New Year (January 1) conjured up long standing pagan associations, focussed around the festival of the god Janus[1]. These new year festivities were markedly pagan and licentious, and as such opposed by the church. Hence the petition to act according to what is pleasing to God, *in beneplacito tuo*. *Reginensis* 316 (I,x), and the sacramentaries of Gellone (XIII) and Angoulême (XII) contain the same Mass *prohibendum ab idolis* set alongside the Masses for the octave of the Nativity[2]. Our collect, H 85, is the collect for an octave Mass in the sacramentaries of Gellone (G 91) and Angoulême (A 91). Part of the oration's historical

---

[1] See F.Cabrol, "Circoncision (Fête de la)," DACL III, 1717-1727.

[2] *Reginensis* 316 (I,viiii), *Gellonensis* (XIIII) and the Sacramentary of Angoulême (XIII)

context, then, is the church's opposition to pagan festivities. The anti-pagan thrust is consistent with the prayer's request to act in correspondence with what is pleasing to God, as well as with the power of the name of the beloved Son, and the liturgical implications of *actus nostri*. As well, *actus nostri* and *bona opera*, when both carried out according to the divine pleasure (*in beneplacito tuo*), contain an implicit rebuke of licentious behaviour.

USE IN OTHER LITURGICAL SOURCES

As noted by Bruylants[3], the prayer is found in these sources: *Dominica infra Octavam Nativitatis*: Pr(11,2), S(85), P(52), COR(15,1)[H 85], OR(164)[Sp 1093], X(11,1), N(26), Q(21), 1474(27), 1570, 1604, and these uncritical editions G(13,1)[G 91], Z(77), PaAug(14,1), PaMon(1,11,1), *Die 5 Januarii, In Uigilia Epiphaniae*: 1474(30), 1570, 1604.

ANALYSIS OF THE PRAYER IN THE ORIGINAL SOURCE

Grammatical structure:[4]

The prayer consists of (a) an address to God, (b) a petition, and (c) the purpose of the petition.

(a) Address: *Omnipotens sempiterne Deus,*
(b) Petition: *dirige actus nostros in beneplacito tuo,*
(c) Purpose: *ut in nomine dilecti Filii tui mereamur bonis operibus abundare.*

The prayer's structure is significant. *Actus in beneplacito tuo* parallels *bona opera in nomine dilecti Filii tui*. Good works, themselves carried out in the name of Christ, correspond to those human actions which are pleasing to

---

[3]Bruylants, II, 761.

[4]For further grammatical analysis see Haessly, Rhetoric in the Sunday Collects of the Roman Missal, 31-32.

God and carried out under his direction. Because the actions of the faithful are done under God's direction, according to his *beneplacitum*, and in the name of the beloved Son, they are worthy of merit (*mereri*).

The sequence of the prayer reveals the oration's meaning. In light of its faith in God's power, the church petitions God to direct all its actions according to his divine disposition. Through this request the faithful desire that their actions may be carried out in the name of the beloved Son, enabling the community to abound in good works.

The collect corresponds quite closely, in structure, content and vocabulary, with the first two chapters of the Vulgate translation of the Letter to the Ephesians, specifically Eph 1:3-2:11. In terms of content and structure, the extended passage sets together the following elements: the divine favour (*beneplacitum*) (1:9), God's guidance of all things (1:11), the power of the name of Christ (1:21), the abundance (*superabundare*) of grace (1:8, 2:7), and the good works designated by God for the faithful (2:10).

The collect also closely echoes a later passage from the Letter to the Ephesians, Eph 5:10-11. The pericope sets unfruitful works (*operibus infructiosis tenebrarum*) in contrast with deeds that are pleasing to God: "*probantes quid sit beneplacitum Deo; et nolite communicare operibus infructuosis tenebrarum ...*" (Eph 5:10-11).

Collect H 95, following much the same model, sets good works, done in the name of the beloved Son, in parallel with actions that are pleasing to God (*in beneplacito tuo*).

Combining the sense of both passages from Ephesians, the freely given, divine *beneplacitum* of Eph 1:9 establishes an order whereby the faithful are called to do what is pleasing to God, the *beneplacitum* of Eph 5:10.

The vocabulary study below lends further weight to an appreciation of the influence of Ephesians on the prayer. This is most noticeable in the terms *beneplacitum* and *bona opera*, as well as in the phrase *dilectus Filius tuus*.

Vocabulary:

Prominent vocabulary: *dirigere, actus, beneplacitum, nomen, dilectus filius tuus, bona opera, abundare, mereri.*

Our analysis will begin with the centrepiece of the prayer, God's *beneplacitum*.

In beneplacito[5] *tuo*

On a number of occasions in the Vulgate translation of the New Testament, *beneplacere* and *beneplacitum* denote that the actions so described are pleasing to God and in accord with this dispensation. They are in accord with the divine will, and as such are said to be good, perfect and fruitful. Key texts are Rm 12:2, 1 Cor 10:5, and the above mentioned Eph 5:10-11[6]. It is this understanding of *beneplacere* that is most commonly encountered in the early liturgical sources[7].

The foundation of what is pleasing to God is set forth in the blessing which opens the Vulgate translation of the Letter to the Ephesians, Eph 1:3-14.

---

[5] For further examples of the use of *beneplacitum* see Deshusses, Concordances III, 1, 189, and for *bene placere*, III, 3, 384-389. See also Blaise, Vocabulaire, § 266 and § 504.

[6] "*Et nolite conformari huic saeculo, sed reformamini in novitate sensus vestri, ut probetis quae sit voluntas Dei bona et beneplacens et perfecta*" (Rm 12:2),
"*Sed non in pluribus eorum beneplacitum est Deo, nam prostrati sunt in deserto*" (1 Cor 10:5),
"*probantes quid sit beneplacitum Deo; et nolite communicare operibus infructuosis tenebrarum ...*" (Eph 5:10-11).

[7] For *beneplacere* see L 1302, V 167, while for *bene placere* see L 1011, L 1112, L 1292 and V 35.

There the noun *beneplacitum*[8] is associated with the mystery of God's saving will in Christ: "*ut notum faceret nobis sacramentum voluntatis suae secundum beneplacitum eius, quod proposuit in eo* [*Christus*]" (Eph 1:9). God's will and favour are believed to be expressed in Christ's work of election, adoption, redemption, remission of sins, inheritance, the coming renewal of all things, and the seal of the Holy Spirit[9]. The ultimate purpose of God's favour is that the faithful may be holy and immaculate in his sight (Eph 1:4), and as well respond to God's love with praise (Eph 1:6,12,14).

The collect H 85 seems to be the only example in the early sources of *beneplacitum* as a noun. There it points to those actions which are pleasing to God, *in beneplacito tuo*, since they correspond to God's underlying favourable disposition towards believers as set forth in Eph 1:3-14. In light of their faith in this economy of divine favour, with its meaning of election, adoption, redemption, remission of sins and abundance of grace in Christ, the church asks God to direct their actions, *dirige actus nostros*, in accordance with this dispensation.

---

[8] The greek text reads εὐδοκία (Eph 1:5,9). This repeated usage serves to indicate the free good pleasure which informs the content of the divine will, counsel and purpose. For commentary see G.Schrenk, "εὐδοκεω, εὐδοκία," TDNT II, 738-751.

[9] While this seal of the Spirit refers to Baptism, it can more broadly denote the designation, appointment and equipment of the saints for a public ministry. See the commentary in Markus Barth, Ephesians 1-3, The Anchor Bible, (New York: Doubleday and Company, 1974), 139-143.

Dirige[10]

The verb *dirigere* has been analysed in the study of the collect for Sunday VIII[11]. There it denoted God's direction of human affairs into righteousness and peace. In H 851, God is asked to direct the actions (*actus*) of the community according to what is pleasing to him. There is some concordance between this petition and the verse Eph 1:11, where God is said to guide all things according to the wisdom of his will: "*qui operatur omnia secundum consilium voluntatis suae*" (Eph 1:11). Note that, as mentioned above, the passage Eph 5:10-11 links the actions of the community with what is pleasing to God, while the Ephesians blessing sees the mystery of salvation as the enactment of God's *beneplacitum* (Eph 1:9). The meaning of *actus* will now be examined.

Actus nostros[12]

As seen above, human actions (*actus*), when directed by God, are themselves good works (*bona opera*). Yet, outside of Christ, these actions are unable to be pleasing to God[13]. Note that the related forms *agere, agenda* and *actio* carry a strong liturgical sense since they are often used to speak of the celebration of the Mass, and the Mass itself[14].

In summary, the prayer's petition calls on God to direct the actions of the community so that they are pleasing to him, and consequently in

---

[10] For further examples of the use of *dirigere* see Deshusses, Concordances III, 1, 505-507.

[11] See above, 195.

[12] For further examples of the use of *actus* see Deshusses, Concordances III, 1, 26-27.

[13] See Col 3:9-10 and H 662.

[14] See Blaise, Vocabulaire, § 5 and § 242.

accordance with the divine favour and kindness underlying his whole economy of salvation in Christ. The dispensation outlined in Ephesians is envisioned here. The purpose of the petition is that, in the name of the beloved Son, the church may abound in good works. This purpose clause will now be examined, commencing with *in nomine dilecti filii tui*. As noted above, to act *in beneplacito tuo* is to perform good works *in nomine dilecti Filii tui*.

In nomine dilecti filii tui

Nomen

The liturgical understanding of the biblical term *nomen* has been discussed in the analysis of the collect for Sunday XII.[15] Summarizing that discussion here, *nomen* points to the being, essence and revelation of whatever is 'named'. In H 85, *nomen* designates Christ, the beloved Son. This use of Christ's 'name' echoes Eph 1:19-23. There Christ, designated as the one in whom God bestows every spiritual blessing (Eph 1:3), is said to have been raised by God to the fullness of power, above every power and name: "*supra ... omne nomen, quod nominatur non solum in hac seculo sed etiam in futuro*" (Eph 1:21). This emphasis on the divine *nomen* fits comfortably into a liturgical setting which seeks to counter pagan practices.

Dilectus filius tuus

The noun *nomen* is qualified by the phrase *dilecti filii tui*. While the title is a further pointer to the inspiration of the oration in Ephesians, it also elucidates the relationship between God's *beneplacitum* and Christ.

The appellation *dilectus filius tuus* is found on only four occasions in the Vulgate translation of the New Testament: Jesus' baptism by John (Mt 3:16-17), the transfiguration (Mt 17:16-17), the parable of the wicked

---

[15]See above, 317.

husbandsmen (Lc 20:13), and Ephesians 1:6. This title points to the special relationship of love between the Father and Jesus[16].

Both the baptism and transfiguration narratives associate Jesus, the beloved Son, his words and deeds, with what is pleasing to God (*complacere*): "*Et ecce vox de caelis dicens: Hic est Filius meus dilectus, in quo mihi complacui*" (Mt 3:16-17)[17],

"*Et ecce vox de nube dicens: Hic est Filius meus dilectus, in quo mihi bene complacui: ipsum audite*" (Mt 17:16-17)[18].

In Ephesians 1:6, the title is associated with God's favour (*gratificare*) towards humanity in Christ:

"*qui praedestinavit nos in adoptionem filiorum per Iesum Christum in ipsum, secundum propositum voluntatis suae, in laudem gloriae gratiae suae, in qua gratificavit nos in dilecto Filio suo*" (Eph 1:5-6).

The liturgical sources furnish further evidence as to the uniqueness of the title[19]. The prayer under consideration appears to be the only example of the appellation in the Deshusses and Darragon concordance, though the more elaborate *dilectissimus filius tuus*[20] is indexed twice.

---

[16]The baptism narratives, with their mention of the descent of the Spirit, have a more trinitarian emphasis.

[17]See also Mr 1:10-11 and Lc 3:22.

[18]See also 2 Pt 1:17, and both Mr 9:6 and Lc 9:35. However, in Mark the pericope reads *Filius meus carissimus*, while neither Mark nor Luke include *in quo mihi complacui*.

[19]For examples of the use of *dilectus* see Deshusses, Concordances III, 1, 503.

[20]See L 552 (a postcommunion) and V 1248 (*Quam oblationem* of the Roman Canon). Note that both prayers associate the title with the eucharistic food, rather than directly with God's pleasure or favour: "*qui nos corporis et sanguinis dilectissimi filii tui domini nostri communione uegetasti*" (L 552).

The name of the beloved Son signifies the fullness and effectiveness of the salvific economy of God's favour. This favour is itself linked to the special relationship of love between God and Jesus. The faithful request that their actions may be carried out in the name, revelation, dispensation and power of Christ, and so may they merit to abound in good works: *mereamur bonis operibus abundare.*

Bonis operibus[21]

In Eph 2:10, good works, *bona opera*, are understood to be those actions, prepared already by God, which enable the believer to walk in God's ways. Through carrying them out, Christians fulfill their calling to be God's works of art (*factura*) in Christ:

"*Ipsius enim sumus factura, creati in Christo Iesu, in operibus bonis, quae praeparavit Deus, ut in illis ambulemus*" (Eph 2:10).

The good works prepared by God are the way in Christ for Christians to live out their election, adoption, redemption, remission of sins and richness of grace bestowed upon them (*superabundare*). Whereas in Eph 1:3-14 the response to the working of God's *beneplacitum* is praise (1:6,12,14), in this passage the response to the abundance of God's grace in Christ over the faithful is good works.

Abundare[22]

The verb *abundare* is used in the Vulgate scriptures to characterise the fruitfulness which flows from the God of the covenant when his people respond in loving obedience. This can be seen in the following passage from

---

[21] For further examples of the use of *opus* see Deshusses, Concordances III, 3, 263-267. For further critical comment on 'good works' in this section of Ephesians see M. Barth, Ephesians 1-3, 242-251; and A. Lindemann, Der Epheserbrief, (Zürich: Theologischer Verlag, 1985), 41-42.

[22] For examples of the use of *abundare* see Deshusses, Concordances III, 1, 15-16.

Deuteronomy. Note that the blessings of the covenant are related to the power of God's *nomen*. The selection reads:

"*Suscitabit te Dominus sibi in populum sanctum, sicut iuravit tibi, si custodieris mandata Domini Dei tui et ambulaveris in viis eius. Videbuntque omnes terrarum populi quod nomen Domini invocatum sit super te et timebunt te. Abundare te faciet Dominus omnibus bonis, fructu uteri tui et fructu iumentorum tuorum, fructu terrae tuae, quam iuravit Dominus patribus tuis ut daret tibi*" (Dt 28:9-11)[23].

This usage is also found in the Vulgate translations of the Pauline letters. Such fruitfulness is associated with the power of Christ's victory over death (1 Cor 15:57-58)[24]. It is also related to the overwhelming generosity of God, which both meets all our needs and enables the faithful to abound in all manner of good works (2 Cor 9:8)[25]. In Eph 1:8, the abundance of grace is associated with the salvation which has come in Christ, itself a part of God's wisdom and insight: "*quae superabundavit in nobis in omni sapientia et prudentia*" (Eph 1:8).

Abundare, then, is typical biblical language connoting the fruitfulness and bounteousness of works done under the direction and grace of God. In H 85 it refers directly to works done in the name of Christ.

---

[23] See also Dt 30:8-10.

[24] "*Deo autem gratias, qui dedit nobis victoriam per Dominum nostrum Iesum Christum. Itaque, fratres mei dilecti, stabiles estote et immobiles; abundantes in opere Domini semper scientes quod labor vester non est inanis in Domino*" (1 Cor 15:57-58). See also Rm 5:15.

[25] "*Potens est autem Deus omnem gratiam abundare facere in vobis, ut in omnibus semper omnem sufficientiam habentes abundetis in omne opus bonum*" (2 Cor 9:8).

Mereamur

Mereri has been studied in the analysis of the collect for Sunday XXV[26]. In H 85, it serves to emphasise the active participation (*actus nostri*) of the faithful in the achievement of good works, which are always under God's direction, within the *beneplacitum* established in the love between God and the Son, and are pleasing to God (*in beneplacito tuo*).

Meaning of the prayer:

The community requests that God direct their actions so that they are in concert with his own disposition of favour, brought about in the beloved Son. When the faithful act in the power of Christ, their actions are pleasing to God and in accordance with his dispensation. Their deeds are good works, meritorious in the power of Christ's name, and characterized by fruitfulness and abundance.

The oration closely parallels the opening sections of the Letter to the Ephesians. The divine favour, *beneplacitum*, denotes the fullness of blessings that have come in Christ, including election, adoption, redemption, remission of sins, inheritance, the renewal of all things, and the seal of the Holy Spirit. Through this salvific dispensation, marked entirely by God's pleasure and favour, the faithful are able to carry out actions which are pleasing to God (Eph 5:10).

The 'name of the beloved Son' connotes not ony the love between God and Christ, but the power of Christ's name, the name which has been raised by God above and beyond all names.

'Good works' points to a life lived in God's will, doing the works that God prepared for his people before creation. Through them, the faithful

---

[26] See above, 142.

become God's work of art (*factura*) in Christ. Both the Ephesians context and the noun *actus* give emphasis to works of praise and worship.

The liturgical context as a prayer for a Sunday in January or, more specifically, eight days after the commemoration of the Birth of the Lord, highlights the divine favour of God through Christ in the salvation of humanity, and the all inclusive power of the name of the beloved Son. The possible pagan New Year setting of the prayer sharpens the sense of the power of Christ's name, while emphasising that Christian deeds and acts ought fall under God's direction, and be in accord with what is pleasing to him.

The new context of the Missal of Paul VI brings no new understandings of the words and phrases in the prayer. The change in liturgical context shifts the focus of the oration to the present acts of the community.

THE RELATIONSHIP OF THE CHRISTIAN PEOPLE TO GOD

The faithful live in the economy of salvation brought about in Christ, the beloved Son. This includes election, adoption, redemption, remission of sins, inheritance, the renewal of all things, and the seal of the Holy Spirit. The primary comment of the oration on this dispensation is that the economy of salvation flows from God's favour and good pleasure. Correspondingly the Christian community desires that their actions may correspond to this dispensation, and so be pleasing to God.

The collect also speaks of the role of Christ in the relationship of the Christian people to God. The title *dilectus filius tuus*, with its Vulgate New Testament background, understands Christ to be not only the beloved one of God, but also the revelation of his power and favour towards believers. Christ's 'name' is synonymous with God's favour, power and salvation.

The faithful abound in good works when they allow God to direct their actions and worship according to the dispensation of his favour. These deeds are meritorious because they are carried out in the power of Christ's name. In the abundance of good works, the faithful live already within the riches of heavenly blessings in Christ, inclusive of the restoration of all earthly and heavenly things in him.

FREER TRANSLATION OF THE PRAYER

Omnipotens sempiterne Deus, dirige actus nostros in beneplacito tuo, ut in nomine dilecti Filii tui mereamur bonis operibus abundare.

All powerful eternal God, guide all our actions in the bounteous mystery of your favour and according to your good pleasure. In the name of your beloved Son, may our lives richly abound with good works.

COLLECT FOR WEEK I[1]

PRAYER

Vota, quaesumus, Domine, supplicantis populi caelesti pietate prosequere, ut et quae agenda sunt videant, et ad implenda quae viderint convalescant.

In your heavenly kindness, Lord, we ask you to accompany the prayers of your suppliant people, so that they may both see what things ought to be done, and grow in strength for carrying out what they will have seen.

ORIGINAL SOURCE

The prayer has come down through the liturgical tradition unchanged. For comment on the origin and sources of the prayer, see the accompanying introductory note and table to this chapter.

USE IN OTHER LITURGICAL SOURCES

As noted by Bruylants[2] the prayer has also been used in these liturgical sources:

Dominica infra Octavam Epiphaniae: Pr(14,1), A(114), S(106), P(66), OR(164)[Sp 1096], X(33,1), N(29), Q(24), 1474(33), 1570, 1604, and in the following unedited sources G(16,1)[G 113], Z(98) B(128), PaAug (17,1).
Item in alia dominica: COR(16,1)[H 86].

---

[1]The feast of the Baptism of the Lord takes place on the Sunday which would otherwise be numbered as the first Sunday of the year in Ordinary Time. The week itself is counted as the first week of the year in Ordinary Time, *Hebdomada I*:
"*Dominica in qua fit festum Baptismatis Domini locum tenet primae dominicae "per annum"; hebdomada tamen quae sequitur computatur prima "per annum"* (MR(1975) "Tempus per annum", 233).

[2]Bruylants, II, 1181.

ANALYSIS OF THE PRAYER IN THE ORIGINAL SOURCE

Grammatical structure[3]:

The prayer consists of (a) an address and petition, followed by (b) two purpose clauses joined in an *et ... et* construction.

(a) Address: *Quaesumus, Domine*
    Petition: *Vota ... supplicantis populi caelesti pietate prosequere.*

(b) Purpose: *ut et quae agenda sunt videant,*
              et ad implenda quae viderint convalescant.

The petition points up the need and humility of the faithful (*vota, supplicans*). This is reinforced by the implication of weakness fostered by the use, in the purpose clause, of the verb *convalescere*.

There are a number of noteworthy features in the purpose clause. The *et ... et* construction makes both sections complementary. Seeing what ought be done is not to be separated from working towards its completion. This is also reflected in the pairing of *agenda* and *implenda*. The pairing of *videre* and *convalescere* is quite unusual in the liturgical sources. As will be shown below, verbs such as *videre* are more frequently set together with *valere*. The force of the petition, then, falls on the strengthening of the community for the task, rather than the completion of the task itself.

Vocabulary:

Prominent vocabulary: *vota, supplicare, populus, caelestis, pietas, prosequi, agere, videre, implere, convalescere.*

Our analysis of the vocabulary will begin with the petition *"vota ... supplicantis populi caelesti pietate prosequere."* Most of these terms have

---

[3]For a more complete analysis see Haessly, Rhetoric in the Collects of the Roman Missal, 32-33.

been studied above in the analyses of earlier collects. The only exception is the verb *prosequi*.

Vota ... prosequere[4]

The verb *prosequi*, when used in the expression *prosequi ... vota*, denotes the faithful's desire that God accompany, assist and favour their petitions to their fulfillment[5]. This expression is linked, in the early Roman sources, with God's loving kindness and fidelity to his people, as well as with the divine inspiration that underlies their prayers and actions. This can be seen in two orations from the *Hadrianum*.

The *ad complenda*, H 474, relates the faithful's petition *vota ... prosequi* to God's ever attentive love and favour towards his people (*pio favore prosequere*). The use of *prosequi* indicates the community's desire that God accompany their request until its fulfillment, in this case the growth in love of God. The prayer reads:

"*Vota nostra quaesumus domine pio fauore prosequere, ut dum dona tua in tribulatione percipimus, de consolatione nostra in tuo amore crescamus*" (H 474)[6],

A similar usage of *prosequi* is found in H 383, the collect for an Easter Sunday Mass (88). The context for the petition is the defeat of death and the opening of the gates of eternal life through the Paschal Mystery, the supreme act of God's ever attentive love. Here *prosequi* expresses the church's desire that God, in his assistance, accompany to completion the

---

[4]For further examples of the use of *prosequi* see Deshusses, Concordances, III, 3, 521-522.

[5]Blaise, Vocabulaire, § 65.

[6]Accompany our prayer, Lord, with your devoted favour, so that, while we receive your gifts in our tribulation, through our consolation we may grow in love of you.

prayers which he himself first inspired in them. The oration reads: *"Deus qui hodierna die per unigenitum tuum aeternitatis nobis aditum deuicta morte reserasti, uota nostra quae praeueniendo adspiras, etiam adiuuando prosequere"* (H 383)[7].

In H 86, *prosequi* is related to God's heavenly loving kindness, *caelestis pietas*. *Caelestis* underscores the divine power of God's *pietas*. The divine *pietas* has been analysed above in the study of the collect for Sunday XXVII[8]. Summarizing that discussion here, in the Vulgate scriptures the divine *pietas* denotes the mystery of God's loving kindness in Christ as he pursues humanity's salvation (1 Tm 3:16). *Pietas* reflects the sense of loving devotion and duty implied when the noun is applied to human actions. There is, then, a certain congruence between the divine *pietas* and the prayer that God accompany their petition to its completion. The community's faith in God's loving kindness and merciful forgiveness is the grounds, in our collect, for their confidence that God will accompany their supplication.

The faithful add a note of humility and need by describing themselves as a suppliant people, *supplicans populus*.

The prayer's petition has a twofold purpose. The community seeks that they may see what ought to be done, and as well grow in strength so that they can carry out what they have seen: *"ut et quae agenda sunt videant, et ad implenda quae viderint convalescant."*

---

[7] God, who on this day through your only begotten Son, with death vanquished, opened the gates of eternal life, with your assistance accompany our prayer, which you first inspired through your prevenient action. Much the same sentiment and phrasing can be seen in V 1165 and H 198. This second oration has been incorporated into the Missal of Paul VI: MR(1975) Fer. V post Cineres, Collecta 181.

[8] See above, 389.

Note that this supplication, necessarily accompanied by God's *pietas*, underlies their seeing (*videre*), growth back to strength (*convalescere*), and the fulfillment of what ought to be done (*implere*).

Various combinations of the words *agere, videre, implere*, as well as *convalescere* and its root *valere*, are found throughout the early liturgical sources. A range of these parallels will be examined in this section in order to exemplify the usage of the terms, and to clarify the meaning of our prayer.

Videre ... agere/implere

Our prayer echoes an admonition situated at the end of the Letter to the Colossians. Here *videre* has the sense of to 'be mindful about', to 'be perceptive about', to 'turn one's attention towards' some task, with the express view of carrying it out (*implere*). Thus the message for Achippus reads: "*Vide ministerium quod accepisti in Domino, ut illud impleas*" (Col 4:17)[9].

A similar sentiment is found in the lenten *super populum* H 183. The prayer sets *agenda* and *recta* in parallel. As well it uses *valere* where H 86 has *convalescere*. Note the connection between the 'light' God offers to the minds of believers, and their ability to have insight, to 'see'. This will be taken up again below. The prayer reads:

"*Mentes nostras quaesumus domine lumine tuae claritatis inlustra, ut uidere possimus quae agenda sunt, et quae recta sunt agere ualeamus*" (H 183)[10].

---

[9]The latin Vulgate translation tends to use *videre* where the greek prefers a variety of terms, each with its own nuance. Here the greek reads βλεπω, a verb which means to see (with the eye) as opposed to being blind. It can also denote intellectual or spiritual perception. For commentary see W.Michaelis, "ὸραω, κτλ.," TDNT, V, 327-328, 343-344. See also 2 Jo 8, where *videre* is similiarly used to translate βλεπω.

[10]Illuminate our minds, Lord, with the light of your radiance, so that we may be able to see what ought be done, and we may be strong to do these upright deeds.

In his commentary on *videre* in H 86, Blaise[11] refers to Canon 4 from a collection of canons from the early 5th century Councils of Mileve. The apposite section of the number is as follows:

"*Item quisquis dixerit eamdem gratiam Dei per Iesum Christum Dominum nostrum propter hoc tantum nos adiuuare ad non peccandum, quia per ipsam [gratiam Dei per Iesum Christum] nobis reuelatur et aperitur intelligentia mandatorum, ut sciamus quid appetere, quid uitare debeamus, non per illam autem nobis praestari ut quod faciendum cognouerimus etiam facere debeamus atque ualeamus, anathema sit ..*"(Canon 4)[12].

The anti-Pelagian tone is clear. God's grace is necessary both for knowing what ought be done, and for carrying it out. Note that *videre* in H 86 has much the same sense as *scire* and *cognoscere* in Canon 4. *Valere* is found where H 86 prefers *convalescere*. Furthermore, *faciendum* (in H 86 *agenda/implenda*) is related to the commandments (*mandata*).

The liturgical context of the prayer as an oration for the Mass of the Sunday after the Epiphany furthers the connection between *videre* and God's light (*lumen*) suggested above in H 183. A dominant symbol of the feasts of the Nativity and Epiphany is that of light, as seen in this prayer for the feast of Epiphany:

"*Deus inluminator omnium gentium, da populis tuis perpetua pace gaudere, et illud lumen splendidum infunde in cordibus nostris quem trium magorum*

---

[11]Blaise, Vocabulaire, § 273, fn 1.

[12]Whosoever will have said that this same grace through our Lord Jesus Christ only helps us not to sin, since through this grace the knowledge of the commandments is revealed to us and their understanding opened to us, so that we might know what we ought to desire and what to avoid, but denies that it is given to us through that grace to be able to know and able to do what we will have known ought to be done, anathema sit.
Canon 4, Concilium Africanum in Milevitana, in C.Munier, ed., Concilia Africae (345 - 525) (Turnhout: Brepols, 1974), 362.

mentibus aspirasti" (H 92)[13].

In view of the Epiphany context of H 86, *videre* has the added sense of perception by the light which shines in our world on account of the incarnation.[14]

The connection between *agenda* and the commandments (*mandata*) is also to be seen when the *super sindonem* (A 115, G 114, S 107) from the same Mass (Dom. I post Theo) as our collect (A 114, G 113, S 106) is taken into consideration. The petition of the *super sindonem* seeks the gift of obedience to God's mandates. The Mass, then, sets the *agenda* of the collect and the divine mandates from the *super sindonem* in parallel. The petition reads: *"Fac nos Domine Deus noster tuis oboedire mandatis ..."* (A 115)[15].

Convalescere/valere ... implere

Convalescere means to grow strong, with the implication of a recovery from weakness and illness. The verb is uncommon in the Vulgate translation of the scriptures[16]. There it also has connotations of growing in strength to do God's work (Js 17:13, Ac 9:22). *Convalescere* is rarely found in the early

---

[13]God, bringer of light to all the nations, grant that your peoples may rejoice in everlasting peace, and pour into our hearts that same splendid light which you instilled into the minds of the three magi.
This prayer is found across the Gallican influenced sources: P 63, G 108, A 110, Sg 102. See also the Christmas preface H 38.

[14]The theme of 'light' is take up in the collect for Sunday XV. There God is addressed as the one who leads those who stray back to his path through the light of his truth. See above, 256. See also the discussion of *lux* and *splendor* in the collect for Sunday XIII, below, 603ff..

[15]Lord our God, make us obey your mandates ...

[16]It is listed ten times in the Dutripon concordance. See Dutripon, <u>Bibliorum Sacrorum Concordantiae</u>, 273.

euchology[17]. The closest parallel to the function of *convalescere* in H 86 is seen in some applications of the root verb *valere*. This has been noted above in the examples H 183 and Canon 4 from the Council of Mileve. Some prayers conjoin *valere* and *implere*, as in the following lenten collect: *"Inquoata [inchoata] ieiunia, quaesumus, domine, benigno fauore prosequere, ut obseruantiam quam corporaliter exercimus, mentibus ualeamus implere senceris"* (V 89)[18].

Note that *implere*, here associated with the observance of the fast, implies sincerity of mind. The verb of petition is *prosequi*, here indicating that God is being asked not only to accompany the faithful's fast but also their internal attitude so that their observance may be beneficial. Furthermore, just

---

[17]*Convalescere* is indexed on only two other occasions in the Deshusses and Darragon concordance. Neither of these two prayers is found in the *Hadrianum, Paduensis*, or the earlier Roman sources. See Deshusses, Concordances, III, 1, 356. One occasion is in the exhortation to the people during the ordination of a bishop. Here the sense of *convalescere* is 'to gain strength':
"... *cuius peruigili cura et instanti sollicitudine ordo ecclesiae et credentium fides in Dei timore melius conualescat...* " (A 2102) (... by whose ever vigilant care and presistant sollicitude may the order of the church and the faith of believers more readily grow strong in the fear of God).
The other is in a blessing of the water during the dedication of a church. Here the sense of *convalescere* is to recover and regain strength following the ravages of sin:
"...*ut omne quod sorde est effugiatur ut [et] tuae pietatis beneficium in omnibus conualescat*" (G 2419) (... so that every detestable thing may be driven out and the favour of your loving kindness may gain strength in all things/in the doing of every good deed).

[18]Lord, favour with beneficent care the fasts which we have begun, so that we may be able to carry out with sincere minds the observances which we perform in our bodies.
This prayer is incorporated into the Missal of Paul VI: MR(1975) Fer. VI post Cineres, Collecta, 182.

as in H 86 God's continuous prompting is linked with his *pietas*, in V 89 it is linked with his gracious favour, *benignus favor*.

In summary, the purpose clause sets out two interconnected requests. Firstly the community asks that they may see (*videre*) what ought to be done (*agenda*). The *agenda* include the commandments, actions that are upright (*recta*) in God's sight, and observances such as the fast. *Videre* denotes the community's desire to both perceive and know, in the light of Christ, what ought be done. The drive to carry out these *agenda*, implicit in *videre*, is taken up in the second purpose clause. There the stress, however, falls not so much on the completion (*implere*) of the mandates but on the strengthing of the faithful (*convalescere*) against weakness and sin, so that they may take up the task of the *agenda*. All implementation and fulfilment of the *agenda*, and hence the necessary growing in strength, must be characterized by sincerity of mind and heart.

Meaning of the prayer:

The oration's first petition requests that God, in his divine loving kindness, accompany, follow up and assist the humble supplication of the community. The verb *prosequi* further connotes that every good petition is inspired by God, and can only be accomplished through God's help. The community makes its request on account of its faith in God's *caelestis pietas*. This expression of God's loving kindness carries both the sense of God's power, *caelestis*, and his devotion and commitment to his people, *pietas* (*pius*).

The purpose of their petition is twofold. Firstly they desire that they may perceive and be mindful of what they ought to do. Such insight, with its imperative sense, comes about when they see things in the light that Christ brings. Secondly they ask that they may grow strong, so that they may bring to completion what they have perceived. Their need to recover and grow in strength attests to the debilitating effect of sin in their lives. The *agenda* themselves include the divine mandates, what is upright in God's sight, and observances such as the fast. However, these are only pleasing to God when carried out in sincerity of heart.

The faithful can only see what ought to be done, and grow in strength to do it, when these actions are continually underpinned by supplication which is itself inspired, upheld and accompanied to its fulfilment by God's assistance.

ANALYSIS OF THE WORDS AND PHRASES IN THE COLLECT IN RELATIONSHIP TO THE MISSAL OF PAUL VI

The collect is the only prayer in the Missal of Paul VI to contain the verb *convalescere*[19]. Our oration also appears to be the only example in the Missal of the expression *vota ... prosequi*[20]. In a number of prayers, however, God is called upon to accompany the actions and works of the faithful. This has already been seen earlier in this analysis in the example V 89, incorporated into MR(1975) as Fer. V post Cineres, Collecta 182[21].

The collect being studied bears some similarity to the collect for Sunday X:

"*Deus, a quo bona cuncta procedunt, tuis largire supplicibus, ut cogitemus, te inspirante, quae recta sunt; et, te gubernante, eadem faciamus.*"[22]

---

[19] See Schnitker and Slaby, Concordantia, 373.

[20] For examples of the use of *prosequi*, see Schnitker and Slaby, Concordantia, 1981-1982. The verb is used on 16 occasions in the Missal.

[21] See also MR(1975) Fer. V post Cineres, Collecta 181, originally H 189. There God's accompaniment is related to his favour, the grace which first inspires the faithful's action, and its being brought to completion.

[22] God, from whom all good things come, grant to your suppliants, both that we might ponder, under your inspiration, what are upright, and that under your guidance, we may do those same things.

The collect for Sunday X stresses that all good comes from God, and all good human actions are done in God's grace (*te inspirante, te gubernante*). Likewise, the collect for Hebdomada I sets all good human actions within God's economy of grace (*caelestis pietas*). This collect gives some accent to the actions of the faithful. They offer prayers (*vota*) and supplication (*supplicans*), they perceive (*videre*), grow strong (*convalescere*), and put into effect (*agere, implere*). Yet the initial petition is that God accompany, *prosequi*, their prayers. The community desires God to remain active in allowing the people to see what ought be done, and to be strong enough to carry it out.

RELATIONSHIP OF THE CHRISTIAN PEOPLE TO GOD

The relationship of the Christian people to God rests in the divine loving kindness (*caelestis pietas*) out of which God inspires and responds to his people's prayer. It is this loving kindness that establishes what the faithful ought to do, and as well provides the light by which they can see and do it. The community is characterized as a suppliant, humble people, in need of strength to recover from their weakness (*convalescere*), and as always supported by God, who keeps their prayer alive and gives the grace to do what the prayer asks.

On the other hand, the prayer emphasizes the active role of the faithful in their life in God. They make supplication and offer prayer, and seek insight. Most particularly, they desire to grow in strength and recover from the ravages of sin, so as to live more fully the divine *agenda*. Yet their supplication itself, and the actions that they seek through it, are only possible, effective and completed when continuously inspired and supported by God's grace.

These *agenda* are perceivable in the light of Christ's incarnation and salvation. When the community carries them out in sincerity, their lives and actions are congruent with God's loving kindness (*pietas*).

FREER TRANSLATION OF THE COLLECT

Vota, quaesumus, Domine, supplicantis populi caelesti pietate prosequere, ut et quae agenda sunt videant, et ad implenda quae viderint convalescant.	In the power of your merciful love, Lord, continually inspire the prayers of your suppliant people, so that by your grace they may see what ought to be done, and grow in the strength to bring these tasks to completion.

COLLECT FOR SUNDAY II

PRAYER

Omnipotens sempiterne Deus, qui caelestia simul et terrena moderaris, supplicationes populi tui clementer exaudi, et pacem tuam nostris concede temporibus.

All powerful eternal God, who govern together heavenly and earthly things, in your clemency hear the supplications of your people and grant your peace in our time.

ORIGINAL SOURCE AND HISTORICAL ORIGINS

The prayer, first encountered in the *Hadrianum* (H 992), has been incorporated into the Missal of Paul VI from the Gregorian sources without any change. For further comment on the original sources of the prayer, see the accompanying introductory note and table.

USE IN OTHER LITURGICAL SOURCES

As noted by Bruylants[1], the prayer is found in these sources:
Dominica II post Epiphaniam: Pr(17,1), A(129), S(121), *OR*(164)[Sp 1099], X(34,1), N(30), Q(25^v), 1474(35), 1570, 1604, and these uncritical editions G(19,1^1)[G 134], Z(113), PaAug(18,1), Par(7).
Incipiunt orationes cotidianae, COR(202,47) [H 922].

---

[1]Bruylants, II, 773.

Grammatical structure:[2]

The collect is made up of (a) an address with motivating clause, and (b) two petitions, set side by side and joined by the conjunction *et*.

(a) Address: *Omnipotens sempiterne Deus,*
    Motivation: *qui caelestia simul et terrena moderaris.*
(b) 1st Petition: *supplicationes populi tui clementer exaudi,*
    2nd Petition: *et pacem tuam nostris concede temporibus.*

The request for God to hear their prayers is associated with the community's belief in God's power in which all things exist, his government of all things earthly and heavenly at the same time, God's clemency, and his choice of them as his people (*tuus populus*).

God's clemency (out of which he is asked to hear the supplications of his people) is set in parallel with his governance of all things. As well, the divine peace is associated with God's power, government and his clemency. There is a certain resonance between the tranquillity and calmness denoted by *clementia* and the sense of governance and measure in the verb *moderari*.

The structure of the prayer explores the relationship between the realms of the divine and the earthly. The motivation clause puts them both under God's rulership, *caelestia simul et terrena*. The second petition shows the congruence between God's peace and earthly existence, *pacem tuam in nostris temporibus*. The first and last words of the prayer, *omnipotens sempiterne Deus ... nostris concede temporibus*, reflect the fittingness of divine action in the world.

---

[2]For a more complete grammatical analysis see Haessly, Rhetoric in the Sunday Collects of the Roman Missal, 33-35, and F.Gerdes, "The Language of the Roman Missal. Part III: Second Sunday after Epiphany to Quinquagesima Sunday" (Ph.D. diss., Saint Louis University, 1958), 82.

Vocabulary:

Prominent vocabulary: *caelestia et terrena, moderari, supplicatio, populus, clementer, exaudire, pax, concedere, nostrum tempus.*

Our study will begin with the motivating clause, and in particular with the idea of God's government of all things in heaven and on earth.

Moderaris[3]

The liturgical usage of the verb *moderari*, along with its cognates *moderamen*, *moderatio* and *moderator*, is analogous to that of *regere* and *gubernare*, as well as *dispensare* and *disponere*[4]. Various aspects of God's government have been examined above in the studies of the collects for Sundays XXIV (*creator et rector*), XVIII (*auctor, gubernator, restaurare, conservare*), VIII (*pacificus ordo, dirigere*), XII (*gubernare, instituare*), IX (*providentia, dispositio*), X (*procedere, gubernare*), and III (*dirigere*).

Summarizing that material here, God's governing follows from his work as creator (*creator, auctor*). Since he never abandons what he establishes in his love, God's government unfailingly reflects his love. As such it is characterized as an order of peace. The scope of the divine government in love and peace extends from the restoration and preservation of all creation in Christ to guiding the local community to carry out the upright deeds God has inspired them to know and ponder. God's government extends to political and civil affairs especially so that the church may worship freely and without hindrance.

---

[3]For further examples of the use of *moderari, moderamen, moderatio*, and *moderator* see Deshusses, Concordances III, 3, 102-103.

[4]See Blaise, Vocabulaire, § 139. For specific examples see V 1493 (*qui prouidencia tua caelestia simul et terrena moderaris*) and L 997 (*Deus, dierum temporumque nostrorum potens et benigne moderator*). L 997 is found, with slight adaptations, in the Missal of Paul VI: MR(1975) Pro seipso sacerd. A, super oblata, 799.

The choice of the verb *moderari* brings a particular nuance to the divine government and rulership. Along with *modus, modulus* and *modestus,* the verb carries a particular sense of ruling, managing and directing within the measure and manner of whatsoever is being governed. It denotes a certain harmony and rhythm. All things, in the first instance, have already received their place and measure from God, their creator. This sense of harmony, proportion and measure sits easily with the concepts of God's clemency (*clementer*) and peace (*tua pax*).

Caelestia simul et terrena

In H 992, God is invoked as the one who governs all that belongs to the the heavens as well as to the earth. The conjunction of the *caelestia* and *terrena*, and its qualification by the adverb *simul*, will now be examined.

The opening verses of the Vulgate translation of the Bible states that the heavens and the earth came from God's will and power:

"*In principio creavit Deus caelum et terram*" (Gn 1:1).

God brought to completion everything in heaven and on earth (Gn 2:1), all of which he pronounced to be good and pleasing to him (Gn 1:31)[5].

The same conjunction of *caelum et terra* is found in the Vulgate translation of the hymn in Colossians (Col 1:15-20). All things in heaven and on earth are declared to have been created through Christ (v.16), and reconciled in him (v.20):

"*quoniam in ipso condita sunt universa in caelis et in terra, visibilia et invisibilia, sive throni sive dominationes sive principatus sive potestates: omnes per ipsum et in ipso creata sunt ... et per eum reconciliare omnia in ipsum,*

---

[5] For further statements of God's power over the heavens and the earth see Es 13:10, Ps 49:4, and Ps 68:35. In Ps 120:4-9 note that the faithfuls' petition for help is predicated on their belief in God's power as the maker of the heavens and the earth, and hence his ever vigilant guardianship over them.

pacificans per sanguinem crucis eius sive quae in terris sive quae in caelis sunt" (Col 1:16,20).

From the scriptural associations it can be seen that God's government of the heavens and the earth, *caelestia simul et terrena moderaris*, points to God's power, in Christ, through which all the heavens and earth were created, pronounced as good, reconciled and continuously watched over in his care.

A collect from a Mass in time of war associates God's governance of the heavens and the earth with his providence. The divine power is believed to be such that no enemy can withstand it. The community's faith in God's providence and government provides the motivation for the faithfuls' petition for God to fight on their behalf. The prayer reads:

"Deus, qui prouidencia tua caelestia simul et terrena moderaris, propiciare romanis rebus et regibus, ut omnes hostium fortitudo te pro nobis pugnante frangatur" (V 1493)[6].

The liturgical sources also suggest that God works through heavenly and earthly things on behalf of the human race. This can be seen in the following collect from a Mass for the dedication, and the anniversary of dedication, of the Basilica of the Archangel Michael and the Angels on the Via Salaria outside the city of Rome. Note that God's governing (*dispensare*) is related to his favour, and is believed to be expressed through the refreshment of the faithful during their suffering and travail on earth (*laborare*):

"Deus qui in auxilium generis humani caelestia simul et terrena dispensas, in inferiore mundi parte laborantes supernorum nos, quaesumus, praesidiis refoue

---

[6]God, who in your providence govern together heavenly and earthly things, look with favour on the things and rulers of the Romans, so that, with you fighting for us, every strength of our enemies may be broken (V 1493).

propitius ministrorum" (L 853)[7].

In summary, the motivation for the petition is the community's faith in God's supreme power over the heavens and the earth. The term *caelestia simul et terrena* indicates the total extent and domain of God's power. As expressed in the scriptures, from this power, working through Christ, all things were created, pronounced good, reconciled and remain under God's constant and faithful love. The use of the verb *moderari* in H 992 signals that God's rulership governs all things in harmony with the being and nature of all that he created in his love. In light of his power, goodness and reconciling love, God is clearly the one to whom to turn to for peace.

The church, confident in its faith in God's government, humbly makes petition, *supplicationes populi tui clementer exaudi*. We will open our examination of this petition with a study of the verb *exaudire*.

Exaudi

The verb *exaudire* is very common in the Vulgate translation of the scriptures as a verb of petition[8]. The opening verse of Ps 4 relates God's hearing petition to his mercy: *"miserere nos et exaudi orationem meam ..."* (Ps 4:2b). The scriptures also associate God's 'hearing' with his offering a favourable response. In Luke's Gospel, Elizabeth's pregnancy is a sign that Zechariah's prayers have been 'heard':

"Ait autem ad illum angelus: Ne timeas, Zacharia, quoniam exaudita est deprecatio tua, et uxor tua Elisabeth pariet tibi filium, et vocabis nomen eius

---

[7] God, who dispenses heavenly and earthly things for the help of the human race, favourably refresh us who toil on earth with the ministrations of your heavenly servants.
The reference to the archangel Michael is found in the *super sindonem* L 854. For *laborare* as earthly travail, see Blaise, Vocabulaire, § 443.

[8] For the many examples of the use of *exaudire* in the Vulgate translation of the scriptures see Dutripon, Bibliorum Sacrorum Concordantia, 449-450.

Ioannen" (Lc 1:13).

The liturgical euchology readily adopted *exaudire* as a verb of petition[9]. Collect L 390 provides a clear example. Here the request for God to attend to the prayers of the community is associated with the divine protection (*Protector*), God's merciful kindness (*misericordia*), and his clemency (*clementer*). From the point of view of the faithful, their petitioning (*aspicere, implorare, exaudire*) is marked by an attitude of humility (*humiliter*). The prayer reads:

"*Protector noster aspice, deus, et misericordiam tuam humiliter inplorantes clementer exaudi*" (L 390)[10].

In H 992, *exaudire* is qualified by the adverb *clementer*, an adverb that commonly qualifies verbs of petition in the early liturgical sources.

Clementer[11]

The cognate form *clemens* is associated, in the Vulgate translation of the scriptures, with God's covenant, propitiation, mercy, patience, compassion and forgiveness. Together, these terms express the community's faith that God never abandons them in spite of their sin and infidelity. This is dramatically seen in the opening dialogue of the meeting between God and Moses at which God renewed the covenant broken by the people's apostasy in the episode of the Golden Calf:

"*Quo transeuente coram eo, ait: Dominator Domine Deus, misericors et clemens, patiens et multae miserationis ac verax, qui custodis misericordiam in*

---

[9] For the many examples of the liturgical use of the *exaudire* see Deshusses, Concordances III, 2, 54-57.

[10] Look upon us, God our protector, and in your clemency hear those who humbly implore your mercy.

[11] For examples of the use of *clementer, clemens* and *clementia* see Deshusses, Concordances III, 1, 267-272. See also Blaise, Vocabulaire, § 63.

milia, qui aufers iniquitatem et scelera atque peccata, nullusque apud te per se innocens est, qui reddis iniquitatem patrum filiis ac nepotibus in tertiam et quartam progeniem" (Ex 34:6-7)[12].

The early euchology's use of *clementia, clemens* and *clementer* is in line with the scriptures. This can be seen in oration L 920:
"Tua nos, domine, quaesumus, pietate dispone: quia nullis egebimus adiumentis, si tuae prouidentiae clementia gubernemur" (L 920)[13].

In the structure of this prayer, *tuae providentiae clementia* parallels *tua pietas*, while *gubernare* parallels *disponere*. The divine clemency denotes the divine mercy and goodness (*pietas*) exhibited in God's providential order and governance (*providentia, disponere, gubernare*).

The prayer asks God to hear, and so respond favourably to, the supplications, *supplicationes*, of the people.

Supplicationes

Supplicatio and its cognate *supplex* appear to have been appropriated into Christian liturgical Latin from their use in pagan cult[14]. There, *supplicatio* was the technical term for the public celebration of thanksgiving and petition during which the temple was opened and the images of the gods brought outside on couches while the *pontifex* performed the *sacra*. As well, *supplex* is frequently found in pagan Roman prayer.

---

[12]See also 2 Es 9:17, 31, and Jn 4:2.

[13]Rule us, Lord, according to your merciful kindness, because we will never be wanting for any assistance if we are governed by the clemency of your providence.
For examples of the use of *disponere*, see Blaise, <u>Vocabulaire</u>, § 139.

[14]Ellebracht, <u>Remarks on the Vocabulary of the Ancient Orations in the Missale Romanum</u>, 148-150.

Both terms are rarely used in the Vulgate translation of the scriptures[15]. Their use in Christian euchology emphasises the humility of those making petition. In H 992, the humility of their petition is related to God's power and government (*omnipotens, moderari*), his clemency, and his covenant choice of the faithful as his own people (*tuus populus*).

In summary, the first petition seeks that God hear and respond favourably to the church's supplications. The supplications, marked by the humility of God's people, are nevertheless made with confidence. This is founded in their belief both in God's harmonious ruling and direction of all things, and in his covenant of gracious clemency and mercy.

Our collect also contains a second, more specific petition. As well as asking for God to hear their supplications, the faithful ask for God's peace in their present lives, *et pacem tuam nostris concede temporibus*.
Pacem tuam[16]

The divine *pax* is a gift of God's love, associated with his merciful propitiation of sin. The term is used to denote the inner peace that is related to freedom from sin, civil peace, and eternal life.

In the collect from a Mass for Charity, the inner peace God bestows is associated with his love. It is set in parallel with that true concord which comes from being at one with God's will, and consequently from being free from the power of sin and temptation:

"*Deus, largitor pacis et amator caritatis, da seruis tuis ueram cum tua*

---

[15]See Dutripon, Bibliorum Sacrorum Concordantia, 1323.

[16]For further examples of the use of *pax* see Deshusses, Concordances III, 3, 313-316. For a short discussion on the liturgical use of *pax*, and a list of references see Ellebracht, Remarks on the Vocabulary of the Ancient Orations in the Missale Romanum, 47. The adjectives *pacificus* and *tranquillus* have been discussed in the study of the collect for Sunday VIII. See above, 185ff.

uoluntate concordiam, ut ab omnibus quae nos pulsant temptacionibus liberemur" (V 1327)[17].

Furthermore, this peace is linked with God's propitiation and mercy. Note that in the embolism to the Lord's Prayer the lack of peace in the present (*in diebus nostris*) is related to sin and disturbance. The prayer reads: *"Libera nos, quaesumus, domine, ab omnibus malis ... da propitius pacem in diebus nostris, ut ope misericordiae tuae adiuti et a peccatis simus liberi semper et ab omni perturbatione securi"* (V 1258)[18].

The divine peace embraces civil peace. It denotes not simply the absence of war but also includes upright living. This can be seen in the collect of a Mass for peace (*Reginensis* 316, III,lvi *Orationes pro pace*):
"Deus, a quo sancta desideria et recta sunt consilia et iusta sunt opera, da seruis tuis illam quam mundus dare non potest pacem, ut et corda mandatis tuis dedita et hostium sublata formidine tempora sint tua protectione tranquilla" (V 1472)[19].

---

[17]God, bestower of peace and lover of love, give to your servants true harmony with your will, so that we may be free from all the temptations which reign their blows upon us.
See also V 1476. A similar invocation to that in V 1258 is found in the Missal of Paul VI: MR(1975) S. Elisabeth Lus., Collecta, 575. The title reads *"Deus auctor pacis et amator caritatis."*

[18]Free us, Lord, from all evil ... propitiously grant us peace in our day, so that aided by the bounty of your mercy, we may be both free from sin and safe from all disturbance.
An abbreviated version of the embolism for the Lord's Prayer, V 1258, serves the same function in the Missal of Paul VI: MR(1975) Ordo M. cum populo, Or. dominica, 472.

[19]God, from whom come holy desires, upright counsel and righteous works, give your servants that peace which the world is unable to give, so that with hearts dedicated to your mandates and, with the terror of the enemy laid aside, the times may be tranquil under your protection.

Here the divine peace is associated with desiring and doing what is holy, with upright counsel and righteous works. The world, of itself, cannot give such peace. Tranquillity under God's protection, the retreat of enemies, and dedication to the divine mandates are set side by side. The oration links God's peace to the whole being, work and environment of the human person; their desires, counsel, works, heart and the age in which they live (*tempus*).

Peace is also a condition for devout religious practice (*religio, devotio*). This has already been seen in the study of the collect for Sunday VIII[20].

Lastly, eternal life is described in terms of peace. The following *super sindonem* from a Mass in a cemetery associates the image of eternal peace with that of light[21], and of fellowship with the saints. Note that those making petition do so as humble supplicants (*supplices*). The prayer reads
"*Inclina, quaesumus, domine, aures tuas ad praeces nostras, pro quibus misericordiam tuam supplices exoramus, ut animas famulorum famularumque tuarum in pacis et lucis regione constituas et sanctorum iubeas esse consortes*" (V 1686)[22].

In H 992, the peace which the community seeks reflects God's love, government, propitiation and clemency. Through this gift, God's people desire

---

[20]See above, 190. This can also be seen in V 1477 (*ut remoto terrore bellorum et libertas securae religio sit quieta*) and V 1473 (*ut in laudibus misericordiae tuae incessabile exultatione laetemur*).

[21]The image of light has been examined in the analysis of the collect for Sunday XV. See above, 256. See also the discussion of *lux* and *splendor* in the collect for Sunday XIII, below 603.

[22]Lord, incline your ears to our prayers on behalf of those for whom we, in supplication, beseech your mercy, so that you may establish the souls of your servants in the place of peace and light, and that you may grant them fellowship with your saints.
See also V 1703. A slightly adapted form of V 1686 is found in the Missal of Paul VI: MR(1975) Pro uno def. 1, Collecta ad lib., 890.

an environment in which they can live in righteousness and harmony with God and neighbour, be free from both sin and civil strife, and be able to worship in security. Life on earth in God's peace is an anticipation of eternal life. The faithful ask the gift of divine peace for the present (*nostris temporibus*).

Meaning of the prayer:

The motivating clause provides the setting from which the meaning of the collect emerges. The community invokes God in light of their faith that he governs everthing in heaven, and at the same time, everything on earth. The verb *moderari* brings out the harmony implied as God rules all things within their own rhythm and measure. God's rulership itself is grounded in his love and fidelity to all that he made. This is exhibited most fully in his work of restoration and preservation of all things in Christ.

The phrase *caelestia simul et terrena* is evocative of the entire domain of God's rule. The totality of all existing things falls under the power of God. In this power, through Christ, all things were made, named as good, restored, and are continually guarded. As well, the pairing of *caelestia* and *terrena* has a secondary sense in that it connotes God's use of heavenly and earthly things for the sake of salvation.

The oration's first petition is that God hear, and respond to, the supplication of his people. This response is related to God's *clementia*. The divine clemency further brings out the fidelity, mercy, compassion and forgiveness of God in the face of human sin, a theme implicit in the liturgical understanding of God's government. God's harmonious rulership and clemency ground the faithful's confidence that they can address their petition to him. At the same time, the faithful temper their confidence with humility.

In a second petition, the community ask God to grant them his peace in the present. God's peace, which is related to his love and is clearly congruent with his moderating rulership, is linked with his propitiation of sin. On earth it includes inner peace, freedom from sin, righteous living, and the absence of civil strife. It is a foretaste of the peace of eternal life, which itself is marked by light, truth and fellowship with the saints.

ANALYSIS OF THE WORDS AND PHRASES IN THE COLLECT WITHIN THE CONTEXT OF THE MISSAL OF PAUL VI

Other than in our collect, the expression *caelestia et terrena* is found chiefly amongst the prefaces in the Missal of Paul VI. There it connotes the united praise of God by both the heavenly and the earthly spheres. This can be seen in the following prefaces:
"*Vere dignum et iustum est, ut te, Deus et caelestia et terrena collaudent*" (MR(1975) Intro. pro praeff., 7, 490)[23],
"*Et ideo, cum Sanctis et Angelis universis, te collaudamus, sine fine dicentes ....*" (MR(1975) Ordo. M. cum populo, Praef. communis V, 437)[24].

The new Missal contains a limited number of references to the church's faith in God's power and rulership of heaven and earth, *caelum et terra*. Amongst the presidential prayers there appears to be only one reference. This is in a blessing over the people at the conclusion of a Mass for the dedication of a church. There God's mastery is associated with the dedication of this his house (*domus*), and invoked over those who have gathered for its dedication. The blessing can also be used at a Mass celebrating the anniversary of the dedication. The apposite section of the prayer reads:
"*Deus, Dominus caeli et terrae, qui vos hodie ad huius domus dedicationem (dedicationis memoriam) adunabit, ipse vos caelesti benedictione faciat*

---

[23] It is right and fitting that together the things of heaven and of earth praise you, God.

[24] And therefore, together with all the saints and angels, we praise you without end saying ....

abundare" (MR(1975) Benedd. in fine M., Bened. soll. in dedic. eccl., 505, 778)[25].

In the order of the Mass itself, the totality of God's power is confessed in the creed[26], and his paternal government of earth as well as heaven petitioned in the Lord's Prayer[27].

As seen in the study of the collect for Sunday VIII, the Missal of Paul VI associates peace not only with righteous and upright behaviour but also with justice[28]. The same collect also, through the adjective *pacificus*, refers God's order of peace to the Cross of Christ, and more immediately to the action of the eucharist[29].

RELATIONSHIP OF THE CHRISTIAN PEOPLE TO GOD

The prayer offers comment on the interrelationship of the heavenly and earthly realms. Both fall under God's governance, a rulership that reflects the harmony in which all creation was made. The conjunction *simul* indicates not only that all things fall under God's rule, but that he is always attentive to all things and concerned about all things, whether heavenly or earthly. Because the faithful live under the divine government, they can be confident that God hears and responds to their petition. This confidence is further underlined by

---

[25] May God, Lord of heaven and earth, who brought you together this day for the dedication of this house, bless you abundantly with his heavenly blessing.

[26] "*Credo in unum Deum, Patrem omnipotentem, factorem caeli et terrae*" (MR(1975) Ordo M. cum populo. Professio fidei, 389).

[27] "*Pater noster, qui es in caelis ... fiat voluntas tua, sicut in caelo, et in terra*" (MR(1975) Ordo M. cum populo, Or. dominica, 472).

[28] See above, 195.

[29] See above, 196.

their trust in God's unwavering clemency. God's relationship to the Christian people, then, is set within his harmonious government, marked by his clemency, and exhibited in his attention to our prayers.

Three further attributes of the Christian relationship to God can be noted in the oration. Firstly, God's rule, clemency and covenant fidelity, constitute the faithful as God's people, *tuus populus*. Secondly, as his people, they make humble petition. Thirdly, their relationship to God, and one another, is to be marked by a peace which embraces the defeat of sin, living according to the righteousness of God, justice and the absence of civil strife. This peace, which can only come from God, mirrors the fellowship of the saints in heaven.

There is also a degree of congruence between the earthly and the divine realms. The divine peace is congruent with earthly existence. At the same time, its very presence in the midst of the community is a foretaste of eternal life. This harmony between the realms legitimates the faithful's petition for divine gifts in the present. The incarnation offers the most complete example of the consonance between the celestial and the earthly, as well as of the presence of divine peace on earth. In response, both the celestial and the earthly realms together offer praise.

FREER TRANSLATION OF THE COLLECT

Omnipotens sempiterne Deus, qui caelestia simul et terrena moderaris, supplicationes populi tui clementer exaudi, et pacem tuam nostris concede temporibus.	Almighty, all powerful God, you direct all that belongs to heaven, and at the same time govern all the things of earth. In your gracious clemency hear the supplications of your people, and, Lord, grant us your peace in our day.

COLLECT FOR SUNDAY V

PRAYER

Familiam tuam, quaesumus, Domine, continua pietate custodi, ut, quae in sola spe gratiae caelestis innititur, tua semper protectione muniatur.

Guard your family we beg Lord, with continuous devoted loving kindness, so that your family, which relies solely on hope of heavenly grace, may be strengthened by your ever present protection.

ORIGINAL SOURCE

The prayer has been incorporated from the Gregorian sources into the Missal of Paul VI with a slight adjustment, in line with the later text A 213. Both P 201 and H 228 read *caelesti etiam protectione muniatur* rather than *tua semper protectione muniatur*. This causes negligible change to the sense of the prayer. Note also that the oration is used as a lenten *super populum* in the *Paduensis* (P 201), the *Hadrianum* (H 228), and MR(1570). For further comment on the original sources of the prayer, see the accompanying introductory note and table for this chapter.

USE IN OTHER LITURGICAL SOURCES

As noted by Bruylants, the prayer is found in these sources[1]: Dominica V post Epiphaniam: Pr(27,1), A (213), S(193), *OR*(165), X(37,1), Q(26'), 1474(39), 1570, 1604, and the uncritical edition Z(155),

---

[1]Bruylants, II, 558. For a more complete list of sources and manuscripts see Moeller, Corpus Orationum IV, E-H, Orationes 2390-3028, oration 2638, 122.

Sabb. post Dom II Quad: P(201), COR(51,4)[H 228], X(59,4mg), N(58), Q(41ᵛ), 1474(84), 1570, 1604,

Sabbato Quatuor Temporum Quadragesimae, Alia oratio [2a], N(51).

ANALYSIS OF THE PRAYER IN THE ORIGINAL SOURCE
Grammatical structure:[2]

The prayer consists of (a) an address with (b) a petition, followed by (c) a clause further qualifying the petitioners (*familia tua*), and (d) a purpose clause.

(a) Address: *Domine, quaesumus,*

(b) Petition: *Familiam tuam continua pietate custodi,*

(c) Qualifying clause: *quae in sola spe gratiae caelestis innititur,*

(d) Purpose clause: *ut tua semper protectione muniatur.*

The prayer is built upon a series of parallels. The descriptive clause *quae in sola spe gratiae caelestis innititur* is in parallel with *familia tua*. Each of the terms in the petition *continua pietate custodi* has a corresponding parallel in the purpose clause *tua semper protectione muniatur*:

continua	*pietate*	*custodi*
semper	*tua protectione*	*muniatur*

The parallel between *continua* and *semper*, as well as the sense of devotion implicit in *pietas*, emphasize the community's belief in their absolute and continuous need to rely on God's *pietas* and protection. The implication is that they are helpless in the face of sin. Similarly, the double use of *in*, as a

---

[2] For a more complete grammatical analysis see Haessly, <u>Rhetoric in the Sunday Collects of the Roman Missal</u>, 38-40, and F.Gerdes, "The Language of the Roman Missal. Part III: Second Sunday after Epiphany to Quinquagesima Sunday," 29.

preposition (*in sola spe*) and as a prefix (*innititur*), serves to intensify the sense of reliance on the hope of heavenly grace alone.

Parallel prayers:

A number of prayers in the early liturgical sources parallel the structure, vocabulary and theme of H 228. What is common to these orations is the relationship drawn between God's ever attentive loving kindness (*pietas*), his protection (*protegere, protectio*), his strengthening (*munire*) of the faithful, and the community's conviction that God's help is needed always (*semper, perpetua*). In the main, the faithful seek protection against sin and its effects. In some of these parallel orations the continuous assistance of the saints is also sought. An examination of a selection of these prayers[3] helps to clarify the framework and vocabulary of our collect.

This conjunction of terms is clear in L 834, a prayer from a Mass for the martyrs Cornelius and Cyprian. The oration relates the divine *pietas*, perpetual protection and strengthening, to God's majesty and power. They are necessary on account of the imperiled state of the faithful (*ad defensionem fidelium*). The continuous intercession of the martyrs is also of assistance: "*Ad defensionem fidelium, domine, quaesumus, dexteram tuae maiestatis extende; et ut perpetua pietatis tuae protectione muniantur, intercessio pro his non desit martyrum continuata sanctorum*" (L 834)[4].

Collect H 472 provides another parallel. The prayer sets *afflictio nostra* in parallel with *adversa omnia*, and *tua pietas* in parallel with *tua semper*

---

[3]See L 526, H 147, H 925, H 995, Sp 1784, and G 1590.

[4]Extend the right hand of your majesty to the defense of the faithful Lord, and, so that they may be strengthened by the perpetual protection of your loving kindness, may the intercession of the holy martyrs on their behalf not be absent.

protectione muniamur. Both *afflictio* and *adversa* point to the power and effects of sin[5], and hence the faithful's need for and trust in God's *pietas*, strengthening and constant protection. The oration reads:

"*Praesta quaesumus omnipotens deus ut qui in afflictione nostra de tua pietate confidemus, contra aduersa omnia tua semper protectione muniamur*" (H 472)[6].

We will now turn from the analysis of this common euchological framework to a more detailed examination of the vocabulary of the prayer H 228.

Vocabulary:

Prominent vocabulary: *familia, pietas, custodire, spes, gratia, caelestis, inniti, protectio, munire*.

Our vocabulary analysis will commence with *familia tua*, a term which both establishes the relationship between God and the baptized and as well grounds the faithful's petition.

Familiam tuam[7]

The origins of the Christian use of the noun *familia* lie in Roman legal terminology. In Roman law the term encompasses the entire household, wife, children, servants and slaves, under the protection of its head, the *paterfamilias*. *Familia*, then, connotes the wealth of associations concerning

---

[5]For *afflictio* see Blaise, Vocabulaire, § 443. *Adversa* has been studied in the analysis of the collect for Sunday XXXII. See above, 422.

[6]Grant all powerful almighty God, that we, who in our affliction trust in your loving kindness, may be strengthened against all opposing things by your continuous protection.

[7]For examples of the use of *familia* see Deshusses, Concordances, III, 2, 103-106. For commentary on the meaning of *familia* see Ellebracht, Remarks on the Vocabulary of the Ancient Orations in the Missale Romanum, 154.

identity, intimacy, protection and role which are bound up with membership of a Roman *familia*.

There appears to be no comparable use of *familia* as God's *familia* in the Vulgate translation of the scriptures[8]. However, in the early euchology, *familia tua* signifies the church. This can be seen in the following *super sindonem* from a Mass for the Pentecost Vigil which sets *ecclesia* and *familia tua* in parallel. Membership of God's family is expressed in terms of both filial belonging (*progenies*) and service (*servire*). The prayer reads:

"*Deus, cuius spiritu totum corpus aecclesiae multiplicatur et regitur, conserua in nouam familiae tuae progeniem sanctificationis gratiam quam dedisti, ut corpore et mente renouati in unitatem fidei feruentes tibi, domine, seruire mereantur*" (V 625)[9].

Sometimes a first person plural verb or pronoun follows *familia*, as in L 746, a post communion from the feast of St Laurence:

"*Satiasti, domine, familiam tuam muneribus sacris. Eius, quaesumus, semper*

---

[8] For examples of the use of *familia* in the scriptures see Dutripon, Bibliorum Sacrorum Concordantiae, 491-493.

[9] God, by whose spirit the whole body of the church is increased and ruled, preserve in the new offspring of your family the grace of sanctification which you have given, so that, renewed in body and mind, they may merit to serve you, Lord, zealous for the unity of the faith (V 625).
The translation follows the text reproduced in *Reginensis* 316. This reading of the text, highlighting the people's fervour for unity, fits with the context of the prayer in the Pentecost Vigil, where unity in faith is contrasted with the variety of tongues (Ac 2:5-13).

However the text in Moeller (Corpus Orationum II, D, orationes 881-1707, 156) reads *in unitate fidei feruentes*. This translates as "[renewed in body and mind,] and fervent in the unity of faith, [they may merit to serve you]." No variant readings are listed for the prayer. In this reading the sense is of the fervour that comes from their new found unity in the faith.

interuentione nos refoue, cuius sollemnia celebramus" (L 746)[10].

Ellebracht noted this as evidence of how intimately the praying community was conscious of being the *familia dei*[11].

By bringing together both the sense of offspring and of service, the liturgical use of *familia* conjoins the faithful's belief that they are the adopted children of God with their designation as his servants (*famulus, servus*). *Familia tua* carries a tone of intimacy and service on the side of the baptized, and of intimacy, protection and obligation from the side of God. Members of God's *familia* are in a unique position from which to make petition to him. In H 228, the petition of God's *familia* is that God guide them with his continuous devoted loving kindness, *continua pietate custodi*.

Continua pietate custodi
Custodire

Custodire has been examined in the study of Collect XXII[12]. Summarizing that discussion here, the guardianship of God is associated with his ruling, cherishing, protecting, visiting and defending the people. Under God's oversight, Christians are able to be pleasing to God, be of one will with him, and walk in his ways. In H 228, God's custodianship is linked with his devoted loving kindness, his *pietas*.

Continua pietate

---

[10] Lord, you have nourished your family with sacred gifts. Refresh us by the everpresent intercession of him whose solemnity we celebrate (L 746).

[11] See Ellebracht, Remarks on the Vocabulary of the Ancient Orations in the Missale Romanum, 155. One of the manuscripts Deshusses consulted in editing a critical text for H 228 exhibits the same characteristic, reading *muniamur* rather than *muniatur*. See the notes to H 228 in Deshusses, Le Sacramentaire Grégorien, 147.

[12] See above, 360.

The divine *pietas* has been analysed in the study of the collect for Sunday XXVII[13]. God's *pietas* is linked with the recreation of what has been damaged by sin, strength for human weakness, pardon, and guidance for sinners. It is associated with the presence and work of Christ and the Spirit. The ordinary sense of human *pietas* already implies a certain devotedness and conscientiousness to duty. Collect H 228 further emphasises this devotedness of God's loving kindness by qualifying it as continuous, *continua*.

The petition *Familiam tuam continua pietate custodi* calls upon God to rule, cherish, defend and protect his family. As members of his household, the faithful are at the same time his progeny and his servants. Because they comprise God's *familia*, the faithful look to him as their protector and sustainer. His guardianship is an expression of his intimate, devoted loving kindness and mercy. The faithful's insistence that his care be continuous, reinforced by their declaration that they are under his protection (*familia tua*), is an indication of their own helplessness and weakness in the face of sin. This is further emphasized in the purpose clause, where the community describe themselves as *quae in sola spe gratiae caelestis innititur*. This clause will now be examined, commencing with the verb *inniti*.

In sola spe gratiae caelestis innititur
Innititur

The verb *inniti* is found rarely in the Vulgate translation of the scriptures, and has an even more restricted currency in the early liturgical sources. The 14 occasions it is used in the scriptures are all from the Old Testament[14]. It is indexed only four times in the Deshusses' concordance,

---

[13]See above, 389.

[14]Dutripon, Bibliorum Sacrorum Concordantiae, 670.

including our collect H 228 and a blessing virtually identical to it (Sp 1784)[15].

The clause echoes a key verse (v.10) in the third servant song of Isaiah (Is 50:4-11)[16]:

"Quis ex vobis timens Dominum, audiens vocem servi sui? Qui ambulavit in tenebris, et non est lumen ei, speret in nomine Domini et innitatur super Deum suum" (Is 50:10).

The passage itself is part of the larger 'book of consolation' which seeks to comfort the exiled community with the word of God's forgiveness (Is 40:1-2), his power over all things (Is 40:12-26), his love for Israel (Is 41:8-16), and their liberation. More specifically, the song belongs to the section which faces up to the disillusionment of the faithful upon their return to Jerusalem and their attempt to rebuild the fragmented community. In the face of the darkness and lack of light, of their exile and dispiriting liberation, the faithful express both their reliance on the God who has called them and given them help, and as well their hope that he will vindicate them.

In H 228, the descriptive clause, with its biblical resonance, further defines the community. As God's *familia* they are under his care and

---

[15]See Deshusses, Concordances III, 2, 367. In a third example, G 2862, *inniti* is a direct reference to the Vulgate translation of the story of Jacob's ladder (Gn 28:13). The fourth reference, G 2020, should possibly read *enixius* rather than *innixius* (Deshusses, Concordances III, 2, 367).

[16]Commentators disagree on the place of vv.10-11 in the song. Westermann (p. 233) relocates them in Ch 51. Other commentators, keeping the text intact, see it as an endorsement of the trust and faith of the Lord's servant: Knight 205, McKenzie 116, Stuhlmueller 340. This is the view followed here. For complete references; G.Knight, Deutero-Isaiah (New York: Abingdon Press, 1965); J.McKenzie, Second Isaiah, The Anchor Bible (New York: Doubleday and Company, 1968); C.Westermann, Isaiah 40-66, Old Testament Library, translated by David M.G.Stalker (London: SCM, 1969); and C.Stuhlmueller, "Deutero-Isaiah and Trito-Isaiah," in R.E.Brown, J.A.Fitzmeyer and R.E.Murphy, eds., The New Jerome Biblical Commentary (Englewood Cliffs N.J.: Prentice Hall, 1990), 329-348.

protection. At the same time, God is their only hope (*in sola spe gratiae caelestis*). No earthly or material help can suffice. The clause serves to intensify their petition for God's continuous, devoted guardianship. Nothing can be relied upon other than God's help alone. This fits well with the lenten context of the prayer in the *Paduensis*, the *Hadrianum*, and MR(1570). The purpose of their petition is that they may be strengthened always by God's ever vigilant protection, *tua semper protectione muniatur*.

Muniatur[17]

The verb *munire* is a Roman military term meaning to 'fortify with a wall.' It came to denote to 'protect' and 'strengthen.' As noted above, a search through the early euchology reveals that *munire* is often found in combination with *pietas, custodire* and *protegere*. Especially common is the association between God's protection and fortifying, as evidenced in the frequent use of the clause *ut in omnibus protectionis tuae muniamur auxilio*[18].

The *ad populum* V 257 from a Mass of the scrutinies for the Fourth Sunday of Lent (I,xxvii) opens up the meaning of *munire* and *protectio*. God's strengthening and protection are associated with his work of salvation. They are sought for the catechumens both as they approach baptism (*regenerandos*) and after baptism (*renatos*). In light of H 228, three further features are of note. Firstly sin remains a constant danger both before and after baptism. Secondly God's protection is qualified as *paterna*. This fits well with H 228's

---

[17] For examples of the use of *munire* see Deshusses, Concordances, III, 3, 127-129. For commentary see Ellebracht, Remarks on the Vocabulary of the Ancient Orations in the Misssale Romanum, 175.

[18] So that we may be strengthened by the help of your protection in all things.
For some examples see V 974, V 1246, V 1575, G 2583. The clause is found in the Missal of Paul VI: MR(1975) Ordo M. cum populo, Prex euch. I, Infra Actionem, 448.

designation of the community as God's *familia*. Thirdly the lenten context of V 257 highlights the lenten associations of H 228. The oration reads:

"*Deus, qui cum salute hominum semper operaris, nunc tamen populum tuum gratia habundantiore multiplicas: respice propitius ad electionem tuam, ut paternae protectionis auxilio et regenerandos munias et renatos*" (V 257)[19].

A post communion links God's fortifying with purification (*purificare*). Both are associated with communion. Note that *purificare* and *munire* are qualified by the adverb *semper*:

"*Huius operatio nos, domine, sacramenti, quaesumus, purificet semper et muniat*" (V 1384)[20].

Tua protectione[21]

The petition in the Vulgate translation of Ps 16:8 sets God's guardianship (*custodire*) and protection (*protegere*) in parallel. The psalm attaches to God's protection a dual sense of great intimacy and of power:

---

[19]God, who work always for the salvation of the human race, now increase your people by even more abundant grace; look favourably on your elect, so that you may strengthen them with the help of your paternal protection both as they approach regeneration and after they have been reborn (V 257). The prayer, with slight modifications, is found in the Missal of Paul VI: MR(1975) Sabb. hebd. V Quadr., Collecta, 223, and Pro elect. seu inscript. nom., Collecta, 729. Note that *paternae protectionis* reads *piae protectionis*.

[20]May the operation of this sacrament continuously purify and fortify us Lord.
Ellebracht makes the observation that the combination of such verbs as *purificare, purgare* and *mundare* with *munire* is evocative of Lc 11:21-26. Because of the power of sin, whatever is purified is also in need of ongoing strengthening and fortification. See Ellebracht, Remarks on the Vocabulary of the Ancient Orations in the Missale Romanum, 176.

[21]For examples of the use of *protectio* see Deshusses, Concordances, III, 3, 526-528.

"*A resistentibus dexterae tuae custodi me ut pupillam oculi: sub umbra alarum tuarum protege me*" (Ps 16:8).

A distant echo of Ps 17:31 can be found in H 228. God is described as the protector of those who hope in him. The divine protection, associated with his way (*via*) and word (*eloquium*), is especially outstanding because of its tried and tested purity. The verse reads:

"*Deus meus, impolluta via eius, eloquia Domini igne examinata: protector est omnium sperantium in se*" (Ps 17:31).

The liturgical sources associate God's protection with a range of divine works. In a secret from a daily Mass (III,xxiii), *protegere* is linked with God's work of cleansing (*mundare*), renewing (*renovare*) and governing (*gubernare*). All these are connected with the eucharistic action:

"*Haec nos oblatio, deus, mundet et renouet, gubernet et protegat*" (V 1310)[22].

In summary, the conjunction of *munire* and *protectio* includes God's work of renewal, purification, government and guardianship. It points to an intimate relationship between God and humanity, in which he uses his power to save his *familia* from sin. The faithful desire God's protection always, another indication of their helplessness in the face of sin. It is in view of this helplessness that they put their hope only in God's grace.

Meaning of the prayer:

The heart of the prayer is the community's petition that God, in his devoted loving kindness, continually guard, protect and strengthen his people. The faithful make their request out of their belief that they are members of God's *familia*. They belong in his household both as his offspring and as his servants, and as such expect that God will always protect them. They further make their petition out of their helplessness in the face of sin. They are the

---

[22] God, may this oblation cleanse and renew us, and govern and protect us.

people whose only hope is to rely on heavenly grace. Hope in anything less than God's help is futile. This is brought out even more strongly by both the biblical resonance of this clause and the lenten context of the prayer.

The combination of God's *pietas*, custodianship, protection and strengthening carries a range of associations. They point to the intimacy with which God relates to his faithful. While this closeness is expressed through belief in God's *pietas*, it is also implicit in *custodire* and *protectio*.

This conjunction of divine actions is broad in scope. It includes God's guarding, protecting, cherishing, ruling defending and strengthening. As well, *munire* is linked with God's purification and cleansing.

The oration insists that the *familia* of God need these gifts continually, as seen in the use of *semper* and *continua*, as well as in the sense of devotedness implicit in *devotio*. This insistence is further testimony to the faithful's weakness, the power of sin, and the community's belief that God is their only hope.

ANALYSIS OF THE WORDS AND PHRASES IN THE COLLECT IN THE CONTEXT OF THE MISSAL OF PAUL VI

Familia tua remains, in the Missal of Paul VI, a significant designation of the church[23]. The following collect from a Mass for the Church provides a clear parallel between *familia tua* and *ecclesia*. The *ecclesia* itself is described as the people gathered together from all nations growing in unity through the Spirit. As well, the church is seen as the leaven and soul of the human community, working in Christ to renew and transform the human family into

---

[23]*Familia* is found in the Missal 68 times, where it generally refers to God's family. See Schnitker and Slaby, Concordantia, 931-934. Most common are *ecclesia*, 284 times (Concordantia, 684-696), and *populum*, 217 times (Concordantia, 1888-1897). *Plebs* is found 60 times (Concordantia, 931-934).

the family of God. Note the two uses of *familia*. This serves to further bind together the church and humankind. The prayer reads:

"Deus, qui in Christi tui testamento ex omnibus gentibus populum tibi congregare non desinis, in Spiritu ad unitatem coalescentem, concede, ut Ecclesia tua, missioni sibi creditae fidelis, cum hominum familia iugiter incedat, et tamquam fermentum et veluti anima societatis humanae in Christo renovandae et in familiam Dei transformandae semper existat" (MR(1975) Pro Eccl, B, Collecta, 786)[24].

The prayer reflects the relationship between God as *paterfamilias* and his *familia*. The members of the church are God's intimate and chosen ones, living in his Spirit. At the same time they are at his service, carrying out his mission. Note further, however, the strong link between God's family and the broader human family. Just as the Spirit works in God's family, bringing them to greater unity, so God's family are to be the leaven and soul of the human community, leading them to renewal in Christ and transformation into the family of God, according to Christ's testament.

The incorporation of the prayer in the Missal of Paul VI is accompanied by the loss of its lenten context. The oration already existed without this context in the Sacramentaries of Angoulême and St Gall, though the Roman Missal of 1570 utilized it both inside and outside of the penitential season. These lenten associations would have heightened the sense of purification linked with *munire*. As well they would have given more focus to the power of sin.

---

[24]God, who in the testament of your Christ never cease to gather together from all the nations a people growing strong into unity in the Spirit, grant that your church, faithful to the mission entrusted to it, may accompany continually the family of humankind, and may it always exist both as a leaven and as the soul of human society which is to be renewed in Christ and transformed into the family of God.

THE RELATIONSHIP OF THE CHRISTIAN PEOPLE TO GOD

The oration describes the faithful as members of God's *familia*. Christians live in the intimacy and protection of God's household as both his adopted offspring and his servants. Their belonging to his *familia*, with its guarantee of protection, ground the church's hope as well as their confidence in making petition. In our prayer, they especially seek protection and strength. As God's servants, the members of his family are instrumental in God's work of renewing all humanity in Christ and of transforming all humanity into members of the church.

At the same time, the collect points to the power of sin. God's *familia* recognize that they can rely only on their hope in his grace. The impossibility of life outside of God is also underlined by their insistence that his protection, guardianship, strengthening and loving kindness be continuous, devoted and always present.

In God's relationship with his people, his power is at work through his love. God's actions towards his people are related to his own *pietas*, and their status as his *familia*.

FREER TRANSLATION OF THE PRAYER

Familiam tuam, quaesumus,
Domine, continua pietate custodi,
ut, quae in sola spe gratiae
caelestis innititur, tua semper
protectione muniatur.

Guard your family, Lord, in your devoted kindness and love. With hope only in your saving grace, may we always be safeguarded and fortified by your protection.

COLLECT FOR SUNDAY VII

PRAYER

Praesta, quaesumus, omnipotens Deus, ut, semper rationabilia meditantes, quae tibi sunt placita, et dictis exsequamur et factis.

Grant, we beg, all powerful God, that, always meditating on spiritual things, we may carry out by words and deeds the things that are pleasing to you.

ORIGINAL SOURCE

The prayer is first encountered in *Reginensis* 316 as a collect for a Mass (III,lxvi) in times of contention: *Orationes in Contencione ad Missas, Item Alia Missa*, V 1521. It is this original form of the text which stands, unmodified, in the Missal of Paul VI.

The oration has been incorporated into the Gregorian and Frankish Gelasian sources in a variety of contexts. It is utilized, virtually unchanged[1], for Masses in times of dissention, Masses for the Sundays after Epiphany, and for daily Mass. In the different sources, and even in the same source, it can be found as a collect, *super sindonem*, or following the prayer *ad complenda*. For details and further discussion, see the introductory note and accompanying table.

USE IN OTHER LITURGICAL SOURCES

As noted by Bruylants[2], the prayer is found in these sources:
Dominica VI post Epiphaniam: A(226), S(206), 1570, 1604, and the unedited sources G(38,2)[G 219], Z(162),

---

[1]The only modifications are found in G 219, which reads *racionabiliter* for *rationabilia* and *sint* for *sunt*.

[2]Bruylants, II, 875.

Dominica V post Epiphaniam: P(112),
Missa in contentione: V(III,66,1p.279) [V 1521], G(410,6)[G 2743], S*(154), OR(202)[Sp 1356],
Incipiunt orationes quotidianae: COR(202,36)[H 911].

ANALYSIS OF THE PRAYER IN THE ORIGINAL SOURCE

Origin:

According to Chavasse[3], the Mass III,lxvi from which our prayer is a collect, is both quite ancient and most probably monastic in origin. Its probable antiquity arises from the fact that it contains two collects and a *super sindonem*.[4] Chavasse detects the monastic setting of the Mass most clearly in the second collect (V 1522), which offers a description of the monastic ideal of unity and harmony in the community: *qui unanimes nos in domo tua praecipis habitare*.[5]

This monastic setting offers an interpretation of the prayer, which, in anticipation of the vocabulary analysis below, will simply be sketched here. The continuous reflection and prayer (*meditari*) on spiritual matters in line with God's law (*rationabilia*), and its consequent enactment in both saying what is pleasing to God and doing what is pleasing to God, acts as a formula for divinely directed harmony and concord in the community. As well, it connotes a whole way of life, reflection and prayer (*meditari*), communication (*dictum*) and action (*factum*), taken up with God's will (*rationabilia, tibi placita*).

---

[3]Chavasse, Le Sacramentaire Gélasien, 437-439.

[4]Ibid., 433.

[5]Who command us to dwell one in heart in your house.
Chavasse discusses more fully this definition of the monastic life, which he sees reflected in a number of the prayers in *Reginensis* 316, in his analysis of Mass III,lxxx. See Chavasse, Le Sacramentaire Gélasien, 440-444.

According to Chavasse, this monastic life has been offset by the disharmony among the monks themselves[6].

Chavasse finds himself somewhat mystified by use of *rationabilis* in both the collect (V 1521) and the *super sindonem* (V 1523) of the Mass[7]. Its presence, however, is a clue to the oration's kinship with a wholly different experience of contention and dissension within the Christian community. Two key terms, *rationabilia* and *et dictis exsequamur et factis*, both relatively rare in the early sources, are quite common in the writings of Pope Gelasius (492-496). They are especially found in his Masses against the Christians who took part in the festival of the Lupercalia.[8]

Together, *rationabile* and *rationabiliter* are found only 14 times in the *Veronensis*[9]. Of these, four are from the Masses of Gelasius against the Lupercalia (L 442, L 432, L 530, L 1080[10]). Coebergh shows that the use of *rationabiliter* was not untypical in Gelasius' writings[11]. The clause *et dictis exsequamur et factis* provides an even stronger parallel of style and vocabulary. As will be seen in more detail below, by far the two clearest parallels to this text are both from prefaces in the Gelasian anti-Lupercalia Masses (L 428 and

---

[6]Chavasse, Le Sacramentaire Gélasien, 438-439 and fn 13.

[7]Ibid, 439.

[8]A discussion of the Lupercalia, Gelasius' reaction to it, and the Masses he authored against it, can be found in the analysis of the collect for Sunday IV. See above, 121ff. For a list of these Masses see Pomarès, Gélase, 191.

[9]See the index in Mohlberg's critical edition, 389.

[10]Chavasse sees this prayer, L 1080, as the source of the apposite clause in the *super sindonem*: *quae animae nostrae conueniunt rationabilia exequamur* (V 1523). See Chavasse, Le Sacramentaire Gélasien, 439 fn 14.

[11]C.Coebergh, "Le pape saint Gélase Ier auteur de plusieurs messes et préfaces du soi-disant sacramentaire léonien," Sacris Erudiri 4 (1952): 65.

L 623). Again Coebergh notes that the conjunction of *dictum et factum* occurs a number of times in Gelasius' writings[12].

While the collect as a whole does not appear in any of the Masses to date recognized as Gelasian, it shows a close relationship to his Masses dealing with the contentious controversy in the Roman Christian community concerning the involvement of the faithful in Lupercalian festivities. This opens the way for a second possible interpretation of the prayer. Here *rationabilia* takes on a sense of the godly and spiritual as opposed to the demonic, while *dictum* and *factum* refer to various aspects of participation in the festival. Unlike in the monastic interpretation, what is at stake is not simply the harmony of the community, but its integrity as an *ecclesia* that offers pure worship to God, rejects paganism in its entirety, and lives in true Christian love of neighbour.

Grammatical structure[13]:

The prayer consists of (a) a simple address, (b) a verb of petition, and (c) an *ut* clause containing the petition and the condition necessary for its fulfillment.

(a) Address: *omnipotens deus*

(b) Verb of petition: *Praesta .. ut*

(c) Petition: *semper rationabilia meditantes,*

Petition: *quae tibi sunt placita,
et dictis exsequamur et factis.*

---

[12]Ibid, 80.

[13]For a more detailed grammatical analysis see Haessly, Rhetoric in the Collects of the Roman Missal, 40-41; and Gerdes, "The Language of the Roman Missal. Part III: Second Sunday after Epiphany to Quinquagesima Sunday," 35.

There are a number of features in the structure of the oration that deserve attention. Speech and action are set side by side in an *et ... et* construction. For both to be pleasing to God, they must be the fruit of constant meditation on the *rationabilia*. In this way, the collect places in tandem the contemplative and active aspects of the life of the community. *Rationabilia* and *tibi placita* are set in parallel. *Semper meditantes* and *exsequamur* are also related. As already noted, reflection is logically prior to and continually undergirds action. As well, the qualification of *meditari* by the adverb *semper* has a parallel in the intensification of the verb through the prefix *ex*. The pair are suggestive of a life characterized by continuous and constant spiritual reflection, holy speech and pleasing actions.

Vocabulary:
Prominent vocabulary: *rationabilis, meditari, placitus,* and the phrase *dictis exsequamur et factis.*

Our analysis of the oration's vocabulary will begin with the qualifying clause of the petition, *semper rationabilia meditantes.*
Meditantes[14]

The Vulgate translation of Psalm 1, which along with Psalm 2 acts as a preface to the Book of Psalms, associates *meditari* with the way of the just and the life of the blessed (*beatus*). Meditation is understood as a continuous activity (*die et nocte*), carried out by a will given over to God. Its object is God's law, and among its fruits are righteousness and prosperity[15].

---

[14]For further examples of the use of *meditari* see Deshusses, Concordances III, 3, 49.

[15]See also Dt 6:7, Ps 70:24 (*lingua mea tota die meditabitur iustitiam tuam*), Ps 118:47 (*meditabar in mandatis tuis*), and Ps 142:2 (*meditatus sum in omnibus operibus tuis*).

The opening verses of the psalm read:

"*Beatus vir, qui non abiit in consilio impiorum et in via peccatorum non stetit et in cathedra pestilentiae non sedit; sed in lege Domini voluntas eius, et in lege eius meditabitur die ac nocte*" (Ps 1:1-3).

The use of *meditari* in the early liturgical sources corresponds to the biblical understanding. This can be seen in L 587, a prayer from either the morning or evening office. Meditation on what are holy (*sancta*) is a basis for life in the divine light. As in V 1521, the qualification of *meditari* by the adverb *semper*, has a parallel in *iugiter vivamus*. The prayer reads:

"*Deus, qui diem discernis et noctem, actos nostros a tenebrarum distingue caligine; ut semper quae sancta sunt meditantes, in tua iugiter luce uiuamus*" (L 587)[16].

In summary, the faithful can only live perpetually in God's way when their lives are characterized by constant and continuous reflection, prayer and meditation on God's law, righteousness, works and holy things. All of these are expressions of God's love. The objects of the community's meditation in collect V 1521 are the *rationabilia*, which will now be examined.

Rationabilia

The adjective *rationabilis* has been analysed in the study of the collect for Sunday IV[17]. It describes the spiritual realities which, as right and pleasing in the sight of God, are in accordance with his law, and which constitute pure worship.

---

[16] God, who sets apart the day and the night, divide our actions off from the shadow of darkness, so that, always meditating on what are holy, we may live perpetually in your light.
See also the two similar prayers, L 888 and L 1118.

[17] See above, 108.

In summary, the outcome of the petition depends on the grace which makes the prayer, reflection and meditation of the faithful continuously and wholly given over to what is right and pleasing in the sight of God. The community is asking the grace to meditate on God's righteousness, mandates and works. Following on from this, the baptized ask that they may carry out in word and deed what is pleasing to God. This will now be examined, beginning with the word *placitum*.

Tibi placita

The adjective *placitus*, discussed in the analysis of the collect for Sunday XI, denotes what is pleasing in God's sight, according to the divine will, in keeping with his mandates. In V 1521, the *placita*, set in parallel with *rationabilia*, are the desired object of the words and works of the faithful.

Et dictis exequamur et factis[18]

Exsequamur

Exsequi has been seen in the study of the collect for Sunday XI[19]. It means to follow or pursue to the end, and so by transference, refers to the accomplishment of an action. In V 1521, what is pleasing to God is to be carried out to the fullest and most complete extent in both what is said and what is done. As noted above, the intensified form of the verb parallels the faithful's petition that they be able to meditate always (*semper*).

Et dictis et factis

As mentioned above, close parallels to the clause *et dictis exequamur et factis* are found in two prefaces from the anti-Lupercalia Masses of Pope

---

[18]For further examples of the use of *dictum* see Deshusses, Concordances III, 1, 476-477, and for *factum*, III, 2, 101-102.

[19]See above, 308.

Gelasius. While the prayer has a certain resonance with Col 3:17[20], there appear to be no other clear parallels in either the Vulgate scriptures or the early liturgical sources. In both prefaces *et dictis et factis* has the same sense. The immoral and diabolical nature of the festivities and rites is clearly shown up by examining what comes from the mouth of the participants (licentious songs, licentious and slanderous denouncing of certain women) and by examining their deeds (nudity, whipping, drunkeness, licentious behaviour, seduction, imprecation of the Roman gods). The apposite section of each preface is as follows:

"*Cum enim idem clamat apostolus: quae secundum faciem sunt, uidete: quaemadmodum se celare posse confidunt, qui, sicut scribtum est, per dulces sermones suos seducentes corda fallacia, et sicut euangelium ait, Christum in cubiles requirentes, palam manifesteque declarant, quid et dictis exsequantur et factis?*" (L 428)[21],

"*Qui hos ispe praui spiritus non dubium est, quo factis probantur et dictis, labem moribus inrogare, dum scilicet uel aguntur crimina uel canuntur*" (L 623)[22].

---

[20] "*Omne quodcumque facitis in verbo aut in opere, omnia in nomine Domini Iesu Christi gratias agentes Deo et Patri per ipsum*" (Col 3:17). The reference to the name of Christ fits well with Pope Gelasius' anti-pagan thrust.

[21] Since as the apostle says, 'look at the evidence of your own eyes' (2 Cor 10:7), in what possible way do they trust to be able to hide themselves, who, as it is written, 'through their sweet words seduce beguiled hearts' (Rm 16:18), and, as the Gospel says, look for Christ 'in hidden chambers' (Mt 24:26), yet who publicly and openly declare what they are pursuing in their deeds and in their words.
The scriptural references are from Pomarès, Gélase, 202-203.

[22] who, by this [participation in the Lupercalia cult] without doubt are depraved spirits, because they are shown to be by their deeds and words, imposing the fall of morals, while evidently either they carry out their crimes or sing about them.

The meaning of the clause is clear. For the Christians, both their speech and their actions must be in accord with God's ways. In effect this summarizes the more detailed admonitions to proper Christian conduct found throughout the New Testament. A good example of such an exhortation is Eph 4:17-5:20, which lists both sins of speech (foul and salacious talk, shouting, malice, empty and deceptive arguments) and of deeds (stealing, immorality, drunkenness).

The conjunction of *dictum* and *factum* evokes a related but secondary meaning. The New Testament consistently calls for congruence between the words and deeds of the faithful. The pharisees are criticized because they do not practice what they speak: "*dicunt enim non faciunt*" (Mt 23:3)[23].

A collect from another of Gelasius' Masses against the Lupercalia (XVIII,xviii) expresses the same thought[24]. Consistency between word and action is set in parallel with a mind faithful to God's will and holy interaction amongst the members of the church. This all-embracing obedience is only possible when the community has been freed from pagan deception. According to Pomarès, *profiteatur verbis* is a reference to the profession of faith at baptism[25]. The prayer reads:

"*Omnipotens sempiterne deus, da nobis uoluntatem tuam fideli mente retinere, et pia conuersatione depromere; ut aeclesia tua a profanis uanitatibus expiata non aliud profiteatur uerbis, aliud exerceat actione*" (L 515)[26].

---

[23]See also the parable of the two sons, Mt 21:28-32, and James dictum concerning faith without works, Jc 2:14-17.

[24]See Pomarès, Gelasius, 216.

[25]Ibid, 217 fn 3.

[26]Almighty eternal God, give to us to keep your will with faithful minds, and express it with pious interaction, so that your church, purified from unholy

In V 1521, the focus of this prayer is the compliance of believers with those things which are spiritual, righteous and pleasing to God. This is done firstly through continuous meditating and reflecting on what are spiritual, and thence through carrying them out in what is said and in what is done.

Meaning of the prayer:

The condition underlying the prayer's petition is the grace to meditate always on spiritual things that are pleasing to God. This denotes a dynamic of continuous, unceasing prayer and reflection upon God's mandates, righteousness, and works. This dynamic of meditation is found repeatedly in the psalms, where it forms the basis of a life in righteousness.

The petition indicates the move from meditation on what is pleasing to God to carrying it out in speech and in deed. The meaning of the prayer is that the whole life of the community, contemplative reflection and prayer first, but communication and action as well, be taken up in what is pleasing to God.

The early liturgical sources offer two contexts for the prayer which affect its interpretation. As a collect from a monastic Mass for times of dissension in the community, the oration reminds the members of the community that the source of their central ideal, true unity and unanimity in Christ and with one another, is found and safeguarded in a whole life given over to what is pleasing to God.

The second interpretation, suggested by the specialized vocabulary of the prayer, concerns the integrity of the faith, deeds and worship of the Christian community before God. When the faithful's reflection and prayer is always conscious of the ways and mandates of God, their worship, deeds and words will have spiritual integrity. Clearly Gelasius' argument was that any

---

falsehoods, does not confess one thing in words, yet do another thing in actions.

reflection on what was done, sung and proclaimed during the Lupercalia festival would show that it is not pleasing to God, nor the fruit of meditating on the things of God.

In applying this anti-Lupercalia vocabulary to dissention in the monastery itself, there is an implicit comment that the presence of disharmony serves notice to the community both that they have committed actions which are not pleasing to God, and that these actions threaten to undermine the integrity of their faith, worship and love of neighbour.

ANALYSIS OF THE WORDS AND PHRASES IN THE COLLECT IN THE CONTEXT OF THE MISSAL OF PAUL VI

Our collect appears to be the only example of the expression *et dictum et factum* in the Missal of Paul VI[27]. However a similar dynamic is operative in the Missal in the pairing of *verbum* and *exemplum*[28]. A collect from an Easter Common of the Blessed Virgin links the spread of the glory of God's name with the words and deeds of Christians. Note that the pair are joined by the conjunction *et* rather than the slightly more binding *et ... et* construction. The prayer reads:

"*Deus, qui Apostolis tuis, cum Maria Matre Iesu orantibus, Sanctum dedisti Spiritum, da nobis, ut, ipsa intercedente, maiestati tuae fideliter servire et*

---

[27] For the 332 examples of the use of *dicere* in the Missal of Paul VI see Schnitker and Slaby, Concordantia, 523-536. For *facere* (which occurs 315 times), 918-931.

[28] For the 89 examples of the use of *verbum* in the Missal of Paul VI see Schnitker and Slaby, Concordantia, 2774-2778. For *exemplum* (which occurs 95 times), 895-899.

nominis tui gloriam verbo et exemplo diffundere valeamus" (MR(1975) Commune B. Mariae VI., temp. pasch., Collecta ad lib., 675)[29].

The *Confiteor* sets word (*verbum*) and deed (*opus*)[30] alongside thought (*cogitatio*) and omission (*omissio*) as possible loci of sin: *"... quia peccavi nimis cogitatione, verbo, opere et omissione"* (MR(1975) Ordo. M. cum populo, Actus paenitentialis, 385)[31].

The new context of the prayer in the Missal of Paul VI brings no new meanings to its vocabulary. The oration's liturgical context in a Mass in Ordinary Time is in line with its presence in the *Paduensis* and the *Hadrianum*, as well as the Sacramentaries of Angoulême, Gellone and St Gall. This context offers the possibility of a broadened interpretation of the prayer. Harmony within the church, and the integrity of its faith, worship and charity, are present in the Christian community at large when the faithful, always meditating on the things that are pleasing in God's sight, carry them out in what they say and do. The corollary to this is that what they say is matched by what they do. This formula for harmony and integrity seems to serve as a description of the Christian life itself.

---

[29]God, who gave the Holy Spirit to your Apostles, gathered in prayer with Mary the Mother of Jesus, give to us, that through her intercession, we may be able to serve your majesty faithfully and, by word and example, spread the glory of your name.
There are a number of prayers where the *verbum et exemplum* of leaders is associated with the building up of the church. See for example, the following orations: MR(1975) Pro papis, Collecta ad lib., 792; and MR(1975) Pro Episc., Collecta ad lib., 794.

[30]For examples of the use of *opus*, which occurs 118 times in the Missal of Paul VI, see Schnitker and Slaby, Concordantia, 1746-1751.

[31]I have sinned in thought, word, deed and omission.

RELATIONSHIP OF THE CHRISTIAN PEOPLE TO GOD

The relationship of the Christian people to God is first of all steeped in prayer and reflection. The faithful ought be continually and unceasingly occupied in turning their hearts and minds to the works, righteousness and mandates of God. Their whole inner being should be oriented to the spiritual things which are pleasing to God. This active meditation forms the base from which can come forth speech and deeds that are pleasing to God.

In line with this, the oration comments on the all embracing nature of the faithful's response to God. It consists in their inner contemplation, and their communication and interaction with one another. All these are to be in accordance with God's mandates. Such harmony in God's will underlies the unanimity of the community and the integrity of their faith, worship and love of neighbour.

FREER TRANSLATION OF THE COLLECT

Praesta, quaesumus, omnipotens Deus, ut, semper rationabilia meditantes, quae tibi sunt placita, et dictis exsequamur et factis.

Grant, almighty God, that in mind and heart we may always reflect and meditate upon what is just and good in your sight. With this as our foundation, may our words always express and our actions exhibit only what is pleasing to you.

COLLECT FOR SUNDAY XVII

PRAYER

Protector in te sperantium, Deus, sine quo nihil est validum, nihil sanctum, multiplica super nos misericordiam tuam, ut, te rectore, te duce, sic bonis transeuntibus nunc utamur, ut iam possimus inhaerere mansuris.

God, protector of those who hope in you, without whom nothing is strong, nothing is holy, increase your mercy towards us, so that, with you as ruler and leader, we may use passing goods now in such a way that we may be able to cling already to the goods that will last.

ORIGINAL PRAYER

As the collect stands in the Missal of Paul VI, it is a composite formed out of two prayers from different early Roman sources. The address, motivating clause and petition are first encountered in the collect from the *Paduensis*, Mass CXVII, ebdomada III <I> post pentecosten, P 517. *Protector in te sperantium, Deus, sine quo nihil est validum, nihil sanctum, multiplica super nos misericordiam tuam, ut, te rectore, te duce, sic transeamus per bona temporalia, ut non amittamus aeterna*[1].

However the purpose clause in P 517, *ut, te rectore, te duce, sic transeamus per bona temporalia, ut non amittamus aeterna* has been largely replaced. The new clause *ut, te rectore, te duce, sic bonis transeuntibus nunc utamur, ut iam possimus inhaerere mansuris*, appears to be borrowed from the

---

[1] God, protector of those who hope in you, without whom nothing is strong, nothing holy, increase your mercy towards us, so that, with you as ruler and leader, we may pass through the good things that are temporal in such a way that we do not lose those which are eternal.

Veronensis preface L 495, whose closing lines read *sic bonis praeteruntibus nunc utimur, ut iam possimus inhaerere perpetuis*[2].

This modification of P 517 is neither found in nor hinted at in any sources prior to the Missal of Paul VI.

USE IN OTHER LITURGICAL SOURCES

As noted by Bruylants[3], the prayer P 517 is also found in these sources: Dominica infra Octavam Sacratissimi cordis Jesu, tertia post Pentecosten: A(1019), S(914), *OR*(169)[Sp 1138], X(254,1), N(138), Q(139ᵛ), 1474(260), 1570, 1604, and these unedited sources G(169,1)[G 1137], Z(684), PaAng(198), FrAug(V,1), Par(23).

The prayer is also found in the *Missale Francorum*[4], *Incipiunt orationes et preces communes cotidianae cum canone,* Mass 19, oration *Ante Nomena,* MF 123. This source is not listed by Bruylants.

ANALYSIS OF THE PRAYER IN THE ORIGINAL SOURCE

Methodological note:

Because the prayer in the Missal of Paul VI is related to two distinct early prayers a slight revision of the usual methodology is in order. The following study will treat P 517 as the original source of the prayer, and so in the analysis below its origins, structure, vocabulary and meaning will be

---

[2]Dumas does not mark this text in his list of sources for the prayers of the Missal of Paul VI. Given the significance of the change, this is perhaps an oversight. See Dumas, "Les sources du nouveau Missel romain," Notitiae 7 (1971): 94.

[3]Bruylants, II, 911.

[4]L.C.Mohlberg, L.Eizenhöfer and P.Siffrin, eds., Missale Francorum, Rerum Ecclesiasticarum Documenta, Series Maior, Fontes II (Roma: Herder, 1957).

studied. The origins and vocabulary of the part borrowed from the preface L 495 will be dealt with in the later section of our study entitled "Analysis of the Words and Phrases of the Collect in the Context of the Missal of Paul VI."

Origin of the prayer:

The prayer appears to be of Roman provenance. It belongs to that primitive layer of the *Paduensis* which consists of those prayers added to adapt the original papal sacramentary to presbyteral usage[5]. Yet even among these prayers P 517 has a distinctive place. It is one of five prayers in this layer of the source that has not been borrowed from *Reginensis* 316, the *Veronensis* or the *Hadrianum*[6]. The original sources of those five prayers remain unknown. There is no indication that they were imported from outside of Rome.

The prayer is also encountered in two other distinct source traditions. It is found as the *oratio ante nomena* of a Mass entitled 19 *Incipiunt orationes et preces communes cotidianae cum canone* from the Gallican Missale Francorum (MF 123). As well it is used as the collect for the Mass of the Fifth Sunday after Pentecost in the Frankish Gelasian Sacramentary of Gellone (G 1137) and Sacramentary of Angoulême (A 1019).

The presence of the prayer in the *Gellonensis* and the Sacramentary of Angoulême is clearly due to borrowing from the *Paduensis*. The following table sets out the sources of the prayers for the Mass, using as a reference the Mass as it stands in the Sacramentary of Angoulême.

---

[5] See Vogel, Medieval Liturgy, 94. For a study of the Masses that comprise these adaptations see Chavasse, Le Sacramentaire Gélasien, 531-546. See also the study of the collect for Sunday XIX, whose source is also a collect from one of these Masses, below 569.

[6] The others are P 94, P 518, P 730 and P 745. Note that P 745 is the original source of the collect for Sunday XIX in Ordinary Time in the Missal of Paul VI. See below, 569.

TABLE 4. THE SOURCES OF PRAYERS A 1019 - A 1023

	Pa	Sp	G	A	S	MF
Col	P 517	Sp 1138	G 1137	A 1019	S 914	MF 123*
Sup Sin	Nil	Nil	G 1138	A 1020	S 915	-
Sup Obl	P 518	Sp 1139	G 1139	A 1021	S 916	-
Preface	-	Sp 1628	G 1051	A 1022	S 917	MF 127**
Post comm	P 519	Sp 1140	G 1141	A 1023 A 1299	S 918	-

* This prayer is the *oratio ante nomina*.
** This preface is a combination of A 1022 and P 870.

From this table the following can be seen. Both the Masses in the *Gellonensis* and the Sacramentary of Angoulême share virtually the same liturgical context (Week V after Pentecost) as the Mass in the *Paduensis* (Week IV after Pentecost). Most tellingly they contain the same collect, secret and postcommunion as the Roman text. Finally the *super populum* in the *Gellonensis* Mass is also borrowed from Roman sources (the Mass in the Sacramentary of Angoulême has no *oratio super populum*). It appears then that the Mass for the Sunday of the Fifth Week after Pentecost in the Sacramentaries of Gellone and Angoulême was imported from the *Paduensis*, and embellished with a mixture of largely Roman, but also some non-Roman, prayers.

A possible alternative to this conclusion emerges from a study of the collect within its context in Mass 19 in the *Missale Francorum*. Since the *contestatio* (MF 127) for that Mass forms the basis of the preface for the apposite Mass in the Sacramentary of Angoulême (A 1022), there is a possiblity that our collect came into the *Paduensis* and the Frankish Gelasians from this Gallican source.

There are, however, good reasons for not supporting such a conclusion. The sharing of the same prayer and preface by the Mass in the *Missale Francorum* and the Mass in the Sacramentary of Angoulême does not explain how the collect, *super oblata* and postcommunion in that Mass in both the *Gellonensis* and the Sacramentary of Angoulême are the same as those in the Mass from the *Paduensis*. With regard to this Mass the Frankish Gelasians show more dependence on the *Paduensis* than on the Gallican *Missale Francorum*. Moreover, the Mass 19 in the *Missale Francorum* is itself largely a compilation of prayers from Roman sources, chiefly from Masses III,i and III,ii in *Reginensis* 316[7]. Furthermore, the preface MF 127 also betrays a strong Roman influence. The prayer has two distinct sections, the first of which is used in our Mass in the Sacramentary of Angoulême (A 1022). Though this section is not found in the earliest Roman sources it is found in the Ambrosian Sacramentary of Milan (Milano 517) and in the Sacramentary of Trent (GregorTc 3782). However, the second section, comprising of that part of MF 127 not included in A 1022, is found in the *Paduensis* Mass entitled CCXVI, *Incipiunt orationes cottidianae Gregorii Papae item alia*, P 870. The preface MF 123 is, then, a composite prayer formed from Roman and (probably) Gallican sources. In conclusion, a close examination of Mass 19 in the *Missale Francorum* neither puts forward compelling reasons for assigning a Gallican origin to our collect, nor undermines the conclusion that the prayer is of Roman provenance.

---

[7]See the table of sources for the prayers of the *Missale Francorum* in Mohlberg, Missale Francorum, 53-54.

Grammatical structure[8]:

The prayer consists of (a) an address with qualifying designator, (b) a motivating clause, (c) a petition, and (d) an extended purpose clause.

(a)   Address: *Deus*

         Qualifying designator: *protector in te sperantium*

(b)   Motivation: *sine te nihil est validum, nihil sanctum*

(c)   Petition: *multiplica super nos misericordiam tuam,*

(d)   Purpose clause: *ut*

         Condition: *te rectore, te duce*

         Purpose: *sic transeamus per bona temporalia, ut non amittamus aeterna.*

In the address and motivating clause, God is invoked as the protector of those who hope in him, and in connection with this, as the one who guarantees strength and holiness. On account of their faith in God's protection and his upholding the strength and holiness of things, the community beseeches God's mercy. In particular they relate this to the hope that God will lead and guide them through the temporal realities of this world.

The oration sets in parallel *sanctum, validum* and the *bona temporalia*. The God who is believed to uphold what is strong and holy, then, is also seen to uphold all that is good. As such he is the one to turn to in hope for protection and guidance amidst what he supports.

The ultimate hope of the community is eternal life, reaching which is related to their use of what God has provided on earth. The faithful believe that they will attain heaven if they use the gifts of this world (*transeamus per*

---

[8] For a more detailed grammatical analysis see M.Haessly, Rhetoric in the Sunday Collects of the Roman Missal, 77-80.

bona temporalia) under the rulership and guidance that comes from God's mercy.

Vocabulary:

Prominent vocabulary: *protector, sperare, validus, sanctus, multiplicare, misericordia, rector, dux, transire, bona temporalia, amittere, aeternus.*

Our word analysis will begin with some additional comments on *protector in te sperantium*, which serves to qualify the address *Deus*.

Protector[9]

The phrase *protector in te sperantium*, which echoes a verse in Ps 17[10], is not uncommon in the early liturgical sources[11]. God's protection has been examined in the analysis of the collect for Sunday V[12]. Summarizing that discussion here, God's protection is linked with his work of cleansing, renewing, strengthening, governing and guarding the church in its battle against sin. Connoting both a sense of power and intimacy, divine protection is connected with God's loving kindness (*pietas*) and, in P 517, his mercy (*misericordia*)[13].

---

[9] For further examples of the use of *protector* see Deshusses, Concordances III, 3, 528-529.

[10] "*Deus meus, impolluta via eius, eloquia Domini igne examinata: protector est omnium sperantium in se*" (Ps 17:31). See also Ps 30:2-5.

[11] See L 35, L 350, L 534, L 1057, V 1548, and G 1900.

[12] See above, 493.

[13] The connection between the divine *pietas* and *misericordia* has been examined in the analysis of the collect for Sunday XXVII. See above, 389ff.

In P 517, the faithful describe themselves as those who hope in God[14]. They call upon him as their *protector* on account of their faith that God protects those who hope in him. Their claim for hoping in him is further based on their belief that without him nothing is strong or holy, *sine quo nihil est validum, nihil sanctum*. These attributes will now be examined.

Validum[15]

The adjective *validus* is quite rare in the early liturgical sources. It is indexed only five times in the Deshusses' concordance, inclusive of our prayer[16].

The only other Roman prayer is V 933, a Vesper prayer for the feast of Sts. Peter and Paul. There the assistance of the apostles is sought so that to the degree the faithful are weak (*fragiles*), they may be given strong assistance (*validiora auxilia*). The prayer reads:

"*Apostolicis nos, domine, quaesumus, beatorum Petri et Pauli adtolle praesidiis, ut quanto fragiliores sumus, tanto ualidioribus auxiliis foueamur*" (V 933)[17].

Examining the prayer within its context in the set of vesper prayers gives some indication of the sense of *validus* and *fragilis*. The particular patronage (V 938) of the two preeminent leaders of the church and founding apostles of Rome connotes fidelity, confession of faith, the apostolic teaching

---

[14]This description, [*Deus*] *in te sperantium* [*fortitudo*] has already been seen in the collect for Sunday XI. See above, 304.

[15]For further examples of the use of *validus* see Deshusses, Concordances III, 4, 420.

[16]The other prayers are V 933, G 1772, G 1988/G 2038, G 2032.

[17]Extend to us Lord the apostolic help of saints Peter and Paul, so that the weaker we are, we may be assisted by stronger helps.

(V 936), and true government (V 934). *Fragilis* however is related to earthly vices (V 931, V 938).

Though from a later source, an episcopal blessing for the Sunday of the fifth week after Pentecost in the Sacramentary of Gellone (G 2032) gives some insight into the adjective *validus*. The blessing shares the same liturgical context in that Sacramentary as our collect (G 1137, *Hebd. V post Pentecosten*)[18]. As Jesus, the Good Shepherd, is asked to convert the errant and bind back the contrite, so he is asked to strengthen the weak (*invalidum*) and safeguard the strong (*validum*). *Validum*, here is associated with strength in Gods' righteousness, itself a gift from God that needs his continual safeguarding. The oration reads:

"*Domine iesus pastur bone qui animam tuam pro ouibus posuisti, sanguinis tui deffende conmercium. - Gregem tuum propitius uisitare dignare, esurientem pasce, sitientem pota. - Quod perit require, quod errat conuerte, contrita conliga, conforta inualedum ualedumque custodi. - Fac eos ante conspectum tuum cum iustitia uiuere et cum misericordia si se custodirent iudicare. Quod ipse*" (G 2032)[19].

In summary, *validum*, when applied to persons signifies those who are strong in Christian virtue and fidelity. When applied to things it denotes those

---

[18]In the Sacramentary of Angoulême this *Gellonensis* prayer is incorporated into a more elaborate blessing (A 1866). This oration is set in a compilation of blessings for the Sunday office, under the heading *Incipiunt benedictiones dominicales: ad matutinas*.

[19]Lord Jesus, the Good Shepherd, who laid down your own life for the sake of the sheep, defend the exchange brought about in your blood. In your favour deign to visit your flock, nourish the hungry, provide drink for those who thirst. Seek out what has perished, convert the errant, bind back the contrite, strengthen the weak, safeguard the strong. make them live in your sight in righteousness, and judge them with mercy if they have kept themselves [in righteousness in your sight].

things that convey such strength. In our prayer it is conjoined with the adjective *sanctus*, which will now be studied.

Sanctum[20]

The adjective *sanctus* denotes what belongs to the divinity itself, or falls under the name and power of God. Holiness is supremely an attribute of God himself.

A covenant renewal ceremony in the Vulgate translation of the Book of Joshua describes God as holy, *sanctus* (Js 24:14-24). The passage links God's holiness with his 'jealousy', in which he fiercely defends and keeps undefiled what is his. The divine holiness is directly opposite to sin, while the covenant context of the passage relates it to his liberating power. The people's response is one of total commitment, fear (*timor*)[21], worship (*servire*), and obedience. The apposite verse reads:

"*Dixitque Iosue ad populum: Non poteritis seruire Domino. Deus enim sanctus et fortis aemulator est nec ignoscet sceleribus vestris atque peccatis*" (Js 24:19)[22].

By extension, everything that is filled with God's power and favour partakes in the divine holiness, and as such is qualified as *sanctus*.

The adjective *sanctus* is found continually in the liturgical sources. Its use as a substantive is less frequent. One case is L 587, a prayer from the Office. In the oration, what are holy, the *sancta*, are set in parallel with what

---

[20] For further examples of the use of *sanctus* see Deshusses, Concordances III, 4, 141-174.

[21] For a study of *timor* (collect for Sunday XII), see above, 318.

[22] See also Os 11:9 and Mt 6:9. The greek text reads $\alpha\gamma\iota o\varsigma$. For commentary see O.Procksch and K.G.Kuhn, "$\alpha\gamma\iota o\varsigma, \kappa\tau\lambda.$," TDNT I, 88-115.

exists in God's light[23]. The *sancta* are diametrically opposed to sin, evil and darkness. They are the subject of that constant prayer and reflection necessary for living in God. The prayer reads:

"*Deus, qui diem discernis et noctem, actos nostros a tenebrarum distingue caligine; ut semper quae sancta sunt meditantes, in tua iugiter luce uiuamus*" (L 587)[24].

Validum and *sanctum* are joined though the construction *sine quo nihil est ... nihil* [*est*]. A similar construct is found in the collect for Sunday XI[25]. The expression emphasises the unsurpassable nature of God's power, as well as our need for it in the face of sin. In doing so it spells out the basis for the faithful's hope in God's protection.

The address and motivating clause in P 517 bring together, on the one hand, God's intimate protection, guardianship, cleansing and strengthening of the faithful, with, on the other hand, his power at work in upholding the strength and holiness in things. Whatever partakes in the holiness of God both is acceptable in his sight and exists within the freedom of his covenant. In a like manner, whatever is strong in God is both strong against sin and powerful in righteousness. It exists within the favour of God and the care of the Good Shepherd. From their faith and hope in God's protection towards them, and his strengthening and sanctification of things, the community makes its petition : *multiplica super nos misericordiam tuam*.

---

[23]For a discussion of God's light, see the analysis of the collect for Sunday XV, 256. See also the discussion of *lux* and *splendor* in the collect for Sunday XIII, below, 603ff.

[24]God, who set apart the day from the night, separate our actions from the gloom of darkness, so that, always meditating on what are holy, we may live continually in your light.

[25]The corresponding clause reads *sine te nihil potest*. See above, 306. See also V 1218 and L 77.

Multiplica super nos misericordiam tuam
Multiplica[26]

In liturgical usage, *multiplicare*, along with verbs such as *largiri*, *tribuere* and *praestare*, means to give or to grant. *Multiplicare* itself has the connotation of giving with abundance[27]. The petition is reminiscent of Ps 35:8: "*Quemadmodum multiplicasti misericordiam tuam, Deus.*"

God's mercy has been analysed in the study of the collect for Sunday XXVI[28]. The divine *misericordia* is the primary expression of God's boundless love in Christ for humanity. Its scope includes salvation from sin and death, restoration, being raised up and the promise of heaven.

This petition for the outpouring of God's *misericordia* is followed by an extended result clause. Its first section contains the conditions which underlie the whole clause. From God's superabundant, merciful kindness, the community first seeks that God be their ruler (*rector*) and leader (*dux*). This conjunction will now be examined.

Te rectore

The application of the title *rector* to God has been discussed in the analysis of the collect for Sunday XXIV[29]. Summarizing that discussion here, *rector* is often paired with the acknowledgement of God as protector, guardian and sustainer of his people. Together these terms are connected with his work of the restoration of fallen humanity, and their entry to eternal life. In P 517, this rulership is set with God's role as leader (*dux*).

---

[26]For further examples of the use of *multiplicare* see Deshusses, Concordances III, 3, 117-118.

[27]Blaise, Vocabulaire, § 67.

[28]See above, 378. The petition parallels that found in the collect for Sunday XXVII, *effunde super nos misericordiam tuam*.

[29]See above, 205.

Te duce

An oration for morning office in *Reginensis* 316, V 1584, associates God's leadership (*dux, princeps*) with his work as originator and founder (*principium, princeps*). The oration reads:

"*Gratias agimus inenarrabile pietate tuae, omnipotens deus, qui nos depulsa noctis caligine ad diei huius principium perduxisti et abiecta ignorantiae caecitatem ad cultum tui nominis atque scientiam reuocasti; inlabe sensibus nostris, omnipotens pater, ut in preceptorum tuorum lumine gradientes te ducem sequamur et principem*" (V 1584)[30].

Note that the prayer plays on the images of origin (*principium*), darkness (*calignas*), and light (*lumen*). These images connote both God's work of creation and salvation. There is also an interplay between leadership (*dux/princeps*) and the idea of origin and beginning (*princeps/principium*). God, the leader and prince of all, is believed to have lead (*perducere*) his people through the darkness of night to the beginning (*principium*) of the day. Similarly the community's faith is that he has also led them back (*revocare*) from ignorance to true worship and knowledge. God's leadership, then, is related to his work as founder, to all that begins in the light, to the defeat of darkness, and to the return of the faithful to the light. Both understandings of God as originator and leader are set within his loving kindness (*inenarrabilis pietas*), and his role as father (*pater*). Following God's leadership involves the whole self, consciousness (*sensus*), worship, knowledge, way of life

---

[30] We give thanks for your indescribable loving kindness, almighty God, who, on repelling the darkness of night, has led us through to the beginning of this day, and who, on casting off the blindness of ignorance, has recalled us to the worship and knowledge of your name: penetrate our consciousness, almighty father, so that, walking in the light of your precepts, we may follow you our leader and our prince.

(*gradiens*), all in tune with God's precepts. God's leadership, however, is active even when the faithful are lost in darkness and blind in ignorance.

A *super populum* associates God's leadership with his guardianship (*custos*), as well as with the community's status as his *familia*. His leadership and guardianship flow from his favour and blessing. Note that the divine leadership extends into all things. The prayer reads:
"*Familiam tuam, domine, benignus inlustra, et benedictionis tuae largitate confirma; ut te in omnibus ducem, te mereatur habere custodem*" (L 549)[31].

Through their desire that God be their ruler and leader, the faithful are asking that God lead, protect, sustain and restore them so as to come to eternal life. They trust that God rules and leads them even when their blindness and ignorance is such that they cannot see or know that he does. The divine rulership and leadership are based in God's loving kindness and favour. The true response to the divine *rector* and *dux* is expressed in worship and obedience. In P 517, the faithful's petition is that, with God as their ruler and leader, they may be able to pass amongst the good things of this life so as not to lose eternal life: *sic transeamus per bona temporalia, ut non amittamus aeterna*. This petition will now be examined.

Sic transeamus per bona temporalia, ut non amittamus aeterna

Two prayers from the liturgical sources shed light on the dynamic operative in this extended purpose clause. Both prayers are concerned with the use of temporal goods on earth so that through them the faithful may reach eternal life.

Collect L 912 is found in a *Veronensis* Mass for the fast of the tenth month (XXVII,x). The prayer sets out an overview of humanity's history in

---

[31] In your favour, illuminate your family, Lord, and strengthen them with the bounty of your blessing; so that it may merit to have you as its leader and guardian in all things.

relation to God's grace. Through their sinful desire when living in God's gracious original creation, humanity lost the original beatitude which was intended to be theirs eternally. In the present time, the sincere are given good, though passing, things on earth (*temporalia beneficia*) such as the fast and the nourishment of the sacrament. Through these they are both sustained on earth and able to recover eternal life (*amissa aeternitas*). Note that alongside the *temporalia beneficia* comes God's aid (*conpetenter instructus*) through which humanity is taught to use the passing things so as to gain eternal life. The prayer reads:

"*Omnipotens sempiterne deus, qui sic hominem condedisti, ut temporalibus beneficiis conpetenter instructum ad caelestia dona prouehis: presta, quaesumus, ut sicut per inlicitos adpetitos de indultae beatitudinis regione decidimus, sic per alimoniam tuo munere destributam et transitoria sustentetur humanitas, et amissa recuperetur aeternitas*" (L 912)[32].

This oration sheds light on a number of terms in our collect. The *temporalia beneficia* of L 912 parallel the *bona temporalia* of P 517. They refer to the good things God provides on earth for humanity, such as the fast and the sacrament. These are of a passing nature, but through them the eternal good things of heaven can be reached. The *Veronensis* prayer also elucidates the sense of *amittere*. The loss of eternal life, and hence of beatitude, is the result of sin. This loss is in contrast with God's original intention for his creation. In L 912 *amittere* is set in parallel with *decidere*, a verb which connotes not only a fall from bliss, but a fall into death. Note also that the

---

[32] Almighty, eternal God, you established the human race in such a way that you might fittingly, lead it, properly instructed through temporal benefits, to the possession of heavenly gifts, grant that, just as through illicit appetites we departed from the place of your gracious beatitude, in that same way through the nourishment distributed by your gifts, may humanity be sustained in its passing reality, and the eternity lost be recovered.

faithful need God's instruction (*conpetenter instructus*) so that they can use the *temporalia beneficia* so as to reach heaven. This parallels the sense of *te rectore, te duce* in P 517.

The preface A 1022 also parallels the dynamics in our collect[33]. Spiritual progress and ultimately the attainment of eternal joy is related to the gifts of the fullness of worship, as well as to an increase of things for earthly life (*augmenta corporea*). Through the use of such mutable gifts (*mutabilia dona*), themselves temporal joys (*temporalis laetitia*), the faithful come to the unchanging good (*immutabile bonus*) and eternal bliss (*sempiterna gaudia*). The prayer reads:

"*UD: Omnipotentiam tuam iugiter implorantes, ut quibus annua celebritatis huius vota multiplicas, plenam divine cultus gratiam largiaris, et per augmenta corporea profectum clementer tribuas animarum, per quod ad immutabile bonum per mutabilia dona veniamus, temporalique laetitiae et gaudia sempiterna succedant*" (A 1022)[34].

---

[33]First of all it should be noted that this preface forms the first section of the *contestatio* (MF 127) in the above mentioned Mass 19 from the *Missale Francorum*, of which the prayer under analysis is the oration *ante nomena* (MF 123). Our prayer and this preface are found together, then, in Masses in the *Missale Francorum*, the Sacramentary of Angoulême, and the Sacramentary of St Gall (S 914, S 917). It seems unfortunate that in the Supplement, this preface is marked down for Sunday V after Pentecost, since in this source our collect (Sp 1138) is set in the Mass for Sunday IV after Pentecost, as is P 517 in the *Paduensis*. Note that the *Gellonensis* employs a different preface (G 1140).

[34]It is right and fitting: Always imploring your power so that for those whose annual prayers of this celebration you favour, you may bestow the full grace of the divine cultus, and, through an increase of corporeal things, you may grant, in your clemency, progress of spirit, through which we come through changeable gifts to the unchanging good, and also, eternal joys may take the place of temporal joy.

Meaning of the prayer:

As seen earlier, the meaning of the prayer emerges from the motivating clause. In view of their hope in God's protection, and its association with the strength, holiness and goodness in things, the faithful implore God's merciful kindness. They desire that, under his rulership and leadership, they may be able to live using transitory goods in such a way that they are in no danger of losing eternal life.

The conjunction of *protector, rector* and *dux* encompasses the broad range of divine actions by which God watches over, and cares for those who hope in him. It denotes God's power and love at work in guarding the people that he created, renews and strengthens.

The substantives *validum, sanctum* and *bona* point to God's continuing presence in created things, by which they can be said to be strong, holy and good. In particular, *bona temporalia* denotes those gifts of the divine order which God gives, such as the fast, the sacraments, worship and corporeal things which lead to spiritual benefits. They are of a passing, transitory nature, yet by using them in accord with God's direction and leadership, the faithful are able to come to eternal life. They are gifts of the divine mercy, which lead the baptized to salvation.

The sense of *non amittamus aeterna* goes beyond a straightforward contrast between eternal and passing goods. More forcefully, *bona aeterna* is in contrast with being closed off eternally from life in God. This implies continued existence in sin, darkness and death, outside any possibility of light, holiness and life.

ANALYSIS OF THE WORDS AND PHRASES OF THE COLLECT IN THE CONTEXT OF THE MISSAL OF PAUL VI

The incorporation of P 517 into the context of the Missal of Paul VI has brought with it two changes. The first, and by far the most radical and important, is the almost complete replacement of the result clause. This will be examined first. The second change, of much less importance, is a slight broadening in the application of the adjective *validus*.

Sic bonis transeuntibus nunc utamur, ut iam possimus inhaerere mansuris

Our first task will be to investigate the origins and early parallels for the revision.

The vocabulary of the new ending contains a slight echo of 1 Cor 7:29-38[35]. In light of his belief in the imminent return of Christ, Paul urges the Corinthians to live their lives is this very transitory present with the parousia firmly in view.

"*Hoc itaque dico, fratres: Tempus breve est: reliquum est, ut et qui habent uxores tanquam non habentes sint, et qui flent tanquam non flentes, et qui gaudent tanquam non gaudentes, et qui emunt tanquam non possidentes, et qui utuntur hoc mundo tanquam non utantur; praeterit enim figura huius mundi*" (1 Cor 7:29-31).

By far the clearest parallel, however, is found in the final lines of preface L 495. The entire oration is as follows:

"*Uere dignum: qui mutabilitatem nostram ad incommutabilia ita iustus et benignus erudis, ut nec fragilitatem destituas et coherceas insolentes: quo pariter instituti pia conuersatione et caelestibus sacramentis, sic bonis praetereuntibus nunc utimur, ut iam possimus inherere perpetuis*" (L 495)[36].

---

[35] It is interesting to note that Blaise refers to these verses when commenting on the very section of P 517 that has been replaced. See Blaise, Vocabulaire, § 403, fn 5.

[36] It is truly right and fitting ... God, who as righteous and beneficent lead our changeable nature to unchanging things in such a way that you neither desert our weakness nor do you forcibly restrain the haughty: by this [leading] may we, established equally by a holy way of life and the heavenly mysteries, use passing goods now in such a way that we may be able to cling already to perpetual goods.

In the prayer, the *bonis praetereuntibus* are set in parallel with the instructive helps (*instituere, erudire*) God gives in his righteousness (*iustus*) and beneficence (*benignus*). These include the holy way of life of the community, *pia conversatio*[37], and the eucharistic mysteries (*caelestia sacramenta*). *Perpetua* is in parallel with *incommutabilia*. While our collect reads *transeuntibus* rather than *praetereuntibus*, and *mansuris* rather than *perpetuis*, these variations are of little consequence to the meaning of the prayer, and seem to be mainly stylistic.

The revision, then, appears to have been borrowed directly from L 495. If this is correct, then further investigation into the historical origins and structure of the preface will shed some light on the meaning of the sentence. The *Veronensis* Mass (XVIII,xiii) for which L 495 was the preface seemed to serve as something of a quarry for the compilers of the new Missal. The motivating clause of that Mass's *super sindonem*, L 493, forms the opening clause for the collect for Sunday XXV[38]. The *super oblata*, L 493, is the offertory prayer for Sunday VIII. As well, the collect from the previous Mass (XVIII,xiii) in the *Veronensis* has been incorporated into the new Missal as the collect for Sunday XXXIII[39].

Both these Masses appear to have the same historical origins[40]. They are attributed to the pen of Pope Vigilius, and seem to have been written for

---

The only other apparent parallel in the early liturgical sources is L 173. Note the parallel between *mansuris* in L 173 and *perpetuis* in L 495.

[37]For *conversatio* as designating conduct or manner of life, see Blaise, Vocabulaire, § 425.

[38]See above, 127.

[39]See above, 116.

[40]See A.Chavasse, "Messes du Pape Vigile (537-555)," Ephemerides Liturgicae 64 (1950): 187-191.

consecutive Sunday liturgies; August 30th (xiii) and September 6th (xiiii), 537. At this time, Rome, in the midst of the siege by the Arian Visigoths, was hopeful that victory would soon be theirs. News had reached them of the imminent arrival of imperial troops. Vigilius, mindful that the siege and its afflictions were associated with the sinfulness of the community, sought in his Masses to press home to the faithful that only in adherence to God's ways is there true and lasting security and peace. Consequently, in the *super sindonem* (L 493) of the Mass XVIII,xiiii, the pope calls them to obey the divine mandates, centred as they are in love of God and neighbour. The *super oblata* sets together God's gifts for worship, the community's meritorious use of them, and eternal reward[41].

In the preface (L 495) from the same Mass, the faithful ask that they may use the passing things given by God as instructive in the present to enable the faithful to cling already to what is eternal. These passing things are God's mandates, the Christian way of life, and the sacraments and worship. They are transitory in that their complete and unchanging state is attained in heaven. Note the similarity here with the meaning of the collect from Mass XVIII,xiii[42]. There Vigilius is reminding the church that their present participation in worship is an anticipation of the perpetual felicity of heaven.

---

[41] "*Omnipotens sempiterne deus, qui offerenda tuo nomini tribuis, et oblata deuotioni nostrae seruitutis asscribis: quaesumus clementiam tuam, ut quod prestas unde sit meritum, proficere nobis largiaris ad praemium*" (L 494). Translation: God, who bestows the gifts being offered to your name, and imputes what has been offered to the devotion of our service, we ask your clemency, so that, because what you grant from these gifts is meritorious for us, you may grant us to advance to the reward.

[42] See above, 123. See also the collect for Sunday XXI (V 551). There, in the midst of the changing things of the world, love of the precepts and desire for the promises are understood to be experiences of the true joys of heaven.

Study of the historical origins and structure of L 495 points up the sense of the *bona transeuntia* and their relationship to the *mansura* in the revised collect. They are divine good things, such as the mandates and worship, which are experienced on earth as transitory, but which in heaven are unchanging, constant joys. The faithful, through participating in them on earth, gain a foretaste of their unchanging perfection in heaven.

A significant change of metaphor is brought about through this borrowing from L 495. The original prayer, P 517, was built around the image of the faithful's journey through life (*transire*), and its consequence for attaining eternal life. The revised collect has dropped this image, in its stead concentrating on the present exercise (*uti*) of divine good things experienced on earth as transitory.

The use of the verb *uti* in the Pauline text, 1 Cor 7:29-31, offers a slightly broader interpretation of the *bona transeuntia*. There the reference is to the use of things of the world in general. However, the clear dependence of the oration's revision on L 495 suggests that this broader reading is not brought into effect by the text.

In line with this change of metaphor, much of the force of the eschatological sense of the original prayer has entirely disappeared through the deletion of the references to the possible loss of eternal life. This is consistent with the Missal's tendency to avoid eschatological language, already noted in the study of the collect for Sunday XIV[43]. There is also a loss of the sense of the power of sin throughout one's life, whereby even when the faithful live amongst what is good, they remain in danger of eternal death. The direction of the new collect is entirely different. The *mansura bona* point to the enduring presence in heaven of things on earth that can only exist as transitory.

---

[43] See above, 248.

The focus of the collect is not the loss of eternal life, but that under God's protection the faithful may enjoy a foretaste on earth of heavenly things.

Validum

The adjective *validus* is used six times in the Missal of Paul VI[44]. On four of these occasions, *validus* is particularly associated with love, whether the love of the martyrs in the Holy Spirit, or that love of Christians which works for justice and peace. This sense is already seen in G 1772, seemingly the only oration in the early sources that qualifies *dilectio* with *valida*[45]. The apposite sections of the prayers read:

"*ut corda nostra ea dilectione valida potiantur, per quam sanctus martyr Vincentius omnia corporis tormenta devicit*" (MR(1975) S.Vincentii, Collecta, 518)[46],

"*et in nostris cordibus eam dilectionem validam operentur, per quam sancti martyres ....*" (MR(1975) Pro pluribus martt., temp. pasch. 2, Super oblata, 687, (G 1772))[47],

"*validum et purum hauriamus amorem ad progredientes populos iuvandos*" (MR(1975) Pro populorum progressione, Post comm., 821)[48],

---

[44] See Schnitker and Slaby, Concordantia, 2761.

[45] Deshusses, Concordances, III, 4, 420.

[46] ... so that our hearts may possess that stong love, through which the holy martyr Vincent overcame all bodily torments.
The original source for this oration appears to be the *Sacramentarium Rivipullense*, 884. The critical edition is A.Olivar, ed., Sacramentarium Rivipullense, Monumenta Hispaniae Sacra, Serie litúrgica, Vol. VII (Madrid-Barcelona: Instituto Enrique Flórez, 1964).

[47] ... and my these gifts being presented work in our hearts that strong love, through which the holy martrys ....

[48] ... may we take to heart a strong and pure love for the sake of helping the developing nations .... [The original source is unknown.]

"*validum hauriamus amorem et ubique tuae pacis operatores efficiamur*" (MR(1975) Pro reconciliatione, Post comm., 825)[49].

From the early liturgical sources it has been shown that *validum* denotes what is strong because it is in God's righteousness and under his guardianship. In the Missal of Paul VI this is particularly applied to Christian love. *Validum* embodies the strength of the love which underpins martyrdom, the work of justice, and the work of reconciliation.

Meaning of the prayer:

The meaning of the revised prayer is quite different from that of the original. The faithful call upon God as protector, ruler and leader to guide their usage of the *bona transeuntia*. These *bona transeuntia*, whose holiness and strength (with its connotation of strength for love, justice and reconciliation) come from God alone, are transitory expressions on earth of the life of heaven. The community desires that, under God's rulership and protection, they may participate in these divine gifts in such a way that they may be able to experience in this present life something of eternal life.

The original siege context of the new clause further emphasises that no matter what else is taking place, whether it is the siege, hope of victory or peace itself, God's merciful kindness is at work providing true and lasting good things for the community.

---

[49] ... may we take to heart a strong love and may we be made workers of your peace everywhere ....
[The original source is unknown.]

THE RELATIONSHIP OF THE CHRISTIAN PEOPLE TO GOD

The original prayer: P 517:

The prayer expresses a number of aspects concerning the relationship of the Christian people to God.

God upholds the strength, holiness and goodness of all things. In P 517 this is particularly so with regard to the *bona temporalia*, gifts given by God such as the fast, the sacraments, worship and corporeal things which lead to spiritual benefits, and the proper participation in which leads to eternal life. Such fitting participation comes when God rules and leads their actions.

Yet the power of sin is such that the community realize that even their engagement in the *bona temporalia*, when not governed by God's guidance, can lead them to the loss of eternal life.

God's intimate protection, strengthening and making holy, rulership and leadership, are all effects of the divine mercy, through which he desires that those who hope in his protection come to share eternal life.

The collect in the Missal of Paul VI:

The prayer as it now stands in the Missal of Paul VI focuses on quite different elements in the Christian people's relationship to God. God, who upholds the strength, holiness and goodness of all things, provides good, though transitory, gifts which, when used according to his rulership and leadership, provide on earth an experience of their expression in heaven.

While the prayer has a sense of partial realization in the present of the eschaton, there is a diminishment of the eschatological perspective in the relationship of the Christian people to God between the original and the present text. The oration has lost its reference to the effect of sin, especially the possible sundering of their relationship through entry to the never ending death that constitutes the loss of eternal life.

FREER TRANSLATION OF THE COLLECT

Protector in te sperantium, Deus, sine quo nihil est validum, nihil sanctum, multiplica super nos misericordiam tuam, ut, te rectore, te duce, sic bonis transeuntibus nunc utamur, ut iam possimus inhaerere mansuris.

God, you are the protector of all who hope in you. Without you nothing is strong, nothing is holy. Pour out upon us your merciful kindness. Under your rulership, and with you as our leader, may we use, here and now, the good gifts we can only grasp passingly so that we may already possess your eternal gifts.

COLLECT FOR SUNDAY XXVIII

PRAYER

Tua nos, quaesumus, Domine, gratia semper et praeveniat et sequatur, ac bonis operibus iugiter praestet esse intentos.

May your grace, Lord, ever precede us and always follow us, and, may it grant us to be continually intent upon good works.

ORIGINAL SOURCE

The prayer is found throughout the Gregorian and Frankish Gelasian sources virtually unmodified[1], and has been incorporated from them into the Missal of Paul VI without any changes. For further comment on the original sources of the prayer, see the accompanying introductory note and table.

USE IN OTHER LITURGICAL SOURCES

As noted by Bruylants[2], the prayer is found in these sources: Dominica XVI post Pentecosten: A(1396), S(1251), Q(146), 1474(279), 1570, 1604, and in the uncritical editions G(244,2)[G 1532] and Z(881). The prayer is found as an oration for the office: COR(204,24)[H 966].

ANALYSIS OF THE PRAYER IN THE ORIGINAL SOURCE
Grammatical analysis[3]:

The collect is made up of (a) a simple address, and (b) two petitions

---

[1] The text in the second clause of G 1532 is slightly corrupt: *hac bonis operibus iugiter posset esse intentus.* A 1396 reads *subsequatur* in place of *sequatur*.

[2] Bruylants, II, 1150.

[3] For a more complete grammatical analysis, see Haessly, Rhetoric in the Sunday Collects of the Roman Missal, 107-108.

joined by the conjunction *ac*.

(a)   Address: *Domine*

(b)   1st Petition: *tua nos gratia semper et preveniat et sequatur,*

         2nd Petition: *ac*   [*nos*] *bonis operibus iugiter praestet esse intentos.*

In the first petition, the verbs *praevenire* and *sequi* are joined in an *et ... et* construction. Both divine actions are sought in tandem. As well, the verbs are both qualified by the adverb *semper* and share the same object, *nos*. The faithful ask that God's grace precede human action and that it follow or continue to inspire it.

The conjunction *ac* designates that the second petition is internally related to the first. In connection with the gift of God's grace inspiring, upholding and bringing their actions to completion, the community request that they may be intent upon carrying out good works. The *opera bona* are set in parallel with God's grace. In the same way that *praevenire* and *sequi* are qualified by *semper*, so too is *esse intentos* qualified by *iugiter*. This provides a neat parallel between God's actions and those of the faithful. Just as the community desires God's grace to inspire and uphold them always, it also wishes to be continually set upon responding appropriately by doing good works.

Note the all-encompassing role of grace, and the typical vocabulary for expressing the theology of grace. Grace comes before (*praevenire*), grants (*praestare*), makes the faithful intent (*esse intentos*), fills their actions (*bona opera*), and follows after the works and the lives of the faithful until their completion (*sequi*).

Vocabulary:

Prominent vocabulary: *gratia, praevenire, sequi, praestare, intentus,* and *bona opera.*

Our analysis of the oration's vocabulary will begin by examining some prayers which parallel the conjunction of *praevenire, sequi* and *gratia* found in H 966.

Tua nos ... gratia semper et praeveniat et sequatur[4]

The collect of a morning Mass for Easter Sunday sets out the faithfuls' belief that their actions, in this case their prayers (*vota*), are only effective when they are preceeded and inspired, upheld and carried through to completion by divine grace (*praevenire, adspirare, adiuuare, prosequi*). These divine graces are placed within the context of the paschal mystery; the resurrection, the defeat of death, and the opening of the way to eternal life. The prayer reads:

"*Deus qui hodierna die per unigenitum tuum aeternitatis nobis aditum deuicta morte reserasti, uota nostra quae praeueniendo adspiras, etiam adiuuando prosequere*" (H 383)[5].

The faithful's belief in their continuous need for God's grace, before, during and following their every action is expressed in the following lenten collect:

"*Actiones nostras quaesumus domine et aspirando praeueni, et adiuuando*

---

[4]For further examples of the use of *praevenire* see Deshusses, Concordances III, 3, 471-473. For the conjunction of *praevenire* and *sequi* see Blaise, Vocabulaire, § 270. For other examples of this typical vocabulary of grace see V 1316 and V 1416. See also the study of the collect for Week One in Ordinary Time (H 86).

[5]God, who on this day, through your only begotten Son, laid open for us the entrance to eternal life by overpowering death, through your help also follow and complete our prayers, which, in anticipation, you inspire in the first place.

prosequere ut cuncta nostra operatio et a te semper incipiat, et per te cepta finiatur" (H 198)[6].

In H 966, the faithful not only request that God's grace always anticipate, sustain and follow the community, but that from this encompassing in grace they may be always intent upon good works: *ac bonis operibus iugiter praestet esse intentos.*

The clause has some resonance with a verse in the Vulgate translation of the Letter to Titus, Tt 3:8[7]. There the faithful's solicitude to carry out good works is set within the community's entirely unmerited salvation in Christ and the Spirit (Tt 3:4-8). We will now turn our attention to the vocabulary of the clause itself, beginning with *praestare*.

Praestet[8]

Praestare, a common verb of petition in the early orations, has the same sense, and is used in the same constructions, as the verbs *dare* and *tribuere*.[9] In H 966, the faithful's request is that they be intent (*intentus*) on good works. The participial adjective *intentus* will first be analysed.

---

[6] Anticipate our actions with your inspiration, Lord, and with your help follow them to their completion, so that each and every one of our deeds may both always begin from you, and once undertaken, be brought to completion through you.
The prayer is found in the Missal of Paul VI: MR(1975) Fer. V post Cineres, Collecta, 181.

[7] *"ut curent bonis operibus praesse qui credunt Deo"* Tt 3:8.

[8] For further examples of the use of *praestare* see Deshusses, Concordances III, 3, 457-467.

[9] Blaise, Vocabulaire, § 67.

Esse intentos[10]

Intentus, found infrequently in the early sources, has the sense of being 'intent upon' an action. This intensity and commitment is evident in the following two prayers. The first, a blessing for Easter Sunday, relates the faithful's sense of being *intenti* to their propitious return to freedom in the resurrection. It is further associated with a range of good works, including knowing God, preaching him, praising him and loving him. The apposite section of the prayer reads:

"[*Deus*] *inclina aures tuas ad uota populi tui propitius ut hinc ad te recuperatorem suum sensus semper attollat intentos. Te cognoscat, se corrigat; te praedicet, se commendet; te colat, se muniat; te diligat, se praeparet ....*" (A 1824)[11].

In a lenten *super populum* God's grace is set in parallel with the intention of the community to enter into the lenten discipline of fasting and prayer:

"*Praesta nobis, domine, quaesumus, auxilium gratiae tuae, ut ieiuniis et*

---

[10] For further examples of the use of *intentere* see Deshusses, Concordances III, 2, 384. Note that the Deshusses' concordance indexes *intentus* under the verb *intentere*, while the adjective is found under *intendere* in Blaise, Ellebracht, Schnitker and Slaby, and the Lewis and Short dictionary. See Blaise, Vocabulaire, § 435; Ellebracht, Remarks on the Vocabulary of the Ancient Orations of the Missale Romanum, 89; Schnitker and Slaby, Concordantia, 1281-1282; and C.Lewis and C.Short, A Latin Dictionary.

[11] ... incline your ears, God, propitiously to the prayers of your people that from this place your people may life up their hearts and desires ever intent towards you, the one who has regained [them from captivity]. May this people know you and correct itself, preach you and commit itself to your care, revere you and strengthen itself, love you and prepare itself ....

orationibus conuenienter intenti liberemur ab hostibus mentis et corporis" (V 179)[12].

Both prayers associate *intentus* with the freedom and salvation that comes from the paschal mystery. Along with the implicit sense of determination, *intentus* also sounds a note of joy and thanksgiving for salvation.

In H 966, the community desires that God's grace lead them to do good works, *bona opera*. *Bona opera* has been discussed in the study of the collect for Sunday III[13]. Summarizing that discussion here, good works are those actions, already prepared by God, which enable the believer to walk in God's ways. Through them the baptized live out their election, adoption and redemption in Christ.

The adverb *iugiter* underlines the strength of their desire to respond continually in grace. Of course, this very response is itself in the first place inspired and supported by divine grace.

Meaning of the prayer:

The first petition sets forth the all-encompassing, all-enveloping role of grace in the life of the faithful. The community ask that God's grace always precede, inspire, uphold and bring to completion every moment and action of their lives. Stemming from this, they further specify that this all-encompassing grace may work in them to make them unceasingly intent on doing good works. This petition is itself inspired by God's grace, and can only come to completion through God's grace.

---

[12]Grant us, Lord, the help of your grace, so that, suitably intent upon the fast and prayer, we may be freed from enemies of mind and body.

[13]See above, 452.

Both *intentus* and *bona opera* fit well together. Good works are those actions prepared by God which the faithful carry out as they live completely in God's way. The sense of intention in the participial adjective *intentus* is a response to the liberation from sin brought about by the paschal mystery. It denotes an eagerness, driven by thanksgiving and joy, to embrace the new freedom won by Christ.

There are no noticeable changes to the meaning of the prayer when it is set in context as a collect for the Missal of Paul VI.

RELATIONSHIP OF THE CHRISTIAN PEOPLE TO GOD

For the community to live in God, their every action must always be preceded, inspired, upheld, carried out and brought to completion by grace. Through this their deeds are good works. The relationship of the Christian people to God is entirely enveloped in God's initiative and grace.

The Christian response to this grace is marked by an eagerness and intention to be continually engaged in good works. This determination, itself inspired, upheld and completed in grace, is a response in thanksgiving to the freedom that comes from salvation in Christ.

FREER TRANSLATION OF THE PRAYER

Tua nos, quaesumus, Domine, gratia semper et praeveniat et sequatur, ac bonis operibus iugiter praestet esse intentos.	May your grace, Lord, always inspire, uphold and follow our every action, thought and desire. May you make us unceasingly eager to accomplish your good works.

COLLECT FOR WEEK XXXIV

PRAYER

Excita, quaesumus, Domine, tuorum fidelium voluntates ut, divini operis fructum propensius exsequentes, pietatis tuae remedia maiora percipiant.

Lord, rouse up the wills of your faithful so that, more eagerly pursuing the fruit of divine work, they may receive even greater remedies of your loving kindness.

ORIGINAL SOURCE

The prayer is found throughout the Gregorian and Frankish Gelasian sources virtually unmodified, and has been incorporated from them into the Missal of Paul VI without any major changes[1].

Two features concerning the original sources will be commented upon here. Firstly the collect is of Roman origin. It does not appear in the Gallican sources[2] but is found in the *Hadrianum* (H 894) and the *Paduensis* (P 748).

The second point is that the Mass of which H 894 is the collect is transmitted as an integral whole throughout the early source tradition. In the *Paduensis*, the Supplement, and the Sacramentaries of Angoulême, Gellone and St Gall, our collect is accompanied by the same *super oblata* and post communion prayer. The same preface belongs to the Mass in the Supplement and in the three Frankish Gelasian sacramentaries. That preface is also found in the *Paduensis*, though for a different Mass. The only real interruption to this pattern is among the prayers *super populum*, where both the Sacramentaries of Gellone and Angoulême use different prayers. The Sacramentary of St Gall has no *super populum* for this Mass. All the prayers

---

[1] The only change is *quaesumus, Domine* for *domine quaesumus*.

[2] The term Gallican Sources here refers to the *Missale Gothicum*, *Missale Bobbiense*, *Missale Francorum*, and the *Missale Gallicanum Vetus*.

of the Mass, including the *super sindonem* and the two prayers *super populum* can be traced back to Roman sources. None are found in the Gallican sources. This information has been set out as economically as possible below. The table does not note when a prayer appears more than once in a given source.

TABLE 5. SOURCES OF THE MASS OF WHICH *H 894* IS THE COLLECT

	L	V	H	P	Sp	G	A	S
Col.	-	-	894	*748*	1198	*1621*	1487	*1334*
Sind.	-	*335*	900	*Nil*	Nil	*1622*	1488	*1335*
Scr.	603	-	-	*749*	1199	*1623*	1489	*1336*
UD.	869	-	859	*Nil*	1690	*1624*	1490	*1337*
Post Comm	1263	*15*	-	*750*	1200	*1625*	1491	*1338*

The *super populum* in the *Gellonensis* Mass, G 1626, is the same as L 79, H 907, A 1966, and G 1761. The corresponding *super populum* in the Sacramentary of Angoulême, A 1492, is very similar to V 1043, A 1382, G 1512, S 1237.

The above discussion has two implications for our study of the collect. The Roman origins of the prayer means that Roman sources are foundational for the study of the vocabulary. However, since the Gallican influenced liturgical sources have safeguarded the integrity of the Mass as a whole, the study of the prayer and its vocabulary in light of the other prayers of the Mass will be of considerable importance[3]. For our purposes, reference will be made to this Mass as it stands in the Sacramentary of Angoulême.

For further comment on the original sources of the prayer, see the accompanying introductory note and table.

USE IN OTHER LITURGICAL SOURCES

As noted by Bruylants[4], the prayer is found in these sources: Dominica XXIV et ultima post Pentecosten: A(1487), S(1334), P(748), OR(177)[Sp 1198], X(276,1), Q(149^v), 1474(298), 1570, 1604, and in these unedited sources G(262,1)[G 1621], Z(939), FrSal 3(40,1), FrSt(XLI,1), *Incipiunt orationes quotidianae*: COR(202,19)[H 894].

ANALYSIS OF THE PRAYER IN THE ORIGINAL SOURCE
Grammatical structure:[5]

The prayer is made up of (a) an address to God, (b) a petition, and (c) two interconnected purpose clauses, the first of which sets out the condition for attaining the second.

(a) Address: *Dominus*

(b) Petition: *excita, quaesumus ... tuorum fidelium voluntates*

---

[3]Interestingly, the collect, secret and post communion prayer still appear together in MR(1570) for the Twenty Fourth Sunday after Pentecost. It is only in MR(1975) that the Mass is disbanded. Only the collect has been retained in the Missal of Paul VI.

[4]See Bruylants, II, 548. For a more complete list of sources and manuscripts see Moeller, Corpus Orationum, IV, E-H, Orationes 2390-3028, oration 2555, 87.

[5]For a more complete grammatical analysis see Haessly, Rhetoric in the Sunday Collects of the Roman Missal, 120-121.

(c) Purpose: *ut*
  Condition: *divini operis fructum propensius exsequentes,*

  Ultimate purpose: *pietatis tuae remedia maiora percipiant.*

A variety of comments can be made concerning the structure of the prayer. The actions of God (*divinum opus*), as set out in the prayer, are God's rousing of the wills of the faithful (*excita voluntates*), and their reception of his remedies (*remedia percipiant*). The phrases *divini operis fructum* and *pietatis tuae remedia* are set in parallel. They are further connected through a play on the verb *percipere*. While in H 894 the object of *percipere* is the *remedia*, the verb can be used for the gathering of fruit (*fructus*)[6].

Propensius (*exsequi*), with its reference to the will, serves as the link between the object of the petition (*excitare*) *voluntates* and the object of the purpose clause *remedia* (*percipere*). The comparative form (*propensius*) of the adverb *propense* and the comparative form (*maiora*) of the adjective *magnus* are central to the dynamic of the prayer. The more willingly the faithful pursue the fruit of divine work, the greater the remedies they obtain.

Finally, the three verbs are all modified by prefixes, intensifying their meaning: <u>ex</u>*citare (cire),* <u>ex</u>*sequi (sequi),* and <u>per</u>*cipere (capio).*

Vocabulary:

Prominent vocabulary: *excitare, voluntas, divinum opus, fructus, propensius, exsequi, pietas, remedia, percipere.*

Our analysis of the vocabulary of the prayer will begin with a study of the petition, *excita ... tuorum fidelium voluntates.*

---

[6]Lewis and Short, A Latin Dictionary, 1879 (1962), s.v. "*percipio*", 1334. For some examples from the liturgical sources see V 600 and V 1048.

Excita .. voluntates

The petition focuses the oration upon the will (*voluntas*[7]) of the faithful. The verb *excitare*[8], an intensified form of *cire*, means to stimulate, to rouse up. It is also used in the *super sindonem* (A 1488) of the same Mass in the Sacramentary of Angoulême, where its object is the hearts of the faithful. In the *super sindonem* three things are brought together, the study of divine teaching, its understanding, and the readiness to follow it. The oration reads: "*Excita Domine tuorum corda fidelium, ut sacris intenta doctrinis, et intellegant quod sequantur, et sequendo fideliter adprehendant*" (A 1488)[9].

Note the link between the church's petition that God rouse their hearts and the faithful's attention to divine teaching, as expressed in the words *intentus* and *exsequi*.

When set together, the collect and the *super sindonem* concern themselves with the willingness and eagerness of the whole inner human, heart and will. Similarly, the two prayers set in parallel the fruit of divine work and the place that divine teaching has in the people's lives, when it is studied, understood, and followed.

In H 894 God is called upon to rouse up the wills of his faithful so that they may more willingly pursue and seek out the fruit of divine works, *divini operis fructum propensius exsequentes*. Our examination of this expression will begin with the phrase *divini operis fructum*.

---

[7] *Voluntas* has been studied in the analysis of the collect for Sunday XXIX. See above, 296.

[8] For further examples of the use of *excitare* see Deshusses, Concordances III, 2, 59. For an example of *excita voluntates* see V 1222.

[9] Lord, rouse up the hearts of your faithful so that, intent upon your sacred teachings, they may both understand what they are attending to, and, by faithfully attending, comprehend it.

Divini operis fructum exsequentes propensius
Divini operis fructum

The scarcity in the early euchology of clear parallels for this phrase has led to some speculation as to its interpretation. It can either refer to the fruit of the work that God does, or to the fruit of those efforts of the faithful which are in line with God's will.

Both Capelle[10] and Brou[11] see it as equivalent to *fructum boni operis*, and understand it to signify the divine fruit of our good works. Brou's argument, based on two supports, is the more fully developed. Firstly he can find no prayer in the early euchology which contains the phrase. This leads him to examine it in the light of the similar expression *fructus boni operis*. The phrase is found in H 180, a lenten prayer that Brou ascribes to the authorship of Gregory the Great. This Gregorian authorship is significant. Brou recognizes that the two main expressions in our collect, *divini operis fructus* and *pietatis tuae remedia*, are typically, and somewhat exclusively, found in the writings of Gregory the Great. Brou's examination of the expression *divini operis fructus*, especially in light of Gregory's use of it in Homily XIX of his Homiliarum in Ezechielem II,[12] leads him to conclude that the phrase refers to the moral fruits of those whom God has chosen to work in his vineyard, that is, the fruits of good works.

Further support for Brou's position can be found in the liturgical use of *fructus*. The noun is commonly used to express the fruit of the good works of

---

[10] Capelle translates the prayer as follows: "*Excitez, Seigneur, les volontés de vos fidèles, pour que, plus assidûment appliqués à produire le fruit divin des bonnes oeuvres, ils reçoivent d'autant plus largement les secours de votre bonté.*" See B.Capelle, Travaux liturgiques I, 265-266.

[11] L.Brou, Les Oraisons des dimanches après la Pentecôte, 122-127.

[12] Gregory I, Homiliarum in Ezechielem II, PL, 76, 1155, § 2.

the faithful, *fructus bonorum operum* (V 722, Sp 1708, Sp 1751, Sp 1742). A rare example of the application of *fructus* to God's work is found in the Gallican blessing G 2020, where God's fruits include freedom from evil and war, tranquility, peace, security and freedom in the present.

However, an alternative, and more probable reading emerges from a study of the structure of the collect, along with an examination of the other prayers of the Mass in the Sacramentary of Angoulême. The prayer, and the Mass itself, seem to indicate that *divinum opus* is a reference to God's work. For their part, the faithful wish to willingly pursue the fruit in themselves (*fructus*) of this divine work. We will first examine the sense of *divinum opus* as God's work.

The collect sets *diuini operis fructum* and *pietatis tuae remedia* in parallel, implying that both *pietas tua* and *divinum opus* refer to God's actions and intentions.

As well, the preface (A 1490) of the Mass in the Sacramentary of Angoulême provides an interpretation of *opus*. The prayer reads:
"*UD. Tuum est enim omne quod uiuimus, quia licet peccati uulnere natura nostra uitiata sit, tui tamen est operis ut a terrena generati ad caelestia renascamur*" (A 1490)[13].

Tuum opus is clearly a reference to God's work, here specified as the rebirth to eternal things of our earthly and wounded human nature[14].

---

[13] It is right and fitting: It is entirely through you that we live, because, although our nature has been corrupted by the wound of sin, nevertheless, it is through your work that we, who have been born of the things of earth may be reborn unto the things of heaven.

[14] For other examples of *tuum opus* as God's work see L 11 and G 1714.

The following schema sets out the parallelism between the collect, *super sindonem*, and the offertory prayer. The preface has already been seen above.

Collect	Super sindonem	Secreta
Excita dne qs tuorum fidelium uoluntates	*Excita dne tuorum corda fidelium*	*... ad te conuerte*
ut propensius exsequentes	*ut intenta*	
diuini operis, pietatis tuae remedia maiora percipiant	*sacris doctrinis*	*ut a terrenibus cupiditatibus liberi*
(divini operis) fructum propensius exsequentes	*et intellegant quod sequantur, et sequendo fideliter adprehendant.*	*in caelestibus desideriis transeamus.*

This internal evidence makes it apparent that *diuinum opus* refers to such divine works as sacred teaching, freedom from earthly temptation, and the rebirth of our earthly and wounded human nature. As well, the divine work is also expressed in the petitions of both the collect and the *super sindonem*, where God is asked to rouse up the wills and hearts of the faithful; *excita ... voluntates, excita ... corda.*

The faithful ask that God rouse their wills so that they may willingly pursue the fruit (*fructus*) of his work. The sense of *fructus* will now be examined.

Fructum[15]

While the prayer asks for the fruit of God's action, the fruit itself appears to be the action of the faithful that God's work produces. As already

---

[15] For further examples of the use of *fructus* see Deshusses, Concordances III, 2, 185-187.

noted, *fructus* is most commonly used to express the fruit of the good works of the faithful. Both the collect and the *super sindonem* from the Mass in the Sacramentary of Angoulême contain a contrast between God's action and the action of the faithful. This contrast can be set out as follows:

	GOD'S ACTION	FAITHFULS'ACTIONS
A 1487	*Excita uoluntates, diuinum opus, remedia percipiant*	*(diuini operis) fructum propensius exsequentes*
A 1488	*Excita corda*	*sacris intenta doctrinis, intellegant quod sequantur, sequendo adprehendant.*

The *diuini fructum operis*, then, appears to point to human actions and fruits which are the result of God's own work. The faithful desire that, with God rousing their wills, they may pursue and follow through on these actions evermore willingly, *propensius exsequentes*. This expression will now be studied.

Propensius exsequentes

Exsequi has already been discussed in the study of the collect for Sunday XI[16]. In A 1487 it is qualified by the comparative form of the adverb *propense*[17]. The adverb, a derivative of *propendere*, signals the inclination and favour of the will. *Propensius*, then, acts as a link between the petition and the final purpose clause. The purpose of the petition to rouse up their wills is that the faithful may follow willingly. The use of the comparative form of the adverb is in parallel with *maiora* (*remedia percipiant*). The more willingly the

---

[16]See above, 308.

[17]For further examples of the use of *propense* see Deshusses, Concordances III, 3, 506-507.

faithful pursue the fruit of divine work in them, the greater the *remedia* the faithful may receive.

The faithful's petition is that, in taking up the fruit of God's work more willingly, they wish to receive the ever more momentous remedies of God's loving kindness, *pietatis tuae remedia maiora percipiant*. This petition will now be examined, beginning with the noun *remedia*.

Remedia[18]

Remedium, with its medical connotations of antidote, refers to the healing aid that God provides. It can point to healing and assistance in the present, and as well has an eschatological dimension as the healing that is eternal life.

The eschatological sense is clear in the lenten collect H 292, where the attainment of eternal remedies is related to participation in the fast. These *remedia* are also connected with the expiatory power of the fast. The prayer reads:

"*Nostra tibi quaesumus domine sint accepta ieiunia quae nos et expiando gratiae tuae dignos efficiant et ad remedia perducant aeterna*" (H 292)[19].

Remedium is used to express the effects of the redemption won by Christ[20]. In a vesper prayer for paschaltide, the expression *pietatis tuae remedia percipere* refers to the reception of the salvation that has come from the paschal mystery. The unceasing reception of these remedies is linked to abstinence from sin and purity of service:

---

[18]For further examples of the use of *remedium* see Deshusses, Concordances III, 4, 56-58. See also Ellebracht, Remarks on the Vocabulary of the Ancient Orations in the Missale Romanum, 186-187.

[19]May our fast be acceptable to you Lord, and through its expiation, may it make us worthy of your grace, and lead us to eternal remedies.

[20]Blaise, Vocabulaire, § 228.

"*Largere, quaesumus, aecclesiae tuae, deus, et a suis semper et ab alienis abstinere delictis, ut pura tibi mente deseruiens pietatis tuae remedia sine cessatione percipiat*" (V 540)[21].

The context of A 1487 within the Mass in the Sacramentary of Angoulême helps elucidate the workings of *pietatis tuae remedia*. The collect itself connects the reception of these remedies with the willing action of the faithful, expressed as *propensius exsequentes*.

In the post communion of the Mass (A 1491), the faithful express their faith in the healing power of communion, which is curative of the corruption of our minds:

"*Concede nobis Domine quaesumus, ut sacramenta quae sumpsimus quicquid in nostra mente uitiosum est, ipsius medicationis dono curetur*" (A 1491)[22].

Note that *remedium* is typically found in post communion prayers, and occasionally in offertory prayers as well[23]. There it points to the healing actions of the sacraments, which is completely gratuitous, and takes evil out of the heart and mind.

There is a further parallel between the collect and the *super sindonem* in the dynamic of both willing and searching which is operative in both petitions. Just as the collect asks that the faithful pursue and seek ever more fully the fruit of the divine work in them, so too the petition in the *super sindonem* is

---

[21]Grant to your church, Lord, always to hold back from transgressions as well as from commiting the offences of heretics/ pagans, so that, serving you with a pure mind, it may unceasingly receive the remedies of your mercy. This relationship of *remedia* to the paschal mystery is also seen in V 517, V 527 and V 537, orations from the same set of paschal vesper prayers.

[22]Grant to us Lord, that the sacraments which we have taken may, by their medicinal gift, heal whatever is corrupt in our minds.

[23]See Blaise, Vocabulaire, § 253.

that the community may be intent upon sacred teachings, follow them, understand them, and faithfully grasp them.

In H 894, the divine *remedia* are described as coming from God's merciful kindness, *pietas tua*. This divine *pietas* will now be examined.

Pietatis tuae

The divine *pietas* has already been discussed in the study of the collect for Sunday XXVII. Summarizing that discussion here, in the Vulgate translation of the scriptures, the divine *pietas* denotes the mystery of God's loving kindness in Christ (1 Tm 3:16). The early liturgical sources associate it particularly with the forgiveness of sin.

Maiora

The *remedia* are further qualified by the comparative adjective *maiora*. The sense is that the more willingly the faithful follow up God's work, the greater the healing they are able to receive. A similar construction *beneficia pociora percipere* is seen in the following post communion prayer from the feast of the Archangel Michael. In this prayer, the reception of the still greater favour of God's grace is linked with the intercession of the Archangel. Note that the sense of *beneficia* is broader than the reception of the sacrament. The prayer reads:

"*Adesto plebi tuae, misericors deus, et ut graciae tuae beneficia pociora percipiat. beati Michahelis archangeli fac supplicem depraecacionibus subleuari*" (V 1036)[24].

---

[24] Be present to your people, merciful God, and so that your people may receive ever more complete benefits of your grace, make our supplication be raised up to you by the intercessions of blessed Michael the Archangel. The text in Moeller reads ... *potiora percipiat, beati* ... See Moeller, Corpus Orationum I, A-C, orationes 1-880, oration 168, 89.

Percipiant[25]

Percipere, meaning to receive, is commonly used in the early sources. Its use in H 894 is in line with the above examples V 540 and V 1036.

Meaning of the prayer:

The faithful petition God to rouse up their wills. This is based in their belief that the greater their effort to bring forth and pursue further the fruit of God's work in them, the greater the response of God in giving healing graces.

The *divinum opus* points to the paschal mystery, through which our earthly and wounded human nature is reborn to eternal things. The *remedia* connote especially the medicinal action of the sacraments, which frees and heals the heart and mind from evil.

Examination of the sources reveals that the prayer is almost invariably placed very close to the beginning of Advent[26]. Our vocabulary study does not seem to point to any specific Advent content in the prayer. There are, however, aspects in the prayer which make it a fitting preparation for the Advent fast and the celebration of the incarnation. As seen in H 292, fasting, which is given an expiatory power, is associated with the attainment of the eternal *remedia*. The divine *pietas* connotes the mystery of God's loving kindness, which is manifested most fully in the Incarnation.

The prayer undergoes no change of meaning when set in its context as a collect in ordinary time in the Missal of Paul VI. It is worth noting that a similar conjunction of God's *opus* and its fruit, *fructus,* is found in the collect for the votive Mass of the Most Precious Blood of Christ. Here the work of God's mercy, *opus misericordiae tuae*, is set in parallel with the mystery of

---

[25]For further examples of the use of *percipere* see Deshusses, Concordances III, 3, 330-334.

[26]See Moeller, Corpus Orationum IV, 87.

salvation, *nostrae salutis mysterium*. The faithful's petition is that they may obtain and pursue the fruit of this mystery in them, *eiusdem fructum*. The prayer reads:

"*Deus, qui pretioso Unigeniti tui Sanguine universos homines redemisti, conserva in nobis opus misericordiae tuae, ut, nostrae salutis mysterium iugiter recolentes, eiusdem fructum consequi mereamur*" (MR(1975) De Pret. Sang. D.N.Iesu Christi, Collecta, 860)[27].

RELATIONSHIP OF THE CHRISTIAN PEOPLE TO GOD

The relationship of the Christian people to God directly involves the willing action of the faithful. The more their will is given over to pursuing the fruit of God's action in them, the more they receive the healing graces of God's loving kindness.

However, the willing response of the church itself is both a response to the mystery of God's loving kindness and takes place within this mystery. The baptized wish to take up ever more fully the healing fruit of the redemption that has come in Christ. This redemption is the ultimate expression of God's *pietas*. At the same time, the community's very desire itself for God's healing comes from God.

---

[27] God, who through the precious blood of your Only Begotten Son redeemed all humankind, preserve the work of your mercy, so that, unceasingly recalling the mystery of our salvation, we may merit to obtain and pursue the fruit of that same mystery.

FREER TRANSLATION OF THE COLLECT

Excita, quaesumus, Domine, tuorum fidelium voluntates, ut, divini operis fructum propensius exsequentes, pietatis tuae remedia maiora percipiant.

Lord, rouse up the wills of your faithful people. May we, following ever more willingly the fruit of your work in us, receive ever more fully the remedies of your loving kindness.

CHAPTER EIGHT
PRAYERS FROM THE AMBROSIAN SOURCES:
THE COLLECTS FOR SUNDAYS XIII, XVI and XIX

INTRODUCTION

According to Dumas, the collects for Sundays XIII, XVI and XIX have been brought into the Missal of Paul VI from the ancient Milanese sacramentaries[1]. The Ambrosian rite, so called after one of Milan's most famous bishops, is itself probably of Roman origin. The city, however, developed its own liturgical forms and texts, though this development did not preclude borrowing texts and feasts from Roman sources[2].

SOURCES OF THE AMBROSIAN RITE

As well as the descriptions and commentaries on the liturgical life of the city found in various patristic sources[3], a number of liturgical texts have survived to the present[4]. The most ancient extant sacramentaries with critical

---

[1] A.Dumas, "Les sources du nouveau Missel romain", Notitiae 7 (1971): 94.

[2] For studies of the Milanese rite see P.Lejay, "Ambrosien (Rit)," DACL I, 1373-1442; Archdale A. King, Liturgies of the Primatial Sees (Milwaukee: The Bruce Publishing Company, 1957), 286-453; and A.Paredi, "Milanese Rite," in The New Catholic Encyclopedia (New York: McGraw Hill, 1967).

[3] See King, Liturgies of the Primatial Sees, 323-324.

[4] For a description of the major extant Ambrosian manuscripts see R.Amiet, "La tradition manuscrite du missel ambrosien," Scriptorum 14 (1960): 16-60. This section is based largely on Amiet.

editions are the *Sacramentarium Triplex* (Triplex), the Sacramentary of Ariberto (Ariberto), the *Sacramentarium Bergomense* (Bergom), the Sacramentary of Biasca (Biasca) and the Sacramentary of Milan (Milan)[5]. These sacramentaries, all quite similar in their prayer texts and sanctoral cycle, most probably were produced following an eighth century revision of the rite. Quite a large number of prayers are held in common with Roman sources, as can be seen in the concordance of Roman and Ambrosian sources in the Paredi edition of the *Bergomense*[6].

The *Sacramentarium Triplex*, thought to have been produced at the monastery in St Gall, is dated by Heiming around 1010[7]. While not the oldest extant Ambrosian manuscript, it is regarded as one of the most ancient

---

[5]O.Heiming, Das Sacramentarium Triplex: Die Handschrift C 43 der Zentralbibliothek Zürich, 1. Teil: Text, 2 Teil: Wortschatz und Ausdrucksformen, Corpus Ambrosiano Liturgicum I, Liturgiewissenschaftliche Quellen und Forschungen 49 (Münster: Aschendorff, 1968);
A.Paredi, "Il Sacramentario di Ariberto: Edizione del ms. D 3,2 della Biblioteca del Capitolo Metropolitano di Milano," in Miscellanea Adriano Bernareggi, (Bergamo: Edizioni Opera B. Barbarigo, 1958), 329-488;
A.Paredi, Sacramentarium Bergomense: Manoscritto del secolo IX della Biblioteca di S.Alessandro in Colonna in Bergamo, Monumenta Bergomensia VI, (Bergamo: Fondazione Amministrazione Provinciale, 1962);
O.Heiming, Das Ambrosianische Sakramentar von Biasca: Die Handschrift Mailand Ambrosiana A 24 bis inf., 1 Teil: Text, Corpus Ambrosiano Liturgicum II, Liturgiewissenschaftliche Quellen und Forschungen 51 (Münster: Aschendorff, 1969);
J.Frei, Das Ambrosianische Sakramentar D 3-3 aus dem Mailändischen Metropolitankapitel, Corpus Ambrosiano Liturgicum III, Liturgiewissenschaftliche Quellen und Forschungen 56 (Münster: Aschendorff, 1974). This sacramentary is sometimes referred to as the Sacramentary of St Simplicius.
   The abbreviations in brackets follow those used by Moeller in the Corpus Orationum series.

[6]Paredi, Sacramentarium Bergomense, 379-553. The table is attributed to G.Fassi.

[7]O.Heiming, Das Sacramentarium Triplex, lx.

witnesses to the Milanese liturgy. As its title seeks to suggest, it is actually composed of three sources, an eighth century Gelasian sacramentary, a Gregorian sacramentary, and an Ambrosian sacramentary. Excerpts from each manuscript have been copied into their apposite place within the framework that is somewhat typical of Gregorian and Milanese sacramentaries. Thus the temporal and the sanctoral are mixed, and are followed by various commons and votive Masses. The text contains only the prayers said by the presider. The different sources are clearly marked in the manuscript as *Gelasiana* or G, *Gregoriana* or GG, or *Ambrosiana* or A. Since the sections marked *Ambrosiana* have been copied from an earlier sacramentary, the *Sacramentarium Triplex* offers a window into the earlier Ambrosian liturgical tradition.

The Sacramentary of Ariberto is also a 'pure' sacramentary, containing only the prayers for the celebrant, with temporal and sanctoral mixed together. In this case the celebrant may well have been Aribert, Archbishop of Milan (1018-1045). It is thought that he may have commissioned the work, which was produced in the first half of the eleventh century.

Unlike the Sacramentary of Ariberto, the eleventh century *Bergomense* is an augmented sacramentary, containing an antiphonary and lectionary. As well, in the sacramentary proper, the priest's prayers are augmented with the Epistles and Gospels. The temporal and sanctoral are together. The manuscript betrays monastic influences and additions, though the particular monastery remains unidentified.

The Sacramentary of Biasca is an earlier text, generally dated at the end of the ninth century. It, too, is an augmented sacramentary, containing formulae for the celebrant, as well as Epistles and Gospels. The temporal and sanctoral are together.

The Sacramentary of Milan appears to have been produced during the eleventh century. Like the *Bergomense* it is of monastic provenance, though the particular monastery remains unknown. It is an augmented sacramentary, with the Epistles and Gospels included in the text. However it is also unique among the texts that we are considering in that the temporal and sanctoral are separate.

A DESCRIPTION OF THE AMBROSIAN RITE

Before examining the texts themselves it is valuable to have an outline of the Ambrosian liturgy. The Sacramentary of Ariberto[8], the Sacramentary of Biasca[9] and the *Bergomense*[10] each gives an order of the Mass. The earliest known actual account of the Ambrosian liturgy appears to be that offered by Beroldus, Archbishop of Milan (1120-1125)[11]. In light of these sources, the Milanese Mass can be set out as follows:

Introductory rites: *Gloria* and *Kyrie*

Incipit Missa Canonica: *Oratio super populum* [Note: this prayer corresponds to the collect of the Mass].
Scripture readings:

Oratio super sindonem:

Offering of the gifts:

Oratio super oblata   [Note: in the *Sacramentarium Triplex* this prayer is named the *secreta*].

---

[8]Ariberto, *Incipit Laus Angelorum* (Ariberto 564-588).

[9]Biasca, XCVI, *Incipit laus angelorum* (Biasca 755-780).

[10]*Bergomense*, 198, *Incipit Laus Missae*, (Bergom 809-828).

[11]M.Magistretti, Beroldus sive Ecclesiae Ambrosianae Mediolanensis Kalendarium et Ordines Saec. XII (Mediolani: Josephi Giovanola et Soc., 1894; reprint Farnborough, England: Gregg International Publishers Limited, 1968), 46-53.

Eucharistic prayer and rite: *praefatio, canon*:

Communion rite:

Post communionem [Note: in the *Sacramentarium Triplex* this prayer is called the *Oratio ad complendum*].

THE AMBROSIAN ORATIONS IN THE MISSAL OF PAUL VI

The collects in the Missal of Paul VI for Sundays XVI (Triplex 1744) and XIII (Triplex 1750) appear to be of Milanese origin. They served as prayers for the Rogation day litanies that preceded the feast of Pentecost[12]. However the prayer cited by Dumas as the source for Sunday XIX, Triplex 1494[13], appears to be a slightly adapted version of a Roman prayer found in the *Paduense*, P 745, collect for the seventh Sunday after the feast of the Archangel Michael. The original Roman prayer is also present in the *Sacramentarium Triplex*, Triplex 2683 (*super sindonem, Dominica XXVI post Pentecosten, Gelasiana*). While the intention of the compilers of the Missal of Paul VI has been to draw an oration from the Ambrosian sources, the prayer is Roman[14].

In view of the Milanese provenance of our orations, though with due provision made for the collect for Sunday XIX, this study will draw on Ambrosian sources as much as possible when elucidating the meaning of the prayers. Roman sources will not be entirely ruled out due to the close textual

---

[12]There is some variance in the early Milanese sacramentaries. In the *Bergomense* and the Sacramentary of Biasca the Rogation days are immediately before Pentecost, while in the *Sacramentarium Triplex* they come before the feast of the Ascension. For commentary on the history and practices of the Ambrosian Rogation liturgy see King, Liturgies of the Primatial Sees, 367-369.

[13]Dumas, "Les sources du nouveau Missel romain", Notitiae 7 (1971): 94. Dumas numbers the orations according to their usage in the *Bergomense*. He cites the prayer as Bergom 634.

[14]The Roman origins of the prayer are discussed below. See 569.

relationship between the two traditions. The vocabulary concordance drawn up for the *Sacramentarium Triplex*[15] will serve as the basic instrument for the word study. No concordance appears to have been developed for the critical editions of the other major sacramentaries. Also helpful is the list of *incipits* for the *Bergomense* and the Sacramentary of Ariberto drawn up by Combaluzier[16]. Due to its accompanying concordance, the *Sacramentarium Triplex* will serve as the main critical edition for our study. When a prayer text is cited as part of the analysis, its place in each of the four sacramentaries will be noted. Where less than four texts are listed, it means that the prayer only appears in those sacramentaries. When an example is also to be found in an early Roman liturgical source, this too will be indicated.

The following tables place the three collects within their original contexts among the four Ambrosian sacramentaries. There are a number of features of interest. The rogation litanies are absent in the Sacramentaries of Ariberto and Milan. However the Sacramentary of Milan utilizes some of the Rogation prayers as either collects or prayers *super sindonem* in Masses outside of Easter and Pentecost. This is another pointer to the flexibility of this style of oration. While a number of the Mass and Rogation prayers are of Milanese origin, they are combined with prayers from the earliest Roman sources, an indication of the close textual relationship between the two rites. This interdependence can be especially seen in the Ambrosian Mass for Easter Saturday where the collect, post communion and vesper prayer correspond to the Gregorian Mass for the Saturday in Easter Week, while our prayer, the *super sindonem*, has been borrowed from another Mass in the *Paduensis*.

---

[15] O.Heiming, Das Sacramentarium Triplex, 2 Teil: Wortschatz und Ausdrucksformen.

[16] F.Combaluzier, Sacramentaires de Bergame et D'Ariberto: Table des matières et index des formules, Instrumenta Patristica 5, (Steenbrugis: In Abbatia Sancti Petri, 1962).

The tables will follow the order of the prayers as they are found in the Ambrosian sources. Brackets denote that an oration is similar. When a prayer appears more than once in an Ambrosian sacramentary, that will also be noted.

The ensuing studies are arranged according to the order of the prayers in the *Sacramentarium Triplex*. The study of the collect for Sunday XIX will be presented first, followed by the studies of the collects for Sundays XVI and XIII.

TABLE 6. SOURCES OF THE COLLECT FOR SUNDAY XIX:
super sindonem Triplex 1494

	Collct	*Sup Sin*	Sup obl	VD	Post comm	Alia	Ad vesp
Trip	1493 1480	*1494*	1495	*1496*	1497 1485	*1498 1436*	1499
Arib	470	*471*	472	*473*	474	*Nil*	Nil
Berg	633	*634*	635	*636*	637	*638 607*	639 607
Biasca	602	*603*	604	*605*	606	*607*	608
Milan	363	*359*	360	*Nil*	362	*Nil*	Nil
Veron	Nil	*Nil*	Nil	*Nil*	L 417 L 1372	*Nil*	Nil
Reg 316	Nil	*Nil*	(V456)	*Nil*	Nil	*Nil*	(V484)
Greg	H 429 P 366	*P 745*	(H384) (H393) (P328)	*Nil*	H 432 P 368	*Nil*	H 434 P 370

TABLE 7. SOURCES OF THE COLLECT FOR SUNDAY XVI:
Final prayer *Orationes in die secondo in laetanie*

Triplex	1739	1740	1741	1742	1743	1744
Aribert	Nil	Nil	Nil	Nil	Nil	Nil
Bergom	714	715	716	717	718	719
Biasca	683	684	685	686	687	688
Milan	428* 599**	Nil	Nil	1238***	Nil	Nil
Veron	L 468	Nil	(L 582)	Nil	Nil	Nil
Reg 316	Nil	V 1323	(V1421) (V1479)	Nil	Nil	Nil
Greg	H 470 P 404	Nil	Nil	Nil	Nil	Nil

* LXXII, *Item alia Missa de Laetania, oratio super sindomen.*

** CV, *Dominica XX Post Octaua Pentecosten, oratio super populum* (opening collect).

*** CCXVIII, *Missa Pro Tribulantibus uel Pressura Sustinentibus, super sindonem.*

TABLE 8. SOURCES OF THE COLLECT FOR SUNDAY XIII:
First prayer *Orationes in die tertio in laetanie*

Trip	*1750*	1751	*1752*	1753	*1754*	1755	*1756*	1757	*1758*
Arib	*Nil*	Nil	*Nil*	Nil	*Nil*	Nil	*Nil*	Nil	*Nil*
Berg	*725*	726	*727*	728	*729*	730	*731*	732	*733*
Biasc	*694*	695	*696*	697	*689*	699	*700*	701	*702*
Milan	*Nil*	Nil	*Nil*	Nil	*Nil*	1242*	*Nil*	Nil	*Nil*
Roman	*Nil*	V1198 P 591 **	*Nil*	Nil	*Nil*	Nil	*Nil*	Nil	*Nil*

* CCXVIIII, *Item alia Missa pro Tribulante,* opening collect.

** This prayer has been included in the Missal of Paul VI as the collect for Sunday XXVI in Ordinary Time. See above, 476.

COLLECT FOR SUNDAY XIX

PRAYER

Omnipotens sempiterne Deus, quem paterno nomine invocare praesumimus, perfice in cordibus nostris spiritum adoptionis filiorum, ut promissam hereditatem ingredi mereamur.

All powerful, eternal God, whom we dare to invoke by the name Father, perfect in our hearts the spirit of adoption as your children, so that we may merit to enter the promised inheritance.

USE IN THE MISSAL OF PAUL VI

This collect for the Mass of Sunday XIX in Ordinary Time is also the opening prayer for the Mass of Monday, Week II in the season of Easter[1].

ORIGINAL SOURCE

Dumas[2] indicates that the collect has been introduced into the Missal of Paul VI from the *Bergomense*:

"*Omnipotens sempiterne deus, quem docente spiritu sancto paterno nomine inuocare praesumimus, effice in nobis filiorum corda fidelium, ut hereditatem promissam mereamur ingredi per debitam seruitutem*" (Bergom 634)[3].

This prayer is found in the Ambrosian sources as the *super sindonem* for the Mass of the Saturday in Easter Week, *Sabbato ad Sanctum Iohannem, item alia eiusdem in Ecclesia Maiore*, (Triplex 1494, Bergom 634, Ariberto

---

[1] MR(1975): Fer II post domm. II, IV et VI Paschae, Collecta hebd., II, 315.

[2] Dumas, "Les sources du nouveau Missel romain," Notitiae 7 (1971): 94.

[3] Almighty all powerful God, whom by the teaching of the Holy Spirit we dare to invoke by the name Father, effect in us hearts of faithful children, so that through the service that we owe to you we may merit to enter the promised inheritance.

471, Biasca 603, Milano 359). The oration, in this form, does not appear to be used in any liturgical sources outside of the Milanese tradition[4]. It is found in the current Ambrosian Missal: *Sabbato octavae paschae, ad complendem liturgiam verbi*, 116/4, 286. Note the substitution of *debita servitute* for *per debitam seruitutem*.

However, the Ambrosian prayer appears to be a modification of the Roman oration P 745, the *super sindonem* for the seventh Sunday after the feast of St Michael[5]. This prayer reads:

"*Deus, quem docente spiritu sancto paterno nomine inuocare praesumimus, crea in nobis filiorum corda fidelium, ut hereditatem promissam adgredi ualeamus per debitam seruitutem*" (P 745)[6].

The set of nine Sunday Masses after the feast of the Archangel Michael form part of the adaptation made to the papal Gregorian sacramentary to accommodate it to presbyteral use[7]. This adaptation was probably completed by the middle of the seventh century. The majority of the formulae for the

---

[4] Note that the relevant edition of Moeller's Corpus Orationum series has yet to be published.

[5] As noted by Moeller, this Roman prayer also appears in the following texts: Engol 1482, Fulda 1690, Gellon 1616, Lateran 134, Phill 1014, Prag 208,1, Rhen 935, Salzb 328, Sangall 1326 and Triplex 2683, as well as Toledo³ 855. It is usually incorporated in a Mass for a Sunday after Pentecost or a Sunday after the feast of the dedication of the Basilica of St Michael. Note, however, that it is used in the *Lateran* as an oratio following a vigil reading: *Sabbato in XII lectionibus post Pentecosten, V oratio*. See Moeller, Corpus Orationum II, D, orationes 881-1707, oration 1320, 212.

[6] Almighty all powerful God, whom by the teaching of the Holy Spirit we dare to invoke by the name Father, create in us hearts of faithful children, so that through the service that we owe to you we may be able to approach the promised inheritance.

[7] See Vogel, Medieval Liturgy, 94. For a study of these particular Masses and their sources see Chavasse, Le Sacramentaire Gélasien, 531-546.

added Sunday presbyteral Masses were borrowed from *Reginensis* 316, though a much smaller number were also taken from the *Hadrianum* and the *Veronensis*. Most often the compiler simply transposed, as a whole, the appropriate prayers from a Mass from *Reginensis* 316 into the modified Gregorian. Our collect, P 745, though, is one of the very few such borrowed Sunday Mass prayers not found in *Reginensis* 316, the *Veronensis* or the *Hadrianum*[8].

This original Roman prayer also stands in the *Sacramentarium Triplex* as the *super sindonem* for the Mass *Dominica XXVI post Pentecosten, Gelasiana,* Triplex 2683. There is only one modification, the Triplex prayer reading *ingredi* for *adgredi*.

Since it seems that the intention of the compilers of the Missal of Paul VI was to model the collect for Sunday XIX on Triplex 1494, and that the vocabulary of the collect in the Missal is closer to Triplex 1494 than to P 745, our study of the structure and vocabulary of the original source will be based on the text of Triplex 1494.

CHANGES TO THE ORIGINAL SOURCE

The prayer has undergone two sets of changes. The first was when P 745 was modified on incorporation into the Ambrosian liturgy. *Crea in nobis* became *effice in nobis*, while *ingredi ualeamus* became *mereamur ingredi*. The import of these changes will be discussed below.

The modifications made to Triplex 1494 for incorporation into the Missal of Paul VI are more far reaching. The reference to the teaching activity of the Holy Spirit, *docente spiritu sancto*, has been deleted. The

---

[8]The others are P 94, P 517, P 518 and P 730. See Chavasse, Le Sacramentaire Gélasien, 544. Note that P 517 has also been incorporated into the Missal of Paul VI as the collect for Sunday XVII. For a study of this prayer see above, 511.

petition has also been revised. *Effice in nobis filiorum corda fidelium* now reads *perfice in cordibus nostris spiritum adoptionis filiorum*. In a third change, the direct relationship between entry to the promised inheritance and worship has been downplayed through the deletion of the phrase *per debitam seruitutem*.

ANALYSIS OF THE PRAYER IN THE ORIGINAL SOURCE

For further comment on the origins of the prayer, as well as the relationship between the Ambrosian and Roman liturgical sources, see the introductory note 'Prayers from the Ambrosian Sources: An Introduction to the Collects for Sundays XIII, XVI and XIX.'

The readings set down for the Mass for the Saturday of Holy Week, either 1 Tm 2:1-7 and Jo 21:1-14 (Biasca, Bergom) or 1 Tm 2:1-7 and Jo 20:1-9 (Milano), are not closely related to the theme, structure or vocabulary of the *super sindonem*. No readings are given in the *Sacramentarium Triplex*.

Grammatical structure:

The prayer is made up of (a) an address to God, (b) a motivating clause, (c) a petition, and (d) a purpose clause.

(a) Address: *Omnipotens sempiterne Deus,*

(b) Motivation: *quem docente spiritu sancto paterno nomine inuocare praesumimus,*

(c) Petition: *effice in nobis filiorum corda fidelium,*

(d) Purpose: *ut hereditatem promissam mereamur ingredi per debitam seruitutem.*

The oration has a number of noteworthy features. There are, firstly, a number of scriptural allusions operative in the collect. The prayer seems to take its main inspiration from Rm 8:14-17. This is particularly evident in part of the motivating clause, *quem ... paterno nomine inuocare praesumimus*, but can also be seen in the use of *filius* and *hereditas promissa*. The teaching work of the Holy Spirit echoes some passages from the Johannine writings, while the phrase *paterno nomine* has Lucan parallels.

A second point is the link between *filiorum corda fidelium* and *per debitam seruitutem*. The hearts of God's faithful children, of those who put their faith in God, are hearts which offer the service due to him. It is through such service that they enter the inheritance promised them.

Further, this parallel contains a play between being adopted heirs (*filii*) and the idea of service (*seruitus*). The Romans' text sets in opposition the fearfilled spirit of being a servant and the spirit of being an adopted child (Rm 8:15)[9]. In our prayer, entry into the promised inheritance comes about through the service of the adopted children.

Vocabulary:

Prominent vocabulary: *docere, Spiritus Sanctus, nomen paternum, inuocare, praesumere, efficere, cor, filius, fidelis, hereditas promissa, mereri, ingredi, debita seruitus*.

Our vocabulary analysis will begin with the descriptive clause *quem docente spiritu sancto paterno nomine inuocare praesumimus*. This expression, as well as the terms *filius* and *hereditas promissa*, appear to take their main inspiration from the Vulgate translation of Rm 8:14-17[10]. The passage reads: "*Quicumque enim Spiritu Dei aguntur ii sunt filii Dei. Non enim accepistis*

---

[9] *Non enim accepistis spiritum servitutis iterum in timore, sed accepistis spiritum adoptionis filiorum in quo clamamus: Abba, Pater* (Rm 8:15).

[10] For commentary see Fitzmyer, Romans, 497-504. Note that Fitzmyer remarks that *spiritum adoptionis filiorum* could mean either a spirit of adoptive sonship (as opposed to the spirit of servitude) or the Spirit of adoptive sonship. It is possible that Paul means both.

spiritum servitutis iterum in timore, sed accepistis spiritum adoptionis filiorum in quo clamamus: Abba, Pater. Ipse enim Spiritus testimonium reddit spiritui nostri, quod sumus filii Dei. Si autem filii, et heredes: heredes quidem Dei, coheredes autem Christi; si tamen compatimur, ut et conglorificemur (Rm 8:14-17)[11].

The pericope discusses central tenets of Christian belief concerning prayer, the Christian relationship to God, the Christian inheritance, and entry to eternal life. It is in the Holy Spirit that Christians both become adopted children and are able to acclaim God as their Father. Furthermore, the Spirit accompanies the prayer and proclamation of the faithful children, and in so doing gives testimony to God that these are indeed the prayers of his adopted children. In this special status as adopted children of the Father, the baptized are heirs to the promises and co-heirs with Christ their brother. Finally, entry into their inheritance, the life of glory, is associated with their configuration to Christ through sharing in his suffering.

According to Romans, the faithful share in Christ's suffering and death through their faith and baptism (Rm 6:5), as well as through their own suffering on earth as they await the fulfilment of all things in Christ (Rm 8:18). This earthly suffering is yet another opportunity for the Spirit to help the faithful in their weakness (Rm 8:26).

The clause carries two other scriptural allusions. In response to a request from one of his disciples, Jesus teaches (*docere*) his followers to invoke God as their Father (*Pater*), and to praise and bless the divine name (*nomen*): "*Dixit unus ex discipulis eius ad eum: Domine, doce nos orare ... Et ait*

---

[11]See also Gal 4:5-7. This Galatians text was studied in the analysis of the collect for Sunday XXIII. See above, 227.

[*Jesus*] *illis: Cum oratis dicite: Pater, sanctificetur nomen tuum, adveniat regnum tuum ..."* (Lc 11:1-2)[12].

This Vulgate translation of the Lord's Prayer, then, has parallels with our prayer. Through the teaching (*docere*) of Jesus, God is invoked by the name (*nomen*) Father (*Pater*). However, neither this Lucan pericope nor Rm 8:14-17 accounts for the attribution to the Spirit of the role as teacher, *docente spiritu sancto*.

The phrase appears to be Johannine. In the Vulgate translation of John's Gospel, the Spirit, sent by the Father (*Pater*) in Christ's name (*nomen*) will teach (*docere*) the faithful all things, and as well remind (*suggere*) them of what Jesus said:

"Paraclitus autem Spiritus sanctus, quem mittet Pater in nomine meo, ille vos docebit omnia et suggeret vobis omnia quaecumque dixero vobis" (Jo 14:26)[13].

The expression *docente spiritu sancto* seems to be found only in P 745 and orations derived from it[14]. The teaching role of the Spirit is found in few other prayers. One of the clearest examples is a collect from a Gelasian Mass for the Sunday in the octave of Pentecost. The prayer reads:

"Timentium <te>, domine, saluator et custus, auerte ab aecclesia tua mundanae sapientiae oblectamenta fallaciae, ut spiritus tui eruditione forma nobis prophetica et apostolica potius instituta quam filosophiae uerba

---

[12]The Vulgate translation of Matthew is quite similar, though the allusion to teaching (*docere*) is absent. The passage reads:
"Sic ergo vos orabitis: Pater noster qui es in caelis, sanctificetur nomen tuum, adveniat regnum tuum ..." (Mt 6:9-10).

[13]See also Jo 16:13 and 1 Jo 2:20-28.

[14]For further examples of *spiritus sanctus* see Deshusses, Concordance III, 4, 272-283, and Heiming, Das Sacramentarium Triplex: 2 Teil: Wortschatz und Ausdrucksformen, 237-238.

delectent, ne uanitas mendatiorum decipiat quos erudicio ueritatis inluminat" (V 676)[15].

The clause in Triplex 1494 is formed through the compilation of these passages. Under the instruction of the Spirit, the faithful invoke God as their Father[16]. The Holy Spirit is the only basis for such boldness (*praesumere*).[17] It is through the Spirit that the baptized are children (*filii*) of the Father, and as such, heirs of the promised inheritance (*hereditas promissa*). The Spirit teaches them to call God their Father, and even prompts their minds to Jesus' own teaching to invoke his Father as their Father. Finally the Spirit brings this teaching to fruition by enabling the faithful to pray to God as their Father, and by testifying to the Father that they are his adopted children.

In light of this the faithful make their petition that God, their Father, bring it about that their hearts may be the hearts of faithful children.

---

[15]Lord, saviour and guardian of those who fear you, turn away from your church the duplicious allurements of earthly wisdom, so that, formed by the instruction of your Spirit, the teachings of the prophets and apostles, rather than the words of philosophy, may delight us, lest the empty deceit of falsehoods deceive those whom the teaching of the truth has illuminated (V 676, Triplex 1909, Bergom 783).
See also P 526, where the Spirit is attributed a role (*illustratio*) in God's teaching (*docere*).

[16]The understanding of God as *paterfamilias* and the faithful as his *familia* has been discussed in the analysis of the collect for Sunday V. See above, 487.

[17]The faithful ought presume nothing good from their own merits, as seen in the following blessing:
"*Adesto domine supplicationbus nostris et nihil de sua conscientia praesumentibus ineffabili miseratione succurre: ut quod non habet fiducia meritorum: tuorum conferat largitas inuicta donorum*"(Triplex 65, Milano 60, V 1283). (Translation: Lord, hear our supplications and hasten to aid with your ineffable compassion we who presume nothing on account of our own conscience, so that that which our presumption does not have of its own merits, the inexorable bounty of your gifts may confer.)

Effice in nobis filiorum corda fidelium

The original prayer, P 745, reads *crea in nobis filiorum corda fidelium*[18]. This clause echoes a petition in the Vulgate translation of Ps 50: "*Cor mundum crea in me, Deus, et spiritum rectum innova in visceribus meis; ne proicias me a facie tua et spiritum sanctum tuum ne auferas a me*" (Ps 50:12-13).

Note the three sets of parallels: *creare* and *innovare*, *cor*, *viscera mea* and *spiritus*, and *mundus* and *rectus*. *Creare* is concerned with the renewal and remaking of the whole inner being (*cor, viscera mea, spiritus*) of the faithful so that they may be pure and upright. The purpose of the petition is important. The faithful desire such complete renewal so as to be able to remain in God's presence and in his spirit.

These verses from the psalm have been adapted to fit the Pauline theme of adoption as God's children. As God's children, and under the inspiration, teaching, accompaniment and testimony of the Spirit, the community request that their Father may completely cleanse and renew their hearts so that they may be the hearts of faithful children. The purpose of their prayer is their desire to enter their promised inheritance.

The petition in Triplex 1494 reads *effice in nobis filiorum corda fidelium*. It represents a weakening of the original sense of *creare*, with its connotations of renewal *innovare*. On the other hand, the modification works to good effect in that it places the petition in parallel with a section of the preface (Triplex 1496) from the same Mass. This preface is found only in Ambrosian sources. The prayer reads:

---

[18]This prayer appears to be the only example of the conjunction of *creare* and *cor* in the prayers indexed by Deshusses' concordance as well as in the concordance to the *Sacramentarium Triplex*. For examples of the use or *creare*, see Deshusses, Concordances III, 1, 388-389, and Heiming, Das Sacramentarium Triplex: 2 Teil: Wortschatz und Ausdrucksformen, 51.

"*VD. Aeterne deus, et nunc maxime gratulari quando dies salutis nostrae et tuae erga nos pietatis mysterium solemniter celebratur quo de tenebris captiuitatis antiquae filii lucis et libertatis efficimur, et terrenis exuti ad celestia regna transimus propterea profusis gaudiis totus in orbe*" (Triplex 1496)[19].

The *super sindonem*'s petition *effice in nobis filiorum cordis fidelium* is in parallel with *filii lucis et libertatis efficimur*. The Mass brings together the theme of adoption in the Spirit and the resurrection imagery of light and freedom. The hearts of the Father's faithful children are those which reflect the light and freedom wrought by Christ's victory over sin and darkness. Both the *super sindonem* and the preface register the faithful's desire for eternal life (*celestia regna, promissa hereditas*).

The purpose of the petition is that the faithful, through carrying out the service owed to God, may merit to enter the promised inheritance: *ut hereditatem promissam mereamur ingredi per debitam seruitutem*. This purpose clause will now be examined, beginning with *debita seruitus*.

Per debitam seruitutem[20]

The expression, commonly found throughout the liturgical sources, denotes the worship due to God[21]. This can be clearly seen in the *secreta* from

---

[19] It is right and fitting to praise you: and now to praise and thank you to the utmost degree when the day of our salvation and the mystery of your loving kindness towards us is solemnly celebrated, by which, liberated from the darkness of the captivity of former times, we are made children of the light and freedom, and freed from earthly things, we pass through to the kingdom of heaven .... (Triplex 1496, Bergom 637, Ariberto 473, Biasca 605).

[20] For the use of *debita* in the Roman sources see Deshusses, Concordance III, 1, 413. For examples of *debita seruitus, debitae laudes* and similar expressions in the *Sacramentarium Triplex*, see Heiming, Das Sacramentarium Triplex: 2 Teil: Wortschatz und Ausdrucksformen, 55.

[21] See Blaise, Vocabulaire, § 1 and § 245.

a Mass for the feast of Thomas the Apostle:

"*Debitum domine nostrae reddimus seruitutis suppliciter exorantes: ut suffragiis beati Thomae apostoli in nobis tua munera tuearis cuius honorando confessionem laudis tibi hostiam immolamus*" (Triplex 112)[22].

Note that the service that is owed is the sacrifice of praise.

In Triplex 1494, entry into the promised inheritance (*promissa hereditas*), eternal life[23], is related to the community's worship. The collect in the *Paduensis* reads *promissam hereditam adgredi ualeamus*. The faithful seek a renewed and cleansed heart so that they may approach the promises. The same prayer in the Ambrosian sacramentary, Triplex 2683, reads *ingredi ualeamus*[24]. The sense of Triplex 1494 is slightly different. The purpose of the petition has shifted from approaching the inheritance to entry into it, *mereamur ingredi*. As can be seen from the context of the prayer in Paul's Letter to the Romans, it is within the context of the work of the Holy Spirit that their worship has merit, *mereamur*[25] *(ingredi)*.

In summary, in Triplex 1494 the praise and worship due God are associated with the faith of his adopted children, which allows them to call him Father. Their *debita seruitus* is understood within both the context of their

---

[22] Entreating you Lord, we humbly give back to you the debt of our service: so that with the help of blessed Thomas the Apostle you may guard your gifts in us; in honouring his confession, we offer the sacrifice of praise (Triplex 112, Biasca 1365, 1408, Milano 844 and V 1089). A similar prayer is found in Ariberto 777 and L 767.

[23] The *hereditas* of God's children has been analysed as part of the discussion of the collect for Sunday XXIII. See above, 228.

[24] Moeller lists two other variations for this verb form: *valeamus pervenire* (Lateran), *mereamur ingredi* (Prag, Toledo³). See Moeller, Corpus Orationum II, D orationes 881-1707, oration 1320, 212.

[25] *Mereri* has been studied in the analysis of the collect for Sunday XXV. See above, 142.

adoption as God's children, and the context of the celebration of the Resurrection. The faithful can only presume to offer their owed worship to the Father because of the Holy Spirit, who has made them adopted children, accompanies their prayer, and teaches them to address God as Father. The fruit of their worship is entry into the promised inheritance (*hereditas promissa*), eternal life.

This last point is an interpretation of Rm 8:14-17. While for Paul the spirit of adoption leads to worship (*clamamus: Abba Pater*), entry into Christ's glory is also related to the various senses of sharing in Christ's suffering. Our oration associates admission to the promises directly with the faithful's response of praise and worship.

Meaning of Triplex 1494:

At the heart of the prayer is the relationship between the faithful and God set out in Rm 8:14-17. Because of the gift of the presence of the Spirit within them, the faithful have a new status. No longer servants, they are God's adopted children, and as such are co-heirs with Christ and heirs to the promised inheritance. Under the teaching and inspiration of the Spirit they invoke God as their Father. This prayer is not only inspired by the Spirit but accompanied by the Spirit as well.

Their petition, then, is that God work in their hearts so that their entire spiritual selves, heart, soul and mind, will be made more perfectly those of faithful children and heirs. They are asking that their hearts, filled with the light and freedom wrought by Christ's resurrection, may overflow with worship and praise in response to their new life as children of the Father.

Through the worship, thanksgiving and praise which characterizes fidelity of heart, they seek to merit to enter their promised inheritance. This worship itself is inspired and accompanied by the Holy Spirit.

It is the Spirit who makes them children by faith, and teaches them to address God as Father. Moreover, the Spirit moves them to the service (*servitus*) which is that of children who live in freedom, so that as heirs they enter into the promise of heaven.

ANALYSIS OF THE WORDS AND PHRASES IN THE COLLECT WITHIN THE CONTEXT OF THE MISSAL OF PAUL VI

The text as it stands in the Missal of Paul VI has been adapted in a number of ways. The direct reference to the teaching role of the Spirit in the community's invocation of God as Father has been dropped. The petition has been rewritten, with *filiorum corda fidelium* replaced by *in cordibus nostris spiritum adoptionis filiorum*. Also deleted is the direct reference to worship as the response which leads to entry into the promised inheritance.

The deletion of *docente spiritu sancto* weakens the prayer in two significant ways. Firstly it obscures the role of the Holy Spirit in the prayer of the community. Secondly the teaching function of the Holy Spirit is similarly obscured, including the role of the Spirit in bringing to the fore the teachings of Jesus.

Both these points are of consequence to the Missal as a whole. Though mentioned 215 times in the Missal, the Spirit is not directly spoken of in any of the Sunday collects or orations *super oblata* in Ordinary Time[26], and is mentioned in only two of the season's postcommunion prayers[27]. The role of the Spirit in the life of the community has been underplayed in the Missal.

The Missal also gives little attention to the teaching role of the Spirit. There appear to be no prayers which directly relate teaching to the work of the

---

[26]See Schnitker and Slaby, Concordantia, 2362-2370.

[27]MR(1975) Dom. IX per annum, Postcomm., 348 and MR(1975) Dom. XXIII per annum, Postcomm., 371.

Spirit. In three orations, however, the work of the Spirit, described by the verbs *afflare, affari*[28] and the noun *illustratio*, supports the teaching of God and the teaching of the doctors of the church. The prayers read:

"*Cordibus nostris, quaesumus, Domine, Spiritum Sanctum benignus infunde, cuius afflatu beatus Ephraem diaconus in tuis mysteriis decantandis exsultavit, eiusque uirtute tibi soli deseruiit*" (MR(1975) S.Ephrem (diaconi et Ecclesiae doctoris), Collecta, 558)[29].

"*Omnipotens aeterne Deus, qui beatum N. (episcopum) Ecclesiae tuae doctorem dedisti, praesta, ut, quod ille divino affatus spiritu docuit, nostris iugiter stabiliatur in cordibus ...*" (MR(1975) Commune doctorum Eccl. 1, Collecta, 705)[30],

"*Deus, qui corda fidelium Sancti Spiritus illustratione docuisti, da nobis in*

---

[28] This use of *affari*, its only presence in the Missal (Schnitker and Slaby, 94), appears to be quite unusual. The verb is indexed once only in the Dutripon concordance of the Vulgate translation of the bible, describing the address of the King to Daniel in Dan 6:20 (see Dutripon, Bibliorum Sacrorum Concordantiae, 46). *Adfatus* is indexed only once in the Deshusses concordance for the prayer L 947, where it describes conversation between God and his privileged servant Moses (Deshusses, Concordances III,1,64). As well the verb or its cognates are not found in Blaise, Vocabulaire. Given the sense of the prayer, and especially the role of the Holy Spirit, *afflatus* would have been the more expected participial adjective. For the use of *flare* and *flatus* in relation to the Holy Spirit, see Blaise, Vocabulaire, § 217, footnote 1. *Adflatus* is indexed only once in the Schnikter and Slaby concordance, for the collect of the Mass of St. Ephrem (Schnitker and Slaby, Concordantiae, 93).

[29] Lord, in your favour and kindness, pour your Holy Spirit into our hearts, by whose inspiration your deacon St. Ephrem delighted in proclaiming your mysteries in song, and by whose power the saint devoted himself to you alone.

[30] Almighty and eternal God, who gave (your bishop) Saint N. to your Church as its teacher, grant that what he, prompted by the divine Spirit, taught, may always remain fixed in our hearts ....

eodem Spiritu recta sapere, et de eius semper consolatione gaudere" (MR(1975) De Spiritu Sancto A, Collecta, 863)[31].

Note, however, that both these prayers stress the relationship between divine teaching and the heart, *cor*.

Perhaps one reason for the omission of *docente spiritu sancto* was to bring the prayer more closely in line with Rm 8:14-17. Evidence for this is found in the replacement of *effice in nobis filiorum corda fidelium* with *perfice in cordibus nostris spiritum adoptionis filiorum*. The new phrase, *spiritum adoptionis filiorum*, is found in the Vulgate translation of the scriptures only in Rm 8:15[32]. The modified prayer, then, reflects more faithfully the text Rm 8:14-17. As such it continues to imply both the presence of the Spirit in which the faithful are made children, and the activity of the Spirit in which the adopted offspring presume to address God as Father.

The change in the purpose clause is also quite far-reaching. In the original prayer, the fidelity of heart of God's adopted children was expressed in their worship, through which they merited to enter the promised inheritance. This has now been enlarged. As the prayer now stands in the Missal of Paul VI, the entry of the faithful into the promises is related to the perfection in their hearts of the spirit of adoption, *spiritus adoptionis filiorum*. The passage from Romans, and a number of orations in the Missal of Paul VI shed light on the phrase. The reference to merit, *mereamur*, has been retained.

As seen above, the Pauline excerpt relates the spirit of adoption to worship and to sharing in Christ's suffering. *Spiritus adoptionis* is also found

---

[31]God, who taught the hearts of the faithful by the enlightening of the Holy Spirit, grant that, in that same Spirit, we may always discern what is upright, and always rejoice in consolation the Spirit brings.
This prayer was originally from the *Hadrianum*, H 521.

[32]"... *sed acceptistis spiritum adoptionis filiorum in quo clamamus: Abba, pater*" (Rm 8:15).

in the collect which follows the Gloria and precedes the Epistle (Rm 6:3-11) during the Easter Vigil. Here the spirit of adoption is related to renewal in both mind and body. From this Easter Vigil context it is also related to Baptism. Both are expressed in pure worship. The oration, then, makes a direct connection between the Spirit and *servitus*. The prayer reads:
"*Deus, qui hanc sacratissimam noctem gloria dominicae resurrectionis illustras, excita in Ecclesia tua adoptionis spiritum, ut, corpore et mente renovati, puram tibi exhibeamus servitutem*" (MR(1975): Vig. pasch., Collecta 280)[33].

The collect from a baptismal Mass associates the Spirit of adoption with walking in newness of life. This is the new life of baptism in Christ, free from sin and death. The prayer reads:
"*Deus, qui nos facis passionis et resurrectionis Filii tui participare mysterium, praesta, quaesumus, ut, adoptionis filiorum Spiritu roborati, in novitate vitae iugiter ambulemus*" (MR(1975): In conferenda Bapt. A, Collecta, 733)[34].

In the prayer as it stands in the Missal of Paul VI, the faithful's petition that God perfect[35] in their hearts the spirit of adoption includes the perfection not only of their worship, but also the perfection of the renewal of their minds

---

[33]God, who illuminates this most holy of nights with the glory of the resurrection of the Lord, arouse in your church the spirit of adoption, so that, renewed in body and mind, we may offer you pure service.
This prayer has been slightly modified for inclusion in the Missal. The original source reads *conserva in nova familiae tuae progeniem adoptionis spiritum quem dedisti.* See V 454, Triplex 1311, Bergam 539, Biasca 503, Milano 317.

[34]God, who enables us to take part in the mystery of the death and resurrection of your Son, grant that, strengthened by the Spirit of adoption as your children, we may walk always in newness of life.
This prayer appears to be found only in MR(1975).

[35]The replacement of *efficere* with *perficere* serves to intensify further the completeness of the renewal that the faithful desire.

and bodies, of their conformity to the sufferings of Christ, and of their walking in God's ways. The phrase continues to reflect the liturgical contexts of the resurrection and of baptism.

RELATIONSHIP OF THE CHRISTIAN PEOPLE TO GOD: THE COLLECT FOR SUNDAY XIX

The prayer reflects the relationship of the Christian people to God as set out in Romans 8:14-17. Because of the presence of the Holy Spirit within them, the baptized are the adopted children of God, their Father. Through their adoption they are co-heirs with Christ and heirs themselves to the promised inheritance, eternal life. The Holy Spirit enables them to pray to God as their Father, accompanies their prayers to the Father, and testifies to the Father that these are the prayers of his adopted children.

Entry into the promised inheritance is associated with the perfection within them of the spirit of their adoption as children. Their baptism is brought to fulfillment in them through pure worship, the renewal of their bodies and minds, living out the new life of baptism, sharing in Christ's sufferings. All this can only be accomplished through the work of the Spirit in them.

The modifications made to Triplex 1494 and P 745 have two implications for the relationship between the faithful and God as expressed in the collect for the Missal of Paul VI. Firstly the original oration's concentration on worship (*per debitam seruitutem*) has been expanded to all aspects of Christian existence. On a more negative note, through the deletion of the expression *docente spiritu sancto* there has been a diminishment in appreciation of the teaching role of the Spirit in the life of the church.

FREER TRANSLATION OF THE PRAYER

Omnipotens sempiterne Deus, quem paterno nomine invocare praesumimus, perfice in cordibus nostris spiritum adoptionis filiorum, ut promissam hereditatem ingredi mereamur.

All powerful, eternal God, we dare to call upon you as our Father. Bring to perfection in our hearts the spirit of adoption as your children, so that through your Spirit, we may enter the inheritance you promised.

COLLECT FOR SUNDAY XVI

PRAYER

Propitiare, Domine, famulis tuis, et clementer gratiae tuae super eos dona multiplica, ut, spe, fide et caritate ferventes, semper in mandatis tuis vigili custodia perseverent.

Be favourable to your servants, Lord, and in your clemency multiply over them the gifts of your grace, so that, fervent in hope, faith and charity, they may, with vigilant observance, always persevere in keeping your commandments.

ORIGINAL SOURCE

"*Propitiare domine famulis tuis et clementer gratiae tuae super eos dona multiplica: ut spei fideique et caritatis amore feruentes semper in mandatis tuis uigili custodia perseuerent*" (Triplex 1744).

The prayer is found under the following headings:

Incipiunt oratio quae dicendae sunt in laetaniis uel in uigiliis cottidianorum dierum:

* CXLII, *Item orationes in die secundo <ambrosianae> (In Basilica Apostolorum*, prayer before *Item ad Missam Oratio Super Populum*), Triplex 1744,

* *Item oratio in die secundo XII* (prayer before *item ad Missam or. sup. pop.*), Bergom 719,

* XCI, *Item orationes die II in letanie XII* (prayer before *Item ad Missam Oratio Super Populum*), Biasca 688.

The prayer served as the final collect for the litanies of the second of the three Rogation days that preceded the feast of Pentecost[1]. It does not appear to be used in any liturgical sources outside of the Milanese tradition[2].

CHANGES TO THE ORIGINAL

The opening section of the purpose clause has been modified, with *spei fideique et caritatis amore (ferventes)* replaced by the simplified *spe, fide et caritate (ferventes)*.

ANALYSIS OF THE PRAYER IN THE ORIGINAL SOURCE

Origin:

The liturgical context of the prayer gives a sense of immediacy to the vocabulary. The Pentecost Rogation days were taken up with fasting, vigils, prayer and petition in preparation for the feast. The oration was well-suited to such an occasion, with its references to the fervour of the community's faith, hope and love, its vigilance and perseverance, and the observance of the divine mandates (fasting, prayer, petition). God's favour and clemency are themselves based in the Paschal mystery, while the petition for the multiplicity of divine gifts has a certain Pentecost flavour.

For further comment on the origins of the prayer, as well as the relationship between the Ambrosian and Roman liturgical sources, see the introduction to this chapter.

---

[1]There is some variance in the early Milanese sacramentaries. In the *Bergomense* and the Sacramentary of Biasca the Rogation days are immediately before Pentecost, while in the *Sacramentarium Triplex* they come before the feast of the Ascension. For commentary on the history and practices of the Ambrosian Rogation liturgy see King, Liturgies of the Primatial Sees, 367-369.

[2]Note that the relevant edition of Moeller's Corpus Orationum series is yet to be published.

Grammatical structure:

The prayer is made up of (a) a simple address, (b) two petitions, and (c) two purpose clauses, in which the first provides the grounds for the second.

(a) Address: *Domine*

(b) First Petition: *Propitiare famulis tuis*

 Second Petition: *et clementer gratiae tuae super eos dona multiplica*

(c) 1st Purpose: *ut spei fideique et caritate amore feruentes*

 2nd Purpose: *semper in mandatis tuis uigili custodia perseruerent.*

There is a parallelism in the purpose clauses between *uigilia custodia* and *spei fideique et caritatis amore feruentes*. The vigilance of the faithful's care and perseverence is related to the fervour of their love of the three virtues. Note that through the use of *-que* and *et* faith, hope and love are to be taken together as a single unit. As such they echo their conjunction in the Vulgate translation of 1 Cor 13:13 and 1 Th 5:12.

The combined effect of the adverb *semper*, the adjective *uigil* and the verb *perseverare* in the second purpose clause reminds the community that there ought be no rest or relaxation of their obedience to God's mandates.

The keeping of the commandments is the particular object of the petition. The context of the prayer as a collect in the liturgy of the Pentecost Rogation days points especially to fervent fulfillment of the prescriptions of fasting, prayer and petition.

The prayer's second petition, based in the community's belief in God's favour and clemency, is quite general; *gratiae tuae dona multiplica*. Its content is filled out by the purpose clauses.

Vocabulary:

Prominent vocabulary: *propitiare, famulus tuus, clementer, multiplicare, gratiae tuae donum, spes fidesque et caritas, amor, feruere, mandata tua, uigil custodia, perseuerare.*

Our vocabulary analysis will begin with the two petitions *propitiare domine famulis tuis et clementer gratiae tuae super eos dona multiplica*. With the exception of the verb *propitiare* the petitions' vocabulary and constructions have been studied elsewhere. Their use in the early Ambrosian sacramentaries does not appear to add any further nuances or perspectives to their meaning. The designation of the faithful as God's *famuli* is quite common[3]. The divine clemency is often invoked in the early euchology. *Clementer* has been analysed above in the study of the collect for Sunday II[4]. Summarizing that discussion here, *clementer* and its cognate forms are associated, in the Vulgate scriptures, with God's covenant, propitiation, mercy and compassion.

The formula *gratiam tuam ... multiplicare*, found in a number of prayers in the Ambrosian sources[5], has been studied in the analysis of the collects for Sundays XVII and XXVI[6]. *Propitiare*, however, has not been discussed previously.

---

[3]*Famulus* has been studied in the analysis of the collect for Sunday XVIII. See above, 194. For examples of the use of *famulus* in the *Sacramentarium Triplex*, see Heiming, Das Sacramentarium Triplex: 2 Teil: Wortschatz und Ausdrucksformen, 90-91.

[4]For examples of the use of *clementer, clemens and clementia* in the *Sacramentarium Triplex*, see Heiming, Das Sacramentarium Triplex: 2 Teil: Wortschatz und Ausdrucksformen, 33-34.

[5]See the collect for the Vigil of the feast of All Saints: "*Domine deus noster multiplica super nos gratiam tuam ....*" (Triplex 3300, Biasca 1381). For a similar prayer see Triplex 522 (Ariberto 886, Bergom 1102, L 394, V 1117).

[6]See above, 522.

Propitiare[7]

Propitiare conveys the faithful's desire that God be favourable to them and receive their petition graciously[8]. This request for God's favour is particularly related to the sinfulness of the community and their desire for forgiveness. The verb *propitiare* often occurs in conjunction with words such as *peccata* (Triplex 3023, V 1503), *iniquitas* (Triplex 1722, Bergom 697, Biasca 666, H 882), and other verbs such as *absolvere* (Triplex 932, Milano 134, V 231).

In the following *super sindonem* God's favour, associated with his mercy, is related to his vigilant protection of the faithful from the falsehood of the devil. This divine favour and protection is seen as a continuation of the work of the incarnation. The prayer reads:
"*Propitiare misericors deus supplicationibus nostris et populum tuum peruigili protectione custodi: ut qui unigenitum tuum in carne nostri corporis deum natum esse fatetur nulla possit diaboli falsitate corrumpi*" (Triplex 334)[9].

Note that in this prayer it is the faithful's humble petitions (*supplicationes nostrae*) which are the object of God's *propitiare*, whereas in Triplex 1744 it is the people themselves (*famuli tui*). In Triplex 1722, a collect from the litany of the first Pentecost Rogation day, the object of God's *propitiare* is the sins of the community (*nostrae iniquitates*).

---

[7] For examples of the use of *propitiare* in the *Sacramentarium Triplex*, see Heiming, Das Sacramentarium Triplex: 2 Teil: Wortschatz und Ausdrucksformen, 203.

[8] Blaise, Vocabulaire, § 69 and §248.

[9] In your favour, merciful God, hear our prayer, and guard your people with your ever vigilant protection: so that the people who confess that your only begotten, the divine one, has been born in the flesh of our bodies may not be misled by any falsehood of the devil (Triplex 334).
For a similar prayer see Milano 59.

The two petitions in Triplex 1744 call upon God's merciful forgiveness and clemency. This is quite fitting in a time of fast, during which the members of the community are especially aware of their sinfulness and need for forgiveness. Together God's merciful forgiveness and clemency bespeak God's goodness and mercy at work in the incarnation, the Paschal mystery and Pentecost. The faithful's desire that God multiply the gifts of his grace over them is amplified in the purpose clause. The primary grace they seek is that the community may be fervent in its love of its faith, hope and charity; *spei fideique et caritatis amore feruentes*.

Spei fideique et caritatis amore feruentes

The conjunction of faith, hope and love has been examined in the analysis of the collect for Sunday XXX[10]. Paul posits them as the most enduring and important of all the spiritual gifts on earth. Together, faith, hope and love are at the heart of the faithful's response to God's covenant love. They form the basis of a vigilant life on earth in peace and charity, as well as in expectation of Christ's coming. In the collect for Sunday XXX the love of what God commands (*praecipere*) is set in parallel with an increase in the three virtues.

(spei fideique et caritatis amore) ferventes[11]

The community prays that they may be fervent in the three virtues of faith, hope and charity. The construction (*spei fideique et caritatis*) *amore feruentes* is somewhat unusual. The construction is found twice in an Ambrosian preface from a Mass for the martyrs Maurice and companions. There it functions to accentuate the sense of fervour of love and faith found in

---

[10] See above, 413.

[11] For examples of the use of *fervere* in the *Sacramentarium Triplex*, see Heiming, Das Sacramentarium Triplex: 2 Teil: Wortschatz und Ausdrucksformen, 92.

these soldiers. The two examples are *tanto caritatis ardore feruebant* and *tuae fidei amore succensus*. Maurice and companions, Christian soldiers belonging to the Theban Legion, were martyred for their refusal to offer sacrifice for the success of an impending military expedition. The prayer appears to be found only in the Ambrosian sources:

"*UD aeterne deus: Cui caterua fidelium ... Sed hi tanto caritatis ardore feruebant: ut eiectis armis flexo poplite passim geniculantes: spiculatorum tela hilare corde susciperent: Inter quos beatus Mauricius tuae fidei amore succensus: decertando martyrii est coronam adeptus*" (Triplex 2534)[12].

Following on from their petition to be fervent in the three foundational virtues that make up the authentic Christian response to God's covenant and love, the community further seek that they may persevere always, with vigilant observance, in God's mandates; *semper in mandatis tuis uigili custodia perseuerent*. This petition will now be examined, commencing with the sense of the divine commandments, *mandata tua*.

In mandatis tuis

The divine mandates and precepts have been discussed in the analysis of the collects for Sunday XXV[13]. Summarizing that discussion here, the divine mandates reflect God's ordering and justice. They are ordained towards love of God and neighbour, and worship of God. The obedience of the baptized has an ecclesial context, whereby it brings peace and harmony to the

---

[12]It is right and fitting: The troop of faithful soldiers ... But they were fervent with such an ardour of love that, on laying down their arms, and everywhere kneeling on bended knee, they received the blows of [the soldiers] looking on with gladness in their hearts. Amongst them was blessed Maurice, who was aroused with love of faith in you, and, in this striving, attained the crown of martyrdom (Triplex 2534, Ariberto 917, Bergom 1129, Biasca 1050, Milano 1153). For a list of manuscripts and sources see Moeller, Corpus Praefationum, Apparatus (A-P), Preface 90, 45.

[13]See above, 132, 140.

community, and enables them to offer pure worship. In such obedience, the church mirrors on earth the life of heaven.

In the *Sacramentarium Triplex*, *mandata* is used for the general sense of keeping God's commandments[14]. It also takes on more specific meanings, such as the laws of fasting[15]. The Rogation context of our prayer would suggest that the *mandata* here refer to the laws and customs surrounding the fast. The faithful request that their observance (*custodia*) of these commandments may be vigilant. This conjunction of *mandata* and *custodia* will now be examined.

Tua mandata ... uigil custodia

The conjunction of *custodia* and *mandatum* is often found in the Vulgate translation of the scriptures. It reflects the ongoing, divinely willed response of the faithful to God's covenant with them.

In making a pact with Abraham (Gn 17:1-22), God admonishes the patriach, along with his descendents, to observe (*custodire*) his covenant:
"*Dixit iterum Deus ad Abraham. Et tu ergo custodies pactum meum, et semen tuum post te in generationibus suis*" (Gn 17:9).

Moses urges the chosen people to fidelity and obedience (*custodire*) towards the mandates (*mandata, praecipere*) of God's covenant:
"*Non addetis ad verbum quod vobis loquor, nec auferetis ex eo: custodite mandata Domine Dei vestri, quae ego praecipio vobis*" (Dt 4:2).

Observance (*custodire*) of the divine mandates exemplifies true love of God, as seen in the First Letter of John:
"*Haec est enim caritas Dei, ut mandata eius custodiamus*" (1 Jo 5:3).

---

[14] See the orations Triplex 2091 (Ariberto 757, Bergom 987, Biasca 923, Milano 1012, Go 378), Triplex 1838 (L 194).

[15] See the oration Triplex 776, Ariberto 272, Bergom 326, Biasca 301, Milano 61, 284, V 173 and Triplex 778, Milano 107.

Our clause, then, echoes the covenant injunction to that loving obedience of the divine precepts and mandates which God desires as the authentic response to his love.

The faithful's loving observance is further qualified as *uigil*. This heightened sense of vigilant observance has previously been seen in the collect for Sunday XXII[16]. As noted above, *uigil* also refers to the community's observance of the Pentecost Rogation practices.

Perseuerent[17]

On a number of occasions in the Vulgate translation of the New Testament the verb *perseuerare* has been applied to the activities of the Christian community. While connoting a sense of steadfast perseverence, it relates the efforts of the faithful to an expectation of God's love and grace.

Two pericopes from the Acts of the Apostles provide a parallel with the Pentecost Rogation liturgy. The first Christian community, gathered in the upper room following the Ascension, are described as steadfast (*perseverantes*) in prayer as they await the Spirit:

"*Hi omnes erant perseverantes unanimiter in oratione cum mulieribus et Maria matre Iesu et fratribus eius*" (Ac 1:14).

Some few verses later in Ac 2:42, the post Pentecost *ecclesia* is described as "*perseverantes in doctrina apostolorum et communicatione fractionis panis et orationibus.*" Here *perseverare* carries the sense of the fidelity of the community in following the teaching of the apostles, in the breaking of the bread, and in prayer.

---

[16]See above, 361.

[17]For examples of the use of *perseverare* in the *Sacramentarium Triplex*, see Heiming, Das Sacramentarium Triplex: 2 Teil: Wortschatz und Ausdrucksformen, 183.

The author of the Letter to the Hebrews encourages the church to persevere in the training (*disciplina*) through which God is putting them (Heb 12:5-13). Their correction is coming from a loving Father treating them as his own children. Ultimately their perseverance will bear rich fruit (v. 11), as the example of Jesus shows (Heb 12:2). The apposite verse reads:

"*In disciplina perseverate. Tanquam filii vobis offert se Deus*" (Heb 12:7).

An Ambrosian[18] lenten preface links sincere perseverance in God's mandates with purification through fasting and the edification of good works. In doing this the preface offers an example of how *mandata* may mean the commandments in a generic sense, even in the context of fasting. As in Triplex 1744, these gifts are associated with God's clemency. The fruit of perseverance is the consolation of full participation in the Easter liturgy, and eventual entry into heaven. The preface reads:

"*UD usque aeterne deus: Et tuam immensam clementiam supplici uoto deposcere: ut nos famulos et ieiunii maceratione castigatos et ceteris bonorum operum exhibitionibus eruditos in mandatis tuis facias perseuerare sinceros et ad paschalia festa peruenire illaesos: Sicque praesentibus subsidiis consolemur quatenus ad aeterna gaudia pertingere mereamur*" (Triplex 883)[19].

---

[18]For a list of manuscripts and sources see Moeller, Corpus Praefationum, Apparatus (A-P), Preface 402, 182.

[19]It is right and fitting: With humble suppliant prayer to beseech your immense clemency so that you may make us, your servants, who are both corrected by the chastening action of the fast and edified by other displays of good works, persevere in sincerity in your mandates, and come through to the paschal feat unharmed. And thus may we be consoled with aid in the present to the extent that we may merit to attain eternal joys (Triplex 883, Ariberto 314, Bergom 376, Biasca 347, Milano 153).

The preface provides the basis for a lenten collect in the Missal of Paul VI: MR(1975): Fer. V hebd. IV Quadr., Collecta, 213.

In summary, the closing petition of the prayer is that God may grant the community steadfast, vigilant and continuous loving obedience in response to his covenant, and in particular in observance of his mandates. The adverb *semper* and adjective *uigil* stress the effort such perseverance requires, and as well the verb *perseverare* also carries a sense of expectation of God's favour.

Meaning of the prayer:

From the merciful forgiveness and clemency of God the community petitions first of all that they may be fervent in the virtues of faith, hope and love. This set of virtues are the most enduring and important of all the spiritual gifts on earth. They express the response to the covenant that God desires from his people, and through which the faithful live in peace, charity and expectation.

Furthermore, the community request that, through their fervour for the virtues they may steadfastly respond with loving obedience to God's covenant, particularly by vigilant observance of his mandates.

The construction (*spei fideique et caritatis*) *amore feruentes*, with its connotations of the passionate and willing obedience of the martyrs, highlights the wholeheartedness of the faithful's love for faith, hope and charity.

The verb *perseverare*, set in combination with the adjective *uigil* and the adverb *semper* signifies not only steadfast effort in obedience to God's mandates, but also the sense of expectation that surrounds conformity to God's will. The liturgical context gives added significance to the terms in the prayer. The community's participation in the fasting, vigils and prayer in preparation for Pentecost is reflected in *perseverare, uigil custodia*, and *tua mandata*. The use of *feruentes* catches something of the fervour associated with the coming of the Spirit. God's merciful forgiveness and clemency are known most clearly in the Paschal mystery, the seasonal celebration of which is being brought to a close with the Pentecost liturgy.

There is some change to the prayer when seen in its context as a collect for a Sunday in Ordinary Time in the Missal of Paul VI. The modifications to the prayer's vocabulary are of minor importance. However the complete change of liturgical context means the prayer loses much of its specificity and immediacy. The *mandata* are interpreted more generally, as is the faithful's perseverance in vigilant obedience and observance. Despite this loss of particularity, the underlying sense of the oration is maintained.

RELATIONSHIP OF THE CHRISTIAN PEOPLE TO GOD

The Christian people's relationship to God involves, at all times, steadfast and vigilant observance of the divine mandates. This obedience, with its effort and expectation, is the church's response to the covenant, a response that is at one with God's will. The strength and persistence which enable their vigilant observance is a product of the passion and ardour for the virtues of faith, hope and love. Both this fervour and perseverance are gifts of God's forgiveness and clemency.

FREER TRANSLATION OF THE COLLECT

Propitiare, Domine, famulis tuis, et clementer gratiae tuae super eos dona multiplica, ut, spe, fide et caritate ferventes, semper in mandatis tuis vigili custodia perseverent.

Look favourably upon us, O Lord, and in your forgiving mercy increase within us the gifts of your grace. Thus may we, in fervent hope, faith and charity, remain always steadfast in vigilant obedience to your commandments.

COLLECT FOR SUNDAY XIII

PRAYER

Deus, qui, per adoptionem gratiae, lucis nos esse filios voluisti, praesta, quaesumus, ut errorum non involvamur tenebris, sed in splendore veritatis semper maneamus conspicui.

God, who through the adoption of grace wished us to be children of the light, grant that we may not be enveloped in the darkness of errors, but that we may always remain bright in the splendour of truth.

ORIGINAL SOURCE

The original prayer is found in the Milanese sources under the following headings:

Incipiunt oratio quae dicendae sunt in laetaniis uel in uigiliis cottidianorum dierum:

* CXLIII, *Item orationes in die tertio <ambrosianae>*, Triplex 1750,
* *Item oratio in die tertio, I*, Bergom 725,
* XCII, *Orationes in laetanie die III*, Biasca 694.

The prayer served as the first collect for the litanies of the last of the three rogation days that preceded the feast of Pentecost[1].

The prayer does not appear to be used in any liturgical sources outside of the Milanese tradition[2].

---

[1] There is some variance in the early Milanese sacramentaries. In the *Bergomense* and the Sacramentary of Biasca the rogation days are immediately before Pentecost, while in the *Sacramentarium Triplex* they come before the feast of the Ascension. For commentary on the history and practices of the Ambrosian Rogation liturgy see A.King, Liturgies of the Primatial Sees, 367-369.

[2] Note that the prayer, Triplex 1750, is not found in Moeller's Corpus Orationum. A number of the prayers for the Pentecost Rogation Days in the Milanese sources seem to have been overlooked in the compilation of the

CHANGES TO THE ORIGINAL

The original prayer has been incorporated unmodified into the Missal of Paul VI.

ANALYSIS OF THE PRAYER IN THE ORIGINAL SOURCE

Origin:

The liturgical context of the prayer as the opening collect for the litany of the third and final Rogation Day before Pentecost gives some specificity to the prayer. The oration resounds with images associated with the feasts of Easter, the Ascension and Pentecost, as well as the baptismal connotations of Easter and Pentecost[3]: *adoptio, filii, lux, splendor, veritas* and *tenebrae*. The Rogation emphasis on prayer, penance and petition is reflected in the petitions' desire for the avoidance of the darkness of error and the grace to abide in the splendour of the truth.

For further comment on the origins of the prayer, as well as the relationship between the Ambrosian and Roman liturgical sources, see the introduction to this chapter.

Grammatical structure:

The prayer consists of (a) an address to God, (b) a motivating clause, (c) and two petitions connected by the conjunction *sed*.

Corpus Orationum series. Also not found are Triplex 1743 from the second Rogation Day and Triplex 1751, 1756 and 1758 from the third Rogation Day.

[3]In the Milanese liturgy Pentecost was considered a suitable time for administering the sacrament of baptism. The heading for the Pentecost Mass Triplex CLI reads *Oratio ad missam post ascensum fontis statio ad Lateranum*. The title for the same Mass in the Sacramentary of Biasca reads *Mane die Sancto Pentecosten in eclesia minore missa pro baptizatis*.

(a)　Address:　*Deus*

(b)　Motivation:　*qui per adoptionem gratiae lucis nos esse filios uoluisti*:

(c)　Petitions:　*praesta quaesumus*

　　　　　　　ut　errorum non inuoluamur tenebris

　　　　　　　sed　in splendore ueritatis semper maneamus conspicui.

The prayer is constructed around the interweaving of four sets of images: *adoptio:filius, filius:lux, lux/splendor:veritas,* and *tenebrae:error*. Amongst the images are two opposite pairs: *lux/splendor:tenebrae, veritas:error*. For the present *lux* and *splendor* are treated together. Their differences are examined below in the vocabulary analysis. These sets of images are freely borrowed from the Vulgate translation of the Johannine and Pauline writings. The verb *manere* is also typical Vulgate Johannine vocabulary. Note further that the text draws a contrast between being enveloped in darkness, *involvamur tenebris*, and remaining bright in the splendour of truth, *maneamus conspicui*.

The connections between the pairings form the basis of the structure of the prayer. Through the adoption of grace (*adoptio*) God has made the faithful into children (*filii*) of the light (*lux*). Those who live in the light (*lux, splendor*) live in the truth (*veritas*). On the other hand, those who do not live in the light live in the darkness (*tenebrae*) of error (*error*). They no longer live as adopted children in accordance with God's desire. The purpose clause, through the conjunction *sed*, sets *tenebrae/error* and *lux/splendor:veritas* in complete opposition: *ut ... non involvere ... sed ... semper manere conspicui*. The focus of this dynamic of opposition falls on the radical discontinuity between *veritas* and *error*. The faithful desire to abide in the splendour of truth rather than to be wrapped in the darkness of error.

The sense of the prayer follows from the interrelationship of these images. Motivated by God's desire that those who are his adopted children be children of the light, the community requests that they may abide always in the light and glory of truth, and also that they may not be taken up in the darkness of error.

The various pairings in the oration, and their scriptural roots, will now be examined more fully.

Vocabulary:

Prominent vocabulary: *adoptio, lux, filius, error, tenebrae, inuoluere, splendor, ueritas, manere, conspicuus.*

A significant portion of the collect's vocabulary reflects its usage in the Vulgate translation of the scriptures. *Adoptio, filius, lux, ueritas, splendor, tenebrae, error* and *manere* are interconnected in a range of ways throughout the Johannine and Pauline writings. A number of these terms have already been analysed in earlier studies. There seems to be little divergence between the Roman and Milanese usages of such deeply scriptural images. However, where possible, similar occurrences in the Ambrosian sources will be noted.

In the main, our vocabulary study will analyse the words of the prayer in light of the way they have been set in pairs. We will begin with the set *adoptio ... filii*.

Adoptio ... filii

The grace of God's adoption (*adoptio*) of the faithful as his children (*filii*) has been studied in the collects for Sundays XXIII[4] and XIX[5]. Our prayer employs these terms in an unusual turn of phrase, *per adoptionem*

---

[4] See above, 227.

[5] See above, 583.

gratiae, the adoption of/by grace. The scriptural basis of adoption is most clearly seen in Rm 8:14-17 and Gal 3-5. Summarizing those discussions here, through the redemption wrought by Christ, God has given the Spirit to those who believe so that they may be his adopted children. As adopted children they are able to call him Father, and are heirs to eternal life. They live in the freedom that Christ brings through the Holy Spirit. This is most especially a freedom to love. Our collect, Triplex 1750, associates adoption with the light (*lux*).

Filius ... lux

Filius lucis is a common way in the Vulgate to translate Johannine and Pauline expressions denoting those who live entirely in the light (*lux, lumen*) of truth that Christ brings. In a passage from the Gospel of John where Jesus is announcing his coming death, the children of light are those who both believe in the light (Jesus himself) and walk in it. While those who walk in the light can see the way, those who are caught up (*comprehendere*) in darkness (*tenebrae*) are lost. The passage reads:

"*Dixit ergo eis Iesus: Adhuc modicum lumen in vobis est. Ambulate dum lucem habetis, ut non vos tenebrae comprehendant; et qui ambulat in tenebris nescit quo vadat. Dum lucem habetis, credite in lucem, ut filii lucis sitis*" (Jo 12:35-36)[6].

Note in this passage the contrast between walking in the light (*ambulare*) and being seized by the darkness (*comprehendere*). The children of light walk, those who fall prey to error are seized by darkness, and so walk

---

[6] See also Eph 5:8 and 1 Th 5:5. For another Ambrosian prayer which combines the images of *adoptio, filius* and *lumen* see Triplex 1559 (Ariberto 480, Bergom 645, Biasca 614, Milano 380). The *secreta* (Triplex 1560, V 553) for that same Mass takes up the theme of *ueritas*. The Mass itself is for a Sunday in Eastertide.

not knowing where they go. This is echoed in the contrast in Triplex 1750 between *involvamur tenebris* and *maneamus conspicui*.

As in our prayer, the New Testament writings often set the metaphor of light, *lux, lumen,* in conjunction with truth, *ueritas,* as well, contrasting it with the metaphor of darkness (*tenebrae*).

Lux ... ueritas

The pairing of *lux* and *ueritas,* as well as their relationship to *error,* has been analyzed in the study of the collect for Sunday XV[7]. Summarizing that discussion here, Christ is the embodiment of all light and truth. Life in his light is characterized by love, goodness, righteousness and truth. There is no compatibility between on the one hand God's light and truth and on the other the ways of darkness and error.

In our collect *lux* is paralleled by *splendor,* a noun which also has scriptural resonance.

Splendor[8] *... ueritas*

The Vulgate translation of 2 Corinthians establishes a relationship between *lux, splendor* (*splendescere*) and *tenebrae.* The apposite verse reads: "*quoniam Deus, qui dixit de tenebris lucem splendescere, ipse illuxit in cordibus nostris ad illuminationem scientiae claritatis Dei in facie Christi Iesu*" (2 Cor 4:6).

From the context of the verse in the larger passage (2 Cor 4:1-6), *lux* and *splendescere* are associated with the dispelling of primordial darkness

---

[7] See above, 256.

[8] For further examples of the use of *splendor* in the *Sacramentarium Triplex* see Heiming, Das Sacramentarium Triplex: 2 Teil: Wortschatz und Ausdrucksformen, 238. Note that quite a number of these examples are from prayers connected with the feasts of the Nativity and the Epiphany.

(*tenebrae*) and the beginning of the creation of heaven and earth (Gn 1:3)[9], the knowledge of God's glory (δόξα) revealed in Christ himself[10], and the true (*veritas*) gospel of Christ. *Tenebrae* is linked to the sinister darkness and emptiness of the formless chaos (Gn 1:2)[11], blind submission to the god of this world (the devil), and the way of destruction. *Splendor*, then, reflects the brilliance of God's light, and as well alludes to the divine glory (δόξα).

The phrase *splendor ueritatis* appears to be found among the early Roman and Ambrosian sources in only two other, closely related prayers. The *super oblata* from a Mass for the Annunciation reads as follows:

"*Oblaciones nostras, quaesumus, domine, propiciatus intende, quas in honore beatae et gloriosae semper uirginis dei genetricis Mariae annua solempnitate deferimus, et quoaeternus* [*coaeternus*] *spiritus sanctus tuus, qui illius uiscera splendore suae graciae ueritatis repleuit, nos ab omni facinore delictorum emundet benignus*"[12].

In the oration, *splendor gratiae ueritatis* refers to the action of the Holy Spirit by which the Word took flesh. It is further related to cleansing the

---

[9] See the commentary on light and creation in the study of the collect for Sunday XIV, 240.

[10] See also Heb 1:3: "*qui* [*Filius*], *cum sit splendor gloriae et figura substantiae* ...."

[11] For commentary on the meaning of the primordial darkness of Gn 1:2, see C.Westermann, Genesis 1-11: A Commentary, translated by J.J.Scullion from Genesis (Kapitel 1-11), Neukirchen-Vluyn: Neukirchener Verlag, 2nd edition 1976 (Minneapolis: Augsburg Publishing House, 1984), 102-110.

[12] Lord, propitiously look upon our oblations, which we offer on this annual solemnity in honour of the blessed and ever glorious virgin Mary, mother of God, and may your co-eternal Holy Spirit, who filled her womb with the splendour of his grace of truth, favourably cleanse us from every act of sin (V 849, Triplex 555, Ariberto 656, Bergom 888, Biasca 814).

faithful from sinful deeds[13].

For collect Triplex 1750, the opposite of *splendor ueritatis* is the *tenebrae errorum*. Both these terms will now be discussed.

Tenebrae[14]

The fundamental sense of *tenebrae*, as seen in the opening verses of the scriptures themselves, has been touched on above. For the New Testament writings, darkness (*tenebrae*) symbolizes existence outside of the truth, light, way, community, forgiveness and salvation in Christ. This can be seen in the following passage from the First Letter of John:

"*Et haec est adnuntiatio, quam audivimus ab eo et adnuntiamus vobis, quoniam Deus lux est, et tenebrae in eo non sunt ullae. Si dixerimus quoniam societatem habemus cum eo, et in tenebris ambulamus, mentimur et veritatem non facimus; si autem in luce ambulamus, sicut et ipse est in luce, societatem habemus ad invicem, et sanguis Iesu Christi Filii eius, emundat nos ab omni peccato*" (1 Jo 1:5-7).

---

[13]The second prayer, from the Sixth Sunday of Advent, is quite similar. It uses *ueritas splendoris* rather than *splendor ueritatis*. While not found in the early Roman sources, it is present in the 8th century Gallican Bobbio Missal (eds. E.A.Lowe and J.W.Legg) as a prayer *ad pacem* for the feast of the Annunciation (Bobbio 127). The prayer reads:
"*Altari tuo domine superposita munera spiritus sanctus assumat: qui beatae Mariae uiscera sui splendoris ueritate repleuit*" (Trans: May the Holy Spirit take up the gifts placed upon your altar, Lord, [the same Holy Spirit] who filled the womb of blessed Mary with the truth of his splendour) (Triplex 151/554, Ariberto 106, Bergom 84, Biasca 84). Note that in the *Sacramentarium Triplex* this prayer also is found alongside V 849/Triplex 555 as one of the two possible *secreta* prayers for the Feast of the Annunciation. For a much weaker connection between *splendor* and *ueraciter* see the prayer H 98 (Triplex 370/385, Milano 11).

[14]For further examples of the use of *tenebrae* in the *Sacramentarium Triplex* see Heiming, Das Sacramentarium Triplex: 2 Teil: Wortschatz und Ausdrucksformen, 247.

In the liturgical sources, darkness is evocative of sin and death. This prayer from a Mass for the dead associates *tenebrae* with eternal death, *mortalitas*[15]. *Lux* is associated with life, hope and healing on earth, as well as eternal life with the saints in heaven. The oration reads:

"*Deus uita uiuentium, spes morientium, salus omnium in te sperantium: praesta propitius ut animae famulorum famularumque tuarum a nostrae mortalitatis tenebris absolutae: imperpetua [in perpetua] cum sanctis tuis luce laetentur*" (Triplex 3547)[16].

Our collect links *tenebrae* with *error*.

Error

The cognate verb *errare* has been studied in the analysis of the collect for Sunday XV[17]. Summarizing that discussion, the verb *errare* and the noun *error* are used to designate departures from God's ways, such as heresy, schism, participation in immoral and pagan practices, and disobedience. Those who stray (*errare*) by following paths other than God's fall into error (*error*), and walk in sin, darkness and death. Yet at the same time associated with the deviation of humanity from God's ways is the divine will that all humanity be saved.

The sense of *error* in Triplex 1750 is left unspecified. The other collects in the Rogation litany for Day III do not offer any precise interpretaton

---

[15] The understanding of *mors* and *mortalitas* as eternal death has been studied in the analysis of the collect for Sunday XIV. See above, 244.

[16] God, life of the living, hope of the dying, salvation of all who hope in you: grant propitiously that the souls of your servants, set free from the darkness of our mortality, may rejoice with the saints in perpetual light (Triplex 3547).
The prayer is not found in the other Ambrosian sacramentaries. However it is found in the later Roman source GregorTC 3061.

[17] See above, 257.

of *error*. They do deal, however, with the effects of sin (Triplex 1755) and the allurements of the devil (Triplex 1758). From the structure of Triplex 1750, then, *error* denotes all that lies outside the light, glory and truth of Christ. It points to a lost existence in darkness, sin and death, and as such is the opposite of a life in the grace of adoption as God's children.

Involvere

Involvere is rarely found in the liturgical sources[18]. From its context in Triplex 1750 the verb conveys being totally enveloped in and overwhelmed by the darkness that comes from error. A similar usage is seen in the preface Triplex 2251, where *involvere peccatis* describes the state of the people mired in abject wretchedness on account of sin:

"*UD aequum et salutare: Ut te postposito uetusti ... Quis te talem non timeat dominum? aut quis tantam maiestatem non prostratus adoret? Nos enim adoramus supplici corde genu deflexo obsecrantes: ut erigas miseros ad te de luto fecis clamantes: et de tantis nos absoluas quibus inuoluimur propitiatus peccatis ....*" (Triplex 2251)[19].

---

[18]*Involvere* is indexed twice in the Deshusses' concordance: V 695 and preface G 1335. The only two occurrences in the Triplex are our collect and the preface Triplex 2251 (which will be discussed below). See Deshusses, Concordances III, 2, 406 and Heiming, Das Sacramentarium Triplex: 2 Teil: Wortschatz und Ausdrucksformen, 127. Note that the prefaces Triplex 2251 and G 1335 are identical, and in fact are part of identical Masses for Sunday XII after Pentecost.

[19]VD ... Who does not fear such a Lord? or, prostrate, adore such majesty? For we adore with suppliant hearts, crying out on bended knee, so that you may raise us up, we wretched ones, shouting out to you from the mire of rot and filth, and [we adore and cry out] so that you may propitiously set us free from the uncountable number (*tantus*) of our sins, by which we are overwhemed (Triplex 2251).
The preface is not indexed in Moeller's Corpus Praefationum, and is not found in the Deshusses and Darragon concordance. Its only appearance in the Milanese sources seems to be in the *Sacramentarium Triplex*.

Semper maneamus conspicui

The remaining expression for analysis is *semper maneamus conspicui*. The verb *manere* is strongly evocative of the Vulgate translation of the Johannine writings, where it translates the greek μενειν[20]. As used in the New Testament, *manere* does not intend mere passive remaining or simple duration. Rather it has the sense of deep-seated abiding, lived out in a vital, active relationship. It also carries a certain Johannine dualism, whereby what abides in the Christian does not abide in their opponents. The corollary also holds. *Manere* implies that where Christians abide in what is of God, their opponents do not abide there. This fits well with the dichotomy in our collect between light and darkness.

For John, the key to abiding in the light (*lumen*) is love of neighbour (1 Jo 2:10). Note that in the following extended passage, light (*lumen*), truth (*verum*), and the love commandment are related. They are the opposite of darkness (*tenebrae*), which in turn is related to hate (*fratrem suum odire*), being lost (*nescire quo eat*), and blindness. The pericope reads:
"*Iterum mandatum novum scribo vobis, quod verum est et in ipso in vobis, quia tenebrae transierunt, et verum lumen iam lucet. Qui dicit se in luce esse, et fratrem suum odit, in tenebris est usque adhuc. Qui diligit fratrem suum in lumine manet, et scandalum in eo non est. Qui autem odit fratrem suum in tenebris ambulat et nescit quo eat, quia tenebrae obcaecaverunt oculos eius*" (1 Jo 2:8-11).

Those who do not live in love abide not only in darkness but in death:
"*Nos scimus quoniam translati sumus de morte ad vitam, quoniam diligimus fratres. Qui non diligit manet in morte*" (1 Jo 3:14).

---

[20]For commentary on μενειν and the related verb εἶναι, see R.Brown, The Epistles of John, Anchor Bible (Garden City, New York: Doubleday and Company, Inc., 1982): 195-196, 259-261.

In Triplex 1750 the community request that they may abide in the splendour of God's truth. *Manere* is qualified by *semper*, emphasizing the continuous nature of their abiding.

Furthermore the faithful wish to be *conspicuus* in the truth. Here the context of light and splendour, along with the contrast of the darkness, indicate that the baptized desire not only to be visible in and by the light, but to abide in it as outstanding, conspicuous, distinguished. A similar emphasis is found in this *ad complendum* for the Mass of the martyr St Lawrence. In the light of heaven his triumph is not simply visible but remarkable and distinguished. Hence it ought to be venerated with appropriately worthy and fervent worship. This was especially so in Milan, where the martyr had special prominence[21]. The prayer reads:

"*Da quaesumus omnipotens deus ut triumphum beati Laurentii martyris tui quem despectis ignibus consummauit in terris: perpetua caelorum luce conspicuum digno feruore fidei ueneremur*" (Triplex 2263)[22].

---

[21] Along with the two basilicas in the city, the Ambrosian sacramentaries mention the church of St Laurence. An example is Triplex Mass CXXVII, whose rubric reads *VII Kalendas Maii, Letanie Maior, ad Sanctum Laurentium*. The church appears to be the oldest in Milan, and probably played a central role in the development of the Milanese liturgy. See P.Lejoy, "Ambrosien (Rit)," DACL I, 1388.

[22] Grant, almighty God, that we may venerate with worthy fervour of faith the triumph of your blessed martyr Laurence, which he, in contempt of the flames, brought to perfection on earth, and which [now] shines outstanding in the perpetual light of heaven (Triplex 2263).
The prayer is not found in the earliest Roman sources, nor in the other Milanese sacramentaries. However it is in the Sacramentaries of Angoulême and Gellone: A 1193, G 1307.

Meaning of the prayer:

The meaning of the prayer emerges from the motivating clause. God, through his adoptive grace, has willed that the faithful, his children, be children of the light. The grace of adoption bespeaks the gift of the Holy Spirit in believers making them children of God, coheirs with Christ, heirs to eternal life and enabling them to call God their Father. The faithful enter this grace through baptism. The image of light is evocative of the great works of the original creation, the incarnation, the resurrection, and Pentecost. On account of these, the children of the light live Spirit- filled lives in the truth and way of Christ, lives marked by love, obedience, goodness and righteousness. The light symbolizes life on earth in hope and healing, as well as the promise of eternal life in heaven. It signals the defeat of darkness, sin and eternal death.

The remainder of the prayer is a petition to live as God has willed. The community are able to make this prayer in confidence because it is in line with God's will for them, and as well, as adopted children it is the Spirit who carries their prayer to the Father. Their petition is twofold. They both do not want to be enveloped in the darkness of error, and they desire to remain always resplendent in the splendour of the truth.

The prayer does not specify the sense of *error*. The expression *tenebrae errorum* points to a wandering existence, lost in sin, consumed by the primordial darkness banished at creation, and leading only to eternal death. It is a state of spiritual wretchedness and misery, which from within affords no means of escape. Within this straying there is no truth. Inside this darkness there is no light.

The community's request is that they abide in the splendour of God's truth. *Splendor* takes up the image of the salvific light of Christ and the Spirit. As well, it connotes the glory of God. The splendour of truth is life in love and righteousness. Yet Christian life in the light is no passive 'bathing' in the light. Just as, through the grace of adoption, God wills the baptized to be fully his children, so the community petitions to actively and wholeheartedly abide in his truth. Abiding in God's light especially denotes both love of neighbour and the rejection of the ways of sin and darkness. God's children desire to abide always and with distinction.

The vocabulary of the prayer expresses a radical dichotomy between life in the light and living in darkness. *Splendor* and *tenebrae*, truth and error, know no common ground. The verb *involvere*, with its connotations of passivity, carries the sense that those in error are fully wrapped and bound in a darkness in which there is no light, and from within which there is no escape. On the other hand, *manere* points to an active, vital relationship which embraces the truth, and willingly and continuously wishes to live in it.

The liturgical context of the prayer further enhances the significance of the vocabulary. The oration was used at a time when the celebration of Easter was drawing to a close, the glory of the Ascension still fresh in the minds of the faithful, the feast of Pentecost was anticipated, and the sacrament of baptism either had been conferred (at Easter) or was about to be conferred (at Pentecost). The ecclesia is in a season of rejoicing over God's will that they be saved.

Further, the Rogation days preceding Pentecost acted as a reminder of the power of darkness and error, and of the faithfuls' continuous need for God's help so that they might ever abide in the divine light and glory.

The immediacy of these dimensions of the prayer is lost when placed in its new context as a collect for the Thirteenth Sunday of Ordinary Time in the Missal of Paul VI. The Paschal and baptismal allusions are no longer as evident. The prayers of the new Missal bring no new interpretations to the oration's vocabulary. Our collect remains the only example of the conjunction of *splendor*[23] and *veritas*.

RELATIONSHIP OF THE CHRISTIAN PEOPLE TO GOD

The Christian people respond to God within a relationship established by God himself. God has invited the faithful to be his adopted children, and to live in the light. Creation, the incarnation, the resurrection, the sending of the Spirit and baptism are divine actions expressing God's will for his people.

The community live according to the divine will when they engage wholeheartedly and continuously in the truth revealed by God's light and splendour. This especially involves love of neighbour and righteous behaviour. It is to live in the Spirit as adopted brothers and sisters of Christ.

This state is totally incompatible with the state of error and darkness. Outside of God's adoption, light, splendour and truth is envelopment in darkness, loss of direction, the abandonment of hope, sin and eternal death. This is not God's will for his people, whom he has rescued from darkness.

FREER TRANSLATION OF THE PRAYER

Deus, qui, per adoptionem gratiae, lucis nos esse filios voluisti, praesta, quaesumus, ut errorum non involvamur tenebris, sed in splendore veritatis semper maneamus conspicui.	God, in adopting us as your offspring, you wished us to be children of your light. Grant that we may not be enfolded and overcome by the darkness of error, but that we may always abide resplendent in the splendour of your truth.

---

[23]*Splendor* is found 19 times in MR(1975). See Schnitker and Slaby, Concordantia, 2373-2374.

PART III
THE RELATIONSHIP OF THE CHRISTIAN PEOPLE TO GOD

PART III
THE RELATIONSHIP OF THE CHRISTIAN PEOPLE TO GOD

INTRODUCTION

The task of this introduction to Part III is to set out the key features that inform the presentation of a specifically liturgical theology of the relationship of the Christian people to God expressed in the collects. Three points are involved. First, this theology is expressed in the form of the *lex orandi* of the church. Second, the structure of the prayers themselves offers a framework for presenting their theology. Third, the interpretation of the meaning of the prayers and their vocabulary needs to take into account the particularity of the vocabulary of Christian euchology. With these points in mind, the outline of the ensuing chapters can be given.

<u>The form of the collects as *lex orandi*</u>:

The theology of the collects is expressed in the form of prayer, and so reflects the living, vital relation of the people to God as they offer him worship and service. The prayers are made through Christ, in virtue of the life of adoption given through him. In the way the faithful address and invoke God, they indicate their belief about who God is and how he wishes to be approached. The orations are motivated by the church's faith in God's actions and its confidence that he will continue to act on its behalf. The petitions of the people identify its needs and expectations as it seeks to respond in loving service to God. Finally, the prayers are offered within a trinitarian structure, expressing the church's fundamental belief in the revelation of the Godhead and the economy of redemption enacted.

Theological implications from the structure of the prayers:

The systematic presentation of a liturgical theology of the relationship of the Christian people to God in the collects can be determined by the structure of the collects themselves. Firstly, as prayers addressed to God, the orations 'name' God, and ascribe to God a range of attributes. Secondly, in the motivating clause, though not only in the motivating clause, the faithful bring to the prayer their belief in God's action towards them and all that God has made. Thirdly, in offering their prayer, the faithful 'name' who they are as a worshipping assembly, gathered before God. Fourthly, confident that God responds to their prayers, the members of the assembly petition God's favour for their own lives, for the church and for the world.

This structure in the prayers suggests that the presentation of their theology of grace can be divided into two broad sections, the theology of God and the theology of the Christian life. Consequently a chapter will be devoted to each of these, beginning, as in the orations, with the theology of God. The chapter on the theology of God, in accordance with the structure of the orations, will examine how the prayers 'name' God, the actions they ascribe to him, and the divine attitudes believed to underlie God's deeds. The chapter on the Christian life, also constructed according to the structure of the prayers, will contain an examination of the theology of church, and of the Christian life lived in grace.

The interpretation of the prayers:

Just as a liturgical theology attempts to take into account the nature of prayer and the structures in prayers, it also respects the specificity of the prayers' vocabulary. The orations construct and exemplify a particular Christian liturgical vocabulary. This has been seen in the vocabulary studies which form a major part of the analysis of each collect.

The vocabulary of the prayers is drawn from the Latin translations of the scriptures and from classical Roman cultic terminology. However, the meaning of words and expressions in Roman Christian euchology is especially determined through an examination of the way they are related, in differing liturgical contexts, to other words, phrases, expressions, symbols and allusions.

The particularity of this liturgical vocabulary is further underlined when three additional points are taken into consideration. The first is that the act of liturgy is a privileged ecclesial, and so hermeneutical, locus. Hence, the vocabulary used in worship assumes added symbolic dimensions not necessarily present in its non-liturgical usage. The second is that prayers, and especially their words and expressions, are continually reused, adapted and reappropriated into other liturgical contexts and prayers. They thus carry a range of connotations within the parameters of their liturgical usage. The third point is that the specific context in which this vocabulary is developed, used and reused is the liturgy itself. The prayers are composed by worshippers for worship.

Our presentation of the liturgical theology in the collects, then, must respect the particularity of the vocabulary of Christian euchology.

The content of the chapters in Part III:

The content of the chapters in Part III is determined by the above three factors, (1) that the theology in the collects is expressed in the form of the church's *lex orandi*, (2) that the structure of the prayers offers a framework for this theology, and (3) that when interpreting prayers the specific nature of a liturgical vocabulary must be taken into account.

Consequently the first chapter in Part III will deal with the theology of God expressed in the collects. It will examine the 'name' by which God is known, and the attributes by which he is described. As well, it will discuss the actions that are ascribed to God, and the qualities that are characteristic of these actions.

The second chapter will examine the theology of the Christian life in grace. It commences with a review of the ecclesiology in the prayers. This is followed by a study of the collects' understanding of various aspects of ecclesial, Christian life. A third chapter will be devoted to an evaluation of the collects for Ordinary Time in the Missal of Paul VI in light of the Christian euchological tradition, and the place of these prayers in the Mass.

CHAPTER NINE
THE THEOLOGY OF GOD

INTRODUCTION

Our presentation of the relationship of the Christian people to God in the collects opens with a discussion of the theology of God contained in the form of address and petition. From the standpoint of a liturgical theology, informed by the structure and content of the prayers themselves, the faithful's relation to God is expressed through the way God is addressed and also through the petitions requested. These show in what God the community believes.

Our synthesis of the study of the collects will commence with an examination of the way God is 'named'. This will be followed by a discussion of the attributes which are predicated of God, the works which are ascribed to him, and the qualities which are said to characterize divine actions.

The theology of the divine 'name':

In the collects, the address to God is linked with the invocation of the divine 'name', *nomen*[1], related back to its manifestation in the scriptures where God names himself, enabling his people to name him. The 'name' of God is a hebraism transposed into the Vulgate translation of the scriptures and commonly found in liturgical texts. *Nomen* signifies the being and essence of a person or deity.

---

[1] For the study of *nomen* see the analysis of the collect for Sunday XII, 317.

The expression and explication of the divine 'name' in the collects can be divided into three categories; (a) the primary expressions of God's name, (b) supplementary 'names', and (c) the trinitarian structure of the prayers' naming of God.

(a) *The primary expressions of God's Name*:

God is usually addressed as either *Deus* or *Dominus*. *Sanctitas, majestas, dilectio,* and *omnipotentia* are four primary expressions associated with the divine 'name'. The adjective *sanctum* and the noun *majestas* both express qualities that are practically synonymous with God's name. The collect for Sunday XII associates the manifestation of God's *nomen* with the revelation of his love, *dilectio*[2]. The collect for Sunday XXII links the revelation of God's *nomen* to his power. Each of these four is foundational for understanding the theology of the 'name' of God expressed in the collects.

(i) *Sanctitas*: The collect for Sunday XII asks for the love and fear of the Lord's holy name, *nomen sanctum*.[3] The adjective *sanctum* is also used as a substantive in the collect for Sunday XVII to express the belief that God is the source of all holiness in things: *Protector in te sperantium, Deus, sine quo nihil est validum, nihil sanctum*. A biblical term, *sanctus* denotes what belongs to the divinity itself, that is, what falls under the 'name' and power of God. By extension, everything that is filled with God's power and favour partakes in the divine holiness, and as such is qualified as *sanctus*.

(ii) *Majestas*: Roman euchology uses both *majestas* and *nomen* as terms of address for God. In the collect for Sunday XXIX, the faithful express their desire to respond to the divine *majestas* with sincere service. The second petition in the collect for Sunday XXIX is that the faithful may serve the divine

---

[2] See also the collect for Sunday XXV, where the holy law is associated with love of God and neighbour.

[3] For the study of the adjective *sanctus* see 520.

majesty, *majestas*, with sincere hearts[4]. *Majestas*, also a biblical term, denotes the reality of God as it is manifested through his power and exacts reverence.

(iii) *Dilectio*: The collect for Sunday XII associates the revelation of God's name with the divine love, *dilectio* in which God establishes all things, governs them and never abandons what he has established[5]. In response to this divine love, the community request the gifts of fear and, in equal measure, love of God's holy 'name'. The verb *diligere* has biblical roots. It is used in the Vulgate translation of John's Gospel to express the mutual love between the Father and the Son (Jo 15:9). *Diligere* also refers to that salfivic love in which God sent the Son into the world (Jo 3:16).

(iv) *Omnipotens, omnipotentia, Deus virtutum*: The collect for Sunday XXII associates the divine name with the divine power through use of the term *Deus virtutum*. The petition of the community for love of the divine 'name' is motivated by their belief in God's power and its expression in goodness, as seen in the title by which God is addressed and the oration's motivating clause: *Deus virtutum, cuius est totum quod est optimum*.

The title *Deus virtutum*, taken from the Vulgate translation of the Old Testament, images God as the victorious cosmic king, surrounded by his heavenly court[6]. At the same time, this king is ever ready and willing to fight on behalf of his people. The same view of the divine power is carried over into the New Testament. There God is described as the one to whom all powers are subject, and the one whose power in goodness is at work in all human affairs. The divine power has Christological overtones in that Christ shares in God's supremacy over all powers.

---

[4] For the study of *majestas* see 299.

[5] See the study of *diligere*, 314.

[6] For the study of *Deus virtutum* see 354.

The faithful's understanding of God's power is related to their belief that God is the source of all that is good (XXII, Jc 1:17). What is also implied here is that God is the source of only that which is good.

In the collects, then, God's power is linked with his goodness, the divine supremacy over all, the power of Christ, creation, and God's ongoing concern for all he created[7].

The orations draw a strong connection between God's power and the exercise of the divine mercy. In the collect for Sunday XXVI, God is said to manifest his power most especially in pardoning (*parcendo*) and showing mercy (*miserando*). This combination of power and mercy points to God's power over sin and death. As well, it points to the power of God's love for humanity in spite of their sin.

Consequently the church confidently invokes the God of power and mercy (*omnipotens et misericors Deus*) to drive out all that is adversarial towards the freedom to serve God (XXXII), and to grant its members the gift of worthy worship (XXXI). These merciful works of God are effected in his power, from which comes forth only that which is good.

In short, in revealing his power and mercy, God reveals his own self.

(b) *Subsidiary titles*:

God is also named by a set of supplementary titles which are more expressive of his activity than of his nature. He is addressed as *creator et rector* (XXIV), *protector* (XVII), and named as *auctor et gubernator* (XVIII) and *rector et dux* (XVII). The first thing to note here is how, in Roman euchology, these titles are interrelated. This is seen in the conjunctions of *creator* and *rector*, and of *auctor* and *gubernator*. The collect for Sunday XVII sets together the titles *protector*, *rector* and *dux*. Since these titles are

---

[7] See also the study of the title *Deus creator et rector* in the analysis of the collect for Sunday XXIV, below 203ff..

related to God's work, they are considered later in this chapter, when these works are set forth.

(c) *The trinitarian structure of 'naming' God*:

In the main, the prayers are addressed to God, *Deus*, *Dominus*, as the first person of the Trinity, but they are addressed through Christ. This is in line with the earliest Roman orations[8]. The name *Pater* is not employed. The collect for Sunday XIX is a partial exception in that the invocation of the first person of the Trinity recalls the name Father without using it directly as a form of address: *Omnipotens, sempiterne Deus, quem paterno nomine invocare praesumimus*. There are also indirect allusions to the fatherhood of God in those prayers which refer to Christ as *tuus Filius*, as in the collects for Sundays III[9] and XIV[10].

Apart from addressing all prayers through Christ, the place and redemptive work of the Son is given particular emphasis in the collects. In the collect for Sunday III there is a theology of the 'name' of Christ as the beloved Son of the Father, as seen in the expression *nomen dilecti filii tui*. The expression contains an echo of the Vulgate translation of Eph 1:19-23. This passage expresses the community's belief that Christ has been raised by God to the fullness of power, above every name and power. It also recalls the Vulgate translation of Jo 17:6, where Jesus declares himself to be the manifestation of God's name to those the Father gave him. From the structure of the collect for Sunday III, Christ's name as the beloved Son is set in parallel with God's favour, power and salvation.

In the collect for Sunday XXIII the redemptive matrix of redemption, adoption, freedom and eternal inheritance is ascribed to God's action through

---

[8] See above, 13 fn 12.

[9] *Deus ... ut in nomine dilecti filii tui ...*

[10] *Deus qui in Filii tui humilitate iacentem mundum erexisti*

Christ. In the collect, those who have been redeemed and become adopted children of God are named as the *in Christo credentes*. This is an important point. This Pauline matrix, and especially Paul's understanding of the grace of adoption, presumes faith in the work of Christ and also the work of the Spirit. The redemptive work of Christ is also recalled in the collect for Sunday XIV, where God's raising of the fallen world is said to be in response to the self-abasement of his Son: *Deus, qui in Filii tui humilitate iacentem mundum erexisti*.

As noted in the study of the collect for Sunday VIII, the Missal of Paul VI gives a more Christological focus to the understanding of God's peaceful order[11], relating it to the life, work and future coming of Christ.

While the Christology of the prayers is well attested, their pneumatology appears somewhat impoverished. Some of the vocabulary of the prayers, such as *procedere*[12] (X) and *adoptio* (XIII, XIX, XXIII), infer the presence and work of the Spirit. Similarly, the vocabulary of filial inheritance evokes Eph 1:13-14 where the Spirit is described as the pledge of the eternal inheritance (*hereditas*, XIX, XXIII). The role of the Spirit in the faithful's invocation of God as Father (Rm 8:14-17, Gal 4:5-7) may be presumed in the motivating clause of the collect for Sunday XIX, but the direct reference to the teaching role of the Spirit (*docente Spiritu sancto*) in the original was deleted when the text was incorporated into the Missal of Paul VI.

A weakness in the collects, then, is their neglect of the pneumatology implied in their vocabulary. Subsequently, there is a lack of balance in the theology put forward by the prayers between the place of the Spirit and the redemptive role of Christ.

---

[11] See above, 196.

[12] See 284.

(d) *Summary*:

The collects contain a theology of the divine name, the name, revealed by God, by which he is invoked. The divine *nomen*, a biblical expression, denotes the being and essence of God. The collects describe God's being and *nomen* in terms of holiness, majesty, love and power, which are primarily biblical ascriptions appropriated into Roman euchology. The orations particularly associate divine love with God's work of creation and his fidelity to what he establishes. They relate God's power to his goodness and mercy.

These ascriptions of the divine *nomen* are complemented by a series of interconnected, subsidiary titles which specify aspects of God's action. Their interrelationship expresses the continuity of God's action in the one divine economy of creation, redemption and completion.

Finally the structure of the prayers evokes the mystery of the Trinity. The collects, in the main, are addressed to the first person of the Trinity, but with infrequent allusions to the Fatherhood of God. The orations give some prominence to the redemptive work of Christ, who is 'named' as the beloved Son. This is the chief way in which the reality of the Trinity is expressed. However the pneumatology implicit in the prayers remains undeveloped.

The divine attributes:

Closely associated with the *nomen* and the titles ascribed to God are the divine attributes to which appeal is made. These do not have the substantive denotation of *dilectio* or *omnipotentia*, but they are closely associated with God and his actions. These attributes further express the people's sense of God's attitude towards them, and so ground their confidence that God will respond to their needs. The attributes characteristically appealed to throughout the collects are God's loving kindness, *pietas*, and mercy, *misericordia*. Associated with *misericordia* are God's propitiation, clemency, and his forgiveness of sin and the remission of its debt. A third attribute, to which appeal is made once, is the divine *fortitudo* (XI).

(a) *Pietas*[13]:

In the Latin of classical pagan Rome, *pietas* designated moral attitudes of fidelity to gods, country and family. When applied in Christian Latin to God, it underscores the 'conscientiousness' and 'diligence' attendant upon God's steadfast, unwavering love. To appeal to God's *pietas* expresses the community's belief that God's concern and devotedness to humanity know no bounds. Christian euchology links the divine *pietas* with the mystery of salvation in Christ (1 Tm 3:16), as well as with the work of the Spirit. In the liturgical sources, the divine *pietas* is associated with the pardon and forgiveness of sin, the recreation of all that has been damaged by sin, and the continuing gifts of strength and guidance for those who have been renewed.

In the collects God's *pietas* is believed to be grounds for his guardianship, protection and stengthening (V), as well as for the remedies (*remedia*) given to the baptized (XXXIV). God's loving kindness is associated with the request that God accompany, follow up and assist (*prosequere*) the humble supplication of the faithful (I).

The attribution of such loving kindness to God is closely associated with the community's belief in God's merciful forgiveness, *misericordia*[14].

(b) *Misericordia, miserari*[15]:

Whereas *pietas*, when applied to God, emphasises the devotedness and concern in God's care for humanity, *misericordia* highlights God's forgiveness

---

[13]The divine *pietas* is found in the collects for Sundays I, V, XXVII, and XXXIV. See especially 389.

[14]For the close connection between God's *pietas* and *misericordia* see the study of the collect for Sunday XXVII, 391.

[15]*Misericordia* and *miserari* are found in the collects for Sundays XVII, XXVI, XXVII, XXXI, XXXII. See especially 378.

of sin. In the Vulgate translation of Eph 2:4-6, God's mercy, *misericordia*, is said to be the primary expression of God's boundless love for humanity. The Christian experience of salvation from sin and death, restoration in Christ, being raised up, and the promise of heaven are sought in appeal to divine mercy.

The liturgical sources repeatedly set grace within the context of God's mercy, including the averting of what sins deserve, the defeat of the enemies and errors of faith, protection from *mortalitas*, and the remedies for sin.

As noted above, God's mercy is closely associated with God's power, *omnipotentia*. It is also related to his propitiation (*propitiatio*), favour (*clementer*), and his forgiveness of sin and the remission of its debt (*dimittere*). The noun *propitiatio* (XXIV) and its cognates *propitiare* (II), *propitiatus* (XXXII) and *propitius* (XI) denote God's favour in view of his forgiveness of their sin and propitiation[16]. *Propitiatio* also carries the sense of God's being propitiated and bestowing merciful favour in response to those acts of worship through which divine forgiveness and favour is sought. Mercy is not without some aspect of just retribution.

The collect for Sunday XVI sets God's propitiation and clemency together: *Propitiare Domine, famulis tuis, et clementer gratiae tuae super eos dona multiplica* (XVI). While the need for propitiation comes from the sin of the community, the adverb *clementer* highlights God's gracious forgiveness[17], in fidelity to his covenant (Ex 34:6-7).

The purpose clause of the collect for Sunday XXVII links the request for God to forgive (*dimittere*) what conscience dreads with the abundance of God's loving kindness (*pietas*) and mercy (*misericordia*). As with *propitiatio*,

---

[16]For the study of *propitiatio* see 210.

[17]See the collect for Sunday II, 475.

the liturgical use of the verb *dimittere* denotes not only forgiveness but also the removal of the debt owed on account of sin.

(c) *Fortitudo*[18]:

The collect for Sunday XI refers to God as the source of moral strength and courage, *fortitudo*, for those who hope in him. In the oration, *fortitudo* is related to God's propitiation (*adesto propitius*), and appealed to in light of the faithful's own mortal weakness (*mortalis infirmitas*) which leaves them unable to will or do what is pleasing to God. The ascription of *fortitudo* to God in the Vulgate translation of the scriptures is associated with the powerful help, protection and guardianship God offers his people. In Roman Latin euchology, God's *fortitudo* is also linked with his consolation.

The work of God:

The people's relationship to God is effected through the works that they, in prayer, ascribe to God. This expression of the *divinum opus* (XXXIV) includes (a) creation, providence and government, (b) redemption, and (c) their completion in eternity. This division should not obscure the fact that, from the standpoint of the prayers, the *divinum opus* is exercised in a single united economy of divine actions, incorporating and interconnecting creation, redemption, restoration, government and fulfillment in eternity.

(a) *Creation, providence and divine government as complementary*:

(i) Creation: As noted above, the titles of *creator*[19] and *auctor*[20] are ascribed to God in the collects.

The Vulgate translation of the scriptures opens with God's creation (*creare*) of all things: *In principio creavit Deus caelum et terram* (Gn 1:1).

---

[18]For the study of *fortitudo* see 304.

[19]For the study of *creator* see 203.

[20]For the study of *auctor* see 161.

The Pauline corpus speaks of the new creation (*nova creatura*) that comes in Christ (2 Cor 5:12-18). In Christian euchology, the title *creator* (XXIV) and the verb *creare* (XVIII) include God's original act of creation, his work of restoration wrought by Christ, and God's continuous creating, sanctifying, blessing and vivifying in Christ. Through the conjunction of *creator* and *rector* God's ongoing rulership is associated with his acts of initial and ongoing creation.

In the liturgical sources, the title *auctor* connotes the faithful's belief that God is the source of all life and goodness. It refers to God's authorship of peace, mercy, goodness and the remedies for sin. The collect for Sunday XVIII associates *auctor* particularly with initial creation. Through the title *auctor*, its conjunction with *gubernator* and association with restoration (*restaurare*) and preservation (*conservare*), God is named as the source of all goodness, continually engaged in the governance, restoration and preservation of what he has made.

God is also named as the originator of all good things, *bonorum omnium auctor* (XXXIII). The *bona* are especially associated with eternal happiness, *perpetua et plena felicitas*. In this the collect further relates the title *auctor* with the entry of the faithful into eternal happiness.

As can be seen, Roman euchology associates God's creative actions, whether initial or ongoing creation, with his work of government, restoration, preservation and completion in eternity in a single economy of grace.

(ii) Providence: The description of God's acts of creation is complemented by a further set of terms which connote his providential ordering: *providentia* (IX), *dispositio* (IX), *ordo* (VIII), *beneplacitum* (III) and *dirigere* (III, VIII)[21].

---

[21]*Cuius providentia in sui dispositione non fallitur* (IX), *mundi cursus pacifico nobis tuo ordine dirigatur* (VIII) and *dirige actus nostros in beneplacito tuo* (III). Note also the motivating clause, collect for Sunday XII: *nunquam tua gubernatione destituis, quos in soliditate tuae dilectionis instituis*.

As expressed in the collect for Sunday IX, the entire divine economy of creation and salvation is directed in God's providence: *cuius providentia in sui dispositione non fallitur*. This belief is also seen in the petition from the collect for Sunday III: *dirige actus nostros in beneplacito tuo*. The ultimate aim of the divine *dispositio* is that all things be returned to their pristine origins and integrity[22]. The use of *beneplacitum* emphasises that this order issues from God's good will and pleasure[23]. The divine *beneplacitum* (Eph 1:3-2:11) encompasses salvation in Christ, inclusive of election, adoption, redemption, the remission of sins, inheritance, the coming renewal of all things, and the seal of the Spirit. While *beneplacitum* means God's own good pleasure, it can also refer to the measure of the acts of the faithful who are called to do what is pleasing (*beneplacitum*) to God (Eph 5:10-11).

The nouns *providentia, dispositio* and *ordo* also express the confidence that God's directing (*dirigere*[24]) of all things is an ordered activity. The orations qualify God's *ordo* with the adjective *pacificus*[25]. The divine *ordo* is directed towards righteousness, civil peace, inner peace and the worship and devotion of the church. When it is said of God's *dispositio, non fallitur*, this encapsulates the community's belief that what God brings about, he upholds until its completion. The divine providential ordering is given effect in God's government and guidance of all things.

(iii) Government and guidance: God's government and guidance are expressed in the collects through a range of interconnected terms which expresses the manifold actions of God in the world. None of these images and titles is meant to stand alone. Some terms have been appropriated from their

---

[22]For the study of *dispositio* see above 370.

[23]For the study of *beneplacitum* see above 447.

[24]For the study of *dirigere* see 181 and 195.

[25]For the study of *pacificus* see 185 and 196.

usage in the Vulgate translation of the scriptures, for example *gubernare* (Sap 14:3), *regere* (Ps 22:1), *dirigere* (Gn 24:56, Ps 5:9) and *custodire* and *protegere* (Ps 16:8). Others are adapted from Roman usage, such as the verb *munire*, which appears to have been borrowed from Roman military vocabulary.

God's governorship is continually attested in the collects through the titles *gubernator* (XVIII), *rector* (XVII, XXIV) and *dux* (XVII), the noun *gubernatio* (XII), as well as the verbs *gubernare* (X), *moderari*, (II) and *dirigere* (III, VIII). They mark the community's belief in God's continuous leadership and governance of what he has created and continues to bring forth. This can be seen where God is invoked as *creator et rector* (XXIV), and described as *auctor et gubernator* (XVIII). God is said to govern what he established in his love *gubernatio ... instituere* (XII), and to govern what he has inspired, *inspirare/gubernare* (X). The use of *moderari*[26] in the collect for Sunday II points to the faithful's belief that God governs according to the measure and rhythm of what he created. As can be seen in the collect for Sunday XVII, God's leadership and rule are closely linked with his guardianship and protection (*protector, te rectore, te duce*).

The community's faith in God's guardianship is expressed by the title *protector* (XVII), the verbs *custodire* (V, XXII) and *munire* (V), and the noun *protectio* (V). The conjunction of *custodire*, *munire* and *protectio* in the collect for Sunday V denotes God's ruling, cherishing, visiting and defending his people[27]. *Munire*, originally a military term meaning to fortify with a wall, is particulary associated in the liturgy with protection from sin[28]. The verb *protegere*, as used in the Vulgate translation of Ps 16:8, attaches to God's

---

[26]For the study of *moderari* see above 471.

[27]See 495.

[28]For the study of *munire* see above 492.

protection a dual sense of intimacy and power[29]. The biblical title *protector* (Ps 17:31) as used in the collect for Sunday XVII, is linked with the titles *rector* and *dux*.

(b) *God's work of redemption*:

God's providential ordering, government and guidance are further complemented in the prayers through references to his work of redemption. This redemptive activity is, as noted earlier, an integral element in the single divine economy of creation, salvation and completion. The prayers contain a series of interrelated images which reflect the church's belief in God's redemptive acts. None of these images and descriptions of God's works is designed to stand in isolation, but rather, by their conjunction, they express the unity of God's manifold actions in the world.

(i) God's relation to his people is expressed in terms of redemption/adoption/freedom/inheritance. The collects approach God's work of redemption mainly through the Pauline matrix of redemption (*redemptio*), adoption (*adoptio*), inheritance (*hereditas*) and freedom (*libertas*)[30], all of which are associated with the justification given in baptism. This is most evident in the collects for Sundays XIII and XXIII. The collect for Sunday XXIII highlights the community's reponse in believing (*credentes*)[31] in these works.

This redemptive matrix serves to emphasise the breadth, totality and intimacy of God's redemptive work in the faithful. As well it points to two central aspects of the life of grace: freedom, *libertas*, and the promised inheritance, *hereditas*. In both Rm 8:14-17 and Gal 4:6 adoption is especially

---

[29] For the study of *protegere* see above 493.

[30] See the Vulgate translation of Galatians 4:6-7, Rm 8:15-17, and Eph 1:3-14.

[31] See the study of the collect for Sunday XXIII. The original prayer read *ut in Christo renatis*. It now reads *ut in Christo credentibus*.

associated with the work of the Spirit. As noted above, the collects in the current Missal, while emphasising the metaphor of adoption, give little attention to the role of the Spirit.

(ii) The collect for Sunday XIII links the image of adoption as children with that of light (*lumen*) and truth (*veritas*). Life as children of adoption, associated as it is with freedom and inheritance, is set in parallel with existence in the light, and hence in truth (*in splendore veritatis*).

These images are present in the collects for Sundays XIII and XV, where light is associated with truth: *in splendore veritatis* (XIII), *veritatis tuae lumen* (XV). The association of *lux* and *splendor* in the collect for Sunday XIII is evocative of the Vulgate translation of 2 Cor 4:1-6. That passage links God's light with the dispelling of the primordial darkness, the revelation of God's glory in Christ, and in that light, the knowledge which guides the life of believers. This last point is especially operative in the collect for Sunday XV, which associates the light of truth, *veritatis tuae lumen*, with God's guidance of sinners back to his way.

(iii) The *divinum opus* is expressed in a third image, that of the raising up of the fallen world by God on account of Christ's free self-abasement, obedience and death. The fallen world, *iacens mundus*, is in a state of ruin, darkness and death[32]. God, however, is believed to have raised the world, and so freed it from its subjection to death.

This image reflects the belief of the faithful in the cosmic dimensions of God's redemptive work in Christ. The whole of creation is raised. The image bespeaks the deadly effects of sin, which reduced the world to darkness and ruin, while also highlighting the enormity of the Son's love, and the acceptance of his actions by God.

The collect for Sunday XV relates the raising of the fallen world to freedom from bondage and servitude to sin.

---

[32] For the study of *iacens mundus* see above, 240.

(iv) Freedom from the bondage of sin is a fourth metaphor of redemption. Christ's work frees believers from the slavery of sin, as expressed in the clause *quos eripuisti a servitute peccati* (XIV). This is a modification of the original prayer, in which the metaphor of redemption was that of rescue from perpetual death, rather than rescue from bondage: *quos perpetuae mortis eripuisti casibus*[33]. The metaphor of sin as death is still present in the collects, but in a much diluted form[34].

The image of the bondage of sin underlines the effects of sin in humanity, and humanity's helplessness before it. The collect for Sunday XIV associated the fallen state of the world with humanity's sin. Freedom from the bondage of sin is linked with free service of God[35].

(v) Also present in the collects is the image of restoration, *restaurare*[36]. The church's euchology commonly associates restoration with baptism, in which humanity is restored to its original goodness. However in the collect for Sunday XVIII, restoration is directed towards all of creation: *et grata restaures et restaurata conserves*. In this the image of restoration parallels the raising of the fallen world, though restoration is associated here with God's work for his people (*his ... restaures*).

The metaphor of restoration of all that is pleasing also points to the cosmic dimensions of salvation. The description of creation's restoration as the restoration of what were *grata* marks a strong connection between God's work of original creation, his work of redemption, and his pleasure in its redemption. Furthermore, the collect for Sunday XVIII provides a good

---

[33]See 243.

[34]See the collect for Sunday XI, where the community describe their state as one of *mortalis infirmitas*, 307.

[35]See also the study of the collect for Sunday XXXII, particularly 428ff..

[36]See the study of the collect for Sunday XVIII, 169.

example of the way the orations set God's actions within a single unified economy of creation (*auctor*), redemption and restoration (*restaurare*), and ongoing help (*gubernator, conservare*), all of which is associated with what are pleasing to God (*grata*).

(vi) The belief in the divine indwelling in the world is given expression in the collect for Sunday VI. Two words are used, *manere*[37], to abide, and *habitare*[38], to indwell. Both *manere* and *habitare* have scriptural connotations. *Manere* is used in the Vulgate translation of the Johannine writings to indicate God's promise to remain in the hearts of believers. In the Johannine corpus, God is said to abide in those who confess Jesus as the Son of God, who believe in God's love for them, and who dwell in God's love (1 Jo 4:15-16). Furthermore, remaining in God's love involves keeping the commandments (Jo 15:10) and sharing with the poor (1 Jo 3:17). *Habitare*, in the Vulgate translation of the Pauline writings, connotes the presence of Christ by faith (Eph 3:17), the presence of Christ's word (Col 3:10) or his power (2 Cor 19:9). It can also mark the presence of the Spirit (Rm 8:8-9). Note that for Paul, without Christ it is sin which dwells (*habitare*) in the inner depth of the human person (Rm 7:17-19), not God.

There is a second metaphor of indwelling in the collects. Using the verb *manifestare*, the petition in the oration for Sunday XXVI is motivated by the belief that the depth and breadth of God's power is revealed in divine pardon and mercy. *Manifestare* is used in the Vulgate translation of the Johannine story of the miracle of Cana, in which the miracle manifests Jesus' glory and elicits the first act of faith mentioned in that Gospel. The verb, then, implies an experience of Christ that is so strong that it calls forth the

---

[37] For the study of *manere* see above, 327.

[38] For the study of *habitare* see above, 328.

response of faith. In the collect for Sunday XXVI, God's power is said to be manifest in the granting of mercy and pardon.

The *divinum opus*, then, includes God's abiding and dwelling in the world. This is a presence in which the divine power is believed to be made manifest as mercy and pardon, calling forth the response of faith. While the verb *habitare* contains an allusion to the role of the Spirit, *manere, habitare* and *manifestare* are used most frequently in the Vulgate translation of the scriptures to point to the presence and action of Christ.

(vii) The belief expressed in the collects concerning the protection of the faithful by God is complemented by the people's faith in God's continuing work in them. This is alluded to in a variety of ways. The collect for Sunday XXII expresses the community's belief that God nourishes (*nutrire*) what is good in the faithful[39], through their worship and participation in the sacraments. What God has nurtured, he is then asked to guard: *quae sunt nutrita custodias*.

The collects for both Sunday XXVIII and XXXIV associate God's work with rousing the will of the faithful to carry out good works. This is seen in the expressions *bonis operibus iugiter praestet esse intentos* (XXVIII), and *excita ... voluntates ut divini operis fructum propensius exsequentes* (XXXIV).

God's work in the faithful perfects the spirit of adoption in believers: *perfice in cordibus nostris spiritum adoptionis filiorum* (XIX). In some cases, the nature of God's work is expresed in the request for God's healing remedies, *remedia* (XXXIV).

(viii) In conclusion, the collects contain an array of interconnected images of redemption, complemented by descriptions of God's ongoing redemptive actions in the community. These images and actions reflect a liturgical theology which views all God's redemptive actions as essentially

---

[39]For the study of *nutrire* see above, 359.

related within a single economy of creation, redemption and fulfillment in eternity.

(c) *God's fulfillment of his works in eternity*:

The belief that God will bring to completion in eternal beatitude his work of creation, salvation and restoration is rendered in a variety of ways.

Through the images of inheritance, *hereditas*,[40] and promise, *promissum, promissio*[41], the collects express their belief in God's covenantal promise. Their faith is that it is God's will that the lives of all the people be brought to completion and fulfillment in him. This sense of completion is seen in the collect for Sunday XIX, which associates entry into the promised inheritance, *promissa hereditas*, with the perfection in the hearts of the faithful of the spirit of adoption.

The completion of God's work in eternity is also expressed in the images that express hope for the *bona invisibilia* (XX) and *vita perpetua* (XXV). The *bona invisibilia* connote the fullness of those good things, the *bona*, that are presently revealed in Christ, the church, the sacraments and worship, and in creation[42]. The image of eternal life, *vita perpetua*, points to life in the immutable God, where there is unchanging perfection and goodness[43].

Along with the sense of completion and fulfillment, there is also the image of participation in the divine happiness, *felicitas* (XXXIII). The faithful

---

[40]See the collects for Sundays XIX and XXIII.

[41]See the collects for Sundays XIX, XX, XXI, XXX, XXXI.

[42]For the study of *bona invisibilia* see above, 344.

[43]For the study of life in God as unchanging perfection and goodness, see the study of *varietas* in the collect for Sunday XXI, 275.

are believed to become full participants with God and with each other, *consortes* (XXVI)[44], in the good things of heaven, *caelestia bona* (XXVI). The entry of the faithful into eternal life, then, signals God's bringing to completion and fulfillment his work of creation, redemption, indwelling and ongoing action in the community. It seems unfortunate that the image of the restoration of all creation and its preservation in that state (XVIII) is not complemented by an image of God's work in the final recapitulation of all things, heavenly and earthly, in Christ, as envisioned in Eph 1:10 and Rm 8:21.

(d) *Conclusion*:

In their prayers, the faithful ascribe to God a range of deeds which further reveal the community's belief concerning God's *nomen* and his attributes. The *divinum opus*, which in the orations encompasses the whole economy of creation, redemption and completion, gives orientation to the people's relation to God. Their trust in this divine work is underlined by the qualities with which they describe it.

Qualities of God's actions:

God's actions are characterized, in the prayers, by a number of qualities which uphold the confidence with which the worshippers address him. There appear to be three such qualities: (a) abundant generosity, (b) perfection in goodness, and (c) providential ordering.

(a) *Abundant generosity*:

The quality of abundant generosity is ascribed to God's acts of redemption, his *pietas*, *misericordia* and promises.

---

[44] For the study of *consortes* see above, 383.

The petition in the collect for Sunday XVIII is that God bestow his unceasing favour, *perpetua benignitas*[45]. The use of *benignitas* in the Vulgate translation of the scriptures (Tt 3:4-7, Rm 2:4) bespeaks God's redemption, compassion and kindness. In this it connotes God's goodness, tolerance and forbearance. The oration relates this bounteous favour to God's initial act of creation, its restoration, continuous government and preservation.

This abundance is also adverted to in the collect for Sunday XXVII. In the motivating clause, the faithful set forth their belief that the abundance of God's loving kindness, *pietas*, exceeds their merits and their prayers. Because of the parallel in the prayer between *pietas* and *misericordia*, the collect also emphasises the abundance of God's mercy.

Furthermore, as seen in the collect for Sunday XX, God's promises too have a richness and abundance that is beyond every human longing: *promissiones tuas, quae omne desiderium superant* (XX).[46]

(b) *Perfection in goodness*:

God's action for his people is also characterized by the goodness and perfection of all that comes from him. God is invoked as the one from whom comes everything that is perfect: *cuius est totum quod est optimum* (XXII). The clause echoes the Vulgate translation of Jc 1:17, whose sense is that everything that is good comes from God, and that only what is good comes from God. As noted above, the oration relates God's goodness to his power.

The motivating clause in the collect for Sunday X describes God as the one from whom all good things come forth: *Deus, a quo bona cuncta procedunt*[47]. The clause alludes to the goodness of initial creation, as well as

---

[45]For the study of *benignitas* see 176.

[46]See also the reference in the collect for Sunday XXXIII to heaven as *plena et perpetua felicitas*.

[47]For the study of the invocation, see 284. See also the use of *profutura* in the collect for Sunday IX, 372f.

to the goodness of all present things. The verb *procedere*, through its use in the Vulgate translation of the scriptures to describe the Father's sending of Christ and the Spirit, connotes both goodness and salvation[48].

(c) *Ordered and provident*:

God's provident disposition (*providentia in sui dispositione*, IX) and peaceful order, *pacificus ordo* (VIII), have been studied above. They are included here to emphasise that quality of provident order which the collects ascribe to God's actions. As expressed in the collects, God's works are described as acts of providence (*providentia*), order (*ordo, dispositio*), and good pleasure (*beneplacitum*), which are unfailing (*non fallitur*), and lead to peace (*pacificus*).

Conclusion:

The task of this chapter has been to present the theology of God in the collects. The relationship of the Christian people to God is reciprocal to their perception of who God is and what God does for them. The community's perceptions are expressed in the way they name and invoke God, and through the petitions made to him.

Our study of the theology of God opened with an examination of the way God is 'named' in the prayers, which in turn is related to God's manifestation of his name, his being and essence, in the scriptures. The collects were seen to contain a theology of the divine *nomen*, expressed through such terms as *sanctitas, majestas, dilectio* and *omnipotentia*. The orations also employ a range of interrelated, subsidiary titles, *creator, auctor, gubernator, rector, dux, protector*, which have to do with divine actions. The study of the divine *nomen* was concluded with a discussion of the trinitarian structure of the collects' naming of God.

---

[48]For the study of *procedere* see above, 284.

Following this, attention was given to the divine attributes ascribed to God in the prayers, and to which appeal is made. These are less closely associated with God's nature than love, *dilectio*, and power, *omnipotentia*, but are qualities shown in his works. The chief attributes are *pietas*, and mercy, *misericordia*. It was noted that God's mercy is inclusive of God's propitiation, clemency, forgiveness and remission. A third attribute, invoked on one occasion, is God's *fortitudo*.

This study of the divine attributes was followed by a discussion of the works, *divina opera*, ascribed to God. These works include creation and providence, redemption, and completion in eternity. However, from the standpoint of the prayers, these are all facets of the one united economy of divine action.

The chapter was brought to a close with an analysis of the qualities by which the faithful describe God's work, and that thereby uphold their confidence and trust in addressing him and making petition. The three fundamental qualities of God's actions were seen to be abundance in giving, perfection in goodness, and provident order.

CHAPTER TEN
THE CHRISTIAN LIFE IN GRACE

INTRODUCTION

The collects, as prayers of the church, offer an interpretation of who God is, and why and how he is to be approached. At the same time, these prayers set forth an interpretation of who the praying community itself is, and how it stands in relation to God, even as it relates to him in worship. In turn, this relation to God motivates and shapes the faithful's prayer.

The orations offer a portrayal of the Christian life in grace. In them the church 'names' itself as it has been named by God in its election, and gives expression to its needs, its faith and hope, as well as to its place in the broader context of all God's works. Our presentation of the relationship of the people to God will commence, then, with an examination of the collects' ecclesiology. This will be followed by a discussion of what lies at the very essence of the community's response to God, and hence determines and orients the whole of Christian prayer and life. The remainder of the chapter will take up the central ideas, images and themes through which the collects characterize the life of the Christian community. The orations express the necessity of grace for doing what is pleasing to God, a necessity which is given further emphasis when viewed in terms of the impediments of sin. They offer a portrayal of the richness, fullness and hope of a Christian life lived in grace. Finally, there is to be found in the collects a perspective on the relationship of the Christian people to the world, setting the Church's relation to God within the broader context of God's entire work.

The community of the church: a people of grace

The collects, as the public prayer of the gathered community, are of their nature prayers of the church and embody an ecclesiology. Our first task is to examine the various 'names' found in the collects for those God has chosen. Each designation contributes something to the community's understanding of who they are before God, and what response is appropriate. The church is named as the *ecclesia* (VIII), and as the people of God, *populus Dei, populi tui* (I, II, XXI). It is referred to as God's family, *familia* (V), and by the related term servants of God, *famuli tui* (XVI, XVIII). The community of believers are the children of God, *filii* (XIII, XIX, XXIII). The collects also refer to the community as those who, through their baptismal profession, bear the 'name' Christian. Each of these designations will now be discussed, beginning with *ecclesia*.

(a) *Ecclesia*:

The designation of the church as *ecclesia* is found in the collect for Sunday VIII[1]. As used in the Vulgate translation of the scriptures, the term denotes the local assembly called together by God. At the same time, it connotes the entire church, in that the local *ecclesia* is itself a representation of the whole *ecclesia* God has called. Because it refers directly to those assembled, the term is eminently suitable for use in worship, as seen in the collect for Sunday VIII.

The term *ecclesia*, then, points to God's gracious action of bringing the faithful together, the unity of the whole church in God's action, and the response of the assembly in worship.

The early collects developed as the prayer of a local church. In the Missal of Paul VI, the prayers are prescribed for churches in all parts of the world. This universal destination of the Missal changes the nuance in the term *ecclesia*.

---

[1] For the study of *ecclesia* see above, 189.

(b) *Populus Dei*:

The faithful pray together as the people of God, *populus tuus* (I, II). The title recalls the community's belief in God's covenant choice of a people from amongst all the nations. In the collect for Sunday II, the *populus tuus*, in seeking its own needs, appeals to God's power over all creation, the heavens and the earth, *qui caelestia simul et terrena moderaris*. As an image which recalls the covenant, the term emphasises God's gracious choice and consequent fidelity to his people, and locates the local community within the whole of God's people.

(c) *Familia tua*:

In the collect for Sunday V, the faithful describe themselves as God's family, *familia tua*[2]. The noun *familia* has been imported into Christian Latin from classical pagan Roman law, in which *familia* designated the membership of an entire household, wife, children, servants and slaves, all under the protection of the head, the *paterfamilias*. As God's *familia*, the faithful express their faith that they truly belong to God and are protected by him. God is asked to guard his *familia* with continuous loving kindness: *Familiam tuam ... continua pietate custodi*.

As seen in the study of the collect for Sunday V, the Missal of Paul VI draws a strong link between God's family and the whole human family. The church is understood to be the leaven and soul of the human community, working in Christ to make of the human family the family of God[3]. This again gives a more universal than local connotation to the word *familia*.

(d) *Famuli tui*:

Closely allied with the metaphor of *familia* is the image of the faithful as God's servants, *famuli tui* (XVI, XVIII). The image particularly connotes

---

[2] For the study of *familia* see above, 487.

[3] See 495.

obedience and due service. This can be seen in the collect for Sunday XVI, where God's *famuli* seek the gift of perseverance in obedience to the divine mandates. However, in the collect for Sunday XVIII the term designates an attitude of rejoicing, along with a sense of divine election[4]. The *famuli* glory precisely because God is their originator and governor: *qui [famuli tui] te auctorem et gubernatorem gloriantur habere.*

Famuli, then, recalls the service and obedience of the faithful. It also connotes their rejoicing in their election to be servants of such a God. As God's servants, the faithful benefit from God's care for all creation, as expressed in the collect for Sunday XVIII.

(e) *Filii*:

The community also refer to themselves as the daughters and sons of God's love and light: *filii dilectionis tui* (XXIII), *filii lucis* (XIII). In both collects the image is related to the grace of divine adoption, *adoptio*. As with the images of *ecclesia* and *populus tuus*, the image of adoption portrays God's loving choice and fidelity. The term especially emphasises the intimacy and fidelity of God's relationship to the church. The bonds of adoption are freely embraced by God, and not easily cast off. *Adoptio* thus points to the dignity of the baptized, who in baptism are made the brothers and sisters of Christ, live in the very freedom of Christ, *libertas*[5], and are heirs to eternal life, *hereditas* (XXIII). The prayer associates this freedom with belief in Christ in the phrase, *in Christo credentes.*

(f) *Those who make Christian profession*:

The community also appeal to their 'name' (*nomen*) as 'Christian', as those who have made Christian profession. This is seen in the collect for Sunday XV. The designation connotes both the baptismal profession of faith,

---

[4] See 157.

[5] For the study of *libertas* see 228.

and its implied commitment to a way of life[6]. It also contains a sense of being judged by the baptismal profession. As with the expression *in Christo credentes*, the focus is on the faithful's profession of faith and consequent fidelity to the commitment asked of them by God's covenant.

(g) *Summary*:

From these various designations of the church, it can be seen that the Christian community is first and foremost a people called together by God. The images of adoption, people, family and *paterfamilias*, *famuli*, and *ecclesia* variously express this truth. The church is the community of those invited to make baptismal profession of faith in Christ and so to enter into an intimate bond of filial adoption, a covenant to which God is always faithful, and which asks a like commitment from the church's members. While in the context of their original composition the prayers express the character of a local church, in the Missal of Paul VI these same terms connote more readily the universal church.

The Christian life as a life of love and service of God expressed in worship:

In keeping with this reality of being God's people, the orations stress the primacy of both love and service, and their fundamental expression as worship.

(a) *Love and service of God's name*:

The place of love as the essential quality of Christian life can be seen in the collect for Sunday XXII. There, in response to their belief in God's power and goodness, the faithful seek the gift of love of the divine *nomen* in the depths of their inner being: *insere pectoribus nostris tui nominis amorem*. The prayer connects the love of the divine *nomen* with service of God through the petition in the purpose clause for an increase in religious observance and practice (*religionis augmentum*). The primacy of the response of love is also

---

[6]See 261ff..

evident in the collect for Sunday XX, where the community seeks the gift of love of God so that they may love God above all things and thus pursue the promises which he has made to them.

In the collect for Sunday XXIX, the people ask for the gift of sincere service of God's *majestas*. As seen above, *majestas* denotes God's 'name', and hence service is related to the reverence due him. This service is also related to love through the qualification *sincero corde*. The collect for Sunday XXXIII depicts full and eternal happiness as the outcome of an unfailing service of the author of all good things. In the collect for Sunday XXIV, heartfelt service (*toto corde tibi servire*) is sought as the proper response to God's work in creation and governance, as well as the proper way to obtain propitiation for sin.

The petition in the collect for Sunday XII is for fear (*timor*) and love (*amor*) of God's holy name (*sanctum nomen*). *Timor* connotes reverential and pious obedience and observance[7]. Together fear and love engender, and are expressed in, a commitment to sincere worship, obedience, wisdom, love of neighbour and building the messianic kingdom[8]. Similarly, the juxtaposition of love for God and veneration of God in the collect for Sunday IV, along with their relation to love of neighbour, set love and service at the centre of the Christian response to God's own love.

(b) *Worship*:

The primary expression of Christian love and service of God's name is worship. Joyful service as worship is seen to be the appropriate response to the community's faith in God's creation, rulership and propitiation (XXIV, XXXIII), his redemption of this people from the bondage of sin and its effects in creation (XIV), and his promise of eternal life (XXXI).

---

[7] See above, 318.

[8] See above, 320.

The theology of worship expressed in the collects is seen through an analysis of their vocabulary of worship, *laetari, gaudere, perfrui, servire, religio, devotio* and *venerari*, and of petition, *supplicatio, vota, invocatio* and *oratio*.

The specific quality of Christian worship is the joy[9] which marks the faithful's response to living within the bounteous effects of God's love, propitiation and salvation in Christ[10]. Joyful worship is an anticipation of the eternal joy given to those whom God has saved from the fallen state of the world and from servitude to sin (XIV). The collect for Sunday XXXIII connects human rejoicing, devotion, service and entry into eternal beatitude with God's authorship of all good things. In light of God's work of creation, salvation and the gifts of eternal beatitude, the service of the faithful ought to be marked by constant and devoted rejoicing and worship. In this, the prayer places worship and rejoicing at the heart of all Christian service, acts of devotion, and all attitudes of devotion.

Roman Christian euchology describes worship as an act of service, *servire*[11], a usage common in pagan religious vocabulary and in the Vulgate translation of the scriptures[12]. The verb indicates that worship is the service due to God in response to his works[13]. Christian euchology associates *servire* not only with worship but with attending to the tasks of church offices,

---

[9] *Laetari* (VIII), *laetitia sancta* (XIV), *gaudere* (XXXIII), *perfrui* (XIV).

[10] See the study of *gaudere*, 118.

[11] See the collects for Sundays XXIV, XXIX, XXXI and XXXIII.

[12] See Ellebracht, <u>Remarks on the Vocabulary of the Ancient Orations in the Missale Romanum</u>, 56.

[13] For a study of the common liturgical expression *servitus debita*, see the analysis of the collect for Sunday XIX, 578.

obedience to the commandments, and deeds of charity[14], thereby closely interconnecting worship, ecclesial life and love.

The noun *religio* is used to denote worship. Its pagan Roman meaning was the performance of religious rites, and by association the word came to evoke attitudes of awe, reverence, and conscientious regard for one's duties. The Vulgate translation of the scriptures relates *religio* with religious observances and good works (Jc 1:26-27). The collect for Sunday XXII links *religio* to the nurturing of what is good in the faithful, specifically the gift of the love of God's name in the hearts of the faithful.

The use of *venerari* in the collect for Sunday IV points to Christian worship as the primary expression of love for God, relates all acts of veneration (the lenten fast, veneration of the saints) to worship of God, and associates worship with love of neighbour[15].

Another word incorporated into Christian euchology from pagan ritual language is the noun *devotio* (VIII, XXXIII), with the adjective *devotus* (XXIX)[16]. They signify, in Christian usage, acts of worship such as the eucharist, penance and fasting, and evoke the affective piety, zeal and dedication out of which the acts of devotion are accomplished.

The terms found in the collects descriptive of prayer and petition are quite limited. *Supplicatio* and *supplex*, appropriated into Christian liturgical language from their use in the pagan cult, particulary emphasise the humility of the faithful as they make petition[17]. *Votum, invocare* and *oratio* are used frequently in the Vulgate translation of the scriptures, especially in the psalms.

---

[14] See the study of the collect for Sunday XXIV, 212.

[15] See 103.

[16] For the study of *devotio* see 189.

[17] For the study of *supplex* see 476.

In the liturgy they point to the petition of the community that they may love and serve the divine name.

In summary, the prayers, as *lex orandi*, first place all Christian life in the context of worship. Roman terms (*servire, religio, venerari* and *devotio*) are used, but placed in relation to the biblical revelation of God's name, and so to the commandments of love of God and neighbour. Public worship does not stand alone, but is related to all human (Christian) activity on the one hand, and gives it its orientation as service of God on the other. Being Christian worship, it carries the quality of joy, and relates present worship and Christian actions to the eternal joy of what is yet to come. Within this context of joyful love and service, the faithful humbly make supplication.

<u>The necessity of grace in the love and service of God</u>:

If the faithful are to love, serve and worship God as he deserves and mandates, this can only be done by divine grace. This absolute dependence on grace is reflected by the collects in a number of ways.

The people's prayer and supplication itself is said to be effective only when it is accompanied, assisted and favoured by God. Thus the petition in the collect for week I reads: *Vota, quaesumus Domine, supplicantis populi caelesti pietate prosequere.* The motivating clause in the collect for Sunday XXI expresses the community's belief that fitting and praiseworthy worship is a gift, *munus*, from God: *Omnipotens misericors Deus, de cuius munere venit, ut tibi a fidelibus tuis digne et laudabiliter serviatur.* Devoted, sincere and loving worship and service are also the object of petition in the collects for Sundays IV, XIV and XXIV.

Grace is said to be necessary so that Christians may use appropriately the good things that God has provided. The collect for Sunday XVII seeks God's mercy so that the faithful may use transitory good things (*bona transeuntia*) in such a way that they already cling to what is lasting. The goodness in these things is associated with God's grace, without which nothing is strong (*validum*) or holy (*sanctum*). The *transeuntia* are divine good things, such as worship and the mandates, experienced on earth in a passing manner but which in eternal life are the source of unchanging joys. Only when used in line with God's guidance and leadership (*te rectore, te duce*) do they provide a foretaste of lasting joy.

Similarly, humans can only do what is good when God's grace precedes, inspires, upholds and brings to completion their actions. This is especially marked in the petition from the collect for Sunday XXVIII: *tua nos, quaesumus, Domine, gratia semper et praeveniat et sequatur*[18].

All Christian responses to God, whether prayer, worship and service or good works, are possible only when inspired, upheld, supported and brought to completion in divine grace.

The impediment of sin:

The faithful's awareness of their need for grace to live according to the divine order and mandates is heightened by their consciousness of sin and its effects in themselves and in the world. The pervasiveness and power of sin affects the people's relationship to God, rousing them to petition for redemptive grace and the waiving of any penalty due their transgression. This is shown first in the motivation of the prayers, and then in the way the collects describe sin, its effects and power.

(a) *The motivation of the prayers*:

Appeals are made to God's mercy, propitiation and clemency because of the sinfulness of the people, and their powerlessness against sin. God's mercy is closely associated with his power over sin and death[19]. *Misericordia*

---

[18] See also the purpose clauses of the collects for week I and Sunday X.

[19] See 377.

is linked with God's loving kindness, *pietas*, relating God's forgiveness to his love[20]. The need for God's propitiation indicates that there is penalty owed due to sin.

In their appeal to God's works, the people in prayer ascribe to him their redemption, *redemptio* (XXIII), healing, *remedium* (XXXIV), forgiveness, *parcere* (XXVI), *dimittere* (XXVII), and protection, *munire* (V). These terms express the reality of sin, its debilitating effects on the faithful, their sinfulness, and their powerlessness against sin. *Dimittere*, in liturgical usage, means not only forgiveness but is associated with the remission of punishment[21].

(b) *The description of sin and its effects*:

The collects contain a range of images and descriptions which put forth the people's understanding of the nature and power of sin, and in so doing, determine their petition.

(i) *Tenebrae*: As applied to human and Christian life, *tenebrae* symbolizes existence outside of the truth, light, way, community and forgiveness that salvation in Christ brings (1 Jo 1:5-7). In the collect for Sunday XIII, the effect of darkness is described using the verb *involvere*[22], suggesting that those who live in the darkness are entirely enveloped by it. They are mired in an abject wretchedness that leaves them totally passive, directionless, and unable to extricate themselves.

(ii) *Error, errare*: Envelopment in darkness is quite close to the sense of *error* and *errare*[23]. The noun and verb mean departure from God's ways, whether through heresy, schism or sin. The image of following paths other

---

[20]See 391.

[21]See 394.

[22]For the study of *involvere* see 608.

[23]For the study of *error* and *errare* see 257.

than God's does not mean following another clear direction, but signifies being lost.

(iii) *Servitus peccati*: In the collect for Sunday XIV[24], the metaphor of bondage connotes a state of disobedient servitude and toil which leads to death. As seen in the Vulgate translation of Rm 6:16, it is the opposite of obedient service of God. The community's belief is that, in response to the *humilitas* of the Son, God raised the fallen world, and loosened the chains of sin: *quos eripuisti a servitute peccati*.

(iv) *Infirmitas*: One of the effects of sin is *infirmitas*, weakness which leaves the faithful unable to carry out their duties towards God[25]. The collect for Sunday XI qualifies it as *mortalis*, as leading to death, *mors*.

(v) *Quae conscientia metuit*[26]: In the liturgical sources, *conscientia* points to the moral sense of what is right and wrong. *Metuere* denotes the fear of judgement that is in the hearts of the faithful. The effect of sin is a state of fear in face of God's impending judgement and consequent punishment.

(vi) The effects of sin in the world: Human sin is such that it involves the whole of creation. This is seen in two closely related images, that of the fallen world, *iacens mundus* (XIV), and of darkness, *tenebrae* (XIII). The *iacens mundus* denotes the state of the world in ruin because of humanity's rejection of God's design[27]. This is also a rejection of the 'light' in which all creation was created, and represents an embracing of the sinister darkness, *tenebrae*, of the formless, chaos-laden abyss (Gn 1:2)[28]. The fallen state due to

---

[24]For the study of *servitus peccati* see 247.

[25]For the study of *infirmitas* see 307.

[26]See the study of the collect for Sunday XXVII, 394ff..

[27]For the study of *iacens mundus* see 240.

[28]For the study of *tenebrae* see 606.

sin is indirectly referred to in the collect for Sunday XVIII, which has a petition for God to restore all that is pleasing to him.

(c) *The intensity of the struggle against sin*:

The language of the prayer for Sunday XXXII is a reminder that the faithful are locked in continuous struggle with the forces of sin and the devil, the *adversantia*. Similarly, the intensity of the struggle is evidenced in the use of such substantives as *noxia* (IX), and *inimica* (XV) to describe those things which oppose loving service, the force of verbs such as *respuere* (XV) and *inhaerere* (XVII) to express the people's grace-given response, and *excludere* (XXXII) and *expedire* (XXXII) to signify the desired freedom from evil.

The portrayal of lived grace:

Upheld by grace and freed from sin, the church is able to fittingly serve God. The collects, especially through their petitions, portray characteristics and qualities of a Christian ecclesial existence of love, service and worship, responsive in grace and conformed to what is pleasing to God. (a) *Following the divine precepts*:

Life in grace is characterized by following the divine precepts, which themselves are ordained towards love and worship of God and love of neighbour[29]. The petitions of the collects for Sundays XXI and XXX stress that Christian obedience is an act of love. It is the response of those whose lives are shaped by the biblical virtues of faith, hope and charity (XVI, XXX). Loving obedience has an eschatological quality, since it is linked with desire for what God has promised (XXI), and leads to entry into eternal life (XXX).

(b) *Good works*:

The accent on following the divine precepts is complemented by an emphasis on doing good works. The biblical basis for an understanding of *bona opera* is found in Eph 2:10. The passage describes them as actions,

---

[29] See the collects for Sunday IV and XXV.

prepared already by God, which enable believers to walk in God's ways. Roman euchology, by using the words *placita*[30] and *recta* (X, VI)[31], qualifies these actions as those done according to his rule, and upright and pleasing in his sight. God's works are carried out in the power and revelation of the *nomen* of the beloved Son (III). Furthermore, they are a fitting expression of the 'name' Christian, professed in baptism (XV).

(c) *What is humanly involved in doing good works*:

The collects offer an account of what is involved, humanly speaking, in responding to God in love and service. As expressed in the prayers, the spiritual faculties of affection and love (*cor, pectus*), mind (*mens*), cognition (*cogitare, meditare, videre*), will (*voluntas, intentus*) and moral judgement (*conscientia*) are operative in living a life of grace[32]. They are often set in conjunction with each other, indicating that the whole of the inner human person is the subject of graced existence[33]. The collect for Sunday XXXII refers to the freedom in mind and body, *mente et corpore pariter expediti*, that comes when God suppresses the forces that oppose the faithful.

Life in grace entails congruence between will and action, since obedience to God's mandates requires that in both we be pleasing to God (XI)[34]. In a parallel construct, the collects for week I and Sundays VII and X

---

[30]*Beneplacitum* (III), *placita* (VI), *placere* (XI) and *quae tua* (XXXII).

[31]For the study of *recta* see 330.

[32]*Cor* (XIX, XX, XXI, XXIV, XXIX), *pectus* (VI, XXII), *mens* (IV, VII, XXI, XXXII), *cogitare* (X), *meditare* (VII), *videre* (I), *voluntas* (XI, XXI, XXIX, XXXIV), *intentus* (XXVIII) and *conscientia* (XXVII).

[33]For example, the collect for Sunday XXI brings together mind (*mens*), will (*voluntas*) and heart (*cor*). The collect for Sunday XXIX conjoins the will (*voluntas*) and the heart (*cor*). In the collect for Sunday IV, *mens* is an allusion to the Vulgate scriptural expression *ex toto corde et in tota anima et in tota mente tua* (Mt 22:37).

[34]*in exsequendis mandatis tuis, et voluntate tibi et actione placeamus*.

posit a close relation between prayerful perception of what is pleasing to God, and its accomplishment[35].

There is quite an emphasis in the collects on an affective response to God's grace. This is expressed in terms of love of God's name[36], love of neighbour[37], joyful worship[38], fervour in faith, hope and charity[39], glorying in God's creation and governance[40], feeling the effects of God's propitiation[41], love for the precepts[42], and desire for the promises[43].

The achievement of good works, then, involves the free, graced engagement of the whole human person, spiritual and corporeal. Upright deeds flow from a will and cognition themselves devoted to what is pleasing to God. Underlying such good works is an all-embracing, affective love for what comes from God and leads to the attainment of eternal life with him.

(d) *Biblical images of life in grace*:

Life in grace is portrayed by the distinctly biblical terms of adoption, *adoptio* (XIII, XIX, XXIII), and light, *lux, lumen, splendor* (XIII, XV).

---

[35] ... *Et quae agenda sunt videant, et ad implenda quae viderint convalescant* (I), ... *semper rationabilia meditantes, quae tibi sunt placita, et dictis exsequamur et factis* (VII), ... *ut cogitemus, te inspirante, quae recta sunt, et, te gubernante, eadem faciamus.*

[36] ... *tui nominis amor* (XXII).

[37] ... *rationabilis affectus* (IV).

[38] ... *sancta laetitia* (XIV, XXXI).

[39] ... *spe, fide et caritate ferventes* (XVI).

[40] ... *te auctorem et gubernatorem gloriantur habere* (XVIII).

[41] ... *tuae propitiationis sentire effectum* (XXIV).

[42] ... *id amare quod praecipis* (XXI).

[43] ... *id desiderare quod promittis* (XXI), ... *ad tua promissa currentes* (XXVI, XXXI).

Adoption, which connotes the intimacy and security of being God's children, *filii*, is associated with freedom, *libertas*, and eschatological hope, *hereditas* (XXIII). The metaphor of light, as used in the Vulgate translation of the scriptures, is conjoined with way, *via*, truth, *veritas*, and life, *vita* (Jo 14:6). Life in light, as reflected in the collects, is marked by avoiding error and remaining in truth (XIII). The divine light of truth, *veritatis tuae lumen*, allows those who stray to return to God's ways (XV).

(e) *Eschatological quality*:

The collects' portrayal of life in grace has a decisive eschatological quality. The community lives in constant expectation and hope of God's promises, a hope which in turn motivates their petition. The redemptive image of adoption is completed by that of inheritance, *hereditas*, just as the biblical designation of the church as God's people of choice, *populus tuus*, is linked with his covenant promise (*promissa* XIX, *promissum* XXVI, *promissio* XX, XXXI, *promittere* XXI, XXX).

Christian life (XX), including loving obedience (XXI) and praiseworthy worship and service (XXXI) is marked by desire for what God promises[44]. The prayers relate current service (XXXIII) and obedience to future happiness[45]. God's revelatory and redemptive deeds and gifts on earth, the *visibilia* (XX), the *restaurata* (XVIII) and the *bona transeuntia* (XVII), themselves presage the fullness of revelation, restoration and joy in eternal life. Consequently, the community seek to persevere in their obedience (XVI), for an increase in devotion (XXII), and to merit to enter eternal life (XXV).

(f) *Summary*:

The love and service of God is given expression in Christian worship, obedience to God's precepts, and in good works. These graced responses

---

[44]See also the expression *ad tua promissa currentes* in the collect for Sunday XXVI, 382-3.

[45]XXV, XXX, XXXIII, as well as XIX.

involve the free, loving engagement of the whole person, spiritual and corporeal, cognitive and affective, mind, heart and will, devoted to what is pleasing to God and intent on its accomplishment. The collects also contain a number of biblical expressions and images which situate the life of grace in God's love, freedom in Christ, the divine promises, light, truth and way. One of the defining characteristics of Christian life is that it is marked by an eschatological hope and expectation of the fulfillment and completion of all life in God's love.

The relationship of the church to the world:

The collects express an attitude towards the world, which sets the church within its larger context. The orations offer comment upon God's power and government over all creation, as well as upon the goodness itself of creation. Within the prayers are to be found various uses of the term *mundus*, especially in relation to the effects of sin in the world. The prayers also give a perspective on the relationship between the church and the world.

(a) *God's power and government over all creation*:

In the collects the community's faith in the power and government of God over all creation is expressed unequivocally. This can be seen in the motivating clause for the collect of Sunday II: *Deus, qui caelestia simul et terrena moderaris*. The conjunction of *caelestia* and *terrena* indicates the totality of all creation. Though the adjective *caelestis* is more usually found in the collects to qualify the divine[46], here it has a more particular meaning that refers to what God has created.

Initial creation itself is filled with the goodness of God. All God's works, both initial creation and all God's continuing acts of creation, are described as good: *Deus, a quo bona cuncta procedunt* (X). Everything that is

---

[46]For example, *caelestis pietas* (I), *gratia caelestia* (V) and *caelestium bonorum consortes* (XXVI).

good, and only what is good, is said to come forth from God: *cuius totum quod est optimum* (XXII). The church's prayer always envisages God's work as a whole, and does not express a view of creation that is separate from an economy of grace.

(b) *The world, mundus*:

The sphere of human existence is designated in the collects as the world, *mundus*. The term is given a variety of meanings in the prayers.

It is used as a neutral term to describe the course of world events, the *mundi cursus* (VIII). At the same time, the 'world' is a place affected by sin. In the collect for Sunday XIV, the world is referred to as the *iacens mundus*, the fallen world. The phrase describes the world as being in a state of ruin because of its rejection of its place in God's design. The image of the fallen world goes with the sinful rejection of the light, which leaves it in the darkness.

The need for ongoing restoration and preservation points to the community's experience of the continuing, threatening presence of the forces of evil in the world. In the collect for Sunday XXXII these are named as the *adversantia*[47]. The substantive denotes temptation, sin and the work of the devil.

The collect for Sunday XXI speaks of earthly realities, the *mundanae varietates*, as changeable, inconstant, and transitory[48]. Their variability is set in contrast with the perpetual nature and unchanging goodness of the true joys that come from God, *vera gaudia*. By implication, what is subject to change is open to sin (Jc 1:17-18). Only God, the unchanging source of all that is good, is the guarantor of true joys.

---

[47] For the study of *adversantia* see 422.

[48] See 275f.

The world is also the field of God's grace, so that grace for humanity is unimaginable without the restoration of the world. The collect for Sunday XIV expresses the belief that God raised up the fallen world on account of the free self-abasement of Christ. The petition in the collect for Sunday XVIII is that God continue the restoration from sin of all that he made in his favour. Once restored, it is kept in that state by God: *et grata restaures et restaurata conserves*.

(c) *The relationship between the church and the world*:

The collects touch on the relationship between the church and the world. As seen above, in the collect for Sunday XVIII, the servants of God, *famuli*, petition God, their originator and governor that he restore the creation which was so pleasing to him, and preserve it as restored. The same concern for the world is exhibited in the collect for Sunday II. The people of God (*populus tuus*) call upon God who rules all creation, the heavens and the earth. Their petition is for divine peace in the present.

The church's concern for the world is also expressed through love of neighbour. All the mandates of God's holy law are ordained towards love of God and neighbour (IV, XXV). The broader context of the Missal itself develops this point in three ways. Firstly, according to the Introduction to the General Instruction, during the Eucharist the faithful bring before God the prayers of the whole human family[49]. Secondly, the church, the *familia Dei*, is said to have a role in the renewal and transformation of the whole world into the family of God. This was seen in the discussion of the meaning of *familia tua* in the Missal of Paul VI[50]. Thirdly, the Missal connects peace and

---

[49] Proemium, § 5. See above, 52.

[50] See the study of the collect for Sunday V, 487.

righteousness with justice[51]. The faithful's petition for divine peace, then, includes justice for all humanity.

The relationship of the world to the church is given expression in the collect for Sunday VIII. The prayer relates tranquil worship and fruitful devotion to conditions of civil peace. Worship and peace are both understood to fall under God's order, with God establishing peace so that the church may worship.

(d) *Summary*:

The collects profess the community's belief that the world, the product of God's goodness, falls under his power and is ruled in his wisdom. As affected by sin, however, it is subject to the forces of sin and the devil. The faithful believe that the fallen world has been raised up by God. They are confident that God will continue in his grace to restore it and uphold what he has restored, since grace for humanity is unimaginable without the restoration of the world.

As the servants of God, the members of the church ask for God's grace for the world. This is motivated by their love for all God's works, and by their sense that it is only where harmony and peace prevail that God can be properly worshipped.

Conclusion:

The purpose of the chapter has been to examine the ways in which the collects have developed and expressed the relation of the Christian people to God. As acts of worship, the orations themselves embody this relationship in that they are expressions in worship of who the faithful are as they stand, gathered by God, naming him as he has revealed himself, and offering prayer and petition. Through their prayer they express their perspectives on the

---

[51] See the study of the collect for Sunday VIII, 195.

Christian life itself, their need for God, and their predicament under sin and its effects.

It was argued that at the core of Christian life is the faithful's response to God in love and service, expressed primarily in worship. The collects offer a range of perspectives on such love and service, in that they present a picture of the qualities and characteristics of graced human life, lived in truth, filial freedom and hope. The church's relation to God is given further context when examined in light of its relation to the world, and the world's relation to the church, and in the light of humanity's sinful condition.

CHAPTER ELEVEN
EVALUATION OF THE MISSAL OF PAUL VI

INTRODUCTION

The final task of this study is to offer an evaluation of the collects in the Sacramentary, and comment upon two sets of questions raised by our examination of the prayers. The evaluation will look at the collation of the prayers, examine their new context in the revised Missal and its effects on their vocabulary, and offer a limited critique of the collects[1]. The chapter will close with some remarks concerning the function of the first presidential prayer in early Roman Latin liturgy, the role of the collect in the Missal of Paul VI, and some proposals for further investigation.

The collation of the prayers as collects for the Sundays of Ordinary Time:

Three processes were used in the collation of the collects for the Sundays of Ordinary Time: adoption from the Missal of Pius V, introduction from the early Sacramentaries, and centonization using ancient orations[2].

---

[1]Much of the data used in this chapter is readily available in Appendix II entitled "Collects for the Sundays in Ordinary Time: Original Source, and Position in MR(1570) and MR(1975)."

[2]These processes are in line with the principles and methods said by Dumas to have governed the selection of texts by the revisors of the Missal. See Dumas, "Les oraisons du nouveau Missel romain," Questions liturgiques 52 (1971), 266-270. See the discussion of these points in Chapter Two, 39.

Twenty five of the prayers are held in common with the Missal of Pius V[3]. Six prayers were introduced into the new Missal from ancient Roman sacramentaries; three from the *Veronensis* (IV, XXIV, XXXIII), two from *Reginensis* 316 (VI and XXIII), and one from the *Paduensis* (XIX). As well two prayers were incorporated from early Ambrosian sources (XIII and XVI). The collect for Sunday XXV, more so than the collect for Sunday XVII, is a product of centonization, composed from two prayers, one from the *Veronensis* and the other from the Mozarabic Sacramentary. Neither of these two was utilized in the Missal of Pius V.

The new context of the prayers in the Missal of Paul VI:

Once incorporated into the new Sacramentary, the orations and their vocabulary are read within a new context, different from their original context and their place in the Missal of Pius V.

Like the Tridentine Missal, the Missal of Paul VI is a liturgical book for the universal church. By contrast, the ancient prayers were written for and utilized in local churches. As seen in the above studies, a number of the ancient collects were composed for specific historical events of local interest only[4]. Even when they were reused in various Masses, they were preserved in liturgical books which served the local church only.

---

[3]These are the collects for Sundays I, II, III, V, VII, VIII, IX, X, XI, XII, XIV, XV, XVII, XVIII, XX, XXI, XXII, XXVI, XXVII, XXVIII, XXIX, XXX, XXXI, XXXII and XXXIV. Note that the collect for Sunday XVII is based on a prayer found in MR(1570), though modified by the substitution of a purpose clause borrowed from the *Veronensis* preface L 495, a prayer not utilized in the Tridentine Missal.

[4]See the collect for Sunday IV, composed by Pope Gelasius in opposition to Christian Rome's celebration of the pagan festival of Lupercalia, as well as the collects for Sundays VIII, XVIII, XXIV, XXV and XXXIII, in which Pope Vigilius has in mind the siege of Rome by the Visigoths. The analyses of these prayers are found in Chapter Four.

Unlike the prayers of the Missal of Pius V, the orations of the new Missal are primarily prayed in vernacular translations, in line with the pastoral principle of the adaptation of the liturgy to contemporary times.[5] Thus precisely as prayers of the universal church, they also undergo a process of inculturation through their translation. While the issues of translation and inculturation are outside the scope of this dissertation, the question can be mentioned here of the suitability of Latin Roman 'collect style' prayers, themselves the product of Roman Christian inculturation[6], as orations for all cultures and languages.

The development in the liturgical meaning of words and expressions comes to light when the collects are examined from within their context in the new Missal as a whole. A number of such developments and diminishments in euchological vocabulary were discovered during the course of the analysis of the orations, and can be conveniently brought together here.

The church itself is understood more as the universal church than as the the gathering of the local community. Though the prayers were composed for a local church, through their inclusion in the Missal of Paul VI, a sacramentary for the whole of the church, they are employed in the particular churches of the universal *ecclesia*. This means the designations for the church, such as *ecclesia, populus, familia,* refer first to the universal church, and then to the local community. This situates the worship of the local community as an action of the univesal church.

Enlarged in the new Missal is the relation of the church to the world[7]. As seen in the study of the collect for Sunday V, the designation of the church as God's *familia* serves to place the church within the context of the entire

---

[5] See MR(1975) Prooemium, § 10 - § 15.

[6] See above, 20-23.

[7] See 495.

human *familia*. In the Missal the church is described as the leaven and soul of the human family, working to bring all its members into God's family.

The study of the collect for Sunday VIII reveals a broadening of the understanding of righteousness and of peace. There it was seen that, in the revised Sacramentary, the meaning of righteousness, *iustitia*, living according to God's law and righteousness, has been enlarged to include the order of justice and peace[8]. In the Missal the adjective *pacificus* is applied to the gifts prayed over at the offertory of the Mass, and to the self offering of Christ on the Cross[9]. The peace of Christ also includes peace for the victims of war and disorder. The expression *pacificus ordo* (VIII) denotes that ordering which brings peace. In the context of the Missal it refers back to the Cross of Christ, more immediately to the action of the eucharist, and can carry reference to the order of peace of which the world stands in need.

The study of *adversantia* and *excludere* (XXXII) in the new Missal points to a change in their meaning[10]. In particular their association with the forces of evil and the devil have been removed, weakening somewhat the metaphor of struggle and contest against sin in life on earth.

A critique of the collects for the Sundays in Ordinary Time:

These shifts in euchological vocabulary already offer material for a critique of the collects. However, any critique of the orations ought to acknowledge the limits inherent in studying such a restricted selection of texts. It must be attentive to the limits of the genre of the collects as prayer. As well, the collects themselves form only one set of 34 orations in the much larger collection of prayers and ritual actions that comprise the Missal and the

---

[8] See 195.

[9] See 196.

[10] See 433.

Mass. As an example, the renewed liturgy as a whole can be evaluated in terms of whether it fulfills the desire of the Vatican Council for a revised liturgy to meet contemporary circumstances and needs[11]. However, such a broad criterion can only be useful in assessing the small number of Sunday collects for Ordinary Time if these prayers are examined in relation to the Mass as a whole. Only then can it be appreciated what contribution the collects offer as the renewed liturgy seeks to meet such needs.

More appropriate criteria for a critique are furnished by the General Instruction of the Missal, which proposes a relation between the collect and the Mass, and by the Dumas' article in which he sets out his understanding of the principles and methods which guided the *Consilium* charged with revising the Missal[12].

(a) *The General Instruction of the Missal*:

In establishing how the collects relate to the Mass, the General Instruction offers two avenues of critique, which themselves have emerged from our study in Chapter Two of the place of the collect in the Mass[13]. Do the collects for Ordinary Time reflect the meaning of Sunday as the celebration of the Paschal mystery? Do the collects express the meaning of Ordinary Time as the season in which all the mysteries of Christ are celebrated?

(i) Sunday as the day of celebration of the Paschal mystery: A small, but not inconsequential, number of prayers have been incorporated into the Sundays of Ordinary Time from a prior context in the season of Easter. The collects for Sundays X, XI, XIV, XV, XIX, XXI, XXIII and XXIX were, in their original sources, prayers said during the Paschaltide liturgies. Furthermore, from amongst these, the collects for Sundays X, XIV, XV and

---

[11]SC § 4.

[12]Dumas, "Les oraisons du Missel romain," Questions liturgiques 52 (1971): 263-270.

[13]See 43.

XXI were utilized as prayers for the Paschal season in the Missal of Pius V. The Paschal sense of the collects of Ordinary Time is also brought out by the use of the collects for Sundays XIV, XV, XIX and XXIII (twice) in Masses for the season of Easter.

This inclusion in the Sundays of Ordinary Time of a number of prayers whose original context was Paschaltide, and the use of some prayers in the Missal of Paul VI for both Sundays in Ordinary Time and Masses in the season of Easter, together contribute to the realization of Sunday as the day of celebration of the Paschal mystery. Through such usage the collects share something of the character of the liturgies during Easter.

This, however, cannot be so fully confirmed from the content of the orations themselves, especially when viewed in light of the theology of the divine 'name' they contain[14]. Present in the collects are a theology of the 'name' of Christ (III), a very small number of direct references to the work of Christ (III, XIV, XXIII), and a number of indirect Christological allusions in the vocabulary. In general, very few of the prayers, even those appropriated from an original Easter liturgical context, give direct expression to the Paschal mystery.

(ii) Ordinary Time as the season in which all the mysteries of Christ are celebrated: Similar remarks can be made about the way in which the collects for Ordinary Time celebrate the mystery of Christ in all its fullness. Examining the original liturgical context of the prayers, not only are a number first encountered in liturgies for Eastertide, but one is associated with the celebration of the Nativity (III), two with the Ascension (VI, XII), and two with Pentecost (XIII, XVI). In the Missal of Pius V, the current collect for Sunday III is utilized twice during Christmastide, and the collects for Sundays X and XXIX are found in the Masses for the vigil of the Ascension and the Sunday within the octave of the Ascension respectively. However, none of the

---

[14]See above, 621ff..

present collects is found in Masses outside of Ordinary Time or Eastertide in the Missal of Paul VI.

Yet the content of the orations, while mentioning the work of Christ, does not overly highlight the mysteries of Christ. As well, repeating here what was noted in the above discussion of God's work of restoration[15], it seems unfortunate that the image of the restoration of all that is pleasing to God and its preservation in that state (XVIII), is not complemented by an image of God's work in the final recapitulation of all things in Christ.

In short, it can be said that while the liturgical context of various collects in their original sources, in the Missal of Pius V, and in the Missal of Paul VI, is reflective of the celebration of the Paschal mystery and the mysteries of Christ, this is generally not found in the content of the prayers.

Rather the prevailing content of the collects appears to centre around the mystery of God's 'name', revealed by him in the scriptures and expressed primarily in the liturgy in terms of holiness (*sanctitas*), majesty (*majestas*), love (*dilectio*) and power (*omnipotentia*)[16]. As well, the collects contain a portrayal of the Christian life in grace, dedicated in love and service to worship of the divine name[17]. In short, it is the veneration of God's name in worship which is brought to expression in the collects for Ordinary Time.

(b) *Critique furnished from Dumas*:

The article by Dumas states that the compilers of the Missal wished to be true to the original liturgical context and best textual witness of the prayers in their earliest known source[18]. This principle itself allows room for critique.

---

[15] See 639.

[16] See Chapter Nine, 621ff..

[17] This is the focus of Chapter Ten, 645f..

[18] Dumas, "Les oraisons du Missel romain," Questions liturgiques 52 (1971): 263-264.

(i) The original liturgical context: Under the heading "*Le nature des textes*", Dumas specifies the differences between the collect, prayer over the gifts and postcommunion, requiring that each type of text be utilized in its proper function[19]. The collects for Ordinary Time do not transgress these divisions, though the collect for Sunday XXIX is found in *Reginensis* 316 as both a collect and a postcommunion.

Beyond this however, the collects have been assembled from a range of liturgical contexts within the variable prayers of the liturgy. A number were originally prayers *super sindonem*[20], and the collect for Sunday V was first a prayer *super populum*, as was probably the collect for Sunday XVIII. The collect for Sunday XXV was created from an *oratio super sindonem* and an *oratio ad pacem*. Other orations were first encountered as prayers from the Office[21], while two orations are from Rogation day litanies[22]. Note that in the Missal of Paul VI, the collect for Sunday XVIII is also utilized in that Missal as a prayer *super populum*.

The compilers of the new Missal, then, have not been overly attentive to the principle enunciated by Dumas. They have respected the original context of orations by ensuring that in the revised Sacramentary the collects for Ordinary Time have not been selected from prayers over the gifts or postcommunion prayers, and that these collects have not been used in those contexts. On the other hand, the texts incorporated into the Missal as collects come from a broad variety of liturgical contexts, and the collect for Sunday XVIII is utilized in two different contexts, as a collect and as a prayer *super populum*.

---

[19]Ibid, 263.

[20]IV, VI, and VIII.

[21]XXIII, XXVIII

[22]XIII, XVI.

This selection, however, is quite typical of western liturgical texts in their adaptation of individual prayers to differing liturgical contexts. The same versatility has been noted above with regard to the liturgical seasons in which the 34 collects have been and are variously used.

(ii) The best textual witness of the original prayer: The majority of texts have been incorporated from the original source into the Missal unchanged. Aside from the two cases where a new prayer was created by centonization (XVII, XXV), there are three ways in which some prayers have been modified.

The original source of the collect for Sunday XV is corrupt, and so the current text is a restored version, reliant on the prayer as found in the Supplement to the *Hadrianum*. This is in line with the principles enunciated by Dumas[23].

The collect for Sunday XVIII is also a revised version of the prayer as found in the original source. In this case, the original has been modified by incorporating into it changes chosen from variant readings of the prayer throughout its manuscript tradition[24]. Somewhat confusedly, in the light of Dumas' principles, the original prayer itself, with only minor changes, is found in the new Missal as an oration *super populum*. The main reworking of the original prayer is in the substitution of *grata* for *creata*, by which some resonance with original creation is lost, but, on the other hand, emphasis is given to the favour in which God holds what he creates[25].

Four other prayers have also been modified. The collect for Sunday XVI now reads *spe, fide et caritate ferventes*, rather than *amore spei, fidei et caritatis ferventes*, a change of little consequence. In the collect for Sunday

---

[23]Dumas, "Les oraisons du Missel romain," Questions liturgiques 52 (1971): 263.

[24]See 149.

[25]See above, 175.

XIV, the clause *quos eripuisti a servitute peccati*, has replaced *quos eripuisti ex perpetuae mortis casibus*. The collect for Sunday XIX reads *quem paterno nomine invocare praesumimus, perfice in cordibus nostris spiritum adoptionis filiorum*, whereas the original read *quem docente spiritu sancto paterno nomine invocare praesumimus, effice in nobis filiorum corda fidelium*. Also deleted is the phrase *per debitam seruitutem*. There are two changes made to the collect for Sunday XXIII. The original petition, *respice in opera misericordiae tuae*, has become *filios dilectionis tuae benignus intende*, and the description of the faithful as the *in Christo renati* has been modified to *in Christo credentes*. The modifications to these collects fall outside the principles and methods of revision outlined by Dumas. They also warrant further attention since they introduce new meanings to the ancient prayers.

The changes made to the collect for Sunday XIV leave a weakened image of the power of sin and its effects[26]. There is a marked loss of the rigorous eschatological perspective of creation, sin, death and salvation. This is also reflected in the changes made to the collect for Sunday XVII subsequent to its incorporation into the new Missal. There the reference to the possible loss of eternal life, *transeamus ... ut non amittamus aeterna*, was deleted. This diminishment of eschatological tension is consistent with the reduction in scope of *adversantia* and *excludere*. As noted in the study of the collect for Sunday XIV, the Missal appears to reflect the same timidity in the face of vigorous eschatological language that is found in the changes made to the euchology of the Ordo Exsequarium[27].

The deletion from the collect for Sunday XIX of the teaching role of the Spirit means that there is no clear mention of the Spirit in the 34 orations, nor are there any direct references to the teaching role of the Spirit in the new

---

[26]See 247.

[27]See 248, fn 24.

Missal as a whole[28]. As remarked above in the section on the Trinitarian dimensions of the collects, a number of images usually associated with Christ and the Spirit have been more directly ascribed to the work of Christ. Moreover, the pneumatology implied in the vocabulary of the orations remains undeveloped. This modification to the collect appears, then, to have contributed to a failure to include the role of the Spirit in the revised Sacramentary, and a subsequent lack of balance in the collects between the place of the Spirit and the redemptive role of Christ.

The second change made to the same prayer represents a broadening in the meaning of the original. Through the modification of the petition, the more clearly Pauline expression *spiritus adoptionis filiorum* has replaced *filiorum corda fidelium*. In the original prayer this petition was particularly related to worship, *debita servitus*, but the Pauline expression denotes worship, the renewal of minds and bodies, the conformity of the faithful to the sufferings of Christ, and the faithful's walking in God's ways[29]. Through this substitution and the deletion of *per debitam seruitutem*, the meaning of life in adoption is enriched, and worship is intimately connected to the whole of the life of the people.

The changes to the collect for Sunday XXIII signify a revision of the theology of baptism in these orations. The sense of baptism as God's work, *opera misericordiae tuae*, has been diminished, though the themes of God's love and adoption have been highlighted. The deletion of the references to baptism, through the term *renatus*, modifies the foundational Pauline matrix, weakening the link in the liturgical text between the pairings redemption/adoption and freedom/inheritance. The description of the faithful as *renati* is now mainly restricted, in the renewed Missal, to prayers during the

---

[28]See 581.

[29]See 583.

seasons of Lent, Easter and Pentecost[30]. On the other hand, the use of *credentes* strengthens the need for faith in the act of baptism, an understanding also present in the collect for Sunday XV (*qui christiana professione censentur*).

In conclusion, the modifications made to the collects for Sundays XVIII, XIV, XIX, XXIII and even XVII do not fit within the principles of revision outlined by Dumas, but bring about significant changes in the meaning of the prayers and the theology of the collects when examined as a whole.

Concluding remarks and proposals for further investigation:

Our study of the collects will be brought to a close with some comments on the origins and functions of the first presidential prayer in early Roman Latin liturgy, the role of the collect in the Missal of Paul VI, and some proposals for further investigation.

(a) *The original function of the first presidential prayer in early Roman Latin liturgy: some concluding remarks*

Our analysis of the origins and history of the opening presidential oration has brought to light little evidence to support the contention of Willis that the prayer is closely related to the readings that follow. The lack of such evidence in the prayers themselves, and the variety of liturgical contexts into which the orations are cast, work against the Willis hypothesis.

There is some evidence that the collects and other variable presidential prayers, on occasion, contain themes which are also found in the readings. This is postulated of some of the six prayers from *Reginensis* 316 entitled *Dominica post clausum paschae*[31]. According to Chavasse, these prayers originally belonged to an early pre-existing set of six Masses for Easter which

---

[30] See 234, fn 29.

[31] These are studied in Chapter Five. The prayers are V 541 (XIV), V 546 (XV), V 551 (XXI), V 556 (XXIX) and V 566 (XI).

were later incorporated as a group into that sacramentary[32]. He compares them with what he considers to be the probable Epistle and Gospel readings for the Sundays after Easter in Rome before the end of the sixth century. Some commonalities become apparent, notably that V 546 (XV) and V 556 (X) have resonances with the respective Epistles of the day. Chavasse finds similar correspondence with other variable prayers, mainly prayers *super sindonem* and prefaces, from these Masses.

In short, our study has turned up no evidence to support Willis' hypothesis as a general principle, but reveals that in the variable presidential prayers of some Masses there were possibly allusions to the readings.

Our research does lend support to a thesis along the lines of that proposed by Jungmann, for whom the first presidential prayer was the climax and closing action in the ceremony of entry[33]. According to our study, the precise historical origins of this opening presidential prayer remain clouded. The 'collect style' prayer itself appears to be the product of liturgical adaptation and inculturation in the city of Rome, through which pagan Roman classical rhetorical forms were reappropriated into the developing Christian Latin liturgy. The result was a thoroughly Christian oration of typically Roman character and appeal. The first presidential prayer, once established in the liturgy, seems to have had two primary functions, both of which are alluded to in discussion of the etymology of the term *collecta*. Reflecting the sense of *collecta* as the *plebs collecta*, the oration brings the introductory rites to a climax and conclusion, gathering those assembled, ministers and people, into a single worshipping community. At the same time, the nature of the oration as a prayer of petition indicates that the prayer gathered the prayer of

---

[32]Chavasse, Le sacramentaire Gélasien, 241-244.

[33]See above, 31-32.

all those in the congregation (*collecta* as *colligere*), and brought it to conclusion.

Secondary functions, such as anticipating the readings or announcing the feast, season or special circumstance, could also accrue to these two primary functions of the prayer.

(b) *The function of the collect in the Missal of Paul VI: some concluding remarks and proposals for further investigation*

In the Missal of Paul VI the collects, as a body, express something of the character of the worship in which the church engages. They express the nature of the church as a community, gathered by God into his people redeemed through Christ and living in expectation of the divine promises. The faithful's response to God's call is one of worship, which is the primary expression of their love and service, and the foretaste of eternal happiness with him and the saints. Christian worship, as reflected in the collects, is first and foremost loving veneration of the divine name as revealed by God, and its invocation for the grace to live in fidelity to God in Christ. Christian worship itself is intimately connected with love of neighbour, obedience to God's mandates and good works, giving them their orientation as service and love of God.

The collects suggest something of the *indoles* of the celebration of the Eucharist. As a topic for further investigation, they could well be compared with the prayers over the gifts, which express something of the nature of the act of worship, and with the postcommunions which express the effects of taking part in it. This would help situate the collect within the broader liturgical theology of the Mass itself, and further illuminate the way in which the collect reflects the character of the celebration.

Our analysis of the collects has already shown that throughout the liturgical tradition Mass collects have been used in the Liturgy of the Hours, and prayers from the Office have been incorporated into the Mass. The collects for Sundays XXIII and XXVIII are first encountered as orations for the

Liturgy of the Hours, and the collects for Sundays VI, IX, X, XI, XII and XV have all been used in various liturgical manuscripts as prayers for the Office[34].

In the present text of the Divine Office[35] the Sunday collects for Ordinary Time are used as the concluding prayers of the Office of Readings, Morning and Evening Prayer, and the Hours during the Day for the Sundays during Ordinary Time[36]. They are said by the presider of the assembly, who can be a layperson in the absence of a priest or deacon[37]. The context of their use in the Divine Office, then, is quite different from that in the Mass. There the collect, as a priestly and presidential prayer, is associated with the gathering of the community, is expressive of the character of the celebration, and is a priestly prayer of petition which mediates the petition, praise and homage of the assembly[38]. A study of this dual usage could lead to a better understanding of the importance of context to the interpretation of the collects.

These two areas of investigation, in shedding light on how the collect reflects the character of the celebration, and the importance of context in the interpretation of the prayer itself, would further extend the work of this dissertation, which has concentrated on the theological import of the content of the orations.

---

[34] See the section entitled "Use in other Liturgical Sources" in the analyses for each of these prayers.

[35] <u>Officium Divinum ex decreto Sacrosancti Oecumenici Concilii Vaticani II Instauratum Auctoritate Pauli PP. VI Promulgatum: Liturgia Horarum, Iuxta Ritum Romanum, Editio Typica Altera</u>, I-IV (Libreria Editrice Vaticana, MCMLXXXV). The General Instruction of the Liturgy of the Hours is found in Volume I, 21-94.

[36] See the General Instruction of the Liturgy of the Hours, § 198-200.

[37] General Instruction of the Liturgy of the Hours, § 256-258.

[38] See above, 66.

APPENDIX I

COLLECTS FOR THE SUNDAYS OF ORDINARY TIME IN MR(1975)[1]

HEBDOMADA I
Vota, quaesumus, Domine, supplicantis populi caelesti pietate prosequere, ut et quae agenda sunt videant, et ad implenda quae viderint convalescant.

DOMINICA II
Omnipotens sempiterne Deus, qui caelestia simul et terrena moderaris, supplicationes populi tui clementer exaudi, et pacem tuam nostris concede temporibus.

DOMINICA III
Omnipotens sempiterne Deus, dirige actus nostros in beneplacito tuo, ut in nomine dilecti Filii tui mereamur bonis operibus abundare.

DOMINICA IV
Concede nobis, Domine Deus noster, ut te tota mente veneremur, et omnes homines rationabili diligamus affectu.

DOMINICA V
Familiam tuam, quaesumus, Domine, continua pietate custodi, ut, quae in sola spe gratiae caelestis innititur, tua semper protectione muniatur.

DOMINICA VI
Deus, qui te in rectis et sinceris manere pectoribus asseris, da nobis tua gratia tales existere, in quibus habitare digneris.

DOMINICA VII
Praesta, quaesumus, omnipotens Deus, ut, semper rationabilia meditantes, quae tibi sunt placita, et dictis exsequamur et factis.

---

[1] Significant changes from the original oration are marked with an *. The original expressions are placed in brackets following the current prayer.

DOMINICA VIII
Da nobis, quaesumus, Domine, ut et mundi cursus pacifico nobis tuo ordine dirigatur, et Ecclesia tua tranquilla devotione laetetur.

DOMINICA IX
Deus, cuius providentia in sui dispositione non fallitur, te supplices exoramus, ut noxia cuncta submoveas, et omnia nobis profutura concedas.

DOMINICA X
Deus, a quo bona cuncta procedunt, tuis largire supplicibus, ut cogitemus, te inspirante, quae recta sunt, et, te gubernante, eadem faciamus.

DOMINICA XI
Deus, in te sperantium fortitudo, invocationibus nostris adesto propitius, et, quia sine te nihil potest mortalis infirmitas, gratiae tuae praesta semper auxilium, ut, in exsequendis mandatis tuis, et voluntate tibi et actione placeamus.

DOMINICA XII
Sancti nominis tui, Domine, timorem pariter et amorem fac nos habere perpetuum, quia numquam tua gubernatione destituis, quos in soliditate tuae dilectionis instituis.

DOMINICA XIII
Deus, qui, per adoptionem gratiae, lucis nos esse filios voluisti, praesta, quaesumus, ut errorum non involvamur tenebris, sed in splendore veritatis semper maneamus conspicui.

DOMINICA XIV
Deus, qui in Filii tui humilitate iacentem mundum erexisti, fidelibus tuis sanctam concede laetitiam, ut, *quos eripuisti a servitute peccati, gaudiis facias perfrui sempiternis.

(*quos eripuisti ex perpetuae mortis casibus, gaudiis ....)

DOMINICA XV
Deus, qui errantibus, ut in viam possint redire, veritatis tuae lumen ostendis, da cunctis qui christiana professione censentur, et illa respuere, quae huic inimica sunt nomini, et ea quae sunt apta sectari.

DOMINICA XVI
Propitiare, Domine, famulis tuis, et clementer gratiae tuae super eos dona multiplica, *ut, spe, fide et caritate ferventes, semper in mandatis tuis vigili custodia perseverent.

(*ut amore spei, fideique et caritiatis ferventes, ...)

DOMINICA XVII
Protector in te sperantium, Deus, sine quo nihil est validum, nihil sanctum, multiplica super nos misericordiam tuam, ut, te rectore, te duce, *sic bonis transeuntibus nunc utamur, ut iam possimus inhaerere mansuris.

(*sic bona temporalia, ut non amittamus aeterna).

DOMINICA XVIII
Adesto, Domine, famulis tuis, *et perpetuam benignitatem largire poscentibus, ut his, qui te auctorem et gubernatorem gloriantur habere, et **grata restaures, et restaurata conserves.

(*et opem tuam largire, ... **creata restaures)

DOMINICA XIX
Omnipotens sempiterne Deus, *quem paterno nomine invocare praesumimus, **perfice in cordibus nostris spiritum adoptionis filiorum, ut promissam hereditatem ingredi mereamur ***.

(*quem docente spiritu sancto paterno ... **effice in nobis filiorum corda fidelium ... *** per debitam servitutem)

DOMINICA XX
Deus, qui diligentibus te bona invisibilia praeparasti, infunde cordibus nostris tui amoris affectum, ut, te in omnibus et super omnia diligentes, promissiones tuas, quae omne desiderium superant, consequamur.

DOMINICA XXI
Deus, qui fidelium mentes unius efficis voluntatis, da populis tuis id amare quod praecipis, id desiderare quod promittis, ut, inter mundanas varietates, ibi nostra fixa sint corda, ubi vera sunt gaudia.

DOMINICA XXII
Deus virtutum, cuius est totum quod est optimum, insere pectoribus nostris tui nominis amorem, et praesta, ut in nobis, religionis augmento, quae sunt bona nutrias, ac, vigilanti studio, quae sunt nutrita custodias.

DOMINICA XXIII
Deus, per quem nobis et redemptio venit et praestatur adoptio, *filios dilectionis tuae benignus intende, ut **in Christo credentibus et vera tribuatur libertas, et hereditas aeterna.

(*respice in opera misericordiae tuae, ut **in Christo renatis ....)

DOMINICA XXIV
Respice nos, rerum omnium Deus creator et rector, et, ut tuae propitiationis sentiamus effectum, toto nos tribue tibi corde servire.

DOMINICA XXV
Deus, qui sacrae legis omnia constituta in tua et proximi dilectione posuisti, *da nobis, ut, **tua praecepta servantes, ad vitam mereamur pervenire perpetuam.

(Deus qui ... *da nobis horum propitius efficientiam mandatorum: quia inpossibile sibi nullus excusat, quod tanta breuitate concluditur, tanta aequitate precipitur:)

(**Placabilis Domine, qui es pax certa et caritas indisrupta, pacem nobis omnibus largire plenissimam: ut pacifici ... perpetuam)

DOMINICA XXVI
Deus, qui omnipotentiam tuam parcendo maxime et miserando manifestas, gratiam tuam super nos indesinenter infunde, ut, ad tua promissa currentes, caelestium bonorum facias esse consortes.

DOMINICA XXVII
Omnipotens, sempiterne Deus, qui abundantia pietatis tuae et merita supplicum excedis et vota, effunde super nos misericordiam tuam, ut dimittas quae conscientia metuit, et adicias quod oratio non praesumit.

DOMINICA XXVIII
Tua nos, quaesumus, Domine, gratia semper et praeveniat et sequatur, ac bonis operibus iugiter praestet esse intentos.

DOMINICA XXIX
Omnipotens sempiterne Deus, fac nos tibi semper et devotam gerere voluntatem, et maiestati tuae sincero corde servire.

DOMINICA XXX
Omnipotens sempiterne Deus, da nobis fidei, spei et caritatis augmentum, et, ut mereamur assequi quod promittis, fac nos amare quod praecipis.

DOMINICA XXXI

Omnipotens et misericors Deus, de cuius munere venit, ut tibi a fidelibus tuis digne et laudabiliter serviatur, tribue, quaesumus, nobis, ut ad promissiones tuas sine offensione curramus.

DOMINICA XXXII

Omnipotens et misericors Deus, universa nobis adversantia propitiatus exclude, ut, mente et corpore pariter expediti, quae tua sunt liberis mentibus exsequamur.

DOMINICA XXXIII

Da nobis, quaesumus, Domine Deus noster, in tua semper devotione gaudere, quia perpetua est et plena felicitas, si bonorum omnium iugiter serviamus auctori.

HEBDOMANA XXXIV

Excita, quaesumus, Domine, tuorum fidelium voluntates, ut, divini operis fructum propensius exsequentes, pietatis tuae remedia maiora percipiant.

APPENDIX II

COLLECTS FOR THE SUNDAYS IN ORDINARY TIME: ORIGINAL SOURCE, and POSITION in MR(1570) & MR(1975)

MR (1975)	ORIGINAL SOURCE		MISSALE ROMANUM MR(1570)
I	H 86 *Note also* P 66	16, Orat. in alia Dom (post Oct. Dom.) item alia (collect) XIII, Dom.I post Epip., collect	Dom. infra Oct. Epip. (M1181)
II	H 922	202, Incip. orat. cottd, alia, (collect).	Dom.II post Epip. (M773)
III	H 85 *Note also* P 52	15, Orat. in alia Dom (post Oct. Nat. Dom.), (collect). X, Orat. in alia Dom. (post Oct. Nat. Dom.), collect.	Dom.infra Oct. Nat. (M761) & Die 5 Jan., In Vigilia Epiphaniae
IV	L 432 XVIII,iiii, Juli.incip. diurnae, super sindonem.		*Not in MR(1570)*
V	H 228 *Note also* P 201 *Note also* H 926	51, Sabb. Quadr. II, super populum. XLVII, Sabb. Quadr. II, super populum. 202, Incip. orat. cottd., alia (collect)	Dom.V post Epip. & Sab. post Dom.II Quad. (M558)

VI	V 587 *Note also* V 1038	I,lxv, Orat. et Prec. Dom. post Ascensa Domini, super sindomen. II,lx, Orac. in Ieiunio Mensis Septimi, super sindonem	*Not in MR(1570)*
VII	V 1521 *Note also* H 911 *Note also* P 112	III,lxvi, Orat. in contencione, ad Missas, Item alia Missa, collect. 202, Incip. orat. cottd., alia (collect). XXVII, Dom. V post Theo., collecta.	Dom.VI post Epip. (M875)
VIII	L 633	XVIII,xxxviiii, Julio, incip. orat. et praec. diurnae, super sindonem.	Dom.IV post Pent. (M170)
IX	V 1186	III,iii, Orat. et Prec. Dominicis Diebus, collect.	Dom.VII post Pent. & Missae pro aliquibus locis, Sab. ante Dom III Nov., BMV Div. Pro. Matris. (M220)
X	V 556	I,xl, Quarta Dom. post clausum Paschae, collect.	Dom.V post Pascha & In Vigilia Ascensionis (M199)
XI	V 566	I,lxii, Sexta Dom. post clausum Paschae, collect.	Dom.I post Pent. (M230)
XII	V 586	I,lxv, Orat. et Prec. Dom. post Ascensi Domini, collect.	Dom. infra Oct. Ssimi Corporis Xti, secunda post Pent. (M1033)
XIII	T* 1750	CXLIII, Item orat. in die tertio [in Laetaniis].	*Not in MR(1570)*.

XIV & Fer. II post domm. II, IV and VI Paschae Collect hebd., IV, 315.	V 541	I,lviii, Orat. et Prec. Dom. post Octabas paschae, collect.	Dom.II post Pascha. (M364)
XV & Fer. II post domm. II et V Paschae Collect hebd., III, 325.	L 75 *Note also* V 546	VIII,xx, April, Item alia, collect. I,lviii, Item II Dom. post clausum Paschae, collect.	Dom.III post Pascha (M336)
XVI	T* 1744	CXLII, Item orat. in die secundo [in laetaniis].	*Not in MR(1570).*
XVII	P 517 & L 495	CXVII, Hebd., IIII, post Pent, collect. Preface	Dom. infra Oct. Sacratissimi Cordis Jesu, tertia post Pent. (M911) *Not in MR(1570)*
XVIII & Orat. sup. pop. 8, 508.	L 887	XXVII,v, Admonitio Ieiunii Mensis Sept. et Orat. et Prec., Item alia, final prayer.	Feria V post Dom. II Quad. (Sup.Pop.) M23

XIX & Fer II post domm. II, IV et VI Paschae Collect hebd., II, 315.	P 745 *Note also* T* 1494	CLXXXV, Dom. VII post Sancti Angeli, collect. CXII, Sabb. post Pasch, super sindonem.	*Not in MR(1570).*
XX	V 1178	III,i, Orac. et Prec. Dominicis Diebus, collect.	Dom.V post Pent. (M323)
XXI & Fer. II post domm. III et V Paschae Collect hebd., V, 325	V 551	I,lviiii, Tertia Dom. post clausum Paschae, collect.	Dom.IV post Pascha (M342)
XXII	V 1182	III,ii, Orac. et Prec. Dominicis Diebus, collect.	Dom.VI post Pent. (M467)
XXIII & Dom. V, Paschae Collect 305, & Sabb. post Domm. II, IV et Vi Paschae Collect hebd., II, 322	V 522	I,lvi, Incip. Orat. Paschales Vespertinales.	*Not in MR (1570).*

XXIV	L 1045	XXVIIII,xiiii, Sept.(of the same type as Orat. et Prec. Diurnae), collect.	*Not in MR(1570).*
XXV	L 493 & LMS 1374	XVIII,xiiii, Iulio Incip. Orat. et Prec. diurnae, item alia 2, super sindonem. CLIV, Mass in VIII Dominico de Quotidiano, prayer ad pacem.	*Not in MR(1570).* *Not in MR(1570).*
XXVI	V 1198	III,vi, Orat. et Prec. Dominicis Diebus, collect.	Dom.X post Pent. (M418)
XXVII	V 1201	III,vii, Orat. et Prec. Dominicis Diebus, collect.	Dom.XI post Pent. (M770)
XXVIII	H 966	204, Orat. vesp. seu matut.	Dom.XVI post Pent. (M1150)
XXIX	V 561 *Note also* V 1209 *Note also* V 1264	I,lxi, Quinta Dom. post clausum Paschae, collect. III,viiii, Orat. et Prec. Dominicis Diebus, collect. III,<xvii>, Incip. canon accionis, post communionem.	Dom. infra Oct. Ascensionis. (M762)
XXX	L 598 *Note also* V 1209	XVIII,xxxiii, Julio, Incip. orat. et praec. diurnae, item alia, collect III,viiii, Orat. et Prec. Dominicis Diebus, collect.	Dom.XIII post Pent. (M759)
XXXI	L 574 *Note also* V 1206	XVIII,xxviiii, Julio, Incip, orat. et praec. diurnae, item alia, collect. III,viii, Orat. et Prec. Dominicis Diebus, super sindonem.	Dom.XII post Pent. (M742)

XXXII	V 1234	III,xv, Orat. et Prec. Dominicis Diebus, collect.	Dom.XIX post Pent. (M751)
XXXIII	L 486	XVIII,xiii, Iulio Incip. orat. et prec. diurnae, collect.	*Not in MR(1570)*.
XXXIV	H 894 *Note also* P 748	202, Incip. orat, cottd., alia, collect. CLXXXVI, Dom VIII post Sancti Angeli, collect.	Dom.XXIV et ultima post Pent. (M548)

* For the sake of space, T here replaces the abbreviation Triplex, the stardard form for denoting the Ambrosian *Sacramentarium Triplex*.

APPENDIX III
THE *CURSUS* IN THE COLLECTS FOR ORDINARY TIME IN MR(1975)

The collects have been set out below according to the layout of the *Editio Typica* of the Missal of Paul VI. The accent marks also follow those found in the text. The table attempts to indicate as precisely as possible the instances of the three chief forms of Roman *cursus* operative in the present Roman collects, the *cursus velox, cursus planus* and *cursus tardus*. However, further examples of the *cursus* may come into play when the text is spoken, possibly due to the elision of syllables by the president.

The operation of the *cursus* in the prayers suggests yet another avenue of inquiry. The collects could well be studied to see what particular features of the prayer are highlighted by the *cursus* itself when the oration is spoken. As this approach is tangential to the focus of the present study of the theological content of the orations, it will not be pursued here.

The three forms of *cursus* in the orations are:

cursus velox: + - - - - + -
cursus planus: + - - + -
cursus tardus: + - - + - -

All three are found in the collect for Sunday XXX:

    Omnípotens sempitérne Deus,
    da nobis fídei, spei et caritátis augméntum,
                           + - -   + -   (*planus*)
    et, ut mereámur ássequi quod promíttis,
                        + - - - - + - (*velox*)
    fac nos amáre quod praécipis.
                + - -   + -- (*tardus*)

HEBDOMADA I
Vota, quaésumus, Dómine,
+ - - + - - (tardus)
supplicántis populi caelésti pietáte proséquere,
          + - - + - -
                (tardus)
ut et quae agénda sunt vídeant,
     + - - + - - (tardus)
et ad implénda quae víderint convaléscant.
     + - - - - + - (velox)

Per Dóminum nostrum Iesum Christum Fílium tuum, qui tecum vivit et regnat in unitáte Spíritus Sancti, Deus, per ómnia saécula saeculórum.[1]
     + - - - - + - (velox)

DOMINICA II
Omnípotens sempitérne Deus,
qui caeléstia simul et terréna moderáris,
supplicatiónes populi tui cleménter exáudi,
          + - - + - (planus)
et pacem tuam nostris concéde tempóribus.
     + - - + - - (tardus)

DOMINICA III
Omnípotens sempitérne Deus,
dirige actus nostros in beneplácito tuo,
ut in nómine dilécti Fílii
tui mereámur bonis opéribus abundáre.
     + - - - - + - (velox)

DOMINICA IV
Concéde nobis, Dómine Deus noster,
ut te tota mente venerémur,
et omnes hómines rationabili diligámus afféctu.
          + - - + -
                (planus)

---

[1] The prayer *Per Dominum* concludes each of the collects for Ordinary Time. It is to be found in the General Instruction of the Roman Missal, § 32. See RM(1975) Institutio Generalis Missalis Romani, § 32, 35.

DOMINICA V
Famíliam tuam, quaésumus, Dómine,
    contínua pietáte custódi,
        + - - + -   (planus)
ut, quae in sola spe grátiae caeléstis innítitur,
                + -   - + - -
                     (tardus)
tua semper protectióne muniátur.

DOMINICA VI
Deus, qui te in rectis et sincéris
    manére pectóribus ásseris,
      + - -   + - -   (tardus)
da nobis tua grátia tales exístare,
    in quibus habitáre dignéris.
           + - - + -   (planus)

DOMINICA VII
Praesta, quaésumus, omnípotens Deus,
           + - -   + -   (planus)
ut, semper rationabília meditántes,
        + -- - - +   -   (velox)
quae tibi sunt plácita, et dictis exsequámur et factis.

DOMINICA VIII
Da nobis, quaésumus, Dómine,
     + - -   + - -   (tardus)
ut et mundi cursus pacífico nobis tuo órdine dirigátur,
                    + - -   - - + -
                         (velox)
et Ecclésia tua tranquílla devotióne laetétur.
                + -   - + -   (planus)

DOMINICA IX
Deus, cuius providéntia in sui
       dispositióne non fállitur,
             + - -   + - -   (tardus)
te súpplices exorámus,
  + - - - +   -   (velox)
ut nóxia cuncta submóveas,
      + - -   + - -   (tardus)
et omnia nobis profutúra concédas.
            + -   - + -   (planus)

DOMINICA X
Deus, a quo bona cuncta procédunt,
        tuis largíre supplícibus,
                    + - - + - - (tardus)
ut cogitémus, te inspiránte, quae recta sunt,
et, te gubernánte, éadem faciámus.
             +- -   - -+ - (velox)

DOMINICA XI
Deus, in te sperántium fortitúdo,
               + - - - - + - (velox)
invocatiónibus nostris adésto propítius,
               + -   - + - - (tardus)
et, quia sine te nihil potest mortális infírmitas,
                     + -   - + - -
                        (tardus)
gratiae tuae praesta semper auxílium,
               + - - + - - (tardus)
ut, in exsequéndis mandátis tuis,
et voluntáte tibi et actióne placeámus.

DOMINICA XII
Sancti nóminis tui, Dómine,
timórem páriter et amórem fac nos habére perpétuum,
                        + - - + - -
                            (tardus)
quia numquam tua gubernatióne destítuis,
               + - - + - - (tardus)
quos in soliditáte tuae dilectiónis instítuis.
                     + -   - + - - (tardus)

DOMINICA XIII
Deus, qui, per adoptiónem grátiae,
        lucis nos esse fílios voluísti,
                    + - - - -+ - (velox)
praesta, quaésumus, ut errórum non involvámur ténebris,
sed in splendóre veritátis semper maneámus conspícui.
                             + -   - + --
                                (tardus)

DOMINICA XIV
Deus, qui in Fílii tui humilitáte
        iacéntem mundum erexísti,
fidélibus tuis sanctam concéde laetítiam,
                + - - + - - (tardus)
ut, quos eripuísti a servitúte peccáti,
                + - - + - (planus)
gáudiis fácias pérfrui sempitérnis.
               + - - - - + - (velox)

DOMINICA XV
Deus, qui erràntibus, ut in viam possint redíre,
                                        + -   - + -
                                                  (*planus*)
veritátis tuae lumen osténdis,
      + -   - + -   (*planus*)
da cunctis qui christiána professióne censéntur,
                                      + -   - + -
                                             (*planus*)
et illa respúere, quae huic inimíca sunt nómini,
                                  + - -   + - -
                                               (*tardus*)
et ea quae sunt apta sectári.
        + - - + -   (*planus*)

DOMINICA XVI
Propitiáre, Dómine, fámulis tuis,
                   + - -   + -   (*planus*)
et cleménter grátiae tuae super eos dona multíplica,
                                             + -   - + - -
                                                 (*tardus*)
ut, spe, fide et caritáte fervéntes,
                      + - - +   -   (*planus*)
semper in mandátis tuis vígili custódia persevérent.
                                          + --   -   - + -
                                                 (*velox*)

DOMINICA XVII
Protéctor in te sperántium, Deus,
                  + - -   + -   (*planus*)
sine quo nihil est válidum, nihil sanctum,
multíplica super nos misericórdiam tuam,
                              + - -   + -   (*planus*)
ut, te rectóre, te duce,
sic bonis transeúntibus nunc utámur,
                     + - -   -   - + -   (*velox*)
ut iam possímus inhaerére mansúris.
                    + -   - +   -   (*planus*)

DOMINICA XVIII
Adésto, Dómine, fámulis tuis,
                + - -   + -   (*planus*)
et perpétuam benignitátem largíre poscéntibus,
                                    + -   - +   - -   (*tardus*)
ut his, qui te auctórem et
             gubernatórem gloriántur habére,
                             + -   - + -   (*planus*)
et grata restáures, et restauráta consérves.
                                + -   - +   -   (*planus*)

DOMINICA XIX
Omnípotens sempitérne Deus,
quem patérno nómine invocáre praesúmimus,
                              + -   - + - -   (tardus)
pérfice in córdibus nostris
      spíritum adoptiónis filiórum,
ut promíssam hereditátem íngredi mereámur.
                          +   - -   - -+ -   (velox)

DOMINICA XX
Deus, qui diligéntibus te bona invisibília praeparásti,
                               + --   -   - + -
                               (velox)
infúnde córdibus nostris tui amóris afféctum,
                        + -   - +   - (planus)
ut, te in ómnibus et super ómnia diligéntes,
                       + --   - - + - (velox)
promissiónes tuas, quae omne desidérium súperant,
                       + - -   + - -
                          (tardus)
consequámur.

DOMINICA XXI
Deus, qui fidélium mentes uníus éfficis voluntátis,
                        + - -   - - + -
                          (velox)
da pópulis tuis id amáre quod praécipis,
             + -   -   + - -   (tardus)
id desideráre quod promíttis,
ut,inter mundánas varietátes,
          + -   - -- + -   (velox)
ibi nostra fixa sint corda, ubi vera sunt gáudia.

DOMINICA XXII
Deus virtútum, cuius est totum quod est óptimum,
ínsere pectóribus nostris tui
      nóminis amórem, et praesta,
ut in nobis, religiónis augménto,
      quae sunt bona nútrias,
ac, vigilánti stúdio, quae sunt nutríta custódias.
                             + -   -   + - -
                               (tardus)

DOMINICA XXIII
Deus, per quem nobis et redémptio venit
      et praestátur adóptio,
                + -   - +   --   (tardus)
fílios dilectiónis tuae benígnus inténde,
                      + -   - +   -   (planus)
ut in Christo credéntibus
et vera tribuátur libértas, et heréditas aetérna.

DOMINICA XXIV
Réspice nos, rerum ómnium Deus creátor et rector,
et, ut tuae propitiatiónis sentiámus efféctum,
         + -   - + - (*planus*)
toto nos tríbue tibi corde servíre.
     + -   - + - (*planus*)

DOMINICA XXV
Deus, qui sacrae legis ómnia constitúta
        + - - -   - + - (*velox*)
in tua et próximi dilectióne posuísti,
da nobis, ut, tua praecépta servántes,
       + - - + - (*planus*)
ad vitam mereámur perveníre perpétuam.
     + - - + - - (*tardus*)

DOMINICA XXVI
Deus, qui omnipoténtiam tuam
     + - - + - (*planus*)
parcéndo máxime et miserándo maniféstas,
grátiam tuam super nos indesinénter infúnde,
        + -   - + - (*planus*)
ut, ad tua promíssa curréntes,
    + - - + - (*planus*)
caeléstium bonórum fácias esse consórtes.
       + - - + - (*planus*)

DOMINICA XXVII
Omnípotens, sempitérne Deus,
  qui abundántia pietátis tuae
et mérita súpplicum excédis et vota,
effúnde super nos misericórdiam tuam,
      + - - + - (*planus*)
ut dimíttas quae consciéntia métuit,
     + -- + - - (*tardus*)
et adícias quid orátio non preasúmit.
    + -- -   - + - (*velox*)

DOMINICA XXVIII
Tua nos, quaésumus, Dómine, grátia
      + - -   + -- (*tardus*)
semper et praevéniat et sequátur,
    + -- -   - + - (*velox*)
ac bonis opéribus iúgiter praestet esse inténtos.
          + -   - + -
           (*planus*)

DOMINICA XXIX
Omnípotens sempitérne Deus,
fac nos tibi semper et devótam gérere voluntátem,
+ - - - - + -
(velox)
et maiestáti tuae sincéro corde servíre.
+ - - - - + - (velox)

DOMINICA XXX
Omnípotens sempitérne Deus,
da nobis fídei, spei et caritátis augméntum,
+ - - + - (planus)
et, ut mereámur ássequi quod promíttis,
+ - - - - + - (velox)
fac nos amáre quod praécipis.
+ - - + - - (tardus)

DOMINICA XXXI
Omnípotens et miséricors Deus, de cuius múnere venit,
+ - - + -
(planus)
ut tibi a fidélibus tuis
digne et laudabíliter serviátur,
+ - - - -+ - (velox)
tríbue, quaésumus, nobis,
+ - - + - (planus)
ut ad promissiónes tuas sine offensióne currámus.
+ - - + -
(planus)

DOMINICA XXXII
Omnípotens et miséricors Deus,
+ - - + - (planus)
univérsa nobis adversántia propitiátus exclúde,
+ - - + - (planus)
ut, mente et córpore páriter expedíti,
+ - - - - + - (velox)
quae tua sunt líberis méntibus exsequámur.
+ - - - - + - (velox)

DOMINICA XXXIII
Da nobis, quaésumus, Dómine Deus noster,
in tua semper devotióne gaudére,
+ - - + - (planus)
quia perpétua est et plena felícitas,
+ - - + - - (tardus)
si bonórum ómnium iúgiter serviámus auctóri.
+ - - + - (planus)

HEBDOMANA XXXIV

Excita, quaésumus, Dómine, tuórum fidélium voluntátes,
                          + - - - - + -
                                        (*velox*)
ut, divíni óperis fructum propénsius exsequéntes,
                    + - - - - + -
                                (*velox*)
pietátis tuae remédia maióra percípiant.
           + - - + - - (*tardus*)

BIBLIOGRAPHY

LITURGICAL SOURCES

Altaarmissaal vor de Nederlandse Kerkprovincie. Nationale Raad voor Liturgie, 1979.

Andrieu, M. ed. Les Ordines romani du haut moyen âge 2. Les textes (Ordines I-XIII). Spicilegium Sacrum Lovaniense 11. Louvain: 1931.

Bannister, A. "Liturgical Fragments." The Journal of Theological Studies 9 (1908): 398-427.

Deshusses, J. ed. Le Sacramentaire Grégorien: Ses principales formes d'après les plus anciens manuscrits I. Spicilegium Friburgense 16. Fribourg Suisse: Éditions Universitaires, 1979.

Dumas, A. and J. Deshusses, eds. Liber Sacramentorum Gellonensis. Textus cura A. Dumas. Introductio, Tabulae et Indices cura J. Deshusses. Corpus Christianorum, Series Latina, 159-159A. Turnhout: Brepols, 1981.

Feltoe, C. L. ed. Sacramentarium Leonianum. Cambridge: At the University Press, 1896.

Férotin, M. ed. Le Liber ordinum en usage dans l'église wisigothique et mozarabe d'Espagne du cinquième au onzième siècle. Monumenta Ecclesiae Liturgica 5. Paris: Librairie de Firmin-Didot et Cie, 1904.

Férotin, M. ed. Le Liber mozarabicus sacramentorum et les manuscrits mozarabes. Monumenta Ecclesiae Liturgica 6. Paris: Librairie de Firmin-Didot et Cie, 1912.

Frei, J. ed. Das Ambrosianische Sakramentar D 3-3 aus dem Mailändischen Metropolitankapitel. Corpus Ambrosiano Liturgicum III. Liturgiewissenschaftliche Quellen und Forschungen 56. Münster: Aschendorff, 1974.

Heiming, O. ed. Das Sacramentarium Triplex: Die Handschrift C 43 der Zentralbibliothek Zürich. 1 Teil: Text, 2 Teil: Wortschatz und Ausdrucksformen. Corpus Ambrosiano Liturgicum I. Liturgiewissenschaftliche Quellen und Forschungen 49. Münster: Aschendorff, 1968.

Heiming, O. ed. Das Ambrosianische Sakramentar von Biasca: Die Handschrift Mailand Ambrosiana A 24 bis inf.. 1 Teil: Text. Corpus Ambrosiano Liturgicum II. Liturgiewissenschaftliche Quellen und Forschungen 51. Münster: Aschendorff, 1969.

Liber Sacramentorum Romae Ecclesiae: Omnium vetustissimus S. Leoni Papae in vulgatis tributus. Migne, J. P. ed. Patrologia Latina, 55, 21-156. Paris: 1846.

Lowe, E. A. ed. The Bobbio Missal: A Gallican Mass-Book (Ms. Paris. Lat. 13246.). The Henry Bradshaw Society, Vol. 58. London: 1920.

Messale Romano: Riformato a Norma dei Decreti del Concilio Ecumenico Vaticano II e Promulgato da Papa Paolo VI. Roma: Conferenze Episcopale Italiana, 1973.

Messbuch. Herausgegeben im Auftrag der Bischofskonferenzen Deutschlands, Österreichs und der Schweiz sowie der Bischöfe von Luxemburg, Bozen-Brizen und Lüttich. Köln: Benziger, 1975.

Misal Romano: Reformado segun las Normas de los decritos del Concilio Ecumenico Vaticano II y Promulgado por el Papa Pablo VI, Edicion tipica aprobada por la Conferencia episcipal Mexicana. México: Conferencia Episcopal Mexicana, 1993.

Missale Romanum ex decreto Sacrosancti Concilii Tridentini restitutum, Pii V iussu editum. Romae, Apud haeredes Bartholomaei Faletti, Johannem Variscum and Socios, 1570. Paris: CIPOL, 197-. Text-fiche.

Missale Romanum Ex Decreto Sacrosancti Oecumenici Concilii Vaticani II Instauratum Auctoritate Pauli PP. VI Promulgatum. Editio Typica Altera. Vatican City: Librera Editrice Vaticana, MCMLXXV.

Missel Romain. Paris: Desclée-Mame, 1974.

Mohlberg, C. Das fränkische Sacramentarium Gelasianum in alamannischer Überlieferung (Codex Sangall. No. 348): St. Galler Sakramentar-Forschungen I. Liturgiegeschichtliche Quellen, Heft 1/2. Münster: Aschendorff, 1939.

Mohlberg, C., L. Eizenhöfer and P. Siffrin. ed. Liber Sacramentorum Romanae Aeclesiae Ordinis Anni Circuli (Cod. Vat. Reg. lat.316). Rerum Ecclesiasticarum Documenta, Series Maior, Fontes IV. Roma: Herder, 1960.

Mohlberg, C., L. Eizenhöfer and P. Siffrin. ed. Missale Francorum. Rerum Ecclesiasticarum Documenta, Series Maior, Fontes II. Roma: Herder, 1957.

Mohlberg, C., L. Eizenhöfer and P. Siffrin. ed. Sacramentarium Veronense. Rerum Ecclesiasticarum Documenta, Series Maior, Fontes I. Roma: Herder, 1956.

Officium Divinum ex decreto Sacrosancti Oecumenici Concilii Vaticani II Instauratum Auctoritate Pauli PP. VI Promulgatum: Liturgia Horarum, Iuxta Ritum Romanum. Vols. I-IV. Editio Typica Altera. Vatican City: Libreria Editrice Vaticana, MCMLXXXV.

Olivar, A. ed. Sacramentarium Rivipullense. Monumenta Hispaniae Sacra. Serie litúrgica, Vol VII. Madrid-Barcelona: Instituto Enrique Flórez, 1964.

Paredi, A. ed. "Il Sacramentario di Ariberto: Edizione del ms. D 3,2 della Biblioteca del Capitolo Metropolitano di Milano." In Miscellanea Adriano Bernareggi, 329-488. Bergamo: Edizioni Opera B. Barbarigo, 1958.

Paredi, A. ed. Sacramentarium Bergomense: Manoscritto del secolo IX della Biblioteca di S.Alessandro in Colonna in Bergamo. Monumenta Bergomensia VI. Bergamo: Fondazione Amministrazione Provinciale, 1962.

Saint-Roch, P. ed. Liber Sacramentorum Engolismensis: Manuscrit B.N. Lat. 816, Le Sacramentaire Gélasien d'Angoulême. Corpus Christianorum, Series Latina, 159 C. Turnhout: Brepols, 1987.

The Sacramentary. Revised according to the second typical edition of the
 Missale Romanum (1975), March 1, 1985, for use in the dioceses of
 the United States of America. Trans. prepared by the International
 Committee on English in the Liturgy. Collegeville: The Liturgical
 Press, 1985.

Wilmart, A. The Psalter Collects: From V-VIth Century Sources (Three
 Series). The Henry Bradshaw Society, No 83. Edited by L.Brou.
 London: 1949.

INSTRUMENTS and DICTIONARIES

Blatt, F. ed. Novum Glossarium Mediae Latinitatis ab anno DCCC usque ad
 annum MCC. M-N. Hafniae: Ejnar Munksgaard, MCMLIX-
 MCMLXIX.

Blaise, A. Dictionnaire latin-français des auteurs chrétiens. Turnhout:
 Brepols, 1964.

Blaise, A. Le vocabulaire latin des principaux thèmes liturgiques. Turnhout:
 Brepols, 1966.

Bruylants, P. Les oraisons du Missel Romain: texte et histoire, Vol. I:
 Tabulae synopticae fontium Missalis Romain indices, Vol. II,
 Orationum textus et usus juxta fontes. Louvain: Centre de
 Documentation et d'Information Liturgiques, Abbaye du Mont César,
 1952.

Combaluzier, F. Sacramentaires de Bergame et D'Ariberto: Table des
 matières et index des formules. Instrumenta Patristica 5. Steenbrugis:
 In Abbatia Sancti Petri, 1962.

Deshusses, J. and B. Darragon, eds. Concordances et tableaux pour l'étude
 des grands sacramentaires: Vol. I Concordance des Pièces; Vol. II
 Tableaux synoptiques; Vol. III pts. 1-4, Concordance Verbale.
 Spicilegii Friburgensis Subsidia, nn. 9-14. Fribourg, Suisse: Éditions
 Universitaires, 1982-83.

Dumas, A. "Les sources du Missel romain." Notitiae 7 (1971):37-42, 74-77,
 94-95, 134-136, 276-279, 409-410.

Ellebracht, M. P. Remarks on the Vocabulary of the Ancient Orations in the Missale Romanum. Latinitas Christianorum Primaeva, Fasc.XVIII, Second Edition. Nijmegen-Utrecht: Dekker and Van De Vegt, 1966.

Facciolati, J., A. E. G. Forcellini, and J. Furlanetti. Lexicon Totius Latinitatis, III. Patavii: Typis Seminarii, MDCCCLXXI.

Haessly, M. Rhetoric in the Sunday Collects of the Roman Missal. St Louis: The Manufacturers Printery, 1938.

Johnson, C. "Sources of the Roman Missal (1975): Proprium de Tempore, Proprium de Sanctis." Notitiae 32 (1-2-3/1996): 7-180.

Lewis, C. and C. Short. A Latin Dictionary. Founded on Andrews' edition of Freund's Latin Dictionary, revised, enlarged, and in great part rewritten. Oxford: The Clarendon Press, 1879/1962.

Moeller, E., J-M. Clément et B. Coppieters 't Wallant, eds. Corpus Orationum. T.1 A-C, orationes 1-880, t.2 D, pars prima, orationes 881-1707, t.3 D, pars altera, 1708-2389, t.4 E-H, orationes 2390-3028, t.5 I-O, orationes 3029-3699. Corpus Christianorum, Series Latina, 160-. Turnhout: Brepols, 1992-.

Moeller, E. ed. Corpus Praefationum. T.1 Étude préliminaire, t.2 Textus (A-P), t.3 Apparatus (A-P), t.4 Textus (Q-V), t.5 Apparatus (Q-V). Corpus Christianorum, Series Latina, 161-161 D. Turnhout: Brepols, 1980-1981.

Schnitker, T.A. and W.A.Slaby. Concordantia Verbalia Missalis Romani. Münster: Aschendorff, 1983.

Siffrin, P. Sacramentarium Veronense (Leonianum): Konkordanztabellen zu den römischen Sakramentarien 1. Rerum Ecclesiasticarum Documenta, Series minor: Subsidia studiorum, 4. Roma: Casa Editrice Herder, 1958.

Siffrin, P. Liber sacramentorum Romanae Aeclesiae (Cod. Vatican. Regn. Lat. 316) Sacramentorum Gelasianum: Konkordanztabellen zu den lateinischen Sakramentarien, 2. Rerum Ecclesiasticarum documenta, Series minor: Subsidia studiorum, 5. Roma: Casa Editrice Herder, 1959.

Ward, A. and C. Johnson. The Prefaces of the Roman Missal: a source compendium with concordance and indices. Roma: Tipografia Poliglotta Vaticana, 1989.

BIBLICAL TEXTS and INSTRUMENTS

Aland, L. et alia, ed. The Greek New Testament. United Bible Societies in cooperation with the Institute for the New Testament Textual Research, Münster/Westphalia. Third Edition (Corrected). Stuttgart: Biblia-Druck GmbH, 1983.

Dutripon, F. P. Bibliorum Sacrorum Concordantiae: Vulgatae Editionis. Editio octava. Paris: Bloud et Barral, 1880; reprint New York: Georg Olms Verlag, 1976.

Fischer, B., I. Gribomont, H. F. D. Sparks, W. Theile, ed. Biblia Sacra Iuxta Vulgatam Versionem. Editio Altera Emendata Tomus II Proverbia-Apocalypsis. Stuttgart: Wüttembergische Bibelanstalt, 1975.

Gramatica, A. Bibliorum Sacrorum Iuxta Vulgatam Clementinam. Nova Editio. Roma: Typis Polyglottis Vaticanis, 1946.

ROMAN DOCUMENTS

Consilium ad Exsequendam Constitutionem de Sacra Liturgia. "Schemata 250 (12/X/1967), 264 (18/XII/1967), 273 (15/II/1968), 282 (21/III/1968), 301 (15/XI/1968)" [photocopy].

Flannery, A. Vatican Council II: The Conciliar and Post Conciliar Documents. New York: Costello Publishing Company, 1975/1986.

Marini, P. "Elenco degli 'Schemata' del 'Consilium' e della Congregazione per il Culto Divino (Marzo 1964 - Febbraio 1975)." Notitiae 18 (1982): 487-539.

Paul VI, motu proprio Sacram liturgiam, January 25, 1964. Acta Apostolica Sedis 56 (1964): 139-144.

Sacra Congregatio pro Cultu Divino. "De editione typica altera Missalis Romani et Gradualis simplicis." Notitiae 11 (1975): 290-337.

Sacrosanctum Concilium, December 4, 1963. Acta Synodalia Sacrosancti Concilii Oecumenici Vaticani Secundi, II, vi, 409-497. Roma: Typiis Polyglottis Vaticaniis, 1973.

Tanner, N. Decrees of the Ecumenical Councils. II. Washington DC: Georgetown University Press, 1990.

WORKS CITED

Ambrose. Expositio Psalmi CXVIII (Litterae XII-XXII). Sancti Ambrosii Episcopi Mediolanensis Opera 10. Milano: Biblioteca Ambrosiana, 1987.

Amiet, R. "La tradition manuscrite du missel ambrosien." Scriptorum 14 (1960): 16-60.

Antonio, W. D. V. "The Euchological Texts of the Ordo Exsequiarum of 1969." Ephemerides Liturgicae 107 (1993): 289-311.

Barth, M. Ephesians 1-3. The Anchor Bible. New York: Doubleday and Company, 1974.

Bastiaensen, A. "Sur quelques oraisons du Missel Romain." In Mélanges Christine Mohrmann: Nouveau recueil offert par ses anciens élèves, 140-163. Utrecht/Anvers: Spectrum Éditeurs, 1973.

Bastiaensen, A. "L'Église a la conquête de sa liberté: recherches philologiques dans le Sacramentaire de Vérone." In Graecitas et Latinitas Christianorum Primaeva, Supplementa III, ed. C.Mohrmann et alia, 121-153. Nijmegen: Dekker & van de Vegt: 1970

Bernhold of Constance. Micrologus de Ecclesiasticis Observationibus. Migne, J. P. ed. Patrologia Latina, 151, 978-1022. Paris, 1853.

Best, E. A Commentary on the First and Second Epistles to the Thessalonians. New York: Harper & Row Publishers, 1972.

Betz, H. D. Galatians: A Commentary on Paul's Letter to the Churches in Galatia. Hermenia, ed. H.Koester. Philadelphia: Fortress Press, 1979.

Bietenhard, H. "ὄνομα, ὀνομαζω, ἐπονομαζω, ψευδώνυμος." In Friedrich, G. ed. Theological Dictionary of the New Testament. Vol. V, 242-283. Translated and edited by Geoffrey W. Bromiley from Theologisches Wörterbuch zum Neuen Testament, Fünfter Band, Stuttgart: W. Kohlhammer Verlag (no date given). Grand Rapids, Michigan: WM. B. Eerdmans Publishing Company, 1967.

Botte, B. and C. Mohrmann. L'Ordinaire de la messe: texte critique, traduction et études. Études liturgiques publiées sous la direction du Centre de Pastorale Liturgique et de l'Abbaye du Mont César, 2. Paris: Les Éditions du Cerf, 1953.

Bourque, E. Étude sur les sacramentaires romains: les textes primitifs. Pt I. Roma: Pontificio Istituto di Archeologia Cristiana, 1942.

Brou, L. "Étude historique sur les oraisons des dimanches après la Pentecôte dans la tradition romaine." Sacris Erudiri 2 (1949): 123-224.

Brou, L. Les Oraisons des dimanches après la Pentecôte: Commentaire Liturgique. Paroisse et Liturgie, collection de pastorale liturgique, 38. Bruges: Apostolat Liturgique Abbaye de Saint-André, 1959.

Brown, R. The Epistles of John. Anchor Bible. Garden City, New York: Doubleday and Company, Inc., 1982.

Brown, R. The Gospel According to John (i-xii). The Anchor Bible. New York: Doubleday, 1966.

Bugnini, A. The Reform of the Liturgy: 1948-1975. Translated by M.J.O'Connell from La riforma liturgica (1948-1975), Roma: Edizione Liturgiche, 1983. Collegeville, Minnesota: The Liturgical Press, 1990.

Cabrol, F. "Circoncision (Fête de la)." In Cabrol, F. and H. Leclerq, eds. Dictionnaire d'Archéologie Chrétienne et de Liturgie III, 1717-1727. Paris: Librairie Letouzey et Ané, 1948.

Capelle, B. "La collecte du troisième dimanche après pâques, dans le missel romain." Revue bénédictine 41 (1929): 171-173.

Capelle, B. "Messes du Pape S. Gélase dans le Sacramentaire Léonien." Revue bénédictine 56 (1945-46): 12-40.

Capelle, B. Travaux liturgiques de doctrine et d'histoire, I, II. Louvain: Abbaye du Mont César, 1962.

Caron, A. M. "Eucharistic mystery: Spring of new Life. A study in Liturgical Theology." Ph.D diss., Drew University, 1987.

Casel, O. "Beiträge zu römischen Orationen." Jahrbuch für Liturgiewissenschaft 11 (1931): 35-45.

Chapman, M. A. The Prayer of Faith: Brief sermon outlines for the Sundays of the year, on the orations or collects of the Mass. St.Louis: B. Herder Book Co., 1928.

Chavasse, A. "Messes du Pape Vigile (537-555) dans le sacramentaire léonien." Ephemerides Liturgicae 64 (1950): 161-213; 66 (1952): 145-219.

Chavasse, A. Le Sacramentaire Gélasien (Vatican Reginensis 316): Sacramentaire presbytéral en usage dans les titres Romains au VIIe siècle. Tournai: Desclée et Cie, 1958.

Coebergh, C. "Le pape saint Gélase Ier auteur de plusieurs messes et préfaces du soi-disant sacramentaire léonien." Sacris Erudiri 4 (1952): 46-102.

Conzelmann, H. 1 Corinthians: A Commentary on the First Epistle to the Corinthians. Hermenia, ed. G. W. MacRae. Translated by J. W. Leitch from Der erste Brief an die Korinther, Göttingen: Vandenhoeck & Ruprecht, 1969. Philadelphia: Fortress Press, 1975.

Dibelius, M. James: A Critical Commentary on the Epistle of James. Hermeneia, ed. H. Koester. Translated by M. A. Williams from Brief des Jakobus, Göttingen: Vandenhoeck & Ruprecht, 1964, 11th revised edition prepared by H. Greeven. Philadelphia: Fortress Press, 1976.

Dibleius, M. and H. Conzelmann. The Pastoral Epistles. Hermeneia, ed. H. Koester. Translated by P. Buttloph and A. Yarbro from the German Die Pastoralbriefe by M. Dibelius, (no publisher given) 4th revised edition by H. Conzelmann, 1966. Philadelphia: Fortress Press, 1972.

Diezinger, W. Effectus in der römischen Liturgie. Bonn: Peter Hanstein Verlag, 1961.

Dix, G. The Shape of the Liturgy. 2nd edition with additional notes by P. V. Marshall. New York: The Seabury Press, 1945/1982.

Dold, A. "Stark auffällige, dem Altgelasianum und dem Pragense nahe Sakramentar-Texte im CLM 28547." Ephemerides Liturgicae 66 (1952): 321-351.

Dudley, M. R. The Collect in Anglican Liturgy: Texts and Sources 1549-1989. Alcuin Club Collection. Collegeville: The Liturgical Press, 1994.

Dumas, A. "Pour mieux comprendre les textes liturgiques du Missel romain." Notitiae 6 (1970): 194-213.

Dumas, A. "Les oraisons du nouveau Missel romain." Questions liturgiques 52 (1971): 263-270.

Fitzmyer, J. A. Romans. The Anchor Bible. New York: Doubleday, 1993.

Foerster. W. "σεβομα, κτλ.." In Friedrich, G. ed. Theological Dictionary of the New Testament. Vol. VII, 168-196. Translated and edited by Geoffrey W. Bromiley from Theologisches Wörterbuch zum Neuen Testament, Siebenter Band, Stuttgart: W. Kohlhammer Verlag (no date given). Grand Rapids, Michigan: WM. B. Eerdmans Publishing Company, 1971.

Fulgentius. Epistola XIV. Migne, J. P. ed. Patrologia Latina, 65, 394-435. Paris: 1861.

Gerdes, F. "The Language of the Roman Missal. Part III: Second Sunday after Epiphany to Quinquagesima Sunday." Ph.D. diss., Saint Louis University, 1958.

Goulburn, E. M. The Collects of the Day: An exposition critical and devotional of the collects appointed at the communion I. New York: E. & J. B. Young and Company, 1881.

Gregory I, Homilarium in Ezechielem II. Migne, J. P. ed. Patrologia Latina, 76, 934-1312. Paris: 1878.

Haessly, M. Reflections on the Sunday Collects of the Roman Missal. St Meinrad's Abbey: A Grail Publication, 1946.

Haunerland, W. Die Eucharistie und ihre Wirkungen im Spiegel der Euchologie des Missale Romanum. Liturgiewissenschaftliche Quellen und Forschungen, Band 71. Münster: Aschendorff, 1989

Holleman, A. W. J. Pope Gelasius I and the Lupercalia. Amsterdam: Adolf M. Hakkert, 1974.

Hughes, K. H. "The Opening Prayers of 'The Sacramentary': A Structural Study of the Prayers of the Easter Cycle." Ph.D. diss., University of Notre Dame, 1981.

Irwin, K. Context and Text: Method in Liturgical Theology. A Pueblo Book. Collegeville: The Liturgical Press, 1994.

Johanson, B. To All the Brethren: A text-linguistic and rhetorical approach to I Thessalonians. Stockholm: Almqvist & Wiksell International, 1987.

Jungmann, J. A. The Mass of the Roman Rite: Its Origins and Development (Missarum Sollemnia) I. Translated by F. Brunner from Missarum Sollemnia, Revised Edition, Vienna: Herder Verlag, 1949. Westminster MD: Christian Classics Inc., 1992.

Jungmann, J. A. The Place of Christ in Liturgical Prayer. Translated by A. Peeler from Stellung Christi im liturgischen Gebet, Münster: Aschendorff, 1925, 2nd German Edition, revised 1962. Staten Island, N.Y.: Alba House, 1965.

Jungmann, J. A. Public Worship: A Survey. Translated by C. Howell from Der Gottesdienst der Kirche, Innsbruck: Verlagsantalt Tyrolia, 1955. Collegeville: The Liturgical Press, 1957.

King, A. A. Liturgies of the Primatial Sees. Milwaukee: The Bruce Publishing Company, 1957.

Kissane, E. J. The Book of Isaiah. Vol 1. Dublin: The Richardson Press, 1941.

Klauser, T. A Short History of the Western Liturgy. Translated by J. Halliburton from Kleine abendländische Liturgiegeschichte: Bericht und Besinnung, Bonn: Peter Hanstein Verlag, 5th German edition, 1965. New York: Oxford University Press, 1969.

Knight, G. Deutero-Isaiah. New York: Abingdon Press, 1965.

Krosnicki, T.A. Ancient Patterns in Modern Prayer. The Catholic University of America Studies in Christian Antiquity, No. 19. Washington: The Catholic University of America Press, 1973.

Leclerq, H. "Cursus." In Cabrol, F. and H. Leclerq, eds. Dictionnaire d'Archéologie Chrétienne et de Liturgie III, 3193-3205. Paris: Librairie Letouzey et Ané, 1948.

Lejay, P. "Ambrosien (Rit)." In Cabrol, F. and H. Leclerq, eds. Dictionnaire d'Archéologie Chrétienne et de Liturgie I, 1373-1442. Paris: Librairie Letouzey et Ané, 1924.

Levine, B.A. Numbers 1-20. The Anchor Bible. New York: Doubleday, 1993

Lindemann, A. Der Epheserbrief. Zürich: Theologischer Verlag, 1985.

Magistretti, M. Beroldus sive Ecclesiae Ambrosianae Mediolanensis Kalendarium et Ordines Saec. XII. Mediolani: Josephi Giovanola et Soc., 1894; reprint Farnborough, England: Gregg International Publishers Limited, 1968.

Manu, T. "Le thème de la vie dans l'euchologie du missel romain de Paul VI: Collectes, Prières sur les Offrandes, Postcommunions." Diss. Pontifico Ateneo S. Anselmo, Roma, 1977.

Martindale, C. C. The Prayers of the Missal I: The Sunday Collects. New York: Sheed and Ward, 1937.

Matera, F. Galatians. Sacra Pagina, Vol. 9. Collegeville: Liturgical Press, 1992.

Mazza, E. The Eucharistic Prayers of the Roman Rite. Translated by M. J. O'Connell from the Italian Le Odierne Preghiere Eucharistiche, Bologna: Centro Editioriale Dehoniano, 1984. New York: Pueblo Publishing Company, 1986.

McKenzie, J. Second Isaiah. The Anchor Bible. New York: Doubleday and Company, 1968.

Miazek, J. "La 'colletta' del 'proprio de tempore' nel 'Missale Romanum' di Paolo VI." Diss. Pontifico Ateneo S. Anselmo, Roma, 1977.

Michaelis, W. "ὁράω, κτλ.." In Friedrich, G. ed. Theological Dictionary of the New Testament. Vol. V, 315-382. Translated and edited by Geoffrey W. Bromiley from Theologisches Wörterbuch zum Neuen Testament, Fünfter Band, Stuttgart: W. Kohlhammer Verlag (no date given). Grand Rapids, Michigan: WM. B. Eerdmans Publishing Company, 1967.

Milgrom, J. Leviticus 1-16. The Anchor Bible. New York: Doubleday, 1991.

Mohrmann, C. "A Propos des collectes du psautier." Vigiliae Christianae 6 (1952): 1-19.

Mohrmann, C. Études sur le latin des chrétiens. Roma: Edizioni di Storia e Letteratura, 1958.

Mohrmann, C. "Le latin liturgique." La Maison-Dieu (1950/23): 1-30.

Mohrmann, C. Liturgical Latin: Its Origins and Character. Washington: The Catholic University of America Press, 1957.

Mohrmann, C. "Quelques observations sur l'évolution stylistique du canon de la Messe romain." Vigiliae Christianae 4 (1950): 1-19.

Morris, L. The First and Second Epistles to the Thessalonians. Revised edition. Grand Rapids, Michigan: William B. Eerdmanns Publishing Company, 1991.

Munier, C. ed. Concilia Africae (345 - 525). Corpus Christianorum, Series Latina 149. Turnhout: Brepols, 1974.

Orr, W. F. and J. A. Walther. 1 Corinthians. Anchor Bible. New York: Doubleday and Company Inc., 1976.

Paredi, A. "Milanese Rite." In The New Catholic Encyclopedia. Vol. 9, 838-842. New York: McGraw Hill, 1967.

Pascher, J. Die Orationen des Missale Romanum Papst Pauls VI, IV Teil, Im Jahreskreis. St Ottilien: EOS Verlag, 1983.

Pomarès, G. Gélase Ier: Lettre contres les lupercales et dix-huit messes du sacramentaire Léonien. Sources Chrétiennes 65. Paris: Éditions du Cerf, 1959.

Procksch, O. and K. G. Kuhn. "ἅγιος, ἁγιάζω, ἁγιασμός, ἁγιότης, ἁγιωσύνη." In Kittel, G. ed. Theological Dictionary of the New Testament. Vol. I, 88-115. Translated and edited by Geoffrey W. Bromiley from Theologisches Wörterbuch zum Neuen Testament, Erster Band, Stuttgart: W. Kohlhammer Verlag (no date given). Grand Rapids, Michigan: WM. B. Eerdmans Publishing Company, 1964.

Rheinfelder, H. "Zum Stil der lateinischen Orationen." Jahrbuch für Liturgiewissenschaft 11 (1931): 20-34.

Ricoeur, P. Interpretation Theory: Discourse and the Surplus of Meaning. Fort Worth: Texas Christian University Press, 1976.

Rordorf, W. Sunday: The History of the Day of Rest and Worship in the Earliest Centuries of the Christian Church. Translated by A. A. K. Graham from Der Sonntag: Geschichte des Ruhe- und Gottesdiensttages im altesten Christentum, Zürich: Zwingli Verlag, 1962. Philadelphia: The Westminster Press, 1968.

Schmidt, K. L. "καλέω, κτλ.." In Kittel, G. ed. Theological Dictionary of the New Testament. Vol. III, 487-536. Translated and edited by Geoffrey W. Bromiley from Theologisches Wörterbuch zum Neuen Testament, Dritter Band, Stuttgart: W. Kohlhammer Verlag (no date given). Grand Rapids, Michigan: WM. B. Eerdmans Publishing Company, 1965.

Schorlemmer, P. Die Kollektengebete mit Texte, Übersetzung und einem Glossar. Gütersloh: Bertelsmann, 1928.

Schrenk, G. "εὐδοκέω, εὐδοκία." In Kittel, G. ed. Theological Dictionary of the New Testament. Vol. II, 38-751. Translated and edited by Geoffrey W. Bromiley from Theologisches Wörterbuch zum Neuen Testament, Zweiter Band, Stuttgart: W. Kohlhammer Verlag (no date given). Grand Rapids, Michigan: WM. B. Eerdmans Publishing Company, 1964.

Searle, M. "Semper Reformanda: The Opening and Closing Rites of the Mass." In Shaping English Liturgy: Studies in Honor of Archbishop Denis Hurley. Edited by P. Finn and J. M. Schellman. Washington: The Pastoral Press, 1990.

Seow, C. L. "Hosts, Lord of." In Freedman, D. N. ed. The Anchor Bible Dictionary. III, 304-307. New York: Doubleday, 1993.

Soubigou, L. A Commentary on the Prefaces and the Eucharistic Prayers of the Roman Missal. Translated by J. A. Otto from the French Les préfaces de la liturgie - étudiés, prêchées, méditées, I, II, Paris: P.Lethielleux. Collegeville: The Liturgical Press, 1971.

Stuhlmeuller, C. "Deutero-Isaiah and Trito-Isaiah." In Brown, R. E., J. A. Fitzmeyer and R. E. Murphy, eds. The New Jerome Biblical Commentary, 329-348. Englewood Cliffs N.J.: Prentice Hall, 1990.

Taft, R. Beyond East and West: Problems in Liturgical Understanding. NPM Studies in Church Music and Liturgy. Washington: The Pastoral Press, 1984.

Thiel, A. Epistolae Romanorum Pontificum Genuinae. Vol. 1. Brunsbergae: Eduardi Peter, 1868.

Vacandard, E. "Le cursus: son origine, son histoire, son emploi dans la liturgie." Revue des questions historiques 78 (1905): 59-102.

Vogel, C. Medieval Liturgy: An Introduction to the Sources. Revised and translated by W. G. Storey and N. K. Rasmussen from Introduction aux sources de l'histoire du culte chrétien au moyen âge, Spoleto: Centro italiano di studi sull'alto medioevo, 1981. NPM Studies in Church Music and Liturgy Washington D.C.: The Pastoral Press, 1986.

Wanke, G and H. Balz. "φοβεω, φοβεομαι, φόβος, δεος." In Friedrich, G. ed. Theological Dictionary of the New Testament. Vol. IX, 189-219. Translated and edited by Geoffrey W. Bromiley from Theologisches Wörterbuch zum Neuen Testament, Neunter Band, Stuttgart: W. Kohlhammer Verlag (no date given). Grand Rapids, Michigan: WM. B. Eerdmans Publishing Company, 1974.

Weiss, L. "Die Orationen im Missale Romanum von 1970." Diss. Albert-Ludwigs-Universität, Freiburg, 1978.

Westermann, C. Genesis 1-11: A Commentary. Translated by J. J. Scullion from Genesis (Kapitel 1-11), Neukirchen-Vluyn: Neukirchener Verlag, 2nd German edition, 1976. Minneapolis: Augsberg Publishing House, 1984.

Westermann, C. Genesis 12-36. Translated by J. J. Scullion from Genesis XII-XXXVI, Neukirchen-Vluyn: Neukirchener Verlag, 1981. Minneapolis: Augsburg Publishing House, 1985.

Westermann, C. Isaiah 40-66. Old Testament Library. Translated by D. M. G. Stalker from Das Buch Jesaia, 40-66, Göttingen: Vandenhoeck & Ruprecht, 1966. London: SCM, 1969.

Williams, D. 1 and 2 Thessalonians. New International Biblical Commentary. Peabody, Massachusetts: Hendrickson Publishers, 1992.

Willis, G. G. A History of the Early Roman Liturgy to the Death of Pope Gregory the Great. Henry Bradshaw Society, Subsidia 1. London: The Boydell Press, 1994.

Willis, G. G. "The Variable Prayer of the Roman Mass." In Further Essays in Early Roman Liturgy. Alcuin Club 50. London: SPCK, 1968.

INDEX ONE

VOCABULARY IN THE COLLECTS FOR ORDINARY TIME

Word	Collect
abundantia	XXVII
abundare	III
actione	XI
actus	III
adesto	XI, XVIII
adicias	XXVII
adoptio	XXIII
adoptionem	XIII
adoptionis	XIX
adversantia (adversare)	XXXII
aeterna (aeternus)	XXIII
affectu (affectus)	IV
affectum	XX
agenda (agere)	I
amare	XXI, XXX
amorem (amor)	XII, XXII
amoris	XX
apta (aptus)	XV
assequi	XXX
asseris (asserere)	VI
auctorem (auctor)	XVIII
auctori	XXXIII
augmento (augmentum)	XXII
augmentum	XXX
auxilium	XI
beneplacito (beneplacitum)	III
benignitatem (benignitas)	XVIII
benignus	XXIII
bona (bonus)	X, XX, XXII
bonis	III, XVII, XXVIII
bonorum	XXVI, XXXIII
caelesti (caelestis)	I
caelestia	II
caelestis	V
caelestium	XXVI
caritate (caritas)	XVI
caritatis	XXX
censentur (censere)	XV
christiana	XV
Christo (Christus)	XXIII
clementer	II, XVI
cogitemus (cogitare)	X
concedas (concedere)	IX
concede	II, IV, XIV
conscientia	XXVII
consequamur (consequi)	XX
conserves (conservare)	XVIII
consortes (consors)	XXVI
conspicui (conspicere)	XIII
constituta (constituere)	XXV
continua (continuus)	V
convalescant (convalescere)	I
corda (cor)	XXI
corde	XXIV, XXIX
cordibus	XIX, XX
corpore (corpus)	XXXII
creator	XXIV
credentibus (credere)	XXIII
curramus (currere)	XXXI
currentes	XXVI
cursus	VIII
custodi (custodire)	V
custodia	XVI
custodias	XXII

da (dare) VI, VIII, XV, XXI, XXV,
XXX, XXXIII
desiderare XXI
desiderium XX
destituis (destituere) XII
Deus . . . .
II, III, IV, VI, VII, X, XI, XIII,
XIV, XV, XVII, XIX, XX,
XXI, XXII, XXIII, XXIV, XXV,
XXVI, XXVII, XXIX, XXX,
XXXI, XXXII, XXXIII
devotam (devotus) XXIX
devotione (devotio)   VIII, XXXIII
dictis (dicere) VII
digne XXXI
digneris (dignari) VI
dilecti (diligere) III
dilectione (dilectio) XXV
dilectionis . . . . XII, XXIII
diligamus (diligere) IV
diligentes XX
diligentibus XX
dimittas (dimittere) XXVII
dirigatur (dirigere) VIII
dirige III
dispositione (dispositio) IX
divini (divinus) XXXIV
Domine . . . .
I, IV, V, VIII, XII, XVI, XVIII,
XXVIII, XXXIII, XXXIV
dona (donum) XVI
duce (dux). XVII

ecclesia VIII
effectum (effectus) XXIV
efficis (efficere) XXI
effunde (effundere) XXVII
erexisti (erigere) XIV
eripuisti (eripere) XIV
errantibus (errare) XV
errorum (error) XIII
exaudi (exaudire) II
excedis (excedere) XXVII
excita (excitare) XXXIV

exclude (excludere) XXXII
exoramus (exorare) IX
expediti (expedire) XXXII
exsequamur (exsequi)   VII, XXXII
exsequendis XI
exsequentes XXXIV
exsistere (exsistere) VI

fac (facere) . . . XII, XXIX, XXX
faciamus X
facias . . . . XIV, XXVI
factis VII
fallitur (fallere) IX
familiam (familia) V
famulis (famulus) . . XVI, XVIII
felicitas XXXIII
ferventes (fervere) XVI
fide (fides) XVI
fidei XXX
fidelibus (fidelis) . . . XIV, XXXI
fidelium . . . . XXI, XXXIV
Filii (Filius) . . . . III, XIV
filiorum XIX
filios . . . . XIII, XXIII
fixa (figere) XXI
fortitudo XI
fructum (fructus) XXXIV

gaudere (gaudere) XXXIII
gaudia (gaudium) XXI
gaudiis XIV
gerere (gerere) XXIX
gloriantur (gloriari) XVIII
grata (gratus) XVIII
gratia (gratia) . . . . . VI, XXVIII
gratiae . . . . . . V, XI, XIII, XVI
gratiam XXVI
gubernante (gubernare) X
gubernatorem (gubernator) . XVIII
gubernatione (gubernatio) . . . XII

habere (habere) . . . . . XII, XVIII
habitare (habito) VI
hereditas XXIII

hereditatem XIX
homines (homo) IV
humilitate (humilis) XIV

iacentem (iacere) XIV
implenda (implere) I
indesinenter XXVI
infirmitas XI
infunde (infundere) . . XX, XXVI
ingredi (ingredi) XIX
inhaerere (inhaerere) XVII
inimica (inimicus) XV
innititur (inniti) V
insere (inserere) XXII
inspirante (inspirare) X
instituis (instituere) XII
intende (intendere) XXIII
intentos (intentus) XXVIII
invisibilia (invisibilis) XX
invocare (invocare) XIX
invocationibus (invocatio) . . . XI
involvamur (involvere) XIII
iugiter . . . . . . XXVIII, XXXIII

laetetur (laetari) VIII
laetitiam (laetitia) XIV
largire (largiri) . . . . . . X, XVIII
laudabiliter XXXI
legis (lex) XXV
liberis (liber) XXXII
libertas XXIII
lucis (lux) XIII
lumen. . . . . XV.

maiestati (maiestas) XXIX
maiora (magnus) XXXIV
mandatis (mandatum) . . XI, XVI
maneamus (manere) XIII
manere VI
manifestas (manifestare) . . XXVI
mansuris (mansurus) XVII
meditantes (meditari) VII
mente (mens) . . . . . . IV, XXXII
mentes XXI

mentibus XXXII
mereamur (mereri) . . . .
III, XIX, XXV, XXX
merita (meritum) XXVII
metuit (metuere) XXVII
miserando (miserari) XXVI
misericordiam . . XVII, XXVII
misericors . . . . . XXXI, XXXII
moderaris (moderari) II
mortalis XI
multiplica (multiplicare) XVI, XVII
mundanas (mundanus) XXI
mundi (mundus) VIII
mundum XIV
munere (munus) XXXI
muniatur (munire) V

nihil . . . . XI, XVII
nobis . . . .
IV, VI, VIII, IX, XXII, XXIII,
XXV, XXX, XXXI, XXXII,
XXXIII
nomine (nomen) . . . . . III, XIX
nomini XV
nominis . . . . XII, XXII
nos . . . .
XII, XIII, XVII, XXIV, XXVI,
XXVII, XXVIII, XXIX, XXX
nostris . . II, XI, XIX, XX, XXII
noxia (noxius) IX
nutrias (nutrire) XXII
nutrita XXII

offensione (offensio) XXXI
omnipotens . . . .
II, III, VII, XIX, XXVII, XXIX,
XXX, XXXI, XXXII
omnipotentiam XXVI
operibus (opus) . . . . III, XXVIII
operis XXXIV
optimum XXII
oratio XXVII
ordine (ordo) VIII
ostendis (ostendere) XV

pacem (pax) II
pacifico (pacificus) VIII
parcendo (parcere) XXVI
pariter . . . . XII, XXXII
paterno (paternus) XIX
peccati (peccatum) XIV
pectoribus (pectus) . . . . VI, XXII
percipiant (percipere) . . . XXXIV
perfice (perficere) XIX
perfrui (perfrui) XIV
perpetua (perpetuus) XXXIII
perpetuam . . . . . . XVIII, XXV
perpetuum XII
perseverent (perseverare) . . . XVI
pervenire (pervenire) XXV
pietate (pietas) . . . . I, V
pietatis . . . . XXVII, XXXIV
placeamus (placere) XI
placita VII
plena (plenus) XXXIII
populi (populus) . . . . I, II
populis XXI
poscentibus (poscere) XVIII
possimus (posse) XVII
possint XV
posuisti (ponere) XXV
potest XI
praecepta (praeceptum) . . . XXV
praecipis (praecipere) . XXI, XXX
praeparasti (praeparare) XX
praesta (praestare) . . . .
VII, XI, XIII, XXII
praestatur XXIII
praestet XXVIII
praesumimus (praesumere) . . XIX
praeveniat (praevenire) . . XXVIII
preasumit (praesumere) . . XXVII
procedunt (procedere) X
professione (professio) XV
profutura (profuturus) IX
promissa (promittere) XXVI
promissam XIX
promissiones (promissio) XX, XXXI
promittis (promittere) XXI, XXX

propensius (propense) . . . XXXIV
propitiare XVI
propitiationis (propitiatio) . XXIV
propitiatus XXXII
propitius XI
prosequere (prosequi) I
protectione (protectio) V
protector XVII
providentia IX
proximi (proximus) XXV

quaesumus . . . .
I, V, VII, VIII, XIII, XXVIII,
XXXI, XXXIII, XXXIV

rationabili (rationabilis) IV
rationabilia VII
recta (rectus) X
rectis VI
rector XXIV
rectore (rector) XVII
redemptio XXIII
redire (redere) XV
religionis (religio) XXII
remedia (remedium) XXXIV
respice (respicere) XXIV
respuere (respuere) XV
restaurata (restaurare) XVIII
restaures XVIII

sacrae (sacer) XXV
sanctam (sanctus) XIV
sancti XII
sanctum XVII
sectari XV
sempiterne (sempiternus) . . . . . .
II, III, XIX, XXVII, XXIX, XXX
sempiternis XIV
sentiamus (sentire) XXIV
sequatur (sequi) XXVIII
servantes (servare) XXV
serviamus (servire) XXXIII
serviatur (servire) XXXI
servire . . . . XXIV, XXIX

servitute (servitus) XIV
sinceris (sincerus) VI
sincero XXIX
sola (solus) V
soliditate (soliditas) XII
spe (spes) . . . . V, XVI
spei XXX
sperantium (sperare) . . . XI, XVII
spiritum (spiritus) XIX
splendore (splendor) XIII
studio (studium) XXII
submoveas (submovere) IX
sui (suus) IX
superant (superare) XX
supplicantis (supplicare) I
supplicationes (supplicatio) II
supplices (supplex) IX
supplicibus (supplex) X
supplicum (supplex) XXVII

tales (talis) VI
te IV, VI, IX, X, XI, XVII, XVIII, XX
temporibus (tempus) II
tenebris (tenebrae) XIII
terrena (terrenus) II
tibi VII, XI, XXIV, XXIX, XXXI
timorem (timor) XII
tota (totus) . . . . IV, XXIV
tranquilla (tranquillus) VIII
transeuntibus (transire) . . . XVII
tribuatur (tribuere) XXIII
tribue . . . . XXIV, XXXI
tua (tuus) . . . .
V, VI, VIII, XII, XXV, XXVI,
XXVIII, XXXII, XXXIII
tuae . . . .
XI, XII, XV, XVI, XXIII, XXIV,
XXVII, XXIX, XXXIV
tuam . II, V, XVII, XXVI, XXVII
tuas . . . . XX, XXXI
tui . . . . II, III, XIV, XX, XXII

tuis . . . .
X, XI, XIV, XVI, XVIII, XXI, XXXI
tuo . . . . III, VIII

universa (universus) XXXII
utamur (uti) XVII

validum (validus) XVII
varietates (varietas) XXI
veneremur (venerari) IV
venit (venire) . . . . XXIII, XXXI
vera (verus) XXIII
veritatis (veritas) . . . . . XIII, XV
viam (via) XV
videant (videre) I
viderint I
vigilanti (vigilare) XXII
vigili (vigil) XVI
virtutum (virtus) XXII
vitam (vita) XXV
voluisti (velle) XIII
voluntate (voluntas) XI
voluntatem XXIX
voluntates XXXIV
voluntatis XXI
vota (votum) . . . . I, XXVII

INDEX TWO

KEY LATIN TERMS

Abundare, 452
Actus, 449
Adesse, 154
Adoptio, 227, 602, 634, 659
Adsequi, 416
Adversari, adversantia, adversus, 422, 433, 670
Aequitas, 134
Affectus, 107, 659
Agere, 308
Amare, 270, 271, 274, 415
Amittere, 525
Amor, 313, 314, 320, 357, 592, 649, 650
Aptus, 264
Asserere, 329
Auctor, 123, 16,1 624, 630, 637
Augmentum, 357

Beneplacitum, 446, 447, 631, 642
Benignus, 156, 176, 641
Bona cuncta, 284, 641, invisibilia, 639, aeternus, 524, mansura, 528, temporalia, 524, 534, transeuntia, 528,
Bonus (optimus), 356

Caelestis, 460, 472, 481, 661
Caritas, 314, 413, 592
Censeri, 261
Christus, 626
Clementer, 475
Cogitare, 285, 658
Collecta, 11, 28, 32, 34

Collectio 10, plebs collecta 11,31.
Colligere, 10
Concedere, 102
Conscientia, 394, 656, 658
Conservare, 171, 631, 637
Consors, 377, 383, 639
Conspectu dei, 59
Convalescere, 460
Cor, 214, 270, 298, 577, 658
Corpus, 427, 658
Creare, 165, 577
Creator, 203, 624, 630
Creatura, 165
Credere, 233, 634, 648
Currere, 377, 382, 406
Cursus (Roman), 16, 22 fn34
Cursus mundi 183
Custodia, 360, 594
Custodire, 489

Debitus, 578
Deprecatio, 59
Desiderare, 270, 271, 273, 274
Desiderium, 348
Destituere, 313, 316
Deus virtutum, 345, 623
Deus pater, 625
Devotio, 121, 189, 349, 651,652
Devotus, 297
Dicere, 504
Digne, 405
Dilectio, 132, 233, 314, 623
Diligentes, 345
Diligere, 106, 113

Dimittere, 394, 629, 655
Dirigere, 181, 195, 449, 631
Dispositio, 370, 631, 642
Docere, 573
Dominus deus noster 102
Dux, 523, 624
Ecclesia, 189, 495, 646, 669
Effectus, 208
Efficere, 577
Erigere, 241
Eripere, 245, 636
Errare, error, 257, 607, 611, 655
Exaudire, 474
Excedere, 392, 393
Excitare, 547
Excludere, 426, 433, 657, 670
Existere, 333
Expedire, 428, 657
Exsequi, 308, 429, 551

Facere, 285, 504
Fallere, 372
Familia, 487, 647, 669
Famulus, 157, 647, 663
Felicitas, 121, 639
Fevere, 592
Fides, 413, 592
Filius, 648
Filius adoptionis, 602, fidelis, 577, lucis, 603
Filius (Xt), 233, 450, 625
Fortitudo, 304, 630
Fructus, 548, 550

Gaudere, 118, 651
Gaudium (sempiternum), 246, vera, 278, 662
Genere, 298
Gloriari, 159
Gratus, 175, 636
Gubernare, 162, 290
Gubernatio, 316
Gubernator, 162, 624, 632, 637

Habitare, 326, 328, 335, 637
Hereditas, 227, 228, 634, 639, 660
Heres, 227, 228
Humilitas, 239

Iacere, 240
Ibi...ubi, 270
Id...quod, 271
Indoles, 44f, 60, 61, 680
Infirmitas, 307, 656
Inhaerere, 657
Inimicus, 264, 657
Initi, 490
Inspirare, 288
Instituere, 313
Institutor, 315
Intendere, 235
Intentus, 540, 658
Invisibilia, 343, 344
Invocare, 573
Invocatio, 651, 652
Involvere, 608
Iustitia, 196, 670

Laetari, 187, 651
Laetitia, 242,
Laudabiliter, 405
Lex orandi, 617
liber, liberare, 227, 228, 420, 430, 634, 660
Lumen, 256, 635
Lux, 604, 659

Maiestas, 299, 622
Mandatum, 308, 593
Manere, 326, 327, 335, 609, 637
Manifestare, 381, 385, 637
Meditare, 502, 658
Mens, 105, 270, 427, 658
Mereri, 142, 416, 454
Meritum, 392
Metuere, 396, 656
Miserari, 377, 378, 391, 399, 400

Misericordia, 156, 232, 393, 628, 641
Misericors, 377, 403
Moderari, 471, 632, 661
Mors, 307, 636, perpetua, 244
Multiplacare, 522
Mundanus, 276, 662
Mundus, 184, 662, iacens, 240, 638, 656
Munire, 492, 632, 655

Nomen, 357, 450
Nomen christianum, 263, 265, 266, 648
Nomen divinum, 621, 678
Nomen paternum, 573
Nomen sanctum, 317
Noxia, 373, 374, 657
Nuncupare, 59
Nutrire, 359, 638

Offensio, 407,
Omnipotens, 377, 403, 623
Opes tuae, 156
Opus, 231, 452, opera bona, 541, 657
Opus divinum, 548, 635, 638
Orare, 11
Oratio presidentialis, 56
Oratio, 11,57, 398, 631, 642, 651, 652
Ordo, 185, 631, 642, 670,

Pacificus, 138, 185, 196, 670
Parcere, 377, 379, 655
Paterfamilias, 647
Pax, 190, 477
Peccatum, 247, 636
Pectus, 329, 357, 658
Percipere, 555
Perfrui, 246, 651
Perpetuus, 176, 245
Perseverare, 595
Pervenire, 142

Pietas, 156, 389, 391, 399, 400, 460, 495, 554, 628, 641
Placitus, 504, 658
Ponere, 131
Populus, 460, dei, 647, 663, 669
Poscere, 158
Posse (nihil potest) 306
Postulatio, 59
Praecipere, 273, 274, 415
Praestare, 539
Praesumere, 397, 573
Praevenire, 538
Precatio, 61
Preceptum, 140, 657
Procedere, 284, 285, 641
Professio (christiana professio), 261
Profutura, 373, 374
Promissio, 347, 382, 406, 639
Promittere, 660
Promittere, 273, 274, 416, 417, 660
Propensius, 551
Propitiare, 590
Propitiatio, 156, 210, 214, 629
Propitiatus, 425
Prosequi, 459
Protectio, 304 fn5, 493, 517, 624
Protegere, 632
Providentia, 368, 631, 642
Proximus, 132

Ratio, 135
Rationabilis, 108, 114, 135, 499, 503
Rector, 205, 330,522, 624, 658
Redemptio, 227, 634, 655
Regere, 632
Religio, 357, 651, 652
Remedium, 552, 655
Renasci, 227, 234
Respicere, 206, 231
Respuere, 264, 657
Restaurare, 169, 631, 636, 637,
Restaurata, 660

Sanctitas, 622
Sanctus, 520, laetitia, 249
Sectari, 264
Sentire, 207
Sequi, 538
Servare, 140
Servire, 122, 212, 215, 298, 404, 651
Servitus, 245, 578, 636, 656
Sincerus, 299, 332
Soliditas, 315
Sperare, 306, 517
Spes, 413, 592
Spiritus adoptionis, 583
Spiritus sanctus, 573, 581, 626
Splendor, 604, 611, 635, 659
Studium, 361
Superare, 347, 446
Supplex, 285, 460
Supplicatio, 476, 651, 652
Susceptor, 304 fn5

Tenebrae, 605, 606, 655
Terrenus, 472, 481, 661
Timor, 313, 318, 320, 650
Tranquilitas, 185, 190, 192
Transire, 524, 528

Validum, 518, 532
Varietas, 275, 662
Velle, 308
Venerari, 103, 113, 651, 652
Veritas, 256, 604, 635, 660
Via, 256, 660
Videre, 461, 658
Vigil, 597
Vigilare, 361
Visibilia, 344, 349, 660
Vita, 660, perpetua, 639
Voluntas, 272, 297, 547, 658
Votum, 59, 393, 459, 651, 652

INDEX THREE

SCRIPTURE (VULGATE) REFERENCES

Genesis
Gn 1: 165, 175 fn60, 284, 472
Gn 1:1; 630
Gn 1:2; 656
Gn 1:2,3; 605
Gn 1:3-4; 240
Gn 1:31; 240
Gn 2:4-24; 288
Gn 3:5; 238 fn7
Gn 3:17; 166
Gn 17:1-22; 594
Gn 24:1-67; 181
Gn 24:56; 633

Exodus
Ex 5:11; 380
Ex 34:6-7; 476

Leviticus
Lv 3:1; 197
Lv 7:11-34; 197
Lv 18:21; 317 fn22
Lv 19:18; 102 fn9; 132
Lv 19:34; 133
Lv 20:3; 317 fn 22

Numbers
Nm 7; 197

Deuteronomy
Dt 4:2; 594
Dt 6:4-9; 102 fn8, 132, 346, 502 fn15,
Dt 9:10; 414

Dt 10:12-13; 318
Dt 28:9-11; 453

Joshua
Js 17:13; 463

Judges
Jd 5:20; 183
Jd 20:26; 197
Jd 21:4; 197

I Samuel
I Rg 11:15; 197
I Rg 10:8; 197

II Samuel
II Rg 6:17; 197

I & II Kings
III Rg 17:1 - IV Rg 2:18; 139 fn 23
III Rg 19:1-8; 138 fn21

Nehemiah
II Es 9:17,31; 476 fn12

Job
Jb 6:11; 304 fn6

Psalms
Ps 1; 502, 503
Ps 2; 502
Ps 4:2; 474
Ps 5:9; 182, 633

Ps 15:18; 59
Ps 16:8; 494, 633, 634
Ps 17:31;494, 517 fn10, 634
Ps 21:24; 318
Ps 22:1; 633
Ps 25; 354
Ps 27:8; 304 fn5
Ps 30:2-5; 517 fn 10
Ps 35;8;376 fn2, 522
Ps 41:2; 273
Ps 50:12-13; 577
Ps 58:6; 354 fn6
Ps 58:17; 304 fn5
Ps 60:4; 304 fn5
Ps 68:17; 231
Ps 70:24; 502 fn15
Ps 79; 354 fn6
Ps 83; 354 fn6
Ps 89:16; 231
Ps 97: 8-9; 134
Ps 102:1-5; 317 fn22
Ps 106:22; 405
Ps 110:10; 319
Ps 110:10; 313
Ps 115:7; 405
Ps 115:13,117; 306
Ps 118; 256, 257
Ps 118:32; 383 fn20
Ps 118:47; 502 fn15
Ps 118:169-170; 59
Ps 126:1; 353, 361
Ps 140:2; 59 fn60
Ps 142:2; 502 fn15

Proverbs
Pro 2:5-6; 319

Song of Songs
Cn 5:12; 110 fn31

Wisdom
Sap 11:21-27; 379
Sap 14:3; 633
Sap 17:10; 398

Ecclesiasticus
Ecli 1:11-40; 319
Ecli 36:18-19; 196

Isaiah
Is 11:1-9; 319
Is 40:491
Is 40:12-26;491
Is 50:4-11; 491
Is 53:6; 258
Is 53:11; 258
Is 59:17; 414 fn8

Jeremiah
Jr 31:33; 414

Ezekiel
Ez 7:4-11; 380 fn11
Ez 8:18; 380 fn11
Ez 9:5,10; 380 fn11
Ez 45:15; 197

Hosea
Os 19:9; 520 fn22

Matthew
Mt 2:37-40; 103, 112, 133 fn4,
Mt 3:16-17;450, 451
Mt 4:4; 284
Mt 6:9-15; 394, 423, 520 fn22
Mt 6:20-21; 270
Mt 7:7-11; 281
Mt 17:16-17; 450, 451
Mt 21:28-32; 506 fn23
Mt 22:37; 106
Mt 23:3; 506
Mt 25:40; 215 fn37

Mark
Mr 1:10-11; 451 fn17
Mr 4:35-41; 313
Mr 6:45-52; 313
Mr 9:2-8; 313, 451 fn18
Mr 12:29-31; 103 fn10, 133 fn11

Mr 12:34; 133 fn12
Mr 24:26; 505 fn 21

Luke
Lc 1:13; 475
Lc 1:78-79; 182, 244
Lc 3:22; 451 fn17
Lc 4:18; 198
Lc 9:35; 451 fn18
Lc 10:25-37; 103 fn10, 107 fn22, 133 fn12
Lc 11:1-2; 575
Lc 11:21-26; 493
Lc 15:7; 390 fn5
Lc 20:13; 451

John
Jo 1:4,9; 256
Jo 1:17-18; 276, 282, 284
Jo 2:11; 381
Jo 3:16; 314, 623
Jo 4:2; 476 fn 12
Jo 5:29; 166 fn41
Jo 6:57; 327 fn6
Jo 8:42; 284
Jo 10:11-16; 255
Jo 12:35-36; 603
Jo 14; 257
Jo 14:6; 660
Jo 14:26; 575
Jo 15:1-17; 306
Jo 15:5-7; 327 fn6
Jo 15:26; 284
Jo 15:9; 106, 314, 623
Jo 15:10;327, 637
Jo 16:13; 575 fn13
Jo 16:23-30; 285 fn8
Jo 17:6; 318, 625
Jo 17:21; 327 fn6
Jo 20:1-9; 572
Jo 21:1-14; 572
Jo 24:14-24; 520

Acts of the Apostles
Ac 1:14; 595
Ac 2:21; 306 fn14
Ac 2:42; 595
Ac 6:8; 304 fn5
Ac 9:22; 463

Romans
Rm 2:4; 176, 641
Rm 5:1-11; 157
Rm 5:12-7:24; 229
Rm 5:12; 238 fn7, 244
Rm 5:15; 453 fn24
Rm 6:3-9; 230
Rm 6:3-11; 583, 656
Rm 6:5; 574
Rm 6:16; 248 fn22
Rm 6: 18-19; 212
Rm 7:17-19;328, 637
Rm 7:19,24-25; 230 fn22, 244
Rm 8; 307
Rm 8:2,6; 230
Rm 8:8-9; 328, 637
Rm 8:14-17; 166, 230, 572, 603, 626, 634 fn30, 635
Rm 8:21; 640
Rm 8:26; 397, 574
Rm 8:32; 379
Rm 8:38-39; 355
Rm 10:13; 306 fn14
Rm 12:1-2; 109, 447
Rm 16:18; 505 fn21

I Corinthians
I Cor 2:9: 348
I Cor 7:29-38; 528, 531
I Cor 7:32-34; 286
I Cor 9:24; 383
I Cor 10:5; 447
I Cor 10:31-33; 407
I Cor 13:8-13; 413, 589

II Corinthians
II Cor 4:1-6; 635
II Cor 4:6; 604
II Cor 5:12-18; 166, 631
II Cor 10:7; 505 fn21
II Cor 12:9; 328
II Cor 19:9; 637

Galatians
Gal 3-5; 603
Gal 3:14,29; 228
Gal 3:27-29; 227
Gal 4:5-7; 227, 626
Gal 4:6-7; 634 fn30, 635
Gal 4:30-31; 227
Gal 5:13-14; 229
Gal 5:17; 423
Gal 5:21; 228
Gal 5:22; 230

Ephesians
Eph 1:3-24; 231, 355, 446, 625, 626, 634 fn30, 640,
Eph 1:3-2:11; 632
Eph 2:4-6; 378, 629
Eph 2:10; 657
Eph 3:17: 328, 637
Eph 3:20; 348, 392, 397
Eph 4:17-5:20; 506
Eph 5:8-9; 257, 603 fn6
Eph 5:10-11; 446

Colossians
Col 1:15-20; 344, 472, 473
Col 3:9-10; 449 fn13, 637
Col 3:11; 328
Col 3:17; 505
Col 4:17; 461

I Thessalonians
I Th 2:15; 423
I Th 3:1-5; 118
I Th 5:2; 413
I Th 5:5; 603 fn6
I Th 5:12; 589
I Th 5:16-18; 119

I Timothy
I Tm 1:5; 395
I Tm 1:9-10; 423
I Tm 2:1-7; 192, 572
I Tm 3:16; 389, 460, 554, 628

Titus
Tt 3:4-8; 176, 378 fn7, 539, 641

Philemon
Ph 1:9-11; 407
Ph 2:6-9; 238 fn6, 240
Ph 4:19; 348

Hebrews
Heb 1:3; 605
Heb 1:8-9; 134
Heb 12; 596

James
Jc 1:17-18; 353, 356, 624, 641, 662
Jc 1:26-27; 358, 652
Jc 2:14-17; 506 fn23

I Peter
I Pt 1:22-2:2; 109
I Pt 2:21-25; 255, 258
I Pt 3:22; 355
I Pt 5:8; 423

II Peter
II Pt 1:2-4; 383, 384
II Pt 1:17; 451 fn18
II Pt 1:21; 289

I John
I Jo 1;1-2; 382
I Jo 1:5-7; 606, 655
I Jo 2:8-11; 257, 609
I Jo 2:20-28; 575 fn13

I Jo 3:14; 609
I Jo 3:17; 297 fn6, 327, 637
I Jo 4:13; 327 fn6
I Jo 4:14-15; 327
I Jo 4:15-16; 637
I Jo 5:3; 594
I Jo 5:12; 327 fn6

II John
II Jo 8: 461 fn9

Jude
Ju 24; 171

Revelation
Ap 15:4; 59 fn60